Communications
in Computer and Information Science 285

Sumeet Dua   Aryya Gangopadhyay
Parimala Thulasiraman   Umberto Straccia
Michael Shepherd   Benno Stein (Eds.)

Information Systems, Technology and Management

6th International Conference, ICISTM 2012
Grenoble, France, March 28-30, 2012
Proceedings

 Springer

Volume Editors

Sumeet Dua
Louisiana Tech University, Ruston, LA, USA
E-mail: sdua@coes.latech.edu

Aryya Gangopadhyay
University of Maryland, UMBC, Baltimore, MD, USA
E-mail: gangopad@umbc.edu

Parimala Thulasiraman
University of Manitoba, Winnipeg, MB, Canada
E-mail: thulasir@cs.umanitoba.ca

Umberto Straccia
ISTI, Italian National Research Council, Pisa, Italy
E-mail: straccia@isti.cnr.it

Michael Shepherd
Dalhousie University, Halifax, NS, Canada
E-mail: shepherd@cs.dal.ca

Benno Stein
Bauhaus University, Weimar, Germany
E-mail: benno.stein@uni-weimar.de

ISSN 1865-0929   e-ISSN 1865-0937
ISBN 978-3-642-29165-4   e-ISBN 978-3-642-29166-1
DOI 10.1007/978-3-642-29166-1
Springer Heidelberg Dordrecht London New York

Library of Congress Control Number: 2012934202

CR Subject Classification (1998): I.2, I.2.11, H.3-4, C.2, D, H.5

Typesetting: Camera-ready by author, data conversion by Scientific Publishing Services, Chennai, India

Printed on acid-free paper

Springer is part of Springer Science+Business Media (www.springer.com)

Message from the Program Chair

It is my pleasure to welcome you to the 6th International Conference on Information Systems, Management and Technology (ICISTM 2012).

The proceedings of the 6th International Conference on Information Systems, Management and Technology contain 38 peer-reviewed papers that were selected for presentation at the conference. These papers were selected after a rigorous peer-review of 85 submissions, which originated from 28 countries, primarily India, the USA, Italy, Nigeria, Germany and France, in response to the call for papers.

An exceptional international multidisciplinary team of 11 scientists and academicians from six countries including the USA, Canada, Italy, Germany, India and Greece served as Co-chairs for the six tracks: (1) Information Systems, (2) Information Technology, (3) Information Management, (4) Business Intelligence, (5) Applications, and (6) Management Science and Education. The conference also featured a workshop on Program Protection and Reverse Engineering (PPREW), which was ably led by two Workshop Co-chairs from the USA. A team of nine Publicity Co-chairs, two Tutorials Co-chairs, and the Publications chair assisted the Track Chairs and the Program Chair in the review process and the organization of the program.

The Track Co-chairs, Workshop Co-chairs and the Program Chair established an international Program Committee consisting of 118 members from 17 countries (primarily from the USA, Canada, Italy, India, Germany and Greece) to assist in the review process. Eight external reviewers also assisted this team. The Track Chairs and the Program Chair made paper assignments to the Program Committee members so that the focus of each paper matched its reviewer's expertise. A total of 237 reviews and reviewer ratings were obtained for the submitted papers. Each reviewer's rating was weighted by his or her confidence in the domain area. The Track Chairs, in coordination with the Program Chair, made the final selection of the accepted papers. The peer-reviewed papers were accepted into two categories: regular papers (up to 12 pages) and short papers (up to six pages).

In addition, the proceedings also have six position papers invited from selected Program Committee members. These papers are in extended abstract format and discuss an expert's opinion on the recent advancements in an area of interest to the conference. The position papers were not peer-reviewed and appear in a separate section in the proceedings.

The proceedings are published in Springer's *Communications in Computer and Information Science (CCIS)* series, and the papers have been reviewed by Springer's editorial team for final publication in this volume. The publication of the proceedings in the CCIS series offers a uniquely formulated and widely available medium for the dissemination of the selected papers.

The conference was a result of a harmonized effort between several people. I would like to thank all these people, as their contributions to the conference organization and proceedings have been invaluable. The General Chairs, Sartaj Sahni, Renaud Cornuemieux and D. P. Goyal, offered their perpetual guidance throughout the process. This conference is a result of their enthusiastic vision and unwavering commitment to the conference. The expertise, leadership and responsiveness offered by our exceptional team of Track Chairs was crucial for the peer-review of the conference papers and, thus, for the final product that is included in this volume. The Publicity Chairs and the Tutorials Chair did a remarkable job in circulating the conference information and generating interest in the project.

I would like to issue a special thanks to our Publications Chair, Pradeep Chowriappa, for the timely and effective preparation of the proceedings, which involved the rigorous task of carefully checking each accepted paper and ensuring compliance with the Springer LNCS/CCIS standards. Alfred Hofmann and Leonie Kunz from Springer and their editorial team skillfully assisted us with the compilation of these proceedings. The organizing team at Grenoble Ecole de Management (Grenoble EM), especially Mark Thomas, Aurore Besson and Thomas Vignoud, deserve sincere appreciation. Grenoble EM provided the venue and made local arrangements for the conference. Finally, I would like to thank the authors and the Program Committee for making this year's program particularly notable and uniquely multidisciplinary.

March 2012   Sumeet Dua

Conference Organization

General Co-chairs

Renaud Cornu Emieux   Grenoble Ecole de Management, France
D.P. Goyal   Management Development Institute (MDI), India
Sartaj Sahni   University of Florida, USA

Program Chair

Sumeet Dua   Louisiana Tech University, USA

Track Chairs

Information Systems

Aryya Gangopadhyay   University of Maryland, USA
Parimala Thulasiraman   University of Manitoba, Canada

Information Technology

Umberto Straccia   Institute of the National Research Council of Italy CNR, Pisa, Italy

Information Management

Michael Shepherd   Dalhousie University, Canada
Benno Stein   Bauhaus-Universität Weimar, Germany

Business Intelligence

Akhilesh Bajaj   University of Tulsa, USA
Huimin (Min) Zhao   University of Wisconsin- Milwaukee, USA

Management Science and Education

Ruppa (Tulsi) Thulasiram   University of Manitoba, Canada
M. Thenmozhi   Indian Institute of Technology, Madras, India

Applications

Panagiotis Bamidis   Aristotle University of Thessaloniki, Greece
Fuxing Yang   Verathon, Inc., USA

Workshop on Program Protection and Reverse Engineering (PPREW)

Arun Lakhotia   University of Lafayette, USA
Jeffery "Todd" McDonald   University of South Alabama, USA

Tutorial Chairs

Lionel Jouffe   BAYESIA, France
Teng Moh   San Jose State University, USA

Publicity Co-chairs

William Acosta   University of Toledo, USA
Travis Atkison   Louisiana Tech University, USA
Theeraphong Bualar   Silpakom University, Thailand
Magdalini Eirnaki   San Jose State University, USA
Nigel Gwee   Southern University and A&M College, USA
Sridhar Hariharaputran   Bielefeld University, Germany
Dipak Misra   Xavier Institute of Management, India
S. Selvakumar   National Institute of Technology,
                                   Tiruchirappalli, India
Sumanth Yenduri   University of Southern Mississippi, USA

Publications Chair

Pradeep Chowriappa   Louisiana Tech University, USA

ICISTM 2012 Program Committee

Information Systems

Jemal Abawajy   Deakin University, Australia
Eid Alabalawi   University of Manitoba, Canada
Li Bai   Temple University, USA
Abhinav Bhatele   Lawrence Livermore National Laboratory, USA
Virendra Bhavsar   University of New Brunswick, Canada
Pim Chaovalit   University of Maryland, USA
Alfredo Cuzzocrea   University of Calabria, Italy
Matthew Doerksen   University of Manitoba, Canada
Wayne Franz   University of Manitoba, Canada
Aryya Gangopadhyay   University of Maryland, USA
Saurabh Garg   University of Melbourne, Australia
Rama Govindaraju   Google, USA
Nigel Gwee   Southern University and A&M College, USA
Zhensen Huang   Precise Software Solutions, Inc., USA
Dongseong Kim   University of Canterbury, New Zealand

Kishore Kothapalli   International Institute of Information
                                    Technology, Hyderabad, India
Navin Kumar   Advisory Board Company, USA
Ming Li   Deakin University, Australia
Xin Li   Georgetown University, USA
Mike McGuire   University of Lafayette, USA
Teng Moh   San Jose State University, USA
Manish Parashar   Rutgers State University, USA
Himani Rana   University of Manitoba, Canada
Stephen Russell   Naval Research Laboratory, USA
Taghrid Samak   Lawrence Berkeley National Laboratory, USA
Justin Shi   Temple University, USA
Iftikhar Sikder   Cleveland State University, USA
Steven Solomon   University of Manitoba, Canada
Parimala Thulasiraman   University of Manitoba, Canada
Vidhyashankar Venkataraman   Yahoo, USA
Dong Yuan   Swinburne University of Technology, Australia

Information Technology

William Acosta   University of Toledo, USA
Giacomo Berardi   ISTI Institute of the National Research
                                    Council, Italy
Fernando Bobillo   University of Zaragoza, Spain
Giovanni Casini   Universitá di Pisa, Italy
Marco Cerami   IIIA-CSIC, Italy
Andrea Esuli   Istituto di Scienza e Tecnologie
                                    dell'Informazione, Italy
Fabrizio Falchi   ISTI-CNR, Italy
Claudio Gennaro   ISTI-CNR, Italy
Nigel Gwee   Southern University and A&M College, USA
Nicolas Madrid   University of Málaga, Spain
Diego Marcheggiani   ISTI Institute of the National Research
                                    Council, Italy
Sheetal Saini   Louisiana Tech University, USA
Fabrizio Silvestri   ISTI-CNR, Italy
Umberto Straccia   Institute of the National Research
                                    Council of Italy, Italy
Antoine Zimmermann   DERI, France

Information Management

Peter Bodorik   University of Manitoba, Canada
Steven Burrows   Bauhaus-Universität Weimar, Germany
Jörg Frochte   Bochum University of Applied Science,
                                    Germany

Meng He   Dalhousie University, Canada
Dennis Hoppe   Bauhaus-Universität Weimar, Germany
Roman Kern   Know-Center GmbH, Austria
Vlado Keselj   Dalhousie University, Canada
Sunny Marche   Dalhousie University, Canada
Evangelos Milios   Dalhousie University, Canada
Oliver Niggemann   Institute Industrial IT, Germany
Srinivas Sampali   Dalhousie University, Canada
Michael Shepherd   Dalhousie University, Canada
Benno Stein   Bauhaus-Universität Weimar, Germany
Henning Wachsmuth   Universität Paderborn, Germany

Business Intelligence

Akhilesh Bajaj   University of Tulsa, USA
Baisakhi Chakraborti   National Institute of Technology, Durgapur,
                             India
Chen-Huei Chou   College of Charleston, USA
Demian D'Mello   St. Joseph Engineering College, India
Tatiana Escovedo   Pontifícia Universidade Católica do Rio
                             de Janeiro, Brazil
Rahul Hakhu   Baddi University, HP, India
Mike Hardin   University of Alabama, USA
Uday Kulkarni   Arizona State University, USA
Kafui Monu   University of British Columbia, Canada
Srinivas Prasad   Gandhi Institute for Technological
                             Advancement, India
Matti Rossi   Aalto University, Finland
Young Ryu   The University of Texas at Dallas, USA
Holger Schrödl   Otto-von-Guericke-Universität Magdeburg,
                             Germany
Vijayan Sugumaran   Oakland University, USA
Parijat Upadhyay   West Bengal University of Technology, Bengal,
                             India
Yinghui Yang   University of California, USA
Limin Zhang   North Dakota State University, USA
Huimin Zhao   University of Wisconsin-Milwaukee, USA
Lina Zhou   University of Maryland, USA

Management Science and Education

S.S. Appadoo   University of Manitoba, Canada
M. Thenmozhi   Indian Institute of Technology, Madras, India
Ruppa Thulasiram   University of Manitoba, Canada
Manish Verma   Memorial University, Canada
Sajjad Zahir   University of Lethbridge, Alberta, Canada

Applications

Christina Athanasopoulou	Aristotle University of Thessaloniki, Greece
Panagiotis Bamidis	Aristotle University of Thessaloniki, Greece
Stathis Constantinidis	Aristotle University of Thessaloniki, Greece
Dimitris Dranidis	CITY College, Greece
Barry Eaglestone	University of Sheffield, UK
Luis Fernandez Luque	Northern Research Institute, Norway
Xiujuan Geng	University of North Carolina, Chapel Hill, USA
Daniela Giordano	University of Catania, Italy
Thanos Hatziapostolou	City College, Greece
Efthyvoulos Kyriacou	Frederick University, Cyprus
Filippo Molinari	Politecnico di Torino: Portale Istituzionale, Italy
Iraklis Paraskakis	South-East European Research Center, Greece
Hongjian Shi	Danaher Imaging, USA
Davide Taibi	Italian National Research Council, Italy
Liyang Wei	Hologic, Inc., USA
Lin Yang	University of Medicine and Dentistry of New Jersey, USA
Fuxing Yang	Verathon, Inc., USA
Yin Yin	iCAD, Inc., USA
Fei Zhao	GE Global Research Center, USA

Workshop on Program Protection and Reverse Engineering (PPREW)

Todd R. Andel	Air Force Institute of Technology, USA
Robert W. Bennington	Air Force Research Laboratory, Sensors Directorate, USA
Mihai Christodorescu	IBM T.J. Watson Research Center, USA
Christian Collberg	University of Arizona, USA
Saumya Debray	University of Arizona, USA
Roberto Giacobazzi	University of Verona, Italy
Michael Grimaila	Center for Cyberspace Research, USA
Sylvain Guilley	TELECOM-ParisTech, France
Arun Lakhotia	University of Louisiana, Lafayette, USA
Jean-Yves Marion	Lorraine Research Laboratory in Computer Science and its Applications, France
Jeffery "Todd" McDonald	University of South Alabama, USA
Milla Dalla Preda	University of Bologna, Italy
Richard R. Raines	Air Force Cyberspace Technical Center of Excellence (CyTCoE), USA
Natalia Stakhanova	University of South Alabama, USA
Clark Thomborson	University of Auckland, New Zealand
Alec Yasinsac	University of South Alabama, USA

Table of Contents

Information Systems

Information Technology

Information Management

Business Intelligence

Management Science and Education

Applications

Workshop on Program Protection and Reverse Engineering

Short Papers

Position Papers

Focused Crawling Using Vision-Based Page Segmentation

Mahdi Naghibi and Adel Torkaman Rahmani

Department of Computer Engineering, Iran University of Science and Technology (IUST),
Narmak, Tehran, Iran
naghibi@comp.iust.ac.ir, rahmani@iust.ac.ir

Abstract. Crawling the web to find relevant pages of the desired topics is called focused crawling. In this paper we propose a focused crawling method based on vision-based page segmentation (VIPS) algorithm. VIPS determines related parts of a web page which is called page blocks. The proposed method considers the text of the block as the link contexts of containing links of the block. Link contexts are terms that appear around the hyperlinks within the text of the web page. Since VIPS algorithm utilizes visual clues in the page segmentation process and is independent from the HTML structure of the page, it can find link contexts in an accurate manner. Our empirical study show higher performance of the proposed focused crawling method in comparison with the existing state of the art results.

Keywords: Web mining, Information retrieval, Focused crawling, Page segmentation, VIPS algorithm.

1 Introduction

The web is big and is growing fast. The indexable web content is estimated as billions of web pages [1]. Also web is highly dynamic. Web pages content and their link structure change rapidly [2]. General surfing tools of the web take snapshots of the whole web and try to keep it up to date, but the characteristic of the web make them inefficient. This necessitates using of methods being able to explore only some specified portions of the web and ignore undesired parts of it. Focused crawlers are effective tools for surfing the web and finding pages belonged to the specific topics while using network resources in an almost optimal way. They begin from some start pages, called seed pages, extract links of these pages and assign some scores to these links based on the usefulness of following these links to reach the on-topic pages. Then crawlers get most scored links and by means of these links navigate to new pages. They repeat this procedure for newly fetched pages until some stop conditions are achieved.

The main issue in design of focused web crawlers is to make it possible for them to predict relevancy of pages which current links will lead to. The crawlers try by using some resources of information inside the current page or by means of analyzing link structure between the web pages, accurately calculate the score of links within the

S. Dua et al. (Eds.): ICISTM 2012, CCIS 285, pp. 1–12, 2012.
© Springer-Verlag Berlin Heidelberg 2012

current pages. One of the richest resources of information for conducting focused crawlers is the *link context* of the hyperlinks. The human users can surf the web because the link contexts have clues to the content of target pages of the hyperlinks. Focused crawlers can emulate behavior of the human users and utilize these valuable cues to conduct their surfing path on the web.

From the early works in focused web crawling, the researchers tried to determine the usefulness of following a hyperlink not only based on its text but by using additional information from the text of the web page containing the link. This effort lead to the concept of link context. According to [3] context of a hyperlink or link context is defined as the terms that appear in the text around a hyperlink within a Web page. While its importance have been demonstrated in variety of web information processing tasks such as web pages categorization [4] and web information retrieval [5] it has a strong role in performance of focused web crawling algorithms. Based on reported results in this area of research, it is not an overstatement to say that link contexts is one of the most effective and efficient parameters in calculating potential of a hyperlink to lead us to relevant pages. The challenging question in link context extraction that needs to be answered is that how around of a hyperlink can be determined. In the other words how can we determine which terms are around a hyperlink and which are not. A human user can easily understand which areas of a web page are related to each other and which areas around a hyperlink form its link context. Yet it is not an easy task for a crawler agent.

In this paper we propose a focused crawling method based on Vision-Based Page Segmentation (VIPS) algorithm. VIPS uses DOM of a web page in addition to some visual clues of the page's layout to detect related parts of the page, which is called page blocks. After the detection of page blocks, the proposed method considers text of a block as the link context of hyperlinks which the block contains. Since VIPS algorithm has been found as an effective method for page segmentation [5], it is expected that considering the block text as the context of links of the block result in higher performance of the proposed method in comparison whit most effective existing approaches. To investigate this expectation we have done some empirical studies based on different metrics.

The rest of this paper is organized as follow. In the next section we take a look at existing focused crawling methods. section 3 describes the proposed method in details. section 4 belongs to experimental results and the last section contains the conclusion.

2   Literature Review

Focused crawling is relatively a new area of research. One of the first works in this field is Fish Search [6] which was proposed in 1994. The title of focused crawling was suggested in 1999 by [7] for this research area. Since link context plays an important role in focused crawling, we categorize focused crawling methods based on their link context extraction strategy.

2.1　Categorizing Focused Crawling Methods Based on Their Link Context Extraction Strategy

We categorize link context extraction methods into four categories: using whole page text and link text, window based methods, DOM based methods and block based methods. In the following we describe them in more details.

Using Whole Page Text and Link Text. The simplest method for link context extraction is considering the whole text of a web page as link context of the links of the page. Fish search used this method to score links of web page and in this way all of links inside a page will have same priority for crawling. Naïve best first method which is another early research in field of focused crawling also uses whole page text as link context of page links. A version of Best first method uses the text of each link as its link context and computes link scores based on the relevancy of link context to the target topic. Another version of this method also uses link text as link context but scores each link using a combination the relevancy of page text and link context to the desired topic, based on the following formula:

$$linkScore = \beta \times \text{Relevancy}(pageText) + (1 - \beta) \times \text{Relevancy}(linkContext) \qquad (1)$$

Where *linkScore* is the score of a link inside a web page, *pageText* is whole page text and *linkContext* is extracted link context for the hyperlink which in this version of Best first method is equivalent to link text. Relevancy(*text*) function computes relevancy of given text to desired topic. The β factor determines impact of each computed relevancies in final link score.

Window Based Methods. Window based methods have proved their efficiency in information retrieval systems [5]. Specially for link context extraction in the field of focused web crawling, these simple methods can deal with varying length of pages and outperformers more complicated methods that use DOM tree information [3] for variety of topics. In this method for each hyperlink, a window of T words around the appearance of a hyperlink within a page is considered as its link context. The window is considered to be symmetric with respect to link text whenever is possible. It means the window will have T/2 words before and T/2 words after the link text. Text of hyperlink will always be included in text window. Shark search algorithm which is an evolved version of fish search algorithm uses this method for link context extraction.

DOM Based Methods. When a web page is considered as an indecomposable entity, a considerable amount of data which is hidden in HTML structure of page, will be eliminated. Document Object Model or DOM of a web page, models a web page as a tree. The Structure of page HTML is considered as the edges and the tags are considered as the nodes of the tree. In [8] based on the idea that texts in different parts of a page and their distances from a hyperlink can be utilized for predicting the relevancy of the target page of the hyperlink, Chakrabarti used DOM tree of a web page to compute distances of words positioned in different leaves of DOM tree from a hyperlink within that page. After fetching target page of an hyperlink its relevancy is computed and the set of related <token, distance> pairs to the hyperlink which was computed in container page of that hyperlink and the relevancy of fetched page, forms a learning instance. This instance is given to the apprentice learner which is responsible for computing links scores.

In [3], Pant an Sirinisavan used DOM tree of a web page to extract link context of hyperlinks having anchor texts shorter than a predefined threshold. Their method traverses tree structure of DOM from the position of a hyperlink to the root of the tree in a level by level manner. If text of a given hyperlink be not long enough, the method traverses to hyperlink parent node and aggregates all of its children nodes text with the hyperlink text. If aggregated text be long enough the method considers it as the hyperlink link context and if not, this procedure is continued.

Block Based Methods. Related parts of a page is called page block and the procedure of extracting page block from a web page is called page segmentation. Link context extraction Methods based on page segmentation use text of page block as link contexts of the hyperlinks positioned in that block. It is expected that link extraction based on page segmentation be more accurate and effective than other introduced methods for focused web crawling. Reported results in [9] encourage this expectation. In that work page segments is called content blocks. Some predefined HTML tags such as heading and table related tags are considered as content block tags which means they are capable to form parts of a content block. A tree structure of these tags which is extracted from DOM tree of a given page is then processed to forms page segments: each sub tree of content block tags tree which have a lower height than a predefined portion of whole tree is considered as a content block. This method is very dependent to HTML structure of a web page and faces challenges similar to challenges of DOM based methods.

The proposed algorithm in [10] which is called VIPS, also utilizes HTML structure of a web page for page segmentation but does not totally relies on it and also utilizes visual clues of a web page for block extraction. To the best of our knowledge VIPS is one of the strongest algorithms for web page segmentation and is successfully applied in variety of web mining and retrieval task such as web search [5]. We utilized VIPS algorithm in the proposed focused crawling method for link context extraction. This algorithm is explained with details in the next section.

2.2   Other Focused Crawling Methods

The focus of this paper is on link context extraction for focused web crawling but to have a survey of focused web crawling methods we briefly discuss about other approaches in this area. Diligenti et al. introduced an interesting data model called context graph [11]. This model maintains contents of some training web pages and their distances form relevant target pages in a layered structure. Each layer represents Pages with same distances to relevant pages. By training a classifier for each layer, the distance between newly visited pages and target pages can be determined. Rennie et al. utilized Q-learning framework for focused web crawling [12]. In their method quality or Q value of links is computed using a naïve base classifier. Researchers of [13] used Hidden Markov Model (HMM) to compute probability of leading current links to relevant pages. This model needs considerable user interactions for making HMM model. An improved version of this method is proposed in [14].

3   Using VIPS Algorithm for Focused Crawling

In previous section we reviewed focused crawling methods and their link context extraction strategies. In the follow, first we discuss about the challenges of non-block based link context extraction methods. This makes clear the reason of using a block based method which is independent from HTML structure of the web page. After that we describe VIPS algorithm in details and explain how this algorithm can helps in link context extraction and computing link scores.

3.1   Challenges of Non-block Based Link Context Extraction Methods

Challenges of Using Whole Page Text and Link Text. It is clear that considering the whole text of a web page as the link contexts of its contained links, will put considerable noisy words in each of extracted contexts. From another point of view we know that considering same score for all of the links inside a page is not a right decision, because different links of a web page have not the same following values. Also Text of a hyperlink has not enough capability for representing the topic of its target page. As the results of [14] show, considering the whole text of a web pages as the link contexts will lead to higher performance than using text of links as contexts. Combining these two i.e. the hyperlink text and the page text, can remedy the mentioned challenges but can't totally overcome them.

Challenges of Window Based Methods. A typical window based method first extracts total text of a web page using a depth first traversal strategy on the DOM tree of the page. Then based on the position of a hyperlink, the method determines the words which are located in the neighborhood of the hyperlink with the distance of T/2 words before an T/2 words after the hyperlink text, if possible. This approach won't be able to locate the appropriate position of a link context for two reasons. First the HTML structure of a web page does not necessarily show the visual layout of a page which a web browser presents to the users, and a typical depth first (or any other blind) traversal of HTML structure of a web page which is not aware of the visual layout of the page, can't put the related texts, in the neighborhood of each other and keep their original locality. Second considering a symmetric text window around a hyperlink, may put noisy words from one side of the window into the link context in many cases. Because for many hyperlinks, appropriate link context is positioned only before or after its text, not both.

Furthermore the suitable size of window for link context extraction is not clear at all [3]. Because web pages of different domains and topics usually have different page layouts and structures. for example political news web pages have different layouts from the academic ones. Thus the optimal size of window varies from one topic to another and has a high influence on the performance of methods.

Challenges of DOM Based Methods. DOM based Methods use HTML tag tree as the source of information for determining link context of a hyperlink. But as we know HTML format is originally proposed for determining a web page layout for web browsers and is not a structured data format such as XML. Thus an HTML page data structure may be very different from what a browser displays and the extracted link context for a hyperlink maybe not the same as the link context that a human user understands for that hyperlink. This emerged use of approaches which are able to detect related areas of a web page not only based on its HTML structure but based on some visual clues and in some way near to how a human user understands related parts of a web page.

3.2   Link Context Extraction Based on VIPS Algorithm

If a block based link context extraction method be totally dependent to the DOM of the web page, it will encounter challenges similar to DOM based methods ones. This indicates the need for a block extraction methods which in somehow be independent from HTML structure of the page. In VIPS algorithm the *vision-based content structure* of a page is obtained by combining the DOM structure and the visual cues of the web page. VIPS uses background colors, font sizes, font styles and many other things that have influence on the layout of the web page and can help in finding related parts of the page which are called the blocks. The segmentation process has three main steps: raw block extraction, separator detection and content structure construction. These three steps as a whole are regarded as a round. The algorithm is top-down. The web page is firstly segmented into several big raw blocks and the hierarchical structure of this level is recorded. For each big block, the same segmentation process is carried out recursively until sufficiently small blocks whose degree of coherence (DoC) values are greater than a predefined degree of coherence PDoC, are produced. Figure 1 shows the pseudocode of VIPS algorithm and its three main steps. After all blocks are processed, the final vision-based content structure of the web page is outputted. All of the leaf nodes of this structure are considered as the final blocks.

After the detection of final blocks, link contexts are extracted from the text of these blocks. In fact we consider text of the block as the link context of its contained hyperlinks. Figure 2 shows the pseudocode of link context extraction process of the proposed method. Since VIPS algorithm is independent from HTML structure of the web page and considers visual aspects of the web page in its segmentation process, it can extract the link contexts more accurately than window base, DOM based and some other block based methods such as [9]. Specifically, considering the text of the block as the link context of its hyperlinks will result in the following advantages:

- Appropriate position of link contexts can be determined.
- For a majority of blocks, appropriate link contexts size is determined.

```
input:   root: root node of DOM tree, in the first step it is the root of the page
output: cStructure: hierarchical vision-based content structure
Vision-Based-Page-Segmentation(root)
    pool ← Extract-Raw-Blocks(root);
    separators ← Detect-Separators(pool);
    cStructure ← Construct-Content-Structure(pool, separators);
    return cStructure;
end
----------------------------------------------------------------------------------
input:   root: root node of DOM tree
output: pool: a set of raw blocks, initialized with Ø
Extract-Raw-Blocks(root)
    if Dividable(root) == TRUE then
        for each child ∈ root.childs do
            pool ← pool ∪ Extract-Raw-Blocks(child);
        end for
    else
        rawBlock ← SubTree(root); //consider subtree as a raw block
        Set-Block-DoC(rawBlock);
        pool ← pool ∪ {rawBlock};
    end if
    return pool;
end
----------------------------------------------------------------------------------
input:   pool: a set of raw blocks
output: separators: a list of raw block separators, initialized with {s₁}
Detect-Separators(pool)
    for each block ∈ pool do
        for each s ∈ separators do
            base on the relationship between block and s:
                Split or Update s in separators or Remove it;
        end for
    end for
    for each s ∈ separators do
        Set-Separator-Weight(s);
    end for
    return separators;
end
----------------------------------------------------------------------------------
input:   pool: a set of raw blocks; separators: a list of raw block separators
output: cStructure: hierarchical vision-based content structure
Construct-Content-Structure(pool, separators)
    separators ← Sort-Ascending(separators);
    //sorting is based on the weight of separators
    for each s ∈ separators do
        mBlock ← Merge(Get-Blocks(s.neighboringBlokcs, pool));
        //gets neighboring blocks of s from pool and Merges them
        Set-Merged-Block-DoC(mBlock);
        Construct-Hierarchy(mBlock, cStructure);
        // puts mBlock into cStructure hierarchy
    end for
    for each leaf ∈ cStructure.leafs do
        if leaf.DoC < PDoC then
            newCStructuer ← Vision-Based-Page-Segmentation(leaf.root);
            Replace((leaf, newCStructure), cStructure);
            //replaces leaf with newCStructure in cStructure
        end if
    end for
    return cStructure;
end
```

Fig. 1. Pseudocode of the VIPS algorithm and its three main steps

Since VIPS algorithm does not use a blind traversal and is aware of visual layout of the web page, it is capable to preserve the original locality of the elements of the page and can transfer these localities to the extracted blocks. Thus we can be very hopeful that the text of the extracted block is truly in the neighborhood of the block hyperlinks and is consistent with the original layout of the segmented web page.

```
input:  link: a hyperlink of the page;
        cStructure: hierarchical vision-based content structure of the page
output: linkContext: link context of the input hyperlink
Extract-Link-Context-Using-VIPS(link, cStructure)
    for each leaf ∈ cStructure.leafs do //leaf is a block
        if link ∈ leaf.links then
            linkContext ← leaf.text;
            break for;
        end if
    end for
    retrun linkContext;
end
```

Fig. 2. Pseudocode of link context extraction process of the proposed method

Also the reported statistics in [5] show that only 19% of blocks contain more than 200 words and a two-third majority of them, contains less than 50 words. These statistics are consistent with what we understand from the web pages as a human. Since most of the web pages have a main content block which typically contains a relatively long text, and some other blocks such as navigation bars and page headers with short texts. This indicates that the VIPS algorithm can determine the appropriate size of many link contexts, in addition to detecting their appropriate position.

4   Experimental Study

In this section, at first we describe evaluation metrics used for performance evaluation. Then we talk about experimental settings of our evaluation. After that, experimental results will be proposed and analyzed based on evaluation metrics.

4.1   Evaluation Metrics

We have used two standard evaluation metrics, Harvest Rate and Target Recall, to describe and compare the performance of different focused crawling methods. These metrics have been used for focused crawling evaluations by many researches [3], [14], [15].

Harvest Rate. The harvest rate for t fetched pages from the start of the crawling process until now, $H(t)$, is computed based on the following formula:

$$H(t) = \frac{1}{t}\sum_{i=1}^{t} r_i \tag{2}$$

Where r_i is the relevancy of page i which is fetched by the crawler. This relevancy is computed based on the binary output of an *evaluator classifier*. We talk more about evaluator classifiers in section 4.2.

Target Recall. To compute this metric, first a set of target pages, T, is specified. If $R(t)$ be target recall of a focused crawler for t fetched pages up to now then:

$$R(t) = \frac{|C(t) \cap T|}{|T|} \tag{3}$$

Where $C(t)$ is the set of crawled pages from the beginning until page t and $|T|$ indicates the number of pages in T.

4.2   Experimental Settings

Compared Methods. The proposed method of this paper is compared with two methods which based on [14] and [3] have been lead to the state of the art results in focused crawling. These two methods are Best first and Text window methods. Reported results of [14] and [3] show better performance for versions of Best first and Text window methods that utilize both link context and page text for computing link scores. Hence we implemented these versions of Best first and Text window methods and we used formula 1 for combining relevancy scores. In this formula, *linkContext* is considered as link text and text of the window for Best first and Text window methods respectively. Also we implemented and evaluated two versions of the proposed method. One version uses block text as link context and computes the link score based on the context relevancy, and the other version combines the relevancy of link context with the relevancy of page text using formula 1. The β factor in formula 1 is set to 0.25 as found to be effective in [3], for all of the methods that combine page text score with link context score. Window sizes for Text window method is set to 10, 20, and 40 same as [3]. PDoC parameter of VIPS algorithm is set to 0.6 according to [5].

Focused Topics. Six distinct topics from different domains are selected from the Open Directory Project (ODP) [16] to evaluate focused crawling methods. ODP is a comprehensive human-edited directory of the web which contains URLs related to a hierarchy of topics in many domains. The selected topics from ODP are: Algorithm, Java, First aids, England football, Olympics and Graph theory. We extracted corresponding URLs to each topic and made a set of URLs for each topic. A portion of each URL set is considered as target set T for computing target recall metric. The reported results for each method are the average of obtained results for focused topics.

Evaluator and Conductor Classifiers. Corresponding pages of URL sets of each topic are fetched and two types of classifiers are trained using fetched pages as learning instances. One type of classifiers, we call *evaluator classifiers*, is responsible for computing relevancy of fetched pages to a topic during the focused crawling process and computing r_i in harvest rate formula. We trained one evaluator classifier for each topic. We considered all pages of the URL set of the topic as positive samples and as a double number of positive samples, we randomly selected pages belonged to other topics of ODP and considered them as negative samples of the evaluator classifier.

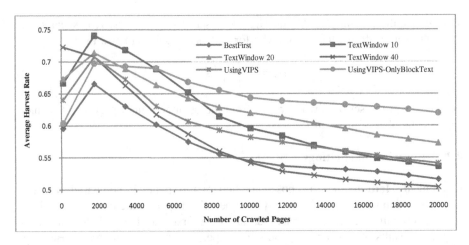

Fig. 3. Performance comparison between two versions of the proposed method, Best first method and three versions of Text window method, based on average harvest rate metric

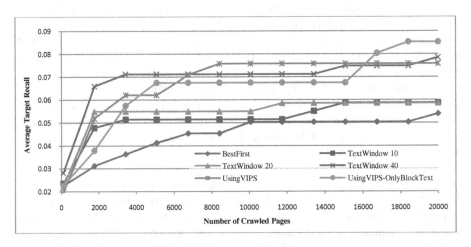

Fig. 4. Performance comparison between two versions of the proposed method, Best first method and three versions of Text window method, based on average target recall metric

The other type of classifiers is used by the crawlers for computing relevancy of different parts of the pages to a topic. We call them *conductor classifiers*. They trained like evaluator classifiers for each topic but they didn't use whole set of positive training sample. They only use positive samples which are not included in the target set T of the topics. Multi Layer Perceptron (MLP) neural network is employed as the classification algorithm which is a good choice for focused crawling [16].

4.3   Experimental Results

We established a relatively long crawling process by fetching 20000 pages for each pair of topics and methods. Figures 3 and 4 illustrate the comparison of two versions of the proposed method with Best first method and three versions of Text window method with different sizes of the windows, based on harvest rate and target recall metrics respectively. Except one version of the proposed method which only uses link context relevancy, all of the compared methods utilize a combination of page text relevancy and link context relevancy based on formula 1 for computing link scores. As can be seen in figure 3, average harvest rate of the proposed method which computes link scores only based on the text of the blocks is more than all of the other compared methods after crawling 20000 pages. The Superiority of the proposed method over its competitor which is the Text window method with window size 20, increases after crawling more number of pages. An interesting point of figure 3 results is the higher harvest rate of the proposed method that only uses block text than the version of this method that in addition to block text, uses page text.

As we can see in figure 4 both versions of the proposed method outperforms the other compared methods based on the target recall metric and they are very close to Text window method with window size 40. We believe that the harvest rate metric can reflect focused crawling performance better than target recall metric. Because harvest rate computes relevancy of each crawled web page by utilizing evaluator classifiers but target recall is only concerned on pages which are in target set T and ignores many relevant pages that are not included in T.

Table 1. Performance evaluation of focused crawling methods after fetching 20000 pages

Focused Crawling Methods	Harvest Rate		Target Recall	
	AVG	STDV	AVG	STDV
Best First	0.52	0.33	0.05	0.05
Text Window 10	0.54	0.30	0.06	0.06
Text Window 20	0.57	0.30	0.06	0.05
Text Window 40	0.50	0.30	0.08	0.09
Using VIPS	0.54	0.29	0.08	0.10
Using VIPS- Only Block Text	**0.62**	**0.23**	**0.09**	**0.09**

To have an overall comparison, average harvest rate and target recall and their standard deviations after crawling 20000 pages are reported in table 1 for different methods. This table shows that the version of the proposed method which only uses text of the blocks, has better performance than the other compared methods based on average harvest rate and average target recall metrics. Also the standard deviation of harvest rate of this method is lower than the others and the standard deviation of its target recall is acceptable in comparison with the others. The reported standard deviations in table 1 are not surprising at all when they are compared to reported standard errors in [3] and [15].

5   Conclusion

In this paper we proposed a focused crawling method which uses VIPS algorithm for link context extraction. Since VIPS algorithm utilizes visual clues in page segmentation process and is independent from HTML structure of the page, it can find the size and the position of link contexts in an accurate manner. The experimental results show that the version of the proposed method which only uses text of the blocks for computing link scores, outperforms the other compared methods based on harvest rate and target recall metrics.

References

1. Gulli, A.: The indexable web is more than 11.5 billion pages. In: International Conference on World Wide Web (2005)
2. Lewandowski, D.: A three-year study on the freshness of Web search engine databases. Journal of Information Science 34(6), 817–831 (2008)
3. Pant, G., Srinivasan, P.: Link contexts in classifier-guided topical crawlers. IEEE Transactions on Knowledge and Data Engineering 18(1), 107–122 (2006)
4. Attardi, G., Gullì, A., Sebastiani, F.: Automatic Web page categorization by link and context analysis. In: Proc. THAI 1999, pp. 105–119 (1999)
5. Cai, D., Yu, S., Wen, J.R., Ma, W.Y.: Block-based web search. In: Proceedings of the 27th ACM SIGIR Conference, pp. 456–463 (2004)
6. De Bra, P.M.E., Post, R.D.J.: Information retrieval in the World Wide Web: Making client-based searching feasible. Computer Networks and ISDN Systems 27(2), 183–192 (1994)
7. Chakrabarti, S., Van den Berg, M., Dom, B.: Focused crawling: a new approach to topic-specific Web resource discovery. Computer Networks 31(11-16), 1623–1640 (1999)
8. Chakrabarti, S., Punera, K., Subramanyam, M.: Accelerated focused crawling through on-line relevance feedback. In: Proceedings of the Eleventh International Conference on World Wide Web, WWW 2002, pp. 148–159 (2002)
9. Peng, T., Zhang, C., Zuo, W.: Tunneling enhanced by web page content block partition for focused crawling. Concurrency and Computation: Practice and Experience 20(1), 61–74 (2008)
10. Cai, D., Yu, S., Wen, J.R., Ma, W.Y.: VIPS: a visionbased page segmentation algorithm. Microsoft Technical Report, MSR-TR-2003-79 (2003)
11. Diligenti, M., Coetzee, F.M., Lawrence, S., Giles, C.L., Gori, M.: Focused Crawling Using Context Graphs. In: Proceedings of 26th VLDB Conference, pp. 527–534 (2000)
12. Rennie, J., McCallum, A.K.: Using reinforcement learning to spider the web efficiently. In: Proceedings of the Sixteenth International Conference on Machine Learning, pp. 335–343 (1999)
13. Liu, H., Janssen, J., Milios, E.: Using HMM to learn user browsing patterns for focused web crawling. Data & Knowledge Engineering 59(2), 270–329 (2006)
14. Batsakis, S., Petrakis, E.G.M., Milios, E.: Improving the performance of focused web crawlers. Data & Knowledge Engineering 68(10), 1001–1013 (2009)
15. Wang, C., Guan, Z.-Y., Chen, C., Bu, J.-J., Wang, J.-F., Lin, H.-Z.: On-line topical importance estimation: an effective focused crawling algorithm combining link and content analysis. Journal of Zhejiang University SCIENCE A 10(8), 1114–1124 (2009)
16. http://rdf.dmoz.org/ (accessed, October 2011)

The Co-design of Business and IT Systems: A Case in Supply Chain Management

Navid Karimi Sani, Shokoofeh Ketabchi, and Kecheng Liu

Informatics Research Centre, University of Reading, UK
{n.karimisani,s.ketabchi,k.liu}@reading.ac.uk

Abstract. The twenty-first century business environment is extremely competitive and challenging. It forces organisations to deploy strategies in order to maintain their position in the marketplace. As a result, they should modify their current practices and transform themselves in a way that they can cope with existing challenges. But they do not reflect these changes in their IT systems. First, the pace of the change is fast, and organisations are forced to change their business rules and processes frequently. But they do not reflect these changes in their IT systems. Second, organisations utilise IT systems without carefully considering its effects on other parts of the organisation. Therefore, the challenge is to organically align IT with business activities in order to improve the overall performance. The solution to this challenge is to co-design the business and IT systems. Co-design of business and IT is a field that concerns with gathering and processing knowledge from different parts of an organisation to transform business processes and IT systems simultaneously. This paper aims to expand co-design theory and also to develop a co-design method to offer practical solutions for aligning business processes and IT systems. The organisational semiotics is the theoretical and methodological foundation of this research.

Keywords: Co-Design of Business and IT systems, Information Systems, Organisational Semiotics, Organisational Onion, Norm Analysis Method, Supply Chain Management.

1 Introduction

Organisations are social entities which are composed of coordinated and structured systems that have a shared goal and interact with their external environment. In any organisation, there are various behaviours that occur more frequently than others. In order to maximise performance and minimise the error, organisations try to capture the pattern of these behaviours and make them standardised [6][16]. Obviously the next step after formalising work processes is to automate them [9][15]. Therefore, regulations, standards, controls, and sometimes tasks should be built into machine instead of being carried out by individuals. This is highly beneficial for firms in the sense that individuals are complex systems, and they have their own agendas which are not necessarily in line with organisational goals. Moreover, individuals are not

S. Dua et al. (Eds.): ICISTM 2012, CCIS 285, pp. 13–27, 2012.

free of errors, because of factors that affect their behaviour such as health, attitude, and emotion. Nowadays business organisations recognise the benefit of IT systems to the extent that they believe it is an indispensable element of their operations.

Organisations change over time to adapt to their external forces, or to improve their organisational performance. However, they do not reflect those changes in their IT systems. In other words, the IT system, which was developed to carry out business activities, tasks and norms, is not able to do so anymore [11]; for the reason that changes are not reflected in IT. As a result, the IT system, which was once supportive, becomes the bottle neck of business activities.

The solution to tackle this issue is to lessen the gap between the application of changes in the business system and IT system. The co-design of business and IT systems is the field which addressed this problem and tries to solve it by gathering, interpreting and using knowledge from different parts of an organisation to transform business processes and IT systems simultaneously in order to support stakeholders in their actions. In fact, co-design is a cross organisational process which people are involved from different parts of the organisation.

This work is motivated by the co-design of business and IT systems theory as introduced by Liu *et al.* (2002) and is the extension to their work [13]. In this theory, they suggest that the IT system should be considered as an integral part of the business system. Therefore, these two systems should be designed together in order to minimise the gap between them. The co-design of business and IT systems is described as a cross organisational processes in which people are involved from different parts of the organisation. The rest of the paper is organised as follows: a brief background on co-design field is presented in section two. Then, the co-design of Business and IT systems (Co-BITS) method is discussed in section three, followed by explaining its application in section four. Finally, the validity of the method is discussed in section five and paper is concluded in section six.

2   Co-design of Business and IT Systems

It is not rare to hear from organisations that the IT system, which could support business activities before, turned into a bottleneck [11][17][18]. By looking closely into these organisations, one can find that shortly after they deployed their IT system, they made some changes in business processes, but they did not reflect the relevant changes into their IT system. The solution to tackle this issue is to lessen the gap between the application of changes in the business system and IT system. The co-design of business and IT systems is the field which addresses this problem and tries to solve it by gathering, interpreting and using knowledge from different parts of an organisation to transform business processes and IT systems simultaneously in order to support stakeholders in their actions.

Several research works have been carried out in recent years which claim to address co-design [20][23]. However, by looking closer, it will be apparent that they simply talk about design as a one-off project. In another work [8], the focus is on problem solving and collaboration between stakeholders. It talks about the co-design and providing a unifying language among stakeholders rather than co-designing systems and sub-systems.

The method that we aim to introduce here is based on the theory of co-design of business and IT systems introduced by Liu *et al.* (2002). This theory is based on organisational semiotics (a branch of semiotics) in which organisations are viewed as information systems; for the reason that information is created, stored, processed and used to facilitate coordination and communication among different parts to achieve organisational goals. Liu *et al.* (2002) argued that deployment of information technology should only changes the way the business is carried out, but not the nature of business [13]. This supports the interrelation and co-design of business system and IT system (as part of the business system).

Liu *et al.* (2002) suggested that activities in organisations which helps towards achieving organisational goals [13]. These actions will normally result in changes physically or socially in an organisation. Stamper (1992) in what he called *organisational onion* [21] suggested that these actions are categorised into three layers (figure 1): *informal, formal* and *technical*.

- Informal: organisations initially launch with a group of people which have a shared goal and try to do some activities together. Communications and rules governing the organisation are informal and unstructured. Individuals start to negotiate on rules, responsibilities, beliefs and values to make a sense of shared goals and culture in the organisation.
- Formal: The bigger become the organisation, it become harder and more costly to manage activities and communications. The only way to decrease the cognitive load of organisations is to bureaucratise some parts that contain repetitive processes, activities, outputs, set of skills and etc.
- Technical: As formal organisations experience bureaucracy, in some aspects human agents can be replaced by machine agents to cut the cost and time of doing the task and de-bureaucratise the human side of organisation and allow the individuals to focus on more creative and innovative tasks.

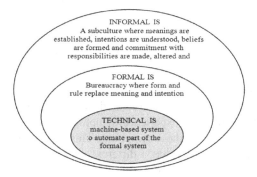

Fig. 1. The organisational onion [10][11]

Next section introduces the Co-BITS method as an approach to design business and IT systems as simultaneously as possible.

3   A Method for the Co-design of Business and IT Systems (Co-BITS)

The proposed method to co-design of business and IT systems (Co-BITS) aims to lessen the gap between the business and I system in the occurrence of change. The method is inspired by the work of Liu *et al.* (2002) in which they introduce the theory of co-design of business and IT systems [13]. Liu *et al.* (2002) emphasises on considering business and IT system as one integral unit; so that, they are designed and evolved together. Co-BITS has also benefited from the research in relevant fields, particularly soft systems methodology (SSM) [5]. On account of the fact that organisations are information systems designed in three layers [10], the assumption in Co-BITS is that the whole process of co-design is happening in an organisation as a three layered information system; informal-formal-technical (figure 2).

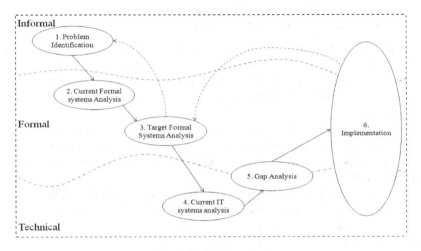

Fig. 2. Co-BITS method

As shown in Figure 2, phases are placed in different layers based on the nature of tasks carried out in each of them. In the following parts, each phase and related tools and techniques are explained.

Phase 1. Problem Identification: The aim of this phase is to identify existing problems and formulate them in a structured way to be investigated and solved. In an organisation, different parts experience symptoms of a problem, but they may not understand the root cause of these symptoms. This issue happens because of two main reasons; first, each individual has a different understanding of the system of work. Second, most people experience some parts of a complex problem. In complex organisational setting, defining the problem requires input from stakeholders who belong to different divisions and work units. Therefore, organisations should bring relevant stakeholders from affected work units to co-design the required changes in business and IT systems. Therefore, the first step is to identify these stakeholders.

Stakeholder identification from MEASUR [12] is used as the analysis technique to find the related stakeholders. This tool (figure 3) identifies stakeholders by their roles: actor, client, provider, facilitator, governing body, and bystander.

Fig. 3. The stakeholder onion [12]

By identifying stakeholders, the power-impact matrix (figure 4) can be used to analyse their influence and the degree of their impact on the system.

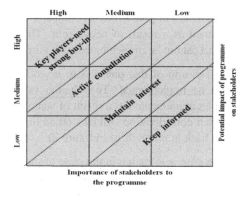

Fig. 4. The power-impact matrix [7]

Then, stakeholders are evaluated regarding the problem situation (table 1):

- Power: represents the importance of stakeholders with regards to the project or programme. It ranges from 1 to 3; 1 stands for low power and rating 3 stands for high.
- Impact: represents the potential impact of the project or programme on stakeholders. It ranges from 1 to 3; 1 stands for low impact and rating 3 stands for high.
- Distance: represents the number of layers between the core and a particular stakeholder in the stakeholder onion. This distance rating shows the level of involvement of stakeholders in the project. It ranges from 1 to 6 in which 6 is Actor, and is 1: bystander.

Phase 2. Current Formal System Analysis: This Phase, current formal system analysis, all business processes, activities and business rules related to the problem situation should be studies and identified. These will demonstrate the current practice of the organisation with regard to the problem.

Phase 3. Target Formal System Analysis: After carrying out phase two, those processes, activities and norms that seem to have problems or cause difficulties to others are determined and explained. It is now time to find proper solutions. These solutions might lead to change in business processes, activities or norms.

There is an arrow going back to phase one (figure 2); this creates a loop between first three phases of Co-BITS in the occurrence of disagreement on the problem(s) and/or solution(s). The loop between phases 1, 2, and 3 (figure 2) tries to solve the weakness of traditional design methods in which a once-only gap analysis identifies the solution to achieve a predefined set of problems [22]. Indeed, this loop creates a continual process that evaluates the fit between amended problems and proposed solutions.

Phase 4. Current IT system Analysis: In this phase, relevant IT systems and their capabilities will be analysed and investigated.

Phase 5. Gap Analysis: In this phase, a comparison is carried out to find out which part of desired changes in the formal system can be implemented into the IT system. The target formal which is the result of phase three is compared against the current IT system's capabilities determined as a result of phase four. The result of this phase shows which solutions can and cannot be implemented with current IT facilities.

Phase 6. Implementation: The aim of this phase is to investigate the changes and identify which ones should be implemented. The change valuation tool helps to identify which solutions can be implemented as a result of stakeholders' participation. Those changes that need further consideration will be studied further by going back to phase three (shown by arrow back tp phase three in figure 2).

Although the desirable situation is to maintain the state of the organisation after all changes are implemented and operations are improved, organisations change to keep up with the external and internal forces. As a result, there will inevitable changes in future while we aim to maintain the integrity of business and IT systems. Therefore, this phase also includes guidelines for future changes in organisations. If some changes are needed, related documentation can be reviewed to find out affected parts of business system, IT system and involved individuals, and then, by discussing it with related stakeholders, it will be either validated through change valuations or exposed to further adjustments which will be again checked by stakeholders. At the end, the documentations should be updated accordingly.

4   The Co-design Method in Action

In the previous section, the proposed method and its theoretical benefits has been discussed. Here, we demonstrate its practice and application in a real world situation.

The case study is based on the practice in a medium size Oil and Gas company focused on oil reserves in Africa. They also have offices in London and Boston and listed on the main board of London stock exchange (LSE). They have been quite successful during recent years by effective asset management during their operations. To maintain this growth, they always reassess their processes and practices. As a result of one of these recent reassessments, they realised that they need better firmer infrastructure to keep up with the growth. One of the main concerns was their relationships with suppliers. Therefore, they decided to review and reassess all the supply chain management activities to solve issues faced. Supply chain management (SCM) includes planning and management of all activities in procurement, logistics, coordinating and collaborating with suppliers, and managing payments. It is a cross-departmental function which aims to integrate main business processes and functions together.

Due to continuous growth during recent years, the volume of company's operations have been extended; hence, the number of their suppliers increased without defining a proper management procedure for dealing with them. Poorly defined SCM processes and activities in combination with their misalignment with IT systems were the main reasons for SCM malfunction. Taking into account these, the company is a suitable candidate for implementing Co-BITS since it can investigate all mentioned issues and offer solutions. In the following section, all phases of Co-BITS are used to study this company and the application of related tools and techniques are explained.

Phase1. The problem identification step seeks to find the roots of the problem described by different people who see different symptoms and look for different solutions. The first step is to find those people who are affected by SCM malfunction. Table 1 shows the result of stakeholder analysis.

Table 1. Stakeholder analysis for SCM

ID	Name	Role	Power rate (1-3)	Impact rate (1-3)	Distance rate (1-6)	Stakeholder Weight
S1	Commercial manager	facilitator	3	3	3	8.57
S2	SCM Manager	actor	2	3	6	10.48
S3	Information Management Consultant	actor	1	2	6	8.57
S4	SAP Consultant	provider	1	3	4	7.62
S5	Senior contract manager	provider	2	2	4	7.62
S6	Contract expert	provider	2	2	4	7.62
S7	Financial Manager	client	3	1	5	8.57
S8	(EHSS)manager	governing body	3	3	2	7.62
S9	App1 Consultant	actor	1	1	6	7.62
S10	App1 User	actor	1	3	6	9.51
S11	Partner A	facilitator	1	2	3	5.71

As a result of communication, brainstorming sessions and workshops with participation of these stakeholders, the roots of problems which caused different symptoms are identified (figure 5) using root-problem analysis tool inspired by [2][3]. Figure 5 shows the root problem analysis of SCM, mainly for requisition procedure.

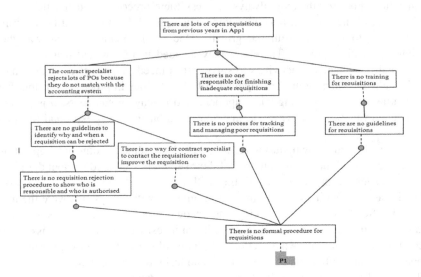

Fig. 5. SCM root problem analysis: requisition root problem

Phase 2. All related processes and activities will be identified and analysed to understand which of them lead to the problem and should be removed, changed or improved. In addition, business rules related to each activity will be studied in this phase to specify the expected behaviour of agents. Figure 6 shows the current practice of SCM using use case diagram. Both processes, 'Purchase' and 'Receive and Invoice', are related to the requisition procedure discussed in root problem analysis (phase 1).

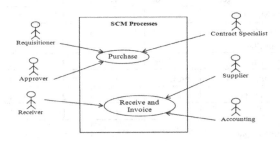

Fig. 6. SCM processes

Phase 3. As a result of the analysis of all processes and activities, some improvements are proposed and a new process model is proposed (figure 7).

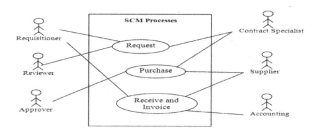

Fig. 7. Proposed SCM processes

As seen in figure 8, a new process is added which is called 'request'; the 'purchase' process is also redesigned. Figure 8 show the activities in the 'request' process which includes initiating a requisition of good(s)/service(s) through investigating their existence before considering the need for a purchase order (figure 8).

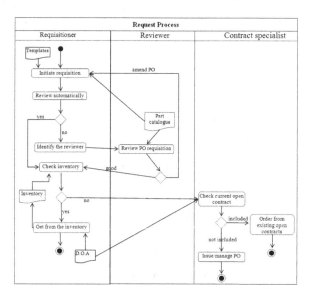

Fig. 8. Proposed 'Request' process

In the desired purchase process, suppliers are identified and activities to buy goods/services are carried out. The procedure for tracking orders and acknowledgements for orders is required to ensure that Suppliers are aware of the order. Moreover, by adding the new "request" process in change 1, all activities and norms for purchase process (and also request process as discussed in change1) should be redefined.

Norm Analysis Method (NAM) is used to specify business rules [10][19]. NAM treats patterns of behaviour and business knowledge as norms which govern people's actions. Identifying the norms will enable us to understand and model the requisition practice in the organisation. The general form for specifying a norm is as follows [10]:

Whenever <context>,if <state>,then <agent>,is <deontic operator>,to <action>

The <context> refers to the situation while the <state> shows the conditions. The <agent> is the actor which this norm is applied to. The <deontic operator> can be obliged, permitted or prohibited. The <action> is the behaviour that the specified agent should carry out. Table 2 shows norms for the proposed request process.

Table 2. Norm analysis for proposed 'Request' process

Process	Activity	ID	whenever <context>	if <statement>	then <agent>	is <operator>	to <action>
Requisition	Initiate Requisition	N1	In Requisition	the requisitioner wants to initiate a requisition	Requisiti oner	obliged	choose the right template for requisition from company's templates
Requisition	Initiate Requisition	N2	In Requisition	the requisition is about a technical good for well operation	Requisiti oner	obliged	choose the required good(s) from the part catalogue
Requisition	Initiate Requisition	N3	In Requisition	the requisition is about a technical good for oil production exploration/operation	Requisiti oner	obliged	choose the required good(s) from the part catalogue
Requisition	Initiate Requisition	N4	In Requisition	requisitioner wants to submit a purchase order for goods	Requisiti oner	obliged	provide information on: (name of the good) AND (technical specification) AND (needed date)
Requisition	Initiate Requisition	N5	In Requisition	requisitioner wants to submit a purchase order for services	Requisiti oner	obliged	provide information on: (name of the good) AND (technical specification) AND (Start and finish date of needed period)
Requisition	Initiate Requisition	N6	In Requisition	requisitioner wants to submit a purchase order requisition	Requisiti oner	permitted	recommend info on (supplier) AND (approximate price)
Requisition	Review automatically	N1	to submit a requisition	the requisitioner is expert in the field	Requisiti oner	permitted	skip the review procedure
Requisition	get from inventory	N1	to receive goods from inventory	the requisitioner request a good from inventory	inventory manager	obliged	update the inventory list

Phase 4. After detailed analysis of processes and activities, target ones are proposed. Now this is the time to see whether the current IT system can support these changes or not. There are two applications to support current business activities and norms. We refer to these applications as App1 and App2. Table 3 presents a list of all applications with their capabilities.

Table 3. Related technical system analysis

Application	Capabilities
App1	• Sourcing of goods and services, Automated workflows, Authorisation of requisitions and orders • Receipting, Invoice registration and matching, Internal supplies and stores management • Full visibility of the cost channels, Automated commitment accounting support • Information Management tools, Addressing indirect spend (e.g employee travel expense claim)
App2	• Financials management containing nominal ledger, payables and receivables ledgers, consolidation, corporate allocations, multi-currency, dual base currency, fixed assets, budget management, and debtor management • Order Management including sales, purchasing, inventory management operations, and easily integrated with partners and customers • Customising processes and their sequence for purchasing, sales, and inventory management

Phase 5. The aim is to find out to what extend the target formal system, developed as a result of third phase, can be implemented into the current IT system. The capabilities of related applications are presented in phase 4 (table 3). It is now time to map the target processes, activities, norms and data model into the IT applications based on their capabilities. In other words, we want to specify which part of the target formal system can be performed by the current technical system.

IT systems can play two roles regarding processes, activities and norms. Table 4 shows in which application business process workflow of the target formal system can be implemented.

Table 4. Mapping target formal into IT capabilities: workflow management system

	App1	App2
Process		
Requisition	√	√
Purchase	√	
Receive/Invoice/Pay	√	√

Table 5 illustrate details of the level of automation for activities and norms of each process.

Table 5. Mapping target formal into current IT capabilities: automation

			IT Application Name	
			App1	App2
Process	**Activity**	**Norm**		
Request	Initiate Requisition	N2,N3,N4,N5	√	
Request	Review Automatically	N1	√	
Request	Get from inventory	N1	√	

Phase 6. All changes and related applications are determined during previous phases. Changes should be evaluated by stakeholders considering several criteria. This valuation will offer a clearer view to changes. Moreover, stakeholders will rate changes based on their perceptions; therefore, all views are taken into account and there will be less worries about unfairness, and political/social pressures [14]. The valuation tool proposed in this paper (table 6) is inspired by the work of Liu *et al.* (2011b). In this template, a list of stakeholders is written on top; they will evaluate the change considering several factors (placed on the first left column of table 6). We use the ID field for each stakeholder to refer to them and stakeholders' weightings are the total weightings calculated in table 1. In this valuation tool, each criterion is weighted according to its significance to the request process. These weightings are not fixed and can be adjusted for each change. Total weightings for stakeholders and criteria each sums to 1 respectively. Stakeholders rate each criterion based on value range -3 to +3. Then, the final rating will be calculated as shown in table 6.

Table 6. Valuation 'Request' process

Change	Change 1: Request Process											
Stakeholders	S_1	S_2	S3	S4	S5	S6	S7	S8	S9	S10	S11	S12
	Stakehol der weight											
	8.57	10.48	8.57	7.62	7.62	7.62	8.57	7.62	7.62	10.48	9.51	5.71
Criteria	Criteria weight											
Core competence	10	2	2	3	3	3	2	1	1	2	3	3	2
Knowledge skill specialisation	3	3	3	3	3	3	3	3	2	3	1	3	2
Learning capabilities	5	2	3	2	3	2	3	3	0	3	2	2	1

Table 6. (*continued*)

Task satisfaction	5	0	-1	-1	-2	0	-2	-1	-1	1	-1	0	0
Social contact	0												
Adaptability	10	2	3	2	3	3	3	2	-2	2	1	2	2
Interaction	5	3	3	3	3	2	3	1	1	2	3	3	2
Transparency	10	1	2	2	1	-1	0	-2	-1	2	3	3	1
Operational risk	0												
Environmental risk	0												
Security Risk	0												
Productivity	10	-1	-1	1	1	3	3	1	-2	1	1	3	2
Quality-timeliness	10	3	2	3	3	3	3	3	2	3	1	3	1
Quality-output	5	-1	-2	1	1	3	3	1	0	2	2	3	2
Financial benefit	6	2	3	2	3	2	1	2	-3	1	2	3	3
Reliability/consistency	6	1	1	2	-1	2	1	2	-2	2	-1	2	2
Cultural benefit	0												
Customer benefit	0												
Sustainability	10	2	3	3	1	2	1	2	1	0	0	1	2
Information security	5	-3	-2	0	1	-2	-2	-3	0	0	-2	-1	-2
	$VSi=Sum(stakeholder\ rate*factors'\ weight)$	122	148	198	183	188	166	108	-34	167	119	224	151
	$V=VSi*Stakeholder\ weight$	104 5.54	1551.04	169 6.86	139 4.46	143 2.56	126 4.92	925.56	-259.08	127 2.54	1247.12	213 0.24	862.21
Total cultural value	Sum(v)/3	48.54656667											

This valuation should be carried out for every change; table 6 is an example of change valuation. The value of 48.55% for this change is discussed with stakeholders and they decided to go ahead with the change. The result of this valuation for every change will be discussed with stakeholders and relevant decisions will be made subjectively. In other words, the implementation of changes is made by direct participation of stakeholders.

5   Validity of the Method for IS Design

Co-BITS is the first attempt at conducting a methodological approach to the field of co-design of business and IT systems. The organisational semiotics is the theoretical foundation which regards organisations as information systems. Long before the existence of technology, there were organisations, human interactions and needed information was captured with other means [1]. We tend to follow the same principle and consider organisations as information systems with three layers; the classification of "informal-formal-technical" provides analysts with a better view of who should be contacted and what should be studied. Those tasks put in the informal layer are concerned with human interaction, organisational culture, employees view towards changes and etc. Consequently, tasks in the formal layer include studying the organisation including human interactions, but repetitiveness and predictability are main features of actions in this layer. Finally, in the technical layer, the main concern is the automation of the business processes and the interaction with machine. This distinction organises the analysts' mentality and helps through the process of co-design.

A well defined design method must have three main elements [4]; (i) a good view of organisation's processes along with activities performed in each process, (ii) business rules which control these activities, and (iii) an information system to capture and feed the necessary information for carrying out activities. The proposed co-design method includes these elements and the applicability has been discussed in detail in section 4. In other words, use case and activity diagrams are familiar modelling techniques in business practice and help to obtain a clear view of current states of an organisation and facilitate communication among different people to reach an agreement for the desired state. This shows that the proposed co-design method has the first main element of a well defined design practice.

Since business rules are identified in a way that it is readable by human and machine and it is specified that which rules are related to which activity and which agent is carrying out that activity, any changes in these rules can be reflected immediately. The root-problem analysis and change valuation techniques are inspired from current literature with strong theoretical and practical background as cited in this paper. The root-problem analysis helps to find roots that cause problems with clear notations. Moreover, the change valuation tool makes it easier to capture stakeholder's view, and reduces unfair decision makings with regards to every change.

In conclusion, the advantages of proposed tools and techniques are to make the co-design process flexible enough to be adaptable to changes. In other words, it will be able to adapt and adjust to future needs. Therefore, the co-design model is well-defined, adaptable and extendable, and helps organisation to manage problems and changes effectively as it did for the supply chain management case.

6   Conclusion

The co-design of business and IT systems as discussed in this paper offers new insightful perspectives towards organisations. The IT system is considered to be an integral part of the formal business systems; as a result, both systems are designed and evolved together. Co-BITS is the first attempt to bring structure and methodological view to the field of co-design. It helps to design a better supply chain management practice by involving people from different disciplines aligned with IT systems. A SCM function from an Oil and Gas company is examined as a case study and findings are discussed. Adopted tools and techniques in the co-design model are industry standardised; it makes the co-design model easily applicable and users can spend time on main and new principles instead of learning new techniques. This also facilitates communications of concerns and objectives. As a result of several follow up interviews with related stakeholders, the benefits of employed system identified and brought here.

The focus of this paper was mainly on the relation between formal and technical layers of the organizational onion. Future work can examine the effects and relations between all three parts with more emphasis on the informal layer of organisations. The topics such as conflict between stakeholders, political power game which results to biased attempts to change the direction of change are some of the topics that can be addressed in informal layer.

References

1. Beynon-Davis, P.: Significant threads: The nature of data. International Journal of Information Management 29(3), 170–188 (2009)
2. Boness, K.: Goal-Refinement Appraisal of Soft Projects (GRASAP). Doctoral Thesis, University of Reading (2011)
3. Boness, K., Finkelstein, A., Harrison, R.: A method for assessing confidence in requirements analysis. Information and Software Technology 53(10), 1084–1096 (2011)
4. Buede, D.M.: The engineering design of systems: models and methods, 2nd edn. Wiley-Blackwell (2009)
5. Checkland, P., Scholes, J.: Soft Systems Methodology In Action. John Wiley & Sons Ltd., Chichester (1990)
6. Daft, R.L.: Organization Theory and Design. South Western Educational Publishing, Hampshire (2007)
7. Department for Business, Enterprise and Regulatory Reform (BERR): Guidelines for Managing Projects, UK (2007), http://www.berr.gov.uk
8. Gasson, S.: A Framework for the Co-Design of Business and IT Systems. In: Proceedings of Hawaii International Conference on System Sciences (HICSS-41), pp. 348–358 (2008)
9. Gustafsson, P., Höök, D., Franke, U., Johnson, P.: Modeling the IT Impact on Organizational Structure. In: Proceeding of the IEEE International Enterprise Distributed Object Computing Conference, pp. 14–23 (2009)
10. Liu, K.: Semiotics in Information Systems Engineering. Cambridge University Press, UK (2000)
11. Liu, K., Karimi Sani, N., Ketabchi, S., Mcloughlin, E.: Co-design of an Adaptable System for Information Management. In: The 13th International Conference on Enterprise Information Systems (ICEIS 2011), Beijing, China (2011a)
12. Liu, K., Sun, L., Tan, S.: Modelling complex systems for project planning: a semiotics motivated method. International Journal of General Systems 35(3), 313–327 (2006)
13. Liu, K., Sun, L., Bennett, K.: Co-Design of Business and IT Systems. Information Systems Frontiers 4(3), 251–256 (2002)
14. Liu, K., Sun, L., Jambari, D., Michell, V., Chong, S.: A Design of Business-Technology Alignment Consulting Framework. In: Mouratidis, H., Rolland, C. (eds.) CAiSE 2011. LNCS, vol. 6741, pp. 422–435. Springer, Heidelberg (2011b)
15. Mintzberg, H.: The Structuring of Organization: A synthesis of the Research. Prentice-Hall, Englewood Cliffs (1979)
16. Mintzberg, H.: Mintzberg on Management: Inside Our Strange World of Organizations. Hungry Minds Inc., New York (1989)
17. Pessman, R.S.: Software Engineering: A Practitioner's Approach, 5th edn. McGraw-Hill (2003)
18. Pessman, R.S.: Software Engineering: A Practitioner's Approach, 6th edn. McGraw-Hill (2007)

19. Salter, A., Liu, K.: Using Semantic Analysis and Norm Analysis to Model Organisations. In: Proceedings of the 4th International Conference on Enterprise Information Systems, Ciudad Real, Spain, pp. 847–850 (2002)
20. Snoeck, M., Michiels, C.: Domain Modeling and the Co-Design of Business Rules and in the Telecommunication Business Area. Information Systems Frontiers 4(3), 331–342 (2002)
21. Stamper, R.K.: Language and Computer in Organized Behaviour. In: van de Riet, R.P., Meersman, R. (eds.) Linguistics Instruments in Knowledge Engineering, pp. 143–163. Elsevier Science, Amsterdam (1992)
22. Simon, H.A.: The Structure of Ill-Structured Problems. Artificial Intelligence 4, 145–180 (1973)
23. Tam, M.M.C., Choi, D.H.L., Chung, W.W.C.: Innovative approach to co-design of information systems: a case study in a small manufacturing business. In: Hawaii International Conference on Information Systems: Collaboration Technology Organizational Systems and Technology, Hawaii, USA (1994)

Cardinality Statistics Based Maximal Frequent Itemsets Mining

Meera M. Dhabu and Parag S. Deshpande

Department of Computer Science,
Visvesvaraya National Institute of Technology, Nagpur, India
{meeradhabu,psdeshpande}@cse.vnit.ac.in

Abstract. Extracting frequent itemsets is an important task in many data mining applications. Since the result set of all the frequent itemsets are likely to be undesirably large, condensed representations, such as maximal and closed frequent itemsets are used. The set of frequent closed itemsets uniquely determines the exact frequency of all itemsets, yet it can be orders of magnitudes smaller than the set of all frequent itemsets. But whenever there are very long patterns present in the data, it is often impractical to generate the entire set of closed frequent itemsets. The only recourse is to mine the maximal frequent itemsets in the domain with very long patterns. In this paper, we propose a new approach for mining all maximal frequent itemsets which introduces and makes use of the compact data structure: *Reduced Transaction Pattern List (RTPL)*, for representing the database. Our implementation exploits the advantages of combining *RTPL* representation with statistical information of cardinality of each item in database. We devise pruning strategy to substantially reduce the combinatorial search space by making use of statistical information of items at two levels. Our experiments using synthetic and real-world standard benchmark dataset shows that the proposed algorithm outperforms algorithms not using cardinality statistical information.

Keywords: maximal frequent itemsets mining, association rules, data mining, cardinality statistics.

1   Introduction

It has been well recognized that frequent pattern mining plays an essential role in many important data mining tasks. These tasks include the discovery of association rules [3,12], strong rules, correlations, sequential rules, episodes [16], partial periodicity [4], multi-dimensional patterns, and many other important discovery tasks [13]. The problem of frequent itemsets mining is formulated as follows [23]: Given a large database of transactions, find all frequent itemsets, where a frequent itemsets is one that occurs in at-least a user-specified percentage of the transactions. However, it is also well known that frequent pattern mining often generates a very large number of frequent itemsets and rules, which reduce not only efficiency but also effectiveness of mining since user has to sift through a large number of mined rules to find useful

S. Dua et al. (Eds.): ICISTM 2012, CCIS 285, pp. 28–39, 2012.

rules. Most pattern mining algorithms have been developed to operate on databases where the longest patterns are relatively short. This leaves data outside the mold unexplorable using most of algorithms.

Most of the pattern-mining algorithms are a variant of Apriori [2]. Apriori employs bottom-up, breadth-first search that enumerates every single frequent itemset. Apriori-inspired algorithms [7, 17, 22] show good performance with sparse datasets such as marketbasket data, where the frequent patterns are very short. However, with dense datasets such as telecommunications and census data, where there are many, long frequent patterns, the performance of these algorithms degrades incredibly. In many real world problems (e.g., patterns in biosequences, census data, etc.) finding long itemsets of length 30 or 40 is not uncommon [6].

There are two current solutions to the long pattern mining problem. The first one is to mine only the maximal frequent itemsets [1, 6, 8, 9, 15]. While mining maximal sets helps understand the long patterns in dense domains, it leads to a loss of information since subset frequency is not available.

The second solution is to mine only the frequent closed itemsets [5, 18, 19, 24]. Closed sets are lossless in the sense that they uniquely determine the set of all frequent itemsets and their exact frequency. At the same time closed itemsets can themselves be orders of magnitude smaller than all frequent itemsets. But, on dense datasets the set of all closed patterns would grow to be too large. The only recourse is to mine the maximal frequent patterns in such domains.

1.1   Problem Definition

The problem of mining maximal frequent itemsets (MFI) can be formally stated as follows: Let $I = \{i_1, i_2, i_3, ..., i_m\}$ be a set of m distinct elements called items. A transactional database TDB is a set of transactions, where each transaction, denoted as a tuple $<tid, X>$, has a unique transaction identity tid and contains a set of items X. A set $X \subset I$ is also called an itemset. An itemset with k items is called a k-itemset. The support of an itemset X, denoted $\sigma(X)$ is the number of transactions in which that itemset occurs as a subset. Thus $\sigma(X) = |t(X)|$. An itemset is frequent if its support is more than or equal to some threshold minimum support (ξ) value, i.e., if $\sigma(X) \geq \xi$, then itemset X is frequent. We denote by F_k the set of frequent k-itemsets, and by FI the set of all frequent itemsets. With these descriptions, we have the following definition:

Definition 1: (Maximal Frequent Itemset): A frequent itemset is called a maximal frequent itemset if it is not a subset of any other frequent itemset and is denoted as **MFI**.

1.2   Related Work

Methods for finding the maximal elements include All-MFS [11], which works by iteratively attempting to extend a working pattern until failure, but it does not guarantee every maximal pattern will be returned. MaxMiner [6] is another algorithm for finding the MFI. It uses efficient pruning techniques to quickly narrow the search.

MaxMiner employs a breadth-first traversal of the search space; it reduces database scanning by employing a lookahead pruning strategy. It also employs item (re)ordering heuristic to increase the effectiveness of superset-frequency pruning. Zaki et al. [25] present the algorithms MaxEclat and MaxClique for identifying MFI. These algorithms are similar to Max-Miner in that they also attempt to look ahead and identify long frequent itemsets early on to help prune the space of candidate itemsets considered. Concurrent to Robert J. et al. work, Lin and Kedem [15] have proposed an algorithm called Pincer-Search for mining long MFI which attempts to identify long patterns throughout the search. The difference between these algorithms is primarily in the long candidate itemsets considered by each. Max-Miner uses a simple, polynomial time candidate generation procedure directed by heuristics, while Pincer-Search uses an NP-hard reduction phase to ensure no long candidate itemset contains any known infrequent itemset.

DepthProject [1] finds long itemsets using a depth first search of a lexicographic tree of itemsets, and uses a counting method based on transaction projections along its branches. DepthProject also uses the look-ahead pruning method with item reordering. It returns a superset of the MFI and would require post-pruning to eliminate non-maximal patterns. FPgrowth [14] uses the novel frequent pattern tree (FP-tree) structure, which is a compressed representation of all the transactions in the database. Nevertheless, since it enumerates all frequent patterns it is impractical when pattern length is long. Mafia [8] is another algorithm for mining the MFI which uses three pruning strategies to remove non-maximal sets. The first strategy is the look-ahead pruning used in MaxMiner. The second is to check if a new set is subsumed by an existing maximal set. The last technique checks if $t(X) \subset t(Y)$. If so X is considered together with Y for extension. Mafia mines a superset of the MFI, and requires a post-pruning step to eliminate non-maximal patterns. Among the most recent methods for MFI are SmartMiner [26] and FPMax [10]. SmartMiner doesn't do explicit maximality checking; rather it uses the information available from the previous combine sets to construct the new combine set at the current node using depth-first search. FPMax mines maximal patterns from the FP-Tree data structure (an augmented prefix tree) originally proposed in [14]. It also maintains the MFI in another prefix tree data structure for maximality checking.

In addition to the pruning strategies used, having a condensed representation of the databases is also vital to achieve good efficiency. Typically, pattern mining algorithms use a horizontal database format, such as the one shown in Table 1, where each row is a *tid* followed by its itemset. Consider a vertical database format, where for each item we list its *tidset*, the set of all transaction *tids* where it occurs. The vertical representation has the following major advantages over the horizontal layout: Firstly, computing the support of itemsets is simpler and faster with the vertical layout since it involves only the intersections of *tidsets* (or compressed bit-vectors if the vertical format is stored as bitmaps [8]). Secondly, with the vertical layout, there is an automatic reduction of the database before each scan. Reduction is achieved by accessing only those itemsets that are relevant to the following scan of the mining process from the disk. Thirdly, the vertical format is more versatile in supporting various search strategies, including breadth-first, depth-first or some other hybrid search.

Despite the many advantages of the vertical format, when the *tidset* cardinality gets very large (e.g., for very frequent items) the intersection time starts to become inordinately large. Furthermore, the size of intermediate *tidsets* generated for frequent patterns can also become very large to fit into main memory. Each representation has its own strengths and limitations. In this paper, we use a *Reduced Transaction Pattern List (RTPL)* representation which leverages some of the positive aspects of existing representations.

2   Proposed Approach

Our general approach is to implement the MFI mining algorithm in the most efficient manner possible, utilizing cardinality statistics of the items present in the database and in minimum run time. The candidate generation and pruning operations are significantly more complicated as they introduce new data in the system at unpredictable intervals. We assume minimal memory requirement and just enough to be able to store all data necessary.

The proposed algorithm can be described using Rymon's generic set-enumeration tree search framework [20]. The Set-Enumeration (SE)-tree is a vehicle for representing and/or enumerating sets in a best-first fashion. The complete SE-tree systematically enumerates elements of a power-set using a pre-imposed order on the underlying set of elements. The idea is to expand sets over an ordered and finite item domain as illustrated in Figure 1 where four items are denoted by their position in the ordering. Figure 1 illustrates an SE-tree for the complete powerset of {1, 2, 3, 4}. The figure assumes a static lexical ordering of the items, but later we describe an optimization that dramatically improves performance by reordering the items.

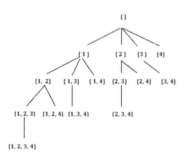

Fig. 1. SE-tree for P ({1, 2, 3, 4})

Proposed algorithm traverses the search space in Depth-first search manner, but always attempts to "look ahead" in order to quickly identify MFI. By identifying a MFI early, it prunes all its subsets from considerations. It returns a superset of the MFI and would require post-pruning to eliminate non-maximal patterns. It also uses heuristics to tune its search in an effort to identify MFI as early as possible. It also uses a technique that can often determine when a new candidate itemset is frequent before accessing the database. The idea is to use the cardinality statistical information gathered at two levels.

2.1   Preprocessing

In this section, we review two data structures used in the proposed MFI algorithm: *Transaction Bit String (TBS)* and *Reduced Transaction Pattern List (RTPL)*.

Similar to several other algorithms for MFI mining, the proposed algorithm preprocesses the transaction database. The transactions in the databases are transformed into bit strings called *Transaction Bit String*, with 1-bits representing the existence of frequent items in the transactions, and 0-bits representing the absence of frequent items. In an initial scan the frequencies of the items are determined. All infrequent items are discarded from the transactions. In addition, the items in each transaction are sorted, so that they are in descending order with respect to their frequency in the database. Experiments showed that it leads to much shorter execution times than a random order.

Table 1. Transaction database D (left), item frequencies (middle), and reduced transaction database after removing infrequent items in transactions & reordering items in descending order of their frequencies

TID	Transaction
10	AB
20	ABE
30	ABCE
40	CD
50	ABE
60	AB
70	ABE
80	ABCE
90	ACE
100	AB

Items	Support Count
{A}	09
{B}	08
{C}	04
{D}	01
{E}	06

TID	Transaction
10	AB
20	ABE
30	ABEC
40	CD
50	ABE
60	AB
70	ABE
80	ABEC
90	AEC
100	AB

This preprocessing is demonstrated in Table 1, which shows an example transaction database on the left. The frequencies of the items in this database are shown in the middle of this table. We obtain the database shown on the right of Table 1 by reordering the items in each transaction decreasingly with respect to their frequencies.

2.2   Condensed Representation of Database

A transaction database is usually huge. If a database can be compressed and only the information related to the mining is kept, the mining can be efficient. Recently, some data compression methods have been devised. FP-tree and Diffset are two typical examples.

In the proposed MFI algorithm, a *TBS* is created for each transaction in the dataset, and each *TBS* has a bit corresponding to each item in the dataset. If item i appears in transaction j, then the bit corresponding to item i of the *TBS* representation for transaction j is set to '1'; otherwise the bit is set to '0'. To enable efficient counting and candidate generation, we are removing duplicate *TBS* patterns from the dataset and maintain a count of each unique *TBS* pattern separately. This preprocessing is demonstrated in Table 2.

After removing duplicate *TBS* from dataset and maintaining count of each unique *TBS* separately, it is transformed into a *Reduced Transactional Pattern List (RTPL)* as shown in Table 3. Bit count accumulates the number of 1-bits in the *TBS*. This list is sorted lexicographically.

Table 2. Transaction Bit String (TBS) of Dataset D

TID	Transaction of Original Dataset	Items arranged in descending order of their frequency count	Bit Map Representation of transaction
10	AB	AB	1 1 0 0
20	ABE	ABE	1 1 1 0
30	ABCE	ABEC	1 1 1 1
50	ABE	ABE	1 1 1 0
60	AB	AB	1 1 0 0
70	ABE	ABE	1 1 1 0
80	ABCE	ABEC	1 1 1 1
90	ACE	AEC	1 0 1 1
100	AB	AB	1 1 0 0

Table 3. RTPL of Dataset D after removing duplicate TBS patterns

Transaction Bit String Representation	Bit count	Frequency of unique TBS pattern
1 1 1 1	04	02
1 1 1 0	03	03
1 1 0 0	02	03
1 0 1 1	03	01

2.3   Item Reordering

In the proposed MFI algorithm, to increase the effectiveness of subset pruning the item reordering policy is implemented. The subset-frequency pruning can be applied when a candidate itemset is found such that $i(x) \cup i_{new}$ is frequent. We therefore want to make it likely that many candidate groups will have this property. A good heuristic for accomplishing this is to force the most frequent items to appear in most candidate itemsets. This is simply because items with high frequency are more likely to be a part of long frequent itemsets. Items that appear first in the ordering will appear in most candidate itemsets. For instance, item A from Table 2 appears in most of the frequent itemsets. Item ordering is therefore used to position the most frequent items first.

The procedure *find_frequent_1-itemsets (D)* in the proposed algorithm, counts the frequency of each item in dataset *D*, removes infrequent *1-itemsets* and reorders items in descending order of their frequency prior to generation of MFI . This strategy tunes the frequency heuristic by considering only the subset of transactions relevant to the given itemset.

2.4   Pruning Techniques

To get all MFI, the usual method is to enumerate all itemsets that are candidates to be a MFI by counting the support of these itemsets and deciding whether they are a MFI. Rymon [20] presents the concept of generic set enumeration tree search framework. The enumeration tree is a virtual tree. It is used to illustrate how sets of items are to be completely enumerated in a search problem.

However, when the number of distinct items is huge, the algorithm that explores the entire search space may suffer from the problem of combinatorial explosion. So the key to an efficient set-enumeration search is pruning techniques that are applied to remove entire branches from consideration [6]. The two most often used pruning techniques: subset infrequency pruning and superset frequency pruning, are based on following lemma:

Lemma 1: A subset of any frequent itemset is a frequent itemset, and a superset of any infrequent itemset is not a frequent itemset.

In this section, we introduce two new pruning techniques used in the proposed MFI algorithm. The first is the look-ahead based on cardinality statistical information of items used for superset infrequent pruning. The second is to check if a new set is subsumed by an existing maximal set. The last technique checks if $i(X) \subset i(Y)$ and Y is present in MFI list. If so, X will not be considered as a maximal frequent itemset.

To reduce search space for superset infrequent pruning, some cardinality statistical information of item is gathered at two levels, viz., Level -1 and Level-2. Bit count is the number of bits having value '1' in each unique *TBS* which gives the information regarding the maximum number of items with which the item in question may occur.

At level-1, using bit count of each unique *TBS* and its frequency count, cumulative cardinality statistics regarding the occurrences of each *1-itemset* with every other *k-itemset* where k ranges from *1* to *(max_freq_items) - 1* is recorded in a 2-D array list *stats_1[][]*. This is demonstrated in Table 4, which shows an example of absolute statistics and cumulative statistics at level-1 on the left & right respectively. Suppose for an item x, if stats_1[x][2] < ξ (i.e. the occurrence of item x with any other *2-itemset* is less than minimum support) then we don't search for *k-itemsets* where x is one of the items and $k \geq 2$.

Similarly, at level-2, cumulative cardinality statistics regarding the occurrence of *2-itemsets* with every other *k-itemsets*, where the value of k ranges from *0* to *(max_freq_items)-1* is recorded in a 3-D array list *stats_2[][][]*. From absolute cardinality statistics, cumulative cardinality statistics are recorded and this information is used to prune the search space. This is demonstrated in Table 5, which shows an example of absolute and cumulative cardinality statistics at level-2 for the itemsets ({AB}, {AE}, {AC}) on the left & right respectively.

As the count of occurrences of each 1-itemset (or 2-itemsets for Level-2) with every other k-itemsets are required to be calculated, the complexity of this operation is very high. We utilize the functionality of the *RTPL* along with the bit count of each *TBS*.

Table 4. Absolute (left) and Cumulative (right) Cardinality Statistics of items at level-1

	0	1	2	3
{A}	0	2	4	2
{B}	0	3	3	2
{E}	0	0	4	2
{C}	0	0	1	2

	0	1	2	3
{A}	8	8	6	2
{B}	8	8	5	2
{E}	6	6	6	2
{C}	3	3	3	2

Table 5. Absolute (left) and Cumulative (right) Cardinality Statistics of items at level-2

	0	1	2
{AB}	3	3	2
{AE}	0	4	2
{AC}	0	1	2

	0	1	2
{AB}	8	5	2
{AE}	6	6	2
{AC}	3	3	2

3   Mining Maximal Frequent Itemsets

The proposed algorithm is composed of two phases: collecting cumulative cardinality statistics at two levels and mining MFI from *RTPL* using stack. Mining MFI phase is further composed of two steps, generating maximal pattern and sub-sequence pruning.

Algorithm for Mining Maximal Frequent Itemsets (MFI) using Cardinality Statistics:
Notation:
    We assume that items in each transaction are kept sorted in lexicographic order. It is straightforward to adopt the algorithm to the case where the database D is kept normalized and each database record is a *<TID, items>* pair, where *TID* is the identifier of the corresponding transaction.

- Input:
    - o D: a transaction dataset;
    - o ξ: the minimum support count threshold;
- Output:
    - o L: list of maximal frequent itemsets in D;
- *find_frequent_1-itemsets (D):* counts the frequency of each item in dataset D, remove infrequent *1-itemsets* and arrange items in descending order of their frequency.
- $L_1 \leftarrow$ *find_frequent_1-itemsets(D)*;
- $N \leftarrow Size (L_1)$: Gives the number of items whose count is great than ξ.
- *BM[][]*: reduced transaction pattern list (RTPL) representation of dataset D
- *Pattern_count[]:* contains count of each unique transaction bit string present in dataset D
- *Stat_1[][]*: contains cardinality statistical information generated at level 1
- *Stat_2[][][]*:contains cardinality statistical information generated at level 2
- *Check_duplicate(string1)* :check whether the *string1* is subset of any string present in L.
- T: Intermediate list of MFI

```
Algorithm
1.  L₁ = {frequent 1-itemset};
2.  T = ∅
3.  for ( x= 0; x < N; x++) do begin
4.    if ( Stat_1[x][0] > ξ)
5.      For all entries t ∈ BM do begin
6.        Push the item  L₁[x] on the stack along with
              start & end indexes  for each intervals;
7.        T=∪ L₁[x]; //Add element to the sequence list
8.        For (y=L₁.start_index;y<= L₁.end_index; y++)
9.          sum = sum + Pattern_count[y];
10.       If (sum > ξ) then Check_sequence(x+1);
12.       Subsequence = Check_duplicate(T);
13.       If (Subsequence == False) then
14.          L=∪T;
15.       Remove top of stack;
16.      End if
17.    End for;

Procedure Check_sequence(x)
Begin
1.  If ( x < N)
2.    Change = False;
3.    Level2=0;
4.    If (stat_1[x][size(T)] > ξ)
5.      For (z= 0; z < size(T); z++) do begin
6.        If (stat_2[z][x][ size(T)-1] > ξ) then
7.          Level2++;
8.      End for;
9.    End if;
10.   If( Level2 == Size(T)) do being
10.     T = ∪ L1[x];
11.     Push the item L1[x] on the stack along with
            start & end indexes for each intervals;
12.     Change = True;
13.     For(i= L₁.start_index;i< L₁.end_index;i++)do
14.       Sum = Sum + Pattern_count[i]
15.     End for;
16.     If(Sum>ξ)then Subsequence = Check_duplicate(T);
17.     If ( Subsequence == false) then
18.        L=∪T;
19.     End if;
20.   End if
21.   If (Change)
22.     Remove top of the stack;
23.   Check_sequence(x+1);
24. End if
End;
```

4   Experimental Evaluation

Our experiments were performed on a 2.66GHz Pentium PC machine with 1GB main memory, running on Microsoft Windows XP. The entire datasets were cached in main memory during the algorithms processing, avoiding hard disk accesses. The next subsections present the performance results achieved using datasets with different densities, followed by the studies on different support thresholds. The proposed MFI algorithm is implemented in Java.

We have tested proposed algorithm on the benchmark datasets namely Mushroom, & Retail and two synthetic datasets T10I4D100K & T40I10D100K . The mushroom [21] dataset is a multivariate, dense dataset with 8,124 transactions, 119 items and an average transaction size of 23. The retail dataset is sparse with 16,470 items, 88,162 transactions and average transaction size of 10 items. In the datasets T10I4D100K and T40I10D100K, the number of distinct item was set to 1,000. The average transaction size is set to 10 & 40 respectively, while the number of transactions in both datasets is set to 1, 00,000.

The performance metrics we have considered are runtime and reduced dataset size.

4.1   Results of Reduced Transaction Pattern List Representation of Dataset

We have tested the results of the data transformation done in the form of *RTPL* representation of datasets with various support levels. *RTPL* representation eliminates data redundancies by maintaning the count of each unique transaction bit string (*TBS*).

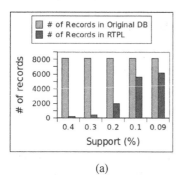
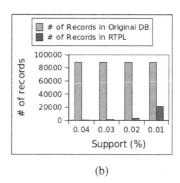

|(a)|(b)|

Fig. 2. Reduction in No. of records for Dataset (a) Mushroom (b) Retail

RTPL further helps in pruning the serach space. Figure 2 shows reduction in number of records for dataset Mushroom and Retail.

4.2   Runtime Evaluation

Figure 3 shows comparison on runtime for the proposed algorithm which uses cardinality statistics and algorithm without cardinality statistics. From the results tabulated in the graph below we can conclude that the proposed algorithm is faster for lower support.

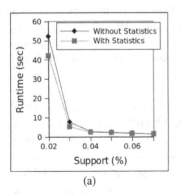 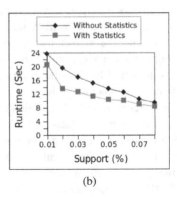

(a)   (b)

Fig. 3. Runtime for (a) T10I4D100K (b) Retail

5   Conclusion

The proposed algorithm intutively reduces memory requirements and improves the runtime efficiency. It has been demonstrated that our approach which uses cardinality statistics of items always takes less time and storage space than an algorithm without cardinality statistics information of items.

The Projected database partitioning technique on items can be adapted to our framework, and an innovative merging technique can be devised to do the merging of the local results extracted from each partition. We leave the discussion on partitioning the database on items as a future work.

Acknowledgements. We are thankful to Rushikesh Pathak for his contribution in the implementation of the proposed algorithm.

References

1. Agrawal, R., Aggarwal, C., Prasad, V.V.V.: Depth First Generation of Long Patterns. In: 7th Int'l Conference on Knowledge Discovery and Data Mining (August 2000)
2. Agrawal, R., Mannila, H., Srikant, R., Toivonen, H., Verkamo, A.: Fast Discovery of Association Rules. In: Fayyad, U., et al. (eds.) Advances in Knowledge Discovery and Data Mining, pp. 307–328. AAAI Press, Menlo Park (1996)
3. Agrawal, R., Srikant, R.: Fast Algorithms for Mining Association Rules. In: Proc. 1994 Int. Conf. Very Large Data Bases (VLDB 1994), Santiago, Chile, pp. 487–499 (September 1994)
4. Agrawal, R., Srikant, R.: Mining Sequential Patterns. In: Proc. Int. Conf. Data Engineering (ICDE 1995), Taipei, Taiwan, pp. 3–14 (March 1995)
5. Bastide, Y., Taouil, R., Pasquier, N., Stumme, G., Lakhal, L.: Mining Frequent Patterns with Counting Inference. SIGKDD Explorations 2(2) (December 2000)
6. Bayardo, R.J.: Efficiently Mining Long Patterns from Databases. In: ACM SIGMOD Conf. Management of Data (June 1998)

7. Brin, S., Motwani, R., Ullman, J., Tsur, S.: Dynamic Itemset Counting and Implication Rules for Market Basket Data. In: Proc. of the ACM-SIGMOD Conf. on Management of Data, pp. 255–264 (1997)
8. Burdick, D., Calimlim, M., Gehrke, J.: MAFIA: A Maximal Frequent Itemset Algorithm for Transactional Databases. In: Intl. Conf. on Data Engineering (April 2001)
9. Gouda, K., Zaki, Z.J.: Efficiently Mining Maximal Frequent Itemsets. In: 1st IEEE Int'l Conf. on Data Mining (November 2001)
10. Grahne, G., Zhu, J.: High Performance Mining of Maximal Frequent Itemsets. In: 6th International Workshop on High Performance Data Mining (May 2003)
11. Gunopulos, D., Mannila, H., Saluja, S.: Discovering All the Most Specific Sentences by Randomized Algorithms Extended Abstract. In: Afrati, F.N., Kolaitis, P.G. (eds.) ICDT 1997. LNCS, vol. 1186, pp. 215–229. Springer, Heidelberg (1996)
12. Han, J., Dong, G., Yin, Y.: Efficient Mining of Partial Periodic Patterns in Time Series Database. In: Proc. Int. Conf. Data Engineering, Sydney, Australia, pp. 106–115 (April 1999)
13. Han, J., Kamber, M.: Data Mining: Concepts and Techniques. Morgan Kaufmann Publishers (2009)
14. Han, J., Pei, J., Yin, Y.: Mining Frequent Patterns without Candidate Generation. In: Proc. 2000 ACM-SIGMOD Int. Conf. on Management of Data (SIGMOD 2000), Dallas, TX (2000)
15. Lin, D.I., Kedem, Z.M.: Pincer-Search: A New Algorithm for Discovering the Maximum Frequent Set. In: 6th Intl. Conf. Extending Database Technology (March 1998)
16. Mannila, H., Toivonen, H., Verkamo, A.I.: Efficient Algorithms for Discovering Association Rules. In: Proc. AAAI 1994 Workshop Knowledge Discovery in Databases (KDD 1994), Seattle, WA, pp. 181–192 (July 1994)
17. Park, J.S., Chen, M.S., Yu, P.S.: An Effective Hash Based Algorithm for Mining Association Rules. In: Proc. of the 1995 ACM-SIGMOD Conf. on Management of Data, pp. 175–186 (1996)
18. Pasquier, N., Bastide, Y., Taouil, R., Lakhal, L.: Discovering Frequent Closed Itemsets for Association Rules. In: Beeri, C., Bruneman, P. (eds.) ICDT 1999. LNCS, vol. 1540, pp. 398–416. Springer, Heidelberg (1998)
19. Pei, J., Han, J., Mao, R.: CLOSET: An Efficient Algorithm for Mining Frequent Closed Itemsets. In: Proc. 2000 ACM-SIGMOD Int. Workshop on Data Mining and Knowledge Discovery (DMKD 2000), Dallas, TX (May 2000)
20. Rymon, R.: Search through Systematic Set Enumeration. In: Proc. of Third Int'l Conf. on Principles of Knowledge Representation and Reasoning, pp. 539–550 (1992)
21. UCI Machine Learning Repositor, http://archive.ics.uci.edu/ml/datasets/Mushroom
22. Savasere, A., Omiecinski, E., Navathe, S.: An Efficient Algorithm for Mining Association Rules in Large Databases. In: Proc. of the 21st Conf. on Very Large Data-Bases, pp. 432–444 (1995)
23. Zaki, M.J., Hsiao, C.-J.: CHARM: An Efficient Algorithm for Closed Itemset Mining
24. Zaki, M.J.: Generating Non-Redundant Association Rules. In: 6th ACM SIGKDD Int'l Conf. Knowledge Discovery and Data Mining (August 2000)
25. Zaki, M.J., Parthasarathy, S., Ogihara, M., Li, W.: New Algorithms for Fast Discovery of Association Rules. In: Proc. of the Third Int'l Conf. on Knowledge Discovery in Databases and Data Mining, pp. 283–286 (1997)
26. Zou, Q., Chu, W.W., Lu, B.: Smartminer: A Depth First Algorithm Guided by Tail Information for Mining Maximal Frequent Itemsets. In: 2nd IEEE Int'l Conf. on Data Mining (November 2002)

Ranked Criteria Profile
for Multi-criteria Rating Recommender

Saranya Maneeroj[1], Pannawit Samatthiyadikun[1], Warat Chalermpornpong[1],
Sasipa Panthuwadeethorn[1], and Atsuhiro Takasu[2]

[1] Department of Mathematics and Computer Science, Faculty of Science, Chulalongkorn
University, Bangkok, 10330 Thailand
[2] National Institute of Informatics, Chiyoda-ku, Tokyo, 101-8430 Japan
{saranya.m,sasipa.c}@chula.ac.th,
{suparvut.s,warat.cha}@Student.chula.ac.th, takasu@nii.ac.jp

Abstract. Recommendation process consists of user profile creation, neighbor
formation and prediction from neighbors' opinion. If user profile can closely
represent user's characteristic, high quality neighbors will be formed and accurate
results will be obtained consecutively. Recently researchers are interested in
multi-criteria user profile to represent user's preference on multiple aspects. Most
of them are created as a vector of the preference valued on each criterion. The
current ranked criteria profile is created based on idea that highly preferred
criterion will get high rank order. However, preference level of criterion may be
opposite to overall score which indicates whether user will select an item. In this
paper, the significance level of each criterion affecting to overall score is
discovered and integrated into ranked criteria user profile. Moreover, either ROC
rank weighting technique or score mapping table is applied to compare a pair of
ranked profiles containing rank value which is an abstract number and could not
be comparable. The experimental results show that incorporating a new ranked
criteria user profile and score mapping table encourages getting better results than
current multi-criteria rating recommendation methods.

Keywords: Single-rating recommender system, Multi-Criteria rating
recommender system, Ranked criteria user profile.

1   Introduction

Recommender system becomes an important module in many web sites to help any
user selects favorite items from the huge database. Generally, recommendation process
consists of three steps [1]; user profile creation, neighbors (group of friends who have
the same taste with the target user) formation, and recommendation generation. Since
recommendations are generated from opinion of neighbors, if high quality neighbors
are derived, high quality recommendation will be obtained. Similarly, if good
representative user profiles are gotten, good neighbors will be formed. Most systems
obtained single overall score as an input to produce user representation.

Recently, Researchers have been attracted by multi-criteria rating recommender
systems, where users give their opinions in terms of a rating score for multiple aspects of

S. Dua et al. (Eds.): ICISTM 2012, CCIS 285, pp. 40–51, 2012.
© Springer-Verlag Berlin Heidelberg 2012

an item. For example, users give multiple scores in relation to the cost, transportation convenience, facility, and service in a hotel rating system.

In current multi-criteria rating recommender systems, the user profile is merely created as a vector whose components are the summarized preference information on corresponding criteria. The main idea of neighbors' formation is to find similarity among a target user and other users. Several works directly find difference between the multi-criteria user profiles of a pair of users [2][7]. Then derived difference value is converted into the similarity values. In some cases, the values of difference between the target user and the other two users are identical that means the other two users get the same level of the similarity values toward the target user. However, if one of them is different from the target user on only one criterion while another one is different from the target user on more than one criterion, both of them should have different level of similarity when compared to the target user. We call this problem as "SDDS" problem (*Same Distance but Different Similarity*).

Because different criteria affect user preferences unequally, there should be a way to assign significance level to each criterion. Therefore, the rank of importance of criteria in the user profile becomes an appropriate way. The basic way to create ranked criteria user profile was proposed in our previous work [3]. It transformed normal preference profile to ranked criteria profile in ascending order in term of summarized preference or rating information on each criterion. However, there are many occasions that a user is very interested in some criteria of a particular movie, but he feels dislike such movie, when considering from his overall score towards that movie. That is, only level of preference cannot be implied to be a rank order of importance of criteria. Since overall score represents level how much a user wants to select each item, the way to measure actual significance level of each criterion affecting to overall score should be considered as a criterion weight.

This paper proposes a new method of ranking criteria of user profile. First, it computes the similarity level of each criterion towards overall score when each user selects an item. Then, for a target user, it calculates the average score of such similarity values on all rated items by such a target user. The average of similarity values becomes the weight of each criterion affecting to a target user's characteristic. This criterion weight is then incorporated to corresponding criterion preference value in order to create the ranked criteria profile. Unfortunately, a rank value is an abstract number which is not comparable. For example, if there are four criteria and the ranked criteria user profile of user A is 4 2 3 1 and user B is 1 2 4 3, how to measure similarity between these two profiles? We resolve this problem by finding the way to convert such rank value to a comparable score. The first way is applying rank attribute weighting scheme "Rank Order Centroid" (ROC) proposed by Barron et al., [4]. The other is score mapping table adapted from our previous work[3]. A new ranked criteria profile is compared to current multi-criteria user profile techniques on benchmark collection; Yahoo Movie database which is a well-known multi-criteria rating recommender with MAE (Mean Absolute Error) metric on 10 fold cross validation.

2   Multi-criteria Recommender

Currently, in recommender systems, both overall and criteria scores come up with more user implication in term of how much and why a user prefers a particular item respectively which means more detailed user's preference is issued. This relates to the fact that a set of criteria takes place in user's consideration when choosing items. To inherit this idea for multiple aspects of preference model, some practical systems have been developed to let users rate on an item toward many aspects, such as, http://movies.yahoo.com, or http://www.hotels.com. These systems were referred to as the "*multi-criteria rating recommender system*".

Many techniques incorporating multi-criteria preference were proposed. Schmit, C., et al., [5] applied the MAUT (Multi-Attribute Utility Theory) on the case study of car recommender system, while Roux F. L., et al., [6] constructed the course recommender based on multi-criteria decision making. Palanivel K., et al., [8] used Fuzzy Multicriteria Decision Making method to list the interesting music for a user.

To sum up, there are three main steps of multi-criteria recommendation process: (1) user profile creation, (2) neighbors formation and (3) prediction generation. In traditional multi-criteria recommendation technique [2], the user profile is created from co-rated items between the target user and other users. After that, the neighbor set of target user is formed using users' similarity methods, which have been extended from single-rating to the multi-criteria rating recommendation technique. It applies the traditional similarity measurement for single rating as either Pearson correlation [2] or Cosine similarity [2] to measure similarity of a pair of users on co-rated items set for k criteria. The similarity on each criterion ($sim_c(u,u')$) is calculated and then similarities of k criteria are aggregated to form overall similarity value($sim(u,u')$) between a pair of users by averaging the similarity values of every criterion as Eq. (1).

$$sim(u,u') = \frac{1}{k} \sum_{c=1}^{k} sim_c(u,u') \tag{1}$$

However, it suffers from *sparsity rating* problem, because each user usually provides rating on a small number of items when compared to the number of items in database. Namely, the co-rated items tend to be found difficultly. In order to eliminate *sparsity rating* problem, many researchers tried to create user profile without using co-rated items. They always create user profile by automatically retrieving multi-attribute content of selected items. Namely, the single ratings of all selected items are converted into the multi-attribute user preference. After that, multi-attribute user preferences of rated items are summarized in the creation of user profile, in order to match the favored attribute content, such as "Comedy" movies, such as in the work of Capphannarungsri, K., et al., [7]. In their work, a pair of user profiles between a target user and other users is usually compared using distance metrics to form a set of neighbors. This causes the SDDS problem which occurs when other two users have the same values of difference from the target user, but they have the different level of similarity toward the target user. Table 1 demonstrates an example of SDDS problem. Both user A and user B have the same value of difference from the target user. If we thoroughly consider the value of each criterion between the target user and other two users, user A should be more similar to the target user than user B since user A has the same values as the target user on three criteria while user B has same value only on two criteria. In order to eliminate the SDDS problem, the significance of each criterion towards each user should be considered. Therefore the rank of the importance of criteria that each user uses in selecting items is the solution of this case. The simple way [3] to create rank of criteria is converting from preference profile in table 1 by ordering the preference value from high to low preference value as shown in table 2.

Table 1. The example of SDDS problem

User ID	Cri.1	Cri.2	Cri.3	Cri.4	Sum
Target user	9	8	7	7	
User A	9	8	7	5	
User B	9	7	7	6	
Diff (Tar, A)	0	0	0	2	2
Diff (Tar, B)	0	1	0	1	2

Table 2. The User profile with criteria-ranking

User ID	Cri.1	Cri.2	Cri.3	Cri.4
Target	R1	R2	R3	R3
A	R1	R2	R3	R4
B	R1	R2	R2	R4

However, in the real situation of selecting items, the criterion which gets high preference may lesser affect a user than low preferred criterion. For example, in case of Yahoo Movies Database, it contains four kinds of criteria, i.e., the story, acting, direction, and visual. Suppose user A gives ratings for the movie "Titanic" as 6, 5, 9, 10, 12 for overall score, story, acting, direction, and visual criteria respectively, where the range of rating is 1-13. Although user A likes visual effect of this movie (score 12), user A dislikes this movie, because the overall score is 6 which is less than 7 (middle score of range of rating 1-13). In contrast, user A dislikes story of this movie(score 5), when he dislikes this movie. It can be implied that, story criterion affects user A in selecting "Titanic" more than visual criterion, even though the visual criterion got the highest preference value, when compared to other criteria. A new ranked criteria profile which compensates this situation should be considered. Namely, the weight of each criterion affecting to characteristic of user in selecting items should be integrated into ranked criteria profile.

Since a rank value is an abstract number which is not comparable, it is difficult to find similarity between each pair of users on their ranked criteria profiles. From Table 2, what is the similarity value between User B and the target user? In the third criterion, what is the similarity value between rank order 3 and 2? Therefore, a way to convert such rank value to be comparable number is also needed.

3   Proposed Method

Since, overall score indicates level of how much a user wants to select an item, a new ranked criteria profile considering on significance level of each criterion affecting to overall score is proposed in this work. Furthermore, in order to convert rank value to be comparable value, we apply two methods. The first is "Rank Order Centroid" (ROC) which is a rank attribute weighting scheme proposed by Barron et al., [4]. The other is the score mapping table (SMT) adapted from our previous work [3].

3.1   Rating Information

Suppose there are m kinds of criteria. Then, for item i, a user a is expected to give rating information represented by the vector R_{ai}.

$$R_{ai} = (r_{ai0}, r_{ai1}, ..., r_{aim}) \qquad (2)$$

where r_{ai0} denotes the overall rating, $r_{aic}(0<c<=m)$ denotes the rating for the cth criterion. For example, the Yahoo Movies Database contains four kinds of criteria, i.e., the story, acting, direction, and visuals. For each movie, a user gives a rate ranging from 1 to 13 to each of these four criteria as well as an overall rating as represented by a vector $(r_{ai0}, r_{ai1}, ..., r_{ai4})$.

3.2   Preference User Profile

When a set of rating information is given, a user profile consisting of the user's preferences is created. This is updated when a user provides more rating information to the system. The user profile is represented as a vector whose components are the average rating values of the corresponding criteria. Let I_a denote the set of items that user a gives rating information. Then, the preference for the jth criterion is defined as

$$p_{aj} = \frac{\sum_{i \in Ia} r_{aij}}{|I_a|} \qquad (3)$$

Where r_{aij}, is the rating value of the jth criterion of item i by user a. Therefore the *preference user profile* of user a is defined as $u_a = (p_{a1}, p_{a2}, ..., p_{an})$, where n is the number of criteria.

3.3   Ranked Criteria User Profile

The basic way to create ranked criteria user profile was proposed in our previous work [3]. In that work, the ranked criteria user profile is created by giving order for all criteria from high to low preference value (p_{aj}). For example, suppose there are 4 criteria as in Yahoo Movies database, if $p_{a2} > p_{a4} > p_{a1} > p_{a3}$, the ranked criteria user profile of user a will be $rp_a = (R_3, R_1, R_4, R_2)$, where the first element of the profile is the rank order of the first criterion which got the third rank order (R_3) in this case, because it got the third order of preference value (p_{a1}).

In this paper, instead of generating ranked criteria profile by converting from preference value directly, the actual significance of each criterion is discovered. It is a weight of each criterion which affects user's characteristic. This kind of weight should be incorporated with corresponding element of preference user profile before converting to be ranked criteria profile.

For each user, a proposed ranked criteria user profile is created by the following steps:

1) For each rated item: similarity value between criterion's rating value and overall rating value is calculated. Since, overall score indicates level of how much a user wants to select an item; a criterion that has deep influence on overall score is a criterion that highly affects user's characteristic. Therefore, when each user gives rating for an item, the similarity level between each criterion score and overall score is computed. We assume that each user gives ratings according to a Gaussian distribution. If a user a gives rating score y for overall score r_{ai0} and score x for criterion c (r_{aic}) to item i, the similarity level between criterion c and overall score of user a on item i is calculated as below.

$$sim_{aic}(r_{aic} = x \mid r_{ai0} = y) \propto e^{-(x-y)^2/2\sigma^2}$$ (4)

where, σ^2 denotes variance of rating information of the user a.

2) For all rated items, significance value of each criterion is calculated. In order to measure which criterion has prior significance than others toward each user, we measure from how much it is influent on overall score for all rated items of such user. Therefore, average value of similarity value that each criterion has toward overall score from the first step is computed as below.

$$sig_{ac} = \frac{\sum\limits_{i \in I_a} sim_{aic}}{|I_a|}$$ (5)

where I_a denotes the set of items that user a gives rating information.

3) For each user, ranked criteria profile is created. The significance level in step 2 shows how much each criterion affects to user's characteristic in selecting items. It is implied as weight of each criterion. Therefore, the criterion weight is incorporated to corresponding element of the *preference user profile* (u_a) as equation below:

$$sp_a = (sig_{a1} \times p_{a1}, \ ..., \ sig_{am} \times p_{am})$$ (6)

The ranked criteria user profile (ru_a) is generated by giving order for all criteria from high to low element values of weighted user profile (sp_a) from Eq. (6). For example, suppose there are 4 criteria as Yahoo Movies database and if $sig_{a3} \times p_{a3} > sig_{a4} \times p_{a4} > sig_{a2} \times p_{a2} > sig_{a1} \times p_{a1}$, the ranked criteria profile of user a is defined by $ru_a = (R_4, R_3, R_1, R_2)$, where the first element of the profile is the rank order of the first criterion which got the forth rank order (R_4) in this case, because it got the lowest value . In contrast, the first order of rank (R_1) is for the third criterion because it has the highest value. The ru_a will be updated when user a gives more ratings by re-calculating the average value of step 2.

3.4   Neighbors Formation

After the ranked criteria user profile of each user is created and updated, the similarity between a pair of users is measured in order to find neighbors. Unfortunately, the ranked criteria user profile contains the rank value which could not be comparable. For example, if there are four criteria and the raked criteria user profile of user a is

$ru_a = (R_4, R_3, R_1, R_2)$, and user b is $ru_b = (R_4, R_2, R_1, R_3)$. The first and the third criteria of both users have the same rank values which are R_4 and R_1 respectively. However, the rank order R_1 has higher significance than R_4, so the similarity value between these two users of the third criterion (R_1) must bigger than the first criterion (R_4). Namely, the difference of the rank order 1 (R_1) should be more important than the difference of the rank order on the lower ranks. Hence, in order to compare between a pair of ranked criteria profiles of any two users, we apply two methods to convert rank value to be a comparable value. The first method is converting each rank value to weighting value using ROC [4]. The other is using a score mapping table (SMT) adapted from our previous work [3].

1) Applying rank attribute weighting scheme called "Rank Order Centroid" (ROC):
We apply the ROC [4] to set weight to each element of the ranked criteria user profile. ROC weights of all criteria are computed from the vertices of the simplex, $w(R_1) \geq w(R_2) \geq ... \geq w(R_n) \geq 0$, restricted to $\sum_{i=1}^{n} w(R_i) = 1$. The defining vertices of this simplex are $e_1 = (1, 0,...,0)$, $e_2 = (1/2, 1/2, 0,...,0)$, $e_3 = (1/3, 1/3, 1/3, 0,...,0)$,..., $e_n = (1/n, 1/n, ...,1/n)$. The weights are computed by averaging the corresponding coordinates of defining vertices. Therefore, the weight of each rank value is computed by the following equation

$$w(R_i) = \frac{1}{n} \sum_{j=i}^{n} \frac{1}{j}, i = 1,...,n \tag{7}$$

where n is number of criteria. If the ranked criteria user profile of user a is $ru_a = (R_4, R_3, R_1, R_2)$, it will be converted to weighted user profile $uw_a = (w(R_4), w(R_3), w(R_1), w(R_2))$. Now, we can find similarity between two users by measuring the distance between them on their weighted user profiles (uw) using the Euclidean distance. For users a and b, the distance $d(a,b)$ between them is the Euclidean distance of their weighted user profiles $|uw_a - uw_b|^2$.
After that, the top N users who have least distance toward a target user will be selected as such a target user's neighbors.

2) Using score mapping table: On the idea that the difference of the rank order 1 (R_1) should be more important than the difference of the rank order on the lower ranks, we proposed score mapping table [3]. Table 3 shows the similarity value between each pair of rank values. Since there are 4 criteria in this work, the highest similarity value is starting from 16 (similarity between R_1 and R_1). This adapted table was created on the basic idea that, the importance value of the first rank order is 4, the second rank is 3, the third rank is 2 and the lowest rank value is 1 respectively from the number of all criteria which is 4. Therefore, when R_1 faces R_1, the similarity value should be 4 ×4 which is 16, or when R_4 faces R_4, the similarity value should be 1 ×1 which is 1. For instance, if the R_1 compares to R_2, it will have similarity value 4 ×3=12, which must be higher than when comparing R_2 and R_3 that has similarity value 3 × 2=6 (see table 3), although the distance of $(R_1$ and $R_2)$ and $(R_2$ and $R_3)$ is the same value which is 1.

Therefore, after we get ranked user profiles of user a and user b, we then look up table 3 to generate similarity value for each criterion ($sim_c(a,b)$). For example, suppose the ranked criteria user profile of user a is $ru_a = (R_1, R_2, R_3, R_4)$, and user b is $ru_b = (R_3, R_4, R_2, R_1)$. The first criterion is R_1 and R_3, then look up the table 3, $sim_1(a,b)$ is 8. For the second criterion, it is R_2 and R_4, $sim_2(a,b)$ is 3. For the third criterion, it is R_3 and R_2, $sim_3(a,b)$ is 6. For the fourth criterion, it is R_4 and R_1, $sim_4(a,b)$ is 4. The overall similarity value between a pair of users (a and b) is summation of similarity value of all criteria as $\sum_{c=1}^{n} sim_c(a,b)$. The overall similarity value of the above example is 21.

After the overall similarity values among a target user and other users in the database are all calculated, the top N users, who have the highest overall similarity value toward a target user, are selected to be the target users' neighbors.

Table 3. The score mapping table (SMT)

Rank of Cri. of user a / Rank of Cri. of user b	R1	R2	R3	R4
R1	16	12	8	4
R2	12	9	6	3
R3	8	6	4	2
R4	4	3	2	1

3.5   Calculation of Similarity Value between a Target User and Other User

After Top N users are selected for a target user from either ROC or SMT methods mentioned above, the actual similarity value between a target user and other user is calculated to be in the range from 0 to 1. According to the following situation, there are totally six users; A, B, X, Y, M, and N. Let set the user A as a target user, and suppose that the rank of similar users is the ordered set $U\_rank(A)=(B,M,N,X,Y)$. Note that sometime two or more users may have the same rank, and this is allowed in our work. If the users N and X are known equally similar to the user A, the rank is obviously given as $(B,M,\{N,X\},Y)$. Therefore, occasionally in this case, user N and X have the same degree of similarity. For a target user a, let $rank_a(u)$ denotes the rank value of the user u in $U\_rank(a)$. For example, $rank_a(B) =1$, $rank_a(M) =2$, $rank_a(N) = rank_a(X) =3$, and $rank_a(Y) =5$ for the above mentioned example. Actual similarity between users a and user u is defined by Eq. (8).

$$actual\_sim(a,u) = \frac{\left|U\_rank(a)\right| - rank_a(u) + 1}{\left|U\_rank(a)\right|} \tag{8}$$

Table 4 shows the example of converting from the order of nearest neighbor list (Top 5 in this case) to the similarity values. The range of similarity is from 0 to 1, where 1 denotes the most similarity.

Table 4. Example of the calculation of similarity value

Neighbor name	Top 5	Similarity value
B	1	(5-1+1)/5 = 1
M	2	(5-2+1)/5 = 0.8
N	3	(5-3+1)/5 = 0.6
X	3	(5-3+1)/5 = 0.6
Y	5	(5-5+1)/5 = 0.2

3.6 Prediction Generation

The prediction is generated by using weighted average on real overall rating of neighbors where actual similarity value between neighbor and a target user from the previous section is assigned as a weight as the following equation.

$$P_{ai} = \frac{\sum_{n \in N} actual\_sim(a,n) \times r_{ni0}}{\sum_{n \in N} actual\_sim(a,n)} \tag{9}$$

where, P_{ai} is the prediction value of movie i for target user a. N is a set of neighbors. r_{ni0} is overall rating of neighbor n for the movie i . For $actual\_sim(a,n)$, it is similarity value between user a and neighbor n calculated by Eq. (8).

4   Experiment

The experiment aims to prove the performance of the proposed ranked criteria user profile technique and the way to generate similarity value between a pair of users from their ranked criteria user profiles. Therefore, we compared the proposed method with the baseline method and the previous ranked criteria profile method.

MCBase: This method is the baseline multi-criteria rating recommendation proposed by Adomavicius, G. et al, [2]. It calculates similarity between any two users by their co-rated items. The multi-criteria rating information obtained from those users are compared using Pearson correlation technique [2] on each criterion. After that, the similarity values on 4 criteria are aggregated using Eq. (1) to form overall similarity value.

PreRank: This method is our previous ranked criteria user profile method [3] which basically created by converting from user preference profile directly.

WeRank: This method is a new ranked criteria user profile proposed in this work. The proposed weight of each criterion is incorporated into user preference profile before converting to ranked criteria profile.

Both PreRank and WeRank use either ROC or SMT to produce similarity value between a pair of ranked criteria user profiles of each pair of users.

In the prediction step, the weighted average technique in Eq. (9) is used for all methods. These all methods are implemented on the same condition and environment and evaluated using MAE metric on 10 fold cross validation.

In this paper, we emphasize 2 parts: a new ranked criteria user profile creation (WeRank), and a way to compare a pair of ranked criteria profiles of each pair of users (SMT). Therefore, the experiments were made based on the following assumptions:

1. PreRank achieves better recommendation results than the baseline multi-criteria rating method (MCBase)
2. SMT is more suitable than ROC in producing similarity value of a pair of users from their ranked criteria user profiles.
3. WeRank provides better results than PreRank.

4.1   Data

We collected data from Yahoo Movie database collected by Yahoo Movie System (http://movies.yahoo.com) which is a widely used database in multi-criteria rating recommender research area. The data consists of 2550 ratings rated by 200 users on 1358 movies. The system requests users to give ratings on the overall rating and four criteria which are story, acting, direction and visual for each movie. The rating values are A+, A, A-, B+, B, ..., D-, F respectively. We converted the rating values to numerical values ranging from 1 to 13 where 1 is F and 13 is A+.

In order to divide data into train and test sets, 10-fold cross validation is used in this experiment to randomly choose different train and test sets. After that, the average of the MAE values is calculated. Parameters used in our experiment are numbers of the nearest neighbors which are 10, 20, and 30 respectively.

4.2   Evaluation Metric

Each method in our experiments is evaluated by Mean Absolute Error (MAE) which is a measure of the recommendation accuracy and given by:

$$MAE = \frac{\sum_{i \in I} |Rc_i - Rp_i|}{|I|},$$

(10)

Rc_i indicates the actual overall rating that user had given on the movie i^{th}. Rp_i is the predicted overall rating generated by each method for movie i^{th}. I denotes the set of the movie items in the test set. Note that lower MAE means better performance.

4.3   Experimental Results

In order to prove the first assumption, we compared PreRank and MCBase methods. Table 5 shows that PreRank with either ROC or SMT outperforms the MCBase method, because of lower MAE value. We also used the pair t-test to test the significance of the difference between each pair of methods by setting the significance level to 0.05 ($\alpha = 0.05$). From Table 5, the average MAE value of 10 fold cross validation shows that the PreRank with ROC or SMT outperforms the baseline method (MCBase) significantly (*p-value* = 0.008 < α= 0.05 and *p-value* = 0.013 < α= 0.05 respectively). Therefore, this can prove the first assumption that, the basic ranked criteria profile, which is created by directly converting from preference profile, with both ways in generating similarity value between a pair of ranked criteria profiles (ROC and SMT) provides better results than the baseline multi- criteria method.

Table 5. The average MAE values of baseline method and basic ranked criteria user profile

Method		Number of Neighbors		
		10	20	30
MCBase		2.8507	2.8208	2.8327
PreRank	SMT	2.5875	2.5646	2.6856
	ROC	2.6543	2.6222	2.7042

For the second assumption, we need to prove our score mapping table (SMT). Therefore, we compare our SMT with the ROC. As shown in Table 6, the average MAE values on 10 fold cross validation of SMT of both PreRank and WeRank are lower than ROC significantly with $p\text{-}value = 0.042 < \alpha = 0.05$ and $p\text{-}value = 0.035 < \alpha = 0.05$ respectively. It can prove the second assumption that SMT is more suitable than ROC for generating similarity value of each pair of ranked criteria user profiles.

Table 6. The average MAE values of basic ranked criteria user profile and the new proposed one

Method		Number of Neighbors		
		10	20	30
PreRank	SMT	2.5875	2.5646	2.6856
	ROC	2.6543	2.6222	2.7042
WeRank	SMT	2.5640	2.5357	2.5584
	ROC	2.6702	2.7026	2.6186

From the second assumption, we considered on only SMT when proving the last assumption in comparing the new proposed ranked criteria profile (WeRank) and the previous one (PreRank). Table 6 shows that the average MAE values on 10 fold cross validation of SMT of WeRank are lower than SMT of PreRank significantly with $p\text{-}value = 0.01 <= \alpha = 0.01$. It can prove the last assumption that a new ranked criteria profile provides better recommendation results than the previous one.

5   Discussion

Since better user profile will provide better neighbors and consecutively better recommendation results. The results show that the ranked criteria profile method outperforms the baseline multi-criteria rating recommendation method [2]. The reason is the user profile of the baseline method is created from co-rated items, which suffers *sparsity rating* problem and this kind of user profile could not represent detailed user's characteristic about how much each criterion affects to a user in selecting items.

The experimental results also show that a new ranked criteria user profile outperforms the previous ranked user profile [3]. It is because the previous one is generated on the idea that highly preferred criterion has high significance level affecting to user's characteristic in selecting items. However, this is not exactly true, because there are many occasions that a user is very interested in some criteria of a movie, but he does not select such movie. Meanwhile, the new ranked criteria profile is created by integrating the significance level of each criterion affecting to overall score (or weight of each criterion), which directly tells whether a user wants to select a movie or not.

Furthermore, the score mapping table (SMT) is more suitable than ROC weight in measuring similarity value between a pair of ranked criteria profiles. The reason is that ROC is used to convert ranked criteria profile to weighted criteria profile to indicate significance level of each criterion affecting to users' characteristic, but distance between two profiles is still calculated in order to measure similarity between a pair of users. Therefore, SDDS problem still remains. In contrast, SMT gives similarity value between each pair of rank values according to importance of ranking order without calculating distance of any two user profiles.

6   Conclusions

In this paper, a new ranked criteria user profile is proposed by integrating significance value of each criterion, which affects each user's characteristic in selecting items. Moreover, the suitable way to compare a pair of ranked criteria user profiles is discovered. It is a score mapping table. From the experimental results, it can be concluded that combining score mapping table and the new ranked criteria user profile can improve accuracy rate of recommendation results.

References

[1] Chen, A.: Context-Aware Collaborative Filtering System: Predicting the User's Preference in the Ubiquitous Computing Environment. In: Strang, T., Linnhoff-Popien, C. (eds.) LoCA 2005. LNCS, vol. 3479, pp. 244–253. Springer, Heidelberg (2005)
[2] Adomavicius, G., Kwon, Y.O.: New Recommendation Techniques for Multicriteria Rating System. IEEE Intelligent Systems 22(3), 48–55 (2007)
[3] Duangjumpa, J., Maneeroj, S., Panthuwadeethorn, S.: A Novel Multi-Criteria User Profile based on Criteria-Ranking for Movie Recommender. In: 2011 International Conference on Engineering and Information Management (ICEIM 2011), pp. 113–119 (2011)
[4] Barron, F.H., Barrett, B.E.: Decision Quality Using Ranked Attribute Weights. Management Science 42(11), 1515–1523 (1996)
[5] Schmitt, C., Dengler, D., Bauer, M.: The MAUT-Machine: An Adaptive Recommender System. In: Proceedings of ABIS Workshop, Hannover, Germany (2002)
[6] Le Roux, F., Ranjeet, E., Ghai, V., Gao, Y., Lu, J.: A Course Recommender System Using Multiple Criteria Decision Making Method, pp. 346–350. Atlantis Press, Chengdu (2007)
[7] Chapphannarungsri, K., Maneeroj, S.: Combining Multiple Criteria and Multidimension for Movie Recommender System. In: Proceedings of the International MultiConference of Engineers and Computer Scientists 2009, Hong Kong, China, pp. 698–703 (2009)
[8] Palabnivel, K., Sivakumar, R.: Fuzzy Multicriteria Decision-Making Approach for Collaborative Recommender Systems. Internation Journal of Computer Theory and Engineering 2(1), 57–63 (2010)

A Graph API for Complex Business Network Query and Traversal

Daniel Ritter and Christoph Herrmann

SAP AG, Technology Development – Process and Network Integration,
Dietmar-Hopp-Allee 16, 69190 Walldorf, Germany
{daniel.ritter,c.herrmann}@sap.com
http://www.sap.com

Abstract. Business Network Management (BNM) provides companies
with techniques for managing their trading partner networks by making
technical integration, business and social aspects visible within a network
view and sets them into context to each other. Therefore, it computationally links data into business and (technical) integration networks as
well as computes semantic correlation between entities of both perspectives. The linked real-world data is then captured in a network-centric
variant of Business Process Modeling Notation (BPMN), which we call
Network Integration Model (NIM). In this paper, we propose a novel concept, which features access to the complex inter-connected business and
technical perspectives in NIM in a standard RESTful architecture style,
called Business Graph API (BGAPI). As foundation we use a powerful
Resource Graph (RG) definition, which is directly computed from the
underlying NIM, and allows simple, uniform, but expressive queries and
traversal on the linked data. We present a novel approach on applying
state of the art RESTful Web-Services to our domain and report on our
experiences with it.

Keywords: Web service, RESTful architecture style, Business Network,
Network-centric BPMN, Graph Query and Traversal.

1   Introduction

Nowadays enterprises are part of value chains consisting of business processes
with intra and inter enterprise stakeholders. To remain compitetive, enterprises
need insight into their business network and ideally into the relevant parts of
partner and customer networks and their processes. However, currently the insight often ends at the borders of systems or enterprises. Business Network Management (BNM) helps to overcome this situation and allows companies to get
insight into their technical, social and business relations [11,12]. For instance,
Fig. 1 shows participants in a sample business network.

In a nutshell, the model used to capture real-world entities that constitute
such a network, is based on network-centric BPMN, called Network Integration Model (NIM) [9,10]. NIM covers all relevant aspects of BNM by extending

S. Dua et al. (Eds.): ICISTM 2012, CCIS 285, pp. 52–63, 2012.

BPMN [10] to the network domain. For that, a *Network* is derived from the BPMN *ConversationDiagram* and consists of specializations of BPMN *Participant*, e.g. *BusinessParticipant* and *CommunicationParticipant*, as well as conversations that abstract BPMN *MessageFlow*, e.g. a business or technical document flow between participants [10]. Further entities are named subsequently while defining our approach.

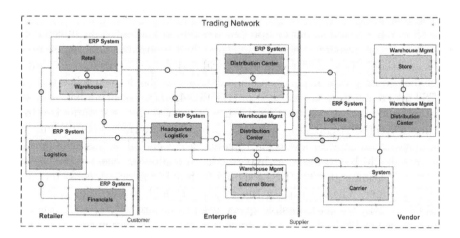

Fig. 1. Sample cross-enterprise Business (Process) Network showing internal and external participants as well as conversations representing business document exchange

Our approach describes how the NIM logical graph can be automatically translated into a form that sufficiently fulfills all requirements for accessing the complete graph, called the Resource Graph (RG). Hereby we show how complex, multi-relational [13], hyper graph structures with nested object hierarchies or forests are represented in a uniform way using an efficient, standardized and easy to use Business Graph API (BGAPI). This approach allows all applications interested in BNM data, i.e. Business Graph Applications (BGAs), to build both visualizations and scalable business applications based on NIM.

Section 2 describes the basic design principles, while section 3 sets the approach into context to related work. In section 4 the Resource Graph is defined while section 5 shows its application within the Business Graph API for complex queries and traversal. Section 5 concludes and outlines future work.

2   Design Principles

The Network Integration Model (NIM) is a representative example for data models that cover structurally and semantically complex, linked data describing real-world technical, business and social entities within a business network. To capture the relevant aspects of these networks with different perspectives on the data, the single networks are semantically linked, e.g. a *Headquarter Logistics* participant is implemented by an *ERP* system instance (see Fig. 1) and the corresponding document flow correlates to e.g. a mediated file to web service communication, and thus creating a multi-relational hypergraph. In addition, the data is structured as deeply nested object hierarchies (tree, forest), e.g. participant with assigned contact person and address information, which leads to multi-value response results (sets of complex data). In this context, applications that access the NIM data for visualizing or processing are called business graph applications (BGA).

To allow a BGA simple, but comprehensive (remote) access to the linked data, an API built on resource oriented concepts shall guarantee uniform, scalable access and should take most recent structural and data changes into account.

For that, at least concurrent, best effort data access should be reached through a RESTful architecture style based on HTTP [4,5,17], a schema-based model evolution, addressable resources via URL and their representation as key to a Resource Oriented Architecture (ROA) [15,16]. The interface shall be built on well-known technology to lower the learning curve and allow faster adoption. Resources should be expressed as hypermedia to enable the client to be the engine of application state. The URLs should be build in a logical, consistent and intuitive manner. The location to the resource should go into the <path> of the HTTP URL, whereas possible query arguments are left for the <query> section of the HTTP URL. All communication with the server must be independent of the previous conversation, i.e. stateless. HTTP requests that are used as described in the standard being safe and idempotent enforce such a stateless design. Possibly large amounts of linked data should be available for BGAs in reasonable time.

The query execution on the data shall be efficient. Changing entities or structure of the data model shall not require any source code changes to the interface. Data should be added, changed, removed and queried in a uniform way. Since large data sets might be requested concurrently, the interface itself shall allow the user to define precise and restrictive queries to avoid sending unnecessary data. For that a query and traversal algebra independent of the source model shall be defined to guarantee for a good ease of use and smart usage, supported by necessary algorithms implemented within the API, e.g. graph traversal. Custom or computed entry points for traversal and queries and additional semantic relationships between entities shall be configurable.

3   Related Work

For network-based, remote APIs, the work of Roy Fielding [4,5] is fundamental, in which architecture styles for resource oriented data access are defined. Fielding's work serves as foundation for the BGAPI defined in this paper. Hence, the definitions of resources, representation, etc are taken as given for the work described in this paper.

Grounded on these concepts, Facebook provides a Graph API [1] and an open graph protocol [2], too. The Graph API allows RESTful access to social media data and is well suited for social applications. The data model is a simple social graph with flat structures and partially connected data containing name, personal information, links to friends, etc. The work follows similar design principles in terms of simplicity, ease of use and addressability [2,3] as our work. However, the open graph protocol focuses exclusively on social aspects. It does not support complex business and integration aspects as well as semantics of complex queries or traversal. The notion of semantic, custom extensions is not foreseen in Facebook's API. The API only allows interaction with the data stored on facebook called the social graph, e.g., people, photos, events, and pages, which is represented as nodes and the connections between them, e.g., friend relationships, shared content, and photo tags, as edges [1]. That means, the model is an undirected, vertex-labeled, vertex-attributed and edge labeled graph. While Facebooks ideas of connections and metadata are considered in the design of the Resource Graph, it does not address the challenges outlined for in the domain of BNM, like the issues of hypergraphs, multigraphs, tree structures and traversal operations.

The notion of accessing connected data is also supported by Rexter [8]. Rexter is a system implemented to access data as web service in graph databases similar to InfoGrid [6]. Contrary to facebook, it therefore works on abstract graphs, which means it is not optimized to work with the semantic meaning of a graph (e.g friendships between people). The specialization on property graphs has two further shortcomings. Property graphs are directed graphs which is an influential part of the rexster design. The Business Network does not have directed edges. Furthermore, property graphs are not hypergraphs as common for multiperspective Business Networks. An important principle of the rexster approach to a graph is its definition of resources and the way of how to expose a graph as a whole. Both are important aids for the BGAPI. However for the BGAPI, Rexter's abstract graph comes short due to complexity and nature of Business Networks.

Our work on traversal on the resource graph is related to graph traversal patterns described in Rodriguez et al. [14]. The different types of graph traversals are formalized on a property graph as operations over power multiset domains and ranges. While we define a general resource graph over different types of structures, like multi-relational (hyper-) graphs, forest, lists, the work on graph traversal is mainly focused on single-step traversal and content-based similarity.

4   The Resource Graph

For defining the Business Graph Interface (BGAPI), the NIM, design principles and related prior art are taken into consideration. The NIM is expressed as a graph of linked data, e.g. connecting participants of different specializations, such as social, business or technical, through message flows of different types. Additionally, there are a variety of supplementary entities, e.g. *Service*, *Group* or *BusinessTerm*. To create the resource graph, it is therefore essential to identify the resources in NIM. Subsequently the Resource Graph (RG), a resource representation of NIM, is introduced as foundation of the BGAPI.

4.1   Defining the Resource Graph

In an abstract view, the business network in the NIM can be seen as a set of participants, e.g. *Distribution Center* or *Store* (see Fig. 1), connected to each others. This cannot be directly found in the actual data, but it represents a logical graph. A simple logical graph is depicted in Fig. 2(a). This graph connects participants (P_0 through P_4) with each other. A more formal definition of the logical graph according to the example is given by

$$G = (V, E),$$
$$\text{with } V = \{P_0, P_1, P_2, P_3, P_4\},$$
$$\text{and } E = \{\{P_0, P_4\}, \{P_0, P_2\},$$
$$\{P_4, P_2\}, \{P_2, P_1\}, \{P_2, P_3\}\}.$$

A simple way to translate such a logical graph into resources would be to take all participants in V and all edges in E and declare them resources. Both, nodes and edges, would know about each other and be addressable as resources. For example, Rexster [8] uses such a representation. Yet this approach is not sufficient to cover NIM. For that, the logical graph is dissolved to form a suitable resource representation, the Resource Graph.

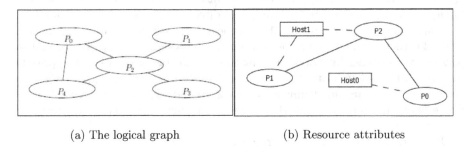

(a) The logical graph   (b) Resource attributes

Fig. 2. Dissolving the logical graph

As first step, *attributes* are introduced to the logical graph. Every node in the Logical Graph could have an associated set of key-value pairs, called attributes. For example *name*, *description* or *location*. Additionally, every node was given the standard attributes of *id* and *type*, which make them identifiable. The *type* would always be in the most specific form. For instance, a *Participant* in the NIM resolves to its real type such as *ApplicationParticipant* or *BusinessParticiantWithApplication*, which are specializations of *Participant*. All attributes are automatically identified from the NIM schema. New attributes are introduced into the model without a need for manual updates on the resource graph.

While attributes are a natural concept for nodes, they could not be applied directly for edges. The logical graph is an abstract concept, which means the edges between the nodes are only an abstract representation of a more complicated matter. Hence, there is no generic way to find attributes in the NIM that could be applied to these abstract edges.

Another type of attribute can be found in sub-objects that specify participants. For instance, Fig. 2(b) shows a graph with the resource attribute *Host*. The so called *resource attributes* can be compared to 1:n relationships in relational databases. A Participant resource does have one host resource assigned for the *host* resource attribute, for example P_0 has $Host_0$, which can be resource attribute of many Participant resources, resp. Consistent with the resource graph, an object that acts as resource attribute can have type-specific normal attributes such as *technicalName*.

Introducing resource attributes leads to semantic differences for edges. While the edge between a *Participant* and a *Host* would be named *host* in accordance with the resource attribute name, the edges between participants could be named *neighbors*. From a data structure perspective, the edge *neighbors* between two participants is more complex than just a "line" between participants. Fig. 3(a) depicts an example of how a possible *neighbors* edge could look like on the underlying data structure of the NIM. This concept is called *connection*, which is indicated by a dotted line that represents the abstract *neighbors* edge, the one that has been drawn as the only edge connecting two participants.

However, there are also two "real" connections between P_0 and P_1. The first one is interrupted by the *MessageFlow* MF_0. Such a flow could be of different types, such as *P2PMessageFlow* or *BusinessFlow*. The second *connection* is more complex, because it connects the participants with the *MessageFlow* MF_1 through *Services* (S_0, S_1) that the participants offer for sending or receiving messages.

For transforming the abstract edges of the logical graph into resources there are two fundamental techniques: (a) to stay consistent with the logical graph, an entity *Edge* could be created that incorporated all the information of all the connections between two participants. This would allow to shape the Resource Graph similar to the Logical Graph or (b) to leave all entities along the connections as independent resources and therefore extend the RG, i.e. the abstract edges of the Logical Graph would have to be abandoned and had to be reconstructed manually. Since (b) does not contradict the requirement of generality, we decided to define all entities as independent resources in the Resource Graph. This leads to the final resource design depicted in Fig. 3(b). The resource attributes $Host_0$ and $Host_1$ are shown by connecting two resources through dashed lines. The straight lines are *connections* in the RG, which indicate that any two resources are adjacent to each other. They do not have any attributes attached to them and are stored in a *connection* list attribute on one or both resources they connect to.

The definition of the NIM allows to create perspectives for business and (technical) integration networks as well as semantic links between participants, and between flows, which builds a hyper graph structure on the logical graph as depicted in Fig. 4(a). However, when using independent resources and connections, the hyper graph can be transformed into a normal graph structure as part of the resource graph.

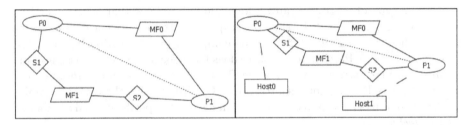

(a) The edges of logical graph dissolved   (b) The final Resource Graph

Fig. 3. From logical graph to resource graph

The concept of *connections* can also be found in the Facebook Graph API [1]. However, it is neither based on a Logical Graph, nor can it handle multi-or hypergraph structures.

Another complex construct within NIM are tree/forest structures. For instance, *MessageFlows* between two participants are grouped by *SubConversation*, which is also able to nest multiple *SubConversation*. All *MessageFlows* are part of at least one *SubConversation*. Fig. 4(b) shows a possible tree structure in the NIM, denoting *SubConversation* as *SC* and *MessageFlows* as *MF*. In the resource graph, tree structures are simply resolved as part of the Resource Graph. All resources in the tree structures have attributes such as *names*, resource attributes such as *parent* and connections such as *children*.

Extending the Resource Graph. The Resource Graph has the shortcoming that the information about the Logical Graph is lost. The connection *neighbors* that was introduced before is an abstract idea that is indirectly part of the Resource Graph and there is no direct information about the *MessageFlows* a *Participant* has. All these abstract edges would need manual information on the graph, that contradicts the design principles of the RG. Therefore, the RG allows to deploy custom rules called *shortcuts* while generating the RG from the schema, which generates specific connections such as the *neighbor* connection. These connections are treated as normal *connections* that exist in NIM. Hence the RG with all resources will always be parsed completely. Thereby shortcuts build a bridge between all the information explicitly contained in the Logical Graph and all the information explicitly contained in the Resource Graph.

For a simplicity and better ease of use, the RG contains metadata associated to the entities, like information about primitive attributes, resource attributes and connections. That is similar to the Facebook API. However for the RG, a semantic description for the entities is added.

Operations on the Resource Graph. The resource graph identifies every single resource by its unique URL, their attributes and connections to further resources. For queries, traversal and filtering on the graph, operators are defined on the RG. While this might be easy to do for small data sets and simple queries, it raises a need to provide functionalities for handling complex requests.

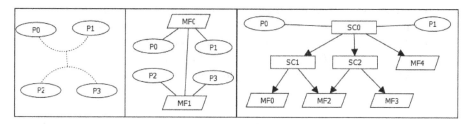

(a) The Logical Graph as a hyper graph   (b) The tree structure in NIM

Fig. 4. More complex structures

Therefore, a formalized approach to traverse and filter the RG was developed as the concepts of *base identifiers*, *operators* and *attribute filters*.

Base identifiers are part of every query. A base identifier is either a single resource identified by its id, */resource.id/*, or a set of resources that is predefined on the RG under a given set name, */:setName:/* , where $setName = \{resource_1, \ldots, resource_n\}$. Such a query would return all resources in the base identifier set, but only in an abstract form showing type and identifier attributes.

Besides the base identifiers, an unlimited amount of *operators* can be applied to them. Operators can be either connections or resource attributes. For example, an *ApplicationParticipant* has the operator *neighbors* and *host* that could be applied to it. Neighbors in this case is a (shortcut) connection, while host is a resource attribute to the *ApplicationParticipant*. This can be written as */:setName:/* `-> neighbors`. Before applying the first operator to the RG, a working set R_0 is created from the base identifier. This working set is then used with the first operator to form the second working set R_1, i.e. $R_0 = resource_1, \ldots, resource_n$, and $R_1 = neighbors(R_0)$. With the working set R_1, the next operator could be used to form the next working set R_2. This would be written as */:setName:/* `-> neighbors -> host` and would return a working set R_2 with $R_2 = host(R_1)$. Since there is no guarantee that $operation_1()$ and $operation_2()$ are inverse functions, the order of operators can not be changed. The overall query result R' of a query with m operators is formed by combining all calculated working sets R_1 up to R_m. In case the base identifier is a set, the resources of R_0 are added to R' as well. In our example, starting with a base identifier set, R is therefore

$$R' = \bigcup_{i=0}^{m} R_i$$

To preserve the graph structure in the result set, R' also needs to be represented as a tree structure. This raises the question of what happens to resources that show up twice in different working sets. For example, $neighbor(A)$ returns (B), and in the next step, $neighbor(\{B\})$ is called that returns $\{A\}$. From a set theoretic perspective, A and B only show up once in the result set R, yet the tree perspective needs to preserve the information that A has a neighbor B and vice versa. This becomes even more problematic when applying the operator a third time, because now we are back to the beginning. For example, consider a graph such as Fig. 5(a), which for the sake of simplicity, does not contain any labels on the connections or attributes on the nodes. Hence connection labels are assumed to be *neighbors*. A sample query for this graph could then be /5/ -> neighbors -> neighbors -> neighbors -> neighbors.

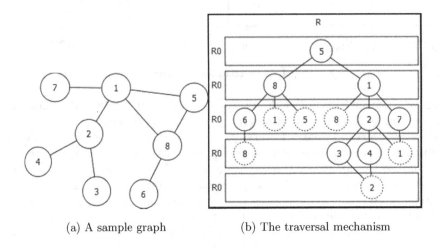

(a) A sample graph   (b) The traversal mechanism

Fig. 5. A sample graph to illustrate the traversal mechanism

Starting from node with label "5", all neighbors of all neighbors would be read until the all connected nodes would be in the result set R'. Fig. 5(b) shows how the query is put into the different working sets according to the mentioned tree structure. The working set R_0 is created from the base identifier "5". From there, the *neighbors* connection is used to find the next working set, consisting of "8" and "1". Moving on from R_1, the next neighbors are determined, which again discovers "1","5" and "8". Since they are already part of the result set R', they are put into the tree as references to the first occurance and marked as a dead end (dashed circle), which eliminates them in the working set R_2. These steps are continued until the tree is traversed. After the evaluation of the operators, R_0 has to be subtracted from R', since the base identifier was a single node, and is therefore not part of the result set.

After applying the operators to the base identifiers, the last part for a formalized query on the RG is to filter the result set. Filtering in this case means showing or not showing particular attributes on resources. Filters are applied as the last part of a query and have a $\sim$ in front of them. A query could therefore look like this

$$/:setName:/$$
$$\text{-> } operation_0$$
$$\sim filter_0$$
$$\sim filter_1.$$

Currently filters are defined for primitive attributes. resource attributes, connections and combination of these three. Two important filters are default: *deref*, shows all available attributes for all resources of result set R, and *meta*, shows the metadata for all resources in set R.

5   The Business Graph API

Given the Resource Graph, the Business Graph API (BGAPI) is defined as RESful style architecture on HTTP, that allows standard GET, POST, PUT and DELETE access to the resource graph. Accordingly, a base identifier query `/SYSTEM1/` would translate to `http://localhost/SYSTEM1/`. The result would be a standard HTTP response returning data containing an resource identifier, the self-url and type specific attributes and resource attributes. For operations on larger sets, base identifier sets are used as entry point for queries, like `/:ALLPARTICIPANTS:/`. That is a custom type and might be defined to return a set of all specializations of type participant.

Simple queries on the linked data graph start with the *search* keyword and concatenate *query*, for search term, *type*, for the type of the recource,

$$\texttt{http://localhost/search?query=term\&type=Host\&...}$$

or *fields*, as field specific search criteria.

$$\texttt{http://localhost/search?location=Sydney}$$

In case of Frind of a Friend (FoaF) queries, like "get all hosts of my neighbors", simple operator graph traversal like

```
/SYSTEM1/
-> neighbors
   -> host
```

translates to `http://localhost/SYSTEM1/neighbors/host/` and results in the required information. In the same way, the result set could be filtered to return only one attribute of the current base identifier, e.g. *location*, and the name of the resource attribute *host*. The corresponding statement

```
/SYSTEM1/
~ meta
~ location
~ host.name
```

translates to

$$\texttt{http://localhost/SYSTEM1/?show=meta,location,host.name.}$$

In a similar way, all modifiying operations on the graph, can be performed by using basic HTTP POST, PUT or DELETE requests.

Althought the usage of the BGAPI on the RG are simple as well as easy to understand and use, the expressiveness and power of this approach becomes obvious, when performing more complex queries. For instance, let us consider a BGA that visualizes the complete business network as graph. It shows basic information on the participants within the network, and wants to keep the number of client-server roundtrips low. In general, there might be at least two ways of doing this with the BGAPI: (a) define a custom search set `everything` that translates to `http://localhost/everything/` and returns resources in the graph or a more selectively (b) starting from a search set,

```
/:businessnetwork:/
     -> neighbors
          -> host
          ~ name
   ~ description
        ~ type
```

which starts from all participants defined as part of the business network, then traverses all neighbors and returns attributes like *name*, *description* and *type* as well as these fields for resource attribute *host* wihtin one request.

6   Discussion and Future Work

In this paper, we presented a novel approach to define resources within a business network for uniform query, traversal and filtering, namely the resource graph. The resource graph is automatically generated from the logical graph of the model and provides rich capabilities for custom semantics. The Business Graph API is defined on the Resource Graph and makes it accessible over a RESTful HTTP interface. We showed how selective queries and traversals on the linked business network resources can be written by exploiting filtering and custom search sets.

Future work will be conducted in generalizing the generic translation to other domains, like social graphs, and in how to compute good entry points in larger networks, possibly by user preferences in a machine learning approach.

Acknowledgments. We thank Ankur Bhatt and Dr. Markus Münkel for concept discussions as well as Gunther Rothermel for sponsorship.

References

1. Graph API, Facebook Inc. (2011),
   http://developers.facebook.com/docs/reference/api/
2. Graph Protocol, Facebook Inc. (2011),
   http://developers.facebook.com/docs/opengraph/
3. Fetterman, D.: Data Grows Up: The Architecture of the Facebook Platform. In: Spinellis, D., et al. (eds.), pp. 89–109. O'Reilly Media, Inc., Sebastopol (2009)
4. Fielding, R.T.: Architectural Styles and the Design of Network-based Software Architectures. PhD thesis, University Of California, Irvine (2000)

5. Fielding, R.T., Taylor, R.N.: Principled Design of Modern Web Architecture. ACM Transactions on Internet Technology 2(2), 115–150 (2002)
6. Infogrid Web Graph Database. Infogrid (November 2011), http://infogrid.org/
7. OMG: BPMN: Business Process Modeling Notation 2.0. Object Management Group (2011)
8. Rexster. Rexster (May 2011), https://github.com/tinkerpop/rexster/wiki/
9. Ritter, D., Bhatt, A.: Modeling Approach for Business Networks with an Integration and Business Perspective. In: De Troyer, O., Bauzer Medeiros, C., Billen, R., Hallot, P., Simitsis, A., Van Mingroot, H. (eds.) ER Workshops 2011. LNCS, vol. 6999, pp. 343–344. Springer, Heidelberg (2011)
10. Ritter, D., Ackermann, J., Bhatt, A., Hoffmann, F.O.: Building a Business Graph System and Network Integration Model Based on BPMN. In: Dijkman, R., Hofstetter, J., Koehler, J. (eds.) BPMN 2011. LNBIP, vol. 95, pp. 154–159. Springer, Heidelberg (2011)
11. Ritter, D., Bhatt, A.: Linked Web Data and Business Network Management. In: International Workshop on Linked Web Data Management (LWDM), Berlin (submitted, 2012)
12. Ritter, D.: From Network Mining to Large Scale Business Networks. In: International Workshop on Large Scale Network Analysis (LSNA), Lyon (submitted, 2012)
13. Rodriguez, M.A., Neubauer, P.: A Path Algebra for Multi-Relational Graphs. In: International Workshop on Graph Data Management (GDM), Hannover (2011)
14. Rodriguez, M.A., Neubauer, P.: The Graph Traversal Pattern. In: Sakr, S., Pardede, E. (eds.) Graph Data Management: Techniques and Applications. IGI Global (2011)
15. Sletten, B.: Resource-Oriented Architectures: Being "In The Web". In: Spinellis, D., et al. (eds.), pp. 89–109. O'Reilly Media, Inc., Sebastopol (2009)
16. Webber, J., Parastatidis, S., Robinson, I.: REST: in Practice: Hypermedia and Systems Architecture. O'Reilly & Associates, Sebastopol (2010)
17. Wilde, E., Pautasso, C. (eds.): REST: From Research to Practice. Springer, Heidelberg (2011)

A Survey of Process Model Reuse Repositories

Mturi Elias and Paul Johannesson

Department of Computer and Systems Science (DSV),
Stockholm University (SU), Stockholm, Sweden
{mturi,pajo}@dsv.su.se

Abstract. Business process modeling is a complex, time consuming and error prone task. However the efforts made to model business processes are seldom reused beyond their original purpose. Rather than modeling of business processes from scratch, analysts can drive process models, by redesigning the existing ones. A repository is, therefore, necessary to store and manage process models for future reuse. In this paper we, discuss requirements for a process model repository that would support reuse of process models, review existing process model repositories based on the requirement. Finally we analyse and point out major challenges of existing repositories that affect reuse. This survey will be a base to develop the future efficient searchable, user-friendly, useful and well-organized process model repositories.

1   Introduction

The rapid growth of Internet technologies over the last decade has supported enterprises in building novel infrastructures, setting up virtual organizations, operating in enlarged geographical spaces, and relying on more complex systems than ever. These developments require that the internal processes of enterprises be streamlined and aligned with partner processes. Furthermore, the IT infrastructures need to be centered around processes so that short lead times and high efficiency can be attained. Therefore, the interest in business process management and workflow systems has been steadily increasing [1].

A business process is a "collection of related, structured activities or tasks that produce a specific service or product (serve a particular goal) for a particular customer or customers", [2]. Business processes can be described by process models that are typically given in a graphical notation. A process model describes the activities, events and control flow of a business process, [3], and may also include additional information such as business goals and performance metrics. Abstracting and making the process logic explicit through such models offer several benefits, including [4, 5]:

- Maintained focus on the business needs. During information systems analysis and design, the focus is kept on the business processes and not their technical realizations.
- Automated enactment. The explicit representation of the business processes through process models can allow their automated enactment in software.

S. Dua et al. (Eds.): ICISTM 2012, CCIS 285, pp. 64–76, 2012.

- Easy change management. When a business process changes, it is sufficient to capture the change in its graphical model, which will trigger synchronization of underlying systems.

While modeling of business processes offers much potential, it is a complex, time consuming and error prone task [6, 7]. One reason for this is the high inherent complexity of many business processes. Another reason is the difficulty of reaching consensus on how the processes shall be run when many stakeholders with different interests and goals are involved in their design. While the second factor can be difficult to address, we believe there are effective solutions for managing process complexity. One possible solution is to collect and share process models and their associated process knowledge through a process model repository. The main benefits of such a repository include process model reuse and knowledge exchange. In addition, a process model repository can play a significant role in fostering innovation. There exist a number of efforts to build process model repositories, e.g. the MIT Process Handbook [8], SCOR [9], SAP's Business Map [10], and IBM's Patterns for E-Business [11]. However, the use of such repositories is still limited and fragmented [12]. Therefore, the main goal of this study is to identify main challenges that limit existing repositories from supporting reuse of process models. In order to investigate the reasons for this limited use, we have formulated a number of requirements on business process repositories and then evaluated and compared a number of existing repositories according to the requirements.

The remainder of the paper is structured as follows. In Section 2, requirements for a process model repository are established based on literature surveys and interviews. In Section 3, the requirements are used for reviewing a number of existing process model repositories. In Section 4, existing process model repositories are analyzed to identify some challenges that affect their usability in supporting reuse of process models. Finally, the paper is concluded in Section 5.

2   Requirements for a Process Model Repository

In order to ensure the success of process model repositories, it is essential to investigate stakeholder requirements. Stakeholders of process model repositories include researchers, practitioners, process owners, and process participants. As there is still a lack of knowledge on requirements for process model repositories, we set out to elicit such requirements from two stakeholder groups, researchers and practitioners. This was done by identifying preliminary requirements through an *exploratory study* and then validating them through a *confirmatory study* [13].

2.1   Requirements Elicitation Process

The requirements elicitation process was divided into two phases, as shown in Figure 1: The first phase is an *Exploratory Study*, which consisted of two processes, Requirements identification and Requirements analysis. The second phase is the

Confirmatory Study, which consisted of Requirements validation and Requirements definition processes. These four processes are briefly described below, while a more complete account can be found in [13].

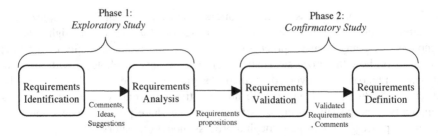

Fig. 1. Requirements Elicitation Process

Requirements Identification. This process was carried out through an exploratory study that aimed at eliciting comments, opinions, suggestions and ideas on process model repositories from both researchers and practitioners. The study was designed to collect as many ideas and suggestions as possible, encouraging the participants not to restrict their responses. Therefore, the study consisted of an open-ended questionnaire that was administered using an oral interview. Since the purpose was to identify potential requirements, we limited the participants to a small number of experts in business process and enterprise modeling.

Requirements Analysis. In this process, the collected responses were analyzed and reformulated into propositions that expressed suggestions for requirements for a process model repository.

Requirements Validation. In this process, the propositions from the previous phase were validated through a confirmatory study. A larger set of participants was asked to judge the validity of the propositions by assessing them using a 5-point likert scale. A total of 30 participants participated in the study while responses from 25 participants (16 researchers and 9 practitioners) were actually used for the study. Incomplete responses and responses from participants who had not marked their profession (researcher and/or practitioner) were omitted.

Requirements Definition. Finally, based on the analysis of the data collected from the confirmatory study, the requirements for a process model repository were suggested. In addition, the requirements definition process also took into account the analysis from the exploratory study.

2.2   Requirements Definitions and Justifications

Primarily based on the analysis of the confirmatory study and secondarily on the exploratory study, the following requirements for a process model repository were defined. These requirements are not claimed to be exhaustive but can be extended and adapted based on the specific purposes of a repository.

Requirement 1 (standard modeling language): The repository should be able to store process models in at least one process modeling language.

While there exists a number of process modeling languages (BPMN, EPC, YAWL, etc.) for modeling business processes, the study indicates that users of one modeling language typically can understand and reuse process models written in another language. Therefore, to provide reusable process models it is not necessary for a repository to store process models in more than one language.

Requirement 2 (domain independence): The repository should allow storing process models regardless of their domain—storing both domain specific and generic process models.

Reuse of process models implies taking a process model from the repository and use it as a starting point for modeling organization specific processes. Process models that are specific to a particular domain may require major customization efforts before they can be reused in a different domain. Therefore, a repository that is not limited to domain specific process models may increase the flexibility of sharing, modifying, and thereby reusing process models.

Requirement 3 (representation): Process models in the repository should be represented in both graphical and textual form.

A graphical notation is considered easier to comprehend than a textual notation [14]. On the other hand, a graphical notation is not as expressive as a textual one, as some aspects of a business process cannot be specified using only diagrams [15]. Therefore, the combination of graphical and textual notations in specifying a business process may build a synergy.

Requirement 4 (business model inclusion): The repository should store both business and process models.

A business model [16] provides a high-level view of the business activities performed by an enterprise—stating *what* is offered by *whom* to *whom*. In contrast, a process model focuses on operational and procedural aspects of these activities—*how* a particular business case is carried out [16]. Business models are said to provide a better starting point for identifying business requirements than process models [17]. Therefore, providing both business and process models in the repository may enable users to more easily identify a process model that meets their requirements.

Requirement 5 (multiple granularity levels): In the repository, a business process should be represented by several process models having different levels of detail.

Granularity of process models may vary depending on the need they fulfill [18]. Top management requires rather large-grained process descriptions, as they want to have a general overview of the time and resources needed to accomplish a process. In contrast, developers, users and analysts often prefer a more fine-grained process model for the details of a business process. Thus, it is important for the repository to maintain several process models (with different level of details) for the same business process.

Requirement 6 (versioning): The repository should allow maintaining multiple versions of a process model.

Differences exist between business processes across business units within one organization as well as across organizations within one industry or across several industries. Therefore, different process models may represent the same business process. Furthermore, the dynamic nature of most business environments requires organizations to continuously adapt their business processes to new conditions [19]. Thus, multiple versions of the same business process need to be defined and managed, and their mutual relationships have to be recorded.

Requirement 7 (annotation): A process model should be annotated with information that can facilitate searching, navigating and interpreting process models.

When the size of a repository is large, it may be difficult for users to find relevant process models. To narrow the area of search we need a way to annotate stored process models [20]. Furthermore, annotation is needed to enhance user understanding of process models in order to decide whether to reuse them.

Requirement 8 (classification scheme): Process models in the repository should be categorized based on widely accepted classification schemes to facilitate navigation.

Classifying business processes in the repository enables users to easily identify processes that meet their business needs by navigating the repository [21]. This requirement was highlighted in the literature review, exploratory study, and was partially affirmed by the confirmatory study.

Some correlation may exist between some of the identified requirements, for example domain independent and classification scheme, i.e. if the repository support storing generic and domain specific process models, the former may save as a classification scheme. Also, in order to support multiple levels of granularity, the repository requires versioning of process models. Therefore support of multiple levels of granularity has a casual effect on versioning i.e. managing process variants.

While the elicitation process has identified specific requirements for a process model repository, there also exist generic requirements for any repository that should be included in the design and implementation of a process model repository. These generic requirements include access control, change control, check-in and check-out, consistency management, content management, configuration management, interoperability with other repositories, etc. [22].

3   Survey of Existing Process Model Repositories

In this sections, we review and analyze a number of existing process model repositories to identify challenges that affect their usability in supporting process model reuse.

The survey of existing repositories is based on publications in academic as well as trade journals and conferences. In order to identify process model repositories, we searched for relevant journal and conference publications by querying Google Scholar using the four keyword phrases "business process model repository", "process model repository", "business process repository", and "process repository". The results from these searches were narrowed down to publications fulfilling the following criteria: (i) The title of the publication explicitly includes or implicitly refers to the area of interest, i.e. business process model repositories, (ii) The publication describes or proposes a business process model repository, (iii) The publication has a citation score of at least five in Google Scholar.

Based on the above criteria, 26 publications were selected, and ten repositories of business process models were identified: (i) MIT Process Handbook [8, 23], (ii) Phios process repository for supply chain (SCOR) [9], (iii) IBM Process Repository [11], (iv) IBM-BPEL Repository [24], (v) Semantic Business Process Repository [25], (vi) Oryx [26], (vii) SAP Process Repository [10], (viii) Prosero Repository [27], (ix) RepoX Repository [28], (x) Advanced Process Model Repository [12].

3.1 Review of Existing Process Model Repositories

In this section, we briefly review the identified repositories. Aspects for reviewing these repositories have been derived from the requirements suggested in the previous section. The aspects include *openness, standard modeling language support (RQ1), representation (RQ3), domain independence (RQ2), business models inclusion (RQ4), classification scheme (RQ8), goal inclusion (RQ7), and versioning (RQ6)*. Openness and goal inclusion are the additional aspects. Openness is the public availability of the repository to its potential users without any proprietary constraints—the ability of users to add, update, delete, or retrieve process models, without any prior legal permission. The cost element has not been considered. Another additional aspect is the goal inclusion. The relationship between *goal inclusion,* and requirement 7 can be traced back from the exploratory study. An aspect related process granularity levels as a requirement, is not included. This is because granularity is the process design intentional, however at the repository level, this is met if the repository supports multiple versions of the same process.

3.1.1 MIT Process Handbook

Openness. The MIT process handbook is a proprietary repository that provides a knowledge base of process descriptions [8, 23]. Therefore, the repository can only be extended and enhanced by its owners.

Standard modeling language. In the MIT repository, business processes are described in natural language, and no standard modeling notation is supported.

Representation. With respect to process representation form, the MIT process handbook only describes business processes in textual form.

Domain independence. The repository is not restricted to any specific domain.

Business models inclusion. The repository does not include business models.

Classification scheme. The process classification scheme adopted by the MIT process handbook is based on two dimensions: generalization-specialization and composition-decomposition, where each process in the repository can be viewed. While browsing of processes is based on the two dimensions of the classification scheme, the repository only provides a keyword-based search for finding processes.

Goal inclusion. Process models stored in the repository are not related to goals.

Versioning. The repository does not manage multiple versions of process models.

3.1.2 Phios Process Repository for Supply Chain (SCOR)

Openness. SCOR, [9], is another proprietary repository similar to the MIT process handbook. It provides a knowledge base of process descriptions related to supply chain management.

Standard modeling language. Like the MIT process handbook, business processes are described in natural language, and no other modeling notation is supported.

Representation. Like the MIT repository, processes are represented in textual form.

Domain independence. SCOR is restricted to supply chain management processes

Business models inclusion. The repository does not include business models.

Classification scheme. Apart from the two dimensions classification scheme, adopted by the MIT process handbook, processes in SCOR are further classified based on four verbs: create, destroy, modify, and preserve. In addition, processes are organized around five management root processes: plan, source, make, deliver, and return.

Goal inclusion. Process models stored in the repository are not related to goals.

Versioning. The repository does not manage multiple versions of process models.

3.1.3 IBM Process Repository (IBM PR)

Openness. The IBM process repository is proprietary to IBM [11].

Standard modeling language. The notation used is not standard but specific to the repository.

Representation. Process models are represented in both textual and graphical form with the aim of providing an explicit control flow.

Domain independence. IBM PR is restricted only to e-commerce business processes.

Business models inclusion. The repository does not include business models.

Classification scheme. Processes are classified into five major groups: B2B direct, consumer direct, demand chain, hosting, and supply chain. In each group, processes are further classified into three sub-groups: direct admin processes, direct starter stores, and direct solution.

Goal inclusion. The repository includes objectives of each process, but not business goals. In contrast to an objective, a goal tends to be longer term, general (rather than specific), qualitative (rather than quantitative), and ongoing.

Versioning. The repository does not handle multiple versions of process models.

3.1.4 IBM-BPEL Repository

Openness. The IBM-BPEL repository is a proprietary repository from IBM for storing and retrieving process models expressed in the Business Process Execution Language (BPEL) format [24].

Standard modeling language. The repository only supports BPEL.

Representation. Processes are represented using a BPEL XML format and stored internally as objects in an ECLIPSE repository.

Domain independence. The repository is not restricted to any specific domain.

Business models inclusion. The repository does not include business models.

Classification scheme. The repository does not include process classification scheme.

Goal inclusion. Process models stored in the repository are not related to goals.

Versioning. The repository does not handle multiple versions of process models.

3.1.5 Semantic Business Process Repository (SBPR)

Openness. SBPR [25] is a non-proprietary repository for storing and managing semantic business process models in SBPM.

Standard modeling language. The repository supports Business Process Modelling Ontology (BPMO), sBPEL, sBPMN, and sEPC, which are the ontological versions of BPEL, Business Process Modeling Notation (BPMN), and Event-Driven Process Chains (EPCs) [25].

Representation. In SBPR, processes are described in graphical form.

Domain independence. The repository is not restricted to any specific domain.

Business models inclusion. The repository does not include business models.

Classification scheme. The repository does not include process classification scheme.

Goal inclusion. Process models stored in the repository are not related to goals.

Versioning. The repository supports (manages) multiple versions of process models.

3.1.6 Oryx

Openness. Oryx [26, 29] is a non proprietary repository that provides a web-based process modeling tool to enable users create, store and update process models online.

Standard modeling language. Oryx supports several process modeling notations, including BPMN, Petri nets, and EPC.

Representation. Business processes are represented in graphical form. Process models are stored in a database and externally represented in RDF format.

Domain independence. The repository is not restricted to any specific domain.

Business models inclusion. The repository does not include business models.

Classification scheme. The repository does not include process classification scheme.

Goal inclusion. Process models stored in the repository are not related to goals.

Versioning. The repository does not manage multiple versions of process models.

3.1.7 SAP Business Map

Openness. The SAP business map, [10], is a proprietary repository.

Standard modeling language. The notation used is not standard but specific to the repository.

Representation. The repository provides process models in a graphical form, which includes its purpose, prerequisites, and activities flows.

Domain independence. The repository is limited to its application products.

Business models inclusion. The repository does not include business models.

Classification scheme. Processes in the SAP business map are classified into eight major business scenarios: interaction centre for automation, make-to-order production in supply chain management (SCM), order-to-delivery, release processing, supplier managed inventory, Radio Frequency Identification (RFID)-enabled returnable transport items, web-based supplier Kanban, and dealer business management.

Goal inclusion. The purpose of each process model is included but not business goals.

Versioning. The repository does not handle multiple versions of process models.

3.1.8 Prosero

Openness. Prosero is a SOA-based semantic repository of business processes and web services [27] meant to be used by an enterprise and its customers.

Standard modeling language. The repository only supports the BPMN notation. For execution, the repository provides a BPEL generator that transforms process models from BPMN into BPEL.

Representation. Business processes are represented in graphical form.
Domain independence. The repository is not restricted to any specific domain.
Business models inclusion. The repository does not include business models.
Classification scheme. The repository does not include process classification scheme.
Goal inclusion. Process models stored in the repository are not related to goals.
Versioning. The repository does not handle multiple versions of process models.

3.1.9 RepoX

Openness. RepoX [28], an XML repository management tool, is a client-server model (not publicly open) repository developed in the METEOR Workflow System environment for the purpose of managing XML-based metadata.
Standard modeling language. Definitions of workflow processes are stored as metadata in the form of XML documents.
Representation. Business processes are represented in graphical form.
Domain independence. The repository is not restricted to any specific domain.
Business models inclusion. The repository does not include business models.
Classification scheme. The repository does not include process classification scheme.
Goal inclusion. Process models are not related to business goals.
Versioning. RepoX supports and manages multiple versions of process models.

3.1.10 Advanced Process Model Repository (APROMORE)

Openness. APROMORE [12] is a SOA-based (non proprietary) repository that offers a rich set of features to maintain, analyze, and exploit the content of process models.
Standard modeling language. In APROMORE, business processes are described in a common format (called canonical format).
Representation. In APROMORE, processes are represented in graphical form.
Domain independence. The repository is not restricted to any specific domain.
Business models inclusion. The repository does not include business models.
Classification scheme. The repository does not include process classification scheme.
Goal inclusion. Process models stored in the repository are not related to goals.
Versioning. The repository supports (manages) multiple versions of process models.

4   Analysis of Existing Process Model Repositories

Based on the above review and the summary shown in Table 1, we analyze the surveyed repositories by identifying challenges to be addressed. Main challenges are the following:

- *Openness*: Most of the repositories, except APROMORE, SBPR and Oryx, are proprietary, i.e. they are the intellectual property of some organizations. The repositories do not allow users outside these organizations to add, update, delete, or retrieve process models, without prior legal permission. This lack of openness can impede the acceptance and consequent use of the repositories, thereby making it more difficult to achieve a critical mass of process models available for reuse.

- *Standard modeling language*: While it is not necessary to support multiple languages in order to provide reusable process models [13], the support of at least one standard modeling notation is necessary. Process models in some of the repositories, such as MIT, SCOR, IBM PR, and SAP are given in non standard modeling notations, which makes it difficult to transform them into executable models or to users' modeling notations of interest for reuse.
- *Domain independence*: Some of the repositories, such as IBM PR, SCOR, and SAP, have a restricted scope, as they are limited to certain domains. The IBM PR is restricted to e-commerce, SCOR is restricted to supply chain management and SAP is restricted to application product. Restricting the repository to certain domain affect the growth of the repository and the reusability of models between business domains becomes restricted.
- *Process representation*: In most of the repositories, processes are represented in either graphical or textual form and not both. Only IBM PR and SAP provides both graphical and textual representation of process models, however they both use non standard notation and their textual format is not well structured to capture important aspects of a business process. This affect understanding of process models by users, which affect reusability.

Table 1. Repositories Review Summary

Requirements \ Repositories	MIT	SCOR	IBM PR	IBM-BPEL	SBPR	Oryx	SAP	Prosero	Repox	APROMORE
Openness	-	-	-	-	+	+	-	-	-	+
Standard modeling language support	-	-	-	+	+	+	-	-	+	+
Domain independence	-	-	-	+	+	+	-	+	+	+
Process representation	T	T	G&T	G	G	G	G&T	G	G	G
Business models inclusion	-	-	-	-	-	-	-	-	-	-
Versioning	-	-	-	-	+	-	-	-	+	+
Goal inclusion	-	-	-	-	-	-	-	-	-	-
Classification scheme	+	+	+	-	-	-	+	-	-	-

Where, T stands for textual representation and G for graphical representation

- *Business models inclusion*: All surveyed repositories do not include business models; therefore a high-level view of the business activities performed by an enterprise is not given. This makes it difficult for users to get a better understanding of process models that could meet their business requirements.
- *Versioning*: Most of the repositories, offer a single process model for certain business process scenario. The repositories, except SBPR, RepoX and APROMORE, do not provide support to manage multiple versions of process models for the same business process. This lack of multiple version support may lead to loss of process knowledge if new ones replace existing models.

- *Goal inclusion*: In most of the repositories, the process models are not related to goals. This makes it difficult for users to gain an understanding of the business goals that are realized by a certain process. As achieving business goals is the purpose of a process, the lack of explicit goal representation also makes it more difficult to understand the process models themselves.
- *Classification scheme*: Searching and navigating across repositories is often a complex and time-consuming task, making it difficult for users to find relevant process models. One reason for this is that most repositories offer their own proprietary process classification schemes instead of utilizing more standard and well-established schemes. As a consequence, users need to understand and learn these proprietary schemes, which makes searching and navigating more demanding.

Some of these challenges are related to the intended use of a repository. In particular, a restriction to a specific domain is typically an intentional design decision. Other challenges are due to economic and organizational factors, such as the decision whether to make a repository proprietary or open. However, the challenge of facilitating search and navigation is common to all repositories. This is because of the lack of standard and well-established classification schemes. Another major challenge is the lack of an efficient version management technique for business processes stored in the repositories. In addition to classification schemes and versioning, another challenge is the difficulty of identifying and understanding business processes that meet users' business need. This is because stored process models are not well described to help user identify process models that might meet their need.

5   Conclusion

In this paper, we have identified some of the challenges that limit existing repositories from supporting the reuse of process models. We first analyzed requirements for process model repositories supporting process model reuse. The requirements were then used to review and analyze existing repositories in order to identify challenges that limit their usage in practice. One of the main challenges is that repositories often lack effective instruments for searching and navigating their contents. Another challenge is the lack of an efficient process version management technique to enable storing multiple process models for the same business process. In addition to that, repositories lack a formal approach to annotate processes stored in the repositories with information such as business goals, business models, business domain, etc.

The long-term goal of this research is to provide a universal process model repository to support reuse of process models. Future research includes, development of a process classification scheme, lightweight process semantic annotation framework and implement a process model repository.

References

1. Kirchmer, M.: Management of Process Excellence. In: vom Brocke, J., Rosemann, M. (eds.) Handbook on Business Process Management 2, pp. 39–56. Springer, Heidelberg (2010)
2. `http://en.wikipedia.org/wiki/Business_process` (last accessed November 6, 2011)
3. Recker, J.C., Rosemann, M., Indulska, M., Green, P.: Business process modeling: a comparative analysis. Journal of the Association for Information Systems 10, 333–363 (2009)
4. Dumas, M., van der Aalst, W.M., ter Hofstede, A.H.: Process-Aware Information Systems: Bridging People and Software Through Process Technology. John Wiley & Sons Inc. (2005)
5. Indulska, M., Green, P., Recker, J., Rosemann, M.: Business Process Modeling: Perceived Benefits. In: Laender, A.H.F., Castano, S., Dayal, U., Casati, F., de Oliveira, J.P.M. (eds.) ER 2009. LNCS, vol. 5829, pp. 458–471. Springer, Heidelberg (2009)
6. Rodrigues Nt, J.A., de Souza, J.M., Zimbrão, G., Xexéo, G., Neves, E., Pinheiro, W.A.: A P2P Approach for Business Process Modelling and Reuse. In: Eder, J., Dustdar, S. (eds.) BPM Workshops 2006. LNCS, vol. 4103, pp. 297–307. Springer, Heidelberg (2006)
7. Markovic, I., Pereira, A.C.: Towards a Formal Framework for Reuse in Business Process Modeling. In: ter Hofstede, A.H.M., Benatallah, B., Paik, H.-Y. (eds.) BPM Workshops 2007. LNCS, vol. 4928, pp. 484–495. Springer, Heidelberg (2008)
8. `http://process.mit.edu/Default.asp` (last accessed November 6, 2011)
9. `http://repository.phios.com/SCOR/` (last accessed November 7, 2011)
10. `http://help.sap.com/saphelp_sm40/helpdata/EN/5e/c8145e3a9d93 40913099159d80fc87/frameset.htm` (last accessed November 6, 2011)
11. `http://publib.boulder.ibm.com/infocenter/wchelp/v5r6m1/ index.jsp?topic=/com.ibm.commerce.business_process.doc/conce pts/processPrice_order.htm` (last accessed November 7, 2011)
12. La Rosa, M., Reijers, H.A., van der Aalst, W.M.P., Dijkman, R.M., Mendling, J., Dumas, M., GarcÌa-BaÒuelos, L.: APROMORE: An advanced process model repository. Expert Systems with Applications 38, 7029–7040 (2011)
13. Shahzad, K., Elias, M., Johannesson, P.: Requirements for a Business Process Model Repository: A Stakeholders' Perspective. In: Abramowicz, W., Tolksdorf, R. (eds.) BIS 2010. LNBIP, vol. 47, pp. 158–170. Springer, Heidelberg (2010)
14. Bauer, M.I., Johnson-Laird, P.N.: How diagrams can improve reasoning. Psychological Science 4, 372–378 (1993)
15. Petre, M.: Why looking isn't always seeing: readership skills and graphical programming. Commun. ACM 38, 33–44 (1995)
16. Bergholtz, M., Jayaweera, P., Johannesson, P., Wohed, P.: Process Models and Business Models - A Unified Framework. In: Olivé, À., Yoshikawa, M., Yu, E.S.K. (eds.) ER 2003. LNCS, vol. 2784, pp. 364–377. Springer, Heidelberg (2003)
17. Gordijn, J., Akkermans, H., van Vliet, H.: Business Modelling Is Not Process Modelling. In: Mayr, H.C., Liddle, S.W., Thalheim, B. (eds.) ER Workshops 2000. LNCS, vol. 1921, pp. 40–51. Springer, Heidelberg (2000)
18. Holschke, O., Rake, J., Levina, O.: Granularity as a Cognitive Factor in the Effectiveness of Business Process Model Reuse. In: Dayal, U., Eder, J., Koehler, J., Reijers, H.A. (eds.) BPM 2009. LNCS, vol. 5701, pp. 245–260. Springer, Heidelberg (2009)

19. Zhao, X., Liu, C.: Version Management in the Business Process Change Context. In: Alonso, G., Dadam, P., Rosemann, M. (eds.) BPM 2007. LNCS, vol. 4714, pp. 198–213. Springer, Heidelberg (2007)
20. Andersson, B., Bider, I., Johannesson, P., Perjons, E.: Towards a formal definition of goal-oriented business process patterns. Business Process Management Journal 11, 650–662 (2005)
21. http://www.uncefactforum.org/TBG/TBG14/TBG14Documents/cbpc-technical-specification-v1_0-300905-11.pdf (last accessed November 7, 2011)
22. Bernstein, P.A., Dayal, U.: An Overview of Repository Technology. In: Proceedings of the 20th International Conference on Very Large Data Bases, pp. 705–713. Morgan Kaufmann Publishers Inc. (1994)
23. Thomas, W.M., Kevin, C., George, A.H.: Organizing Business Knowledge: The MIT Process Handbook. MIT Press, Cambridge (2003)
24. Jussi, V., Jana, K., Frank, L.: Repository for Business Processes and Arbitrary Associated Metadata. In: 4th International Conference on Business Process Management, Austria, vol. 203, pp. 25–31 (2006)
25. Ma, Z., Wetzstein, B., Anicic, D., Heymans, S., Leymann, F.: Semantic Business Process Repository. In: CEUR Workshop Proceedings, Innsbruck (2007)
26. http://bpt.hpi.uni-potsdam.de/Oryx/WebHome (last accessed November 6, 2011)
27. Elhadad, M., Balaban, M., Sturm, A.: Effective business process outsourcing: the Prosero approach. International Journal of Interoperability in Business Information Systems 3 (2008)
28. John, M.: Arpinar: RepoX: An XML Repository for Workflow Design and Specifications (2001)
29. Decker, G., Overdick, H., Weske, M.: Oryx – An Open Modeling Platform for the BPM Community. In: Dumas, M., Reichert, M., Shan, M.-C. (eds.) BPM 2008. LNCS, vol. 5240, pp. 382–385. Springer, Heidelberg (2008)

The Dynamics of Implementation
of Finance Information Systems

David Kiwana and Björn Johansson

Department of Informatics, School of Economics and Management,
Lund University, Ole Römers väg 6,
SE-223 63 Lund, Sweden
{David.kiwana,bjorn.johansson}@ics.lu.se

Abstract. In this paper we present an investigation on dynamics of implementing finance information systems (FISs) and how the implementation relates to usage. A case study based on implementation of a finance information system at Makerere University, Uganda between 2004 and 2007 was conducted from February to June 2011. Current literature shows that how to implement information technologies (ITs) successfully is still a challenging factor. In this paper we aim at answering the research question: What factors related to social context influence the implementation and further usage of finance information systems? Data was gathered through face-to-face interviews with staff from the finance and IT departments. The analysis which was based on human environmental model supports findings of 7 lessons learnt that can help decision-makers in guiding implementation processes of large enterprise systems especially in the accounting and finance management disciplines.

Keywords: Case Study, Enterprise Systems, Finance Information System, Human Environment Model, IS Implementation.

1   Introduction

In this paper we present research conducted in order to investigate dynamics of implementing finance information systems (FISs) and how implementation relates to usage of the systems. The investigation builds on a retrospective case study that describes implementation of a finance information system at Makerere University (Mak) in Uganda between 2004 and 2007. The study was conducted from February to June 2011. The finance information system is a component of an integrated enterprise system called Integrated Tertiary Software (ITS), a South African software product that was installed at the university to manage finances/accounting, students' records and human resource functions.

Without doubt finance resources are among the key pillars needed to support all enterprises. Unfortunately their use and allocation can easily be abused if there are no adequate tools and mechanisms to effectively manage them. Presently it is increasingly becoming clear that many social tasks that include financial records management are greatly being improved and enhanced through the use of information systems.

S. Dua et al. (Eds.): ICISTM 2012, CCIS 285, pp. 77–88, 2012.
© Springer-Verlag Berlin Heidelberg 2012

Usually when an information system is introduced in an organization, an implementation process has to be carried out. The process must be carried out in the right way if the desired objectives are to be realised. This should include ensuring that all the necessary inputs are available, all the desired outputs can be generated, and above all that all the people designated to use the system fully embrace it. Kumar and Van Hillegersberg [9] say that many large organizations have made significant investments of both time and capital to implement Enterprise Resource Planning (ERP) systems, however not all implementations go as well as intended. It is on this basis that this research was conducted in order to generate more knowledge about how social context factors influences IS implementations and from that be able to gain a better understanding about how IS implementations can be done more successfully. Mak was chosen for the case study because at the time of doing the investigation it had been only four years after they had completed an implementation process of a big enterprise information system that included a finance subsystem as well. So it was assumed that most of the issues that had transpired were still fresh in the people's minds. In addition Mak being a big institution with an enrolment of about 40,000 students it would provide a good ground for a wide range of issues that would be relevant for the investigation.

The research question is as follows: What factors related to social context influence the implementation and further usage of finance information systems (FISs)?

The rest of the paper is organized as follows: It begins by providing a short literature review on some earlier studies in the research area. This is followed by a description of the study including research method and the human environment model which is used for analyzing the data. The section thereafter presents the findings gained from the analysis. The penultimate section then presents lessons learnt, and the final section finally gives some conclusions.

2   Implementation of Information Systems

Presently there must be many computer based information systems implementations that are on-going all over the world in various organizations. Usually some implementations move on well and some get a variety of problems. Markus [10] said that no one knows how many computer-based applications, designed at great cost of time and money are abandoned or expensively overhauled because they were unenthusiastically received by their intended users. Leaving aside the need for proper functioning of the system as a prerequisite, there are many other factors that can be attributed to the success or to failure of a given implementation. One of the factors that have been mentioned as being of critical importance is the factor of people's willingness to use the systems. Orlikowski and Robey [13] pointed out that for IT to be utilized, it has to be appropriated by humans, and that in this exercise of human agency, there is always a possibility that humans may choose not to use the technology or to use it in ways that undermine its 'normal' operation. Cordoba and Midgley [1] argue that information systems planning can generate situations of marginalisation of people when certain groups of people privilege their interests at the expense of other groups. Therefore it is important that the processes and goals of information systems planning are subjected to criticism by those groups of individuals who are to be involved and affected by the implementation plans and designs. Galliers [6] says that the participation of people enables continuous communication between stakeholders and facilitates adequate choice of planning and strategies to develop sustainable advantages. Howcroft [8] argues that interpreting information systems in terms of social action and meanings is becoming more popular as evidence grows that development and use of technology is a social as well as a technical process. Walsham [15] mentions that the recognition of the essentially social nature of information systems has led some researchers to adopt research approaches which focus primarily on human interpretations and meaning. Orlikowski and Baroudi [13] mentions that an increasing amount of information systems research that takes place is concerned with the relationship between organizations, individuals that work within those organizations, and information technology. From this it can be concluded that implementation still seems to be problematic and that social context factors in relation to implementation would be of interest to do more research on. The following sub sections present a review on some specific implementations of information systems.

2.1   Implementation of ERP Financial Subsystems

Zhuqiang [17] investigated the implementation of ERP financial subsystems using data on ERP implementation in a number of Chinese enterprises. Two aspects of implementations were investigated, one was the issue of optimizing the use of the systems and the elements, and the other was the issue of better integration of the systems with their environment. One of the interesting aspects that were found was that financial subsystems do not respond to the working processes in the different enterprises consistently because financial management issues are usually varied from enterprise to enterprise. Zhuqiang gave the following as the specific implementation issues: Problems related to software which include difficulties in scalability and integration with other systems, problem of short falls in human resource in some of the desired areas, problem of target not being clear because of failing to define the problem at hand clearly, problems of insufficient attention from senior management i.e. lack of ownership by senior management. All these problems are concerned with the issue of the social behavior of people in relation to information systems and this is one of the issues that this study is addressing.

2.2   Enterprise Systems Implementation Project

Yahaya et al, [16] investigated an enterprise systems implementation project that implemented the ERP system SAP in Rolls-Royce in US. The activities that took place during implementation included: bridging the legacy systems and cleaning up data, training people and running workshops (that involved senior management), managing effective relationships amongst team members and manufacturing simulation exercises. There were implementation problems that were encountered and these mainly included: matching the business process to the software configuration, training people to accept change, teaching employees how to use the modern IT equipment, data clean-up problems and delays in procurement and installations. In addition one of the critical issues that emerged from the study was that a successful ERP implementation must be managed as a program of wide-ranging organizational change initiative rather than as a software installation effort, and that such initiatives require change of the organization's socio-economic system, which is usually intertwined with technology, tasks, people, structure and culture.

Yahaya et al, [16] listed a number of precautionary points which have to be guarded against during implementation among which the following particularly appear to touch the behaviour aspects of people and would need to be studied further: (1) possible failure to align goals through conflicting directions within the organization, (2) resistance to change to new process methods by management, (3) treating the project merely as an IT implementation, rather than change in process methods, and (4) inadequate training.

2.3   Critical Success Factors and ERP Implementations

Holland et al, [7] developed a critical success factors framework for ERP implementations after making studies of EPR implementations at two firms namely: Threads which was a textile firm that had many legacy systems, and Statco which was a European stationery supplier whose business was comprised of autonomous companies each with its own IT system. The factors they developed included: (1) an issue of legacy systems which determines the amount of organizational change required to successfully do an implementation and also which dictates the starting point of implementation, (2) the issue of availability of a clear business vision with quantifiable objectives that can be achieved, (3) the issue of the strategy to use in implementation i.e. whether to implement a fully functional system or just skeletons, (4) the issue of whether top management fully understands what is involved in implementing an ERP project.

Fiona et al, (2001) carried out a study that aimed at theorising the important predictors for initial and ongoing ERP implementation successes, and emerging from the study, they developed a list of critical factors which included the following: (1) team management and nature of team composition, (2) top management support, (3) availability of clear business plan and vision, (4) effective communication at all levels, (5) availability of a committed project leader, (6) change management program and culture, (7) business process reengineering (BPR).

The above literature shows that a good amount of research has been carried out on implementation of enterprise systems and a number of critical factors have been identified. However, as indicated above several implementations of enterprise systems still do not go on as well as they should, and at the same time it could be claimed that there is a lack of knowledge on how social context factors influence implementation. The question that arose therefore is: *What factors related to social context influence the implementation and further usage of finance information systems?*

3   Research Method and Case Organization

The investigation was carried out through field study visits, gathering data on aspects of implementation and use of a finance information system at Makerere University (Mak). The technique that was used was in-depth face-to-face interviews. The reason for choosing this technique was because face-to-face interviewing provides direct contact with the actors which provided additional benefit of providing the opportunity to recognise and process non-verbal communication as well.

The respondents were chosen based on their relevance to the conceptual questions and closeness to the subject of study rather than their representativeness. This was guided by the philosophy of social construction of technology which advises that sampling and data gathering be conducted amongst relevant social groups rather than aiming at a representative sample of the total population [14]. Therefore the people who were interviewed were from the finance and IT departments.

A total of 5 interviews with 10 participants (for some interviews there were more than one participant) were held and in order to make sure that the respondents do not digress during interviews and also that they are well versed with the issues that were to be asked, the key issues of the questions for the scheduled interview were prepared and sent to the respondents before the interviews.

The questions that were asked were mainly in four areas including: general information about the organization, information about the system, information on how the implementation was done, and information on how the system was being run and managed.

The analysis of collected data was based on Human Environment Model (HEM) developed by Du Plooy [3]. HEM is composed of six social context components or characteristics, namely: environment, organizational, group, task, innovation and individual contexts. Macome [11] says that understanding the factors that influence the implementation and use of ICT initiatives in an organization implies making sense of the ICT initiatives in their human and social context. The environment according to Macome consists of external and internal factors that influence technology, individuals, organizational activities and tasks as well as their philosophical viewpoints on communities, organizations and ICT. This is what constitutes HEM and makes the model very appropriate for this analysis. It is on this basis that HEM was chosen and section 4 below gives some brief description of it.

4   Human Environment Model

The human environment model for ICT adoption and use is seen as an integration of the social context of individuals, organizations, groups, tasks, environment and innovation [4]. It represents the local context within which the IT-related initiative is introduced, adopted and used. It must be noted that on the one hand, IT related initiatives influence an organization in different ways, and on the other hand organization determines and shapes the IT-related initiatives, therefore it is important to have the relationship between organization and IT-related initiative encapsulated within the HEM for the adoption and use of IT-related initiatives [11]. Du Plooy and

Roode [4] say that because the HEM is a whole, it cannot be separated into parts, but should be seen as a totality; therefore the binding factor or integrating agent between the various characteristics is their social contexts. They add that the model only makes sense when considered in its totality, as a single environment interacting recursively with information technology during its implementation and use. Table 1 shows the constitution of each of the six characteristics. According to Du Plooy and Roode [4] all six characteristics are related to the adoption process of information technology.

Table 1. The six characteristics of the HEM model [4]

Characteristics	What is included in the characteristics
Environmental Characteristics	Influence of unions, competition from outside IT suppliers, influence of institutions, industry institutions
Organizational Characteristics	Organizational – culture, politics, learning, norms and values, information politics, emergence
Task Characteristics	Changes in work content
Innovation Characteristics	Determining capabilities of IT, influence of IT on values and judgement, business processes, organizational learning, internal communication, e.t.c.
Group Characteristics	Shared understanding, technological frames, partnership, resistance to change, ethnic culture, attitudes towards management, users and the IT division, user ownership of systems.
Individual Characteristics	Ethnic culture, power bases, empowerment and disempowerment

5   Presentation and Analysis of the Findings

This section provides the analysis of the Mak case. It begins by giving a short background of the case and then presents the analysis which is structured after the six HEM characteristics.

Mak, a public university in Uganda procured and installed an integrated information system called Integrated Tertiary Software (ITS) developed in South African. This took place in 2004, and the system was to be used in financial management, students' academic records management and human resource management. During the implementation period which was to last for three years, the system was to be tailored to the local environment, data was to be gathered and captured, and users were to be trained on using the system. Five years after the beginning of the project, a report on the on-going ICT activities in the university by then for the period 2005-2009 showed that while the implementation period had ended and the system was being used, there were still problems in getting it fully operationalised [2]. It indicated that apart from the fact that the system still had some system shortfalls in some functionalities due to incomplete customisation, there were still other key factors that were greatly contributing to in-adequacies that were existing. The factors that were mentioned included: (1) issue of persistent failure by various people to abide by the university set policies and regulations, (2) issue of lack of adequate preparedness in a number of areas, e.g. availing all the required raw data, (3) issue of persistent mind set amongst several staff members.

When the above mentioned factors are closely examined, a conclusion that there was no adequate knowledge and understanding of how the system was to optimally fit into the social setting can be drawn. From this it can be stated that making this knowledge available would be beneficial for future implementation projects.

In order to do this, a systematic study and analysis of the implementation of the system was required to be carried out. In this case the study was restricted only to financial information systems as this is the area this research was focussing on and the investigation aimed at answering three main research questions namely: (1) What factors related to social context influence the implementation and use of FISs and why. (2) What is the relationship between implementation and use of FISs? (3) How should implementation of FISs be done so that problems related to social context during usage can be avoided? In this paper we focus only the first question: *"what factors related to social context influence the implementation and use of FISs"*. It goes ahead to describe the findings, discuss them and give lessons that were learnt.

5.1   Environment Characteristics

This represents influence of unions, competition between IT suppliers, industry innovations, influence of institutions, e.t.c [3]. Fndings from the Mak case showed that the need to establish an efficient system to manage fees collections from private students was the principal driving factor that instigated Mak to procure the entire ITS system. This is exemplified by comments of the head of implementation who said that: *"the privatisation scheme that was introduced in 2001 brought up an increase in the students' population. Makerere could no longer accurately know how much money was being received, how much a student paid and how much was the balance, so we could not give timely reports"*.

The private scheme in which classes are mostly held in evenings (17 - 22 hours) was started as an innovation to enable the university generate its own income instead of depending solely on government funding. It was this innovation that subsequently unfolded the principal driving factor (the need to efficiently manage fees collections) that instigated the implementation project.

5.2   Organization Characteristics

This represents organizational culture, politics, learning, norms and values, and information politics [3]. In the Mak case it was found that while the system performed quite well on students' fees payment, several other functionalities were not being used. This is exemplified by a comment that was made by the head of implementation who said that: *"reconciliations could not be done, expenditure accounts were being captured on other systems, the response times from the vendor were always not very good, I pushed for closing of the many banks but this was not being bought by the head of finance, nobody took the initiative to operationalise the system".* The accounts team also said that: *"Support was always not timely so this rendered people to fall back to their original methods of work in order to meet targets. Secondly training which was given was theoretical and whole sale".* They added on that: *"The implementation started in the middle of the year, so users could not easily access opening balances and this became a big challenge. Also the fees structure was both in local and foreign currency, so there were always arguments on how to apply the conversion rates".*

The critical issue that emerges from the above comments is that there was lack of initiative and commitment to operationalise the system in its entirety. This can be adduced from the following:

i.   At the time of procurement Mak's critical problem was to manage student fees payments, but they went ahead and procured many more modules. So it is not surprising that they could not genuinely operationalise all of them.

ii. There was an administrative problem in the project. This is exemplified by the comment: *"nobody took the initiative to operationalize the system"* made by head of implementation.

iii. Some people had alternative solutions that could solve their problems. This is exemplified by the comment: *"expenditure accounts were being captured on other systems"* that was made by head of implementation.

5.3   Task Characteristics

This is related to changes in work content due to ICT initiatives [3]. According to the data that was gathered, change in work content at Mak was achieved in at least three areas. These included: 1) Capturing of revenues which evolved from manual to electronic downloads via bank interfaces, 2) Generating students' accounts statements which evolved from manual to electronic. Students also could serve by themselves, 3) Transferring of funds from fees collected to various receiving units which evolved from semi electronic (using spreadsheets) to full electronic on ITS. These were positive changes as exemplified by comments from the accounts team who said that: *"the university has benefited from these changes because now non paying students are greatly minimised, and also there are no more queues when clearing students for graduation"*

However there were some changes that were not positive as well. One of these for example was in connection with the screen interface for capturing data whereby a user would have to navigate through several screens when capturing just a single transaction. This was alluded to by the accounts who said that: *"The system is not user friendly. For example to capture data, one has to move through several blocks".*

5.4   Innovation Characteristics

This represents influence of IT on values and judgement, business processes, organizational learning, internal communication, e.t.c [3]. In the Mak case the following innovations were realised:

iv.   Sharing of a common data source by all the major subsystems, i.e. finance, students' academic records and human resources.
v.   Interfacing the finance system with various banks.
vi.   Providing a web interface through which students could access their own account statements.

"Anyone can pay from anywhere in the country, people have access to their financial statements and transfer of money to faculties is now more efficient", commented the accounts team.

5.5   Group Characteristics

This represents shared understanding, partnership, and resistance to change, ethnic culture, and attitudes towards management and user ownership of systems [3]. The first thing to understand is that institutionalisation of a specific ICT-based initiative is often related to a particular group [11]. In Mak case this group constituted of the entire finance department. In addition, two other teams were formed to directly drive the project. One was an internal team within the finance department constituting of all unit heads, and the other was an all encompassing team constituting of members from finance, as well as academic registrar, and human resource departments.

5.6   Individual Characteristics

This includes elements of ethnic culture, power bases, empowerment and disempowerment [3]. Macome [11] says that in the process of creating the human environment for adoption and use of IT-related initiative there is need to prepare users not only through training but also within the human environment perspective by for example informing them about changes that can occur in their jobs. Mak held several IT awareness workshops in which the role of the new technologies was explained to staff. This was alluded to by the head of implementation who said that: *"IT awareness workshops were carried out and were run by the IT department."*

Training of staff that was also done was not very well empowering because first of all people were pulled together in one big group. This made it very difficult for each of the trainees to get one-on-one attention from the trainers whenever they so desired. Secondly after training the trainers immediately went back to South Africa (where they came from) keeping very far away from users who were just maturing. Commenting on this the head of implementation said: *"the whole department was trained together as one group for two months, but in addition the trainers should have also done individualised training, and they should have remained in close proximity"*. The accounts team also said that: *"the training which was done was theoretical and whole sale. Implementation also should have been phased"*.

What is observed here is that individuals were not empowered as they should have, and this caused many to gradually drop off from usage of the system.

6   Lessons Learnt and Discussion

Based on the description above the following seven factors were found influencing implementation from a social context perspective: 1) **Implementation plan should be tagged on problems at hand**. Implementation of a complete finance information system should be done in a phased manner such that various modules are implemented only when actual need to use them arises. In Mak case, the students' fees module picked up successfully because it was being used to solve an identified critical problem. However other modules like expenditure accounts failed to pick because the problems they were targeting were not critical to many people at that time. When ITS was introduced many people had other solutions for capturing expenditures. This made the specific module on ITS not to be priority. 2) **Organisations that opt to decentralise financial management must ensure that the supervisory control from the centre remains firm.** In the Mak case, it was found that some level of financial autonomy was granted to faculties/departments and this gave a leeway to faculties to always easily open new bank accounts whenever they felt it was necessary. The big number of bank accounts that was realised could not be efficiently managed on the single system because of administrative issues. For example for the system to produce a complete set of financial reports all postings in all the various cash books would have to be complete first. Administratively this could not be achieved because the different people who were in charge of the various cash books could not all do the work at the desired speed and finish up within the set timelines. 3) **There should be strategy of how to handle existing software systems before the new installation and implementation.** Software systems found on ground before a new installation is done can compromise a new implementation especially if there is no clear strategy on how incorporate or phase them out. This can further be aggravated if the new system fails to stabilise quickly. In Mak many people reverted back to the systems they were using previously whenever they encountered difficulties on ITS. 4) **Continuous evaluations of staff performance.** Staff performance evaluations should be used to regularly assess staff on the project and wherever necessary institute interventions earl enough. In the Mak case there was an administrative problem to the extent that nobody took the initiative to operationalize the ITS fully. Staff performance evaluations if they existed should have awoken up the people. 5) **Show case of increased efficiency and simplicity in using the system.** The system must be seen to improve efficiency, and at the same time it must be simple to use. In the Mak case the interface between ITS and the various banks eased greatly the task of capturing revenues. This was a big motivating factor. On the other hand the data capturing technique which would require a user to move through several blocks when capturing a single record was found to be very cumbersome and became a big de-motivating factor. 6) **Forming implementation teams that can closely drive the implementation**. Forming implementation teams sharpens the implementation process because it enables smaller groups of people to work very closely with the consultants to ensure that perfect delivery is achieved. In the Mak case necessary teams were established to perform this task. 7) **Well packaged training and quick support service.** During training people may initially be gathered in one or about at most 2 groups (depending on their number), and in addition the trainers must allow time for one-on-one interactions with the trainees as they (trainees) gain maturity. In the case that trainees are far too many compared to the number of trainers then a roll out strategy could be used. In addition a schedule of response times to support calls (that is practically workable) must be provided by the consultants. In the Mak case none of these happened and the result was that many users gradually dismissed the usage of the system.

7   Conclusion

The aim of this study was to contribute towards understanding dynamics of implementation of financial information systems and how the implementation relates to further usage of the systems. Focus was put on interpreting and finding out how the process of implementation was influenced by the social context in which the system operates. Through this study seven lessons that can help to guide implementation process of a finance information system have been identified and described. The lessons show that implementation must be done in a phased manner and should be based on solving the problems at hand, a clear strategy of how to handle software systems before the new implementation must clearly be provided, organisations that opt to decentralise financial management must ensure that supervisory control from the centre remains firm, evaluation of staff performance on the project should be included in the project activities, increased efficiency in service delivery must clearly be seen as the implementation progresses, implementation teams that can drive the project must be formed early enough and the training must include one-on-one interactions between the trainees and the trainers.

It is of high hope therefore that these lessons will be beneficial to many organizations and users who may wish to implement large enterprise systems especially in the area of accounting and finance management discipline.

References

1. Cordoba, J., Midgley, G.: Broadening the boundaries: an application of critical systems thinking to IS planning of critical systems thinking to IS planning in Colombia. Journal of the Operational Research Society 57, 1064–1080 (2006)
2. DICTS, Makerere University ICT Report 2005-2009, Makerere University, Uganda (2009)
3. Du Plooy, N.F.: An analysis of the Human Environment for the Adoption and Use of Information Technology. PhD Thesis, University of Pretoria S.A (1998)
4. Du Plooy, N.F., Roode, J.D.: The Social Context of Implementation and Use of Information Technology, Working paper Department of Informatics, University of Pretoria, SA (1999)

5. Fiona, F.H.N., Janet, L.S.L.: Critical Factors for successful Implementation of Enterprise Systems. Business Process Journal 7(3), 285–296 (2001)
6. Galliers, R.: Reflections on information systems strategizing. In: The Social Study of Information and Communication Technology, pp. 231–262. Oxford University Press, Oxford (2004)
7. Holland, C.H., Light, B.: A Critical Success Factors Model for ERP Implementation. IEEE Software (1999)
8. Howcroft, D., Trauth, E.: Handbook of Critical Information Systems Research: theory and application. Edward Elgar, Cheltenham (2005)
9. Kumar, K., Hillegersberg, J.V.: ERP is now considered to be the price of entry for running a business, and at least at present, for being connected to other enterprises on a network economy. Communications of the Arch. 43(4) (2000)
10. Markus, M.L.: Power, Politics, and MIS Implementation. Communications of the ACM 26(6) (1983)
11. Macome, E.: The dynamics of the adoption and use of ICT-based initiatives for development: results of a field study in Mozambique. PhD Thesis, University of Pretoria, S.A (2002)
12. Orlikowski, W.J., Baroudi, J.J.: Studying Information Technology in Organizations: Research Approaches and Assumptions. Institute of Management Sciences (1991)
13. Orlikowski, W.J., Robey, D.: Information Technology and the Structuring of Organization. The Institute of Management Sciences (1991)
14. Sahay, S., Palit, M., Robey, D.: A Relativist Approach to Studying the Social Construction of Information Technology. European Journal of Information Systems 3(4) (1994)
15. Walsham, G.: The Emergence of Interpretivism in IS Research. Information Systems Research 6(4), 376–394 (1995)
16. Yahaya, Y., Gunasekaran, A., Mark, S.A.: Enterprise information systems project implementation: a case study of ERP in Rolls-Royce. Int J. Production Economics 87, 251–266 (2004)
17. Zhu, Z.: A Systems Approach to Developing and Implementing an ERP Financial Subsystem. John Wiley & Sons, Ltd. (2006)

Profiting from IT Investments in Small and Medium Enterprises: How Does the Industry Environment Influence the Returns of IT-Based Capabilities?

Paolo Neirotti and Elisabetta Raguseo

Politecnico di Torino, Department of Management and Production Engineering,
Corso Duca degli Abruzzi 24, 10129, Torino
{paolo.neirotti,elisabetta.raguseo}@polito.it

Abstract. Thanks to the software commoditization and the rise of the cloud computing, today Information Technology (IT) may have far-reaching effects upon different industries. Small and Medium Enterprises (SMEs) may however encounter several obstacles in using IT to enrich their base of capabilities. This paper examines the diffusion patterns of IT-based capabilities in SMEs and - drawing on the resource-based-view and contingency theory - it analyzes how the industry environment influences the impact of capabilities on performance. Data are gathered through a survey conducted among 238 firms in Italy in 2009. Results show that outcomes of IT investments related to internal efficiency improvements are more diffused than uses of IT enhancing the capabilities related to the firm's external orientation, that in more dynamic industries firms enjoy lower returns on profitability from their IT-based capabilities, and that in more munificent industries firms enjoy superior returns from enriching their capabilities base through IT.

Keywords: Profitability, munificence, dynamism, IT-based based capabilities, SMEs.

1 Introduction

In the last few years the rise of the cloud computing paradigm for Information Technology (IT) sparked interest in studying how diffusion of these technologies and their impact on performance are evolving. There is broad consensus that the decreasing price and the commoditization of enterprise systems and some other information technologies (e.g. RFID, wireless sensor networks) that is now occurring may favor a dramatic acceleration in the diffusion of IT among firms, providing thereby many enterprises with increased opportunities for innovations in business models, products, and organizational processes. With the reduction of costs and technology barriers to IT deployment in firms, differences in IT adoption and use may become more nuanced across industries. Accordingly, IT may become for many firms less strategically important, being for them increasingly difficult to achieve differentiation from competitors through IT use.

S. Dua et al. (Eds.): ICISTM 2012, CCIS 285, pp. 89–100, 2012.
© Springer-Verlag Berlin Heidelberg 2012

In such a scenario it is important to understand whether in Italy Small and Medium Enterprises (SMEs) will continue to under exploit the potential value of IT assets, as they have been doing so far [1]. Despite information systems are an enabler of more internal transparency and better coordination practices in the stage of business growth of small firms [2], SMEs usually under invest in IT due to some of their structural weaknesses. Specifically, SMEs' managers and external consultants usually lack appropriate expertise and absorptive capacities on applying IT effectively to innovate internal routines and business processes [3]. Because of this weakness, these firms rarely approach IT as a strategic lever. Furthermore, the lower human capital and the greater barriers that SMEs face in investing in human resources respect to their larger counterparts may impede them to undertake the complementary investments in the organizational capital that are fundamental for the IT payoff to manifest [4]. These flaws are particular evident in Italy, where in the last few years SMEs have exhibited limited innovation capacity, less educated labor and one of the slowest productivity growth in the European Union [5].

The arguments discussed above highlight that - despite emerging IT may have far-reaching effects upon different industries - in SMEs the diffusion of the capabilities that are based on use of IT (henceforth IT-based capabilities) may lag behind the adoption of IT resources and may show significant industry-level differences. Indeed, the development of these capabilities may depend on industry-specific effects such as institutional norms affecting managers' decisions about IT investments, availability of industry "vertical" IT solutions, specificities in information processing requirements, maturity of the demand. These factors influence firms' capacity to invest in IT and in the related human and organizational capital. In this regard, despite the evolving nature of IT has significantly inspired empirical research on the business value of IT [6], Information Systems (IS) research has overlooked how IT-based capabilities are actually diffused among SMEs and how industry characteristics affect the impact on performance due to such organizational capabilities. This limit is in part due to the difficulties in building rich data sets that can collect extensive information about how firms support their business functions through IT. This problem has led many IS studies [7] to analyze the economic and organizational impact of IT by focusing on measures of IT that consider input measures (i.e. expenditures in the technology) or very aggregate views on IT-based capabilities. The limited attention upon studying industry influence on IT business value is reflected at the managerial level in difficulties SMEs experience on the following issues: 1) readapting standardized IT solutions and complementary practices to the operational specificities of a sector, 2) ineffective managerial decision-making in the selection of information systems according to industry-specific requirements, 3) uncertainties in assessing the economic returns that IT investments may generate depending on a firm's environment.

This study represents a first attempt to bridge the above-mentioned research gap and it undertakes the following research questions: (1) Which are the diffusion patterns of IT-based capabilities in SMEs? (2) Do industry environmental conditions moderate the relationship between IT-based capabilities and performance? In considering the industry environmental influence on IT diffusion and returns, the focus is upon the level of dynamism and munificence. Dynamism refers to the rate of instability in an industry (i.e. changes in customers preference, the pace with which firms develop new products and technologies). Munificence refers to the extent to which the environment can support sustained growth. To investigate these research questions, the study formulates some hypotheses grounded on contingency theory and the resource-based view. The hypotheses are tested on a sample of 238 Italian SMEs.

2   Theoretical Background and Hypotheses

Following a common approach in Information Systems literature, in this study we draw on a definition of IT-based capabilities as "complex bundles of IT-related resources, skills and knowledge, exercised through business processes, which enable firms to coordinate activities and make use of the IT assets to provide desired results" [8]. The development or the enrichment of firms' capabilities through innovative use of IT reflect the outcome of IT assimilation processes, through which firms become able to incorporate and routinize IT resources into their business processes to enhance performance. Accordingly, firms may develop two types of IT-based capabilities: (1) "externally-oriented" or (2) "internally-oriented" capabilities [8]. The former allows firms to respond in a timely way to changes in markets and shifts of customers and suppliers. The latter originates in the use of IS for improving their internal efficiency and the managerial control on operations. This definition of capabilities reflects a focus on the outcome of IT adoption processes, rather on its antecedents [9]. Indeed, a part of past studies [10 and 2, in particular] interprets capabilities related to IT as the preconditions for its successful assimilation. These studies therefore refer to coordination mechanisms between business functions and the IT staff, governance systems for IT decisions, technical skills and absorptive capacities in the IT domain. Given this focus, they fail to assess whether IT is actually a General Purpose Technology that generate economic growth in the majority of industries.

Following the discussion above, our focus on IT-based capabilities may allow to investigate the competitive value of IT more in-depth. In this perspective, the resource based view [11] and the contingent theory provide appropriate arguments to understand how IT may impact a firm's profitability.

According to the contingent position, the profitability returns of firms capabilities are contingent on what the environment requires as critical success factors. Dynamism and munificence are the most important environmental factors influencing how firms create resources and the competitive value of the capabilities that they develop from their use. For example, capabilities affecting a firm's external orientation towards its customers and suppliers may be more valuable in more dynamic industries, as environments where new threats can appear suddenly and opportunities may be short-lived require superior market responsiveness. By the same token, in munificent industries - due to higher demand growth and greater market opportunities - firms exhibiting greater product development capabilities, superior market knowledge and entrepreneurial capacities are more likely to improve their performance. Conversely, "internally-oriented" capabilities might be more critical for performance in more mature and stable industries, being such environments less forgiving on operational inefficiency.

H1.A The lower the environmental dynamism, the higher is the impact of internally-oriented capabilities on firm performance.

H1.B The lower the environmental munificence, the higher is the impact of internally-oriented capabilities on firm performance.

H2.A The higher the environmental dynamism, the higher is the impact of externally-oriented IT-based capabilities on firm performance.

H2.B The higher the environmental munificence, the higher is the impact of externally-oriented IT-based capabilities on firm performance.

Contingent theory does not however take into account that some of the capabilities that firms develop from IT investments might have minor returns on profitability, due to fact that the related technologies are widely diffused on the open market and their implementation do not offer particular obstacles. Thus, as the resource-based-view (RBV) suggests, the returns from IT investments are more likely to be lower in industries exhibiting high competition, high market turbulence and rapid responses from competitors in introducing new technologies. Where these conditions occur, firms may not fully appropriate returns from their IT-based capabilities, as the productivity growth enabled by IT-based innovation is transferred to greater consumer surplus and not to higher firms' profitability [12]. Furthermore, in industries with high dynamism and competition, barriers to imitate IT resources may be weak because these industries have historically attracted a great number of vendors offering industry-specific IT solutions. This fact may have favored a greater number of firms to adopt IT assets in the earlier stage of their diffusion curve, thus at a higher cost (and at a lower "appropriability rate") respect to firms in other industries.

H3. The higher the dynamism and IT adoption rates within an industry, the lower is the impact of a firm's IT-based capabilities on its profitability differentials respect to competitors.

Figure 1 shows the conceptual model followed for the hypotheses validation and highlights that IT-based capabilities may mediate the relationship between firm's preconditions and performance. The empirical validation of this position requires to consider the endogeneity that may affect the linkage between capabilities and performance. Indeed, unobserved firm-specific factors due to superior management capabilities or some other idiosyncratic factors may co-determine both the development of IT-based capabilities and superior profitability. If firms that develop IT-based capabilities are in general better managed, Ordinary Least Square regression model may overstate the impact of IT investments on profitability. Thus, we use a two steps treatment regressions models because they allow to deal with correlation among firm-specific unobserved factors and IT-based capabilities.

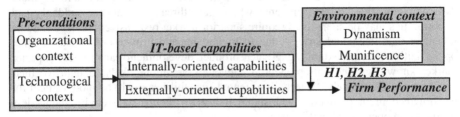

Fig. 1. Conceptual model

3   Research Methodology

3.1   Sample and Data Collection

The data used for this study are the output of a survey carried out between February and April 2010 in the Piedmont region (Italy), which is conducted every year since 2002 on a population of 5,600 SMEs. The survey was carried out on four industry groups: 1) manufacturing, 2) trade; 3) business services; 4) transportation and logistics. About 2,000 companies in the population were randomly selected and were contacted by phone to identify key respondents within the managerial cadre. Then an online questionnaire was delivered, which was built after case studies conduction. A representative sample of 360 firms provided usable responses. The limited availability of data on financial performance from the AIDA database (Bureau Van Dijk) reduced the sample to 238 firms (table 1).

Table 1. Sample composition (number and percentage of firms)

Industry	Small	Medium	Total
Manufacturing industries	71 (29.83%)	51 (21.43%)	122 (51.26%)
Wholesale and retail trade	48 (20.17%)	10 (4.20%)	58 (24.37%)
Transportation and logistics	8 (3.36%)	6 (2.52%)	14 (5.88%)
Business services	27 (11.34%)	17 (7.14%)	44 (18.49%)
Total	154 (64.71%)	84 (35.29%)	238 (100.00%)

3.2   Measures

Capabilities. As theory suggests, capabilities are hard to imitate or buy on strategic factor markets, and thus they are also difficult to observe in quantitative research. As capabilities are an intermediate step between input resources and output, we infer on a firm's ability to convert one to the other by observing the IT resources a firm use and the outputs it achieves. Using a five-point Likert scale with responses ranging from "strongly disagree" (-2) to "strongly agree" (+2), respondents had to evaluate IT impact on a series of items related to the firm's internal and the external orientation. We asked respondents to base their assessment on the impacts observed over the previous 4 years (between 2006 and 2009). Principal Component Analysis (PCA) was applied to these items. The analyses separated four types of capabilities (results are not reported to conserve space). The first factor refers to internally-oriented IT capabilities as it reflects improvements in internal efficiency that were derived from IT use. The second factor refers to the impact of IT in new product/service development processes. As such, it represents an externally-oriented IT capability, as well as the third factor, which refers to the improvement of market capabilities through improvements in knowledge of customers' behaviour and service-levels in sales and after-sales activities ("improved market capabilities"). The fourth factor reflects the use of IT to increase the firm's revenues volume, by allowing the entry in new segment markets or an increased penetration in the current market segments. To operationalize these measures we dichotomized them (1 for high and 0 for low-value sets), based on the median value.

Environmental Conditions. Dynamism and munificence were assessed using national accounting data from Istat. For each industry segment (defined at a 3-digit level of NACE codes), the industry-level total sales for 5 years were regressed on the year variable. Dynamism was operationalized as the variability in annual industry sales and was measured as the standard error of the regression slope coefficient of annual industry sales divided by the industry mean for the 5 year period. Munificence was measured as the growth rate in annual industry sales for 5 years, measured as the regression slope coefficient divided by the average industry sales. For each industry characteristic, we ranked the values by year and split the industries into two sets (high and low), based on the median value for the measure.

To validate hypothesis H3 we also defined a dummy variable IND_IT_INT that includes industries that are expected to be intensive users of IT. As such, this dummy includes firms in medium and high-tech industries (for manufacturing) and in information services (software, consulting and professional services).

Profitability Growth. The profitability impacts were operationalized by measuring changes in profitability differentials between 2006 and 2009. Specifically, for each year and each firm we considered the differences in ROA and the EBITDA/Revenue ratio respect to the median value in a peer group composed by all the Italian firms in the same industry segment (defined at a 3-digit level of NACE codes). This procedure allowed to assess whether in the period under analysis a firm has achieved a competitive edge (or disadvantage) or has bridged (or increased) a former competitive delay. This measure of profitability also controls indirectly for economic cycles (and thus the shift to a recession phase in 2008) and other macroeconomic factors such as industry concentration. Moreover, to measure the impact of IT on labor productivity, we examined changes in the value added per employee ratio between 2006 and 2009, deflating the nominal values to the year base 2000. The value added deflators estimated by Istat for each industry aggregation were used for this purpose. We used the same approach for estimating the growth rates of sales revenues over the period 2006-2009.

Preconditions. The preconditions related to the state of IS adoption was measured by considering whether the firm had adopted three types of enterprise systems: 1) ERP packages; 2) CRM systems; 3) product data management (PDM) or product lifecycle management (PLM) systems. Concerning the organizational preconditions, we took into exam firm size (number of employees in logarithmic form) and the horizontal coordination routines in the IT planning process ("IT-business horizontal integration" mechanisms). Specifically respondents were required to evaluate on a Likert scale the degree of involvement for the top management team in the following tasks: (1) definition of the business requirements for the new IS; (2) decision-making process for business strategy choices; (3) change management endeavours induced by IT adoption projects; (4) management accounting system.

4   Findings

Table 2 shows descriptive statistics and highlights that the improvements in internal efficiency (IIE) have been the most experienced outcome of IT investments in the sample (median value equal to 0.33). By contrast, product development capabilities, market capabilities and business growth capabilities resulted particularly rare (the median values of the scales measuring these capabilities were 0). This fact reflects the rare diffusion of the information systems that are expected to affect the development of these capabilities. Indeed, only 14% of the sample adopted CRM packages in sales and marketing, and only a 3% used PDM or PLM solutions supporting the product development process. Instead ERP systems exhibited a higher adoption rate (about 38%), which is consistent with the fact that the improvement of internal efficiency was perceived as the most diffused IT-based capability.

It is worth noticing that few firms exhibited formalized horizontal coordination mechanisms between business functions and the IT staff. Specifically, more than 50% of firms did not show any type of a manager's involvement in decisions related to information systems (the median value of the IT_B_INT variable is equal to 0).

Table 2. Descriptive statistics

	Variables	Name	Mean	Median	S.D.
Technological Context	ERP	*ERP*	0.38	0.00	0.49
	CRM	*CRM*	0.14	0.00	0.35
	PDM	*PDM*	0.03	0.00	0.16
Organizational context	IT-business horizontal integration	*IT_B_INT*	0.74	0.00	0.94
	Size	*SIZE*	1.55	1.51	0.37
IT-based capabilities (internally-oriented)	Internal efficiency growth	*IIE*	0.19	0.33	0.82
IT-based capabilities (externally-oriented)	Improved new product development capabilities	*NPD_CAP*	-0.25	0.00	0.81
	Improved market capabilities	*MKT_CAP*	0.05	0.00	0.88
	Business growth	*BG*	-0.47	0.00	0.95
Environmental context	Munificence	*MUN*	0.64	1.00	0.04
	Dynamism	*DYN*	0.38	0.00	0.48
Profitability	Δ ROA	*ΔROA*	0.42	0.19	5.84
	Δ EBITDA/Revenue	*ΔEB/REV*	1.22	0.43	7.26
	Revenue growth rates	*REV_GR*	0.02	-0.10	0.91
	Value added per employee change	*ΔVA/Emp*	-5.83	-4.65	18.56

Table 3 reports a synthesis of the results of the second step of the treatment regression models (for simplicity we do not provide the first step) by showing the treatment effects and their interaction with the dummies measuring dynamism and munificence. In the main equation we included control variables and the performance level of 2006. To conserve space, we have not included these effects in table 3.

Table 3. Effects on profitability differentials (second step of the treatment regression model)

Mo del	Dep. Var.	Type of treatment effect (CAP)	DYN	MUN	DYN x CAP	MUN x CAP	MUN x DYN	MUN x DYN x CAP
1	ROA		7.96***	2.32**	-1.23	-2.44†	0.45	....	....
2	EB/Rev	IIE	8.69***	1.59	0.31	0.18	0.55	....	....
3	VA/Emp		28.58***	0.71	-0.16	-2.22	-4.33	....	....
4	REV_GR		0.44	0.03	-0.21	-0.43†	0.04	....	....
5	ROA		8.30***	2.14**	-2.37**	-4.52**	4.33**	....	....
6	EB/Rev	NPD_CAP	7.72***	1.99*	-0.49	-2.94†	3.75*	....	....
7	VA/Emp		25.74***	2.93	-3.17	-12.92**	7.69	....	....
8	REV_GR		1.124***	-0.03	-0.33*	-0.73**	0.78**	....	....
9	ROA		8.72***	1.02	-1.12	0.72	-0.48	....	....
10	EB/Rev	MKT_CAP	6.47**	2.23*	0.39	-0.71	-0.34	....	....
11	VA/Emp		8.05	-0.86	1.14	2.86	-5.98	....	....
12	REV_GR		0.47	-0.12	-0.15	-0.19	-0.02	....	....
13	ROA		2.42	1.37†	-0.50	-0.02	-3.14†	....	....
14	EB/Rev	BG	5.12†	0.325	0.50	-2.06	-6.35**	1.05	8.13†
15	VA/Emp		22.44*	-0.67	0.58	3.17	-11.34*	....	....
16	REV_GR		1.05***	-0.12	-0.30*	-0.28	0.50†	....	....

***p-value<0.1%; **p< 1%; *p<5%; †<10%. Blank cells denote lack of a significant effect

Overall, we found that the development of each IT-based capabilities had a positive impact on performance and that industry environmental characteristics significantly moderate this impact. Improvements in internal efficiency are positively and significantly correlated with improvements in the two profitability differentials under consideration (model 1). However, dynamism negatively moderates the relationship between internally-oriented capabilities and ROA, with the development of internally-oriented capabilities leading to a greater profitability differential in more stable (less dynamic) industries. Moreover, in more dynamic industries improvements in internal efficiency had a negative impact on revenue growth rates (model 4). Also, the interaction of this capability type and dynamism on labor productivity is negative, although not significant. These results provide some degree of support H1.A. By contrast, we did not find any negative interaction between munificence and improvements in efficiency (H1.B is not supported).

Considering hypotheses H2.A and H2.B, table 3 shows that externally-oriented capabilities have almost systematically positive effect on performance. The only exception are the impact of market-based capabilities on labor productivity and revenue growth rates (models 7 and 8) and the effect of business growth capabilities on ROA differentials (model 13). In contrast with hypothesis H2.A, we found multiple evidence that dynamism negatively moderates the performance impact on profitability differentials due to product development capabilities. The interaction of product development capabilities and dynamism impacts negatively on the ROA and

EBITDA/Revenues differentials (models 9 and 10). A similar effect occurs with labor productivity and the revenue growth rate (models 11 and 12).

Hypothesis H2.B finds some degree of support. Market munificence positively moderates the impact of product development competencies and business growth capabilities on firms' profitability differentials. The interaction effect due to the presence of product development capabilities and munificence is positive and significant on ROA and EBITDA/Revenue differentials (models 9 and 10). Moreover in environments that exhibit both turbulence and dynamism firms that developed business growth capabilities had a higher positive impact on profitability differentials with respect to firms that achieved this outcome in industries with other conditions. Indeed, when the treatment effect on firms' differentials in the EBITDA/revenue ratio are estimated, the three order interaction between business growth capabilities, dynamism and munificence is positive and significant (model 14 of table 3). This result thus sounds as a confirm of the lower "destructive" nature of competition in less mature and more munificent industries, being competition in these sectors more likely based on product innovation rather than on price wars.

Furthermore hypothesis H3 is partially supported and advances some arguments in contrast with the ones inspiring hypothesis H1. The fact that dynamism negatively moderates the impact of product development capabilities on profitability differentials sound as an argument in support of hypothesis H3. To provide support to this hypothesis, in other models we estimated separately the interaction effects due to IT-based capabilities and the dummy for IT intensive industries (Table 4). Models 5 and 7 highlighted that in IT intensive industries returns on ROA differentials from product development and business growth capabilities were less salient.

Table 4. Effects on profitability differential. Moderating effects of IT intensive industries.

Model	Dep. Var.	Type of treatment effect (CAP)	IT_INT_IND	IT_INT_IND x CAP	MUN	DYN
1	ROA	IIE	7.24***	0.75	-1.27	-1.22†	1.20†
2	EB/Rev		8.96***	0.97	-0.62	0.41	1.60*
3	ROA	NPD_CAP	8.94***	-0.42	0.94	-1.15†	1.16†
4	EB/Rev		6.54***	0.25	1.35	0.06	1.54†
5	ROA	MKT_CAP	8.29***	0.60	-2.33†	-1.38*	1.18†
6	EB/Rev		8.08***	0.30	-0.14	0.27	1.35†
7	ROA	BG	3.67	1.77*	-3.29*	-1.30†	1.02
8	EB/Rev		2.32	1.27	0.46	0.04	1.51†

***p-value<0.1%; **p< 1%; *p<5%; †<10%.

5   Conclusions

Our study investigates the effects of IT-based capabilities on performance. Findings provide some degree of support to arguments from RBV and to contingency approaches to management of IS. Consistently with contingency theory, we found evidence supporting that in more munificent industries returns from IT investments are higher when firms use IT to develop product development capabilities and for supporting its relationships with customers and suppliers in this process. However, our evidence also confutes in part contingency theory, by showing that in less dynamic industries capabilities that support a firm's external orientation have a greater strategic value. Instead, according to contingency theory, these capabilities would be less critical in more stable environments respect to improvements in operational efficiency. A reason for this result may lie in a classical RBV argument. Indeed, in industries exhibiting less discontinuities, firms are more likely to sustain superior economic returns when they differentiate their competencies base respect to competitors in a way where IT is used to execute "proactive" strategies based on enhancing their products development processes. In stable environments, this choice may be more successful in generating competitive advantages respect to "defensive" strategies focused only on efficiency improvements.

Another argument for explaining the lower returns from IT investments in turbulent industries may lie in SME's particularities and in the inherent nature of information systems. Despite IS research [13] emphasizes that in turbulent environments IT potentially allows firms to improve their strategic flexibility and to undertake a greater number of competitive actions, in SMEs' information systems may decrease their operational and strategic agility. Indeed, the more firms have achieved business processes integration through IT, the harder is to reconfigure their structure around new "organizational architectures" to respond to environmental changes [14]. Reconfigurations of organizational structures based on intensive use of IT may imply complex adjustments dynamics, especially in smaller firms where IT investments generate critical sunk costs. This argument appears consistent with recent evidence [4] showing weak complementarities in SMEs in combining IT expenditures with investments in human capital and in organizational transformations. Given the simplicity of SMEs' organizational structures, it appears that an intensive use of IT associated with skilled people and new organizational practices may unnecessarily overburden the educated employees. In other words, following the discussion above, we can posit that when SMEs deploy information systems in their organizational routines, the rigidity of such technologies may impede them to fully grasp their benefits. This occurs as under high environmental turbulence SMEs have to sustain considerable adjustment costs to reconfigure their IT solutions and the associated routines. By contrast, when firms have to reconfigure frequently their routines, informal coordination channels and "labour intensive" control heuristics may result more flexible than information systems.

A natural concern in relation to these results is whether the current evolution of IT may actually remove part of the obstacles to adoption and economic returns of IT discussed above. Specifically, evolution of IT towards Service Oriented Architecture and "Software as a Service" delivery models for enterprise systems promises companies to dramatically reduce the total cost of ownership and the flexibility of information systems, thereby removing the constraints to IT use related to the inherent rigidity of IT solutions.

The paper offers three types of implications for managers involved in the selection of IT solutions in SMEs. First, our findings reinforce the idea that firms should consider carefully their unique industry conditions before adopting emerging IT. More specifically, the negative moderating impact of industry dynamism on the relationship between IT-based capabilities and performance emphasizes the need of enhancing the flexibility of information systems to respond to market turbulences. With the regard to the role of IT in firms innovation heuristics, the paper suggests that IT may have a role in favouring ambidexterity, by supporting firms in the creation of both internal capabilities aimed to efficiency improvements and external capabilities favouring the development of new product (and increased effectiveness in their development process) and/or the entry in new market segments. With this regard, the paper however shows that just a very small percentage of firms are able to use IT to support their ambidexterity. Finally, results - by showing that in munificent industries the development of IT-based capabilities can produce higher economic returns - stress the importance for SMEs in mature industries of a strategic repositioning in market segments with greater growth opportunities.

Besides these issues, the paper presents stimuli for further studies, which mainly originate in some weaknesses of this research. In this regard, it may be useful to highlight some weaknesses which may raise some concerns. First, SMEs could be isolated by the environmental conditions occurring in their industry as they may be positioned in market niches that are "protected" by the competitive forces occurring at the industry level. To overcome this problem, future studies could check measures of dynamism and munificence at the macro-economic level with managers' perceptions about the environmental forces occurring at the firm level. Second, some concerns can be raised on how much our results can be generalized given our focus on Italian SMEs, and on the Piedmont region, in particular. With this regard, some particularities of the regional industrial system (e.g. a high specialization on automotive, the lack of large firms pushing their small suppliers towards an integration of information systems for supply chain management) may make our sample biased in terms of IT adoption respect to the population of firms localized in other European regions (e.g. the Lombardy area in Italy) with a high economic development and a considerable presence of large enterprises. An extension of the survey to SMEs in other regions could overcome this limitation. Finally, the data were collected from a single respondent at single point in time rather than observed directly through field-based study. This is currently the standard methodology in strategy research, but it has certain drawbacks. We tried to correct these drawbacks through our selection of respondents who were sufficiently knowledgeable about the business. Moreover, in SMEs this approach may present lower drawbacks respect to larger enterprises, as in SMEs CEOs and other managers are usually more generalists and may be thus more knowledgeable about IT-related issues.

Acknowledgment. The authors acknowledge the regional ICT Observatory of Piedmont for its financial support for this research study.

References

1. Fabiani, S., Schivardi, F., Trento, S.: ICT adoption in Italian manufacturing: firm-level evidence. Industrial and Corporate Change 14(2), 225–249 (2005)
2. Street, C.T., Meister, D.B.: Small Business Growth and Internal Transparency: the Role of Information Systems. MIS Quarterly 28(3), 473–506 (2004)
3. Thong, J.Y.L., Chee-Sing, Y., Raman, K.S.: Top Management Support, External Expertise and Information Systems. Information Systems Research 7(2), 248–267 (1996)
4. Giuri, P., Torrisi, S., Zinoyeva, N.: ICT, skills and organizational change: evidence from Italian Manufacturing Firms. Industrial and Corporate Change 17(1), 29–64 (2008)
5. Hall, B., Lotti, F., Mairesse, J.: Innovation and productivity in SMEs: empirical evidence for Italy. Small Business Economics 33(1), 13–33 (2009)
6. Melville, N., Gurbaxani, V., Kraemer, K.: The productivity impact of information technology across competitive regimes: The role of industry concentration and dynamism. Decision Support Systems 43, 229–242 (2007)
7. Santhanam, R., Hartono, E.: Issues in Linking Information Technology Capability to Firm Performance. MIS Quarterly 27(1), 125–153 (2003)
8. Dale, M.D., Muhanna, W.A.: IT capabilities and firm performance: A contingency analysis of the role of industry and IT capability type. Information & Management 46(3), 181–189 (2009)
9. Wade, M., Hulland, J.: The Resource-Based View and information Systems Research: Review, Extension, and Suggestions for Future Research. MIS Quarterly 28(1), 107–142 (2004)
10. Piccoli, G., Ives, B.: IT-Dependent Strategic Initiatives and Sustained Competitive Advantage: A Review of Literature. MIS Quarterly 29, 747–776 (2005)
11. Barney, J.: Firm resources and sustained competitive advantage. Journal of Management 17(1), 99–120 (1991)
12. Hitt, L.M., Brynjolfsson, E.: Productivity, Business Profitability, and Consumer Surplus: Three Different Measures of Information Technology Value. MIS Quarterly 20(2), 121–142 (1996)
13. Sambamurthy, V., Bharadwaj, A., Grover, V.: Shaping agility through digital options: reconceptualising the role of information technology in contemporary firms. MIS Quarterly 27(2), 237–263 (2003)
14. Brandyberry, A., Arun, R., White, G.P.: Intermediate performance impacts of advanced manufacturing technology systems: an empirical investigation. Decision Sciences 30(4), 993–1020 (1999)

Item's Characterization for Model's Development in Information Retrieval System Evaluation

Bernard Ijesunor Akhigbe, Babajide Samuel Afolabi,
and Emmanuel Rotimi Adagunodo

Department of Computer Science & Engineering,
Obafemi Awolowo University, Ile-Ife, Nigeria
{biakhigbe,bafox,eadagun}@oauife.edu.ng,
benplus1@yahoo.com

Abstract. The purpose of this paper is to introduce the concept of Item's Characterization (IC) in the search for usable measures for use at the user-centered level of the evaluation of IR systems. However, after identifying items for use to assess measures either to evaluate the system or propose them for use in the system's evaluation as done in this study, it is appropriate to adequately characterize the items using the right method. The survey and Factor Analytic (FA) methods were used in this experiment. Results obtained from the experiment underscored the robustness of the concept of IC as well as the FA method used. It also showed that both IC and FA will impact on the process of IR system evaluation especially from user's perspective. But a larger sample size and a parallel method of data collection are required for future study, in order to further confirm the model's validity.

Keywords: Item characterization, Evaluation, User-centered level, Factor analytic method and Information Retrieval System.

1   Introduction

Information Retrieval (IR) is a paradigm, which allows users to locate documents with the goal of helping the users find information in carefully curated collections, such as the ones available in libraries [1], and nowadays in the internet. IR has also been referred to as a branch of computer science that deals with tasks such as gathering, indexing, filtering, retrieving, and ranking of content from a large collection of information-bearing items [1]. Systems, which demonstrate these abilities, are referred to as Information Retrieval Systems (IRS) [2]. Today, web search engines are the most visible IR applications, hence its use in this study. Other examples in which the IR paradigm has been introduced are: Question and answering systems, Natural language processing systems and even recommender systems [3], [4]

S. Dua et al. (Eds.): ICISTM 2012, CCIS 285, pp. 101–111, 2012.
© Springer-Verlag Berlin Heidelberg 2012

and [5]. It has also become an everyday technology for many web users, since it has to do with the storage and representation of knowledge and the retrieval of information relevant to a specific user problem [6] or information need.

The concept of Item's Characterization (IC) in IR community could be conceived as being at the infant stage. However, there are two recommended approaches to IR system evaluation: The System-Centered Approach (SCA) and the User-Centered Approach (UCA). In IR literature, the SCA has been successfully used at the processing level, but the measures applied are weak and failed to address issues of user-system interactivity. These measures are: Precision and Recall [2], [7] and [10]. Their variants include: Relative Recall (RR), Ranked Half-Life (RHL) and (Discounted) Cumulated Gain ((D) CG) [28], [29] and [30]. Therefore there is a need to suggest measures for use to address issues that has to do with user-system interactivity in IR systems. In order to achieve this goal, the UCA was employed considering the specific objectives earlier presented. With this, validated and usable measures were suggested for use in the evaluation of IR systems from user's perspective. However, a major challenge with the use of UCA has to do with the issue of methods. These are: the method to use for data collection from users; the method to use for the analysis of data elicited from users and so on.

However, the focuses in this study are more on the issue of IC. Firstly, for use in the suggestion of usable measures for IR system evaluation from user's perspective, and secondly for use whenever the user-centered approach is employed for IR system evaluation. This paper also, seeks to recommend the incorporation of IC in the process of IR system evaluation, from user's perspective.

This is underscored by the fact that items as the underlying structure of factors are the building blocks and foundation of measures (factors). Thus, what they contribute to the factors (measures) especially from users' end (perspective) is fundamental in estimating the strength or weakness they add to the factors that describe them. While section 2.0 discusses the aim and specific objectives of the paper, section 3.0 contains the paper's motivation based on related works. In section 4.0, the study's experiment is presented, with section 5.0 containing results and the paper ends with a discussion and conclusion in section 6.0.

2   Aim and Specific Objectives of Study

This study seeks to describe the process of IC as a starting point to: (i) the assessment of measures for use in user-related studies, (ii) the use of usable measures for IR system evaluation from user's perspective and (iii) the evaluation of IR system at the user-centered level of IR system evaluation. Each of the goals within the IR system evaluation in (i) to (iii) above may have as its product a measurement model. Furthermore, the study's aim was achieved using the following specific objectives: (i) Identify usable items; (ii) Characterize each item; (iii) test the IC in (ii); (iv) formulate a model base on result from (iii) and (v) test the model.

3   Study's Motivation Based on Related Works

In [7], [2] and [8], multiple items (closed questions) were used as the underlying construct for the proposed factors (measures) to be suggested for use in the user-centered level of IR system's evaluation. All three studies utilized items validated and used in other related studies. The Factor Analytic (FA) methods were therefore employed to investigate the study's aims and objectives. While [7] did not report an initial characterization of the items used with respect to the study's aim and objective, [2] and [8] took exception to this. Thus in [2], IC was one of the objectives of the paper. Although IC was not one of the objectives of the paper in [8], the result presented showed the benefit of IC.

The studies of [9], [10] and [11] are other examples of similar user-related studies. [9] investigated the factors influencing user satisfaction in IR. The study revealed that user satisfaction is a subjective variable. This can be influenced by several factors such as system effectiveness, user effectiveness, user effort, and user characteristics and expectations. Although the study investigated the factors influencing user satisfaction, IC was absent. In [10], the effort has to do with the description of the various quality measures for search engines and to ask whether the qualities were suitable. The study was especially focused on user needs and their implication for the design of IR systems (Web Search Engines). However, the use of IC was also absent.

The study of [11] also omitted the use of item based investigation, which is the focus of this study. Instead [11] used the Logic Scoring of Preference method. This method uses a process which takes into account desired logic relationships of inputs, and their relative importance. With this, the extent to which a given system satisfies a set of requirements specified by a human decision maker (evaluator) is determined. This implies that the evaluated system was developed to satisfy the need of users, when used by them for one task or the other. Apart from the absence of the concept of IC, users' evaluation of the system is excluded. They are assumed as just abstractions. Thus, there is deficiency in terms of user's requirement.

The inclusion of IC is important, especially in user-related studies since it provides the opportunity to know the level of contribution of items. This is in terms of the strength of measures as it relates to the evaluation of a system, from user's perspective. In terms of techniques for data collection, data analysis and model's formulation, this study derives its motivation mostly from that of [7], [2] and [8].

4   Study's Experiment

The experiment reported in this study was conducted with a view to empirically examine items with the aim of uncovering their underlying influence on the factors (measures) they contribute to. The experiment was inspired by a need to examine the appropriateness of using items. These items were characterized (assessed) for the purpose of suggesting usable measures for the evaluative purpose of IR system evaluation.   As a result, a resultant model was formulated. This was meant to demonstrate the usefulness of IC for model's development, especially in IR system evaluation. Therefore, results from the experiment provided information regarding the examination of IR system's effectiveness from user's perspectives. In addition, statistics from this experiment is meant to recommend the UCA and the use of IC within the context of the user-centered paradigm. This is an alternative, particularly for user-related studies, and not to disregard the SCA in IR evaluation.

4.1   Methodology

The procedures followed in this experiment are in line with that of [2], [5], [7], [12] and [13]. For instance, all the items used in this study were adopted from already validated scale. This was necessary to fulfill the first objective of this study. In order to proceed with a view not to stray from the study's intention, it was important to conduct a pilot study. The result of internal consistency showed that all the items were > = 0.7 using the Cronbach Alpha test. This suggested that the items selected for use met recommended criteria. Thus, all the items put together were suitable to achieve the study's goal. Therefore, a five point Likert Scale of 1 to 5 (indicating strongly agree to strongly disagree) were used to present the items administered to users using a survey questionnaire. For a more detailed description of these procedures, the works of [2], [5], [7], [12] are presented for further reading.

4.2   Participants (Subjects and Sample)

Subjects for this study were users, who have had the opportunity to use any three search engines (IR systems). These users included: Students, Workers, Lecturers and Researchers. Data were collected using both online and hard copy questionnaire, which were administered randomly to selected users. About two hundred and fifty (250) questionnaires were received and presented for statistical analysis. This number, based on the aim this paper, was sufficient to perform the necessary inferential statistics needed for data analysis, as suggested by [14] and [15].

4.3   Items (Variables) Tested in the Experiment

The Table 1 presented, contains the lists of variables (items) with their qualitative descriptions. As earlier reported, these items were selected based on prior research in related and relevant areas within information systems, and the field of IR, which includes: End-user Computing Satisfaction [16]; Perceived Usefulness, Perceived Ease of Use [17]; User Acceptance of Information Technology [18]; User Satisfaction and success [19]; User satisfaction [20] and [9]; Information system success [21]; Usability and other relevant Information system and IR system related articles [22], [23] and [24]. A detailed definition of each of these domains, which provided the required theoretical basis for their adoption and use in this experiment, are found in [9], [16], [17], [18], [19], [20], [21], [22]; [23] and [24] for further reading.

Table 1. Showing the Items (Variable) used for the Experiment using IN and their Descriptions

IC	Description	IC	Description
i1	I feel the output's format is useful	i11	The system provides prompt services to users
i2	The information is clear	i12	The system is supported by up-to-date SW/HW
i3	I am satisfied with the overall system	i13	The system supports inexperience (naïve) users
i4	The system is successful	i14	Information provided by the system is easy to understand
i5	It is easy to use since I was taught how to use it	i15	Information provided in the system is relevant
i6	No prior knowledge of a similar system is needed to use the system	i16	Information provided by the system is complete
i7	But for my level of skill and ability the system would have been difficult to use	i17	Often, information provided by the system meets my information need
i8	I get the information I need on time		
i9	The system provides up-to-date information		
i10	The system is dependable		

*IC (**Item Code**)

5   Results

There are four subsections in this section. The subsections are: Result of Communality Values (CVs); Result of Exploratory Factor Analysis (EFA) for resultant model's formulation; Result of reliability and validity of Model; and Result of overall validity of Model. Therefore, the details of the essence of each of these results as they border on emphasizing the need for IC are presented as follows.

5.1   Results of Communality Values

The result in Table 2 answers to the second objective of this experiment. It also quantitatively sheds light on each of the items presented in Table 1. The value of communality is the amount of variance in each variable that is accounted for. Thus, the initial CVs were used to estimate the variance in each variable accounted for by all latent factors. In any standard experiment, it is necessary to initially assume that all variances are common. Hence, before extraction all items are set to the variance of 1(one) as shown in Table 2. The results in the column labeled Extracted Value (EV) reveals the common variance in the data structure. In practice, items (observed variables) with small values indicate that they do not fit well with the factor solution. Thus, such items are dropped from the analysis as in [25]. In [26], it was suggested that CVs starting from between > = 0.40 to 0.70 is satisfactory. As a result, this

experiment adopted CV > = 0.50 Threshold Point (TP). Therefore, every item in the
EV column is above the TP, except i6, which is a little above 0.50.

Table 2. Showing Communality values using IN, IV and EV

IN	IV	EV	IN	IV	EV
i1	1	.631	i10	1	.613
i2	1	.609	i11	1	.618
i3	1	.749	i12	1	.684
i4	1	.784	i13	1	.674
i5	1	.621	i14	1	.673
i6	1	.541	i15	1	.749
i7	1	.789	i16	1	.681
i8	1	.710	i17	1	.706
i9	1	.706			

IN (**Item number**), IV (**Initial value**),

EV (**Extracted value**)

5.2   Results Used for Model's formulation

In Table 3, the summary of resultant patterns from the data experimented with is
presented. Each latent factor (parameter) is assumed to affect every observed variable
(item). So, the weight of each item is shown using its Factor Loadings (FLs) arrived at
from the EFA test conducted.

Table 3. Showing summary of Factor loadings using IN, CM and FLs

IN	CM	FLs
i(1-2)	F	.595, *
i(3-4)	GI	.648, .656
i(5-7)	UTC	.584, .596, .871
i(8-9)T	T	* ,.558
i(12-13)	SQ	*, *, .728, .731
i(14-17)	1Q	.595, .670, .651, .604

IN (Item Number), CM (**Corresponding Measures**),

FLs (**Factor Loadings**), F (**Format**), GI (**Global Issue**),

UTC (**User's Technical Capability**), T (**Timeliness**),

SQ (**Service Quality**) and IQ (**Information Quality**)

With these FLs a hypothesized factor structure (model) was estimated. As a result,
objectives (iii) and (iv) were fulfilled. While objective (iii) was fulfilled by the test that
resulted in the FLs, objective (iv) was realized by the resultant model, which was put up
for further analysis. This extra investigation was with a view to determine the reliability
as well as the validity of the model as demonstrated in [12], [13], [2], [5] and [7].

5.3   Result of Model's Reliability and Validity

The outcome from the test of the models reliability demonstrated reasonable confidence. This is because both results of Individual Item Reliability (IIR), Composite Reliability (CR) and Average Variance Extracted (AVE), were above the Recommended Standard (RS) of > = 0.4, > 0.6 and > 0.5 respectively. These RSs are the same with the ones in [12], [13], [2] and [7]. While IIR values range from GI (0.42, 0.44), UTC (0.34, 0.40, 0.76), SQ (0.53, 0.53), to IQ (0.40, 0.45, 0.42, 0.40); CR values range from GI (0.77), UTC (0.70), SQ (0.67), to IQ (0.78). The values of AVE for each factor (parameters/measures) were also dependable, and range from: GI (0.82), UTC (0.73), SQ (0.76), to IQ (0.68). Besides, the Confirmatory Factor Analysis (CFA) approach of the FA technique was used to arrive at all the results presented in this section.

5.4   Result of Models Overall Validity

The purpose of the test carried out on the produced model, was to ensure that its reliability is not in doubt. This was important, since the model is a measurement model, and is expected to be reused. As a result, if reused, the model should be able to produce the same result as already established in section 5.3 based on the result arrived at. Even over time, the model should remain stable whenever used. This was determined by the model's validity as the result in this section demonstrates. In order to substantiate this validity, the structural equation modeling technique was applied and the result got showed that the model will live up to (in terms of consistency) any time used.

The statistics generated for this purpose are: x^2/df (Chi Square/Degree of Freedom): 2.78; GFI (Goodness of Fit Index): 0.910; NFI (Normed Fit Index): 0.893; NNFI (Non-Normed Fit Index): 0.911; CFI (Comparative Fit Index): 0.891; RMSR (Root Mean Square Residual): 0.035 and RMSEA (Root Mean Square Error of Approximation): 0.066. This result is underpinned by the standard recommended criteria in [27]. These criteria have also been used in similar studies, such as: [2], [7], [8], [12] and [13]. They are: x^2/df: < = 3.00; GFI: > = 0.90; NFI: >= 0.90; NNFI: >= 0.90; CFI: >= 0.90; RMSR: <= 0.05 and RMSEA: <= 0.08. Thus, the measurement model has a good fit with the data set and demonstrates constancy. This is shown in Table 4.

Table 4. Showing Result of Overall Model's Validity using the GoFS with other parameters presented in the table

Goodness-of-fit statistics (GoFS)						
G.Par.	**X²/df**	**GFI**	**NFI**	**NNFI**	**CFI**	**RMSR**	**RMSEA**
SrViL	< = 3.00	> = 0.9	> = 0.9	> = 0.9	> = 0.9	< = 0.05	< = 0.08
VoMr	2.78	0.910	0.893	0.911	0.891	0.035	0.066

G.Par (**Goodness of Fit Indices Parameters**);

SrRViL (**Standard Recommended Value in Literature**)

and VoMr (**Value of Model's Reliability**)

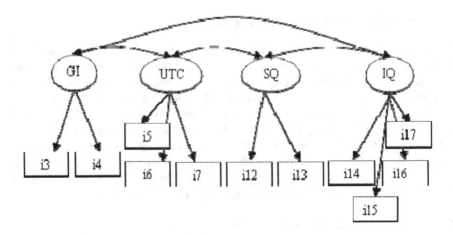

Fig. 1. The resultant model from Item's Characterization

6   Discussion and Conclusion

At the inception of this paper, seventeen items (observed variables) were identified. These items were presented for the experiment carried out in this study. The result of the experiment showed the emergence of four measures (factors): GI, UTC, SQ, and IQ. These four factors were the factors that survived the statistical rigour of the FA technique used for the experiment. Apart from these four measures, two others: F and T, were excluded after the initial experiment. This is because they could not cope with the statistical rigour that was evident in the experiment. Both of these latent factors (F and T) had two observed variables each. But as revealed in Table 3, only one item in each of the factors scored above the TP. Thus both F and T were dropped on the ground of parsimony from the overall factor structure (model). Parsimony is a principle, which does not allow any factor with only one item serving as its underlying structure to be retained. One of the four factors - SQ, has a factor structure of four observed variables (items). Two of the items could not score up to the TP and were dropped. However, SQ was retained since its factor structure does not negate the principle of parsimony. That is despite dropping two of its items as earlier explained, the remaining two items allowed it to be retained in the model, as provided in [5], [2], [7] and [13]. As a result of this process, a 4 - factor and 11- item model are presented.

The statistics generated to examine the presented model's reliability and validity have also been used in literature [5], [12], [7], [13] and [2] for the same purpose. While AVE has been used to assess a model's validity, both IIR and CR have also been used to gauge each item's and factor's reliability respectively. Therefore, the result obtained completely confirmed that the purpose of the experiment carried out in this study has been achieved. This is because both the reliability and validity of the resultant model in Figure 1 showed that each of the items was adequately characterized. Hence, the various goodness-of-fit statistics of the model reveals a good fit to the data set.

The FA is a widely used method for situations in which a small set of unobserved (latent) variables are believed to inspire (explain) a larger set of observed (manifest) variables. As a result, before items are presented for EFA test, a follow-up investigation using FA to characterize them is necessary. With this, the right items that will contribute in thoroughly identifying the right structure from the data set will be uncovered. Thus, generating hypotheses without imposing any restrictions will come easily. Another advantage with the practice of IC is that fewer items will be presented for the process of evaluation. As a result, the workload on the machine's processor to be used for the statistical analysis will be reduced. Besides, the statistical software to be employed for the analysis will be spared unnecessary algorithmic challenges. This would be in terms of time complexities with respect to the type of data structure involved in the proposed data manipulation exercise. For instance, imagine a survey sample size with a data set of $> = 500$ and item size of $> = 50$. Obviously, without first characterizing these items, time complexity would be an issue. However, this remains an issue for future investigation.

Finally, more data in terms of sample size is needed to confirm the validity of the model presented. This is with a view to substantiate further the goodness-of-fit result shown from the experiment described. Thus, there is the need to ascertain whether, with the use of a larger sample size a better goodness-of-fit would be realized for the measurement model.

Acknowledgement. This work is being partly sponsored by the STEP-B (Science and Technologoy Education at the Post-Basic Level) funding through a World Bank grant for the establishment of Center of Excellence in Software Engineering, Obafemi Awolowo University, Ile-Ife. Nigeria. (Grant No. 4304-UNI).

References

1. Castillo, C., Davison, B.D.: Adversarial Web Search. Foundations and Trends in Information Retrieval 4(5), 377–486 (2010),
   http://dx.doi.Org/10.15-61/1500000021
2. Akhigbe, B.I., Afolabi, B.S., Adagunodo, E.R.: Assessment of Measures for Information Retrieval System Evaluation: A User-centered Approach. International Journal of Computer Applications (0975 – 8887) 25(7), 6–12 (2011)
3. Wikipedia. Information Retrieval (2011), http://en.wikipedi-a.org/wiki/ -Information_retrieval (retrieved on May 24, 2011)
4. Pasca, M., Harabagiu, S.: High Performance question/answering. In: Proceedings of the 24th International Conference on Research and Development in Information Retrieval, pp. 366–374 (2001)
5. Ong, C.-S., Day, M.-Y., Hsu, W.-L.: The measurement of user satisfaction with question answering systems. Information & Management 46, 397–403 (2009)
6. Mandl, T.: Recent Developments in the Evaluation of Information Retrieval Systems: Moving Towards Diversity and Practical Relevance. Informatica 32, 27–38 (2008)
7. Akhigbe, B.I., Afolabi, B.S., Udo, I.J., Adagunodo, E.R.: An Evaluative Model for Information Retrieval System Evaluation: A User-centered Approach. International Journal on Computer Science and Engineering (IJCSE) 3(7), 2627–2634 (2011)

8. Akhigbe, B.I., Afolabi, B.S., Adagunodo, E.R.: An Empirical Model for Information Retrieval System Evaluation: The User's perspective. Computer Engineering and Intelligent Systems 2(4), 34–45 (2011)

9. Al-Maskari, A., Sanderson, M.: A Review of Factors Influencing User-satisfaction in Information Retrieval. Journal of the American Society for Information Science and Technology (2010),
http://dis.shef.ac.uk/mark/publications/
my_papers/2010_JASIST_Azzah.pdf (retrieved on March 18, 2010)

10. Lewandowski, D., Hochstotter, N.: Web Searching: A Quality Measurement Perspective. In: Spink, A., Zimmer, M. (eds.) Web Search. Springer Series in Information Science and Knowledge Management, vol. 14, pp. 309–340. Springer, Heidelberg (2008)

11. Dujmovic, J., Bai, H.: Evaluation and Comparison of Search Engines Using the LSP Method. ComSIS 3(2), 3–56 (2006), UDC 004.738.52

12. Wu, J.-H., Shen, W.-S., Lin, L.-M., Greenes, R., Bates, D.W.: Testing the technology acceptance model for evaluating healthcare professionals' intention to use an adverse event reporting system. International Journal for Quality in Health Care 20(2), 123–129 (2008)

13. Nauman, S., Yun, Y., Suku, S.: User Acceptance of Second Life: An Extended TAM including Hedonic Consumption Behaviours. In: 17th European Conference on Information Systems. ECIS2009-0269.R1, pp. 1–13 (2009)

14. Suhr, D.D.: Statistics and Data Analysis Paper 203-30. Principal Component Analysis vs. Exploratory Factor Analysis. In: The Proceedings of the 30th Annual SAS Users Group International Conference. SAS Institute Inc., Cary (2005)

15. Suhr, D.D.: Statistics and Data Analysis Paper 200-31. Principal Component Analysis vs. Exploratory Factor Analysis. In: The Proceedings of the 31st Annual SAS Users Group International Conference. SAS Institute Inc., Cary (2006)

16. Doll, W.J., Torkzadeh, G.: The Measurement of End-User Computing Satisfaction. Journal of End-User Satisfaction, Published in MIS Quarterly 12(2), 259–274 (1988),
http://www.jstor.org/stable/248851 (accessed on October 16, 2009)

17. Davis, F.D.: Perceived Usefulness, Perceived Ease of Use, and User Acceptance of Information Technology. Journal of IT Usefulness and Ease of Use, Published in MIS Quarterly 13(3), 319–340 (1989a), http://www.jstor.org/stable/249008 (accessed on June 18, 2010)

18. Davis, F., Bagozzi, R.P., Warshaw, P.R.: User Acceptance of Computer Technology: A Comparison of Two Theoretical Models. Management Science 38(8), 982–1003 (1989)

19. Islam, A.K.M.N.: Developing a Model to Measure User Satisfaction and Success of Virtual Meeting Tools in an Organization. In: Filipe, J., Cordeiro, J. (eds.) ICEIS 2009. LNBIP, vol. 24, pp. 975–987. Springer, Heidelberg (2009)

20. Ong, C.-S., Day, M.-Y., Hsu, W.-L.: The measurement of user satisfaction with question answering systems. Information & Management 46, 397–403 (2009)

21. Al-adaileh, R.M.: An Evaluation of Information Systems Success: A User Perspective - the Case of Jordan Telecom Group. European Journal of Scientific Research 37(2), 226–239 (2009) ISSN 1450-216X

22. Nielsen, J.: Usability Engineering. Academic Press, Boston (1993)

23. Shneiderman, B., Plaisant, C.: Designing the User Interface: Strategies for Effective Human-Computer Interaction (4th international ed.). Addison Wesley, Boston (2005)

24. Meuronen, A.: Development of a Tool for Measuring User Experience of Customers of Nordea's Internet Bank. Unpublished M. Sc. Thesis (2005)
http://ethesis.helsinki.fi/julkaisut/kay/
psyko-/pg/meuronen/developm.pdf (retrieved on November 24, 2010)

25. Field, A.: Discovering Statistics Using SPSS, 2nd edn. Sage, London (2005)
26. Costello, A.B., Jason, W.O.: Best Practices in Exploratory Factor Analysis: Four Recommendations for getting the most from your Analysis. Practical Assessment Research and Evaluation 10(7) (2005)
27. Hair, J.F., Black, W.C., Babin, B.J., et al.: Multivariate Data Analysis. Prentice Hall, NJ (2005)
28. Borlund, P.: Experimental components for the evaluation of interactive information retrieval systems. Journal of Documentation 56(1), 71–90 (2000)
29. Voorhees, E.: Evaluation by highly relevant documents. In: Proceedings of the 24th Annual International ACM SIGIR Conference on Research and Development in Information Retrieval, pp. 74–82. ACM, New York (2001)
30. Järvelin, K., Kekäläinen, J.: Cumulated gain-based evaluation of IR techniques. Submitted to ACM Transactions on Information Systems (2002)

Knowledge Contribution in Social Media: Exploring Factors Influencing Social Taggers' Acceptance towards Contributing and Sharing Tags

Hesham Allam[1], James Blustein[2], Michael Bliemel[3], and Louise Spiteri[4]

[1] Interdisciplinary PhD Program
[2] Faculty of Computer Science & School of Information Management
[3] School of Business Administration
[4] School of Information Mangement Dalhousie University, Halifax, Canada
{Hesham,M.Bliemel,Louise.Spiteri}@dal.ca, jamie@cs.dal.ca

Abstract. Based on a thorough literature review of social tagging and on technology acceptance models, we developed and empirically validated a motivational model to predict users' acceptance to add and share tagging content. Four factors successfully predicted users' intention to add and share metadata tagging content. Unlike previous studies on virtual communities, Reciprocity was found to be positively related to attitude whereas, in line with previous research, Ease of Use and Personal Productivity were confirmed to have substantial influence on users' attitude, which in turn affects the intention towards creating and sharing tagging content. Our findings are expected to shed light on developing strategies to understand and promote tagging content contribution and sharing which have the potential to increase the collective power and intelligence of the community.

Keywords: Knowledge sharing, social tagging, social media, collaborative tools, theory of reasoned action, technology acceptance model, extrinsic motivators, social exchange theory, social-psychological forces.

1 Introduction

Users' tagging or social tagging is a Web 2.0 phenomenon that enables users to use keyword descriptors to label web content for the purpose of personal and shared organization of information resources [1]. Social tagging offers a promising social environment that uses a range of tools to create, aggregate, and share dynamic content in creative and interactive ways that are more rich than transactions previously conducted on the Internet [2]. We attribute the greatly increased popularity of tagging in recent years to the social nature and flexibility of tags. Tag users can add tags to various types of information resources including images, bookmarks, blogs, and videos; furthermore, individuals can add tags through web-based services such as Flickr, del.icio.us, Technorati, YouTube, etc. The importance and popularity of tagging are attributed, at least in part, to the benefits users gain from effective sharing and organization of very large amounts of information [3, 4].

S. Dua et al. (Eds.): ICISTM 2012, CCIS 285, pp. 112–123, 2012.
© Springer-Verlag Berlin Heidelberg 2012

Although the benefits of social tagging are promising, much effort is required to sustain tag contribution and sharing. This requires not only an active tag administrator to update and monitor quality tagging content regularly, but also necessitates enough contribution and sharing from users to harvest the collaborative benefits offered by tags. In particular, the lack of sustained tagging content inside systems makes these systems obsolete as it fails to harness intended group benefits. However, knowledge sharing, in general, cannot be forced, it can only be encouraged and facilitated [5]; attempting to amend users' behavior positively towards sharing is generally considered the greatest challenge facing those who recognize the potential benefit from knowledge contribution and sharing behavior. An interesting question is: what are the factors that are likely to encourage, and otherwise induce, a positive attitude to add and share content in social media sites? This paper discusses our ongoing research into understanding the factors that increase users' tendencies to engage in adding and sharing tagging content to online tagging tools. Our investigation is focused on the factors of Ease of Use, Personal Productivity, Reciprocity, and Social Norms.

This paper is organized into six sections. The next section surveys the salient literature to identify antecedents to users' attitudes regarding knowledge sharing, and describes the theoretical background of the model. The third section presents the research model and develops the research hypotheses characterizing the relationships depicted in the model. The fourth section describes the research methods. The final sections discuss the results, their implications for research and practice, study limitation, and future research.

2 Theoretical Background

In investigating users' attitude towards using social tagging systems as a dependent variable of this study, we began with the Technology Acceptance Model (TAM)[6]. TAM has been effective in explaining individual use of information technology in many studies (e.g. [7–10]). However, in regards to knowledge contribution (in our case, tag content contribution), we find that TAM can only partially explain knowledge contribution given that it does not account for social costs and benefits experienced by knowledge contributors which can influence their usage of online collaborative tools [11]. To further explain social costs and benefits and their contextual determinants, social exchange theory provides a useful framework [12, 13]. Accordingly, this study uses TAM and social exchange theory as theoretical bases for the proposed model.

2.1 Technology Acceptance Model and Knowledge Sharing Belief

The impact of users' perception and experience of information technology in general, and in social tagging application in particular, may evolve during their participation and interaction with applications. To explain users' experience and behavior with information technology, two major factors come into play as part of the Theory of Reasoned Action (TRA). These two factors are Perceived Usefulness (PU) and Perceived Ease of Use (PEOU). The TRA affirms that these two factors have an influence on users' attitude which, in turn, predicts users' behavioral intention to use information systems [14].

Social exchange theory explains knowledge-sharing behavior from a cost-benefit dimension. Like economic exchange theory, social exchange theory assumes that exchange takes place when the benefit that individuals gain outweighs the cost of acquiring that benefit. However, social exchange focuses more on both intangible costs and benefits [15]. In their exploratory study of attitudes about knowledge sharing, Bock et al. [16] combined social exchange theory with social cognitive theory to test their exploratory factors: expected contribution, expected rewards, and expected social association. They found significant effects of attitude on knowledge sharing.

3 Conceptual Model and Hypotheses

Our basic explanatory model (Figure 1) shows that effective contribution and sharing in tagging tools would lead to potential benefits only if we clearly identify the key factors impacting users' participation. The proposed factors include: (1) System dimension, which includes the construct of Perceived Ease of Use; (2) Personal dimension, which includes the construct of Personal Productivity and (3) Social dimension, including Reciprocity and Social Norm.

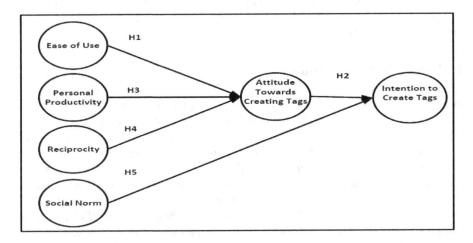

Fig. 1. Conceptual Model

3.1 Ease of Use, Attitude, Intention to Tag

Based on previous studies of TAM [6,10,14,18], we define Perceived Ease of Use as the extent to which an individual perceives that creating and sharing in a tagging system would be effortless. Attitude was defined as the users' preference to add and share tagging content. With regard to Intention, we define it as the extent to which the users of tagging systems would like to create and share tagging content in the future. Previous study confirmed the positive significance of Ease of Use on attitude which, in turn, impacts Intention to use technology [6,10,14,18]. This leads to the following hypotheses:

Hypothesis 1: The ease of use of a tagging system will impact users' attitude to create and share tags; and

Hypothesis 2: Users attitude to create and share tags will impact users' intention to create and share tags in the future.

3.2 Personal Productivity

Personal productivity refers to the capability of the system to offer benefits to help users become more productive in their daily tasks. Many studies confirmed that users of tagging systems participate in the tagging activities because of the personal and collaborative benefits these tools bring. Ames & Naaman [20] ran a comprehensive study on users' incentives to tag in Flickr and ZoneTag. The results showed that participants were motivated by the usefulness of tags to self promote their photo collections and by self organization to organize their photos for future retrieval. Velsen & Melenhorst [21,58] found that users mainly tag their video material for indexing and personal organizational purposes. Suchanek et al. [22,24] indicated that tags help users browse, categorize, and find items. Further, tags are used as a form of information discovery, sharing, and social ranking. Together those conclusions lead to our next hypothesis.

Hypothesis 3: Personal Productivity will affect users' attitude to create and share tags.

3.3 Reciprocity

Following Wasko & Faraj [28], we define Reciprocity as the degree to which a person believes he or she could obtain mutual benefits through knowledge and tag sharing. In their study of why people participate in commerce sites, Wasko & Faraj [29] suggested that online users expect to share their knowledge because they believe in reciprocity. Bock et al. [7] indicated that reciprocal relationship among online users has a positive impact on their attitude towards contributing to the system. In their empirical study of how to motivate users to contribute to blog systems, Hsu & Lin suggested that expected reciprocal benefits have a positive impact on the attitude towards using a blog system [14]. Accordingly, we hypothesize:

Hypothesis 4: Users attitude to create and share tags is positively related to the reciprocal benefits expected from contributing and sharing tags.

3.4 Social Norm

Based on Vankatesh et al. [8], we define Social Norm as the person's perception that most people who are important to him/her think he/she should or should not create and share tagging content. Ellis & Fisher [30] noted that social norm plays a major factor in users' socialization. They noted that social norm is common standards for group members' behavior. When people participate in a social system, they assume a role in it and they usually behave as expected by other members. Vankatesh et al. [8] confirmed that people are affected by the way they believe others will view them vis-a-vis their use of the technology. Teo et al. [31] conducted an empirical study on the adoption of a WAP-enabled mobile phone and they found a strong connection between social norms and users' behavior in utilizing technology. Accordingly, we hypothesize:

Hypothesis 5: Social norm will affect users' intention to create and share tags.

4   Methodology

4.1   Survey Administration

Data from five online social tagging systems were obtained by using an online questionnaire asking respondents of their experience when interacting with online tagging tools. An invitation to participate (with an hyperlink to the questionnaire) was posted on the discussion board of an online tagging tool. Although users reported five online tagging systems, most respondents come from three tagging systems: LibraryThing, Delicious, and Flickr. The online survey yielded a total of 87 responses of which 72 were valid and 15 were incomplete. Although there is no single standard for determining the relationship between sample size and model complexity, there seems to be the following consensus. Using PLS, Chin [33] recommended using ten times the greater of the construct with the greatest number of either (a) formative indicators; or (b) structural paths leading to it. We opted for the former. In our case, Personal Productivity was the construct with the greatest number of indicators (6 items). Based on Chin's recommendation, our sample size should be approximately 60 respondents. Our model uses 72 respondents. The issue of sample size is further discussed in the Study Limitations section (at the end of this article). Of the respondents: 80% were male and 20% were female. The age categories are distributed as follows: 21–25 (5%), 26–30 (19%), 31–35 (45%), 36–40 (23%), and 41–45 (8%). Regarding education: 90% of participants had at least an undergraduate degree and 89% were employed full-time. Most respondents reported solid experience in using and creating tags.

4.2   Measurement Development

The questionnaire was developed from material discussed and tested previously. The list of items used is displayed in Appendix A. The items were slightly modified to suit the context of tagging. Our scale items for Perceived Ease of Use, and Attitude were based on previous studies [6, 9, 11,19]. Reciprocity was measured by items adapted from Hsu & Lin [14]. Each item was measured on a seven-point Likert scale, ranging from "Strongly Disagree" (1) to "Strongly Agree" (7).

5 Data Analysis and Results

5.1 Analytic Strategy for Assessing the Model

In order to verify the proposed model, we used Structure Equation Modeling (SEM) as the data analysis method since the goal of the research is to explore the relationship and the outcome of interactions of the four dimensions [33,39]. SEM is a powerful second-generation multivariate technique for analyzing causal models with an estimation of the two components of a causal model: measurement and structural models [34]. Smart PLS was chosen as the analytical software to explain the measurement and the structural models [35].

5.2 Measurement Model

Construct Validity

Construct validity determines the extent to which a scale measures a variable of interest. Many different aspects have been proposed in the psychometric literature [36]. In this study, we follow Chin's processes [33] of validating instruments in MIS research in terms of convergent and discriminant validity. The following evidence collectively suggests acceptable measurement properties of all of the variables involved in the study. Table 1 shows the composite reliability, Cronbach's alpha, and average variance extracted (AVE) (shown in shaded diagonal elements in table 1). The fact that the values of Cronbach's alpha and composite reliabilities are all higher than the recommended 0.707 by Nunnally [37] and that the values of AVE are all above 0.50 suggested by Fornell & Larcker [38] indicate high internal consistency and convergent validity of our measurements.

Table 1. Psychometric Properties

	AVE	Composite Reliability	Alpha
Attitude (ATT)	0.72	0.91	0.87
Ease of Use (EOU)	0.79	0.92	0.86
Reciprocity (RECP)	0.76	0.90	0.84
Social Norms (SN)	0.80	0.89	0.89
Personal Productivity (PP)	0.72	0.94	0.92
Intention (INT)	0.78	0.88	0.78

Discriminant Validity

Discriminant validity is the degree to which measures of different constructs are distinct: if two or more constructs are unique, then measures of each construct should correlate well among themselves and should not correlate well with other measures from other constructs. Table 2 shows evidence of discriminant validity of all the constructs, as (a) the value of the square root of AVE for each variable correlated with itself (shown in shaded diagonal elements) is higher than its correlation with any other variable; and (b) questions' loadings on their own variable are higher than the cross loadings with other variables [33]. Loadings of 0.45 to 0.54 are considered fair, 0.55 to 0.62 are considered good, 0.63 to 0.70 are considered very good, and above 0.71 are considered excellent [39]. Table 2 shows the correlations for each construct with all the items of other constructs. Item loadings are not presented here due to space limitations. However, all questions loading for all constructs scored .71 and above.

Table 2. Constructs' Correlation

	ATT	EOU	RECP	SN	PP	INT
ATT	**0.85**					
EOU	0.77	**0.89**				
RECP	0.65	0.51	**0.87**			
SN	0.16	-0.05	0.21	**0.90**		
PP	0.83	0.70	0.56	0.04	**0.85**	
INT	0.73	0.24	0.46	-0.01	0.67	**0.88**

Note: The shaded diagonal elements are the square root of AVEs and the off-diagonal elements are the correlations among constructs.

5.3 Structure Model

Two approaches were used to measure the impact of the latent variables on Attitude towards creating and sharing social tags. The first approach is by measuring the path coefficient of each construct and weighs its influence on Attitude. The second approach is using the using the T-test to make sure that results from the structural model are correct and that the R^2 that was produced on the dependent variable is not misleading. We used the bootstrapping approach to assess the t-values significance. Based on the recommendation by Hair et al. [35], we used 5,000 samples with a number of cases equal to our observation of 72.

Figure 2 illustrates the structural model with R^2 value for each endogenous constructs. According to Hair et al. [35], an R^2 value of 0.75, 0.5, or 0.25 for the affected constructs in the structural model is described as substantial, moderate, or weak, respectively. As seen from the above Figure, Ease of Use, Personal Productivity, and Reciprocity explain 80% of Attitude. Additionally, Attitude and Social Norm contributed 0.532 of the variance of Intention to Use. Personal Productivity, Ease of Use, and Attitude, scored path coefficients of 0.49, 0.342, and 0.730 respectively with t-values of 4.376, 3.07 and 12.76 respectively which is significant at 2.64 ($p \leq 0.01$). Further, Reciprocity tested significant on Attitude with a path coefficient of 0.173 and a *t*-value of 1.89 at 1.66 (for *p*≤0.10). Finally Social Norm was not found to have a significant effect on Intention, scoring a path coefficient of only 0.059.

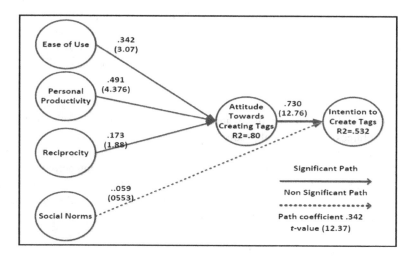

Fig. 2. PLS Results of the Research Model

6 Discussion

The study contributes to knowledge sharing in virtual communities by testing (1) the effect of Ease of Use, Personal Productivity, and Reciprocity on the users' attitude towards creating and adding tags; and (2) the influence of Attitude and Social Norm on the Intention to create and share tags. Contrary to the initial hypothesis, social norm did not significantly affect Intention to tag. This confirms previous studies that showed statistical significance from Social Norms on the Intention to use information systems. This means that people who tag and share their tags with others are not affected by how much their online friends and peers are tagging, or how much they think they should be tagging. We conclude that the lack of close ties in virtual communities makes peer influence on virtual members less substantial and rather weak.

The influence of personal productivity is the most significant on taggers' attitude. In other words, users prefer to contribute and share their tags because it helps them increase and enhance their personal productivity when retrieving information resources. This corresponds with the benefits of creating tags: namely, for the user, to accomplish information search tasks more quickly, improve the performance of information search tasks, and enhance the effectiveness of information search tasks. This is also in line with our original hypothesis that users of an information system will use it if the system helps them in their daily tasks.

The relationship between Ease of Use and Attitude is also substantially significant. Tag users will be more likely to create and share tag metadata if the tagging system is easy to use. This finding extends previous studies on TAM that confirm Ease of Use as a main contributor of the attitude towards using technology.

Reciprocity has a significant impact on attitude. As hypothesized, when users feel that creating and sharing tags will yield mutual benefits to them and the other users, they will feel positive about their attitude in creating and sharing tags. This is consistent with the sentiment often expressed, "why would I share my tags if no one is sharing his." These findings directly contradict prior research in online communities, where it is consistently found that reciprocity is not critical for sustaining supportive relationships and collective action [14, 28].

6.1 Implications for Practice

1. The results argue for more attention to be paid to the individual needs (usefulness and personal productivity) of tagging applications to entice users to add more tagging content. Thus, collecting, displaying, and updating tagging content are critical for encouraging viewing tagging activities among community members. This also suggests the need to educate users of online tagging systems of the real benefits of tagging, which includes increased productivity in retrieving information resources.

2. The findings underscore the importance of Ease of Use as an influential factor in determining users' attitude towards creating Meta data to the tagging systems. This suggest that managers of tagging system should focus on maintaining a user friendly system to encourage taggers to add and share content especially for new users who are not familiar with tagging features.

3. The study argues that the reciprocal benefits perceived by users when contributing content to tagging tools motivates them to create and share content. One way could be to offer recommendation of related tags to those who are frequent tag contributors to reinforce the notion of giving back to those who give.

6.2 Study Limitation and Future Research

First, results of this study must be interpreted in the context of its limitations. Although our sample of 72 respondents resulted in significant results, a larger sample of respondents brings more statistical power and predictability to the proposed model. The next step is to secure a larger sample of respondents that will provide data including more social factors which will add more depth to the current factors. Second, the study depended on one method of measuring the impact of different factors on users' attitude. A qualitative interview with those who create tags could be will enrich the understanding gathered from the survey data. Thirdly, although three factors explained 80% of the variance of Attitude towards creating and sharing tags, these factors are not exhaustive and we acknowledge the possible existence of other factors that could contribute to the Attitude variance. Fourth, since our respondents reported mainly three tagging system, the result cannot be generalized to all social tagging systems. Testing our refined model with a different set of online tagging systems would add more creditability and generalizability to our conclusions. An interesting next step is to investigate the same factors and their influence on the actual behavior of tag contribution and sharing instead of Attitude and Intention. For example, measuring the influence of reciprocity on the creating and contributing behavior seems a logical next step given that some of our initial results that contradict previous research.

Acknowledgments. We express our special thanks to Dr. Ann-Barbara Graff for her contributions in editing the final version of this article. We also thank Drs. Carolyn Watters and Elaine Toms for their contribution in the early stages of the work described herein.

References

1. Trant, J.: Studying Social Tagging and Folksonomy: A Review and Framework. Journal of Digital Information 10(1) (2009)
2. Connor, E.: Medical Librarian 2.0. Medical Reference Services Quarterly 26(1), 1–15 (2006)
3. Nov, O., Naaman, M., Ye, C.: What drives content tagging: the case of photos on Flickr. In: Proceeding of the Twenty-Sixth Annual SIGCHI Conference on Human Factors in Computing Systems. ACM, Florence (2008)
4. Golder, S.A., Huberman, B.A.: Usage patterns of collaborative tagging systems. J. Inf. Sci. 32(2), 198–208 (2006)
5. Gibbert, M., Krause, H.: Practice Exchange in a Best Practice Marketplace. In: Davenport, T.H., Probst, G.J.B. (eds.) Knowledge Management Case Book: Siemens Best Practices, Erlangen, Germany, pp. 89–105. Publicis Corporate Publishing (2002)
6. Davis, F.D., Bagozzi, R.P., Warshaw, P.R.: User acceptance of computer technology: a comparison of two theoretical models. Management Science 35, 982–1003 (1989)
7. Bock, G.-W., Zmud, R.W., Kim, Y.-G., Lee, J.-N.: Behavioral intention formation in knowledge sharing: Examining the roles of extrinsic motivators, social-psychological forces, and organizational climate. MIS Quarterly 29(11), 87–111 (2005)
8. Venkatesh, V., et al.: User Acceptance of Information Technology: Toward a Unified View. MIS Quarterly 27(3), 425–478 (2003)
9. Moon, J.W., Kim, Y.G.: Extending the TAM for a world-wide-web context. Information & Management 38, 217–230 (2001)
10. Venkatesh, V.: Determinants of Perceived Ease of Use: Integrating Perceived Behavioral Control, Computer Anxiety and Enjoyment into the Technology Acceptance Model. Information Systems Research 11(4), 342–365 (2000)
11. Kankanhalli, A., Tan, B.C.Y., Wei, K.K.: Contributing Knowledge to Electronic. Knowledge Repositories: An Empirical Investigation. MIS Quarterly 29(1) (2005)
12. Jarvenpaa, S.L., Staples, D.S.: The use of collaborative electronic media for information sharing: an exploratory study of determinants. The Journal of Strategic Information Systems 9(2-3), 129–154 (2000)
13. Hsu, C.-L., Lin, J.C.-C.: Acceptance of blog usage: The roles of technology acceptance, social influence and knowledge sharing motivation. Information & Management 45(1), 65–74 (2008)
14. Blau, P.M.: Exchange and power in social life. John Wiley & Sons Inc., New York (1964)
15. Bock, G.W., Kim, Y.G.: Breaking the Myths of Rewards: An Exploratory Study of Attitudes about Knowledge Sharing. Information Resource Management Journal 15(2), 14–21 (2002)

16. Chang, C.-C., Chiu, H.-C., Keng, N., Chou, S.-Y.: A study on the knowledge sharing behavior on blogs and forums. Journal of e-Business 10(4), 885–908 (2008)
17. Preece, J.: Online Communities: Designing Usability and Supporting Sociability. John Wiley & Sons, Chichester (2000)
18. Liao, C.-H., Tsou, C.-W., Shu, Y.-C.: The Roles of Perceived Enjoyment and Price Perception in Determining Acceptance of Multimedia-on-Demand. International Journal of Business and Information 3(1) (2008)
19. Ames, M., Naaman, M.: Why we tag: motivations for annotation in mobile and online media. In: Proceedings of the SIGCHI Conference on Human Factors in Computing Systems. ACM, San Jose (2007)
20. van Velsen, L., Melenhorst, M.: Incorporating user motivations to design for video tagging. Interact. Comput. 21(3), 221–232 (2009)
21. Suchanek, F.M., Vojnovic, M., Gunawardena, D.: Social tags: meaning and suggestions. In: Proceeding of the 17th ACM Conference on Information and Knowledge Management. ACM, Napa Valley (2008)
22. Melenhorst, M., et al.: Tag-based information retrieval of video content. In: Proceeding of the 1st International Conference on Designing Interactive User Experiences for TV and Video. ACM, Silicon Valley (2008)
23. Sinha, R.: A cognitive analysis of tagging. In: Sinha, R. (ed.) Rashmi Sinha's Weblog (2005)
24. Golder, S.A., Huberman, B.A.: The Structure of Collaborative Tagging Systems. HP Labs technical report (August 18, 2005), http://www.hpl.hp.com/research/idl/papers/tags/ (cited October 25, 2009)
25. Cialdini, R.: Influence: Science and Practice, 5th edn. Allyn and Bacon (2001)
26. John, A., Seligmann, D.: Collaborative Tagging and Expertise in the Enterprise. In: Proc. WWW 2006, Edinburgh, UK (2006)
27. Wasko, M., Faraj, S.: Why Should I Share? Examining Social Capital AND Knowledge Contribution IN Electronic Networks OF Practice. MIS Quarterly 29, 35–57 (2005)
28. Wasko, M., Faraj, S.: It Is What One Does: Why People Participate and Help Others in Electronic Communities of Practice. Strategic Information Systems 9(2-3), 155–173 (2000)
29. Ellis, D.G., Fisher, B.A.: Small Group Decision Making: Communication and the Group Process. McGraw-Hill (1994)
30. Teo, T.S.H., Pok, S.H.: Adoption of WAP-Enabled Mobile Phones Among Internet Users, vol. 31, pp. 483–498 (2003)
31. Moore, G.C., Benbasat, I.: Development of an instrument to measure the perceptions of adopting an information technology innovation. Information Systems Research 2(3), 192–222 (1991)
32. Chin, W.: Commentary: Issues and opinion on structural equation modeling. MIS Quarterly 22, 7–16 (1998)
33. Maccallum, R.C., Austin, J.T.: Application of Structural Equation Modeling in Psychological Research. Annual Review of Psychology 51, 201–236 (2000)
34. Hair, J.F., Ringle, C.M., Sarstedt, M.: PLS-SEM: Indeed a Silver Bullet. Journal of Marketing Theory and Practice 17(2), 139–151 (2011)
35. Bagozz, R.P., Yi, Y., Philips, L.W.: Assessing construct validity in organizational research. Administrative Science Quarterly 36, 421–458 (1991)
36. Nunnally, J.C.: Psychometric Theory, 3rd edn. McGraw-Hill, New York (1994)
37. Fornell, C., Larcker, D.F.: Evaluating Structure Equation Modeling With Observable Variables and Measurement Errors. Journal of Marketing Research 18(1), 39–50 (1981)
38. Comrey, A.L.: A First Course in Factor Analysis. Academic Press, New York (1973)

Appendix: A List of Items by Construct

Ease of Use
EOU1: Learning to create tags is easy for me
EOU2: I find it easy for me to become skillful at creating tags
EOU3: I find creating tags easy for me

Personal Productivity
PP1: Creating tags enables me to accomplish my information retrieval (search) tasks more quickly
PP2: Creating tags makes it easier to perform my information retrieval (search) tasks
PP3: Creating tags enhances the effectiveness of my information retrieval (search) tasks
PP4: Creating tags increases the productivity of my information retrieval (search) tasks
PP5: Creating tags improves the performance of my information retrieval (search) tasks
PP6: I would find creating tags useful in my daily tasks

Reciprocity
REC1: I find creating and adding tags to share with others can be mutually helpful
REC2: I find creating and adding tags to share with others can be advantageous to me and others
REC3: I think that creating tags to share with others improve mutual benefit

Social Norm
SN1: People who influence my behavior think that I should create add tags to the tagging system(s)
SN2: People who are important to me think that I should create and add tags to the tagging system(s)

Attitude
ATT1: Creating and sharing tags is beneficial for me
ATT2: Creating and sharing tags is desirable for me
ATT3: Creating and sharing tags is a good idea

Mitigation of Random Query String DoS
via Gossip

Stefano Ferretti and Vittorio Ghini

Department of Computer Science,
University of Bologna
Bologna, 40127 Italy
{sferrett,ghini}@cs.unibo.it

Abstract. This paper presents a mitigation scheme to cope with the
random query string Denial of Service (DoS) attack, which is based on
a vulnerability of current Content Delivery Networks (CDNs), a storage technology widely exploited to create reliable large scale distributed
systems and cloud computing system architectures. Basically, the attack
exploits the fact that edge servers composing a CDN, receiving an HTTP
request for a resource with an appended random query string never saw
before, ask the origin server for a (novel) copy of the resource. This request to the origin server is made also if the edge server contains a copy of
the resource in its storage. Such characteristics can be employed to take
an attack against the origin server by exploiting edge servers. In fact,
the attacker can send different random query string requests to different
edge servers that will overload the origin server with simultaneous (and
unneeded) requests. Our strategy is based on the adoption of a simple
gossip protocol, executed by edge servers, to detect the attack. Based
on such a detection, countermeasures can be taken to protect the origin server, the CDN and thus the whole distributed system architecture
against the attack. We provide simulation results that show the viability
of our approach.

1 Introduction

In two recent papers, a Denial of Service (DoS) attack has been discussed that
exploits a vulnerability of current Content Delivery Networks (CDNs) [12,15].
CDNs are considered as a useful solution to store contents that can be employed
to build distributed information systems and by services hosted on cloud computing architectures [3,4,10]. They are widely exploited in many Web applications
and indeed, a major portion of the today's Internet traffic passes through some
CDN.

A CDN is composed of several *edge servers* that are utilized to answer users'
requests. Usually, a request to a Web site (*origin server*) employing CDN technologies is invisibly routed to these other nodes that maintain replicated contents geographically distributed across the CDN. Typically, the choice of the
edge server selected for delivering content to a given user is based on a measure

S. Dua et al. (Eds.): ICISTM 2012, CCIS 285, pp. 124–134, 2012.
© Springer-Verlag Berlin Heidelberg 2012

of network proximity. For instance, among those available in the CDN, the selected edge server is the one with the fewest network hops or with the quickest response time. This approach has the advantage of distributing the load [2,14]. Moreover, user's proximity to the edge server has an impact on user response times, hence improving the quality of the service.

CDNs are commonly believed to offer their customers protection against application-level DoS attacks [11]. In fact, it is well known that, due to its vast resources, a CDN can absorb typical DoS attacks without causing any noticeable effect to users. However, authors of [15] have found an attack where the presence of a CDN actually amplifies the attack against a customer Web site.

Upon a request routed to an edge server, if this server does not have the content, which might be a large file, it retrieves such content from the origin server where the Web site is hosted. Then, the edge server passes that resource to the user. From that moment, the edge server maintains a copy of the resource; this way, subsequent requests for that content might be successfully completed without retrieving again that resource from the origin server. This operation mode enables to distribute the workload and protects the origin server from being swamped with requests.

According to [15], the basic problem is that based on the current implementation of CDNs, edge servers are not allowed to manage "query strings". A query string is a string that is appended to the URL the client is targeting; these strings are usually employed to communicate parameters to the server during some HTTP request. Now, since edge servers do not contain any logic related to the Web site, but they simply maintain replicated resources to distribute the load, when they receive some HTTP request with a random query string which is added to a URL, they treat such a request as new and pass it on to the origin server. The problem is that if the origin server is not expecting a query string, it removes it from the HTTP request and supplies the file. Summing up, if an attacker asks an edge server for a resource and appends to that request a random query string, the edge server will request such a resource to the origin server in turn, even if it already has it. For this request, the origin server sends such a resource to the edge server.

This way, an attacker can force an edge server to retrieve a copy of a large file from the origin server several times. Not only, it has been noticed that if the attacker cancels the connection immediately after requesting the resource, that resource transmission from the origin server to the edge server continues anyway. A DoS attack can thus be implemented as follows [15]. The attacker can retrieve a list of edge servers and send HTTP requests (with random query strings appended to such requests) to a large number of edge servers from a single machine. For each single request, the connection can be canceled after a while; hence, each single request requires little computing power.

Such random query string DoS attack is directed towards the origin server, that spends a lot of its work and its bandwidth to send such resources to several, distinct edge servers. Needless to say, a single attack can have a long-lasting effect on the origin server.

To cope with such a random query DoS attack, approaches such as data mining would at most enable to understand that an attack has been done to a server, ex-post. Some mitigation schemes are outlined in [15], that nevertheless do not solve completely the problem. For instance, to protect against the random query string vulnerability, a content provider can setup its CDN service so that only URLs without query strings are accelerated by the CDN. However, this limits the flexibility of the CDN. In response to the identification of such a threat of CDNs, it seems that no modifications are going to be accomplished [12].

To prevent the attacker from hiding behind a CDN, the edge server can pass the client's IP address to the origin server any time it forwards a request to the origin. This can be done by adding an optional HTTP header into the request. Of course, the attacker can still attempt to hide by coming through its own intermediaries, such as a botnet, or public Web proxies [1,15].

In this work, we propose a simple strategy to face this attack. The idea is to resort to a simple gossip protocol among edge servers (and the origin server). Every time a request with a false query string is received by the origin server from an edge server, the origin server answers by sending the requested resource, as usual. However, it informs the edge server (via some additional information) that the query string was a false one. Of course, such information does not mean that the user is a malicious node, the request might be malformed for a number of other reasons. In any case, the edge server transmits an alert of an such erroneous request to other edge servers, via a gossip algorithm. This way, edge servers can become aware of a random query string DoS attack, if more edge servers notice that a high number of erroneous query string requests have been generated for a particular origin site. Upon detection of the attack, appropriate schemes may be adopted to solve the problem. For instance, edge servers can stop sending requests containing appended query strings to the origin server. We provide some simulation results that confirm that such a simple approach can be adopted to detect a random query string DoS attack, by just adding such a gossip algorithm between servers, without altering the basic behavior of the origin site and edge servers.

A final remark is related to the use of CDNs within clouds, and in general to the integration between these two worlds [3,4,8]. These types of attacks may represent a possible threat for cloud technologies, where the allocation of the number of nodes (e.g. edge servers) is optimized based on the traffic and the workload the service is subject to. Our solution can be viably exploited within these kinds of architectures.

The remainder of the paper is organized as follows. Section 2 outlines the random query string DoS attack and its functioning. Section 3 presents the approach proposed in this work to cope with this DoS attack. Section 4 describes the simulation scenario and provides an analysis of the obtained results. Finally, Section 5 provides some concluding remarks.

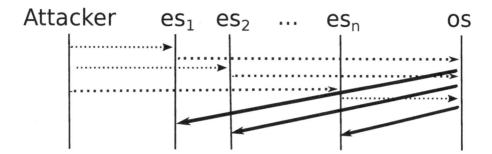

Fig. 1. Random query string DoS attack

2 Random Query String DoS Attack

Figure 1 shows how the random query string QoS attack works. For a detailed discussion the reader may refer to [15]. First, the attacker needs to collect the addresses of edge servers es_i. There are several mechanisms to obtain their IP addresses, as those suggested in [13,15]. Then, the attacker starts to make HTTP requests for some resources belonging to the origin server os to edge servers; it appends random query strings to such requests, so that each es_i will ask os to provide it the resource. After a while, the attacker can cancel the HTTP request by closing the connection with es_i. For each received request, os will send the requested resource to the corresponding es_i nevertheless.

In the figure, requests from the attacker to the edge servers and requests from the edge servers to the origin server are depicted as horizontal lines, differently to resource transmissions from the origin server, to stress the fact that requests are lightweight, almost instantaneous messages, while file transmissions can take a while to be completed.

As shown in the figure, the attack is quite simple. Nevertheless, clearly enough it may waste computational and communication resources of the origin server, and may cause a DoS.

3 Coping with Random Query String DoS

The target of a random query string DoS attack is the origin server. In fact, nodes in the CDN (edge servers) are exploited by the attacker to create a burst of requests towards it. There are several problems concerned with mechanisms that simply try to detect such an attack at the origin server. For instance, one might try to determine the attacker by looking at the source of the request. However, the attacker may resort to mechanisms to vary the IP address, or it can hide behind some public proxy. Another problem is that the attacker may change the file requested through edge servers; hence the origin server should look at all incoming requests. This implies a high computational load for the control. Summing up, the origin server cannot do much by itself.

On the other hand, to tackle the problem it is probably better to avoid some complicated coordination scheme that involves all the edge servers for each request. In fact, this could easily slow down the responsiveness of edge servers and strongly impact the effectiveness and the general performance of the whole CDN [9].

In this sense, the use of gossip dissemination algorithms could be of help [6,7]. Indeed, it has been recognized that gossip schemes are simple solutions to easily spread information through networks. In this section, we propose a scheme that employs a gossip algorithm among edge servers to detect a random query string DoS attack.

3.1 The Approach

The scheme requires a simple extension at the origin and edge server and works as follows. Any time the origin server os receives a request with a false query string from an edge server es_i (as made during the attack), os replies as usual by discarding the invalid query string and sending the resource. But in addition, os alerts es_i that the query string was invalid. Such an additional information can be included as an option within the HTTP message containing the resource and piggybacked to es_i, or it might be sent as a different message as well.

Upon reception of the alert from the origin server os, the edge server es_i gossips it to other edge servers, including other alerts (if any) it received previously from os or from other edge servers. This allows edge servers to understand if more that an edge server has received a false query string directed to the same origin server os. If so, then maybe os is under a random query string DoS attack, and then some more accurate investigation is needed.

It is worth mentioning that the reception of an erroneous query string does not imply that the origin server is under a random query string DoS attack. Such kinds of requests can be received for a variety of reasons, including human errors and incorrect implementations of external mashups that exploit some kind of Web resources coming from the origin server. These external factors should not affect the behavior of the origin server and false positive detections must be avoided. Thus, the identification of a possible attack should happen only after a "sufficient" number of occurrences. Then, appropriate counter-measures can be employed such as, for instance, alerting (through a broadcast) all edge servers, which from that moment will process only HTTP requests without any appended query strings.

A central point of the approach is to quantify the "sufficient" number of alerts to suspect that an origin server is under a random query string DoS attack. Considering the percentage of erroneous requests over the total number of requests on a given time interval probably does not represent an appropriate choice, since such metric would take into consideration the popularity of the Web service hosted on the origin server. Instead, we employ the following simple heuristics. Each edge server collects all the alert messages coming from the origin server or from the gossip protocol executed among edge servers in the CDN. This number is divided by the number S of edge servers. When this value exceeds

---

Algorithm 1. Gossip Protocol executed at e_i

---

function initialization()
  $v \leftarrow$ CHOOSEPROBABILITY()

function gossip(os)
  $msg =$ collect all suspected activities towards os during Δ
  for all $es_j \in$ CDN $\setminus \{e_i\}$ **do**
    if RANDOM() $< v$ **then**
      SEND(msg, es_j)
    end if
  end for

main loop behavior
on reception of an alert **or** timeout idle status
  $os =$ select the origin server to control
  GOSSIP(os)

---

a given threshold, then a random query string DoS attack is suspected. Such a measure is an estimation of the number of erroneous query string received per edge server during a time interval Δ. Indeed, an erroneous query string is assumed to be a rare event. Hence, a non-negligible value of these received requests, when considered globally, for the whole CDN, may clearly indicate a possible attack.

3.2   Gossip Algorithm

The gossip protocol is shown in Algorithm 1 in pseudo-code [6]. It is a very simple push dissemination scheme that exploits a constant probability v to spread information (see the INITIALIZATION() function in the algorithm). The term "push" means that nodes decide to send information to other ones via independent and local decisions. Unlike pull based schemes, no direct requests are performed by receivers. In substance, when an alert must be propagated, the edge server es_i randomly selects the receivers using a probability value $v \leq 1$. In particular, each edge server $es_j, i \neq j$ is gossiped based on a probability determined by v (see the loop in the GOSSIP() function, in the algorithm). On average, the alert is thus propagated from es_i to $v(S-1)$ edge servers, if S is the number of edge servers in the CDN.

A DoS attack is accomplished during a limited time interval, since the goal is to overflow the origin server with a huge number of requests that should waste all the origin server's resources and saturate its network bandwidth. This claims for a rapid detection of a random query string DoS attack. For this reason, each edge server sends gossip messages to others not only after a reception of an alert from an origin server, but also periodically (as reported in the main loop of the algorithm). The origin server os to consider is determined based on the source of the received alert message (if any has been received), or randomly chosen among those for which an alert message has been received previously.

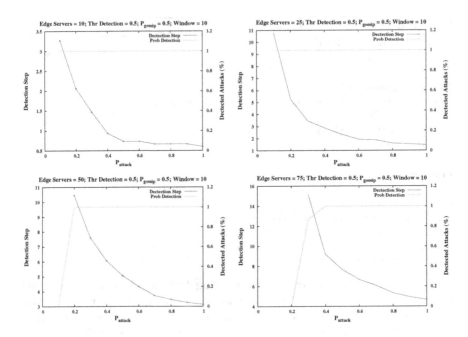

Fig. 2. Average detection step and percentage of detection when varying the number of edge servers and the rate of generation of a random query string

Then, es_i executes the GOSSIP() procedure to disseminate information related to os. We remark that the entity under attack is the origin server. Thus, edge servers exchange information related to os and not to the requested resource. In fact, an attacker might vary the resource specified in different requests, which nevertheless are stored on the origin server os.

Another consequence, which is concerned with such a sudden spike in the requests to the origin server, is that the activity of edge servers can be monitored taking into consideration limited time intervals. For this reason, edge servers exchange suspected activities monitored during a moving time window Δ. This reduces the amount of data to be managed, processed and exchanged among edge servers. Gossip messages are thus limited in size and the control procedure executed at edge servers requires limited computational efforts.

4   Experimental Evaluation

In this section, we report on a simulation we performed to assess whether the approach is able to detect random query string DoS attacks, when varying the configuration of a CDN, and to assess if the scheme is subject to false positives, i.e. if some random query string DoS is erroneously identified, due some almost simultaneous malformed HTTP requests received by edge servers.

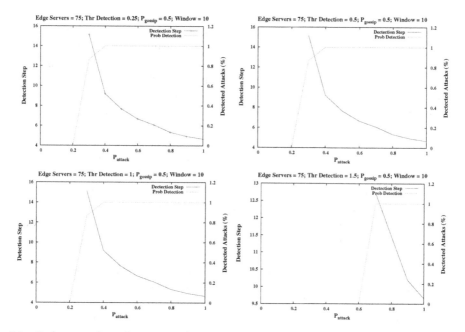

Fig. 3. Average detection step and percentage of detection when varying the threshold to suspect a random query string DoS attack

4.1 Simulator Details

We developed our own simulator to assess the proposed scheme. It was a discrete-event simulator written in C code; pseudo-random number generation was performed by employing the GNU Scientific Library [5]. The simulator allows us to test the behavior of a given amount of edge servers for a settable number of time steps. The attacker is simulated as a random process that sends random query strings to some of the edge servers during the simulation. Such a query is transformed into a resource request, and in turn into an alert generated by the origin server to the edge server. The simulator allows also to simulate non-malicious requests containing erroneous query strings towards some edge servers. Also these requests are generated by a random process (whose generation probability can be varied).

The behavior of edge servers in the CDN was implemented as detailed in the previous Section 3. In particular, the simulator permits to vary all the parameters related to the protocol, such as the dissemination probability v for gossiping messages, the threshold for suspecting that an origin server is under attack and the size of the time window Δ employed to consider the aggregate of received alerts.

4.2 Metrics of Interest and Configuration

We performed a time-stepped simulation of duration $T = 200$ steps. We varied the size of the moving time window. We varied the probability of generation of a novel random query string request by the attacker to a given edge server P_{attack} from 0.1 up to 1, while keeping the probability of a honest erroneous query string at a constant lower value (when not differently stated, its value is set equal to 0.01).

In the following charts we show outcomes obtained when the probability of gossip P_{gossip} among edge servers was set equal to 0.5. We varied such value up to 0.9 obtaining very similar results. Another varied parameter is the size of the time window exploited to include alerts within gossip messages. We varied such value from 10 up to 100 time steps. Also in this case, we did not notice significant differences worthy of mention. In the following, we show outcomes with a window size set equal to 10 time steps (a lower value might have some impact on results).

A delicate aspect related to the success of the attack is concerned with the hardware configuration of the origin server, its computational capacity and network bandwidth, as well as the dimension of the resources requested by the edge servers to the origin server. Due to the extreme variability of these parameters, we decided to not exploit these metrics as those which determine if the attack succeeded. Rather, we exploited the already mentioned threshold to determine if the amount of received alerts at a given edge server enables to detect the attack. We varied the value set for such threshold from 0.25 up to 1.5. As discussed in the previous sections, we assume that when the system is not under attack, an erroneous query string is a rare event. The value compared against the threshold is an estimation of alerts received on average by each edge server during the considered time interval. Thus, given the typical number of edge servers S in a CDN, the selected values represent non-negligible thresholds that might indicate an attack.

For each configuration setting, we run a corpus of 15 different simulations using different seed numbers. Results shown in the charts are obtained as the average of outcomes from the different simulation runs. The metrics we measured are mainly the number of steps needed by edge servers to detect that the origin server is under a random query string DoS attack, and the percentage of detected attacks.

4.3   Results

Figure 2 shows the results of four different configuration scenarios in which we varied the number of edge servers in the CDN. In particular, the four charts refer to a configuration with $10, 25, 50, 75$ edge servers. Each chart reports the average step of detection after the beginning of the attack (red continuous line, y-axis on the left) and the percentage of detected attacks (green dashed line, y-axis on the right). As shown in the charts, the higher P_{attack} (i.e. the stronger the attack to the origin server), the lower the number of steps required for detecting it and the higher the probability of detection.

It is clear that with an increased number of edge servers, more steps of interaction among these nodes are required to detect an attack. Moreover, in certain configurations the system is not able to detect all the attacks, when P_{attack} has a low value, as shown in the figure.

Figure 3 shows the average detection step and percentage of detection obtained when the threshold employed to suspect a random query string DoS attack was varied from 0.25 to 1.5. In this cases, the number of edge servers was set equal to 75 and the probability of gossip among edge servers was 0.5. Charts show that, as expected, the tuning of this parameter influences the outcomes of the distributed scheme. In fact, we have very similar results when such parameter is kept below 1; above it, results change and it becomes more difficult to detect an attack, mostly when a low probability of gossip P_{gossip} is employed among edge servers.

It is worth mentioning that when we simulate the system not being under attack, but with possible generation of non-malicious erroneous query string requests, the system does not detect any DoS. In particular, we varied the rate of generation of such erroneous requests using a probability of a novel generation at each step, for each edge server, varying from 0.01 up to 0.05, with $P_{attack=0}$ and varying all other parameters as in the scenarios mentioned above. In this case, the CDN would behave normally.

5   Conclusions

This paper presented a scheme that may be effectively employed to mitigate random query string DoS attacks employed on CDNs. The attack exploits the behavior of edge servers composing a CDN to force the origin server to transmit contents to these edge servers. This might cause a serious overload for the origin server. To cope with this DoS attack, the idea proposed in this paper is to exploit a gossip protocol executed by edge servers to detect if some origin server is under attack. The distributed scheme is simple and does not require particular efforts for the coordination among edge servers. Outcomes from simulations showed the viability of the proposed approach.

Coping with these kinds of attacks may improve the robustness of distributed services and cloud architectures exploiting CDNs to store and manage their Web resources.

References

1. Ager, B., Mühlbauer, W., Smaragdakis, G., Uhlig, S.: Comparing dns resolvers in the wild. In: Proceedings of the 10th Annual Conference on Internet Measurement, IMC 2010, pp. 15–21. ACM, New York (2010)
2. Al-Qudah, Z., Lee, S., Rabinovich, M., Spatscheck, O., Van der Merwe, J.: Anycast-aware transport for content delivery networks. In: Proceedings of the 18th International Conference on World Wide Web, WWW 2009, pp. 301–310. ACM, New York (2009)
3. Broberg, J., Buyya, R., Tari, Z.: Metacdn: Harnessing 'storage clouds' for high performance content delivery. J. Network and Computer Applications, 1012–1022 (2009)
4. Chiu, C., Lin, H., Yuan, S.: Cloudedge: a content delivery system for storage service in cloud environment. Int. J. Ad Hoc Ubiquitous Comput. 6, 252–262 (2010)

5. Contributors, G.P.: GSL - GNU scientific library - GNU project - free software foundation (FSF) (2010), http://www.gnu.org/software/gsl/
6. D'Angelo, G., Ferretti, S.: Simulation of scale-free networks. In: Simutools 2009: Proc. of the 2nd International Conference on Simulation Tools and Techniques, pp. 1–10. ICST, Brussels (2009)
7. D'Angelo, G., Stefano, F., Moreno, M.: Adaptive event dissemination for peer-to-peer multiplayer online games. In: Proceedings of the International Workshop on DIstributed SImulation and Online Gaming (DISIO 2011) - ICST Conference on Simulation Tools and Techniques (SIMUTools 2011), pp. 1–8. ICST, Brussels (2011)
8. Ferretti, S., Ghini, V., Panzieri, F., Pellegrini, M., Turrini, E.: Qos-aware clouds. In: Proceedings of the 2010 IEEE 3rd International Conference on Cloud Computing, CLOUD 2010, pp. 321–328. IEEE Computer Society, Washington, DC (2010)
9. Lee, K.-W., Chari, S., Shaikh, A., Sahu, S., Cheng, P.-C.: Improving the resilience of content distribution networks to large scale distributed denial of service attacks. Comput. Netw. 51, 2753–2770 (2007)
10. Leighton, T.: Akamai and cloud computing: A perspective from the edge of the cloud. Akamai White Paper (2010)
11. Poese, I., Frank, B., Ager, B., Smaragdakis, G., Feldmann, A.: Improving content delivery using provider-aided distance information. In: Proceedings of the 10th Annual Conference on Internet Measurement, IMC 2010, pp. 22–34. ACM, New York (2010)
12. Schneider, D.: Network defense gone wrong. IEEE Spectrum 48, 11–12 (2011)
13. Su, A.-J., Choffnes, D.R., Kuzmanovic, A., Bustamante, F.E.: Drafting behind akamai: inferring network conditions based on cdn redirections. IEEE/ACM Trans. Netw. 17(6), 1752–1765 (2009)
14. Su, A.-J., Kuzmanovic, A.: Thinning akamai. In: Proceedings of the 8th ACM SIGCOMM Conference on Internet Measurement, IMC 2008, pp. 29–42. ACM, New York (2008)
15. Triukose, S., Al-Qudah, Z., Rabinovich, M.: Content Delivery Networks: Protection or Threat? In: Backes, M., Ning, P. (eds.) ESORICS 2009. LNCS, vol. 5789, pp. 371–389. Springer, Heidelberg (2009)

Public Verifiable Signcryption Schemes with Forward Secrecy Based on Hyperelliptic Curve Cryptosystem

Shehzad Ashraf Ch, Nizamuddin, and Muhammad Sher

Department of Computer Science International Islamic University Islamabad, Pakistan
{shahzad,m.sher}@iiu.edu.pk, sahibzadanizam@yahoo.com

Abstract. Signcryption is a process of combining encryption and signature into a single logical step. Traditional signcryption schemes provide message confidentiality and sender authentication, sender authentication can only be provided after unsigncryption of signcrypted text, so the third part can only verify the sender after breaching the confidentiality. In public verifiable signcryption schemes a third party or judge can verify authenticity of sender without breaching the confidentiality and without knowing the receiver private key, the judge just needs the signcrypted text and some additional parameters. In this paper, we proposed a resource efficient Hyperelliptic curve cryptosystem based signcryption schemes to provide message confidentiality, authentication, integrity, unforgeability, non-repudiation, along with forward secrecy and public verifiability. In case of dispute the judge can verify signcrypted text directly without sender/receiver private parameters. Our schemes are resource efficient and can be applied to any resource constrained environments.

Keywords: Hyperelliptic curve cryptosystem, Jacobian group, genus, Signcryption, Public Verifiability, Forward Secrecy.

1   Introduction

One of the main interests of information security on shared media such as wireless is to transmit information in confidential and authentic manner [19]. These two distinct operations of encryption and digital signatures are combined into a single operation named signcryption by Y. Zheng [3], which opened new dimensions of research. Forward secrecy and public verifiability are needed along with signcryption, forward secrecy implies that even if private key is compromised, it will cause no effect on session key, A scheme is said to be public verifiable if a third party can verify the authenticity of message without revealing the secret information.

In this paper we have reviewed signcryption schemes based on elliptic curve and hyper elliptic curve, then two signcryption schemes are proposed which are based on hyper elliptic curve with added feature of forward secrecy and public verifiability, we have analyzed and compared the efficiency of our proposed schemes with schemes proposed by Hwang[5], Toorani[6] and Mohapatra[7]. The efficiency of our proposed algorithms is evident from these results.

S. Dua et al. (Eds.): ICISTM 2012, CCIS 285, pp. 135–142, 2012.

2   Related Work

Y. Zheng [3] proposed the first signcryption scheme to combine encryption and signature operation into a single unit named signcryption, which reduced computation and communication overhead of separate and distinct encryption and signature schemes.

Y. Zheng [4] Proposed first signcryption scheme based on elliptic curve cryptography. The scheme of [4] used small key size to provide equivalent security as compared to ElGamal and RSA Elliptic curve cryptosystems, which make it attractive for resource constrained environment. The proposed scheme reduces the computation cost up to 58% and communication cost up to 40% when compared with Signature-Then-Encryption schemes based on elliptic curve cryptography. The scheme is not public verifiable and there is no proof forward secrecy.

Hwang et al [5] Proposed public verifiable and forward secure signcryption scheme based on ECC, the confidentiality of information sustain even if the sender private key disclosed. Trusted third party can verify the plaintext using (m, r, s). The scheme has less computational cost for sender side so more suitable for mobile devices. The verification is possible only after breaching the confidentiality of   the message.

Toorani et al [6] proposed signcryption scheme based on elliptic curve to decrease the computation and communication cost. The proposed scheme also provides public verifiability and forward secrecy, so it became suitable for store/forward applications and resource-constrained devices. In the verification phase the session key is provided to the judge which becomes a serious threat to confidentiality. The hyper elliptic curve is stirring from academics to real time industrial applications, as it provides same security while using very less base fields [16].

In [12-14] authors proposed security schemes for banking and e-commerce application using Hyperelliptic curve encryption and HEC-ElGamal technique [9]. These schemes do not provide authenticity of messages. In [15] authors proposed generalized equations for digital signature algorithms defined over hyper elliptic curve (HECDSA). In [16] author proposed signcryption schemes based on HECC, these schemes are resource efficient, these schemes reduced significant amount of high computation and communication costs as compared to signature-then-encryption techniques. The schemes of [16] are not public verifiable and there is no forward secrecy. Nizam et al. [17] proposed signcryption schemes based on HECC with forward secrecy. These proposed schemes need zero knowledge protocol for public verifiability and there is no direct verifiability.

3   Proposed Schemes

We have used hyper elliptic curve cryptosystem in two proposed signcryption schemes; these schemes are based on the shorthand digital signature standard. The schemes work as follows

Let C be hyper elliptic curve of genus $g \geq 2$ defined over finite field F_q and defined by equation 1

$$y^2 + h(x)y = f(x) \bmod q \qquad (1)$$

$h(x) \in F[x]$ is a polynomial and degree of $h(x) \leq g$
$f(x) \in F[x]$ is a monic polynomial and degree of $f(x) \leq 2g+1$
    Primarily a jacobian group JC (Fq) is formed, then select a divisor D, where D is the generator of the group and its Mumford form is

$$D = (a(x),b(x)) = (\sum_{i=0}^{g} a_i x^i, \sum_{i=0}^{g-1} b_i x^i) \in J_C(F_q) \qquad (2)$$

Let φ: J_C (F$_q$)→Z$_q$ is a function which maps Jacobian group element to an integer.
    Let D be devisor of order n. d_a, and P_a be private and public key of sender and d_b and P_b be private and public key of receiver, h represents hash function, E_k/D_k represent Symmetric Encryption / Decryption.

3.1   Signcryption

Sender perform signcryption by obtaining receiver public key P_b from certificate authority and use a routine Signcryption (k,P_b,P_a,d_a,m) to compute signcrypted text.

3.1.1   Scheme One
Signcryption(k,P_b,P_a,d_a,m)
        Select an integer k $\in$ {1,2,3.........n-1} randomly
        Compute Bob (sender) public key scalar multiplication kP_b
        $(K_1) = h(\varphi(kD))$
        $(K_2) = h(\varphi(kP_b))$
        $C = E_{K_2}(m)$
        Compute $r = h_{k_1}$ (c ‖ bind_info)

        Compute $s = \left(\dfrac{k}{(r+d_a)}\right) \bmod n$

        Compute R= rD
        Transmit Signcrypted text (c, R, s)

3.1.2   Scheme Two
Signcryption(k,P_b,P_a,d_a,h,m)
        Select an integer k $\in$ {1,2,3.........n-1} randomly
        Compute Bob (sender) public key scalar multiplication kP_b
        $(K_1) = h(\varphi(s^{-1}(P_a+R)))$
        $(K_2) = h(\varphi(s^{-1}(d_b(P_a+R)))$
        $C = E_{k_2}(m)$

Compute r= h_{k_1} (c ‖ bind_info)

Compute   s $= k^{-1} (d_a + r)$ mod n

Compute R = rD

Transmit Signcrypted text (c, R, s)

3.2   Unsigncryption

Bob receive signcrypted text, to obtain plain text and verify, the Unsigncryption(k,P_b,P_a,d_b,h,c,R,s) routine is used.

3.2.1   Scheme One

Unsigncryption (P_b,P_a,d_b,h,c,R,s)

Compute (K_1,K_2)

(K_1) $= H(\varphi(s(P_a+R)))$

(K_2) $= H(\varphi(s(d_b (P_a+R)))$

Compute r = h_{k_1} (c ‖ bind_info)

$$m = D_{K_2}(c)$$

Check rD = R if true accept the message, otherwise reject

3.2.2   Scheme Two

Unsigncryption (P_b,P_a,d_b,h,c,R,s)

Compute (K_1, K_2)

(K1) $= H(\varphi(s^{-1} (P_a+R)))$

(K2) $= H(\varphi(s^{-1} (d_b (P_a+R))))$

Compute r = h_{k_1} (c ‖ bind_info)

$$m = D_{K_2}(c)$$

Check rD = R if true accept the message, otherwise reject

4   Security Analysis

The proposed schemes fulfils the security notions presented by Zheng [3], confidentiality, unforgeability and non repudiation, additionally provide the feature of forward secrecy and direct public verifiability.

4.1   Confidentiality

The use of symmetric encryption (AES) ensures the confidentiality of the message the private key used for encryption is K_1, K_1can be calculated by finding d_b from $P_b=d_bD$ which is infeasible as it is hyper elliptic curve discrete log problem (HECDLP).

4.2   Unforgeability

An attacker needs K and private key of sender to generate legitimate signcrypted text, finding d_a and K from equation $P_a = d_a D$ is infeasible (HECDLP).

4.3   Non-repudiation

In our proposed schemes any trusted third party can resolve the dispute between sender and receiver.

4.4   Forward Secrecy

Forward secrecy implies that even if private key is compromised, it will cause no effect on session key. In our proposed schemes if an adversary get da for calculating session key k also need r which is computational hard problem.

4.5   Public Verifiability

In proposed schemes if sender denies the transmission of signcrypted text, a judge can verify the signature without revealing the contents of message.

4.6   Judge Verification

In case of dispute between sender and receiver the judge can resolve the dispute as: Judge wants bob to provide (c, P_a, s, R) and following steps to adjust the receiver claim.

4.6.1   Verification Phase of Scheme One
Compute $(K_1) = h(\varphi(s(P_a+R)))$

Compute $r = h_{k_1} (c \parallel bind\_info)$

Check $rD = R$ if satisfied the signcrypted text is valid, otherwise not

4.6.2   Verification Phase of Scheme Two
Compute $(K_1) = h(\varphi(s\text{-}1\ (P_a+R)))$

Compute $r = h_{k_1} (c \parallel bind\_info)$

Check $rD = R$ if satisfied the signcrypted text is valid, otherwise not

5   Cost Analysis

One of the major concerns of a cryptosystem for resource constrained environments is cost, The cost can further bifurcated into computation cost and communication cost, the proposed schemes are analysed with respect to both aspects which are computation and communication.

5.1   Comparative Computational Cost Analysis

The most expensive operation in the existing and proposed signcryption schemes is (ECPM) and (HECDM). Comparative computational costs analysis is based on these most expensive operations.

Computation time of one scalar multiplication is 4.24 ms for elliptic curve point multiplication (ECPM)   and 2.2 ms for hyper elliptic curve devisors scalar multiplication (HECDM) on a PC with Intel Core 2DUO CPU T6400@2.00GHz with 4GB RAM and windows vista operating system using jdk1.6[14].

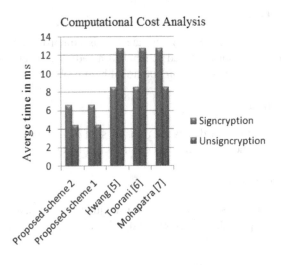

Fig. 1. Computational cost Analysis

5.2   Comparative Communication Cost Analysis

The communication overhead is one of major issue and communication cost analysis is of greater importance.
Communication cost of signature and encryption technique is as in eq 3

$$(|c'| + |H(u)| + |n|) \qquad (3)$$

Communication cost of our proposed signcryption schemes are shown in eq 4

$$(|c| + |D| + |n|) \qquad (4)$$

Generalized formula for communication overhead reduction i s shown in eq 5

$$\frac{(|c'| + |H(u)| + |n|) - (|c| + |D| + |n|)}{(|c'| + |H(u)| + |n|)} \qquad (5)$$

Overhead reduction depends on the choice of parameters and amount of data. The proposed schemes reduce communication overhead from 30-49%.

6   Conclusion

Traditional Asymmetric cryptosystems are infeasible for resource constrained environments while due to its low base field Hyperelliptic curve cryptosystem proved its worth to be used instead of traditional asymmetric cryptosystems as it provides confidentiality, unforgeability, non-repudiation, forward secrecy and public verifiability while utilizing low resources, but hyper elliptic performs double expansion of message and its results are probabilistic, Signcryprion schemes can overcome this problem by providing significant reduction in cost.

Our proposed public verifiable signcryption schemes defined over Hyperelliptic curve cryptography fulfill all the security requirements of signcryption and in addition also provide forward secrecy and public verifiability. In case of dispute judge or any third party can verify signcrypted text without disclosing secret parameters. The proposed scheme can reduce 30 to 49% communication overhead as compared to existing signature and encryption approaches, which makes it more suitable for all resource constrained environments.

References

1. Paul, C., Menezes, J., Vanstone, A.: Handbook of Applied Cryptography. CRC Press (1996)
2. Diffie, W., Hellman, M.: New directions in cryptography. IEEE Trans. Inform. Theory 22(6), 472–492 (1976)
3. Zheng, Y.: Digital Signcryption or How to Achieve Cost (Signature & Encryption) < < Cost(Signature) + Cost(Encryption). In: Kaliski Jr., B.S. (ed.) CRYPTO 1997. LNCS, vol. 1294, pp. 165–179. Springer, Heidelberg (1997)
4. Zheng, Y., Imai, H.: How to construct signcryption schemes on elliptic curve. Information Processing Letters 68, 227–233 (1998)
5. Hwang, R.-J., Lai, C.-H., Su, F.-F.: An efficient signcryption scheme with forward secrecy based on elliptic curve. Applied Mathematics and Computation 167(2), 870–881 (2005)
6. Toorani, M., Beheshti Shirazi, A.A.: An Elliptic Curve-based Signcryption Scheme with Forward Secrecy. Journal of Applied Sciences 9(6), 1025–1035 (2009) ISSN 1812-5654
7. Mohapatra, R.K., Majhi, B.: Signcryption Schemes with Forward Secrecy Based on Elliptic Curve Cryptography. M Tech Thesis Department of Computer Science and Engineering National Institute of Technology Rourkela Rourke
8. Koblitz, N.: Hyperelliptic cryptosystems. Journal of Cryptology 1(3), 139–150 (1989)
9. Zhou, X.: Improved Ring Signature Scheme Based on Hyper-Elliptic Curves. In: IEEE International Conference on Future Information Technology and Management Engineering, FITME, pp. 373–376 (2009)
10. Zhou, X., Yang, X., Wei, P.: Hyper-elliptic curves based group signature. In: Control and Decision Conference, CCDC 2009, Chinese, pp. 2280–2284 (2009)
11. Zhou, X., Yang, X.: Hyper-Elliptic Curves Cryptosystem Based Blind Signature. In: Pacific-Asia Conference on Knowledge Engineering and Software Engineering, KESE 2009 (2009)
12. Ganesan, R., Vivekanandan, K.: A Novel Hybrid Security Model for E-Commerce Channel. In: International Conference on Advances in Recent Technologies in Communication and Computing (2009)

13. Ganesan, R., Vivekanandan, K.: A Secured Hybrid Architecture Model for Internet Banking (e-Banking). Journal of Internet Banking and Commerce 14(1) (April 2009)
14. Ganesan, R., Gobi, M., Vivekanandan, K.: A Novel Digital Envelope Approach for A Secure E-Commerce Channel. International Journal of Network Security 11(3), 121–127 (2010)
15. Lin, Y., Yong-Xuan, S.: Effective generalized equations of secure hyperelliptic curve digital signature algorithms. The Journal of China Universities of Posts and Telecommunications 17(2), 100–108 (2010)
16. Nizamuddin, Ch., S.A., Nasar, W., Javaid, Q.: Efficient Signcryption Schemes based on Hyperelliptic Curve Cryptosystem. In: ICET 2011 (September 2011)
17. Nizamuddin, Ch., S.A., Amin, N.: Signcryption Schemes with forward secrecy based on Hyperelliptic Curve Cryptosystem. In: HONET 2011 (December 2011)
18. Chatterjee, K., De, A., Gupta, D.: Software Implementation of Curve based Cryptography for Constrained Devices. International Journal of Computer Applications (0975–8887) 24(5) (2011)
19. Wang, G., Bao, F., Ma, C., Chen, K.: Efficient authenticated encryption schemes with public verifiability. In: Vehicular Technology Conference, VTC 2004 (2004), doi:10.1109/VETECF.2004.1404665

Analytical Modelling of Fluid Credit Congestion Control Scheme in MultiProtocol Label Switching (MPLS) Networks

Adebayo Oyekan, Ifetayo Ojiwusi, Ayodeji Oluwatope, Adesola Aderounmu,
and Emmanuel Rotimi Adagunodo

Comnet Laboratory, Center of Excellence in Software Engineering
Department of Computer Science and Engineering
Obafemi Awolowo University, Ile-Ife. Nigeria
{aoluwato,gaderoun,eadagun}@oauife.edu.ng
adebayo.oyekan@yahoo.co.uk, luv03real@yahoo.com

Abstract. The service needs of the present and future Internet requires Quality of Service (QoS) provisions and Traffic Engineering (TE) with minimal congestion capabilities. Congestion is a common feature of networks caused by low bandwidth, buffer overflow etc. Internetworks have grown colossally from delivering best effort QoS services to support new traffic classes which require minimal delay and high throughput with more variations in load. This created the need for effective traffic management with the required QoS. MPLS, a label swapping and connection-oriented switching mechanism with high-performance offers new possibilities with its cutting-edge traffic control mechanisms but not without the need to manage congestion. This proposal presents a fluid credit congestion control scheme which manages traffic in MPLS internetwork and predicts congestion.

Keywords: MPLS networks, congestion minimization, and QoS.

1 Introduction

Resources and information users need are not uniformly located. Users also cannot have all what they need at a particular point in time. Network, an interconnection of computers, Information and Communications Technology (ICT) installations and their peripherals came handy to make resource and information sharing a possibility. Networks have grown colossally over the years. An interconnection of various network types with heterogeneous technologies spanning vast geographical locations linking together over millions of end-users and still counting is the Internet. Internet, an almost infinitely sized Internetwork connects various network types such as LANs (Local Area Networks), PANs (Personal Area Networks), WANs (Wide Area Networks), MANs (Metropolitan Area Networks) and lately, PSTNs (Public Switched Telephone Networks) and Global System for Mobile communications (GSM) networks etc. via network layer devices (OSI layer 3) commonly called routers with a

S. Dua et al. (Eds.): ICISTM 2012, CCIS 285, pp. 143–151, 2012.

logical addressing scheme called IP (Internet Protocol) address through a protocol which is the IP protocol. Internet services are provided by interconnected, hierarchical and heterogeneously located ISPs (Internet Service Providers) who connect various intending users. Internet, an IP-based network does traditional best effort QoS services which became unsuitable to deliver the QoS required for new and newer applications such as video streaming and VOIP (Voice Over IP) [2][10]. More so, networks possess varying discrepancies in load and resource requirements [10]. ITU and ETSI define QoS as "the collective effect of service performance which determines the degree of satisfaction of a user of the service" [4]. QoS is a broad term characteristically defining network performance thus, imposing and establishing a service with the appropriate network path. The combination of techniques managing latency, jitter and packet loss is regularly termed QoS [4][6][7][10]. IETF (Internet Engineering Task Force) proposed three QoS architectures namely [2]: Integrated services (Intserv) [13], Differentiated services [11] and Multiprotocol Label Switching (MPLS) [9].

MPLS is a label-based switching method used for transportation of packets across various hops [2][5][10]. Labels can stand for conventional IP destination networks, source address, OSI layer 3 VPN (Virtual Private Network) recipients, data-link circuit, egress interface on the exit router, QoS [5]. MPLS design supports routing of multiple protocols and non-IP protocols [5][10]. MPLS is a technology useable everywhere irrespective of the physical layer media and data-link protocol [1][5][10]. Frame mode MPLS encapsulates a 32-bit label field within OSI Layer 2 and Layer 3 headers to form Layer 2.5 label switched network on layer 2 switching functionality without layer 3 IP routing [1][5][10]. Cell mode MPLS or MPLS over ATM (Asynchronous Transfer Mode) employs the ATM header as its label [5]. MPLS is majorly about traversing packets hop by hop, which hop a packet pass through can be determined by IGP (Interior Gateway Protocol) routing or by MPLS TE (Traffic Engineered) [2][7]. In MPLS, Label Switch Paths (LSPs) are established using signaling Protocols between MPLS-tuned Label Switch Routers (LSRs) [2][5]. Edge LSRs label the packets as they enter the MPLS domain and also remove the labels as the packets leave the MPLS domain after which conventional IP routing continues [1][5]. LSRs then forward the labeled packets across the LSPs which can either be the traditional router-determined shortest paths or TE LSP which is explicit and probably different from the shortest path [1][2][5][7]. Traffic engineering is traffic transportation through a given network in the most efficient, reliable, and expeditious manner possible [1]. TE is used for effectively managing the networks for efficient utilization of network resources [1][10]. QoS with reference to IP network is a packet treatment technique used in choosing how packets are served. These three IETF QoS architectures can be combined to exploit their merits [5].

Congestion occurs when traffic to be transferred is greater than the amount the data communication path can carry. Congestions are inevitable in Internetworks due to diverse causes such as queuing delay as a result of overloading the buffer, unstable flow of bandwidth, etc. Thus, there exists a need for a congestion reduction mechanism to improve performance and reduce packet loss in Internetworks with MPLS not being an exception. This paper presents a fluid credit scheme that manages traffic in the MPLS domain and predicts congestion. This paper contributes significantly in that it seeks to provide a predictive congestion approach from the parameters: mean number of packets and the available bandwidth with a buffer minimization algorithm. The rest of the paper is arranged as follows: Section II discusses related research works; Section III contains the proposed scheme which contains the description of proposed system. Section IV presents the concluding remarks and future work direction.

2   Research Works

MPLS as an emerging and growing technology on the Internet with fast switching and minimal delay has been attracting researches done in many dimensions. One of such researches was the performance comparison of OPNET simulation of VOIP packets traversing MPLS and IP domains [1]. OPNET modeler 14.5 was used to simulate both MPLS and IP networks with comparisons based on the metrics such as voice jitter, voice packet end-to-end delay, voice delay variation, voice packet sent and received. Analysis of simulation results showed that MPLS based solution provides better performance in implementing the VOIP application. The major strength of this paper is the voice packet end-to-end delay performance metric used to estimate the maximum number of VOIP calls that can be maintained in MPLS and conventional IP networks with acceptable quality which can serve as a decision parameter for service providers and administrators.

The performance of MPLS TE queues in order to maximize network resources is another subject of such researches [7]. TE queues were created on all the routers in the MPLS cloud to minimise ISP's job of implementing complex bandwidth broker Operation Support System to map allowed tunnel bandwidth and available queues in the network during provisioning time therefore ensuring an IP network delivers the required QoS needs to carry real time traffic such as VoIP. The scheme was simulated and analyzed with a generalized processor sharing (GPS) system with results.

Another study by [8] was a congestion control model which allows the evaluation of QoS features using MPLS features. FATE (Fast Acting Traffic Engineering) method was realized in the model which dynamically manages network traffic flows by re-balancing streams during periods of congestion. It also gave an analytical model of LSR, which estimates QOS parameters: delay and loss probability. The analytical formulas were made on imitation network model with simulation results.

3   Proposed Scheme Descriptions

3.1   Fluid Credit Scheme

Fluid credit scheme is the modelling of MPLS QoS architecture using the markov-modulated feedback fluid queue theory [12]. The traffic from the source domains get to the MPLS Edge Router (MER/ Edge LSR (Label Switch Router)) where the label assignment is done as depicted in figure 1. The traffic is mapped to a Label Switch Path (LSP) across the MPLS core routers. The proposed scheme is implemented on the routers in the MPLS cloud. The fluid credit scheme becomes the TE queues implemented in the MPLS tuned routers. The TE queues are modeled with Markov-modulated and feedback fluid queues. The input traffic forms a fluid reservoir such that the current state of the fluid reservoir influences the behaviour of the regulating queuing system which is the feedback. The queue system is single server, finite buffer, multiple input and single output. There are source domains where traffic originates from to traverse the MPLS cloud en route their destinations. The technique is implemented within the MPLS cloud alone.

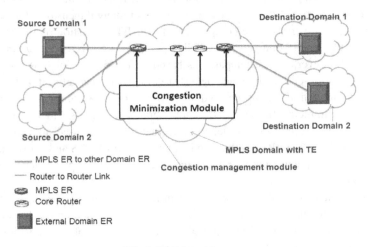

Fig. 1. MPLS architecture

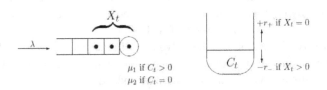

Fig. 2. Interaction process between the processes (X_t) and (C_t) [12]

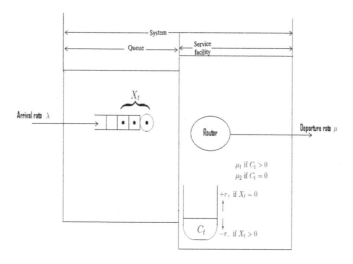

Fig. 3. Adapted schematic representation of a Single-Server fluid queuing system with the processes (X_t) and (C_t) with a server

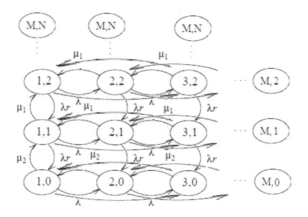

Fig. 4. Flow diagram of the markov process

The proposed scheme is modeled using birth-death fluid model with feedback. The mathematical model is built using Markov-modulated feedback fluid model [12].

The fluid credit scheme is implemented on all routers in the MPLS cloud. This leads to a single-server queuing system where packets arrive according to a Poisson process with rate λ. Packets arriving while the router is busy get to wait until they get served since in the buffer. When the router is idle, the bandwidth with its discrete nature ignored modeled as a fluid commodity called *credit* accumulates in a reservoir at a constant rate $r_+ > 0$. The credit reservoir depletes when the router gets busy at a constant rate $r_- > 0$ only if the reservoir is non-empty. The services packets require in the presence of credit are independent and exponentially distributed random variables with mean $1/\mu_1$ with departure rate μ_1 so far as packets are in the system and the reservoir is non-empty. When the reservoir becomes empty, the router slows down with departure rate going down to $\mu_2 \leq \mu_1$. If $\mu_1 = \mu_2 = \mu$ then it's a Markov-modulated fluid model without feedback [12].

The model used Kendall's notation [3] (M|M|1): (GD|∞|∞). The parameters considered were arrival rate λ, departure rate μ the number of packets X_t and C_t the content of credit reservoir at time t. Figure 3 depicts the schematic diagram of the interaction process between the processes X_t and C_t [12] where the two-dimensional process (X_t, C_t) in figure 2 forms a Markov process which under a suitable condition possess a unique stationary distribution. The two-dimenional process (X_t, C_t) is used to predict congestion arising from buffer overflow and also form the input into the buffer overflow minimization algorithm via simulation. This model assumes the waiting room (buffer) is bounded with N - 1 waiting positions so that the state space $\mathcal{N}$ of the process X_t is given by $\mathcal{N} = \{0, 1, ..., N\}$. The stationary probability of the server being idle with arrival rate λ and departure rate μ is given by

$$P = \left\{ 1 + \frac{\lambda}{\mu_1} + \frac{\lambda}{\mu_1}^2 + \cdots + \frac{\lambda}{\mu_1}^N \right\}^{-1} \tag{1}$$

given the Condition that $\frac{\lambda}{\mu_1} > \sigma_N$. This condition is referred to as condition 1.

Where $\sigma_N \equiv \sigma_N(r_+, r_-)$ is the unique positive solution of the equation $x + x^2 + \cdots + x^N = \frac{r_+}{r_-}$ [12].

Let's assume that condition 1 holds, then

$$F_i(t, y) \equiv P[X_t = i, C_t \leq y], t \geq 0, y \geq 0, i \in \mathcal{N} \tag{2}$$

Therefore the Kolmogorov forward equations for the process (X_t, C_t) are given by

$$\frac{\partial F_0(t, y)}{\partial t} + r_+ \frac{\partial F_0(t, y)}{\partial y} = -\lambda F_0(t, y) + \mu_1 F_1(t, y) - (\mu_1 - \mu_2)F_1(t, o)$$

$$\frac{\partial F_i(t, y)}{\partial t} - r_- \frac{\partial F_i(t, y)}{\partial y} = -\lambda F_{i-1}(t, y) - (\lambda + \mu_1)F_i(t, y) + \mu_1 F_{i+1}(t, y) +$$
$$(\mu_1 + \mu_2)\big(F_i(t, 0) - F_{i+1}(t, 0)\big) i \in \mathcal{N}\{0, N\} \tag{3}$$

$$\frac{\partial F_N(t, y)}{\partial t} - r_- \frac{\partial F_N(t, y)}{\partial y} = \lambda F_{N-1}(t, y) - \mu_1 F_N(t, y) + (\mu_1 + \mu_2)F_N(t, 0).$$

At equilibrium, $F_i(t, y) \equiv F_i(y)$ and $\frac{\partial}{\partial t} F_i(t, y) \equiv 0$ $\forall i \in \mathcal{N}$.

Therefore,

$$r_+ F_0'(y) = -\lambda F_0(y) + \mu_1 F_1(y) - (\mu_1 - \mu_2)F_1(0)$$

$$-r_- F_i'(y) = \lambda F_{i-1}(y) - (\lambda + \mu_1)F_i(y) + \mu_1 F_{i+1}(y) + (\mu_1 - \mu_2)\big(F_i(0) -$$
$$F_{i+1}(0)\big), \quad i \in \mathcal{N}\{0, N\} \tag{4}$$

$$-r_- F_N'(y) = \lambda F_{N-1}(y) - \mu_1 F_N(y) + (\mu_1 - \mu_2)F_N(0).$$

Whenever the router is idle, the credit content (bandwidth) remains. The solution to equation (4) satisfies the boundary condition

$$F_0(0) = 0 \tag{5}$$

Letting

$$p_i \equiv \lim_{y \to \infty} F_i(y) = \lim_{t \to \infty} P[X_t = i], \quad i \in \mathcal{N}, \tag{6}$$

The limiting distribution of the (non-Markov) process X_t must have

$$\sum_{i \in \mathcal{N}} p_i = 1 \tag{7}$$

The solution to (4) should satisfy the rate balance equations

$$\lambda p_i = \mu_1 (p_{i+1} - F_{i+1}(0)) + \mu_2 F_{i+1}(0), i \in \mathcal{N}\{N \tag{8}$$

By letting y→∞ in (4) then the balance equations is equivalent to

$$\lim_{y \to \infty} F_i'(y) = 0, \quad i \in \mathcal{N}, \tag{9}$$

Differentiating (4) gives a homogenous system of differential equations for the derivatives

$$f_i(y) \equiv F_i'(y) \quad i \in \mathcal{N} \tag{10}$$

Written in matrix notation as

$$f'(y) = R^{-1} Q^T f(y). \tag{11}$$

where,

$$f(y) \equiv \big(f_0(y), f_1(y), \dots, f_N(y)\big)^T,$$

R and Q are the $(N + 1) \times (N + 1)$ matrices

$$R \equiv diag(r_+, \overbrace{-r_-, -r_-, \dots, -r_-}^{N}). \tag{12}$$

$$R = \begin{pmatrix} -\lambda & \lambda & 0 & \cdots & & \\ \mu_1 & -(\lambda + \mu_1) & \lambda & 0 & \cdots & \\ \cdots & \cdots & \cdots & \cdots & \cdots & \\ \cdots & 0 & \mu_1 & -(\lambda + \mu_1) & \lambda \\ & \cdots & & 0 & \mu_1 & -\mu_1 \end{pmatrix} \tag{13}$$

3.2   Proposed Fluid Credit Scheduling Algorithm

c_t: credit content in the router (bandwidth)
x_{lp}: number of low priority packets in the ingress buffer
x_{hp}: number of high priority packets in the ingress buffer
s_t = Sojourn time
b_t = Buffer size
c_1;
c_2;
X_t;
Input: uneven arrival of packets
Output: Uneven departure of packets

$$c_1 = x_t / s_t;$$
$$c_2 = c_t / s_t;$$
$$b_t = 0 + b_t;$$

begin

%LIR

if (c_1 && $c_2 > 1.0$ and $b_t > 0.75* b_t$)
$$x_t = 0.4*x_{lp} + 0.6*x_{hp};$$
elseif (c_1 && $c_2 > 1.0$ and $b_t = 0.90* b_t$)
$$x_t = 0.35*x_{lp} + 0.65*x_{hp};$$
end

%LSR

if (c_1 && $c_2 > 1$ and $b_t = 0.75* b_t$)
$$x_t = 0.3*x_{lp} + 0.7*x_{hp};$$
end

%LER

if (c_1 && $c_2 > 1.0$ and $b_t = 0.75* b_t$)
$$x_t = 0.4*x_{lp} + 0.6*x_{hp};$$
elseif (c_1 && $c_2 > 1.0$ and $b_t = 0.90* b_t$)
$$x_t = 0.2*x_{lp} + 0.8*x_{hp};$$

end

continue

3.3   Discussions

The MPLS cloud contains two categories of routers by function namely LER (Label Edge Router) and LSR (Label Switch Router). The algorithm works on the input queue in the routers' ingress buffers. LIR (Label Ingress router) is the ingress LER and the first contact for ingress packets where label assignment is done. The algorithm starts prediction at seventy five percent utilization (75%) but the nature of the LIR stipulates that the scheduling and dropping be reduced since it's the ingress.

LSRs forward labeled packets across LSPs (Label Switch Paths) being MPLS interior routers. The nature of LSRs allow for further dropping since the assumption is that only TCP (Transmission Control Protocol) packets are considered and TCP allow for retransmission.

The egress LER is the exit point in the MPLS domain so further dropping is allowed since the assumption is that only TCP packets are considered which allows for retransmission.

The Eigen value from the solution of matrix R is used to calculate the sojourn time that is the input to the algorithm.

4 Conclusion

Fluid queuing models are applicable in packet switching where data streams are always broken down and transferred in many smaller-sized data cells called packets [12]. Thus, the proposed fluid credit scheme is analytical, empirical and formulative. It predicts congestion in the ingress buffer of the MPLS routers aiming at improved QoS efficiency and performance. Presently, efforts are on-going to validate the fluid credit scheduling algorithm viz mean queuing delay and packet loss metrics via a comparison with and without the algorithm in MPLS.

Acknowledgements. This work is being partly sponsored by the STEP-B(Science and Technologoy Education at the Post-Basic Level) funding through a World Bank grant for the establishment of Center of Excellence in Software Engineering, Obafemi Awolowo University, Ile-Ife. Nigeria. (Grant No. 4304-UNI).

References

1. Jannu, K., Deekonda, R.: OPNET simulation of voice over MPLS with Considering Traffic Engineering. Master thesis, Electrical engineering, thesis no: MSE-2010-5311, School of Engineering, Blekinge institute of technology, box 520, SE-372 25 Ronneby, Sweden (2010)
2. Mahmoud, O., Anwar, F., Salami, M.J.: Simulation and analysis of an admission control mechanism for MPLS DS-TE. Computer Communication 31(10), 2178–2184 (2008) ISSN: 0140-3664
3. Taha, H.A.: Operation Research: An introduction, 8th edn., Upper Sadle River, New Jersey, U.S.A., pp. 568–574 (2008)
4. Olmos, J., Ferrus, R., Sallent, O., Perez-Romero, J., Casadevall, F.: QoS architecture and functionalities: AROMA's perspective. In: Workshop Trends in Radio Resource Management, 3rd edn., Barcelona (2007)
5. Cisco Systems Inc.: Implementing Secure Converged Wide Area Networks of version 1.0, vol. 1. Cisco System Inc., San Jose (2006)
6. Cisco Systems Inc.: Optimizing Converged Cisco Networks of version 1.0, vol. 1. Cisco System Inc., San Jose (2006)
7. Li, Y., Panwar, S.: Performance Analysis of MPLS TE Queues for QoS Routing. In: Proceedings of Advanced Simulation Technologies Conference (ASTC 2004), Arlington, VA (2004)
8. Dekeris, B., Narbutaite, L.: Congestion Control Mechanism within MPLS Networks. In: Scientific Proceedings of RTU. Series 7. Telecommunications and Electronics, vol.3 (2003)
9. Rosen, E., Viswanathan, A., Callon, R.: Multiprotocol Label Switching Architecture. RFC3031 (2001)
10. Holness, F.M.: Congestion control mechanisms within MPLS networks. PhD Thesis, Department of electronic engineering, Queen Mary and Westfield College, University of London, UK (2000)
11. Blake, S., Black, D., Carlson, M., Davies, E., Wang, Z., Weiss, W.: An Architecture for Differentiated Service. RFC 2475 (1998)
12. Scheinhardt, W.: Markov-modulated and feedback fluid queues. Ph.D Thesis, Faculty of Mathematical Sciences, University of Twente, Enschede, The Netherlands (1998)
13. Braden, R., Clark, D., Shenker, S.: Integrated Services in the Internet Architecture: an Overview. RFC 1633 (1994)

Efficient Semi-supervised Learning BitTorrent Traffic Detection with Deep Packet and Deep Flow Inspections

Raymond Siulai Wong, Teng-Sheng Moh, and Melody Moh

Computer Science Department
San Jose State University
San Jose, CA 95192-0249, USA
rlswong@yahoo.com, {teng.moh,melody.moh}@sjsu.edu

Abstract. The peer-to-peer (P2P) technology has been well developed over the Internet. BitTorrent (BT) is one of the most popular P2P sharing protocols; BT network traffic detection has become increasingly important and yet technically challenging. In this paper we propose a new detection method that is based on an intelligent combination of Deep Packet Inspection (DPI) and Deep Flow Inspection (DFI) with semi-supervised learning. Comparing with existing methods, the new method has achieved equally high accuracy with shorter classification time. We believe that this highly effective BT detection method is not only significant to the BT community, but is also very useful to other groups that need to efficiently and correctly detect single applications.

Keywords: Deep Flow Inspection, Deep Packet Inspection, Classification, BitTorrent, Traffic Detection, Peer to Peer Traffic.

1   Introduction

Peer-to-peer (P2P) has been one of the major technologies that contributed to the success and popularity of the Internet. Among the P2P technologies, BitTorrent (BT) has clearly been one of the most widely used ones. It has been demonstrated that BT accounts for approximately 45-78% of all P2P traffic and 27-55% of all the Internet traffic [3]. Given such enormous traffic flows, Internet service providers (ISP) and enterprise network administrators often want to control their network bandwidth by detecting and limiting the bandwidth of P2P activity, in order to provide enough bandwidth for other critical applications. However, P2P traffic detection has become challenging in recent years due to the development of many intelligent P2P applications. For example, port detection, one of the existing techniques, does not work any longer since many new P2P applications now use user-defined, non-standard ports or even dynamic ports.

Detecting P2P traffic is important and it can be seen in different aspects from different people. For an enterprise network, the administrators may want to rate-limit the P2P traffic such that it has enough bandwidth for other critical applications. For a local broadband ISP, they may want to limit the cost charged by the upstream ISP. For

S. Dua et al. (Eds.): ICISTM 2012, CCIS 285, pp. 152–163, 2012.

regular home users, most users today have asynchronous Internet connection service from their ISP, meaning that the upstream rate and downstream rate are not equal and upstream rate is usually lower than downstream rate. If the upstream is congested, it will affect the overall Internet experience.

In this paper, a new detection method, named *Intelligent Combination,* based on Deep Packet inspection (DPI) and semi-supervised learning Deep Flow Inspection (DFI) is proposed. By carefully observing the packet pattern a BT flow, we choose to arrange DPI to be ahead of DFI in the module. This arrangement has greatly speeded up the classification process. From the conducted experiments, the mechanism gives a promising accuracy rates of over 90 percent while improving the classification time over Double Layer, an existing combined DFI/DPI method [7], by 15-20%. Some preliminary results have been reported in an earlier publication [10].

The rest of the paper is organized in the following manner. Section 2 presents the related studies. Section 3 describes our new, improved approach, *Intelligent Combination.* In section 4 we show the simulation results of our proposed system along with three existing methods. Finally Section 5 concludes the paper.

2   Related Works

This section gives a brief overview of the most relevant works; each of their technical details can be found from the original papers. There are three major classes of techniques to detect P2P traffic: 1) port-based, 2) DPI or DFI, and 3) some combination of DPI and DFI techniques. The first class is port-based. This method is based on TCP and/or UDP ports. It has recently become obsolete due to the fact that many new BT clients use new techniques such as utilizing user-defined port, random port, changed port or camouflage port to avoid port detection mechanisms.

The second class is DPI or DFI. In general, DPI looks at packet payload to detect BT packets. For example, Liu et al. [5] proposed a simple DPI algorithm to detect BT traffic. Their algorithm is based on the handshaking messages among the BitTorrent peers.

DFI, on the other hand, detects BT packets by inspecting the entire TCP flows. Le and But [4] used a DFI algorithm to classify traffic. They focused on the packet length statistics as the feature for their classifier. Similar, Liu et al. [6] used packet length to detect P2P packets based on statistical analysis. There are other DFI papers utilizing various popular classification techniques to detect P2P traffic. In particularly, Erman et al. [2] proposed a *semi-supervised learning* DFI algorithm to classify Internet traffic. Their algorithm involves a two-step approach to train their classifier: clustering and mapping. based on the estimation of the labeled sample probabilities within each clusters. This DFI method has been simulated and used for performance comparison (Section 4).

The third class combines the two techniques (DPI and DFI) to increase detection rates. Chen et al. proposed to use both DFI and DPI to detect BT packets [1]; they also suggested executing DPI and DFI in parallel to speed up the overall process. Wang et al. [7] claimed that using both DFI and DPI makes both detection algorithms to comprise each other; thus, the detection rate will increase. Their proposed scheme, named *Double Layer* method, used three steps sequentially: first the port-based detection, then a DFI method to detect P2P traffic, and lastly a DPI method to classify the P2P traffic type. Even though the detection rate is high, the system is complex, and the classification time is long (see Section 4.2).

Our proposed system, Intelligent Combination, is also based on both DPI and DFI methods. While achieving an equally high accurate rate, based on BT packet flow pattern it arranges DPI to come before DFI, and thereby successfully shorten the classification time. We will be presenting our proposed system in the next section with detailed explanation. A table comparing various major algorithms including DPI [5], DFI [4, 6], learning-based DFI [2], Double Layer of combining DFI and DPI [7], and the new proposed Intelligent Combination is given in Table 1.

Table 1. Comparison of major approaches for detecting BT packets

Methods	Scheme (or Steps)	Implementation Strengths	Implementation Limitation
BT header lookup method [5]	Simple DPI	Simple	
Packet/ Flow length statistics method [4, 6]	DFI	Avoid complex per-packet DPI overhead	Difficult to determine suitable thresholds
Learning algorithm [2]	DFI	Avoid complex per-packet DPI overhead	Initial off-line training required
Double Layer [7]	1) Port-based, 2) DFI, then 3) DPI	Possible (though unlikely) quick classification through port-based	1) Difficult to determine suitable thresholds for DFI and 2) Very complex
Intelligent Combination (proposed)	**1) Simple DPI, then 2) DFI**	**1) Use simple DPI, 2) possible quick classification through simple DPI, 3) simpler than Double Layer [7]**	**Initial off-line training required**

3   Proposed System: Intelligent Combination

The main goal is to classify each packet flow as either BT or non-BT. The proposed system, *Intelligent Combination*, is depicted in Figure 1. The system can be divided into two major parts, namely the online classification module and the offline training module. Below is an overview of the system; detailed description is given in the following subsections.

(1)   The *on-line classification module*: It is an intelligent combination of DPI and DFI.

    a.   DPI: The module starts with a simple DPI that quickly detects packets with BT character strings, while at the same time records the host names of these BT packets and updates the BT hostname database.

    b.   DFI: The rest of the packets then go through the DFI portion, which is classifier based on a semi-supervised learning system [8, 2]. It will perform a detailed flow inspection of the features of the unclassified packet flows and classify each as either BT or non-BT.

(2)   The *offline training module*: It provides for the DFI portion a reliable trained classifier based on K-means algorithm [2, 9] for detecting BT flows.

The careful arrangement of the order of DPI and DFI, with first a simple DPI followed by a semi-supervised learning DFI classifier, is based on the following rationale: We observe that a BT packet flow typically begins with handshake messages. These messages often include some simple string pattern such as "BitTorrentprotocol". If such pattern is found (matched), obviously a BT flow is to be expected. A simple DPI may be used for such a straight-forward pattern matching, and a successful matching can then eliminate the need for a long DFI classification for this flow.

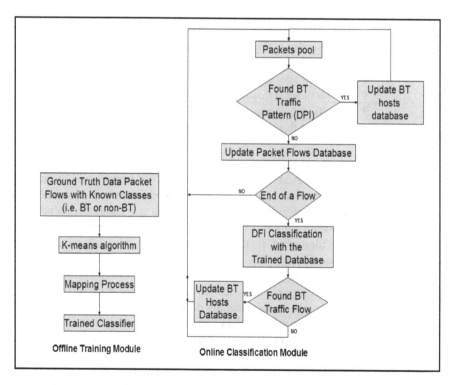

Fig. 1. Proposed *Intelligent Combination* system to classify BT packet flows

3.1   Offline Training Module

The block diagram of the offline training module is given on the left side of Figure 1. The module uses the *K-means algorithm* [9, 2], a well-known algorithm in the area of clustering and machine learning, for mapping data objects (in our case features of packet flows) to classes (BT and non-BT). The module is described below.

The offline training module begins with *the ground truth* as the input to the K-means algorithm. The ground truth consists of packet flows with *known classes* (BT and non-BT). We use ten features to characterize each packet flow, as listed in Table 2. These features are extracted from each of the packet flows within the ground truth.

Table 2. Flow characteristics used in the semi-supervised learning of the offline training module

No.	Features
1	Total number of packets
2	Average packet size
3	Total bytes
4	Total header (transport plus network layer) bytes
5	Number of flow initiator to flow responder packets
6	Total flow initiator to flow responder payload bytes
7	Total flow initiator to flow responder header bytes
8	Number of flow responder to flow initiator packets
9	Total flow responder to flow initiator header bytes
10	Total flow responder to flow initiator header bytes

Next, the *K-means algorithm* divides the packet flows into *clusters* according to the similarities of their ten features. Flows that exhibit closer features will be grouped into the same cluster. At the end of the K-means algorithm, there will be a total of K clusters. Note that even though using K-means may result in a contradiction between a cluster and a ground-truth flow in that cluster, in the classification step we use a majority-win principle (described in the next paragraph); this will minimize the chance of causing a contradiction.

The subsequent step uses *mapping process* as the classification algorithm to label incoming flows. This process is to map each clusters into a given class (in our case, BT or non-BT). The principle for the mapping decision is simple: Given a cluster, if the number of BT packet flows is larger than that of non-BT packet flows, we marked it as BT cluster. Similarly, we mark a cluster as non-BT if there are more non-BT packet flows within the cluster.

When the mapping process is completed, we will have the *trained classifier* (also known as *trained database*), mapping each cluster (or more specifically, each set of ten flow features) into a class. The trained classifier is then used by the DFI of the online classifier module to detect if a packet flow is BT or non-BT.

3.2   Online Classification Module

The main goal of the online classification module is to discover all the *BT hosts*. In the following, we first describe the databases needed, and then the detailed steps of the module.

3.2.1   Databases

There are two databases needed. The first is the *BT host database* for all the classified BT hosts. This database is updated whenever a packet or a flow is being classified as BT. The second is the *packet flow database*, which is for keeping track of all the packets that we have seen during the classification process. It is continuously updated as packets are received, so that at the end of a packet flow it has the complete ten-feature information of this packet flow. This information is then fed into DFI for classification if needed.

3.2.2 Online Classification Module Description

The block diagram of the online classification module is given on the right side of Figure 1. Initially, a packet flow of unknown class is input to the simple *DPI module*. It is based on the match of a simple string pattern (such as "BitTorrentprotocol"). This is used to determine if the encountered packet is of BT class. If it is a BT packet, the *database of BT hosts* will be updated immediately.

If no BT string pattern is matched, then the corresponding packet flow information (i.e. total number of packets in flow, average packet size, etc., features in Table 1) will be extracted, and input to the corresponding entry of *packet flow database*. If that packet is at the *end of the flow*, we have the entry with completed flow information updated in the packet flow database.

This new packet flow information will then be applied to the *DFI classification with the trained database*. Relying on the trained database and based on the ten flow features, the DFI classifier will then determine if the new input flow is BT. Recall that the trained database (also called trained classifier) is obtained from the offline training module as described in Section 3.1. Once the classification decision is made, and if *the flow is found to be BT*, the BT host database will also be updated accordingly.

Finally, note that the above design is based on its main goal – to discover all the BT hosts. This goal is chosen since BT hosts are often the most important information requested by an enterprise network or an ISP. Alternatively, we can set the goal as to discover all the *BT flows*. Note that our classification system (mainly the online classification module) can be easily modify for this alternative, or other similar purposes.

3.3   Strengths of Intelligent Combination System

In this section we note some major advantages in this approach:

(1) *Accuracy*: By employing both DPI and DFI modules, the accuracy of the classification is greatly increased [1, 7]. If one module fails to detect, the other module can have a chance to look at the packet flow.

(2) *Security*: Like most existing DPI modules, our simple DPI does not handle encrypted packets. Yet, the subsequent DFI module will be able to handle them since it does not depend upon reading packet payload (it only needs its features such as payload size).

(3) *Efficiency*: Unlike other combined DPI/DFI methods (such as the Double Layer system by Wang et al [7]), our system first uses simple DPI to quickly determine if a packet is a BT. DFI is used only if the BT packet pattern cannot be found. The major advantage of this improved arrangement is that we do not need to wait until the end of the flow to determine the flow type if the BT pattern can be matched in the DPI stage. In other words, we can quickly identify a flow as BT without waiting for the entire flow to complete. This advantage is also clearly demonstrated in the performance evaluation section (Section 4.5) when the classification time of the proposed system is shorter than both the Double Layer and the DFI.

(4) *Further Speedup*: Since we store the BT hosts in our database, we could further speed up the classification process by first checking if a host is BT. (If there is a match then both DPI and DFI may be skipped.) This will also avoid repeating the tasks that have been done. For instance, if the DFI module has already classified a host as a P2P host then DPI can safely skip packets from that host.

4   Performance Evaluation

This section evaluates the performance of the proposed method with three existing methods: *DPI* [5], *semi-supervised learning DFI* [2], and *Double Layer* of combining DFI and DPI [7].

An initial experiment is used to capture BT and non-BT packets. There can be one or more PCs behind a router. Inside the PC, BitComet 1.21 is installed as the BT client. A sample torrent file was downloaded for BT packet capturing purpose. Note that a torrent file contains information about the tracker server while the tracker server contains the peers' information about shared files.

The *ground truth* in this project is the packet flows of known classes (i.e., BT and non-BT). In order to train a classifier, two types of packet flows (BT and non-BT) needed to captureTo capture BT packets, we start a sample torrent file, and the BT client will automatically start downloading/uploading its contents. At the same time, we start a packet-capturing program to obtain these packets. Similarly, to capture non-BT packets we create non-BT network activities such as HTTP, FTP and SSH.

4.1   DFI-Classifier Training

The DFI module used is based on a semi-supervised learning classifier that would accurately classify BT packet flows. This classifier is first trained with the ground truth generated, then tested against other BT packet flows to observe the accuracy.

We conduct an experiment to estimate the number of packet flows needed to train a reliable classifier for the DFI module, using K=400 in the K-means algorithm, for a fair comparison as the same value was used in the related work [2]. Figure 2 shows the classifier accuracy with increasing number of BT packet flows used in training the classifier. As expected, the more BT packets used to train the classifier, the better the accuracy is. As the number of BT packets increases, however, the classifier will be saturated at some point. After that, even when more packets are supplied, the accuracy will not increase significantly. From Figure 2, one can see that the saturation point occurs around 2,500 packet flows. Thus, in the following experiments, the number of BT packet flows used for training the DFI classifier should be at least 2,500 to ensure a high accuracy.

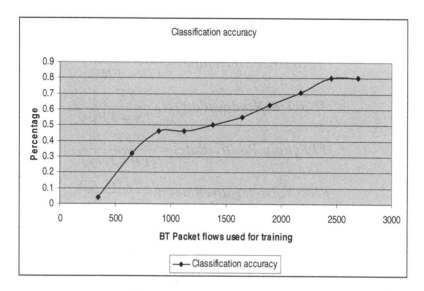

Fig. 2. Classifier accuracy versus the number of BT packet flows used in training classifier in the DFI module

4.2   Classification Accuracy

In this experiment, we compare the classification accuracy results. Based on the results obtained in training the DFI module classifier (Section 4.1), we train the classifier with the ground truth of 8,000 TCP packet flows of which approximately 3,500 are BT TCP packet flows.

In order to obtain a fair comparison of the four methods, we design two statistically different test cases for the experiments. In test case 1, there are 60% BT packet flows and 40% non-BT packet flows. In test case 2, there are about 70% BT and 30% non-BT packet flows.

4.2.1   Accuracy Measurements and Metrics
For a just comparison of the four methods, it is important to take note of both the *positive* as well as the *negative* results. We therefore collect the following four measurements [9]:

Four Measurements:

- *True Positive (TP):* The number of BT packet flows correctly detected.

- *False Negative (FN):* The number of BT packet flows that have *not* been detected.

- *False Positive (FP):* The number of non-BT packet flows that have been falsely identified as BT packet flows.

- *True Negative (TN):* The number of non-BT packet flows that have been correctly identified as non-BT.

Performance Metrics

Based on the above collected data, the following metrics are calculated [9]:

$$TPR(TruePositiveRate) = \frac{TP}{(TP + FN)}$$

$$TNR(TrueNegativeRate) = \frac{TN}{(TN + FP)}$$

$$FPR(FalsePositiveRate) = \frac{FP}{(FP + TN)}$$

$$FNR(FalseNegativeRate) = \frac{FN}{(TP + FN)}$$

In the above, the true positive rate (*TPR*) or *sensitivity* is defined as the fraction of positive examples (BT packet flows) correctly classified. Similarly, the true negative rate (*TNR*) or *specificity* is the fraction of negative examples (non-BT packet flows) classified correctly. Furthermore, the false positive rate (*FPF*) is the portion of negative examples (non-BT packet flows) falsely classified as BT packet flows. Finally, the false negative rate (*FNR*) is the portion of positive examples (BT packet flows) falsely classified as non-BT.

In addition, two widely-used metrics [9] are also employed:

$$Precision,\ p = TP\ /\ (TP+FP)$$

$$Recall,\ r = TP\ /\ (TP + FN)$$

Precision determines, out of the total packet flows that have been classified as BT, the fraction that are actually BT (true or correct classification). Obviously, the higher the precision is, the smaller the number of false positive errors done by the classifier. On the other hand, *recall* measures, out of all the BT packet flows, the portion that have been correctly classified as BT packet flows. A large recall implies a system with very few BT packet flows been falsely classified as non-BT. To simply put, the larger these two metrics are, the more accurate the system is.

4.2.2   Accuracy Results

Tables 3 and 4 show the classification results of the four algorithms, *DPI* [5], *semi-supervised learning DFI* [2], *Double Layer* [7], and the proposed *Intelligent Combination* method, for the two test cases, respectively.

First, comparing Tables 3 and 4, it is clear that they are similar and consistent. Thus, we can trust that the results presented are reliable. Below we discuss results of each of the four methods.

Table 3. Classification Accuracy Results (*Test Case 1*)

Scheme	TPR	TNR	FPR	FNR	Precision p	Recall r
DPI [5]	0.31	1.00	0.00	0.69	1.00	0.31
DFI [2]	0.78	0.86	0.14	0.22	0.89	0.78
Double Layer [7]	0.87	0.86	0.14	0.13	0.90	0.87
Intelligent Combination	0.87	0.86	0.14	0.13	0.90	0.87

Table 4. Classification Accuracy Results (*Test Case 2*)

Scheme	TPR	TNR	FPR	FNR	Precision p	Recall r
DPI [5]	0.35	1.00	0.00	0.65	1.00	0.35
DFI [2]	0.73	0.87	0.13	0.27	0.93	0.73
Double Layer [7]	0.85	0.87	0.13	0.15	0.94	0.85
Intelligent Combination	0.85	0.87	0.13	0.15	0.94	0.85

Simple DPI has very high TNR (100%); i.e., it has achieved 100% accuracy to detect non-BT traffic flows (including HTTP, FTP and SSH). It is because the DPI method searches for the BT pattern string ("BitTorrentprotocol") explicitly inside the packets, which obviously cannot be found in non-BT flows. On the other hand, it has unfortunately very low TPR (31% and 35% in test cases 1 and 2, respectively); i.e., it has a very low rate of successfully identify BT packet flows. It is because the BT pattern string happens mainly in the handshaking messages and it may not appear during the BT data transfer. Because of its simple, straight-forward method, it has very high precision rate (100% - it does not confuse non-BT as BT), but unfortunately a very low recall rate (31% and 35% in the two test cases), this shows that it does confuse many BT as non-BT.

DFI on the other hand has a reasonably high TPR (78% and 73%) – it is able to correctly detect a good portion of BT traffic, and a higher TNR (86% and 87%) – it is also able to correctly detect quite a lot of non-BT traffic. While its precision rate is high (89% and 93%), it does not confuse non-BT as BT); it however has a slightly lower recall rate (78% and 73%), it does sometimes confuse BT as non-BT.

Both our proposed Intelligent Combination method and the Double Layer method [7] have exhibited equally highly accurate results. Their main difference is in the classification time (to be discussed in the next section). We will therefore discuss these two methods together here. They have very high TPR (87% and 85%in the two test cases) and TNR (86% and 87%). These have resulted in high values of both precision and recall rates. Note that their recall rates (87% and 85%) are the highest among the four methods, which implies that both methods do not easily confuse BT with non-BT packet flows (as DPI and DFI do). This is an important strength both methods.

4.3   Classification Time

Figure 3 shows the packets classification time for various classification methods. Note that the proposed Intelligent Combination method has the second shortest execution time (only longer than the simple DPI); this is one of the most important performance metrics, discussed in detail below.

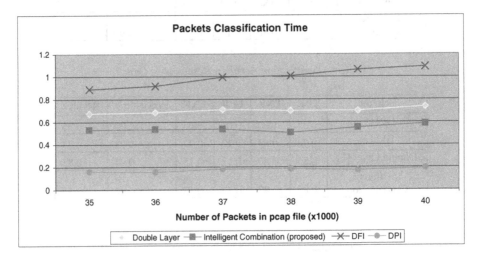

Fig. 3. Packet Classification Time

We first note that the simple DPI has the fastest classification time due to the fact that its classification is purely based on string comparison (whereas the other three methods are more computational intensive). DFI, on the other hand, requires the longest execution time. It is a purely flow-based method, each classification theoretically needs to wait till the entire packet flow is completely received and analyzed. The Double Layer method [7] has the second longest execution time. It is faster than DFI since, before DFI, it applies a simple port-based classification. This step can quickly filter out some BT flows that used popular P2P ports, and therefore speeds up the average execution time.

The proposed Intelligent Combination method is faster than both the Double Layer [7] and DFI. In particular, it is 15-20% faster than the Double Layer method. This is because it first uses the simple DPI (which has the fastest execution time), and if there is a match, it records its BT host names into the BT host database systems, which not only shortens the current flow classification (a quick BT-flow detection), but also helps speed up the future classification time.

5   Conclusion

By recognizing the packet pattern of BT flows, this paper proposed a new BT traffic identification method that is both accurate and fast. Simply put, combining both DPI and DFI makes it accurate; arranging DPI before DFI makes it fast. The simulation results further support its superior performance. They have shown that, by combining the simple DPI with the semi-supervised learning DFI, the BT detection rate is as high as that of the comparable method by Wang et al [7]. In addition, applying intelligent combination of these two techniques further increases the execution speed, 15-20% faster than that of one of the comparable methods [7]. For future works, the semi-supervised learning method may be further improved and refined, and alternative learning algorithms be explored, with the ultimate goal to apply the proposed algorithm onto live-network flows. The principle of putting simple DPI ahead of a more complex DFI may be applied to other systems that aim to quickly and effectively detect single applications.

Acknowledgments. The authors would like to thank many helpful comments Provided by the four anonymous reviewers, especially Reviewer 1.

References

1. Chen, H., Hu, Z., Ye, Z., Liu, W.: A New Model for P2P Traffic Identification Based on DPI and DFI. In: Int. Conf. on Inf. Eng. and Computer Science, ICIECS 2009, pp. 1–3 (2009)
2. Erman, J., Mahanti, A., Arlitt, M., Cohen, I., Williamson, C.: Offline/Realtime Traffic Classification Using Semi-Supervised Learning. IFIP Performance (October 2007)
3. Klemm, A., Lindemann, C., Vernon, M.K., Waldhorst, O.P.: Characterizing the query behavior in peer-to-peer file sharing systems. In: IMC 2004: Proceedings of the 4th ACM SIGCOMM Conference on Internet Measurement, pp. 55–67. ACM Press (2004)
4. Le, T., But, J.: Bittorrent traffic classification, CAIA Technical report 091022A, October 22 (2009), http://caia.swin.edu.au/reports/091022A/CAIA-TR-091022A.pdf
5. Liu, B., Li, Z., Li, Z.: Measurements of BitTorrent System Based on Netfilter. In: Int. Conf. on Computational Intelligence and Security, pp. 1470–1474 (2006)
6. Liu, F., Li, Z., Yu, J.: Applications Identification Based on the Statistics Analysis of Packet Length. In: Int. Symp. Information Engineering and Electronic Commerce, IEEC 2009, pp. 160–163 (2009)
7. Wang, C., Li, T., Chen, H.: P2P Traffic Identification Based on Double Layer Characteristics. In: Int. Conf. Information Technology and Computer Science, ITCS 2009, pp. 593–596 (2009)
8. Chapelle, O., Scholkopf, B., Zien, A. (eds.): Semi-Supervised Learning. MIT Press, Cambridge (2006)
9. Tan, P.-N., Steinbach, M., Kumar, V.: Introduction to Data Mining. Pearson Addison Wesley, USA (2006)
10. Wong, R.S., Moh, T.-S., Moh, M.: Efficient Semi-supervised Learning BitTorrent Traffic Detection - An Extended Summary. In: Bononi, L., Datta, A.K., Devismes, S., Misra, A. (eds.) ICDCN 2012. LNCS, vol. 7129, pp. 540–543. Springer, Heidelberg (2012)
11. Karagiannis, T., Papagiannaki, K., Faloutsos, M.: BLINC: Multi-Level Traffic Classification in the Dark. In: Proc. ACM SIGCOMM 2005, Philadelphia, PA (August 2005)

An Intelligent Multi Agent Framework
for E-commerce Using Case Based Reasoning
and Argumentation for Negotiation

Pooja Jain and Deepak Dahiya

Jaypee University of Information Technology, Waknaghat, Solan
{pooja.jain,deepak.dahiya}@juit.ac.in

Abstract. A multi agent system is composed of a number of agents, communicating, collaborating, coordinating and negotiating with each other to solve a complex problem. The work discusses an intelligent multi agent system which can be used effectively in e-commerce. The agents work on behalf of the user, and help him in buying a product directly or through auction. Case based reasoning makes the system intelligent and help the agents to reach conclusions. The negotiation is done though argumentation. The communication between the agents is done through ACL, also specifying the required ontology. Implementation of the system is done in JADE.

Keywords: Multi agent systems, case based reasoning, negotiation, argumentation, ontology, ACL.

1 Introduction

With the expansion of the internet, e-commerce has also seen a rapid growth. To keep pace with its growth, it's necessary to use a multi agent system, which provides a promising field for the approach of agent and artificial intelligence technology[1]. Steps are being taken to automate ecommerce business processes. Agent technology is often claimed to be the best approach for automating online shopping transactions. Intelligent agents are reactive, proactive and have social ability. Agents should be intelligent enough to work on behalf of the user[2]. An ecommerce system can be best realized through a multi agent system. Nowadays, when there are a large number of sites available for online shopping, its really becoming very tough for the people to choose the desired product at the right price. A multi agent system will help the user in reducing his burden in finding out the right product at the right place.

Most of the papers dealing with multi agent e-commerce systems, create as many buyer agents as there are buyers and as many seller agents as there are products to be sold [3,4]. As the number of products increase, the seller agents also increase, making the system hard to realize in real time scenarios. Nowadays, there are thousands of products being sold on every e-commerce site. Creating a seller agent for each of the products is quite cumbersome. This paper proposes an approach to have one seller agent per each e-commerce site. The second issue dealt in this paper is to have one common portal for all the e-commerce sites instead of having one MAS for one

S. Dua et al. (Eds.): ICISTM 2012, CCIS 285, pp. 164–175, 2012.

e-commerce site. Such a common portal is designed using a multi agent knowledge management system.

A key problem with all the first generation e commerce systems is that they are too focussed on one aspect of the transaction i.e price [5]. In direct buying also, there are many factors that need to be concerned apart from the price. This paper talks about a multi modal search of the products, keeping many factors in mind like the quality, quantity, color, price etc. In the case of auctions, when faced with the need to reach agreement on a variety of issues, humans make use of negotiations. The same can be achieved by automated negotiations performed by a multi agent system.

This paper talks about a multi agent system for e-commerce that uses case based reasoning and argumentation based negotiation. The remainder of this paper is organized as follows: Section 2 provides background in the areas of multi agent systems, agent communication, case based reasoning, and argumentation based negotiation. Section 3 deals with the proposed architecture in detail. It also briefly describes the agent communication through ACL Section 4 deals with the partial implementation of the system in JADE. Section 5 deals with the results and observations. Section 6 concludes the paper and section 7 talks about the future work.

2   Related Work

In a multi agent system(MAS), the agents need to cooperate, coordinate with each other to performs tasks which are not possible by stand slone systems. For effective communication between the agents, three things are of utmost importance [6]:-

- Communication language
- Communication protocol and
- Shared ontology

The internet and advancements in the technologies have revolutionized the way in which business and commerce is conducted nowadays. A lot has changed since the traditional retail shops of brick and mortar to the electronic form of trade[7].

Lasheng Yu talks about a Multi-Agent Automated Intelligent Shopping System (MAISS), but the problem in this architecture is that there is one seller agent for each product[8]. As the number of products to be sold increases, the number of seller agents also increases. With the growth of internet, the e-commerce sites have also increased incredibly and with them the number of products sold. Its almost unrealistic to have so many seller agents.

CBR is a method of making use of past experience to solve newly encountered problems. The past experience is recorded in the case base[9]. Pierre De Loor talks about decision-making in autonomous agents in interactive simulations with the help of CBR [10].

Agents need to cooperate with each other in a multi agent system. Communication among agents and facilitators is typically achieved through an agent communication language, such as the Knowledge Query Manipulation Language (KQML) or FIPA Agent Communication language (ACL) [11]. The semantics of these ACLs have been defined in terms of conditions on the mental state of agents which is supposed to have beliefs, intentions and so on [12,13].

Various interaction and decision mechanisms for automated negotiation have been proposed and studied. These include game-theoretic analysis [14, 15],heuristic-based approaches[16]andargumentation-based approaches[17]. In this paper, argumentation-based approach is discussed. as it allows more sophisticated form of interaction as compared to game-theoretic and heuristic approaches.

3   Architecture of the Proposed System

There are six stages of e-commerce as described by Pattie Maes et al [18]. The phases considered in this paper are depicted in the figure 1.

Fig. 1. Phases of e-commerce

The proposed multi agent knowledge management system for e-commerce has two modules- buy module and the auction module. The two modules are different because there are certain sites which do not have auction facility and there are some which do not have direct buy option. On the contrary there are some which fall into both categories, i.e depending upon the product, there are both options available of buying and auctioning. The working of both the modules is the same till the merchant brokering phase. The buy module doesn't have the negotiation phase. The flowchart of the system workflow can be depicted as in the figure 2.

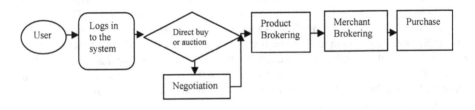

Fig. 2. E-commerce phases flowchart

3.1   Detailed Design of Buy Module

Buy module is the one in which there is no room for negotiation. Very few papers talk about this aspect. It happens many times that the user doesn't want to waste time in auctions or negotiations and want to purchase the item directly. In such cases its important to give the best possible results from all the sites to the user, and then he may decide amongst them.

Whenever a person attempts to buy a product, there are certain measures which helps him to decide to buy the product like price, quantity, quality, delivery area, delivery charges, time taken for delivery etc. All these factors well help to decide the site from which the product is to be purchased. Thus there will be a multi modal search by the system.The architecture of the buy module is depicted in the figure below

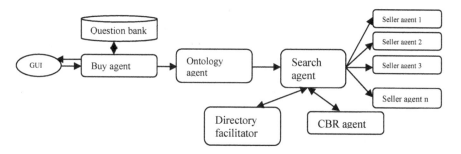

Fig. 3. Buy module

3.1.1 Product Brokering and Merchant Brokering

Product brokering is the method of selection of a product that suits the needs of the customer. Merchant brokering phase is almost automated with the help of an intelligent multi agent system. The agent on behaf of the user decides the merchant/ seller from which the product is to be bought. The merchant is an ecommerce site selling a product as identified by the product identification and product brokering phases.The buyer agent maintains a database of the different products classified into proper headings like Men, Women, Kids, Home and travel, Gift ideas and Fragrances and beauty. Then apparels, jewellery etc inside Women's category. Now, when one of the sub-category is chosen, the user is given sub-sub category. E.g. Men's apparel can be further sub-divided as Shirts,Trousers, Jeans t-shirts etc. Suppose the user chooses Jeans. This query is forwarded to the ontology agent. The responsibility of the ontology agent is to prepare ontology of the product as chosen by the user. If two agents are to communicate about some domain, then it is necessary for them to agree on the terminology that they use to describe this domain [19]. An ontology is a specification of a set of terms, intended to provide a common basis of understanding about some domain [19]. The description about the product should be common to both the buyer agent and the seller agents. There are three ontology languages that can be used, OWL, KIF and XML [19]. Here XML is used.

Now there may be a large number of sites selling jeans. There must be some other details as well which can help in filtering the results. It has a questionaire agent which asks questions from the user which helps it to decide the product from one specific site. This questionairre agent maintains a questionnaire bank,which is updated from time to time. There are specific questions for different products. For instance, in the above discussed case when the user is searching for jeans, the questions asked can be like Color of the jeans,Brand,Size,Regular fit /skinny fit/ slim fit,Low waiste/ high waiste,Delievry city etc.

The ontology would now look like

```
<catalogue>
    <Category name="Men">
        <Sub-category name="Apparels">
            < Sub-sub-category name="Jeans">
                <Brand>Levis</Brand>
                <Color>Blue<Color>
                <Delivery-date>10</Delivery-date>
                <Delivery-area>NCR</Delivery-area>
                <Size>30</Size>
                <Fit>Regular</Fit>
                <Price-range>1000-1500</Price-range>
            </Sub-sub-category>
        </Sub-category>
    </Category>
</catalogue>
```

This ontology is then transferred to the search agent. Search agent works on the principle of cooperative distributed problem solving (CDPS) [20]. Cooperation is necessary as no single agent has sufficient expertise for solving the problem of information retrieval. The agents in the search module share a common goal, and thus there is no potential for conflict between them. The search agent advertises the existence of the task to other agents in the search module with a task announcement, and then acts as the manager of that task for its duration.

Each agent corresponds to one of the e-commerce site registered with the directory facilitator (DF). The directory facilitator agent behaves like yellow pages. It contains the details of all the sites related to e-commerce. It's necessary that the sites register themselves with the DF agent. The DF agent creates an agent for each subscribed e-commerce site and give them names like 1_seller_agent, 2_seller_agent etc. The search agent takes the information from the DF agent, and then sends the request for the product to the seller agents. It may issue a general broadcast to all the agents, or it can announce the task to some of the agents which it feels may solve its task. It takes the help of the case based reasoning (CBR) agent for this. CBR agent acquires knowledge about selling agents' task solving capabilities by CBR and then the tasks can be assigned more directly without the broadcast of task announcements.

The CBR cycle consists of 4 phases namely Retrieve, Reuse, Revise and Retain. Since a problem is solved by recalling a previous experience suitable for solving the new problem, the case search and matching processes need to be both effective and reasonably time efficient.

The basic problem that arises is that of representation of knowledge in case base. If the representation is clear and crisp then the retrieval is efficient and less time consuming. The case base can be represented by using an ontology. Ontology based case based reasoning has been discussed by Yuh-Jen-Chen et al [21]. All the cases should be transferred into a standard format in order to solve the heterogeneous problems. The CBR agent maintains a database of domain ontology and the case ontology. Whenever the search agent receives a query from the buy agent, it transfers this query to the CBR agent to find out a similar case which was solved earlier. If the CBR agent finds such cases/case, then that result is passed to the search agent, which may give the specific seller agent/s which was selected earlier to purchase a similar item. Thus the broadcast of task announcement is replaced by the task announcement to some specific few agents.

Only the case ontology is not sufficient because a case in one domain is different from the case in a different domain. So both the case ontology and domain ontology need to be matched by the CBR agent. During the Retain phase, useful experience is retained for future reuse, and the case base is updated by a new learned case, or by modification of some existing cases. Learning makes the case base expand quickly, which increases the search time a lot. To avoid this, there is a need to maintain the case base so that it doesn't become so large, that it becomes tough to manage. So, the unused cases need to be deleted. Or, instead of adding a new case every time, better to modify the existing similar case. There are many ways of case base maintenance. Here fuzzy logic is used in similarity measuring function to retrieve the similar cases. Fuzzy Similarity -measuring function is defined as follows [22].

$$\text{Similarity}(T_1, T_2) = \sum_{i=1}^{m} \sum_{j=1}^{n} \text{Dist}(A_{1i}:V_{1i}, A_{2j}:V_{2j}) \tag{1}$$

where

$$T1: (A_{11}:V_{11}, \ldots, A_{1m}:V_{1m}) \quad \text{and}$$
$$T2: (A_{11}:V_{11}, \ldots, A_{1n}:V_{1n})$$
$$\text{Dist}(A_{1i}:V_{1i}, A_{2j}:V_{2j}) = W(A_{1i}, A_{1j}) * \text{Equal}(V_{1i}, V_{1j}) \tag{2}$$

The different seller agents listen to the task announcement and evaluate them with respect to their own specialized hardware and software resources. The seller agents compare the ontology given by the search agent with the product ontologies stored in their database. When any seller agent finds a match, then it submits a bid. A bid indicates the capabilities of the bidder that are relevant to the execution of the announced task. A bid may contain information like Price, Brand, Delivery date, Delivery area etc

The seller agents which didn't have an exact match between their product ontology and that of the search agent also place a bid. E.g. a seller agent selling a black jeans instead of blue jeans, also place a bid. The search agent analyses the bids and finds the perfect match. If it doesn't find a single perfect match, then it selects the agents which have bids with almost same properties of the product as the ones asked for. The selection is communicated to the successful bidders through an award message.

As depicted in the figure, 3 and 4 seller agents are chosen and the jeans sold by them are displayed to the user. The user can choose any one of them.

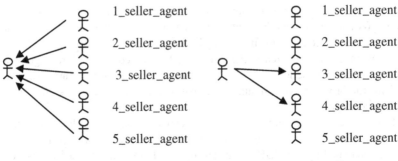

Fig. 4. Bidding   **Fig. 5.** Awarding

The search agent sends the results to the user. The user may select one of the selected agents. Then a direct link is formed between the user and the selected e-commerce site. The payment agent will next take care of the payments.

The buyer agent manages knowledge. It keeps track of all the orders placed by the user. It also keeps a check on the choices made by the user. E.g. the user prefers wearing a regular fit jeans, and then the system won't ask it from the user and will assume the choice of the user to be regular fir, although the user can edit his choice if he wants to. The same examples holds true with the size of the jeans. In such a way, the time of the user is saved and the system thrives to become intelligent. After every successful purchase, the feedback agent stores the feedback of the user. If the user is not happy with the products with one of the sites, then that site can be de-registered by the directory facilitator.

Once the selection is made by the user, the payment agent takes care of the payment made by the user. The payment should be completely secured using either MasterCard or Visa gateway. The information of the user is stored in a confidential database and cannot be showed to any other customer. The database stores the credit card number of the user, so that the user doesn't have to enter the 16 digits of its card again and again. For security reasons, the CVV number and the MasterCard or visa secure code will not be stored.

3.1.2   Communication between the Agents

There is a need of effective communication between the agents. The search agent needs to talk to the seller agents, the CBR agent needs to communicate with the search agent and so on. The communication language used in this paper is FIPA ACL which can be easily implemented in JADE. KQML message between the search agent and the seller agents is

```
ACLMessage msg = new ACLMessage(ACLMessage.cfp);
Jeans j = new Jeans
    ("levis","blue","7","NCR","30","Regular","1000-1500")
msg.addReceiver(new AID("Seller-agent", AID.ISLOCALNAME));
msg.setOntology("Product-ontology");
msg.setContentObject(j);
send(msg);
```

A "Jeans" object contains all the information that the search agent need to pass to the seller agents. The brand is levis, color blue, delivery date is within 7 days, delivery area is NCR, the size is 30, the fit is regular fit and the price range is 1000-1500.

This message is received by all the seller agents in the following format

```
ACLMessage msg = receive();
if (msg != null) {
// Process the message
}
```

3.2   Detailed Design of the Auction Module

As described earlier, e-commerce system has five phases. Negotiation phase is optional. In the case of negotiation, the ecommerce system goes through all the phases uptil merchant brokering. The only difference is that the DF agent will deal with only auction sites. The search agent will send the task announcement to them. Now the negotiation agent will start a negotiation with the selected seller agents.

(negotiation
        (id auction-12)
        (bid-increment 5)
        (terminator-window 10min)
        (highest-bid 1500)
        (current-highest-bid 10))

The first four fields are constant and the last field will be updated regularly. This is the case when the negotiation is single modal, i.e the negotiation is on only one property i.e. the price. It may happen that the person is not ready to negotiate on price but it can negotiate on color or the delivery date. In that case, the framework becomes multi modal. Argumentations mainly include   reward,   threat and appeal[23]. The process of negotiation proceeds by the exchange of proposals, critiques and /explanations. A proposal is a kind of a solution to a problem that the agent has to solve. The search agent puts a proposal to the seller agents in the following format:-

A: I propose that you provide me a product X
The seller agent can respond in two ways:-

B: I accept   acceptance
Or B:I don't have product X   reject

The first scenario is an Award when the search agents gives a reward message to the seller agent B.In the second case the search agent can recommend the product to the seller agent B and then it will be a Threat message. In addition to rejecting a proposal, the seller agent can offer a critique of the proposal, explaining why it is unacceptable.

E.g

B: I can provide X, provided you change your choice to "Grey color" or

This scenario is an Appeal. Such a critique is important in the case of multi modal negotiations. Mathematically stated, when there are 'm' criteria and 'n' alternatives, there are k pairwise comparisons to run a full fuzzy analytical network process(FANP) solution[24]

$$K= [(m*n \, (n-1)) \, /2]$$

4   Implementation

Once the architecture of the multi agent ecommerce system is ready, then its implementation can be done in JADE [25]. JADE is a middleware that facilitates the development of multi-agent systems. Due to time constraints, only the buy module has been implemented. The buy module consists of the search-agent and the seller-agent along with the directory facilitator agent and CBR agent helping the search agent in its operations. The screen shots show the buy agent taking options from the user. The user has selected to buy a jeans. The search agent contacted the questionnaire agent and came out with the specific questions to be asked to the user regarding the jeans.Once the search agent has the options, it adds the details to the catalogue.

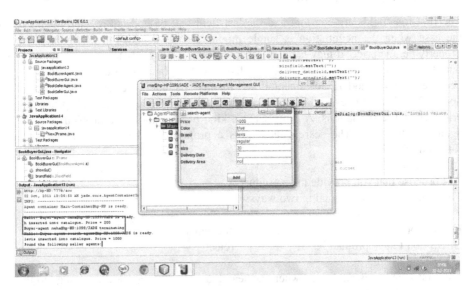

The seller agent is created and the product that it sells is also entered.

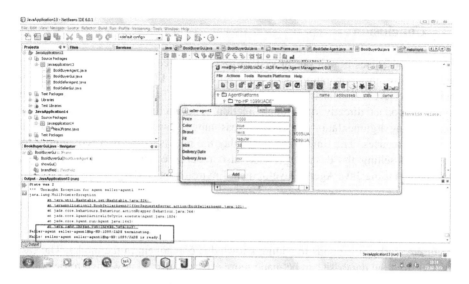

Finally the product is brought from the seller agent with the help of purchase agent.

5   Results and Observations

As stated in the previous section, the proposed multi agent system was implemented in JADE. There were certain results and observations. They are as follows:-

1. The negotiation module considers 'm' criteria and 'n' alternatives and k pairwise comparisons, this makes the process quite comple. The time complexity also increases.

2. This system aims to give the desired product to the user, being selected from a number of sites registered with the directory facilitator agent. Generally, a user searches for a product on different sites separately. He may get the product, but will have to compromise on some or the other factor due to time contraints. But the proposed system searches for the product on all the sites available and give the best deal to the user.

3. There is a need of the e-commerce site to register to the directory facilitator agent so that the system can search the site for a product. This requires a third party subscription. The e-commerce site may be sceptical about its security and may be hesitant to subscribe. In that case convincing it for subscription can be tough. Moreover, some of the well established   sites doesn't want to have a third party subscription at all.

4. The product ontology needs to be stored with the seller agents. If there are some thousands of products, then such thousand ontologies need to be stored in a database attached to the seller agent. This may make the seller agent heavy and costly.

6   Conclusion

This paper discusses a multi agent system for ecommerce. The system incorporate a number of agents cooperating with each other using FIPA agent communication language i.e. ACL and sharing a common ontology. The agents help the user in buying a product directly or through auction. The auction is multi modal and is realized using argumentation. Case based reasoning is used so that the complexity of the system reduces. The time taken to display the results to the user, containing the list of sites selling the desired product; also reduces considerably. The system is implemented using Java Agent Development Environment (JADE).

7   Future Work

The future work corresponds to adding knowledge component in the model. The case retrieval from the database can be made more effective using knowledge retrieval and knowledge re-use. Right now it has been assumed in the buy module that the user is giving only single value for all the parameters. The future work will give more options to the user, i.e. he can enter more than one choice for a parameter. Secondly the negotiation module need to more cost and time effective. The negotiation between the agents should go on smoothly giving various options to the user. The auction module needs to be implemented in JADE.

References

1. Xu, B., Yu, Y.: Multi-agent Based Approach to Collaborative Shopping. IEEE (2010) 978-1-4244-7974-0110/$26.00 ©2010
2. Jain, P., Dahiya, D.: Architecture of a Library Management System Using Gaia Extended for Multi Agent Systems. In: Dua, S., Sahni, S., Goyal, D.P. (eds.) ICISTM 2011. CCIS, vol. 141, pp. 340–349. Springer, Heidelberg (2011)
3. Chavez, A., Maes, P.: Kasbah: An agent marketplace for buying and selling goods. In: Proceedings of the First International Conference on the Practical Application of Intelligent Agents and Multi-Agent Technology (PAAM 1996), London, UK, pp. 75–90 (1996)
4. Badica, C., Badita, A., Ganzha, M., Paprzycki, M.: Developing a Model Agentbased E-commerce System. In: Lu, J., et al. (eds.) E-Service Intelligence—Methodologies, Technologies and Applications, pp. 555–578. Springer, Berlin (2007)
5. Lomuscio, A., Wooldridge, M., Jennings, N.R.: A classification scheme for negotiation in electronic commerce. Internat. J. Group Decision and Negotiation 12(1), 31–56 (2003)
6. Peng, Y., Finin, T., Labrou, Y., Chu, B., Long, J., Tolone, W.J., Boughannam, A.: A multi-agent system for enterprise integration. In: Proc. of PAAM 1998, London, UK, pp. 155–169 (1998)
7. Ferreira, C., Goncalves, R., Babo, R.: Evaluating functionalities of eCommerce websites for emigrants. In: 6th Iberian Conference on Information Systems and Technologies, CISTI (2011)

8. Yu, L., Masabo, E., Tan, L., He, M.: Multi-Agent Automated Intelligent Shopping System (MAISS). In: The 9th International Conference for Young Computer Scientists. IEEE (2008) 978-0-7695-3398-8/08 $25.00 © 2008

9. Wan, W., Zhang, J., Wang, M.: A Multi-agent Negotiation Protocol based on Extended Case Based Reasoning. In: Fourth International Conference on Fuzzy Systems and Knowledge Discovery (FSKD 2007) (2007) 0-7695-2874-0/07 $25.00 © 2007

10. De Loor, P., Bénard, R., Pierre, C.: Real-time Retrieval for Case-Based Reasoning in Interactive Multiagent-Based Simulations. Expert System with Applications (July 2011)

11. Jain, P., Dahiya, D.: Knowledge Management Systems Design using Extended Gaia. Paper Published in the International Journal of Computer Networks and Communications (IJCNC) 3(1), 140–152 (2011) ISSN 0975 – 2293 (Special Issue)

12. Bagherzadeh, J., Arun-Kumar, S.: Flexible Communication of Agents based on FIPA-ACL. Electronic Notes in Theoretical Computer Science 159, 23–39 (2006)

13. DiPippo, C., Fay-Wolfe, V., Nair, L., Hodys, E., Uvarov, O.: A real-time multi-agent system architecture for e-commerce applications. In: Intl. Symp. on Autonomous Decentralized Systems, pp. 357–364 (March 2001)

14. Rosenschein, J.S., Zlotkin, G.: Rules of Encounter: Designing Conventions for Automated Negotiation among Computers. MIT Press, Cambridge

15. Kraus, S.: Strategic Negotiation in Multi-Agent Environments. MIT Press, Cambridge (2001)

16. Fatima, S.S., Wooldridge, M., Jennings, N.R.: Multi-issue negotiation under time constraints. In: Proceedings of the First IJCAAMS: Part 1, Bologna, Italy, July 15-19 (2002), doi:10.1145/544741.544775

17. Kraus, S., Sycara, K., Evenchik, A.: Reaching agreements through argumentation: a logical model and implementation. Artificial Intelligence 104, 1–69 (1998)

18. Maes, P., Guttman, R.H., Moukas, A.G.: Agents That Buy and Sell. Communications of the ACM 42(3) (March 1999)

19. Wooldridge, M.: An introduction to multi agent systems. Wiley publications, ISBN 978-0-470-51946-2

20. Aamodt, A., Plaza, E.: Case-based reasoning: Foundational issues, methodological variations, and system approaches. AI Communications 7(1), 39–52 (1994)

21. Chen, Y.-J., Chen, Y.-M., Su, Y.-S.: An Ontology-Based Distributed Case-Based Reasoning for Virtual Enterprises. In: CISIS 2009 (2009) ISBN: 978-1-4244-3569-2

22. Wan, W., Zhang, J., Wang, M.: A Multi-agent Negotiation Protocol based on Extended Case Based Reasoning. In: FSKD 2007 (2007)

23. Dong, T.-T., Feng, Y.-Q.: An Argumentation-Based Negotiation System. In: 2010 3rd International Conference on Information Management, Innovation Management and Industrial Engineering (2010)

24. Ahmadi, K., Charkari, N.M.: Multi Agent based Hybrid E-negotiation System in E-commerce. IJIPM 2(2), 88–96 (2011)

25. Bellifemine, F., Caire, G., Greenwood, D.: Developing multi-agent systems with JADE. Wiley Series in Agent Technology (February 2007) ISBN 978-0-470-05747-6

Pair-Wise Time-Aware Test Case Prioritization for Regression Testing

Prem Parashar[1], Arvind Kalia[1], and Rajesh Bhatia[2]

[1] Computer Science Department, Himachal Pradesh University, Shimla, India
[2] Computer Science Department, Deen Bandhu Chotu Ram University, Murthal, India
{prem.parashar,arvkalia,rbhatiapatiala}@gmail.com

Abstract. After maintenance, software requires regression testing for its validation. Prioritization of test cases for regression testing is required as software is tested under strict time and other constraints. A Pair-wise time-aware Test Case Prioritization (PTCP) technique has been proposed in this paper that determines the effectiveness of a test case on the basis of total number of faults present in software, number of faults detected till time, and the time of execution of different test cases. It selects that test case which determines maximum new faults, not yet detected, within minimum time. Thus prioritized test suite contains those test cases which are effective and tend to minimize repetitive faults detection. Through two comparative studies, it has been observed that with least wastage of time, the proposed technique performed equally well as other two parallel prioritizing techniques, Average Percentage of Fault Detection (APFD) based prioritization, and Optimal Test Case Prioritization (OTCP).

Keywords: Regression testing, prioritization, fault detection, redundancy, random selection.

1 Introduction

Software testing is one of the very expensive stages of software development life cycle [22]. It is an important part of the software development irrespective of the programming paradigm used. It is a broad term containing a wide spectrum of different activities. It starts from the testing of small unit of software to the post implementation and maintenance of software. The main activities involved in software testing are preparing test cases and their respective test oracles [12]. Since both these tasks are very tedious, therefore even after preparing test cases and test oracles with utmost care, some bugs remain uncovered. Software may malfunction due to uncovered bugs. The consequences of such errors may be nominal or catastrophic depending upon the type of software application [13, 14, 15, 22]. In order to avoid such situations, the system is tested with sufficient number of test cases and the gap between expected value and actual value is observed. Any difference between these values declares the system as erroneous.

S. Dua et al. (Eds.): ICISTM 2012, CCIS 285, pp. 176–186, 2012.
© Springer-Verlag Berlin Heidelberg 2012

Regression testing has always remained a challenge for maintenance team. As maintenance is not a regular or periodic activity for most of the software[13], it is very difficult to make prediction about software maintenance time. For some software systems like business applications, frequency of maintenance may be very high whereas in other types like scientific application, it may be low. When software is brought for maintenance , it is very difficult to reconstitute the same team which had developed and tested it. The formation of new maintenance team makes this process complex.

One of the most important constraints in regression testing is time budget [6]. With the maintenance of software, the size of test cases usually grows making it difficult to execute all the existing test cases and new test cases with in the specified time limit. Prioritization of test cases is even significant if the time budget and total time for the execution of a test suite are equal. After modification, when new changes are incorporated in existing software, software need to be tested well by using a test suite that covers change impact set (all modified components of software and the other components affected by this change). Generally, due to limited time constraints, it is impossible to execute all test cases of a test suite [11, 20, 22]. Under such circumstances, a test case prioritization technique is required which can generate an optimum subset of test cases that covers all or almost all changes. It is not an easy task to construct such subset of given test suite, especially if the number of changes made is very large. Researchers have developed different types of test case prioritization techniques. In this paper it is evident that those techniques also prove to be effective under given time constraints. Pair-wise Test Case Prioritization (PTCP) technique has been presented in this paper, which prioritizes test cases such that test cases selected from test suite (i) will always run within given time limit, (ii) will have the highest potential for fault detection, and (iii) will have the minimum wastage of time.

2   Review of Literature

Rothermel [16,17] et al. described different test case prioritization techniques and compared their relative results through empirical studies. The average percentage of fault detection (APFD) and total fault-exposing potential (TFEP) measures proposed by them have become benchmarks for making comparisons with other techniques. Dalal [3, 4] et al. proposed that automatic test cases that are generated by using combinatorial approach of pair wise interaction between the input fields are highly effective in detecting the failures as compared to traditional approach of software testing. By using this approach, number of test cases required for testing software can be reduced considerably.

Zang [23] et al. used integer linear programming (ILP) method for prioritizing test cases. They represented the test case prioritization problem as an integer linear programming of operations research constructing objective function with the help of number of faults detected by test cases and constraints by taking time of execution of test cases into consideration. The optimum solution of ILP gives the set of feasible test cases for the software and they are prioritized by implementing any of the available test case prioritization techniques. Test cases can be prioritized on the basis of total coverage techniques such as total statement coverage, additional statement coverage, total fault expose potential (TFEP), total function coverage, and additional function coverage. The success of a test case does not only depend on whether it covers the statements that contain faults but also on its ability to surface out the possible faults [17, 19, 22]. In latest studies, it has been observed that various prioritization techniques like prioritization based on random ordering, optimum rate of fault detection, number of branches covered by a test case, and number of methods covered by a test case, are playing significant role in reducing the cost of software testing [5]. The main advantage of all these techniques is that they are general prioritization techniques and can be applied to any type of software application.

Arcuri A.,and Yao Xin [1] have proposed a memetic algorithm that tests container classes of object-oriented software. The main objective of this algorithm is to reduce the search space for object-oriented software. The objective has been achieved by dynamically eliminating those functions from search space that have already been covered. They compared their algorithm to a Hill climbing and a Genetic Algorithm through empirical study and showed that memetic algorithm outperforms the other two types of algorithms.

Corel [2] et al. proposed automatic test data generation for regression testing. The chaining method for test data generation has been implemented in the proposed approach. This test data generation has mainly focused on the common functionality of old and the new system. In this method a pair of equivalent output variables has been identified from old and new system. A software system is erroneous if for a given input its equivalent output variables produce different outputs. The empirical studies conducted by them on systems of different domain have shown that this method of regression testing is most successful in version-specific software. A similar study conducted by Xie and Notkin [21] considered value spectra to see the difference between old and new version of software. They also performed root cause analysis of the deviation by using some heuristics, the main variants of which have been deviation follower and deviation container. The study conducted has shown encouraging results to locate the deviation in the behavior of system at regression testing. Li [9] et al. considered greedy algorithm, additional greedy algorithm, 2-optimal algorithm, hill climbing algorithm, and genetic algorithm for prioritizing test cases. The results of empirical study conducted by them showed that though genetic algorithms do not produce best results all the times but they perform better as compared to greedy algorithms and optimal algorithms most of the times. Jiang [7] et al. proposed a genetic time aware test case prioritizing algorithm in which all permutations of the test cases of a test suit that fit in the given time constraints have been considered. Those test cases have been selected for final execution which exposed maximum faults within minimum time. The algorithm has also kept an eye on the redundancy of the test cases.

Software operational profile plays vital role in prioritizing test cases. While prioritizing the test cases, the operation which is most important is given the highest priority in software testing irrespective of its probability of occurrence [5, 8]. In continuous integration, the developers integrate the software artifacts with the continuous integration agent frequently. Usually, the continuous integrated agent gets a number of modules for integration at a time due to different teams of developers. The main objective of continuous integration is that a developer gets bug report at early stage of software development and can be fixed at earliest. By conducting various empirical studies on different types of software, it has been observed that coverage-based strategies for prioritizing test cases of a test suite outperforms the other strategies in continuous integration testing [7].

Mei [10] et al. proposed a technique for prioritization of test cases for regression testing of business-oriented application. This study has taken into account the erroneous attempts performed by process engineers unknowingly while maintaining some of the artifacts of a system [18]. These faults are unexpected for a test manager and hence are not covered by traditional test suite due to its limited vision. In such cases, coverage based testing is needed. In this study, series of such prioritizing techniques have been implemented. The results of experimental study have shown that the importance of an artifact plays significant role in test case prioritization.

3   Research Methodology

One of the main objectives of regression testing is to test the software within given time budget. The PTCP technique proposed in this paper, is based on two assumption,(i) the reordering of test cases in a test suite is an acceptable ordering i.e. the test cases are independent from one another and hence can be executed in any order, and (ii) reordering of test cases does not make any change in their behavior i.e. the test case will take same time for the execution and will reveal the same faults irrespective of its position in the test suite.

Let time budget assigned to test a software for regression testing is TB, and there are n test cases in a test suite T with times of execution $t_1, t_2, \ldots, t_n$ respectively. Even in ideal time conditions, the prioritization of test cases is required,i.e, if the following inequality holds true, still there is need of prioritization, either for saving time or for additional testing.

$$\sum_{i=1}^{n} t_i <= TB$$

In PTCP, while selecting a test case, number of new faults detected (fd) by it, its time of execution(t), and number of repetitive faults detected(rfd) by it are taken into consideration. The effectiveness (et) of a test case has been calculated as:

$$et = \frac{fd}{t * rfd} \qquad if\ rfd \neq 0\ and$$

$$et = \frac{fd}{t} \qquad\qquad if\ rfd == 0$$

A test case that has maximum value of *et* is considered as most effective. A tie is broken arbitrarily and one of the test cases is included in the prioritized list if two or more test cases have same maximum et value. The algorithm used for the purpose is shown in Table A.

3.1   PTCP Algorithm

Input: A test suite (T), permissible time budget (TB), set of faults not yet detected (TF) and set of faults detected (ft_i) after execution of test case T_i.
Output: a) P: Prioritized list of test cases. b) FD: set of faults detected

In Table A, different mathematical set operations i.e. A U B, A ∩ B, |A|, and A-B have been considered to make proposed algorithm simple and understandable. Test suite T stores test case number. For test case T_1, it stores 1, for T_2, it stores 2, and so on.

After implementing the algorithm given in Table A, it has been observed that number of random selections of test cases in PTCP is always lesser than or equal to APFD based and OTCP techniques. *et*, computed in this algorithm, stores the effective potential of a test case to detect the new faults.

Table A. PTCP Algorithm

```
1.    max=0;
2. for i=1 to n
3. {if ((|ftᵢ |/tᵢ  ≥  max) and (tᵢ ≤ TB)
4. {i) max=| ftᵢ |/ tᵢ;    ii)      p=i;}
5. }
6. i) t=tₚ;         ii) FD=FD U ftₚ;
7. iii)TF=TF-ftₚ;       iv)P=P U Tₚ;
8.   v)  Tₚ=0;
9.while ((TF ≠ Φ) and ((t ≤ TB))
10.{      max=0;
11.        for i=1 to n
12.          {if ((Tᵢ ≠ 0) and ( t+ tᵢ  ≤ TB))
13.             {fd=|TF∩ ftᵢ | ; //pairing( for new faults)
14.               if (fd>0)
15.                {rfd=|FD∩ ftᵢ|    //pairing(redundancy)
16.                  if (rfd≠0)
17.                       et=fd/(tᵢ*rfd);
18.              else
19.                       et=fd/tᵢ;
20.            }
21.          if (et>max)
22.            {
23.               i)  p=i;    ii)   max=et;
24.            }
25.        }
26.    }
27. t=t+tₚ;         ii)        FD=FD U ftₚ;
28. iii) TF=TF-ftₚ;    iv)        P=P U Tₚ;
29. vi)   Tₚ=0;
30.}
```

4   Objectives

The broad objective of the comparative study conducted in this section is to identify those factors which are associated with time-aware test case prioritization. The specific objectives of the comparative study are :

1. To analyze which technique makes optimum utilization of permissible time budget for regression testing.
2. To Analyze which technique minimizes the overlapping of faults detected.

5   Major Findings

The results of the comparative study are based on two examples of test suites tabulated in Table 1 and Table 4 respectively. It has been supported from the results of study that PTCP performs equally well as other two techniques (APFD,OTCP) with least wastage of time. In proposed study,the time taken to detect repetitive fault(s) has been considered a wastage, which should be minimized in regression testing if not avoided. This time can be utilized to test some other modules (which are not included in change impact set) which will boost the confidence in software testing. It has also been found that PTCP technique has strong tendency to minimize repetitive fault detection. The evaluation metrics considered in the study have played significant role in comparative study.

5.1   Analysis

A comparative study of proposed technique has been conducted with two parallel techniques APFD and OTCP proposed by different researchers. The comparative study has been conducted by taking two examples.In Example 1, a test suite(Table 1) with six test cases($T_1,T_2,...,T_6$) and ten known faults ($f_1,f_2,...,f_{10}$), has been taken. Column T of Table 1 contains the respective times of execution(in second) of test cases. Let time limit allowed for regression testing be 20 seconds. The evaluation metrics proposed in this study are:

(i) **Total Faults Exposed(TFE):** It represents the total number of faults exposed by prioritized test suite. It also includes the repetitive faults detected by the test suite, if any. The value of TFE may be greater than the total number of distinct faults present in the software.

(ii) **Distinct Faults Detected(DFD):** It represents the distinct faults detected by prioritized test suite. If T_1,T_2 are two test cases that constitute the prioritized test suite and detect faults f_1, f_2, f_3, f_5 and f_2,f_5, f_6 respectively, the DFD value for the test suite will be 5. DFD ignores the repetitive faults detected by prioritized test suite.

(iii) **Effective Time for execution of test cases(ET):** It represents the total time taken to execute all test cases of prioritized test suite.

(iv) **Percentage of Test Suite Failure (TSF):** It represents the percentage of faults not detected by the prioritized test suite. for example. if the total number of faults present is 10 and the prioritized test suite detects 9 faults , the value of TSE will be 10.

(v) Percentage of Time Wastage (TW): It represents the percentage of total time wasted in detecting repetitive faults. If repetitive faults take m units of time and total time allowed is n units, then TW will be calculated as *(m/n*100)*.

(vi) Percentage of Time Saving (TS): The detection of all faults before given time limit has been considered as time saving. It is calculated as (m/n*100), where m represents the units of time saved and n represents time budget.

Table 1. Test suite and list of faults exposed (Example 1)

'X' represents fault detected

	f_1	f_2	f_3	f_4	f_5	f_6	f_7	f_8	f_9	f_{10}	T
T_1	X	X	X				X	X			6
T_2		X	X				X		X		6
T_3	X			X	X					X	5
T_4						X					3
T_5		X			X		X		X		6
T_6	X		X		X			X		X	6

First row of Table 1 represents that test case T_1 exposes 5 faults(f_1,f_2,f_3, f_7 and f_8) in 6 seconds. The remaining rows of Table 1 can be interpreted in similar way.

After implementing the PTCP algorithm (Example 1), the results obtained are tabulated in Table 2.

Table 2. Prioritized set of test cases(Example 1)

Time Limit: 20 sec.	
APFD	T_1,T_6,T_3,T_4
OTCP	T_1,T_3,T_2,T_4
PTCP	T_1,T_3,T_4,T_5

In Table 2, for APFD, the test cases selected are T_1,T_3,T_4,T_6 and their order of execution is T_1, T_6, T_3, T_4. The results for remaining techniques can be interpreted in similar way.

In Table 3, the results of evaluation metrics for different techniques are tabulated.

Table 3. Metrics values analysis (Example 1)

	TFE	DFD	TSF (%)	ET	TW(%)	TS(%)
APFD	15	9	10	20	40	0
OTCP	14	10	0	20	28.6	0
PTCP	14	10	0	20	28.6	0

In Table 3, for APFD, total number of faults exposed is 15 (5+5+4+1),distinct number of faults detected is 9 ($f_1,f_2,f_3,f_4,f_5,f_6,f_7,f_8,f_{10}$), effective time is 20 seconds (6+6+5+3), test suite failure is 10% (f_9 is undetected), time wastage is 40% (6 faults are detected more than once in 20 seconds), and there is no time saving. The results for other techniques tabulated in Table 3 can be interpreted in similar manner.

In Example 2, a less organized test suite has been taken into consideration. The test suite contains test cases T_1, and T_3, that reveal the same faults and total faults exposed by all its test cases are approximately three times the number of distinct faults present. Therefore, there is a strong possibility of overlapping in fault detection. The time allowed in this case has been considered as 12 seconds. The example is tabulated in Table 4.

Table 4. Test suite and list of faults exposed (Example 2)

'X' represents fault detected

	f_1	f_2	f_3	f_4	f_5	f_6	T
T_1	X		X			X	5
T_2		X		X	X		7
T_3	X		X			X	6
T_4		X			X		3
T_5				X	X		4
T_6	X	X	X		X	X	5

The prioritized test suites generated by applying different techniques have been tabulated in Table 5 and can be interpreted in similar way as for Table 2.

Table 5. Prioritized set of test cases (Example 2)

Time Limit: 12 sec.	
APFD	T_6,T_4,T_5
OTCP	T_6,T_2
PTCP	T_6,T_5

The evolution metrics results for Example 2 have been tabulated in Table 6.

Analysis of both examples revealed that PTCP technique performs equally well as other two techniques, APFD and OTCP with least number of repeated faults.

Table 6. Metrics values analysis for different techniques (Example 2).

	TFE	DFD	TSF (%)	ET	TW(%)	TS(%)
APFD	9	6	0	12	33	0
OTCP	8	6	0	12	25	0
PTCP	6	6	0	9	0	25

5.2   Results and Discussion

The results of Example 1 and Example 2 are shown graphically in Figure 1 and Figure 2 respectively.

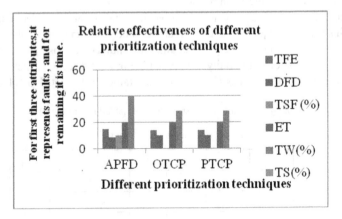

Fig. 1. Relative effectiveness of various techniques (Example 1)

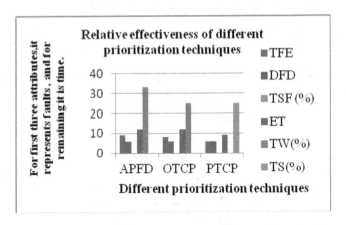

Fig. 2. Relative effectiveness of various techniques (Example 2)

From the results of two comparative studies, it is evident that by taking time and number of effective faults detected by a test case together into consideration, time budget can be managed efficiently. After comparing the results of Figure 2 and Figure 3, it has been observed that PTCP technique is very effective if the test suite is not properly organized. Though results of OTCP are very close to that of PTCP but still PTCP technique is better than OTCP as the number of random selections of test cases required in former is always less than or equal to the later. In case of OTCP, an optimal selection of set of test cases requires the knowledge of all permutations of test cases. It becomes complex if the size of test suite is very large. In such situation, the proposed technique will certainly help the maintenance team to perform regression testing efficiently. Since time effectiveness and reduction in redundancy of faults detection are given highest priority while forming prioritized set of test cases, the proposed technique outperforms under tight time constraints.

5.3   Threats to Validity

Internal Validity. One of the main threats to internal validity is that this study is based upon two main assumptions (i) the test cases of a test suite are independent from each other and (ii) their positions in the test suite do not make any difference in their behaviors. The assumption in all the cases may not be true. The correlation to find the effectiveness of a test case requires further verifications and validations.

External Validity. Threats to external validity are that the study is based on the results of two examples that contain test cases with known faults. In real practice it is difficult to predict test cases and their respective associated faults. When the proposed technique is implemented on subject examples, the results are satisfactory, but in order to generalize it, more experimental studies are needed.

Construct Validity. The evaluation metrics considered in this study may be threats to its construct validity. The mentioned evaluation metrics have appeared in very few researches. Though, through the comparative study, it has been concluded that these metrics play vital role in prioritization, still their relevance to the objectives requires more exploration.

6   Conclusion and Future Work

The proposed technique for the prioritization of test cases has shown encouraging results in maximizing fault detection and minimizing wastage of time as compared to other techniques (APFD and OTCP). The proposed algorithm reduces the possibility of random selection of test cases for execution. PTCP technique can be extended further by conducting empirical study on different software. Although, the metrics proposed in this paper are very effective, still, their generalization needs exhaustive studies of different software domains. The present study can be extended further by considering the behavior of faults instead of test cases.

References

1. Arcuri, A., Xin, Y.: A memetic algorithm for test data generation of object oriented software. In: IEEE Congress on Evolutionary Computation (CEC) (2007)
2. Corel, B., Al-Yami, A.M.: Automated Regression test Generation. In: ISSTA (1998)
3. Dalal, S.R., Jain, A., Karunanithi, N., Leaton, J.M., Lott, C.M., Horowitz, B.M.: Model-Based Software Testing of highly programmable system. In: ISSRE 1998 (1998)
4. Dalal, S.R., Jain, A., Karunanithi, N., Leaton, J.M., Lott, C.M., Horowitz, B.M.: Model-Based Testing in Practice. In: ICSE 1999. ACM Press (1999)

5. Sebastian, E., Malishevsky, A.G., Gregg, R.: Test case prioritization: A family of empirical studies. IEEE Transactions on Software Engineering 28(2) (2002)
6. Graves, T.L., Harrold, M.J., Kim, J.M., Porter, A., Rothermel, G.: An empirical study of regression test selection techniques. ACM Trans. On Software Engineering (2001)
7. Jiang, B., Zhang, Z., Tse, T.H., Chen, T.Y.: How well do test case prioritization techniques support statistical fault localization. In: ICSAC 2009 (2009)
8. Kumar, K.S., Babu, M.R.: Software Operational Profile Based test Case Allocation Using Fuzzy Logic. International Journal of Automation and Computing 04(4), 388–395 (2007)
9. Li, Z., Mark, H., Hierons, R.M.: Search algorithms for regression test case prioritization. IEEE Transaction on Software Engineering 33(4) (2007)
10. Mei, L., Zhang, Z., Chan, W.K., Tse, T.H.: Test case prioritization for regression testing of service –oriented business applications. In: WWW 2009 (2009)
11. Memon, A., Banerjee, I., Hashmi, N., Nagarajan, A.: DART: A framework for regression testing "nightly/daily builds" of GUI applications. In: ICSM (2003)
12. Bertrand, M., Ilinca, C., Andreas, L., Lisa, L.: Automatic testing of object-oriented Software. In: SOFSEM (2007)
13. Parashar, P., Bhatia, R., Kalia, A.: Change Impact Analysis: A Tool for Effective Regression Testing. In: Dua, S., Sahni, S., Goyal, D.P. (eds.) ICISTM 2011. CCIS, vol. 141, pp. 160–169. Springer, Heidelberg (2011)
14. Parashar, P., Kalia, A., Bhatia, R.: Fault-based time-aware test case prioritization for regression testing. In: The Proc. Indian Science Congress 2011, pp. 94–103 (2010)
15. Philippe, G., Segla, K., Filippo, R., Giuliano, A.: Evolution and Search Based Metrics to Improve Defects Prediction, pp. 23–32. IEEE Society (2009)
16. Gregg, R., Untch, R.H., Chu, C., Jean, H.M.: Prioritizing test cases for regression testing. IEEE Transactions on Software Engineering (2001)
17. Gregg, R., Untch, R.H., Chu, C., Jean, H.M.: Test case prioritization: An Empirical study. In: ICSE 1999 (1999)
18. Mark, S., Mike, L., Laurie, W.: Prioritization of regression tests using singular value decomposition with empirical change records. In: ISSRE (2007)
19. Voas, J.: PIE: A dynamic failure-based technique. IEEE Transaction on Software Engineering, 717–727 (1992)
20. Walcott, K.R., Kapfhammer, G.M., Soffa, M.L., Roos, R.S.: Time-aware test suite prioritization. In: ISSTA 2006 (2006)
21. Xie, T., David, N.: Checking Inside the Black Box: regression testing by Comparing Value Spectra. IEEE Transactions on Software Engineering 31(10) (2005)
22. Yoo, S., Harman, M.: Regression Testing Minimization, Selection, and Prioritization: A Survey. Softw. Test. Verif. Reliab. (2007)
23. Zang, L., Hou, S.S., Guo, C., Xie, T., Mei, H.: Time-Aware Test –Case Prioritization using Integer Linear Programming. In: ISSTA 2009 (2009)

Is Technology Universal Panacea for Knowledge and Experience Management? Answers from Indian IT Sector

Neeraj Sharma[1], Kawaljeet Singh[2], and D.P. Goyal[3]

[1] Department of Computer Science, Punjabi University, Patiala - 147002, Punjab, India
[2] University Computer Centre, Punjabi University, Patiala - 147002, Punjab, India
[3] Management Development Institute, Gurgaon - 122007, Haryana, India
sharma_neeraj@hotmail.com, director@pbi.ac.in, dpgoyal@mdi.ac.in

Abstract. The field of knowledge and experience management has witnessed rapid changes mainly as a result of the dramatic progress in the domain of information technology and partly because of the Internet revolution. Accumulation and sharing of experiences is facilitated with efficiency as internet-enabled technologies allow movement of information at unimaginable speed. It has also made the storage of experiences in varied forms like Experience Bases possible. Moreover, learning has accrued over time in the area of social and structural mechanisms, such as through mentoring and retreats that enable effective experience sharing. This in turn has enabled the development of KM/EM applications that best leverage these improved mechanisms by deploying sophisticated technologies. Therefore, it will not be an exaggeration to state that technology has provided a major impetus for enabling the implementation of KM/ EM processes in organizational settings. The present paper discusses the role and the relevance of latest technology in the field of knowledge and experience management and uncovers the state of technology-mediated KM/ EM in Indian IT sector through a survey.

Keywords: Information technology, KM, Experience Management, Software Engineering.

1 Introduction

Experience is defined as previous knowledge or skill one obtained in everyday life [24], [25]. Commonly experience is understood as a type of knowledge that one has gained from practice. In this sense, experience or experiential knowledge can be regarded as a specialization of knowledge consisting of the problems encountered and successfully tackled in the past. Experience management (EM) systems refer to a class of knowledge management (KM) systems applied to managing organizational experiential knowledge. That is, they are IT-based systems developed to support and enhance the organizational processes of knowledge creation, storage/retrieval, transfer, and application [2]. Common EMS technologies include intranets and extranets, search and retrieval tools, content management and collaboration tools, data

S. Dua et al. (Eds.): ICISTM 2012, CCIS 285, pp. 187–198, 2012.
© Springer-Verlag Berlin Heidelberg 2012

warehousing and mining tools, and groupware and artificial intelligence tools like expert systems and knowledge based systems. Many EM initiatives rely on IT as an important enabler. It has often been stated that while IT does not apply to all of the issues of experience management, it can support EM in sundry ways (ibid.). Examples of such support range from finding an expert or a recorded source of knowledge using online directories and searching databases; to sharing knowledge and working together in virtual teams; to accessing information on past projects; and learning about customer needs and behavior by analyzing transaction data. The fact remains that as there is no single technology comprising EMS, there is no single role of technology in experience management.

When we talk of IT applications to organizational EM initiatives, we find three common applications of IT, viz., the coding and sharing of best practices, the creation of corporate knowledge directories, and the creation of knowledge networks. One of the most common applications is internal benchmarking with the aim of transferring internal best practices [16]. The creation of corporate directories, also referred to as the mapping of internal expertise, is another common application of EM. Mapping the internal expertise is a potentially useful application of EM as much experience in an organization remains uncodified [21]. A third common application of EM systems is the creation of knowledge networks (ibid.). Knowledge networks are formed by providing online forums for communication and discussion.

The paper focuses on the applications that result from the use of the latest technologies to support EM mechanisms. The role and relevance of technology in managing accumulated experience of organizational members is also discussed. The paper also analyses the results of a survey carried out with software managers and engineers drawn from Indian software organizations in order to investigate empirically the role of technology in managing experience.

2   Literature Review

There is a wide divergence in the literature about the role of information technology in the success of EM projects. Information technology is regarded as a critical enabler for experience management [2], [8]. They explain that while IT may not guarantee the success of EM as such but it contributes significantly in supporting the EM processes. IT bridges the temporal and spatial distance between members of an organisation, streamlines the knowledge flow and eases collaboration among organisational members. However, they also warn that if you start with technology-centered solutions (for example, a database) and ignore behavioral, cultural, and organisational change, the expected advantages never materialize [8]. The major reason cited for this failure is not incorporating the knowledge capturing process into the engineering processes or not supported by the structures of the organisation [5]. EMS's ability to store, process and transmit experience is not given by technology itself; it is given by the users of the knowledge networks [11]. Studies also point out that when creating IT-based knowledge networks put the human at the center, since the people who will be using the network must see the value in the system; otherwise they will not use it [12]. In this connection, the growth and adoption of Intranet technologies is regarded as a major catalyst for knowledge and experience sharing though with caution that technology can either support or counteract the sharing of knowledge [16]. Therefore, it is important to first figure out what to share, how often and for what reason, and then choose the technology that makes it possible. It is also important to note that the right technology can make the connections between employees possible, but it does not make the experience sharing happen [27].

Information Systems (IS) infrastructure has also been considered as a key factor for the success of EM. IT can provide an edge in harvesting knowledge and an effective IS infrastructure is necessary for the organisation to implement the EM process [6], [22]. According to [7], structural capital includes the databases, organisational charts, process manuals, strategies and routines and anything whose value to the company is higher than its material value. Furthermore, the two most critical factors for the successful EM project are the establishment of a broad IS infrastructure based on desktop computing and communications and the utilization of the network technology infrastructure such as the Internet, Lotus Notes and global communications systems for effective transfer of knowledge and experience [9]. Studies report that experience bases and Intranets are the most popular ways of implementing experience management [10]. On the other hand, there are views that technology can no longer be regarded as a universal panacea for EM and stress that rather the expensive information technology has led to the cynicism surrounding the introduction of new EM strategies in organisations [14]. We also find a suggestion that the success factors people, process and technology need to be balanced in a 50/25/25 relation [21], which further suggests that people factor needs to be the major focus with 50% of the time and budget of an EM implementation project while process and technology factors only need 25% each in terms of the efforts, cost and other infrastructure [ibid.]. The major reason cited for this overemphasis on people element is that leveraging individuals' existing knowledge and experience in an organisation is the most critical job in managing organisational knowledge.

3   IT in KM/ EM: The Positive Side

The varied forms and flexibility of modern IT help enhance the modes of knowledge creation in organizations. For example, information systems designed for support of collaboration, coordination, and communication processes can facilitate teamwork and thereby increase an individual's contact with other individuals [2]. It is found that electronic mail and group support systems increase the number of weak ties in organizations, which in turn speeds up the growth of knowledge creation [15]. Corporate intranets facilitate greater exposure to vast amounts of on-line organizational knowledge, both horizontally and vertically, than what were previously possible. Advancements in storage technology coupled with sophisticated knowledge retrieval techniques like query languages, multimedia databases, and database management systems, have resulted in effective tools for incrementing organizational memory or knowledge repository. Accessing the organizational knowledge repositories with these tools becomes faster. Technology like Groupware systems not only makes it possible for organizations to create intra-organizational memory and but also enables them to share this memory across time and space [20], [26]. IT can play a very significant role in the improvement and expansion of both semantic and episodic organizational memory. Technology such as Document management system allows an organization's past knowledge to be stored efficaciously and made accessible without any complications [23]. There are numerous success stories which have created corporate knowledge repositories and experience bases about customers, projects, competition, and the industries they serve using these technologies [1]. Also a huge cache of tools and techniques comprising a variety of search and retrieval approaches (e.g., browsers and search engines) to access organizational knowledge captured in data warehouses and knowledge repositories are offered by modern information technology.

The use of intelligent software agents is another example of the IT used for transfer of knowledge and experiences among organizational members. Software agents create interest profiles of the individuals in an organization to determine the ones who could be the interested recipients of electronic messages [16]. Knowledge transfer and experience exchange is extended beyond formal communication channels through these technologies. Without the provision of such technology, the reach of individual members of an organization remains confined to co-workers. In this set-up, individuals are unlikely to encounter new knowledge through their close-knit work networks because individuals in the same coterie tend to possess similar information [20]. Furthermore, individuals are usually unaware of what the other members of the network are doing [13]. Platforms provided by IT such as computer networks, and electronic bulletin boards and discussion-groups etc. bridge the gap between the knowledge seekers and the knowledge bearers. Often such metadata (knowledge about where the knowledge resides) turns up to be as important as the original knowledge itself [3], [4]. Organizational knowledge maps or the taxonomies allow organizational members to rapidly locate either the knowledge itself or the knowledge bearers, more efficiently than would be possible without the existence of such technology support [17].

The use of knowledge and application of experience can also be supported by information technology. This is made possible by embedding experiential knowledge into organizational processes. Culture-bound procedures can be embedded into information technology so that the systems themselves become examples of organizational norms. IT can facilitate the capture, updation and dissemination of organizational directives. This will further promote knowledge application. IT can also speed up the knowledge integration and application process by codifying and automating organizational routines.

4   IT in KM/ EM: The Negative Side

There are mainly two approaches to experience management in organizations. These approaches are called people-centered and technology-centered approaches [19]. The people-centered approaches are more humane approaches and are built around the idea of assessing, modifying and improving individual skills and behaviour. On the other hand, technology-centered approaches focus on the establishment of information management systems, artificial intelligence and groupware solutions. Placing more emphasis on technology than human element is bound to fail EM initiatives in organizations. Therefore, a balance between the two approaches is required. The people possessing knowledge need technology for storing, retrieving and sharing it. Thus, wide knowledge and experience transfer cannot happen in large organizations without the tools support provided by technology. However, the values, norms, and culture of an organization are the principal determinants of how successfully important knowledge is transferred [8]. Therefore, the involvement of other organizational units can not be downgraded in comparison to the IT department when addressing the EM. It is opined that EM systems involve more than technology but rather a culture in which new roles and constructs are created [18]. The knowledge management system's ability to store, process and transmit knowledge is not given by technology itself; it is given by the users of the knowledge networks [11]. Therefore, the most critical consideration during the design of IT mediated experience management systems is to place the people component at the centre since the people who will be using the system must see the value in the system; otherwise they will not use it [12]. There is another problem with such knowledge networks. Due to the lack of proper updation and maintenance systems in place, more often than not, such knowledge networks fail and people stop using them or contributing to them.

5   Survey of Indian IT Sector

A survey consisting of a questionnaire was administered to 120 software managers and engineers drawn from 30 software engineering organizations registered with the NASSCOM using random sampling technique. The sample included a mix of large, medium and small software companies dealing in software development, maintenance and consultancy services. The findings of the survey are presented below.

5.1   Instruments Used for Sharing and Distributing Knowledge

Software organisations were asked to rank in order of the usage the instruments used for sharing and distributing knowledge in their organisations. Emails as an instrument for knowledge sharing and distribution was ranked at number one by SE organisations. Company Intranet and groupware systems are another channels used for sharing and distributing knowledge within software organisations. The simple reason for the use of technological instruments like emails, Intranets or groupware systems (Lotus Notes) could be the nature of SE organisations where these technologies are widely and easily available to almost every member of the organisation. That is the reason that formal communication and paper are the least preferred methods of knowledge-sharing within these organisations. Surprisingly the use of informal communication within the members for knowledge transfer is the least used method in SE organisations with an average score of 33.47 (cf. Table 1).

Table 1. Instruments Used for Sharing and Distributing Knowledge

Instruments for Sharing Knowledge	Average Rank	Average Score	Overall Rank
Papers	3.93	42.80	5
Emails	2.91	59.85	1
Company Intranet	3.04	57.70	2
Groupware systems (e.g. Lotus Notes)	3.13	56.19	3
Informal communication	4.49	33.46	6
Formal communication	3.51	49.87	4

5.2   Technical Components of KM System

Technology in itself does not constitute a KM system; rather it facilitates one. Accordingly, organisation respondents were asked about their use of technology to manage knowledge. 88% had implemented Internet technologies. 72% had a corporate-wide Intranet, 67% used a document management system. 32% used data mining and knowledge discovery tools and 24% use teleconferencing/ videoconferencing. One interesting finding was a very low use of Groupware technologies (21%), but 54% of the organisations with a KM strategy in place were planning to implement Groupware in the near future (cf. Table 2).

Table 2. Status of KM Tools

KM Tools	Implemented	Planning to Implement	Not Planned
Internet Technologies	88	12	0
Corporate Intranet	72	19	9
Data Mining/ Knowledge Discovery Tools	32	20	48
Document Management Systems	67	33	0
Groupware Systems	21	54	25
Data Repositories	11	60	29
AI/ BI Techniques	0	15	85
Extranet	18	46	36
Teleconferencing/ Videoconferencing	24	20	56
Workflow Management Systems	0	8	92

Another interesting finding was that organisations with a KM strategy in place are currently at a preliminary level. This is because the use of Artificial Intelligence/ Business Intelligence based techniques for making pertinent knowledge available in a most accurate manner was not on the corporate planning agenda for majority of the organisations (85%). This is due to the fact that techniques like artificial intelligence are used at the system implementation stage. In context to technology, respondents were looking at implementing Data Repositories and Extranet to develop a strong external and internal flow. In context to the current scenario, developing a strong internal information backbone is of primary interest. This resulted in Document Management Systems being the third most effective technology helping respondents in managing knowledge (67%) and the rest of the respondents planning to implement it in the near future. Workflow management systems do not find place in the current bundle of KM technologies and the software organisations did not seem to be enthusiastic about it either (cf. Figure 1).

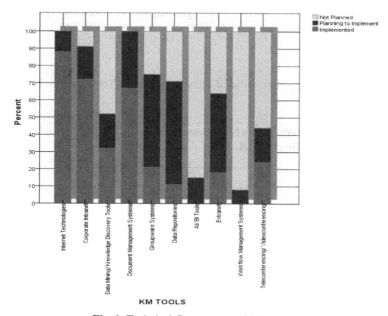

Fig. 1. Technical Components of KM system

5.3   KM Technologies

The software engineers were asked about the technology support tools existing in their organisations for knowledge management. The respondents were asked to rate the various KM technologies in terms of their frequency of use as well as their effectiveness in helping them manage their knowledge. As it is clear from Table 3, the majority of the respondents (83%) reported the Internet Browsers and Search Engines as the most frequently used KM tools in their organisations, followed by Email and Groupware systems (76.5%). Corporate Intranet/ Extranet and Communities of Practice are the other frequently used IT tools for managing the knowledge by employees in software organisations. 74% of the respondents stated Multimedia Repositories to be the least frequently used tool, followed by Teleconferencing/ Videoconferencing reported by 69% respondents to be either used with very low frequency or not used at all by them in managing their knowledge. Also half the respondents reported that they never use Agents/ Filters for KM in their organisations. External Server Services also find very low usage (8.7%). Workflow Management

Systems and Data mining and knowledge discovery tools are other technology components which find deplorable use by software engineers in their routine knowledge management activity.

Majority of the respondents (78.8%) feel that Best Practices Repositories are the most effective technology support tool for knowledge management (cf. Table 4). E-mail and Groupware Systems are the next technology perceived to be very effective in managing knowledge by 77.8% of the respondents. 74% of the software engineers surveyed stated Communities of Practice to be another effective KM technology support tool. On the other hand, majority of the respondents (79.4%) feel that External Server Services are less effective in managing knowledge in organisations, followed by WWW Server/ Communication Software which is perceived to be less effective KM tool by 67.7% respondents.

Table 3. Frequency Distribution of Technology Support Tools Used for KM

Frequency (%age)

Technology Support Tools for KM	Very High	Fairly High	Moderate	Fairly Low	Very Low	Not At All	Can't Say
Corporate Intranet/ Extranet	97 (31.3)	90 (29.0)	47 (15.2)	23 (7.4)	10 (3.2)	28 (9.0)	15 (4.8)
Browsers/ Search engines	190 (61.3)	67 (21.6)	20 (6.5)	15 (4.8)	3 (1.0)	0	15 (4.8)
Search and retrieval tools	93 (30.0)	3 (1.0)	75 (24.2)	15 (4.8)	2 (0.7)	115 (37.1)	7 (2.3)
Agents/ Filters	53 (17.1)	20 (6.5)	50 (16.1)	10 (3.2)	10 (3.2)	155 (50.0)	12 (3.9)
E-mail and groupware systems	186 (60.0)	51 (16.5)	10 (3.2)	30 (9.7)	3 (1.0)	0	30 (9.7)
WWW server/ Communication software	20 (6.5)	47 (15.2)	27 (8.7)	29 (9.4)	47 (15.2)	128 (41.3)	12 (3.9)
Data repositories	112 (36.1)	8 (2.6)	77 (24.8)	20 (6.5)	2 (0.7)	85 (27.4)	6 (1.9)
Multimedia repositories	13 (4.2)	10 (3.2)	23 (7.4)	8 (2.6)	215 (69.4)	15 (4.8)	26 (8.4)
Best practices repositories	30 (9.7)	25 (8.1)	38 (12.3)	30 (9.7)	165 (53.2)	12 (3.9)	10 (3.2)
Data mining and knowledge discovery tools	32 (10.3)	67 (21.6)	47 (15.2)	27 (8.7)	32 (10.3)	95 (30.6)	10 (3.2)
External server services	17 (5.5)	10 (3.2)	47 (15.2)	27 (8.7)	62 (20.0)	132 (42.6)	15 (4.8)
Document management	8 (2.6)	110 (35.5)	62 (20.0)	20 (6.5)	8 (2.6)	100 (32.3)	2 (0.7)

Table 3. (*continued*)

systems							
Workflow management systems	8 (2.6)	7 (2.3)	12 (3.9)	128 (41.3)	82 (26.5)	67 (21.6)	6 (1.9)
Teleconferencing/ Videoconferencing	15 (4.8)	15 (4.8)	43 (13.9)	12 (3.9)	9 (2.9)	205 (66.1)	11 (3.5)
Communities of Practice (CoP)	105 (33.9)	60 (19.4)	56 (18.1)	15 (4.8)	15 (4.8)	52 (16.8)	7 (2.3)

Table 4. Frequency Distribution of Effectiveness of KM Technology Tools

	Frequency (%age)						
Technology Support Tools for KM	Highly Effective	Fairly Effective	Moderately Effective	Less Effective	Very Less Effective	Not At All Effective	Can't Say
Corporate Intranet/ Extranet	136 (43.9)	84 (27.1)	34 (11.0)	29 (9.4)	27 (8.7)	0	0
Browsers/ Search engines	162 (52.3)	60 (19.4)	35 (11.3)	5 (1.6)	15 (4.8)	0	33 (10.6)
Search and retrieval tools	100 (32.3)	13 (4.2)	52 (16.8)	11 (3.5)	4 (1.3)	113 (36.5)	17 (5.5)
Agents/ Filters	46 (14.8)	38 (12.3)	41 (13.2)	61 (19.7)	16 (5.2)	102 (32.9)	6 (1.9)
E-mail and groupware systems	201 (64.8)	40 (13.0)	12 (3.9)	8 (2.6)	8 (2.6)	30 (9.7)	11 (3.5)
WWW server/ Communication software	32 (10.3)	40 (12.9)	16 (5.2)	45 (14.5)	65 (20.9)	100 (32.3)	12 (3.9)
Data repositories	140 (45.2)	86 (27.7)	27 (8.7)	30 (9.7)	6 (1.9)	15 (4.8)	6 (1.9)
Multimedia repositories	31 (10.0)	74 (23.9)	109 (35.2)	58 (18.7)	18 (5.8)	10 (3.2)	10 (3.2)
Best practices repositories	131 (42.3)	113 (36.5)	46 (14.8)	16 (5.2)	4 (1.3)	0	0
Data mining and knowledge discovery tools	6 (1.9)	99 (31.9)	67 (21.6)	36 (11.6)	76 (24.5)	16 (5.2)	10 (3.2)
External server services	11 (3.5)	15 (4.8)	20 (6.5)	74 (23.9)	81 (26.1)	91 (29.4)	18 (5.8)
Document management systems	146 (47.1)	14 (4.5)	48 (15.5)	17 (5.5)	30 (9.7)	38 (12.3)	17 (5.5)
Workflow management	104 (33.5)	16 (5.2)	62 (20.0)	18 (5.8)	15 (4.8)	60 (19.4)	35 (11.3)

Table 4. (*continued*)

systems							
Teleconferencing/ Videoconferencing	23 (7.4)	69 (22.3)	90 (29.0)	68 (21.9)	39 (12.6)	6 (1.9)	15 (4.8)
Communities of Practice (CoP)	119 (38.4)	110 (35.5)	33 (10.6)	23 (7.4)	17 (5.5)	0	8 (2.6)

6   Conclusions

Majority of the Indian software engineering organisations had implemented internet technologies, corporate-wide intranet and document management system. Groupware technologies are low in use but a vast majority of the respondent organisations with a KM/ EM system in place are planning to implement it. Also the use of Artificial Intelligence/ Business Intelligence based techniques for making pertinent knowledge available in a most accurate manner was not on the corporate planning agenda for majority of the organisations. The use of workflow management systems is also dismal in software organisations. Also majority of the respondents reported the internet browsers and search engines as the most frequently used KM tools in their organisations, followed by email and groupware systems. Corporate intranet/ extranet and Communities of practice are the other frequently used IT tools for managing the knowledge by employees in software organisations. Multimedia repositories and teleconferencing/ videoconferencing are the least frequently used tools for managing their knowledge by employees. The survey also revealed that majority of the respondents are of the opinion that the 'Best Practices Repositories' are the most effective technology support tool for experience management. E-mail, Groupware systems and Communities of practice (CoP) are the next technology components perceived to be very effective in managing knowledge by the respondents. This is an important finding for the people involved in technology implementation in software organisations. They should implement knowledge repositories and provide convenient channels for access to various domain-specific CoPs as part of their KM/ EM technology plan. In nutshell, we can conclude that Information Technology is considered as a critical enabler for knowledge and experience management. Technology facilitates in supporting KM/EM processes, connecting people regardless of temporal and spatial distance, streamlining knowledge and experience flow, and facilitating collaboration among organizational members. But still it is not sufficient by itself to guarantee the success of KM/ EM initiatives. The cynicism surrounding the introduction of new EM strategies in organizations can partly be attributed to the development of expensive technology systems that have failed in their attempts to foster knowledge creation and experience transfer in organizations. The growth and adoption of intranet technologies is a catalyst for knowledge sharing. However, technology can either endorse or sabotage the sharing of knowledge. Therefore, it is important to first plan meticulously what to share, how often and for what purpose, and then discern the technology that will make it possible. The technology also influences the outcome of the knowledge transfer process. The appropriate technology

can make the connections between individuals possible but it does not make the knowledge sharing happen. Hence, technology can no longer be regarded as a universal panacea for KM and EM.

References

1. Alavi, M.: KPMG Peat Marwick U.S.: One Giant Brain. Harvard Business School Case 9-397-108 (1997)
2. Alavi, M., Leidner, D.E.: Review: Knowledge Management and Knowledge Management Systems: Conceptual Foundations and Research Issues. MIS Quarterly 25(1), 107–136 (2001)
3. Allee, V.: The Knowledge Evolution: Expanding Organizational Intelligence. Butterworth-Heinemann, Washington (1997)
4. Andreu, R., Ciborra, C.: Organizational Learning and Core Capabilities Development: The Role of Information Technology. Journal of Strategic Information Systems, 117–127 (1996)
5. Basili, V.R., Caldiera, G., Rombach, H.: The Experience Factory. In: Marciniak, J. (ed.) Encyclopedia of Software Engineering, ch. X, vol. 1, pp. 468–476. John Wiley & Sons, NJ (1994)
6. Bhatt, G.D.: Knowledge management in organisations: Examining the interaction between technologies, techniques and people. Journal of Knowledge Management 5(1), 68–75 (2001)
7. Bontis, N., Chua, C.K., Richardson, S.: Intellectual capital and business performance in Malaysian industries. Journal of Intellectual Capital 1(1) (2000)
8. Davenport, T.H., Prusak, L.: Working Knowledge: How Organizations Manage What They Know. Harvard Business School Press, Boston (1998)
9. Davenport, T.H., De Long, D., David, W., Beers, M.C.: Successful Knowledge Management Projects. Sloan Management Review 39(2), 43–57 (1998b)
10. Despres, C., Chauvel, D.: Knowledge management. Journal of Knowledge Management 3(3) (1999)
11. Ericsson, F.: IT as an Enabler of Knowledge Management. In: Proceedings of the 24th Information Systems Research Seminar in Scandinavia, Norway (2001)
12. Hogberg, C., Edvinsson, L.: A design for futurizing knowledge networking. Journal of Knowledge Management 2(2), 81–92 (1998)
13. Kogut, B., Zander, U.: What Firms Do? Coordination, Identity, and Learning. Organization Science 7(5), 502–518 (1996)
14. Kutay, C., Aurum, A.: Knowledge transformation for education in software engineering. International Journal of Mobile Learning and Organisation 1(1), 58–80 (2007)
15. Nonaka, I.: A Dynamic Theory of Organizational Knowledge Creation. Organization Science 5(1), 14–37 (1994)
16. O'Dell, C., Grayson, C.J.: If Only We Knew What We Know: The Transfer of Internal Knowledge and Best Practice. The Free Press, New York (1998)
17. Offsey, S.: Knowledge Management: Linking People to Knowledge for Bottom Line Results. Journal of Knowledge Management 1(2), 113–122 (1997)
18. Pan, S.L., Scarbrough, H.: Knowledge Management in Practice: An Exploratory Case Study. Technology Analysis & Strategic Management 11(3), 359–374 (1999)
19. Ponelis, S., Fairer-Wessels, F.A.: Knowledge Management: A Literature Overview. South African Journal of Library and Information Science 66(1), 1–9 (1998)
20. Robertson, M., Swan, J., Newell, S.: The Role of Networks in the Diffusion of Technological Innovation. Journal of Management Studies 33, 335–361 (1996)
21. Ruggles, R.: The State of The Notion: Knowledge management in practice. California Management Review 40(3), 80–89 (1998)

22. Savary, M.: Knowledge management and competition in the consulting industry. California Management Review 41(2), 95–107 (1999)
23. Stein, E.W., Zwass, V.: Actualizing Organizational Memory with Information Systems. Information Systems Research 6(2), 85–117 (1995)
24. Sun, Z., Finnie, G.: Brain-like architecture and experience based reasoning. In: Proceedings of the 7th JCIS, Cary, North Carolina, USA, pp. 1735–1738 (2003)
25. Sun, Z., Finnie, G.: Intelligent Techniques in E-Commerce: A Case-based Reasoning Perspective. Springer, Heidelberg (2004)
26. Vandenbosch, B., Ginzberg, M.J.: Lotus Notes and Collaboration: Plus a Change. Journal of Management Information Systems 13(3), 65–82 (1996-1997)
27. Walsham, G.: Knowledge Management: The Benefits and Limitations of Computer Systems. European Management Journal 19(6), 599–608 (2001)

A Review of Coupling and Cohesion Measurement in OO Systems Using Program Slicing

Sunint Kaur Khalsa[1], Rajesh Kumar Bhatia[2],
Jitender Kumar Chhabra[3], and Maninder Singh[4]

[1] GNDEC, Ludhiana
[2] DCRUST, Murthal
{kaursunint,rbhatiapatiala}@gmail.com
[3] NIT Kurukshetra
jitenderchhabra@rediffmail.com
[4] Thapar University, Patiala
msingh@thapar.edu

Abstract. This paper gives an overview of various studies regarding static and dynamic Cohesion and Coupling measurement. This study has extrapolated that static measures are insufficient to measure dynamic coupling and cohesion and in order to obtain accurate results dynamic measures are required. Further the current work dwells into the fact that coupling and cohesion calculated with the help of dynamic program slicing yields better results than those calculated by conventional means. One approach to obtain static or dynamic program slicing is making dependence graphs of the system. We have also performed a comparative study on the various dependence graph required to obtain Cohesion and Coupling measurement using static and dynamic Program Slicing.

Keywords: Coupling, Cohesion, Program Slicing, Dependence Graphs, Object Oriented Paradigm, Unified Modeling Language.

1   Introduction

Coupling refers to the degree of interdependence between the modules and Cohesion refers to the functional strength of the module i.e. degree to which the functions of a module are related. Coupling and Cohesion define the modularity of a system and can be measured statically or dynamically taking the actual execution of the system into consideration.

As stated by Weiser [1], Program Slicing is the process of automatically decomposing the program on the basis of their data flow and control flow. Slicing reduces the program to a minimal form which still intacts the desired behaviour of the program. It is a technique to analyze the program for the purpose of debugging, testing, measuring cohesion and coupling etc.

Coupling and Cohesion for a system can also be measured using Program Slicing. Rilling et al. in [2] mentioned that the coupling calculated using slices gives better results than conventional methods. The author gives the statement: "slice based

S. Dua et al. (Eds.): ICISTM 2012, CCIS 285, pp. 199–210, 2012.
© Springer-Verlag Berlin Heidelberg 2012

coupling measures consider only those part of the class that are included in the computed slice, slice based measures can capture both direct and indirect and import and export coupling". So, in this paper more emphasis has been given to slice based coupling measures rather than the conventional measures.

2   Object Oriented Coupling and Cohesion

Briand et al. in [3] has given a unified framework for the measurement of coupling proposed by various authors in object oriented systems. They compared several coupling measures on the basis of various criteria like import and export coupling, types of connection etc and gave a unified framework. Arisholm et al. in [4] described how coupling can be defined and precisely measured based on dynamic analysis of systems. This type of coupling has been named dynamic coupling. The authors states that because of polymorphism and dynamic binding the static metrics for calculating coupling is insufficient. Various measures of dynamic coupling are then used to indicate the change proneness which was otherwise less accurate with the help of static metrics. The measures for import and export coupling have been proposed in this paper and are collected from UML models.

Yacoub et al. in [5] finds out that dynamic metrics have been proposed for the object level coupling. The metrics proposed till date is for the class level coupling. In this paper dynamic metrics have been proposed which can be obtained at the early phases of the software development. The authors have proposed export object coupling and import object coupling. The author has also proposed dynamic complexity metrics which can be obtained from the state chart behavior of the objects. The operational complexity of the object is based on the static McCabe's cyclomatic complexity which is obtained from the control flow graph.

Zhou et al. in [6] proposed a method to find polymorphism in UML based models. As UML sequence diagram cannot describe polymorphism so the authors in this paper have proposed class sets of polymorphism methods (CSPM). The CSPM can be identified in class diagrams based on OCL constraints. The approach transforms sequence diagram into polymorphism class object method acyclic graph (PCOMDAG) for generating test cases.

Briand et al. in [7] has proposed a unified framework for the comparison, evaluation, and definition of cohesion measures in object oriented systems. The authors compared various cohesion metrics on the criteria like types of connection, direct and indirect connections, polymorphism, constructors etc. This framework is intended to be exhaustive and integrates new ideas with existing measurement frameworks in the literature.

Varun et al. in [8] introduced dynamic cohesion metrics which provides scope of cohesion measurement up to object level and takes into account important and widely used object-oriented features such as inheritance, polymorphism and dynamic binding during measurement. A dynamic analyser tool is developed using aspect-oriented programming (AOP) to perform dynamic analysis of Java applications for the purpose of collecting run-time data for computation of the proposed dynamic cohesion measures. Further, an experiment is carried out to shows that the proposed dynamic cohesion metrics are more accurate and useful in comparison to the existing cohesion metrics. As a result the proposed metrics are found to be better indicators of change-proneness of classes than the existing cohesion metrics.

The modularity of a program is measured by its coupling and cohesion. A system should have high cohesion and low coupling, reducing errors [9] and simplifying maintenance and understanding [10]. According to Yourdon et al. [11] if the code is highly cohesive it will not be strongly coupled and vice versa. Program slices offer a basis for measuring module cohesion and coupling.

In order to calculate Coupling and Cohesion using Program Slicing an intermediate program representation called dependence graph has to be created. The dependence graph will be required for performing static or dynamic program slicing. The literature for various types of dependence graphs has been mentioned in the next section.

3   Object Oriented Slicing

The object oriented slicing can be done either by slicing the object oriented programs or by slicing the UML diagrams as the UML diagrams are used to design the object oriented systems.

3.1   Object Oriented Program Slicing Using Dependence Graph

Object oriented program slicing can be of two types: static slicing and dynamic slicing. The static slices are computed for all possible values as a result of which they contain more statements than required. Dynamic slicing on the other hand uses the information about a particular execution resulting in small sizes. Static slicing of object-oriented programs has been reported in [12, 13, 14, 15, 16, 17]. The representation of a program during slicing is an important issue. Taking this challenge into consideration various types of dependence graphs have been suggested by various researchers. Horwitz et al.[12] suggested a system dependence graph (SDG) for the procedural systems. But no graph was made for the object oriented systems. Larson and Harrold [13] extended the SDG of Horwitz et al. [12] to represent the object-oriented programs. Larson et al. suggested Class Dependence Graphs for each class in an object-oriented program and named it CIDG. CIDG captures the control and data dependence relationships about a class without knowing about the calling environment. They also suggested a procedure dependence graph to represent each method in CIDG. To represent derived class, Larson et al. constructed a procedure dependence graph for each method of the derived class and reused the representation of all the methods of the base class and hence constructed a CIDG.

Liang et al. [14] further improved the SDG to add data members of the objects. They suggested a tree representation of the parameter object. They also introduced object slicing, to inspect the effects of a particular object on the slicing criterion. Object slicing gives a better hold for debugging and program understanding for large programs.

Krishnaswamy [15] proposed a dependence-based representation called the object oriented program dependency graph (OPDG) to represent the object-oriented programs. An OPDG is constructed as the classes are compiled to capture the complete class representation. The OPDG represented control flow, data dependencies and control dependencies. The OPDG representation is constructed in three layers: Class Hierarchy Subgraph (CHS), Control Dependence Subgraph (CDS) and Data Dependence Subgraph (DDS).

Chen et al. [16] also proposed an intermediate representation for object oriented programs called Object-Oriented Dependency Graph (ODG). The ODG was a multidiagraph which was derived from a directed graph by adding multiple edge, vertex properties, and property relations to the directed graph. On the basis of ODG, Chen et al. [16] presented an algorithm for slicing of object-oriented programs. Chen et al. in [17] described two types of program slices on the basis of state and behaviour of the system. State slice is based on the message and control slices and behaviour slice is based on attribute and method affecting the behaviour of the class.

Precise calculation of cohesion and coupling cannot be done using static slicing. In [20] Gupta et al. concluded that cohesion calculated by the dynamic slices given better and accurate results than the static slices.

Dynamic slices of object oriented programs have been reported in [21, 22, 23, 24]. Agrawal and Horgan in [21] discussed four approaches for computing dynamic program slices. The first two are based on static program slicing using Program Dependence Graph. The third approach uses Dynamic Dependence Graph (DDG) to compute accurate dynamic slices. Since the size of DDG can be excessively large the author proposed Reduced Dynamic Dependence Graph. In this graph a new node is created only if it can cause a new dynamic slice to be introduced.

Zhao [22] extended the DDG of Agrawal and Horgan [21], with dynamic object-oriented dependence graph (DODG) to represent various dynamic dependencies between statement instances for a particular execution OO program. Song et. al. [23] proposed Dynamic Object Relationship Diagram (DORD). A method was further proposed to compute forward dynamic slice of object-oriented programs DORD. This method returns the dynamic slices of the statements as the statements are executed. The execution of the last statement returns the dynamic slices of the complete system.

Mohapatra et al. [26, 27] proposed extended system dependence graph (ESDG) as an intermediate representation for dynamic slicing of object-oriented programs. The ESDG is constructed once before the execution of the program. The algorithm proposed by them marks or unmarks the edges of ESDG when the dependencies arise and stops during run time. The algorithm is named Edge marking dynamic slicing (EMDS) algorithm for object-oriented programs.

The comparative study of various dependency graphs which are used for performing static and dynamic slicing is shown in table 1. These dependence graphs acts as one of the methods for performing slicing and hence deriving cohesion and coupling of the system.

Table 1. Comparative study of dependency graph for static and dynamic slicing

S. No.	Proposed by	Advantages	Disadvantages
1	S. Horwitz et al. [12]	Introduced the system dependence graphs for procedural systems	No SDG for object oriented systems
2	L. D. Larson et al. [13]	Enhanced the System Dependence Graph to incorporate the object oriented features, which can represent a class hierarchy, data members and polymorphism	It cannot distinguish data members for different objects instantiated from the same class; thus, the resulting slices may be unnecessarily imprecise. It does not handle cases in which an object is used as a parameter or as a data member of another object Not fit to represent larger programs
3	D. Liang et al.[14]	Removed Larson's limitation. Their modified SDG represents the data members of the objects. They represented parameter object and polymorphic object and inheritance as a tree structure. They also introduced the concept of object slicing	Slicing with this technique is expensive, Not fit to represent larger programs
4	C. Hammer et al [28]	It does not represent polymorphic object as a set of tree but as one merged tree so the size of SDG is reduced not affecting its precision	The technique is more expensive Not fit to represent larger programs
5	A. Krishnaswamy et al. [15]	Introduced object oriented program dependence graph (OPDG). OPDG represents control flow, data dependencies and control dependencies. It captures complete class representations which are generated only once during the entire life of the class.	Not fit to represent larger programs
6	D. Kung et al. [18,19]	It models the relationship that exists between the classes such as inheritance, aggregation and association. It improves the structure and control flow info.	Not fit to represent larger programs
7	M. J. Harrold et al. [29]	Concept of call graph is introduced. The nodes represent individual method and the edges represent the call sites.	Does not represent object oriented concepts like inheritance, polymorphism and dynamic binding, not fit for large programs
8	J. Chen et al. [16]	Introduced object oriented dependency graph (ODG)	

Table 1. (*continued*)

9	J. Chen et al. [17]	Described program slices on the basis of state and behaviour.	
10	H. Agrawal et al. [21]	Proposed a method for dynamic dependence graph	
11	J. Zhao et al. [22]	Extended the method by Agrawal et al. by proposing dynamic object oriented dependence graph (DODG). DODG was based on dynamic analysis of control flow and data flow. Supported object oriented features such as method calls, polymorphism, inheritance, dynamic binding etc	The dynamic slicing created are not executable, size of DODG becomes unbounded for many loops
12	Y. Song et al. [23]	Dynamic object relationship diagram (DORD)is proposed , it is executable	
13	Durga Prasad Mohapatra et al.[26]	Proposed extended system dependence graph (ESDG) as the intermediate representation. They have statically constructed the ESDG only once before the execution of the program starts. With ESDG no new nodes are created and added during run time to the intermediate representation. Another advantage is that when a request for the slice is made it is already available	

3.2   Slicing of UML Diagrams

Lallchandani and Mall in [30] state that the traditional slicing is usually performed solely based on data and control dependency relationships among program statements. In order to perform the slicing of UML diagrams it is important that firstly an intermediate representation is formulated of the various classes, objects or methods involved in the architecture and the relationships between them. The authors in this paper have proposed an intermediate representation of class diagram called class dependency graph and sequence diagram called sequence dependency graph. This intermediatory representation is then joined to form Model dependency graph (MDG). This MDG is then used for performing the static slicing of UML architectural models using a tool named Static Slicer for UML Architectural Models (SSUAM).

In [31] Lallchandani and Mall enhanced the previous paper and proposed an intermediate representation for software architecture by integrating various UML diagrams into a single system model. The representation is been named Model Dependency graph (MDG). To construct an intermediate representation an intermediate representation of class diagram, sequence diagram and state chart diagram called Class Dependency Graph, Sequence Dependency Graph and State Trans is created and joined on the basis of certain criteria. An algorithm is then proposed to compute dynamic slice on the basis of MDG proposed. The algorithm is named state based dynamic slicing of UML architectural models (SDSUM). The authors in [31] have also named various applications of MDG e.g calculating metrics for UML models on the basis of behavioral complexities, coupling among interactions, cohesiveness of an interaction etc. Various slice based metrics can be computed from SDSUM e.g. model coverage, model overlap, tightness etc

In [32, 33] Bae and Chae have proposed an approach to manage the complexity of the UML metamodel by modularizing the metamodel into a set of small metamodels for each UML diagram type. The authors have then proposed a slicing algorithm for extracting diagram-specific metamodels from the UML metamodel. To verify the extracted metamodel a modeling tool has been built based on diagram-specific metamodels and its interoperability has been investigated with other UML modeling tool. The authors have sliced the UML metamodel on the basis of its respective diagrams.

Kagdi et al. [34] introduce the concept of model slicing as a means to support maintenance through understanding, querying, and analyzing large UML models. Kagdi et al. constructed model slices from UML class models. Their slicing approach extracts parts of a class diagram in order to construct sub-models from a given model of a system. However, class models are devoid of explicit behavioral information and depict only structural behavior.

Ray et al. in [35] have proposed the conditioned slicing of activity diagram for test case generation. The method first builds a flow dependence graph from an ordinary UML activity diagram and then applies conditioned slicing on a predicate node of the graph. It helps to automatically generate test data, which can be used by a tool to automatically test a program. The approach achieves complete path coverage by boundary testing criterion and divides the test input domain into sub domains using conditional predicates.

4   Coupling and Cohesion Using Program Slicing

Weiser [36] discussed five slice-based complexity metrics. *Overlap* is a measure of how many statements in a slice are found only in that slice, measured as a mean ratio of non unique-to-unique statements in each slice. *Parallelism* is the number of slices that has few statements in common. *Tightness* is the number of statements in every slice, expressed as a ratio over program length. Programs with high overlap and parallelism but with low tightness would decompose nicely. *Coverage* compares the length of the slice to the length of the entire program. Clustering reveals the degree to which slices are reflected in the original code layout.

Longworth in [37] was first to conclude that some of the slice based metrics suggested by Weiser [36] might be used as indicators of cohesion. He concluded that coverage provides a good indicator for either high or low levels of cohesion, while overlap and tightness can be considered to confirm the level suggested by coverage.

The metrics by Weiser and Longworth were further extended by Ott and Thuss in [38]. They improved the behaviour of the metrics by using metrics slices. A metric slice takes into account both the uses and used by data relationship. The Ott and Thuss metrics are Coverage, MinCoverage, MaxCoverage, Overlap and Tightness. A slice based method for measuring functional cohesion was suggested by Bieman and Ott [39]. The author talks about glue and super glue tokens which were found out in a program. Glue tokens are tokens which are shared by more than one slice. Super Glue tokens are tokens which are common to all slices. The strong functional cohesion is given as the ratio of Super Glue tokens to the total token and is similar to tightness measure given by Ott and Thuss [38]. The week functional cohesion is given as the ratio of glue tokens to the total tokens in the procedure. Another measure for cohesion is adhesiveness which is the relative number of slices that each token glues together. A token that glues more slices together is more adhesive and vice versa.

Krinke [40] introduces two types of metrics, slices based and chop based for calculating cohesion at the statement level. In slice-based metric, the cohesion for a statement is the sum of the sizes of the slices in which the statement appears divided by the sum of the sizes of all slices in the module. The chop on the other hand is the influence of one set of points on another between the source and the target point. The chop based metrics calculates cohesion by dividing the number of chops in which the statement appears by the total number of chops.

Meyers and Binkley undertook the broadest study of slice-based cohesion metrics [41, 42] which researches baseline metric values and its relationship with size based metrics, code quality and with each other. When comparing the metric values with each other, they found a very strong correlation between tightness and minCoverage and strong correlation between minCoverage and overlap; tightness and overlap; maxCoverage and coverage. These correlations suggest that it may not be necessary to calculate all of the metrics to characterize the code.

Coupling between modules or components is their degree of mutual interdependence. Traditionally, coupling was calculated in terms of Henry and Kafura's information flow metrics [43] which are defined in terms of the total information flowing in to a module (inflow) and the total information flowing out of a module (outflow).

Harman et al. in [44] define the flow between modules f and g, as the ratio of the number of elements from f included in interprocedural slices with respect to the principle variables of g to the number of elements in f. Coupling is then computed as a normalized ratio of the flow in both directions. This is generalized to the coupling for a given module, which is computed as the weighted average of its computed values with all other modules.

Rilling et al. in [2] proposed a framework of program slicing based coupling measurements to evaluate software quality. The proposed framework combines the well known coupling measurement, CBO (coupling between object classes), RFC (response from classes), and MPC (message passing coupling), with slicing based source code analysis.

Bixin Li et al. in [45] proposed an approach to discuss software coupling conditions in object-oriented programs based on program slicing and information-flow analysis techniques. Firstly the dependence edges are made and then forward and backward slices are used to find coupling. The various coupling conditions discussed by the author are No coupling, Import coupling, Export coupling, I/O coupling and Unidirectional coupling.

Bixin Li in [46] proposed a hierarchical slice based model for the measurement of coupling. Computation of variable related coupling, information related coupling and inheritance coupling is done. A hierarchical model is created comprising of four levels from the object oriented systems by using abstract techniques. The coupling is then proposed between statements, methods, class and modules.

Table 2. Summary of Findings

Topic	References	Advantages	Disadvantages
Program Slicing using Dependence Graphs	[14, 12, 21, 15, 18, 16, 17, 13, 24, 22, 23, 26, 27]	Various techniques for static or dynamic slicing have been proposed with the help of graphs for systems using the source code.	No detailed dependence graph has been proposed for the UML diagrams. The dependence graphs have been constructed from object oriented or procedural source code which is obtained in the coding phase so no emphases is made to improve the quality in the design phase.
UML Slicing	[30]	Slicing of UML Class diagram and sequence diagram proposed	State and activity models for accurate behavioral implications not included. No proposal for coupling and cohesion or any other applications.
	[31]	Slicing using class diagram, sequence diagram and state chart diagram	UML diagrams like activity and use case etc not included in the slices.
	[32, 33]	A slicing algorithm for extracting diagram-specific metamodels from the UML metamodel has been proposed.	Each diagram measures diagram specific characteristics. There are no methods for verifying inter-diagram consistency.
	[34]	Introduced model slicing from class UML models	Class models are devoid of explicit behavioral information and depict only structural behavior in system

Table 2. (*continued*)

Coupling and Cohesion	[1]	Showed importance of slices in coupling	Only static slices were used
	[4, 5]	Dynamic coupling proposed	No reference to dynamic slicing
	[8]	Dynamic cohesion proposed	No reference to dynamic slicing
	[36]	Introduced slices and slice based complexity metrics and its applications for debugging	No relation of slices with cohesion and coupling proposed
	[37, 38, 39, 40, 41, 42]	Related the slice based metrics with cohesion and further improved the cohesion metrics	
	[43,44, 45,46]	Suggested slice based coupling metrics	

5   Conclusion

This paper is a review on the various static and dynamic program slicing techniques. It summarizes the various dependency graphs which have been proposed by researchers for the static and dynamic slicing. This representation is further used for measuring coupling and cohesion. A brief summary of findings for dependence graphs, UML slicing and coupling and cohesion is shown in table 2.

References

1. Weiser, M.: Program slicing. IEEE Trans. Software Eng. 10(4), 352–357 (1984)
2. Rilling, J., Meng, W.J., Ormandjieva, O.: Context Driven Slicing Based Coupling Measures. In: Proceedings of the 20th IEEE International Conference on Software Maintenance (ICSM 2004), Washington DC, USA, p. 532 (2004)
3. Briand, L.C., Daly, J.W., Wüst, J.K.: A Unified Framework for Coupling Measurement in Object-Oriented Systems. IEEE Transactions on Software Engineering 25(1), 91–121 (1999)
4. Arisholm, E., Briand, L.C., Føyen, A.: Dynamic Coupling Measurement for Object-Oriented Software. IEEE Transactions on Software Engineering 30(8), 491–506 (2004)
5. Yacoub, S.M., Ammar, H.H., Robinson, T.: Dynamic metrics for object oriented design. In: Proc. 6th International Symposium on Software Metrics, Boca Raton, FL, pp. 50–61 (1999)
6. Zhou, H., Huang, Z., Zhu, Y.: Polymorphism Sequence Diagrams Test Data Automatic Generation Based on OCL. In: The 9th International Conference for Young Computer Scientists, pp. 1235–1240 (2008)
7. Briand, L.C., Daly, J.W., Wüst, J.K.: A Unified Framework for Cohesion Measurement in Object-Oriented Systems. Empirical Software Engineering 3(1), 65–117 (1998)
8. Gupta, V., Chabbra, J.K.: Dynamic cohesion measures for object oriented software. Journal of Systems Architecture 57(4), 452–462 (2011)

9. Selby, R.W., Basili, V.R.: Analyzing error-prone system structure. IEEE Transactions on Software Engineering 17(2), 141–152 (1991)
10. Horwitz, S., Reps, T.: The use of program dependence graphs in software engineering. In: ICSE 1992: Proceedings of the 14th International Conference on Software Engineering, New York, NY, USA, pp. 392–411 (1992)
11. Yourdon, E., Constantine, L.: Structured Design: Fundamentals of a Discipline of Computer Program and System Design. Prentice Hall (1979)
12. Horwitz, S., Reps, T., Binkley, D.: Interprocedural slicing using dependence graphs. ACM Transactions on Programming Languages and Systems 12(1), 26–61 (1990)
13. Larson, L.D., Harrold, M.J.: Slicing object oriented software. In: Proceedings of the 18th International Conference on Software Engineering, Berlin, Germany, pp. 495–505 (March 1996)
14. Liang, D., Harrold, M.J.: Slicing objects using system dependence graphs. In: Proceedings of International Conference on Software Maintenance, pp. 358–367 (November 1998)
15. Krishnaswamy, A.: Program slicing: An application of program dependency graphs. Technical report, Department of Computer Science, Clemson University (August 1994)
16. Chen, J., Wang, F., Chen, Y.: An object oriented dependency graph. In: Technology of Object-Oriented Languages and Systems Tools, Beijing, China (1997)
17. Chen, J.T., Wang, F.J., Chen, Y.L.: Slicing object-oriented programs. In: Proceedings of the APSEC 1997, Hongkong, China, pp. 395–404 (December 1997)
18. Kung, D., Gao, J., Hisa, P., Toyoshima, Y.: Change impact identification in object-oriented software maintenance. In: Proceedings of International Conference on Software Maintenance, pp. 202–211 (September 1994)
19. Kung, D., Gao, J., Hisa, P., Toyoshima, Y., Chen, C.: Design recovery for Software Testing of Object Oriented Systems. In: World Conference on Reverse Engineering, pp. 201–211 (May 1993)
20. Gupta, N., Rao, P.: Program execution based module cohesion measurement. In: Proceedings of 16th Annual International Conference on Automated Software Engineering (ASE 2001), pp. 144–153 (2001)
21. Agrawal, H., Horgan, J.: Dynamic program slicing. In: Proceedings of the ACM SIGPLAN 1990 Conference on Programmimg Lanuages Design and Implementation, SIGPLAN Notices, Analysis and Verification, White Plains, NewYork, vol. 25, pp. 246–256 (1990)
22. Zhao, J.: Dynamic slicing of object-oriented programs. Technical report, Information Processing Society of Japan (May 1998)
23. Song, Y., Huynh, D.: Forward Dynamic Object- Oriented Program Slicing. In: Application Specific Systems and Software Engineering and Technology (ASSET 1999). IEEE CS Press (1999)
24. Xu, B., Chen, Z.: Dynamic slicing object-oriented programs for debugging. In: SCAM 2002, pp. 115–122 (2002)
25. Malloy, B.A., McGregor, J.D., Krishnaswamy, A.: An extensible program representation for object oriented software. In: Proceedings of ISFST, pp. 105–112 (2004)
26. Mohapatra, D.P., Mall, R., Kumar, R.: An edge marking dynamic slicing technique for object-oriented programs. In: Proceedings of 28th IEEE Annual International Computer Software and Applications Conference, pp. 60–65. IEEE CS Press (September 2004)
27. Mohapatra, D.P.: Dynamic slicing of objectoriented programs. PhD thesis, Indian Institute of Technology, Kharagpur, India (2005)
28. Hammer, C., Snelting, G.: An improved slicer for Java. In: Proceedings of PASTE, pp. 107–112 (2004)

29. Harrold, M.J., Rothermel, G.: Performing data flow testing on classes. In: Second ACM SIGSOFT Symposium on the Foundation of Software Engineering, pp. 154–163 (December 1994)

30. Lallchandani, J.T., Mall, R.: Static slicing of UML architectural models. Journal of Object Technology 8(1), 159–188 (2009)

31. Lallchandani, J.T., Mall, R.: Integrated state-based dynamic slicing technique for UML models. IET Softw. 4(1), 55–78 (2010)

32. Bae, J.H., Lee, K.M., Chae, H.S.: Modularization of the UML metamodel using model slicing. In: Proc. Fifth Int. Conf. on Information Technology: New Generations, pp. 1253–1254 (2008)

33. Bae, J.H., Chae, H.S.: UMLSlicer: A Tool for Modularizing the UML Metamodel using Slicing. In: The 2008 IEEE 8th International Conference on Computer and Information Technology, pp. 772–777 (July 2008)

34. Kagdi, H., Maletic, J.I., Sutton, A.: Context-free slicing of UML class models. In: Proc. 21st IEEE Int. Conf. on Software Maintenance (ICSM 2005), Washington, DC, USA, pp. 635–638 (2005)

35. Ray, M., Barpanda, S.S., Mohapatra, D.P.: Test Case Design Using Conditioned slicing of Activity Diagram. POSTER PAPER International Journal of Recent Trends in Engineering 1(2) (May 2009)

36. Weiser, M.: Program slicing. In: Proc. 5th Int. Conf. Software Eng., pp. 439–449 (May 1981)

37. Longworth, H.: Slice based program metrics. Master's thesis, Computer Science, Michigan Technical University, Michigan, USA (1984)

38. Ott, L.M., Thuss, J.J.: Slice based metrics for estimating cohesion. In: IEEE-CS International Metrics Symposium, pp. 78–81 (1993)

39. Bieman, J.M., Ott, L.M.: Measuring functional cohesion, 0098-5589. IEEE Transactions on Software Engineering 20(8), 644–657 (1994)

40. Krinke, J.: Statement-level cohesion metrics and their visualization. In: SCAM 2007 Seventh IEEE International Working Conference on Source Code Analysis and Manipulation, Paris, France. IEEE Computer Society Press (2007)

41. Meyers, T., Binkley, D.: An empirical study of slice-based cohesion and coupling metrics. ACM Transactions on Software Methodology (TOSEM) 17(1), 1–27 (2007)

42. Meyers, T.M., Binkley, D.: Slice-based cohesion metrics and software intervention. In: Proceedings of 11th Working Conference on Reverse Engineering, Netherlands, pp. 256–265 (2004)

43. Henry, S., Kafura, D.: Software structure metrics based on information flow. IEEE Transactionson Software Engineering 7(5), 510–517 (1981)

44. Harman, M., Okulawon, M., Sivagurunathan, B., Danicic, S.: Slice-based measurement of function coupling. In: 8th International Software Quality Week (QW 1995), San Francisco CA, paper 4-T-4 (1995)

45. Li, B., Zhou, Y., Mo, J., Wang, Y.: Analyzing the Conditions of Coupling Existence Based on Program Slicing and Some Abstract Information-Flow. In: Proceedings of the Sixth International Conference on Software Engineering, Artificial Intelligence, Networking and Parallel/Distributed Computing and First ACIS International Workshop on Self-Assembling Wireless Networks (SNPD/SAWN 2005), pp. 96–101 (2005)

46. Li, B.: A Hierarchical Slice-Based Framework for Object-Oriented Coupling Measurement, TUCS Techl. Report, Turku Centre for Computer Science, TUCS Technical Report No.415, Finland (July 2001)

Fast On-Line Summarization of RFID Probabilistic Data Streams

Razia Haider, Federica Mandreoli, Riccardo Martoglia, and Simona Sassatelli

DII - University of Modena and Reggio Emilia
Via Vignolese, 905, 41125, Modena, Italy
`firstname.lastname@unimore.it`

Abstract. RFID applications usually rely on RFID deployments to manage high-level events. A fundamental relation for these purposes is the location of people and objects over time. However, the nature of RFID data streams is noisy, redundant and unreliable and thus streams of low-level tag-reads can be transformed into probabilistic data streams that can reach in practical cases the size of gigabytes in a day. In this paper, we propose a simple on-line summarization mechanism, which is able to provide small space representation for massive RFID probabilistic data streams while preserving the meaningful information. The main idea behind the proposed approach is to keep on aggregating tuples in an incremental way until a state transition is detected. Probabilistic tuples are processed as they arrive, hence avoiding the use of expensive offline disk based operations, and the output is stored in a probabilistic database in such a way that, as we also experimentally prove, a wide range of probabilistic queries can be applicable and answered effectively.

Keywords: RFID, probabilistic tuple aggregation, location detection.

1 Introduction

In the last several years, RFID technology has gained significant popularity due to its ability of detecting objects and people carrying small RFID tags in an environment equipped with RFID readers. RFID applications usually rely on RFID deployments to manage high-level events such as tracking the location that products visit for supply-chain management [4], monitoring the location and status of patients in hospital environment [9], localizing intruders for alerting services [2], and so on.

A fundamental relation for these purposes is the location of people and objects over time. However, the nature of RFID data stream is noisy, redundant and unreliable and thus streams of low-level tag-reads such as "Tag 101 was seen at antenna 12 at 10:00" must be transformed into meaningful relation instances such as "Tag 101 entered office 1-10 at 10:00". To this end, a common approach for real-time applications is to use an Hidden Markov Model (HMM) that continuously infers locations based on sensor readings [2]. Such a relation, therefore, is a probabilistic relation `At(tagID,location,time,prob)` that is usually stored

S. Dua et al. (Eds.): ICISTM 2012, CCIS 285, pp. 211–223, 2012.

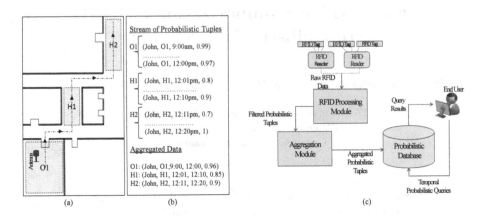

Fig. 1. (a) A visual representation for John movements; (b) The stream of probabilistic tuples before and after applying the summarization mechanism; (c) Architecture for RFID Probabilistic Data Stream Aggregation System

in a (probabilistic) database table and queried to detect complex events meaningful to applications [13]. An example tuple is (101,1-10,10:00,0.7), which indicates that tag 101 at time 10:00 was in office 1-10 with probability 0.7.

RFID tags continually send out their IDs at pre-programmed intervals (few seconds) and for each tag read, the number of probabilistic tuples equals the number of reference locations. Therefore, an HMM for RFID deployments produces huge volumes of uncertain data that can reach in practical cases the size of gigabytes in a day. Storing all these probabilistic tuples in the probabilistic database is extremely expensive and, even more important, it is not always useful. For instance, Fig.1 (a,b) depicts one sample scenario, having a total duration of 3 hours and 20 minutes. In Fig.1(a), John, a user wearing an RFID tag that transmits every second, works in his office for three hours. Then, John goes to the coffee room (H2) by passing through the hall (H1), where he stays for some minutes talking with one of his colleagues. Since the number of locations in this scenario is three, $32,400=(60$ seconds $* 180$ minutes $* 3$ locations) probabilistic tuples are produced for the first three hours which report more or less the same location information for him (stay in office). This represents a rather realistic scenario, as usually person or good movements are noticeably slower than RFID transmission rates.

In this paper, we propose a simple on-line summarization mechanism, which is able to provide small space representation for massive RFID probabilistic data streams while preserving the meaningful information. The mechanism draws inspiration from the field of clustering [8]. The main idea behind the proposed approach is to keep on aggregating tuples until a state transition is detected. This can be seen in Fig.1(b): only one tuple shows John location from 9:00am to 12:00pm i.e. in his office O1. An object or person is said to have state transition if its location changes from one to other, as in Fig.1(b) where John moves from O1 to H1 and consequently to H2. In this case, the proposed summarization method stores only 3 probabilistic tuples instead of $36,000 = (60$ seconds $*$ 200 minutes $*$ 3 locations) probabilistic tuples, while these 3 stored probabilistic tuples give enough information about John's movements. The approach has been implemented in an RFID probabilistic data management system whose architecture is shown in Fig.1 (c). The aggregation module processes probabilistic tuples as they arrive, hence avoiding the use of expensive and offline disk based operations such as sorting and summarization, and promptly stores the output in the probabilistic database MayBMS [7] in such a way that a wide range of probabilistic queries can be applicable and answered effectively.

The rest of the paper is organized as follows. In Section 2, we introduce our aggregation method with its implementation details and different boundary condition tests. Section 3 reports the experimental results. Finally, in Section 4, we briefly discuss about related works and give some concluding remarks.

2   Aggregating Tuples

In this section, we describe the details of our on-line aggregation algorithm (see Algorithm 1) that is implemented in the *aggregation module* shown in Fig.1 (c).

Given m tags and n locations, the *RFID processing module* performs inference on an HMM to produce a stream of timestamp ordered probabilistic tuples:[1]

$$X_1^{T_1}, X_1^{T_2}, \ldots, X_1^{T_m}, X_2^{T_1}, \ldots, X_2^{T_m}, \ldots$$

where each tuple X_t^T has the form:

$$(T, t, P_{T,t}(L^1), P_{T,t}(L^2), \ldots, P_{T,t}(L^n))$$

and each $P_{T,t}(L^i)$ is a score representing the probability that the considered tag T is in location L^i at time t. This is received in input by the aggregation algorithm that in turn outputs a stream of probabilistic tuples of the form:

$$X_{[t_s,t_e]}^T = (T, t_s, t_e, P_{T,[t_s,t_e]}(L^1), P_{T,[t_s,t_e]}(L^2), \ldots, P_{T,[t_s,t_e]}(L^n))$$

such that:

- for each pair of tuples on the same tag T, $X_{[t_{s_1},t_{e_1}]}^T$ and $X_{[t_{s_2},t_{e_2}]}^T$, $[t_{s_1}, t_{e_1}] \cap [t_{s_2}, t_{e_2}] = \emptyset$;
- for each source tuple X_t^T, a result tuple $X_{[t_s,t_e]}^T$ exists such that $t \in [t_s, t_e]$.

The aggregation algorithm works on the intuition that if a person wearing a tag T is stationary or resides at the same location for a period of time $[t_s, t_e]$, the corresponding probabilistic tuples $X_{t_s}^T, \ldots, X_{t_e}^T$ should show "similar" probability distributions. Therefore, in order to derive $X_{[t_s,t_e]}^T$ it draws inspiration from the large dataset clustering field [5] in that it incrementally groups together consecutive "similar" tuples. To this end, at each timestamp t the algorithm maintains

---

[1] For ease of presentation and without loss of generality, we assume that tuples arrive in tag order. For the same reason, the discrete probability distribution of the location random variable is represented as one tuple instead of n different tuples.

at most m clusters, one for each tag T, and for each cluster c_t^T, it treats the tuple region collectively through some statistics $stat^{c_t^T}$ providing a summarized description for the cluster. When a new tuple X_{t+1}^T arrives, the algorithm tries to add it to the cluster associated to the corresponding tag c_t^T by updating the corresponding $stat^{c_{t+1}^T}$ values (see lines 3–5 of algorithm 1). Then, a boundary condition is checked (line 6) and, if it is the case, the tuple is inserted into the cluster by replacing its statistics with the newly computed ones $stat^{c_{t+1}^T}$ (line 7). On the other hand, if a violation is detected:

- c_t^T is closed and discarded from the set of current clusters S (line 10);
- a tuple $X_{[t_s,t]}^T$ describing the behavior of the tag T in the period in which the cluster c_t^T was active is stored in the database (line 11);
- a new cluster for T is created including tuple X_{t+1}^T only, its statistics is computed and it is added to S (lines 12 and 13).

Algorithm 1. Tuple aggregation algorithm

Require: n number of locations, p number of tags , B critical boundary
1: $S = $ current set of clusters; $//S$ contains at most p elements
2: **repeat**
3:      receive the next stream point X_{t+1}^T
4:      $c_t^T = $ identifyCluster(X_{t+1}^T, S) $//stat^{c_t^T}$ is extracted from c_t^T
5:      $stat^{c_{t+1}^T} = $ updateStatistics$(stat^{c_t^T}, X_{t+1}^T)$
6:      **if** testBoundaryCondition$(stat^{c_{t+1}^T})$ **then**
7:          $c_{t+1}^T = $ add(X_{t+1}^T, c_t^T); $//stat^{c_t^T}$ is replaced with $stat^{c_{t+1}^T}$
8:          update S with c_{t+1}^T;
9:      **else**
10:         close and discard c_t^T from S;
11:         insert $stat^{c_t^T}$ in the database;
12:         $c_{t+1}^T = $ createNewCluster(X_{t+1}^T);
13:         add $X_{[t_s,t]}^T$ to S;
14:     **end if**
15: **until** data stream ends

Until now, we intentionally left our aggregation model generic. In the following, we show how output tuples and cluster statistics are computed.

2.1   Output Tuples

In many clustering applications, the resulting clusters have to be represented or described in a compact form to achieve data abstraction. Basically, the most typical compact description of a cluster is given in terms of cluster prototypes or representative patterns such as the *centroid* [8]. The centroid is the logical center of the cluster, usually computed as the average of all cluster points. The use of the centroid to represent a cluster is a very popular schema and works well when the clusters are compact, as in our case.

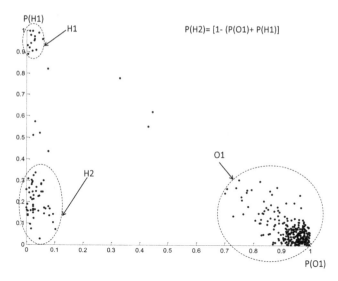

Fig. 2. Cartesian Space representation of the probabilistic tuples of our sample scenario

Therefore, we represent tuples in the n-dimensional Cartesian space as points whose coordinates are the probability values for the n locations. This tuple representation actually exhibits tight clustering as long as the state does not change and a good separation in case of state transition. Fig.2 shows the cartesian plane representation of the sample scenario discussed in Section 1. Since the number of locations is three in this scenario, each tuple generated by the *RFID processing module* is a point in a 3-dimensional space whose coordinates are the probability values for the locations O1, H1 and H2 (the graph shows only the first two dimensions since the third is linearly dependent from the others). We can see that, since John is residing at a same place (his office) for a long period, a large number of points are concentrated in the O1 region; all these points can be aggregated in one point which will be representative of the behavior of all of them. Instead, as John moves from O1 to H1 and consequently to H2, there is a transition that can be seen in the form of some scattered points on the graph plane. Hereinafter, whenever the context is clear, we will use X_t^T to denote either a probabilistic tuple $(T, t, P_{T,t}(L^1), P_{T,t}(L^2), \ldots, P_{T,t}(L^n))$ or its representation in the Cartesian space $(P_{T,t}(L^1), P_{T,t}(L^2), \ldots, P_{T,t}(L^n))$.

Then, we incrementally compute the centroid $V_{c_t^T}$ of each cluster c_t^T while it evolves and, when it is closed, we store $X_{[t_s,t]}^T$ as $(T, t_s, t, V_{c_t^T})$.

2.2   Boundary Conditions

The main objective of the boundary condition test, is to be able to discriminate when a cluster has to be closed in order to avoid distortion. To this end, we draw inspiration from techniques at the state of the art for cluster validity measurement [11]. Two measurement criteria are typically used for evaluating a clustering schema [11]: compactness and separation. While the former expresses the requirement that the members of each cluster should be as close to each other as possible, the latter refers to the fact that the clusters themselves should be widely separated and it is not particularly interesting for our scenario; we thus focus on compactness and consider three different methods for quantifying it. The three models, which provide different indices that can be used in the boundary condition test, are:

- *Maximum Probability Change (MPC)*: it monitors the probability distribution trends. To this end, let $\overline{L}_{X_t^T}(\overline{L}_{c_t^T})$ be the location with the maximum probability value in $X_t^T(c_t^T)$. For each cluster c_t^T, MPC maintains $\overline{L}_{c_t^T}$ as statistics, and the boundary condition is satisfied when $\overline{L}_{c_t^T} = \overline{L}_{X_{t+1}^T}$. The main disadvantage of this method is that it is very sensitive to noise and thus makes more clusters with fewer points in it;
- *Diameter-oriented (DM)*: it measures how large the cluster shape is. To this end it uses the cluster diameter as statistics and checks whether the latter is within a threshold B: $\max_{X,Y \in c_{t+1}^T}\{d(X,Y)\} \leq B$. The main disadvantage of this approach is the time and space complexity, due to the fact that the distance between all pairs of points have to be computed and constantly kept updated on the arrival of new data elements. This function is also very sensitive to noise, since the maximum cluster diameter can quickly become large in a noisy environment;
- *Centroid Vs Latest Reading Comparison (CLRC)*: it gives a measure of the mutual distance between the centroid $V_{c_t^T}$ and the latest point X_{t+1}^T. To this end, it checks whether $d(V_{c_t^T}, X_{t+1}^T) \leq B$. The main advantage of this method w.r.t. the DM model is that computations are less time and space consuming, as $V_{c_t^T}$ can be computed incrementally.

Regarding distance $d(\cdot, \cdot)$ between tuples, our approach is independent from the actually adopted function. Several alternatives are possible for its implementation since we only require it is applicable in a n-dimensional space. In our experiments we adopted the Euclidean distance. Finally, note that for both DM and CLRC, we can control the quality of the clustering process by properly selecting the threshold B: low values of B produce a high number of small and tight clusters, while we have an opposite behavior for high values of B.

3   Experimental Evaluation

In order to evaluate the performance of the presented approach, we have conducted several experiments in different scenarios, collecting data from persons wearing RFID tags. The experimental scenarios are all set in three indoor locations (denoted L1, L2 and L3) and capture different possible movement behaviors: (i) "No Stay", where people rapidly move between locations without staying on any specific one; and (ii) "Stay", where people move between locations and spend some time on each of them. Both types of scenarios have been tested with

Table 1. Performance Evaluation of (a) MPC, (b) DM and (c) CLRC

EXP	Scenario	#Tags		#Locs	#Clusters	%SP	%TAL	AvgLocError
			(a) MPC					
1	No Stay	1		3	3 (=)	0.033	98.91	0.0136
2	Stay	1		5	13 (+160%)	0.026	95.93	0.0452
3	No Stay	2	Tag 1	5	9 (+80%)	0.080	86.61	0.1549
			Tag 2	5	11 (+120%)	0.097	83.04	0.1957
4	Stay	2	Tag 1	4	8 (+100%)	0.033	92.89	0.0707
			Tag 2	4	10 (+150%)	0.041	95.82	0.0453
5	Stay	2	Tag 1	4	16 (+300%)	0.053	82.16	0.1929
			Tag 2	4	13 (+225%)	0.043	86.96	0.1495
Mean					+141%	0.050	90.29	0.108

EXP	Scenario	#Tags		#Locs	#Clusters	%SP	%TAL	AvgLocError
			(b) DM					
1	No Stay	1		3	3 (=)	0.033	98.91	0.0136
2	Stay	1		5	5 (=)	0.010	96.95	0.0383
3	No Stay	2	Tag 1	5	5 (=)	0.044	88.39	0.1419
			Tag 2	5	5 (=)	0.044	85.71	0.1739
4	Stay	2	Tag 1	4	5 (+25%)	0.020	94.14	0.0608
			Tag 2	4	8 (+100%)	0.033	95.82	0.0445
5	Stay	2	Tag 1	4	6 (+50%)	0.020	84.95	0.1696
			Tag 2	4	8 (+100%)	0.026	87.96	0.1374
Mean					+34%	0.040	91.60	0.0975

EXP	Scenario	#Tags		#Locs	#Clusters	%SP	%TAL	AvgLocError
			(c) CLRC					
1	No Stay	1		3	3 (=)	0.033	98.91	0.0136
2	Stay	1		5	5 (=)	0.010	96.95	0.0383
3	No Stay	2	Tag 1	5	5 (=)	0.044	88.39	0.1410
			Tag 2	5	5 (=)	0.044	85.71	0.1739
4	Stay	2	Tag 1	4	4 (=)	0.016	94.14	0.0596
			Tag 2	4	5 (+25%)	0.020	96.65	0.0393
5	Stay	2	Tag 1	4	4 (=)	0.013	88.63	0.1190
			Tag 2	4	5 (+25%)	0.016	89.97	0.1185
Mean					+6%	0.024	92.41	0.0879

one/multiple tags. In all the experiments, we apply the aggregation methods we propose to the stream of tuples generated by the *RFID Processing Module*.

The goal of our evaluation studies is two-fold: (i) to validate and compare the effectiveness of each method in precisely summarizing the movement behaviors which actually took place in the scenarios (Section 3.1); and (ii), to evaluate the best performing method on a possible target application, i.e. to compare the results which can be obtained by querying the RFID data via a temporal probabilistic database with and without applying the aggregation method to the involved data (Section 3.2).

3.1 Effectiveness of Aggregation Methods

In this subsection, we analyze the performance of the presented aggregation methods by means of five experiments conducted on different movement scenarios types (stay/no stay) and with a varying number of actually visited locations and tags. The experimental setup and the obtained results are summarized in the left and right parts of Table 1, respectively. For each experiment, we measure the effectiveness of the methods based on four parameters: (a) number of output clusters

Table 2. Probabilistic Query Results for Aggregated and Non-Aggregated data

	EXP1					EXP2				
	Actual	Aggregated Data	conf	Non-Aggregated Data	conf	Actual	Aggregated Data	conf	Non-Aggregated Data	conf
Q1	P1	P1	0.983	P1	0.996	–	P1	0.027	P1	0.004
Q2	L2	L1	0.105	L1	0.482	L3	L2	0.213	L2	0.606
		L2	0.831	L2	0.518		L3	0.786	L3	0.394
		L3	0.062							
Q3	2:09:34	2:09:34	0.983	2:09:34	0.78	5:20:55	5:20:55	0.984	5:20:55	1
Q4	L1,P1	L1,P1	0.983	L1,P1	0.994	L1,P1	L1,P1	0.975	L1,P1	1
Q5	N/A	N/A	N/A	N/A	N/A	N/A	N/A	N/A	N/A	N/A
Q6	2:09:35	2:09:35	0.817			5:14:44	5:14:48	0.879		
		2:09:46	0.022	*	*		5:16:47	0.005	*	*
							5:19:50	0.0001		

	EXP3					EXP4				
	Actual	Aggregated Data	conf	Non-Aggregated Data	conf	Actual	Aggregated Data	conf	Non-Aggregated Data	conf
Q1	P1	P1	0.981	P1	1	–	P1	0.033	P1	0.016
	P2	P2	0.988	P2	1		P2	0.004	P2	0.04
Q2	L2	L1	0.026	L2	0.976	L2	L1	0.053	L1	0.216
		L2	0.944	L3	0.024		L2	0.898	L2	0.784
		L3	0.03				L3	0.048		
Q3	4:41:24	4:41:24	0.94	4:41:24	0.516	6:05:10	6:05:10	0.989	6:05:10	0.801
Q4	L1,P1	L1,P1	0.988	L1,P1	1	L1,P1	L1,P1	0.996	L1,P1	1
	L1,P2	L1,P2	0.981	L1,P2	1	L1,P2	L1,P2	0.989	L1,P2	1
Q5	L1	L1	0.998	L1	1	L1	L1	0.987	L1	1
	L2	L2	0.974	L2	1	L2	L2	0.991	L2	1
	L3	L3	0.686	L3	0.999	L3	L3	0.654	L3	1
Q6	4:40:03	4:40:04	0.701			6:05:11	6:05:12	0.882		
		4:40:20	0.028	*	*		6:06:08	0.001	*	*
		4:41:03	0.001							

	EXP5				
	Actual	Aggregated Data	conf	Non-Aggregated Data	conf
Q1	–	P1	0.037	P1	0.002
		P2	0.021		
Q2	L3	L2	0.166	L2	0.146
		L3	0.833	L3	0.854
Q3	6:26:45	6:26:39	0.988	6:26:56	0.518
Q4	L1,P1	L1,P1	0.998	L1,P1	1
	L1,P2	L1,P2	0.988	L1,P2	1
Q5	L1	L1	0.988	L1	1
	L2	L2	0.969	L2	1
	L3	L3	0.73	L3	1
Q6	6:26:46	6:26:40	0.842		
		6:28:02	0.022	*	*

(#Cluster); (b) percentage of occupied space w.r.t. non-aggregated data (%SP); (c) percentage of time at actual location (%TAL); and (d) average location error (AvgLocError) between clustered and actual locations. The basic intuition for (a) is that the nearer it is to the number of actually visited locations, the more effective is the method; (b) provides a clear quantification of the space required by the aggregated tuples (the smaller the percentage the higher the saved space); beyond these "overview" approaches, (c) and (d) provide us with more detailed information on the actual contents of the generated clusters. More specifically, the %TAL is the percentage of time for which aggregated data reports the same location as of ground truth; besides correctness, this gives us an idea about the promptness of each method to adjust the output to the ground truth over the experiment duration (the higher the value the better). Moreover, average location error takes into account how much the summarized description of each generated cluster is near to the actual ground truth values. We devised the measure so to highlight what we really think is crucial in this evaluation, i.e. how long and how much each method differs from the ground truth: It is calculated by means of an average Euclidean distance between the ground truth and the aggregated summarized descriptions over the total time span, only considering those time instants when a "wrong" location is reported values of AvgLocError are between 0 and 1, therefore the lower the value the better the estimate).

From the obtained experimental results (right part of Table 1 (a, b, c)), we found that MPC is very sensitive to noise and thus performs poorly in the presence of noisy data. On average it makes 141% more clusters than expected (up to 300% more in EXP5), while average location error is quite high, for instance with values of 0.19 for EXP3 and EXP5 (0.108 on mean for all the experiments). TAL is about 90% on mean, with the lowest values being 83% (EXP3) and 82% (EXP5). DM performs better than MPC but its diameter can quickly become very large in presence of noisy data. DM has an average location error of 0.0975 and average TAL of approximately 92%, while it makes 34% more clusters than expected. CLRC shows superior performance to MPC and DM, giving good results even in noisy environments. The average TAL is about 92%, whereas the average location error is approximately 0.0879; on average, it only makes 6% more clusters than expected, which, together with the other figures, represents a very encouraging result. The same holds for the very consistent space savings produced by all methods (ranging from 0.05% of the space required by non-aggregated data to the most compact 0.024%, given by MPC and CLRC, respectively).

3.2   Temporal Probabilistic Query Processing

After having evaluated the goodness of the output data *per se*, we now want to assess the performance of a probabilistic DBMS in answering some typical queries over the summarized versus non-summarized data of our five experiments. For the tests in this section we will exploit the CLRC method, since it has been proven the best performing one (see Section 3.1).

As mentioned earlier, the output of the *RFID Processing Module* is a probabilistic stream of tuples where we keep the probabilities of each object being on a specific location at a specific instant. In order to handle the uncertainty associated to these probabilistic streams, we use the MayBMS database management system [7] and validate the results obtained on the aggregated and complete data over a number of queries. The queries contain constraints (interval or snapshot) over the temporal history of the RFID data and are used to identify and track RFID objects in the test environment.

In the following, we discuss six of the most significant queries, named Q1 to Q6, that we used in the tests. For each query, we will show its plain text form, its MayBMS (SQL) form shown in Fig.3, and discuss the obtained results

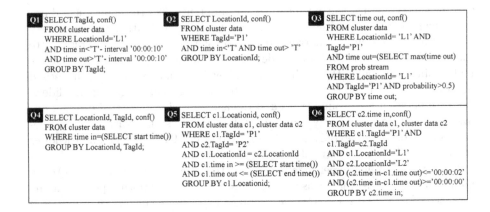

Fig. 3. MayBMS (SQL) form of selected Queries

as summarized in Table 2. In particular, the table shows, for each of the five experiments (columns) and of the six queries (rows), from left to right, the actual (expected) and computed output results over aggregated and non-aggregated data. The MayBMS SQL code of each query is shown in Fig. 3.

Q1. *"Find who was at loacation 'L1' 10 seconds ago?"* Note that conf() is the MayBMS function for calculating the confidence of the answer. Further, in some of the experiments (EXP1, EXP4 and EXP5) the actual answer to this query should be "no one" ("-" in Table 2). In all cases, we can see that the results on summarized data are correct and with a confidence which is very near (almost identical) to the non-aggregated data results; this shows that, even if data in aggregated form contain less detailed information, they provide accurate answers to the queries.

Q2. *"Find where was person 'P1' at time 'T'?"* Again, all the answers on the aggregated data are correct. Moreover, from this and some of the following queries we can see that the confidence of the correct answer is higher on the summarized data, due to the noise that is present in the non-summarized data.

Q3. *"Find when 'P1' was seen last time at location 'L1'?"* Note that start_time() is a user-defined function for retrieving the startup time of the used data set.

Q4. *"Find where and which persons are detected at the first moment?"*

Q5. *"Whether it happened that two persons are together at the same location at the same time? Where?"* Note that this queryis not applicable to EXP1 and EXP2, since only one tag is used.

Q6. *"Find when 'P1' moved from location 'L1' to 'L2'?"* This is an interesting case involving transition detection between two locations. As expected, the results we got from the DBMS experimentally prove that transitions are much easier to identify on the aggregated data, since the complete data contain a lot of "noise" producing a very large quantity of irrelevant and/or incorrect results ("*" in Table 2).

4   Related Works and Concluding Remarks

The efficient management of RFID data involves a large number of issues in a wide range of applications. One of the main concerns for data management is that the rate of RFID data streams is quite fast and, therefore, the resulting volume of the stream is quite huge. For these reasons, clustering becomes one of the more challenging tasks to perform. While, to the authors' knowledge, no specific works exist on RFID data stream aggregation, in the database community various algorithms have been proposed for a number of clustering problems and several methods working on very large amounts of data gained popularity, such as DBSCAN [3], CURE [5] and BIRCH [16].

Besides purely deterministic approaches, the vague and uncertain nature of the data stream has recently captured a lot of research attention and many clustering algorithms have been proposed which also take into account the probabilities associated to the involved data. In this context, a fuzzy version of DBSCAN has been presented as FDBSCAN [10]. This algorithm, instead of finding regions with high density, identifies regions with high expected density, based on the probability distributions of the objects.

Another probabilistic extension is P-DBSCAN [14], which takes advantage of the probability distribution information of the object locations in the definition and computation of probabilistic core object and probabilistic density-reachability.

In [12], an extension of the K-means algorithm is proposed, named as UK-means algorithm, which considers expected distance between the object and the representative of the cluster.

As UK-means is based on classical K-means algorithm, it can be sensitive to noise. UMicro [1] uses a general model of the uncertainty and keeps track of the standard errors of each dimension within each cluster, showing that the use of even general uncertainty model during the clustering process is enough to improve the quality of results over purely deterministic approaches. Other similar related approaches are the two-phase clustering algorithm discussed by Zhang et al. in [15], named as LuMicro, and PWStream [6], which has been proposed for the specific problem of sliding windows.

The objective of most of the methods discussed above is to analyze the incoming data and judge on their "certainty", thus producing the highest quality possible clusters both in terms of compactness and high probability, discarding low quality ones. Further, they work on the assumption of knowing specific information characterizing the uncertainty, such as having the entire probability density function or standard error data available. The number of clusters to be produced is also usually known in advance. On the other hand, our methods are targeted for a different objective, i.e. a summarization task in a location tracking context, and are thus designed to work on a different perspective. More specifically, our ultimate goal is to correctly identify and highlight state transitions, while avoiding redundant information produced in stable states. In this context, not only one active cluster per tag suffices but, even more importantly, we never have to judge on the quality (probability) of the created clusters; instead, we purely and "objectively" summarize the received data in order to make it available to subsequent modules in a more compact but equally meaningful way. In this way, as experimentally proven, a probabilistic database such as MayBMS can effectively answer a wide range of probabilistic queries on the summarized version of the data, which only take up a fraction of the original space.

References

1. Aggarwal, C., Yu, P.: A framework for clustering uncertain data streams. In: Proceedings of the 24th International Conference on Data Engineering, pp. 150–159. IEEE (2008)
2. Cucchiara, R., Fornaciari, M., Haider, R., Mandreoli, F., Martoglia, R., Prati, A., Sassatelli, S.: A Reasoning Engine for Intruders' Localization in Wide Open Areas using a Network of Cameras and RFIDs. In: Proceedings of 1st IEEE Workshop on Camera Networks and Wide Area Scene Analysis. IEEE (2011)
3. Ester, M., Kriegel, H., Sander, J., Xu, X.: A density-based algorithm for discovering clusters in large spatial databases with noise. In: Proceedings of the 2nd International Conference on Knowledge Discovery and Data Mining, vol. 1996, pp. 226–231. AAAI Press, Portland (1996)
4. Gonzalez, H., Han, J., Li, X., Klabjan, D.: Warehousing and analyzing massive RFID data sets. In: 22nd International Conference on Data Engineering, ICDE 2006. IEEE Computer Society (2006)
5. Guha, S., Rastogi, R., Shim, K.: CURE: an efficient clustering algorithm for large databases. In: ACM SIGMOD Record, vol. 27, pp. 73–84. ACM (1998)
6. Hu, W.C., Cheng, Z.L.: Clustering algorithm for probabilistic data streams over sliding window. In: Proceedings of the 9th International Conference on Machine Learning and Cybernetics (ICMLC), pp. 2065–2070. IEEE (2010)
7. Huang, J., Antova, L., Koch, C., Olteanu, D.: MayBMS: a probabilistic database management system. In: Proceedings of the 35th SIGMOD International Conference on Management of Data, pp. 1071–1074. ACM (2009)
8. Jain, A.K., Murty, M.N., Flynn, P.J.: Data clustering: a review. ACM Compututing Survey 31, 264–323 (1999)
9. Kim, D., Kim, J., Kim, S., Yoo, S.: Design of RFID based the Patient Management and Tracking System in hospital. In: 30th Annual International Conference of the IEEE Engineering in Medicine and Biology Society, EMBS, pp. 1459–1461. IEEE (2008)
10. Kriegel, H., Pfeifle, M.: Density-based clustering of uncertain data. In: Proceedings of the Eleventh ACM SIGKDD International Conference on Knowledge Discovery in Data Mining, pp. 672–677. ACM (2005)
11. Legány, C., Juhász, S., Babos, A.: Cluster validity measurement techniques. In: Proceedings of the 5th WSEAS International Conference on Artificial Intelligence, Knowledge Engineering and Data Bases, pp. 388–393 (2006)
12. Ngai, W., Kao, B., Chui, C., Cheng, R., Chau, M., Yip, K.: Efficient clustering of uncertain data. In: Proceedings of the 6th International Conference on Data Mining (ICDM), pp. 436–445. IEEE (2006)
13. Ré, C., Letchner, J., Balazinksa, M., Suciu, D.: Event queries on correlated probabilistic streams. In: Proceedings of the ACM SIGMOD International Conference on Management of Data, pp. 715–728 (2008)

14. Xu, H., Li, G.: Density-based probabilistic clustering of uncertain data. In: Proceedings of International Conference on Computer Science and Software Engineering, pp. 474–477. IEEE (2008)
15. Zhang, C., Gao, M., Zhou, A.: Tracking high quality clusters over uncertain data streams. In: 25th International Conference on Data Engineering, ICDE 2009, pp. 1641–1648. IEEE (2009)
16. Zhang, T., Ramakrishnan, R., Livny, M.: BIRCH: an efficient data clustering method for very large databases. In: ACM SIGMOD Record, vol. 25, pp. 103–114. ACM (1996)

An Efficient and Highly Available Distributed Data Management System

Nobuhiko Matsuura[1], Seiji Suzuki[1], Maki Ohata[2], Ken Ohta[2],
Hiroshi Inamura[2], Tadanori Mizuno[3], and Hiroshi Mineno[4]

[1] Graduate School of Informatics, Shizuoka University, Japan
[2] Research Laboratories, NTT DOCOMO, Japan
[3] Faculty of Information Science, Aichi Institute of technology, Japan
[4] Faculty of Informatics, Shizuoka University, Japan

Abstract. Because context-aware services, such as those for home and building energy management systems, need many sensors to enable us to understand our surrounding environment, the use of sensors has been increasing all over the world. We can obtain vast amounts of information with these sensors, but they raise one serious problem that is how to collect, store, and analyze data. Although a key-value store (KVS) is a newer way than a traditional relational database (RDB) of constructing database management system, the KVS involves optimized write processing and the RDB involves optimized read processing. In this paper, we propose an efficient and highly available distributed data management system (DDMS) that consists of three components of a PUCC node, stream manager, and data manager. We evaluated the query-processing performance with YCSB and revealed that the performance could be improved by combining the data manager with the stream manager.

Keywords: distributed data management system, data-stream processing, key-value store.

1 Introduction

The number of sensors is increasing all over the world due to their usefulness. There are many sensors even in homes, and they are only used for various automatic functions in individual devices. However, current developers are trying to integrate sensors into single services, and there are many services that use them, such as those for home energy management systems (HEMS) [1], building energy management systems (BEMS) [2], and monitoring systems for the elderly [3]. These are called context-aware services and they take user locations and conditions into account.

Context-aware services collect, store, and analyzes sensor data to understand our surrounding environment. There are client-server architectures to construct these systems because anyone can obtain computer resources inexpensively due to the introduction of cloud computing, which has been widely studied [4]. However, it is too difficult for server to manage all work from two viewpoints. As

S. Dua et al. (Eds.): ICISTM 2012, CCIS 285, pp. 224–234, 2012.

the point of view of the collecting, the server must be accepting of differences in sensor specifications, such as a data format. As the point of view of the storing and analyzing, the server also must process the vast amount of write request and process the read request as soon as possible to maintain freshness of the sensor data. So, there are three requirements when systems are constructed with this architecture: common format access method, high-write and high-query-processing performance. A specialized system for the sensor data management is required to support the three requirements. Therefore, we propose an efficient and highly available distributed data management system.

The rest of the paper is organized as follows: Section 2 discusses related works; Section 3 presents our proposed system, and Section 4 presents the experimental results and a discussion. Finally, Section 5 concludes the paper and discusses future work.

2   Related Work

2.1   Data Management System

Peer-To-Peer (P2P) Networks. P2P networks are used to construct virtual logical networks called overlay networks on existing physical networks, and P2P nodes can communicate on the overlay networks. The nodes have IDs and a neighbor node list on P2P networks. Communication requests include the target node ID and are delivered by continuously choosing the nearest neighbor node.

On the other hand, P2P networks are also used to construct distributed hash tables (DHT). DHT is ways of distributed data management and they store data constructed from pairs of keys and values. Well known algorithms to construct DHT are Chord [5] and Skipgraph [6]. The data in these algorithms are stored in nodes with the same ID as the hash value of the key. When one node wants to obtain data, it can easily find the stored node using the hash value of the key as the target ID. DHT is highly scalable and load-balancing because data are stored in random nodes by using hash values. However, DHT cannot store complex data like those sensors from because they only have a simple data model.

Database Management System (DBMS). Fig. 1 outlines a database server architecture using a database management system (DBMS). A key-value store (KVS) is a newer way than the traditional relational database (RDB) of constructing DBMS. KVS interconnects many nodes using P2P networks and it can decentralize management. Table 1 compares KVS. The CAP theorem in the table means that it is impossible for a distributed computer system to simultaneously provide all three guarantees of consistency, availability, and partition tolerance. In terms of the CAP theorem, all systems include "P", which is first letter of "partition tolerance" and is highly scalable because it guarantees tolerance against partitions.

On the other hand, there has been a paper that has evaluated DBMS from the point of view of throughput and latency [7]. It describes a developed evaluation tool and presents the results from evaluating from four systems: Cassandra [8],

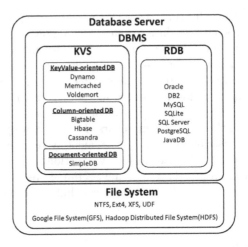

Fig. 1. DBMS architecture

Table 1. Kinds of KVS

Name	Data model	CAP theorem	Distribute model	Persistence model
Cassandra	Column-oriented	AP	Consistent hash	Memtable/SSTable
HBase	Column-oriented	CP	Sharding	Memtable/SSTable on HDFS
CouchDB	Document-oriented	AP	Consistent hash	Append-only B-tree
Riak	Document-oriented	AP	Consistent hash	?
MongoDB	Document-oriented	CP	Sharding	B-tree
Tokyo cabinet	KeyValue-oriented	AP	Consistent hash	Hash or B-tree
Voldemort	KeyValue-oriented	AP	Consistent hash	Pluggable
Redis	KeyValue-oriented	CP	Consistent hash	In-memory with background snapshots
Scalaris	KeyValue-oriented	CP	Consistent hash	In-memory only

HBase [9], PNUTS [10], and MySQL. The conclusion from the results was that RDB (PNUTS, MySQL) involves optimized read processing and KVS (Cassandra, HBase) involves optimized write processing. As previously explained, KVS is suitable for constructing systems that cause frequently data collection and storage like those in the sensor data management systems. However, KVS has a major problem in that query processing is poor because reading is poor.

Data-Stream Management System (DSMS). DSMS [11,12,13] is a system that controls the maintenance and querying in data streams. DSMS uses a continuous query (CQuery) against a data stream to obtain some records. The query is executed once and it obtains some records in traditional RDB. In contrast, the CQuery continues to execute querying when new data appear. DSMS has an advantage in query processing and a disadvantage in that it cannot store data.

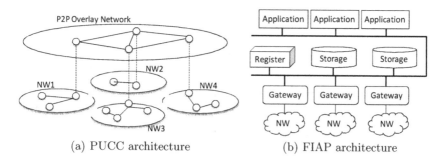

Fig. 2. Architecture for PUCC and FIAP

2.2   Heterogeneous Network Convergence Protocol

PUCC. Fig. 2(a) outlines the P2P Universal Computing Consortium (PUCC) architecture, which adopts the P2P architecture and supports cooperation across heterogeneous networks by using overlay networks. The PUCC node provides an application program interface (API) and event notification according to the publish-subscribe model. There are two ways of sending and receiving the sensor data. The first way is to obtain or set data from a node API as in "getSensorData or "setSensorDa" using an invoke message. The second way is to subscribe to a notification from a published node using the subscribe and notify messages. As previously stated, the PUCC architecture has a master node like a gateway at an under layer network and it constructs the P2P networks between these gateway. The message is sent on above the structure to achieve heterogeneous convergence.

FIAP. Fig. 2(b) outlines the Facility Information Access Protocol (FIAP) architecture, which adopts a traditional internet architecture and has four components. Each component plays its own role: register resolves names of other components those in domain name service, storage stores data from a gateway, the gateway relays data from behind networks to public networks, and applications provide useful services using the stored data. FIAP receives and sends data using a fetch message, a write message, and a trap message. As stated above, the gateway fills an important role to achieve heterogeneous convergence because the gateway manages communication between behind networks, such as sensor networks, and other components.

3   An Efficient and Highly Available Distributed Data Management System (DDMS)

We propose an efficient and highly available distributed data management system (DDMS) in this section. Fig. 3 outlines our proposed system for the sensor management system, which has three features of a common format access method and high-write and high-query-processing performance.

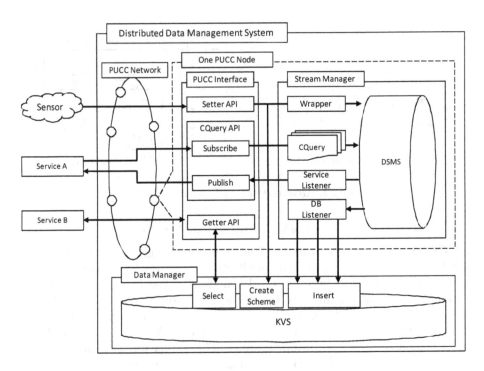

Fig. 3. Distributed data management system (DDMS)

The proposed system consists of three components of a PUCC node, stream manager, and data manager. The PUCC node constructs the overlay networks using the P2P technique and responds to a sensor network with the same sensor network ID as the PUCC node ID. Thus, the PUCC node processes the data from one or more sensor networks and a service sends requests to the corresponding PUCC node. The PUCC node provides the common format access method by the PUCC protocol to reduce differences in sensor specifications. Every PUCC node has some API and the sensor data is processed at the stream manager. The stream manager continues to execute querying by CQuery against the sensor data stream to provide high-query-processing performance. On the other hand, the stream manager also sends the data to the data manager. The data manager receives the data and stores into the KVS that provides high-write performance.

For instance, the following is a flow of a security service constructed by the proposed system. We assume there are motion sensors that send sensor data to a Setter API of the PUCC node. The data through the Setter API reaches the stream manager via a wrapper that converts them to objects optimized for the stream manager. And then, the data manager automatically creates new schema if the data manager has no scheme for received sensor data. The stream manager bundles these data as a stream to execute processing later. On the other hand, the CQuery is sent from the security service to the stream manager via a Subscribe operation of the CQuery API. The stream manager continues to execute querying by CQuery against the sensor stream and sends the result to a service listener. The service listener has a subscribed node information and sends the result using a publish operation of CQuery API. In parallel with above process, the stream manager sends all data to the data manager via a DB listener. The data manager stores the received data to obtain the data later. The proposed system has two kinds of node that is the PUCC nodes and KVS nodes, and both node constructs cluster by many node to provide high availability.

As we previously mentioned, the number of APIs for the obtaining data is two and they are both used by the kinds of queries. Queries requested by the service can be categorized into three types. The following describes when queries are used and how they are executed.

- The query to obtain newest single data (SQuery)
  These queries are used for tracking sensor data or suggest user actions, such as those in checking weather conditions or monitoring the elderly. The system executes these queries on the CQuery API and obtains a datum every certain period.
- The query to obtain recent multi-data (MQuery)
  These queries are used for providing data on real-time statistics or state predictions, such as visualizations of power consumption to assist with energy savings and traffic jam expectations. The system executes these queries on the CQuery API and obtains all data in certain periods.
- The query to obtain previous multi-data
  These queries are used for data mining, such as detecting user habits or providing advice to improve our lives. The system executes these queries on the getter API and obtains all data in certain periods.

By combining the data manager with the stream manager, the system can provide a way of creating a data stream to the external service with the stream manager before the data are stored into the data manager. The proposed system basically focuses on storing all data into the data manager for processing later. The created data stream can provide on additional function that is difficult to achieve in the system with only the data manager, such as SQuery and MQuery. The stream manager can also reduce the read request of the data manager because it executes many read requests before sending the data manager. Thus, the data manager can focus entirely on string the data.

4 Evaluation

We evaluated write and query-processing performance by comparing our system with a system with RDB or KVS. Our main target application was a context-aware service, such as BEMS or HEMS. We selected BEMS for the evaluation environment because it is operated under harsher conditions than HEMS from the point of view of the number of requests and load testing.

We have already constructed a sensor data collecting environment as a testbed to study sensor networks, platforms, and services. This environment covered half the floor of a building that housed our laboratory at Shizuoka University,

Table 2. Node specifications

OS	CentOS 5.7
CPU	2.66GHz
RAM	512MB
HDD	50GB
RDB	PostgreSQL 8.1.23
KVS	Cassandra 0.8.6
DSMS	StreamSpinner 1.0

Table 3. YCSB parameters

Key size	10 bytes (max)
Value size	20 Kbyte
Record count	20,000,000
Operation count	100,000

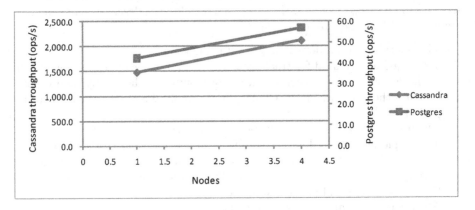

Fig. 4. Results for write-performance and scalability

which had six floors. We used 50 sensors, and the testbed collected about 50 data per second. Therefore, we needed 600 sensors to obtain information for the whole building and total write requests of 600 operations per second from the sensors. This environment is a standard size for BEMS in Japan and we used this throughput as an important metric in the evaluation. Table 2 summarizes the specifications for nodes that were used in the test evaluation.

4.1 Write Performance and Scalability

We evaluated write throughput to find the fundamental performance with the Yahoo! Cloud Serving Benchmark (YCSB) tool [7] that measures performance by continuously sending write or read requests to DBMS. The upper bound for write throughput in our system was determined by storage performance. If the write throughput was lower than 600 ops/s, there was not enough machine power for processing data with our application. We chose PostgreSQL with sharding as traditional RDB and Cassandra as KVS. At the above paper, the evaluation already done with respect to the comparison of the write performance of a traditional RDB with KVS. However, the evaluation uses read and write complex request and not use only write request. In particular, most load of the data manager is caused by write request because most of the read request is processed by the stream manager in the proposed system. Thus, we needed to demonstrate the write performance of both DBMS using only write request.

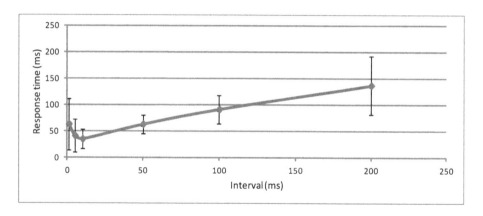

Fig. 5. Relation between interval and response time

Fig. 4 plots the results for write throughput and Table 3 lists the parameters for YCSB. The figure shows Cassandra has the same rate of increase against the number of nodes as PostgreSQL, and this rate is scalable. DBMS with sharding is one of the best ways of improving write performance if it is not considered to be a disadvantage where it is necessary to process data on the client side. This means that there are few systems that have greater scalability than Cassandra. In addition, from the point of view of system requirements, our system requires at least 600 ops/s, while PostgreSQL's throughput is 56.8 ops/s, which does not satisfy our requirements when there are less than four nodes. However, Cassandra's throughput is 2113.0 ops/s, which satisfies our requirements. The difference in performance between both systems is up 37.2-fold. The results indicate that KVS is more suitable for a sensor data management system than RDB with sharding.

4.2 Query-Processing Performance

We evaluated query-processing performance for SQuery and MQuery. As we mentioned in Section 3, SQuery and MQuery require expeditious processing. We used the response time as the evaluation metric and it denotes the time between writing and obtaining by query. In the evaluation, SQuery obtained a datum every 10 seconds and MQuery obtained all data in 10 seconds.

First of all, we must decide a interval of processing CQuery to evaluate query-processing performance. The proposed system can define the processing CQuery interval freely. Fig. 5 plots the relation of the interval between response times with variance. A small interval is better because there is a shorter response time, and a large interval is better because communication and write costs are reduced. However, the shortest response time is very unstable from the point of view of variance, and a stable system is the best. We must consider the availability of processing, acceptable response times, reduced loads, and stability when constructing the system. In this case, we define the interval time as 10 milliseconds.

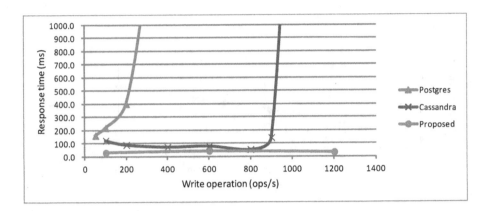

Fig. 6. SQuery response time

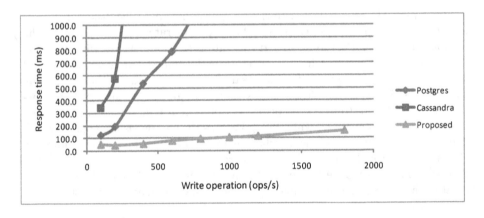

Fig. 7. MQuery response time

Fig. 6 plots the results from evaluating SQuery. The points that begin to rise in the figure denote that the load from queries reaches a limit. Performance was ranked in the following order: Proposed, Cassandra and PostgreSQL. The reason the limit for PostgreSQL was reached was only poor write performance, and the reason it was reached for Cassandra was poor read performance. The difference between both systems was caused by the balance of write and read performance, and write performance was more important than read performance in the evaluation. There is a reason that the proposed system has best performance at combination of the data manager and stream manager. The stream manager virtually acts as the entrance of system for the data and processes the write requests at first. Because the stream manager also acts as temporal storage, it could reduce communication and storing costs by packing data.

Fig. 7 plots the results from evaluating the MQuery. The points that begin to rise in the figure also denote the performance limit. Read performance was more important than write performance in this evaluation, and PostgreSQL's performance is better than Cassandra's. In contrast, the proposed system has a low stable rate of increase against write operation.

We demonstrated the performance of our system by evaluating it. The proposed system could dramatically improve performance by combination of the data manager and stream manager. However, we need to be careful about the interval of processing CQuery because it involves a trade-off and affects the whole system.

5 Conclusion

We propose an efficient and highly available distributed data management system (DDMS) that consists of three components of a PUCC node, stream manager, and data manager. We evaluated the query-processing performance with YCSB and revealed that the performance could be improved by combining the data manager with the stream manager.

But we also need to be careful about processing interval because it involves trade-off. About appropriate processing interval time for CQuery, it is better to automatically adjust it according to the number of write and read requests in practice. We will try to find an effective way to utilize the combination of the data manager and stream manager. We will aim at improving the performance of DDMS in the future.

Acknowledgements. This research was partially supported by the Ministry of Education, Science, Sports and Culture, Grant-in-Aid for Young Scientists (A) 21680007, and Challenging Exploratory Research 22650012.

References

1. Lu, J., Sookoor, T., Srinivasan, V., Gao, G., Holben, B., Stankovic, J., Field, E., Whitehouse, K.: The Smart Thermostat: Using Occupancy Sensors to Save Energy in Homes. In: Proc. ACM SenSys (November 2010)
2. Mineno, H., Kato, Y., Obata, K., Kuriyama, H., Abe, K., Ishikawa, N., Mizuno, T.: Adaptive Home/Building Energy Management System Using Heterogeneous Sensor/Actuator Networks. In: Proc. CCNC (January 2010)
3. Tabar, A., Keshavarz, A., Aghajan, H.: Smart home care network using sensor fusion and distributed vision-based reasoning. In: Proc. ACM International Workshop on Video Surveillance and Sensor Networks (VSSN 2006) (October 2006)
4. Baker, J., Bond, C., Corbett, J., Furman, J., Khorlin, A., Larson, J., Leon, J., Li, Y., Lloyd, A., Yushprakh, V.: Megastore: Providing Scalable, Highly Available Storage for Interactive Services. In: 5th Conference on Innovative Data Systems Research (CIDR) (January 2011)
5. Stoica, I., Morris, R., Karger, D., Kaashoek, M., Balakrishnan, H.: Chord: A Scalable Peer-to-Peer Lookup Service for Internet Applications. In: Proc. ACM SIGCOMM, pp. 149–160 (2001)

6. Aspnes, J., Shah, G.: Skip Graphs. ACM Transactions on Algorithms (November 2007)

7. Cooper, B., Silberstein, A., Tam, E., Ramakrishnan, R., Sears, R.: Benchmarking Cloud Serving Systems with YCSB. In: Proceedings of the 1st ACM Symposium on Cloud Computing, SoCC 2010 (2010)

8. Lakshman, A., Malik, P.: Cassandra: a decentralized structured storage system. In: 3rd ACM SIGOPS International Workshop on Large Scale Distributed Systems and Middleware, LADIS 2009 (2009)

9. HBase, http://hbase.apache.org/

10. Cooper, B., Ramakrishnan, R., Srivastava, U., Silberstein, A., Bohannon, P., Jacobsen, H., Puz, N., Weaver, D., Yerneni, R.: PNUTS: Yahoo!'s hosted data serving platform. In: Proc. 34th VLDB (2008)

11. StreamSpinner, http://www.streamspinner.org/

12. Abadi, D., Carney, D., Cetintemel, U., Cherniack, M., Convey, C., Lee, S., Stonebraker, M., Tatbul, N., Zdonik, S.: Aurora: a new model and architecture for data stream management. The International Journal on Very Large Data Bases (2003)

13. Abadi, D., Ahmad, Y., Balazinska, M., Cherniack, M., Hwang, J., Lindner, W., Maskey, A., Rasin, E., Ryvkina, E., Tatbul, N., Xing, Y., Zdonik, S.: The design of the borealis stream processing engine. In: Second Biennial Conference on Innovative Data Systems Research (CIDR 2005) (January 2005)

Quo vadis: Descriptive and Thematic Analysis on IT Outsourcing

Stefan Bensch

Department of Business Informatics and Systems Engineering, Augsburg University,
Universitätsstraße 16, 86159 Augsburg, Germany
stefan.bensch@wiwi.uni-augsburg.de

Abstract. IT outsourcing is highly prioritized in science and practice. The number of scientific publications is increasing as rapid as market growth. Technological and market-related developments in scientific research and economic reality provide the motivation to conduct a literature review and give an outlook about future considerations of IT outsourcing. Overall, in the last decade back to 2000, 283 articles were analyzed. A systematic classification of research in IT outsourcing helps to categorize the wide range of topics in this field. Thematic developments, subject areas, research theories and industry sectors are analyzed in a systematic manner.

Keywords: IT outsourcing, offshore-outsourcing, analysis framework.

1   Introduction

In the last decade, both practice and academic research in the discipline of IT outsourcing (ITO) has changed significantly. Companies sign strategic, global contracts and the research field is growing fast. Hence, there is a need and a challenge for a holistic view, to handle the big amount of new research results in a systematic manner. Four earlier papers that examine ITO in a full [11] or partial [16, 22, 24] manner, however, give no specific insight into the publication landscape in information systems research. The paper at hand tackles this need by conducting a literature review. It is a systematically attempt to categorize and analyze the academic literature in the field of ITO with the following research questions:

1. How ITO has been explored in the past in information systems research?
2. What are the implications for the strategic ITO?

For practical contribution the number of research for certain industries is measured. Therefore, criteria should be to determine for the practice as a contribution in accordance with the literature. For scientific purposes it will be determined which main themes in current research topics and which research methods in the field of ITO are treated and what issues and publication outlets occupy an important future role.

For this purpose, the structuring of research outcomes is necessary. A publication pool is derived from a total of 16 internationally ranked journals and conferences,

S. Dua et al. (Eds.): ICISTM 2012, CCIS 285, pp. 235–246, 2012.
© Springer-Verlag Berlin Heidelberg 2012

investigated over the years 2000 to 2010. Articles with a direct thematic relation to ITO are identified and systematically evaluated.

The contribution follows the recommendations of a literature review in structure, as a scientifically recognized and accepted method in Information Systems (IS) research [9]. First, in section 1, the need for a new weighting literature review is motivated. In Section 2, key terms are defined and identified in the conceptual context. In Section 3, the literature review process is described. Section 4 characterizes the research field as well as the main findings based on the body of literature. The paper concludes with a summary and conclusion in section 5.

2   IT Outsourcing

This section shows a general overview of ITO and explains basic terms. The concept matrix is described.

2.1   Terminus Technicus - Outsourcing

The concept of outsourcing is not a specific phenomenon of the Research in Information Systems (IS). Outsourcing is evolving away from dyadic partnerships in which a customer buys a service of a third-party provider. A service provider offers its customers a service portfolio with complex arrangements [11]. Although ITO is subject to a high complexity, the market is growing increasingly and companies also pass critical business processes to providers. Until the mid-90s, the cost-effectiveness was the main driver of the outsourcing decisions. The immense and sustained growth and the use of different specialized IT service providers are mainly due to strategic intentions. The management of relations and access to highly specialized personnel and expertise are the focus of the strategic network [18].

ITO has been consolidated into the IS research field. The topic is titled in numerous workshops, conferences and journals. In science and practice currently there is an attempt to establish a precise definition for the ITO phenomenon. However, there is no commonly accepted definition for this term. Recent articles accumulate for these purpose systematically scientific publications, expert opinions and pragmatic descriptions of practice and attempt a comprehensive definition (e.g. [1, 2]). The procedure turns out basic concepts and general objectives. The definitions are often in agreement that the term ITO addresses *total- and partial- outsourcing* and - *insourcing* in combination with geographical location layers like *domestic/nearshore* and *offshore* (fig.1). A modern definition to apply in a broader research framework as a reference is from Gartner Group. It focuses on the management of outsourced IT services.

„ITO is a method of purchase for buying IT services for the management of IT infrastructure and business applications. ITO contracts are differentiated from project services in that they are multiyear, performance-based contracts to deliver day-to-day IT operations and management, versus one-off discrete efforts" [15].

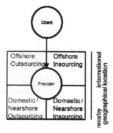

Fig. 1. IT outsourcing classification

2.2   Concept Matrix

In the last decade a large number of studies were conducted. In the literature analysis thematically relevant articles will be structured and evaluated. For this purpose is a methodological system used, the concept-based matrix, developed from the scientific literature, which extract all relevant information and helps to organize [38]. The concept matrix is also used to determine subject-specific information's and to bring the research methods in relationship. Based on an in-depth and systematic analysis, research topics can be synthesized and discussed. For this purpose a distinction is made in the paper at hand, between quantitative and qualitative criteria (fig. 2).

The quantitative part, the descriptive analysis, covered for each article next to the year of publication, issue, the journal or conference name and the culture of the publisher. Furthermore, the matrix includes the concept of search (forward or backward) and the search process (used keywords (outsourc * OR * offshore)) [38].

The qualitative analysis classified the identified articles on the research methods of information systems research, and research topics of ITO. Furthermore, there is a mapping to the industrial sector.

Basically, meta-data are a description of documents, and contain information about their content, structure or form. The characteristics of the descriptive analysis can be derived from the articles meta-data. For qualitative analysis, the content discussion is required. Also requires the classification process a qualitative interpretation skill of the reviewer [11].

Reference [40] develops a classification framework, that the research methods classified according to their degree of formalization, qualitatively or quantitatively, and the underlying paradigm, behavioral or constructive science. The classification has been included with the references [33, 4] with regard to the calibrated contained methods. The category paradigm is replaced by the logical approach, referred as logic. A portfolio approach is derived which includes all the research methods of the IS research.

The research priorities were determined by a indexing of the articles. In the first iteration, 133 content terms have been assigned. Terms were therefore grouped. After 7 iterations of the procedure: structuring - restructuring - synthesis, 12 research topics are identified. These in turn were assigned to four structuring major areas. A useful guide for categorizing design is used by Evangelopoules et al. [12] and could be adapted for the article at hand. Furthermore, the classification of research methods can draw conclusions about the way of information obtaining in the research field.

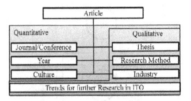

Fig. 2. Analysis framework

3   Literature Review

ITO is an established research field in information systems. The large number of official publications in the field of computer science and business information system (IS) [29]; makes a systematic selection of high quality scientific publication outlets necessary. Publication outlets are therefore to bring into a ranking of quality or other criteria for the current research [14]. For the challenge, a systematic comparison of internationally accepted literature rankings was conducted. An order of criteria according to literature rankings was derived. To include the current state of research and past research and the attempt, to qualify the literature review as complete within the literature corpus, articles were systematically selected in known publication outlets between 2000 and 2010 and examined. The claim for the historical completeness flows in with the consideration of identified reviews, covering the period prior to 2000. These include the references [11, 24]. Furthermore, the challenge of the approach through the consistent use of methods of recognized frameworks, has been stabilized [9, 10, 19, 29, 34, 35, 37, 38].

In the development and execution the work at hand follows vom Brocke et al. [9], which is a reflection of existing scientific publications and is a scientifically recognized procedure. The procedure follows the typical structure of literature reviews and based on the proposed 5 phases: (1) definition of review scope, (2) conceptualization of topic, (3) literature search, (4) literature analysis and synthesis, and (5) research agenda.

The procedure also includes the ongoing debate on "rigor vs. relevance" [13, 31, 32]. With the systematic selection of official publications and articles on one hand and the scientifically based methodology which describes how the results can be derived (rigor) on the other hand can be taken into account that publications are accepted publication outlets (relevance).

3.1   Analyzed Publications

Published and referenced articles on ITO was collected using an extensive literature review. We examine articles in the literature rankings: (1) MIS JOURQUAL ranking [3], (2) VHB- JOURQUAL 2-listing (sub-ranking: Business Information Technology and Information Management) [36], (3) WKWI-listing, the WI Commission Guidelines [39].

With this approach, the objective of transparency is pursued. It creates a reliable basis of valuation of the conglomerate of internationally comparable literature rankings and takes into account different geographical areas of influence. With the process leading European journals and especially renowned North American and international literature sources of the IS will be collected. In a systematic manner by chosen publication outlets, national rankings of other differences can be compensated [9]. Reviews of the MIS Journal Rankings and the JOURQUAL 2 ranking were prioritized for the effective range of the IS due to the higher overlap with other rankings of the scope of the IS research.

In a first step the 20 most prominent journals of the MIS ranking and the JOURQUAL 2 (A +, A and B") ranking (= 26) and respective the "Top 20" of the WKWI-listing for journals and conferences (= 40) were compared and brought into a sequence. The principle of the intersection is an appropriate statistical tool for the process. For the work at hand the top 16 publications were explicit analyzed.

3.2   Literature Search

The literature search systematized the process of article identification and selection. The process can divide in the 3 steps (1) semi-automated keyword search, (2) manual archival research and (3) reverse search methods [38].

Phrases such as (outsourc * OR * offshore), has been searched in singular and plural, in English language. Articles were identified by the search fields title, abstract and keywords. The procedure provides results with the words "outsource", "outsourced", "outsourcing" and "outsource" or "offshore", "offshored", "offshoring" and "offshore". Furthermore, all archives of publication outlets in a second pass were reviewed for relevance by title, abstract and keywords. By means of respective work packages of graduate business students was the procedure supported. The work packages were supervised by the author of the work at hand. Inaccuracies in the semi-automatic keyword search have been fixed by this.

3.3   Limitations

The chosen method of literature review has scientific criticisms. The weaknesses were well known to the authors. The contribution is one part influenced by the choice of research method. To observe the outlets in the IS, reference [34] identified 326 journals. There are currently over 800 journals relating to IS [26]. Even with a systematic approach is a comprehensive literature review not possible. In the rapidly growing field of IS, the possible publication outlets are versatile. Thus, different facets of a research field will be placed not only in their typical official publication outlets. For example, it is observed that increased with the popularity of the Internet and e-commerce, IS researchers publish in marketing and other journals that are not directly attributable to the IS publication outlet [20]. Furthermore, for the systematic analysis of identified publication output are added problems of the effect size. The classification of the articles is effected by the researchers [21]. Other researcher can be come to similar or other categorizations of the studied publications. Remain business practices, far as not covered in the literature, are without reflection.

4   Analysis and Synthesis

In the last two decades several studies and articles on the facets of the ITO have been published. In context of the literature review and research questions, it is important to recognize trends and dynamic changes [33]. Thereby were four earlier papers that examine ITO explicitly [11] or in a partial [16, 22, 24] manner. The claim to the historical integrity is ensured by the inclusion of reviews that examine the period before 2000 (cf. [11, 24]).

4.1   Meta-analysis

Between 2000 and 2010, 283 articles are identified with the forward search procedure, of which 85 articles were rejected for lack of reference to the research question. Another 13 articles were added to the reverse search method. Total of 211 scientific publications were found, 4 articles are literature reviews. These 4 articles are not arranged thematically, as they deal with several issues. So, 211 articles are analyzed (fig. 3). With the search word "outsource *" 135 articles were found and with the search word "offshore *" we identified 49 articles in the selected publications by elected e-libraries [23]. The other articles were manuel identified.

The number of publications sorted by year shows figure 3. Significant is the rapid increase in the publications from 2008. The increase does not come from one or a few publishers. The increase can be interpreted as a permanent or demand-driven trend (here shown as a moving average value). The last 3 years of the review period takes a proportion of 48.3 percent (102/211), based on all classified articles. Critical should be noted when a lot of publications arise about an issue this is in general not the moment of the biggest impact of this method/technique in real life or in the scientific community. For this purpose is noted, the hype cycle, which ensures that publications can appear temporally distorted ad the delay effect. The presumed trend can be observed particularly in the areas of relationship and contract management. In this topics is much published in this time. The years before 2000 shows backward search results and are not representative.

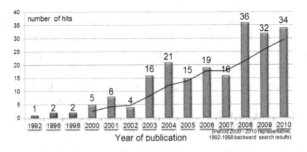

Fig. 3. Articles by year

Striking is a large number of Anglo-American (Canda & USA) publications (fig. 4). Almost, half of all publications come from this region. The fact is explained by the selection of the analyzed publisher by ranking. Only two publishers are dominated from European research institutions (EJIS, Information and Management) [11]. 8 publisher are Anglo-American origin (AI Magazine, CACM, Decision Sciences, ISR, JMIS, Management Science, MISQ, SIAM Journal on Computing). Six of them have published articles in the area. From 6 global IS publisher (ACM CSUR, ACM TODS, Artificial Intelligence, DSS, IEEE Software, Mathematical Programming and Mathematical Programming Computing, ICIS) have 3 publisher articles. With the reverse search procedure 13 articles in global and Anglo-American regions was collected. The large number of international articles comes from the ICIS conference outlet (61 of the 81 publications of the global area).

Fig. 4. Articles by publication

The investigation of the average number of articles per publisher for cultures shows that come 12 articles (23/2, and 24/2 (12) with reverse search hits) from European region, 17 (100/6, and 106/8 (13 with reverse search hits)) from the Anglo-American and 25 (75/3, and 84/6 (14 with reverse search hits)) from the global publication outlets. The issue of ITO is therefore increasingly represented in the Anglo-American publications (fig. 4).

4.2   Thematic Developments

Within the ITO there is an abundance of research topics. Research topics in ITO are numerous and not assessed in a uniform regulatory framework. Previous works differ in the analysis of research areas in the approach and the classification. A classification by the authors of articles by key words will only partially correct results. Here is a holistic perspective developed on the research area. An exploratory, inductive approach to structure outcomes is used. Research topics are clustered repeated by the authors for a systematic evaluation of the relevant articles. The uniformed procedure seems suitable to gain knowledge about the hierarchical articles. A multi-iterative clustering with 7 steps was taken. Identified clusters were tested for differences, congruence's, integrity and completeness. Articles could then be placed in a hierarchical structure. The indexing (see 2.2) leads to representative subject areas within the range. Each subject area exclusively assigned articles. There are articles dealing with several themes, or investigate a thematic interface. These articles have been assigned to the section which is represented by the most intense arguments. The classification is completely within the literature corpus, since all the identified articles will be referred. The process of analyses were done as long as could be derived articles to topics. The synopsis shows an aggregated view of the main characteristics in fig. 5.

Most of the contributions of ITO research explain the theme group *decision support* (70 of 207 articles, 33.8%). Within the category may 25 articles (35.7% or 25/70) be classified into motives, 16 articles in risks and success factors (22.8%) and 13 articles (18.6%) are in effect on employment and prospects. A prominent research area focuses on *soft factors*, (74.2% or 46/62). A less significant part of the work has a tangible, controlled management of the relationships (hard factors) on the subject (25.8% or 16/62). The Client-Provider relationship management is examined with 62 articles second most frequently (30%, 62/207). The category of IS Organization investigate fifth (20.3% or 42/207) of the articles. 19 articles (9.2% or 19/207) study the issue of sourcing, business process outsourcing is represented with 10 articles (4.8% or 10/207) and the area Application service providing have 13 articles (6.3% or 13/207) assigned.

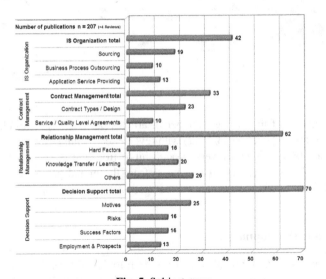

Fig. 5. Subject areas

A consideration of the time distribution shows that articles appear to BPO since the year 2004 and the number of articles already in 2005 is slightly decreasing. The theme ASP follows the same trend. Most articles will be published in 2003 and between 2006 and 2010 were only 2 articles found. The weakest theme class, contract management is represented with 33 articles (15.9% or 33/207). In the category analyze 23 articles (70% or 23/33) the subfield contract types and their design. 10 articles in the category (30.3% or 10/33) investigate Service / Quality Level Agreements.

Furthermore, the analysis gives insights into the used research methods (fig. 6). A separation between the formalization shows that 110 of 211 articles use a quantitative research method. 99 articles follow a qualitative research method. Two articles using a plurality of methods of modeling and prototyping. So there is a slight overhang to formal, numerical studies. The separation according to the logical approach shows that the knowledge discovery process in the ITO in particular conducted by explicitly inductive and empirical research.

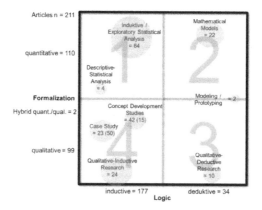

Fig. 6. Research methods

4.3   Qualitative Analysis by Industry Sector

The literature pool contains a total of 51 articles that are clearly classified in an industry sector (fig. 7). The distribution of industry sectors is a result of content analysis. One problem is to determine which industry sector is assigned to an article. Not all research contributions explicate the industrial sector. Other works are independently valid or view multiple industry sectors. The most common cited industry, with 20 points, is represented by the software industry. In 10 articles, the authors indicate that they have collected the data specifically within the Indian software development. The second largest sector is the field of banking / finance. It represents 12 publications or 23.5% (12/51) of all considered empirical analysis. The third place is occupied by the IT service industry. It is notable that China will evolve in the business to the market leader that India today is for software development. Considering also the dates of relevant publications, we recognize that development must be considered quite as "groundbreaking". The range of IT services industry comprises a total of 11 articles. 4 articles thereof explicitly address the area of e-commerce. Only one article examines the Web Services section. It seems as if the trend still hesitant processed by the academic research (cf. [25]). A similar result occurs also Gonzales et al. (cf. [16]). They post only a single counter in the category e-commerce. One possible explanation for this probably lies in the nature of the information gain of the research field of ITO. Most of the empirical analysis applies knowledge from empirical data. It is conceivable that already occur practices in the discipline of e-commerce, the data but not yet collected and been scientifically studied. Such works will be found increasingly in the future contributions. 4 statistical analyses occur from the public sector. These articles examine contract management, knowledge transfer and the motives of ITO. Of the 4 remaining articles, three articles belong to the manufacturing sector and one to the medical sector.

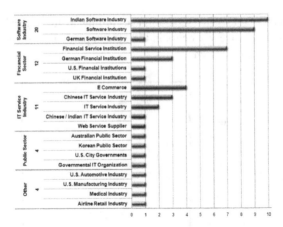

Fig. 7. Articles by industry sector

5   Conclusion

Outsourcing comprises a wide range of topics in various research fields. This shows the systematic analysis of academic and practical development of research-related fields, over a period of 10 years. The research field was hierarchically structured in 7 categories and 12 sub-groups in systematic way. For this purpose, 283 recognized articles with thematic relevance were analyzed. Articles with similar or same topics were grouped into thematic categories. The review analysis shows: (1) Research articles and market development are equally ascending. (2) International journals publish on average more articles than Anglo-American outlets and these in turn have a higher publication output than European publication outlets. (3) The main drivers of ITO are the client-provider relationships, wherein currently more informal, soft design options have been published. Specifically, the articles deal with decision support. In particular, the parts of motives, risks and success factors are represented. (4) Outsourced IT service functions are hardly considered scientifically. (5) Surprisingly, there is a lack of procedural approaches in the area of ITO.

For future research in the discipline of ITO more options are emerging. On the one hand, business surveys and detailed theoretical studies of outsourcing models are recognized [27], on the other hand, the possibility of the success factors and the risks of ITO on the determinants of the contract or the client-provider relationship are due. [30]. There is lack of statistical tests to measure dependencies. Criteria for the design of a questionnaire can be found for example in references [5, 17, 28]. E-commerce issues are comparative examined slightly during ongoing globalization in ITO. Furthermore, for this paper, a process-driven analysis is planned for the ITO (as a method of purchase IT services such as cloud computing services). Established and proven reference models and processes are found also in the procurement literature and can, in terms of IT-industrialization, supplement the younger stages of ITO. Procurement processes and the reference models are discussed differently in the literature [8]. The analysis and comparison of these processes can determine the state-of-the-art. Identified reference models cover parts of the procurement processes. For further research investigation, we will use explicit reference models and extract the purchase perspective in combination with ITO overall [6]. It is especially important to investigate the vendor identification and vendor selection for the formation of interorganizational value networks [7]. It has to be explored how existing ERP systems must be designed to support and implement the procurement-process for ITO in value networks.

References

1. Agerfalk, P., Fitzgerald, B.: Outsourcing to an Unknown Workforce: Exploring Open-sourcing as a Global Sourcing Strategy. MISQuarterly 32(2), 385–409 (2008)
2. Agerfalk, P., et al.: Open-Sourcing in the Celtix Project: A Case of Outsourcing to an Unknown Workforce. In: ICIS 2006 Proc., Paper 1 (2006)
3. AIS: AIS: MIS Journal Rankings,
   `http://ais.affiniscape.com/displaycommon.cfm?an=1&subarticle nbr=432`
4. Backlund, P.: On The Research Approaches Employed at Recent European Conferences on Information Systems (ECIS 2002 - ECIS 2004). In: ECIS 2005 Proc., Paper 6 (2005)
5. Balaji, S., Brown, C.: The Effects of Client Governance Mechanisms and Relational Exchange on IS Outsourcing Effectiveness. In: ICIS 2010 Proc., Paper78 (2010)
6. Bensch, S.: How to Procure Cloud Computing Solutions:A Manageable Value Network Approach. In: Proc. of the Int. Conf. on Man. of Emergent Digital EcoSystems., Paper 32 ACM Digital Library, San-Francisco (2011)
7. Bensch, S.: Technical and Organizational Potentials of Value Networks for Ubiquitous Information Products and Services: Exploring the Role of Cloud Computing. In: The 4th Int. Conf. on Ubi-media Computing, pp. 1–6. IEEE Computer Society, Sao Paulo (2011)
8. Bensch, S., Schrödl, H.: Purchasing Product-Service Bundles in Value Networks - Exploring the Role of SCOR. In: The 19th European Conference on Information Systems – ICT and Sustainable Service Development, Helsinki, Finland, pp. 1–10 (2011)
9. vom Brocke, J. et al.: Reconstructing the Giant: On the Importance of Rigour Documenting the Literature Search Process. In: Proc. of the 17th European Conference on Information Systems, Verona, Italy, pp. 3226–3238(2009)
10. Cooper, H.M.: A Taxonomy of Literature Reviews. American Educational Research Association (1985)
11. Dibbern, J., et al.: Information Systems Outsourcing: A Survey and Analysis of the Literature. The DATA BASE for Advances in Information Systems 35(4), 6–102 (2004)
12. Evangelopoulos, N., et al.: Uncovering the Intellectual Core of the Information Systems Discipline. Management Information Systems Quarterly 32(3), 467–482 (2008)
13. Frank, U.: Einige Gründe für eine Wiederbelebung der Wissenschaftstheorie. DBW Die Betriebswirtschaft 3, 278–292 (2003)
14. Frick, N.: Quo vadis, B2B? Eine Literaturuntersuchung von Journal-Publikationen inden Jahren 2000 bis 2008. In: 10th Int. Conference on Wirtschaftsinformatik, Zurich, Switzerland, pp. 262–271 (2011)
15. Gartner Inc.: IT Term Definition: IT Outsourcing,
   `http://www.gartner.com/technology/research/it-glossary/#8_0`
16. Gonzalez, R., et al.: Information Systems Outsourcing: ALiterature Analysis. Information and Management 43(7), 834–871 (2006)
17. Gopal, A., Gosain, S.: Research Note-The Role of Organizational Controls and Boundary Spanning in Software Development Outsourcing: Implications for Project Performance. Information Systems Research 21(4), 960–982 (2010)

18. Grover, V., et al.: The effect of service quality and partnership on the outsourcing of information systems functions. J. Management Information Systems 12, 89–116 (1996)
19. Jackson, G.B.: Methods for Integrative Reviews. Review of Educational Research 50(3), 438–460 (1980)
20. Katerattanakul, P., et al.: Consistency and Concern on IS Journal Rankings. JITTA 7(2), 1–20 (2005)
21. King, W.R., He, J.: Understanding the Role and Methods of Meta-Analysis in IS Research. Communications of the Association for Information Systems 16, 665–685 (2005)
22. King, W.R., Torkzadeh, G.: Information Systems Offshoring: Research Status and Issues. MIS Quarterly 32(2), 205–225 (2008)
23. Knackstedt, R., Winkelmann, A.: Online-Literaturdatenbanken im Bereich der Wirtschaftsinformatik. Wirtschaftsinformatik 48(1), 47–59 (2006)
24. Lacity, M.C., et al.: A review of the IT outsourcing literature: Insights for practice. Journal of Strategic Information Systems 18, 130–146 (2009)
25. Lacity, M.C., et al.: Global outsourcing of back office services: lessons, trends, and enduring challenges. Strategic Outsourcing: An International Journal 1(1), 13–34 (2008)
26. Lamp, J.: The Index of Information Systems Journals, http://lamp.infosys.deakin.edu.au/journals/index.php
27. Lee, J.-N., et al.: Multi-Vendor Outsourcing: Relational Structures and Organizational Learning From a Social Relation Perspective. In: ICIS 2009 Proc. pp. 1–8. AIS (2009)
28. Levina, N., Ross, J.W.: From the Vendor's Perspective: Exploring the Value Proposition in Information Technology Outsourcing. MIS Quarterly 27(3), 331–364 (2003)
29. Levy, Y., Ellis, T.J.: A systems approach to conduct an effective literature review in support of information systems research. Informing Science: International Journal of an Emerging Transdiscipline 9, 181–212 (2006)
30. Mani, D., et al.: An Empirical Analysis of the Impact of Information Capabilities Design on Business Process Outsourcing Performance. MIS Quarterly 34(1), 39–62 (2010)
31. Österle, H., et al.: Memorandum on design-oriented information systems research. European Journalof Information Systems 20(1), 7–10 (2010)
32. Österle, H., et al.: Memorandum zur gestaltungsorientierten Wirtschaftsinformatik. Zeitschrift für betriebswirtschaftliche Forschung 6(62), 664–672 (2010)
33. Palvia, P., et al.: Management Information Systems Research: What's There in a Methodology? In: CAIS, vol. 11, Article 16 (2003)
34. Peffers, K., Ya, T.: Identifying and evaluating the universe of outlets for information systems research: Ranking the journals. Journal of Information Technology Theory and Application 5(1), 63–84 (2003)
35. Rowley, J., Slack, F.: Conducting a literature review. Management Research News 27(6), 31–39 (2004)
36. Schrader, U., Hennig-Thurau, T.: VHB-JOURQUAL2: Method, Results, and Implications of the German Academic Association for Business Research's Journal Ranking. BuR – Business Research 2(2), 180–204 (2009)
37. Torraco, R.J.: Writing Integrative Literature Reviews: Guidelines and Examples. Human Resource Development Review 4(3), 356–367 (2005)
38. Webster, J., Watson, R.T.: Analyzing the past to prepare for the future: Writing a literature review. MIS Quarterly 26(2), xiii–xxiii (2002)
39. WI-Association: WI-Orientierungslisten. Wirtschaftsinformatik 50(2), 155–163 (2008)
40. Wilde, T., Hess, T.: Forschungsmethoden der Wirtschaftsinformatik. Wirtschaftsinformatik 49(4), 280–287 (2007)

Energy Analysis of Services through Green Metrics: Towards Green Certificates

Mariagrazia Fugini[1] and José Antonio Parejo Maestre[2]

[1] Dipartimento di Elettronica e Informazione
Politecnico di Milano
Piazza L.daVinci, 32, I-20133 Milano, Italy
fugini@elet.polimi.it
[2] Dpto. de Lenguajes y Sistemas Informáticos
E.T.S. de Ingeniería Informática
Avda. Reina Mercedes, s/n.41012 Sevilla, Spain
japarejo@us.es

Abstract. Energy-awareness in services can be obtained through annotations regarding energy consumption. In this paper, annotations are given as *Green Performance Indicators* (GPIs). A service is annotated in terms of its structure, of the used IT platform, and of development costs, human resources, and environment impact. GPIs relate to service development, deployment, and maintenance. An approach is proposed based on monitoring the GPIs so as to enable the analysis of services from their energy consumption viewpoint. Our approach allows estimating energy efficiency of services through a comparison of behaviorally similar services (e.g., an on-line purchasing service) through the analysis of their GPIs. By collecting details from GPIs, we propose a model for an energy certificate, called *Green Certificate*, aimed at classifying services at given energy efficiency levels according to the energy they consume during their lifecycle.

Keywords: Energy consumption, Green computing, Service Systems, Performance Indicators, Metrics, Service Energy Accounting, Green Certificate.

1 Introduction

Under a green IT approach, services can be described in terms of the energy they consume. Energy depends of software/hardware resource employed by the service to run and of the resources they require along their lifecycle, even from an organizational viewpoint. Energy-related issue are gaining attention in academia and industry by developing services that can be tuned to consume less energy in terms of power, IT resources, employed human resources or consumable/supply chains, and so forth [2, 13].

To sustain this attention, it is necessary to stress the importance of designing, developing, and executing service-based applications along the perspectives of energy awareness [3, 8]. This means that services can be characterized by metrics regarding

S. Dua et al. (Eds.): ICISTM 2012, CCIS 285, pp. 247–258, 2012.
© Springer-Verlag Berlin Heidelberg 2012

which resources and of what type (e.g., processor, memory, but also consumables or human resources) required by the service to run, as well as how much effort (e.g., in terms of costs, to consider a unique standard metric) it requires during development, deployment, execution, and maintenance along its lifecycle.

In this paper, we characterize services in terms of properties featuring their energy consumption in data centres. These properties are specified as energy-awareness parameters or annotations called *Green Performance Indicators* (GPIs). We show how a service can be annotated with GPIs describing the service in terms of the IT resources it uses (CPU, memory, storage, and so on), of the organizational factors, e.g., human resources, involved in its development and management, and in terms of its impact on the environment, such as consumables directly or indirectly produced within the service lifecycle. We also refer to energy consumption vs Quality of Service (QoS) as an indicator of to which extent a consumer is willing to accept, e.g., lower response time in front of energy saving.

The paper shows that, through a GPI annotation, the service can receive an energy certificate, called *Green Certificate* (GC), which is a tradable commodity for service providers and consumers. The GC shows the energy consumption level of a service from various viewpoints: from the technical side (IT or provider's perspective) and from the organizational side (business or customer's perspective). The ultimate purpose of the GC is to support service selection form service registries taking into account also energy criteria, besides service behavior and service non-functional issues (e.g., response time, availability, QoS, security level).

We rely on our previous work on GPIs for the definition of a comprehensive set of GPIs providing a global view of energy consumption along the service provisioning model, from service strategy, design and development, to execution, control and monitoring. In fact, this research is carried out in the EU-FP7 GAMES Project[1]. GAMES develops methodologies, software tools, and innovative metrics for an energy-aware design and management of service centers [2]. It proposes guidelines for designing and managing service-based applications along the perspectives of energy awareness. The approach focuses on: a) *co-design* of energy-aware applications and their underlying services and IT architectures in order to satisfy users, context, and Quality of Service (QoS) requirements, addressing energy efficiency and controlling emissions. This is carried out through the definition of GPIs to evaluate if and to what extent a given service and workload configuration will affect the carbon footprint emission levels; b) *run-time management* of IT service centre energy efficiency, exploiting an adaptive system behavior at run time. GAMES relies on web services as a suitable support to *adaptivity* to different system states and requirements in front of energy policies. GAMES defines a *green lifecycle* for development of adaptive, self-healing, and self-managing application systems able to reduce energy consumption. In particular, in GAMES, we have defined GPIs and have shown the results of monitoring complex service applications using a monitoring technique based on the analysis of GPIs at the IT infrastructure level. This paper makes a step forward in the definition of a Green Certificate out of GPIs. To this aim we consider a subset of all the defined GPIs and show their WS-* compliant specification to be stored in a registry of service descriptions.

---

[1] http://www.green-datacenters.eu/

The paper is organized as follows. Section 2 reviews related work. Section 3 describes GPIs and how we analyze energy efficiency for a given service. Section 4 introduces the fundamentals of a GC specification and use. Section 5 concludes the paper.

2   Related Work

Research on metrics for green IT and data centres are in progress with the vision of achieving economic, environmental, and technological sustainability. Several sets of metrics are available to measure data centre efficiency, proposed by Green Grid[2], Uptime Institute[3], Transaction Performance processing Council (TPC)[4] and others. However, there is no widely accepted metric set [12], allowing for easy measuring and monitoring of energy consumed and wasted by a data center. In [10] a set of server energy efficiency measures and metrics is presented. It envisions the requirements for new metrics considering Green IT as a technology to be harmonized as a hardware, software, architecture, and QoS solution. The research towards energy efficient software began with estimating the energy consumption of the processor by instruction level power models [14]. Earlier research studies on energy efficiency of software addressed methodologies that target memory related power consumption [15]. However, in all these research works, the energy consumption of a given application is estimated upon the given hardware architecture. In [8], we have presented energy efficiency metrics for a single service, which maps directly the relationship between energy consumption and execution time. In this way, we can compute both quality and energy metrics for each service and design a novel constraint-based quality and energy-aware service composition. In our current approach, we have considered green metrics for service applications from the hardware usage, the service lifecycle, as well as for the environmental and organizational factors perspectives. Energy efficiency is defined as the ratio between the energy used to reach the goal and the total energy consumed. For instance, one of the most used metric to measure electrical efficiency in Data Centers in the Data Center infrastructure Efficiency (DCiE), calculated by dividing IT equipment power by total   facility power. DCIE was developed by members of the Green Grid, an industry group focused on data center energy efficiency. Here, we consider energy consumption by a service as a factor that depends on processor usage, data storage usage, and I/O peripheral usage, as well as from organizational factors. We say that a service performs in a "green way" if it delivers the expected results according to given Quality of Service (QoS) requirements consuming less processor and/or less storage and/or less I/O or less organizational elements. Our approach is ultimately an adaptation of the Activity Based Costing (ABC) approach [3], tailored to the specific characteristics of services based activities and applied to the evaluation of the energy consumption through costs. ABC identifies activities in an organization, and assigns

---

[2] www.thegreengrid.org
[3] www.uptimeinstitute.org
[4] www.tpc.org

the cost of each activity with resources related to all services, according to the actual consumption by each. ABC has been criticized because of the high costs of modeling and inefficiency when manually driven, which had historically leaded to the adoption of alternative approaches [5]. However, current IT services infrastructure capabilities for monitoring and automated data capturing make it affordable and viable. The convenience of ABC for the analysis of service-based economic activities has been pointed-out in literature [5] due to its holistic view of the process of service provision, taking into account the total costs.

3   Green Performance Indicators (GPIs)

GPIs as design-time annotations of a service are aimed at providing information that allows designers to provide a better design for activities (e.g., lowering the amount of used data or of human resources needed to design and to fix the code/tune the deployment). The approach in this paper aims at obtaining a tool supporting the *analysis of energy efficiency* through analysis of GPIs. GPIs can be examined to identify energy peaks and their reasons by comparing *similar* services (namely, services having the same functional behavior with possibly different non-functional properties, e.g., with higher response time or lower availability). The purpose is to discover whether, by using a different service, for instance a less processing-intensive service, the same activity can be executed with the same functional results, under a customer-accepted response time, and with *less energy consumption*.

GPIs are structured in four clusters:

- *IT resource usage metrics*, related to the use of the IT platform;

- *Lifecycle metrics,* describing the process lifecycle expenditures (costs of modelling, analysis, design, development, deployment, maintenance, and evolution) and QoS metrics.

- *Energy impact metrics*, related to the impact of the application lifecycle on the environment (considering electricity, power supply, consumed material, and emissions).

- *Organizational metrics*, taking into account human factors involved in running and managing applications, and the standardizations and compliance efforts to obtain more energy-efficient systems.

As detailed in [7], the GPIs are layered according to a classical pyramid of information and business systems [9], namely at the strategic, tactic/control, and operational level, as reported in Fig. 1. At the *strategic level* [4], we insert GPIs able to drive high-level decisions about a system organization in terms of used human resources, impact on the environment, outsourcing of non-core services, guidelines for system development according to eco-related laws and regulations (such as policies of Energy Star[5], United Nations Global Compact[6] etc.), and so on.

---

[5] ENERGY STAR http://www.energystar.gov/
[6] United Nations Global Compact http://www.unglobalcompact.org/

GPIs at the *tactic/control level* denote how the service will consume less energy if its development is enhanced, e.g., through the use of mature platforms, which will improve the system quality in terms of service delivery versus customers' expectations and in terms of less complexity of the service interfaces. Decommissioning of unused services and data is a GPI at this level, controlling the recovering of system resources. GPIs about consumables measure to what extent the system is wasting in terms of paper, toners, materials, and so on. At the *operational level*, we insert GPIs for monitoring the energy related to usage of IT resources, such as the processor, the memory, the I/O, and the storage. We consider these factors as a characterization of energy needs that keep GPIs independent of physical configurations of machines and storage devices.

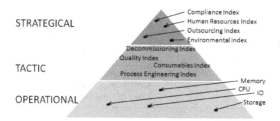

Fig. 1. Layered GPIs

In order to set the principles for obtaining a GC, in this paper, we make the following hypothesis. First we will consider a subset of the GPIs defined in GAMES [8] in order to simplify the formulation of the GC and the computation of the costs. We have selected a set of GPIs which are listed in Table 1. The selection has been performed on a pure sampling basis, avoiding the most complex GPIs. For Units, we consider costs units as a uniform measurement basis. Secondly, GCs regard services, not complex business processes, whole applications or products. The motivation is that we aim at having a clear boundary for factors to be measured to compute the values of the GPIs. Third, the proposed method for creation and use of the GC is intended for *comparisons* and *selection* of services. In particular, we consider *functionally equivalent services* and provide criteria for analyzing energy consumption in a *comparative way*.

3.1   Comparison-Based Approach for Energy Analysis of Services

The approach *compares* similar services considering their energy-related annotations. GPIs are considered for pairs of services (or service groups). We separate the *technical* annotations (*IT view*) of a service from its *organizational* annotation (*business view*), in order to take into account the total energy consumption related with service provisioning. As stated, for the sake of simplicity, in what follows we express energetic consumption as costs. This allows us to aggregate measurements related to different activities, and provides a single significant value for groups of related GPIs (named henceforth *GPI Clusters*). The importance of the annotation of services for energy analysis has been expressed in our previous work [5, 3].

Table 1. A subset of GPIs which has been selected for illustration of GC

GPI Cluster	GPI	Definition (expressed as costs)
Strategic	Human Resources Index (HR)	Cost of human involvement in service development, deployment, execution and management.
	Environmental Index (E)	Costs associated to CO2 emissions, water, energy consumption, etc. caused by production, transportation, logistics, etc. involved in service lifecycle.
Tactic/Control	Decommissioning Index (D)	Cost associated to the energy that can be re-generated by non-usage, versioning, or substitution of services.
	Consumables Index (C)	Costs associated to printouts and material produced by the service during execution.
Operational	CPU (cpu)	Cost of power consumption by CPU
	IO (IO)	Cost of power consumption by I/O operations
	Memory (M)	Cost of power consumption by Memory
	Storage (S)	Cost associated to the energy consumption of the long term storage subsystem (can be independent of the main I/O and even be replicated).

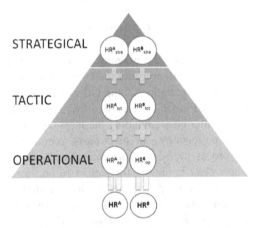

Fig. 2. Splitting the values of the *Human Resources* GPI into its level components: comparing two services A and B

To compute the values of the GPIs, we consider that a service is exposed through its WSDL (Web Service Definition Language) enriched with GPIs at the three levels, as an in *information systems for service management*. Subsequently, we relate GPIs at one level with the *technical metrics* that contribute to obtain that GPI. By considering the same three levels also for the technical metrics of the services, we support the analysis of an *organizational GPI* into its *technical metrics*.

An example is the Human Resources (HR) GPI, related to monitoring how much programmers, or service maintenance personnel "consume" in terms of man/hours to keep services on line and available (this is a tactic/control-level GPI). This example is depicted in Fig. 2. By checking this GPI, an organization manager can explore the technical causes determining the energetic cost related to HR. He can than decide that endowing a programmer with automatic maintenance tools can help saving energy since the maintenance is less expensive, hence the service has higher energy performance. More precisely, the HR GPI considered from an organizational viewpoint can be analyzed in its three-layer (operational, tactic/control, strategic) technical components, going in depth about the factor(s) which most heavily contribute to energy consumption. This analysis can be performed by automated tools (outlined in Sect. 4) by decomposing the HR down to its elementary components. These components can be simply summated as follows to create the global HR value:

$$HR\ (service\_A) = HR_{op} + HR_{tct} + HR_{strat}$$

Other GPIs are not so simple to be split, since their global value cannot be obtained as a summation but is sometimes a means or even requires weighted combinations.

An issue to be taken into account in the computation of GPIs values is that some of the *costs* must be *distributed* and *balanced* over a *set of services* (e.g., using weights). Moreover, the cost computation should be linked to a *time dimension* namely be time-framed observation interval (monthly, annually, etc., depending on the specific GPI). Consequently, cost accounting should focus on the appropriate period. For instance, the total cost associated to the consumables index could be computed on a per-year basis, by dividing the total consumables cost of the infrastructure supporting the services of an organization, and dividing it by the number of services hosted, and the number of invocations (along this year) to which the certificate refers. CPU times, conversely, refer to nanoseconds time frames: hence the time-frame should be made consistent for all the GPIs in a GC if global and per-GPI-cluster costs need be provided.

Providing a full formulation for computing the values for each one of the selected GPIs is out of the scope of this paper, but will be addressed in future work. Of course, the huge volume of data to deal with and the wide range of aspects included in GPIs can be a source of uncertainty, since most of the data that has to be included is hard to measure. Consequently, the propagation of the uncertainty related to those measurements should be done in order to demonstrate that an index of abstract level with this wide range and data is able to really measure something in real life problems. Two examples concerning this problem are as follows. 1) The human Resources Index, for instance, is still hunted by the problems described in [6]. Beyond these old problems, the question arises e.g. how to distribute the energy wastes between small teams working at home with low travel cost or employees working miles away or distributed teams using a lot of communication technology etc. 2) What if a strategy implies a waste of resources on the operation level in one project context, and in the other contexts this effect is quite small and so the advantages of this particular strategy lead to a low use of energy?

As 2) shows, our GPIs should also deal with the question of unique measurability and with the problem of a kind of "Bullwhip-Effect" in the composed index values which might occur by escalating uncertainties. As 1) indicates, it should be studied further how GPIs are assumed to be measured as abstract index values without too wide uncertainties. These aspects will be addressed when dealing with composed services, which are currently out of the scope of this paper. Namely, it may be not simple to apply the additive property given here, and hence a discussion about the questions above can extend the approach to energy measures presented in this paper.

4   Specifying and Using Green Certificates

The *Green Certificate* (GC) is proposed as a document that qualifies a service at a given level of "greenness". It has three main sections: *Issuer Declaration*, *GPI Catalog* and *Valuation*. Fig. 3 shows the UML meta-model of its structure. The *IssuerDeclaration* section is a placeholder where the issuer of the certificate can insert his name, the address of his web site or contact mail, and a signature for the certificate such that the integrity and authenticity of the valuations section could be guaranteed. To this purpose, we have integrated the GC definition with the XML Data Signature W3C standard http://www.w3.org/TR/xmldsig-core/). This paves the way for the specification certificates whose issuers can be different organizations, such as the service developers and owners of the platform where the service is deployed. These organizations could play the role of a trusted third party in charge of monitoring and auditing the values of the GPIs.

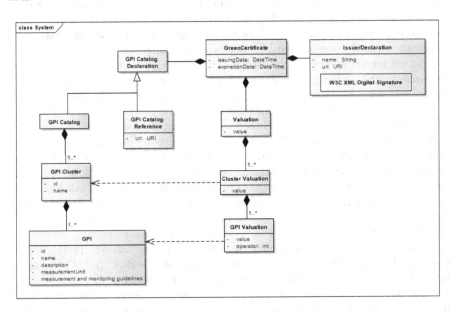

Fig. 3. UML meta-model of Green Certificates

The *GPI Catalog* section contains the definitions of GPI Clusters and of GPIs in the clusters that will have an assigned value in the GC. We left open the possibility of specifying the Catalog of GPIs by creating a global reference through an URL. This allows for the separation between the definition of the catalog of GPIs and the definition of the GC. This also allows for the reuse of *GPI Catalogs*. In this sense, catalogs can be stored in separate documents and referenced from multiple certificates. To demonstrate this feature, we have created a GPI catalog named "*The GAMES Canonical GPI Catalog*", where our chosen set of GPIs is defined. New GCs can use this basic GPI catalog as a starting point. For each GPI, the catalog can define: an identifier, a name, a unit of measurement, a description, and monitoring and measurement guidelines written in natural language. The *Valuation* section of the GC specifies the costs for the GPI, its aggregation by clusters and even the global cost value are provided.

4.1   Use of the Green Certificate: Provider and Consumer Perspectives

Providers have access to all the details of GPIs for cost computation and can perform analysis on them based on the hierarchical diagrams of GPIs shown in Fig.2. We also offer the possibility of using Kiviat diagrams, which display multivariate data in a two-dimensional chart of three or more quantitative variables represented on axes starting from the same point. Authors consider that this kind of chart are especially useful, since they allow to simultaneously evaluate the global cost as the area of the polygon shown in the chart and the specific costs of concrete GPIs in its corresponding axis. Moreover, when GPI clusters are present, authors recommend the use of an additional separator axis between them, which allows the graphical displaying of the global cost of each GPI Cluster as an independent polygon. In Fig. 4 these two kinds of Kiviat diagrams are shown. In this case, they are used for comparing the GPIs of two different services.

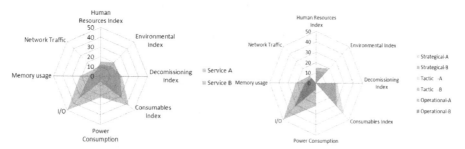

Fig. 4. Two Kiviat diagrams. The left-hand-side diagram shows the whole cost of services. The right-hand-side one uses additional separator axes in order to show global costs per GPI Cluster.

Service Providers expose a certificate with Green values for clusters and, on demand, for single GPIs. *Service Consumer* can use the Certificate in different ways, namely, "Select the service":

1. Having a "better" Certificate in terms of global cost.
2. According to an analysis of costs of the clusters (e.g., select service with lowest cost for IT cluster).
3. According to an analysis of cost of the single GPI, e.g., select service that has lowest cost in storage occupancy.

We notice that a cost is always related to an acceptance *range* from the customer (not related to an absolute point or exact value) because an absolute category of service costs for all kinds of application domains cannot be created. Moreover, even for a given category of services (e.g., scientific computation services), costs cannot be evaluated for the single service in an absolute way but rather only in a *comparative* way, by comparing services having the same functionality. In order to select the most suitable service for the specific customer, some more detailed analysis of the causes of a cost can be performed at the cluster level or even at the single GPI level. The level of analysis the customer can perform depends on the *provider/customer relationship* and on market considerations. For example, the level can depend on the consumer's goals in terms of cost reduction. So, for instance a provider can expose a Green Certificate analyzable at the global level only if he wants to provide the service as a black box executed at his site on his IT infrastructure. Conversely, if he allows a service to be deployed on the customer's site, he should expose the Green Certificate with details at the strategic and tactic levels only, while providing no details of the GPIs regarding the operational level.

Finally, some customers might want to know the details of the area where they are expending for energy: so the detail of analysis level will be eventually decided on a market convenience basis. A contract negotiation will be the basis for admitted/available levels of analysis.

In order to support and aid the creation of green certificates, an XML schema has been created. This schema specifies the structure and acceptable values of the elements of GCs and can be used by editors to validate them. Moreover, we have created two XSLT transformations for the green certificates. XSLT transformations allow the automated generation of HTML or PDF documents from XML. On the one hand, we have created a "document XLST", that transforms a GC into a human readable document with a set of tables where the values of the GPIs are shown. On the other hand, we have created a "Graphical Representation XSLT" that shows the Kiviat diagram of this certificate using a set of APIs and functions for image generation provided online freely by Google as a service.

A sample GC with the results generated by the transformations can be found at: http://www.isa.us.es/uploads/GAMES/TranformationDemo.html.

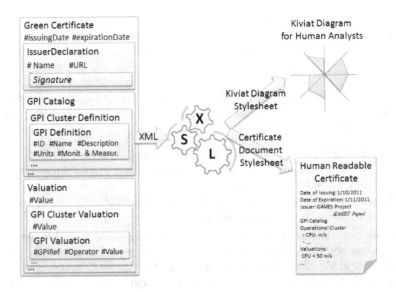

Fig. 5. Structure of GCs and transformations through XSLT to different document formats

4.2   Integration of the Green Certificate with the WS-* Standards Stack

A set of standards have been promoted by different organizations (such as the W3C, or OASIS) for the specification of functional and non-functional properties of services. On the functional side, the main standard is WSDL, that allows describing the set of operations, and input/output data formats of services. On the non-functional side, there are various proposals usually called the WS-* standards stack, but we will focus on WS-Policy and WS-Agreement. On the one hand, WS-Policy [11] is a W3C recommendation that provides a framework for expressing domain-specific capabilities, requirements, and general characteristics of web services, named policies. Those policies can be inserted in the WSDL contract of the service allowing providers to advertise specific non-functional properties of their services. From the client perspective, those policies allow for a more precise and enriched discovery and selection of services based on such non-functional properties. On the other hand, WS-Agreement [1] is a specification by the Object Grid Forum that aims at enabling the creation of offers and electronic contracts between service providers and customers. WS-Agreement documents contain a set of *guarantee terms*, which specify guarantees on the values of the non-functional properties of the services affected by the agreement. The specific XML language in which guarantee terms are expressed is left open in the specification, thus GCs could be used to specify the energy consumption costs associated to the service as a guarantee of the contract or offer.

The use of XML as the underlying format for GCs and the specification of an XML schema for describing their structure enable a seamless integration of our proposal with the WS-* standards stack we have created an the creation of Green Certificates.

As a demonstration of the applicability of the proposal and its compatibility with WS-Agreement and WS-Policy, a sample WS-Agreement contract and WSDL interface definition enriched with GCs for specifying non-functional properties of services are available at http://www.isa.us.es/uploads/GAMES/Agreement-GC.xml and http://www.isa.us.es/uploads/GAMES/WSDL-GC.xml respectively. Those examples demonstrate that the framework proposed in this paper can be applied to service selection scenarios. However the integration of the GC into current selection algorithms and tools and its application on simulations scenarios is proposed as future work.

5   Conclusions

The paper has described a method for energy consumption analysis, and developed the concept of Green Certificate. GPIs have been presented which enable evaluating energy consumption in services starting from the analysis of the overall resources used/required by the service. The organizational factors related to a service lifecycle have also been considered, analyzing in particular the case in which services selection from the providers/customers can be augmented by using analysis tools to evaluate the GC exposed for the service as an energy certificate. The concepts of GPIs and GC for energy-awareness can be pursued in several directions. First, the GC schema can be related to service in a more complex yet significant way by providing formulas to split costs of GPIs into elementary costs. In GAMES, further work will also consider tagging the services provided by data centers with their technical and business characteristics, form the IT infrastructure and facilities, to strategic and control issues contributing to energy consumption associated to a service.

Acknowledgments. We received support by the European Commission (FEDER) project SETI (TIN2009-07366), by the project ISABEL (P07-TIC-2533) funded by the Andalusia local Government, and by the GAMES project (http://www.green-datacenters.eu/), partly funded by the European Commission's IST activity of the 7th Framework Program (contract ICT-248514). This work expresses the opinions of the authors and not necessarily those of the European Commission. The Commission is not liable for any use that may be made of the information contained in this work.

References

1. Andrieux, A., Czajkowski, K., Dan, A., Keahey, K., Ludwig, H., Nakata, T., Pruyne, J., Rofrano, J., Tuecke, S., Xu, M.: Web services agreement specification (ws-agreement). Specification from the Open Grid Forum (OGF) 03 (2007)
2. Bertoncini, M., Pernici, B., Salomie, I., Wesner, S.: GAMES: Green Active Management of Energy in IT Service Centres. In: Soffer, P., Proper, E. (eds.) CAiSE Forum 2010. LNBIP, vol. 72, pp. 238–252. Springer, Heidelberg (2011)
3. Cappiello, C., Fugini, M.G., Gangadharan, G.R., Ferreira, A.M., Pernici, B., Plebani, P.: First-Step toward Energy-Aware Adaptive Business Processes. In: Meersman, R., Dillon, T., Herrero, P. (eds.) OTM 2010. LNCS, vol. 6428, pp. 6–7. Springer, Heidelberg (2010)
4. David, F.R.: How companies define their mission. Long Range Planning 22(1), 90–97 (1989)
5. Drucker, P.F.: Management Challenges in the 21st Century, 1st edn. HarperBusiness (1999)
6. Brooks, F.P.: The Mythical Man-Month: Essays on Software Engineering. Anniversary Edition. Addison-Wesley (1995)
7. Fugini, M., Gangadharan, G.R., Pernici, B.: Designing and managing sustainable IT service systems. In: Competitive and Sustainable Manufacturing, Product and Services (APMS) Conference, Cernobbio, Italy, October 11-13 (2010)
8. Kipp, A., Jiang, T., Fugini, M.: Green metrics for energy-aware IT systems. In: CISIS, pp. 241-248 (2011)
9. O'Brien, J.A., Marakas, G.M.: Management Information Systems. McGraw-Hill (2011)
10. Sekiguchi, S., Itoh, S., Sato, M., Nakamura, H.: Service aware metric for energy efficiency in green data centers (2009),
    http://www.iea.org/work/2009/standards/Sekiguchi.pdf
11. Vedamuthu, A.S., Orchard, D., Hirsch, F., Hondo, M., Yendluri, P., Boubez, T., Yalçinalp, Ü.: Web services policy 1.5 framework. W3C Recommendation (September 2007)
12. Williams, J., Curtis, L.: Green: The new computing coat of arms? IT Professional 1(10), 12–16 (2007)
13. Harizopoulos, S., Shah, M., Ranganathan, P.: Energy efficiency: The new holy grail of data management systems research. In: Proc. 4th Biennial Conference on Innovative Data Systems Research, CIDR (2009)
14. Tiwari, V., Malik, S., Wolfe, A.: Power analysis of embedded software: A first step towards software power minimization. IEEE Trans. on VLSI Systems 2, 437–445 (1994)
15. Ferreira, A.M., Kritikos, K., Pernici, B.: Energy-Aware Design of Service-Based Applications. In: Baresi, L., Chi, C.-H., Suzuki, J. (eds.) ICSOC-ServiceWave 2009. LNCS, vol. 5900, pp. 99–114. Springer, Heidelberg (2009)

Uncertainty Interval Temporal Sequences Extraction

Asma Ben Zakour[1,2], Sofian Maabout[1],
Mohamed Mosbah[1], and Marc Sistiaga[2]

[1] LaBRI, University of Bordeaux, CNRS UMR 5800, France
[2] 2MoRO Solutions, Bidart, France

Abstract. Searching for frequent sequential patterns has been used in several domains. We note that times granularities are more or less important with regards to the application domain. In this paper we propose a frequent *interval time sequences* (ITS) extraction technique from discrete temporal sequences using a sliding window approach to relax time constraints. The extracted sequences offer an interesting overview of the original data by allowing a temporal leeway on the extraction process. We formalize the ITS extraction under classical time and support constraints and conduct some experiments on synthetic data for validating our proposal.

1 Introduction

Frequent sequence extraction was introduced by Agrawal and Srikant in [3] by extending their *Apriori* algorithm for computing frequent sets proposed in [2]. For the frequent sequences extraction process, events occurrence chronology is more or less important with regard to the knowledge to extract or to the application domain. Sometimes, relaxing time constraints extraction allows bringing forward useful information. We propose to *merge* temporally close and consecutive events (associated to a discrete timestamp) into an unique set of simultaneous events associated with an interval timestamp. This interval reflects an uncertainty on the occurrence time of events. It is managed by a window size fixed by users. This work is motivated by an industrial application. It concerns the prediction of aeronautic equipments maintenance tasks by analyzing aircrafts lives data. For example, for an aircrafts lives data on which V_i refers to the flight i and M_j refers to the maintenance task j, we consider $\mathcal{S} = \{S_1, S_2\}$ a set of historic sequences such that: $S_1 = \langle (0, V_1)(1, V_2)(2, V_3)(5, M_1) \rangle$, $S_2 = \langle (0, V_1)(1, V_3)(2, V_2)(6, M_1) \rangle$ and a minimal support constraint equal to 2 sequences and a window size equal to 1. Our method will bring forward the following frequent sequence: $\langle ([0,0]V_1)([1,2]V_2 \ V_3)([5,6]M_1) \rangle$. It means that "When the flight V_1 is done, the flights V_2 and V_3 are done *in any oder* between one and two time unit after V_1, *i.e.*, they occur in the time interval $[1, 2]$. Then, the maintenance task M_1 is done in the time interval $[5, 6]$ after V_1". So merging of V_2 and V_3 are at the coast of an *uncertainty* of events occurrences. Related methods (some of them are presented in section 2) do not allow extracting such information. For instance, the

S. Dua et al. (Eds.): ICISTM 2012, CCIS 285, pp. 259–270, 2012.

GSP algorithm proposed in [13] applied on the sequences of the previous example with equivalent support constraint and window size, extracts the following frequent sequence: $\langle (V_1)(V_2\ V_3)(M_1) \rangle$. It has the same events chronology as us, but does not provide any temporal information and means: " The flight V_1 is done, it is followed by flights V_2 and V_3 done in any order on a 1 depth time interval, they are themselves followed by the application of the maintenance task M_1". This frequent sequence cannot be efficiently used by an aeronautic expert which aims to reduce maintenance cost and aircraft interruptions by predicting maintenance task application moment since the sequence does not provide any temporal information.

Paper Organization. The following section presents a concise overview of related works, especially the difference between our method and other approaches extracting interval timestamped sequences. Then, we formally define the semantics of sequences with uncertainty time intervals. Section 4 details the extraction process. We conclude our work by comparing our approach with an existing method (i.e the *GSPM* algorithm proposed in [9]). Finally, we present some avenues for future works.

2   Related Work

Several works found in the literature deal with grouping events and frequent interval sequences extraction. The method proposed in [11] groups some sequences events by using a sliding window. Grouping is performed during a pre-processing step, and then an extraction algorithm is applied on the merged sequences. However, grouped events are timestamped with a discrete time reference that is an arbitrary choice motivated by treatment simplicity. We consider that a group's discrete timestamp is a loss of events occurring information. Moreover, applying the sliding window on a pre-processing phase increases the size of initial sequences (several grouping possibilities for the same sequence) which sets an ambiguity on support counting. Several works have been proposed extracting such frequent sequences considering interval timestamped sequences as initial data. It is important to note that all approaches described below consider an interval timestamp as a during time which event occurs. That is the point which distinguishes those methods from ours which considers the timestamp interval as an *uncertainty* of the exact moment of event occurrence it is associated with.

The method presented in [6] extracts frequent sequences by using an *A Priori* like algorithm. It first identifies frequent patterns apart from timestamps. Then, for an extracted frequent pattern, it intersects intervals events occurrences in order to provide a succession of intervals associated with the frequent sequence.

In [8], a timestamped sequence is represented by a hypercube whose axes are the sequence events. The similarity between sequences is expressed by hypercubes intersection volume. Sequences are grouped using this similarity. If enough sequences are grouped, then a representative sequence is extracted and considered frequent pattern.

Extraction algorithms presented in [14,4] use Allen's interval theory [1] which identifies thirteen interval relationships. A *PrefixSpan* algorithm [10] like extraction is applied on discrete timestamped sequences. Both algorithms results consist in relationships sequences between events and not on timestamped sequences. The closest work to ours is [9]. The authors extract frequent sequences with interval timestamps from discrete timestamped sequences. They use a *level function*, which is actually a non sliding window, so that temporally close events are grouped by applying that function.

Concerning the extraction technique itself, we note two main procedures: the first one is levelwise, or breadth first, like *A priori* and has been used, for instance, in [13,6] and [12]. The second one uses a *divide to conquer* strategy by progressively reducing the search spaces and selecting at each step the frequent 1-patterns. Each such selected 1-pattern is concatenated to a frequent k-pattern to build a frequent k+1-sequence. This second strategy has been used in e.g., [9,10,4,5,14] and [7]. It turned out to be more efficient on data parsing and on computing time. We adopt this second method for applying our algorithm which is inspired by *PrefixSpan* proposed in [10].

3   Definition

First we define simple temporal sequences as formulated in several works dealing with extraction of frequent sequences, for instance [9,5,10].

Consider $\omega = \{e_1, e_2, \ldots, e_k\}$ a set of events. A transaction is defined as a set of simultaneous events. A temporal sequence is a succession of chronologically ordered transactions. On a temporal sequence each transaction is associated with a discrete timestamp. It is denoted by $S = \langle (t_1, I_1), (t_2, I_2) \ldots (t_n, I_n) \rangle$, $n \in \mathbb{N}$ where $\forall 1 \leq i \leq n$, where I_i is a transaction and t_i its timestamp. A timed sequences database is a set of temporal sequences where each of them is identified by a unique identifier denoted by *id_sequence*. The support of a sequence S' in a database sequences D is the percentage of sequences from D which contain S'. It is denoted by $support_D(S')$. S' is said frequent if its support is greater than a minimum threshold *minsupp* fixed by users.

Now, we define interval temporal sequences. We recall that sequences with interval timestamps consider the transaction's interval as an uncertainty during which the transaction's events can occur. If we consider for example the 1-sequence $S = \langle ([t_b, t_e], e) \rangle$, intuitively S means that: "the event e occurs punctually between moments t_d and t_e in time".

Definition 1 (Interval Temporal Sequences (ITS)). *A n length interval temporal sequence S (ITS) is denoted by:*

$$S = \langle ([m_1, M_1], I_1), ([m_2, M_2], I_2) \ldots ([m_n, M_n], I_n) \rangle$$

where $([m_i, M_i], I_i)$ is a transaction with interval timestamp such that:

- $\forall 1 \leq i \leq n : m_i \leq occurrence\_time(e_j) \leq M_i$. *for all $e_j \in I_i$;*
- *An interval temporal sequence is coherent if for each successive transactions I_i and I_{i+1}, $m_i \leq m_{i+1}$ and $M_i \leq M_{i+1}$.*

Example 1. Consider a ITS $S1 = \langle([0,1], A)([2,2], BC)\rangle$ it means that: "A occurs with a random occurrence in the interval $[0,1]$, and B and C occur simultaneously at the earliest 1 temporal unit after A and at the latest 2 temporal units after". $S2 = \langle([0,3], A)([1,2], B)([2,5], C)\rangle$ is not a coherent STI since the upper bound of the second interval is lower than the upper bound of the first interval$(2 < 3)$.

Simple temporal sequences have discrete timestamps, so transactions are associated with *punctual* temporal point on which events occur without any uncertainty. Then, we can say that each temporal sequence with discrete timestamps $S = \langle(t_1, I_1) \ldots (t_n, I_n)\rangle$ can be considered an interval temporal sequence with null interval depths (null uncertainty) and is denoted by:

$$STI(S) = \langle([t_1, t_1], I_1), \ldots, ([t_n, t_n], I_n)\rangle$$

In order to fit temporal parameters on extracted sequences and patterns formulation needs, we consider temporal constraints. They aim to: set a maximum threshold of uncertainty, to control minimum and maximum temporal delay between successive transactions and to control the whole pattern length.

Let SI be an n length ITS. SI satisfies the temporal constraints: *mingap*, *maxgap*, *min_whole_interval*, *max_whole_interval* and the sliding window ws if and only if $\forall\ 1 \le i \le n$:

- *Gap* control minimum and maximum temporal delay between two successive transactions such that:

$$mingap \le (m_i - M_{i-1}) \le maxgap$$

- *Whole_interval* control minimum and maximum whole sequence length such that:

$$min\_whole\_interval \le |m_1 - M_n| \le max\_whole\_interval$$

- *Sliding Window* enable grouping successive transaction's events into a same one timestamped with an interval. The size of the sliding window fixes a maximum group spreading and so the maximum interval width. So the window size regulates a maximum uncertainty threshold such that:

$$|M_i - m_i| \le ws$$

Example 2. Consider the ITS $SI = \langle([0,1], A)([2,3], BC)([6,10], D)\rangle$ and the time constraints *mingap* and *maxgap* respectively equal to 2 and 3. SI does not satisfy *mingap* because of $m_2 - M_1 = 2 - 1 = 1 \le 2$. On the other hand, SI satisfies *maxgap* since for all its successive transactions the maxgap constraint is satisfied $(m_2 - M_1 = 2 - 1 \le 3\ ; m_3 - M_2 = 6 - 3 \le 3)$. For a sliding window size equal to 3, SI is not a valid sequence since $M_3 - m_3 = 10 - 6 \le 3$. For a sliding window constraint fixed to 4, SI satisfies it by all its timestamps.

Those temporal constraints allow to managing temporal parameters into an ITS; They control minimum (respectively maximum) temporal leeway between two successive transactions since the correlation between both of them can be meaningful. Actually, minimum (respectively maximum) gap avoids considering too close (respectively too far) transactions successive. In the same way, the *whole_interval* constraint fixes a minimum (respectively maximum) threshold for the whole sequence duration in order to maintain the meaningful correlation between all sequence's transactions. On the other hand, the sliding window manages events grouping and uncertainty of their occurrences.

In the following, we define a $\Diamond$ operator that merges successive transactions in a sequence. For an ITS sequence, $\Diamond$ starts from a position j and merges spreading transactions into a window size. The operator provides an ITS sequence in which transactions contain merged events and are timestamped with grouped transaction's union intervals.

Definition 2. Let $SI = \langle([m_1, M_1], I_1)([m_2, M_2], I_2) \ldots ([m_n, M_n], I_n)\rangle$ be an ITS, $j < n$ an integer and a window size ws. Then the $\Diamond_{ws}$ operator is defined by:

$$\Diamond_{ws}(SI, j) = SI' = \langle([m'_1, M'_1], I'_1)([m'_2, M'_2], I'_2) \ldots ([m'_n, M'_n], I'_k)\rangle$$

- where $\forall 1 \leq i < j: ([m'_i, M'_i], I'_i) = ([m_i, M_i], I_i)$;
- $\exists 1 \leq l_j \leq l_{j+1}, \ldots l_i \ldots \leq l_{k-1} \leq n$ such that:

  - $I'_j = \cup_{p=j}^{l_j} I_p; \ldots I'_i = \cup_{p=l_{i-1}+1}^{l_i} I_p; \ldots I'_k = \cup_{p=l_{k-1}+1}^{l_n} I_p,$
  - $m'_j = m_j, M'_j = M_{l_j}, \ldots, m'_i = m_{l_{i-1}+1}, M'_i = M_{l_i}, \ldots m'_k = m_{l_{k-1}+1},$
    $M'_k = M_n$
  - $|m_j - M_{l_j}| \leq ws; \ldots |m_{l_{i-1}+1} - M_{l_i}| \leq ws; \ldots |m_{l_{k-1}+1} - M_n| \leq ws.$

Example 3. Consider $SI = \langle([0, 2], A)([1, 2], B)([3, 5], C)([4, 6], D)\rangle$ and a window size $ws = 3$. Then $\Diamond_3(SI, 1) = \langle([0, 2], AB)([3, 6], CD)\rangle$. Th Events from the first (respectively last) couple of transactions are grouped and their intervals merged. Since both transactions are spread into the window size and $(2 - 0) \leq 3$ (respectively $(6 - 3) \leq 3$)). We note that $\Diamond_3(SI, 2) = SI$. Actually, for the start grouping position 2, the second and third transactions cannot be merged since their unified interval is too large regards to the window size. Finally, $\Diamond_3(SI, 3) = \langle([0, 2], A)([1, 2], B)([3, 6], CD)\rangle$ and $\Diamond_3(SI, 4) = SI$.

Now we define the $\overset{\frown}{\Diamond}$ operator which for a n length ITS and a sliding window size ws provides a set of ITS's. It is the set of results of all $\Diamond$ operator applications on a n length for j's values varying into $[1, n - 1]$. Intuitively $\overset{\frown}{\Diamond}$ merges successive transactions by sliding the window size along the input sequence. It provides the set of all summarized sequences that contain the input one.

Definition 3. *Consider* $SI = \langle([m_1, M_1], I_1) \ldots ([m_n, M_n], I_n)\rangle$ *and ws a window size. Then,* $\forall 1 \leq i \neq n$ *and* $SI_i = \Diamond_{ws}(SI, i)$ *we define* $\widehat{\Diamond}_{ws}$ *such that:*

$$\widehat{\Diamond}_{ws}(SI) = \{SI_1, SI_2, \ldots, SI_{n-1}\}$$

Example 4. Consider $SI = \langle([0,2], A)([1,2], B)([3,4], C)([4,6], D)\rangle$ and $ws = 3$. Then $\widehat{\Diamond}_3(SI) = \{\langle([0,2], AB)\ ([3,6], CD)\rangle, \langle([0,2], A)([1,4], BC)\ ([4,6]D)\rangle, \langle([0,2], A)([1,2], B)([3,6]CD)\rangle\}$.

Now we define the containment relationship between ITSs. Intuitively, an interval temporal sequence SI contains another interval temporal sequence SI', if and only if events of each transaction of SI' are contained in one (or successive) transaction(s) of SI and the SI''s transaction's interval implies the (the combination of) SI transaction(s) interval(s). Note that the transactions chronology order must be preserved.

Definition 4. *Let SI and SI' be two interval temporal sequences. Let $SI = \langle([m_1, M_1], I_1), \ldots, ([m_n, M_n], I_n)\rangle$ and $SI' = \langle([m'_1, M'_1], I'_1) \ldots ([m'_k, M'_k], I'_k)\rangle$. Let ws be a window size. SI' contains SI, denoted by $SI' \sqsupseteq SI$ iff:*

- $\exists 1 \leq l_{d1} \leq l_{f1} \leq l_{d2} \leq l_{f2}, \ldots, \leq l_{dk} \leq l_{fk} = n$;
- $\exists 1 \leq i1 \leq i2 \ldots \leq in \leq k$;
- $I'_{i1} \supseteq \sqcup_{p=l_{d1}}^{l_{f1}} I_p, \ldots I'_{iu} \supseteq \sqcup_{p=l_{du}}^{l_{fu}} I_p, \ldots I'_{in} \supseteq \sqcup_{p=l_{dn}}^{n} I_p$;
- $[0, (M_{f1} - m_{d1})] \supseteq [0, (M'_{i1} - m'_{i1})], \ldots [(m_{du} - M_{f(u-1)}), (M_{fu} - m_{d(u-1)})] \supseteq [(m'_{iu} - M'_{i(u-1)}), (M'_{iu} - m'_{i(u-1)})], \ldots [(m_{dn} - M_{f(n-1)}), (M_{fn} - m_{f(n-1)})] \supseteq [(m'_{ip} - M'_{i(p-1)}), (M'_{in} - m'_{i(n-1)})]$.

Example 5. Consider $SI_1 = \langle([0,2]A)([3,4], B)([5,6]C)\rangle$, $SI_2 = \langle([0,4]AB)\rangle$ and $SI_3 = \langle([0,2]A)([3,6]BC)\rangle$. $SI_1 \sqsupseteq SI_2$ since $[0,4]$ implies $[0,2]$ and $[3,4]$ and $SI_1 \sqsupseteq SI_3$. However, $SI_1 \not\sqsupseteq SI_4 = \langle([0,3]A)([2,6]BC)\rangle$ since $[0,2]$ does not imply $[0,3]$.

Proposition 1. *Let ws be a window size, a discrete timestamped sequence S and an ITS SI. S contains SI if and only if there exist $SI' \in \widehat{\Diamond}_{ws}(STI(S))$ and $SI' \supseteq SI$. Where $\subseteq$ is the commune inclusion relation between sequences (e.g. [3]).*

Now, we will define the interval temporal sequence support into a simple sequences database. Intuitively, it is the number of sequence in the collection that at least contain once the interval sequence.

Definition 5. *The support of a STI SI in a collection D is defined by:*

$$supp_D(SI) = |\{S \in D \mid S \sqsupseteq SI\}|$$

For simplification reason, $supp_D(SI)$ will be denoted by $supp(SI)$.

4   ITS Extraction

This section describes the extraction process of frequent interval temporal sequences from discrete temporal sequences. We detail the *ITS-PS* (interval temporal sequences- PrefixSpan) algorithm. It gradually groups close events into a single transaction by applying a sliding window. This merging allows to joining dissociated events and associates to the group an interval that sweeps all their dissociated occurrences. The algorithm applies a *pattern growth* [10] approach using a vertical search based on database projection. First, *ITS-PS* identifies the set of 1-sequences (frequent events) denoted by $L_1 = \{S; S = \langle([m = 0, M = 0], e)\rangle; support(e) \geq minsupp\}$. Then, recursively frequent $i + 1$-sequences are extracted from a i-sequence. Each recursive step i applies two steps:

- First step compute a new projection of the sequences database D' by each 1-ITS of L_1 (L_1 the set of frequent 1-ITS computed at the $i-1$ iteration). D' is the new search space for the possible continuations of the pattern extracted at the previous iteration.
- Second step identifies the set of frequent 1-ITS in the search provided by the first step. Each 1-ITS is concatenated to the pattern extracted at the $i - 1$ iteration to provide a frequent i-pattern. Then, a new iteration is executed.

The recursive process continues until one of the two following conditions is satisfied: (1) the projection (first step) provides an empty search space (2) No frequent 1-ITS is identifies (second step 2: L_1 is empty).

As the algorithm *GSPM* [9], our algorithm uses the pattern growth strategy. However, *ITS-PS* applies the sliding window and makes a difference on two points: (1) the identification of frequent 1-ITS and (2) the search space projection. Concerning the 1-ITS identification, the application of the sliding window allows associating shifted occurrences of the same event (occurring in different sequences), if the delay between the two farthest occurrences is at the most equals to the window size. This modification relaxes grouping time constraint and is managed by the sliding window.

Example 6. If we consider the following frequent sequence $SI = \langle([0, 0]A)\rangle$, a *minsupp* constraint equal to 2, $ws = 2$ and a search space $\mathcal{D}$ projection over SI equal to $\mathcal{D}|_{SI} = \{\langle(1, B)(2, CD)\rangle, \langle(2, D)(3, B)(4, F)\rangle\}$, two frequent events are identified: $([1, 3]B)$ and $([2, 2]D)$. Actually, the pattern $([1, 3]B)$ means that event B is frequent in $\mathcal{D}$ and B appearance varies over 2 temporal units $(3 - 1)$ after A.

Concerning search space projection, we extend the process by using a restricted (to the window size) backward projection in order take into account the slide of the window and consider the backward exploration of events. Such projection allows considering locally (with regard to the window size) disordered events. In order to avoid multiple extraction of the same ITS k-pattern from an

ITS (k-1)-pattern, the backward exploration does not take into account event already processed as the last element of a k-pattern from the same $(k-1)$-pattern. So we define a sequence projection over a 1-ITS.

Definition 6. *Let* $\omega = \{e_1, e_2 \ldots e_m\}$ *be an ordered set of events,* $S = \langle (t_1, I_1) \ldots (t_n, I_n) \rangle$ *be a temporal sequence and* $([t_m, t_M], e_r)$ *an 1-ITS. Assume there exists* $(1 \le j \le n)$ *such that* $e_r \in I_j$ *and* $t_j \in [m, M]$. *Then:*

– *The prefix on* S *w.r.t* $([m, M], e_r)$ *is the subsequence of* S *appearing before e It is denoted by:*

$$wprefix(S, e_r, t_j) = \langle (t_1, I_1), (t_2, I_2) \ldots (t_j, I_j) \rangle$$

– *The suffix of* S *w.r.t* $([m, M], e_r)$ *is the subsequence of* S *containing the possible continuities of* $([m, M], e_r)$

$$wsuffix(S, e_r, [m, M]) = \langle (t_k, I'_k) \ldots (t_p, I'_p \setminus \{e_r\}) \ldots (t_u, I'_u) \ldots (t_n, I_n) \rangle$$

such that:
1. $t_p \in [m, M]$;
2. $e_r \in I_p$;
3. $t_k \le (t_i - ws)$ *and* $t_{k-1} \le (t_i - ws)$;
4. $t_u \le (t_i + ws)$ *and* $t_{u+1} \le (t_i + ws)$;
5. $I'_l = I_l \setminus \{e_1, e_2, \ldots, e_{(r-1)}\}$ $(k \le l \le u)$.

Let $\mathcal{D}$ *be a temporal sequences database and* $\alpha = \langle ([m, M], e) \rangle$ *be a frequent 1-sequence. The* $\mathcal{D}$ *projection over* α *is defined by:*

$$\mathcal{D}|_\alpha = \{SI \mid SI = wsuffix(S, e, [m, M]), S \in \mathcal{D}\} \text{ and } ([m, M], e) \sqsubseteq S$$

Example 7. In the previous example, if we consider the frequent event $([1, 3]B)$, the extracted pattern will be $SI = \langle ([0, 0]A)([1, 3]B) \rangle$. The projection defined by our method takes into account all events around the last one of SI, it provides the following search space: $\mathcal{D}|_{SI} = \{\langle (1, CD) \rangle, \langle (-1, D)(1, F) \rangle\}$. In the new database, the 1-ITS $([-1, 1]D)$ is considered as frequent since the associated event D appears in two sequences and the timestamps associated with both occurrences are close w.r.t the window size: $1 - (-1) = 2 \le 2$. And then, the pattern extracted became $SI' = \langle ([0, 0]A)([2, 2]D)([1, 3]B) \rangle$ which is represented by the following sequence $SI' = \langle ([0, 0]A)([1, 3]BD) \rangle$. In the other hand, during the extraction of the pattern $\langle ([0, 0]A)([2, 2]D) \rangle$, the event B is not taken into account on the backward projection so as not to be extracted twice SI'.

This section presented the *ITS-PS* that provides frequent temporal interval sequences using a *pattern growth* strategy. The algorithm extracts $(k+1)$-sequences from a k-sequence by progressive reduction of the search database. The temporal intervals are made by using the sliding window on two level of the extraction process: the identification of frequent events and the search space projection.

5   Experiments

In this section we compare patterns extracted by our method with patterns extracted by the *GSPM* algorithm presented in [9]. Both algorithms are based on the *PrefixSpan* method. They are different because of the application of distinctive grouping method. Actually, *GSPM* is based on the application of an increments function unlike the *ITS-PS* which uses a sliding window. For a meaningful comparison, when the sliding window is fixed to a *ws* value, the *GSPM* step function is set to $f(t) = \lfloor 1/ws \rfloor$. The following example explains the *GSPM* process. More details can be found in [9].

Example 8. Consider the database $\{S_1 = \langle (0, A)(1, B) (2, C)(3, F)(4, B) (6, G) \rangle,$ $S_2 = \langle (0, A)(1, C)(2, B)(3, D)(4, F)(5, G) \rangle\}$, a threshold support $minsupp = 2$, a sliding window $ws = 2$ and a step function $f(t) = \lfloor t/2 \rfloor$. Timestamps interval provided by *GSPM* are in the form $[2 \times f(t), 2 \times (f(t) + 1)[$. The extraction algorithm identifies first the following frequent 1-sequences A, B, C, F and G (They are timestamped with null intervals). If we consider the frequent B, the projection provides: $\{S'_1 = \langle (1, C)(2, F)(3, B)(5, G) \rangle, S''_1 = \langle (2, G) \rangle, S'_2 = \langle (2, F)(3, G) \rangle\}$. In this search space, the pattern $([2, 4[, F)$ is identified as frequent since (1) F appears twice: in S'_1 and in S'_2 and (2) for the both occurrences, $f(t) = \lfloor t/2 \rfloor = 1$. Then, in order to identify the interval timestamp to be associated with F, we apply $[2.f(t), 2.(f(t) + 1)[$ which provides $[2, 4[$. In the same projection, G appears in 3 sequences. In S''_1 and S'_2 with $f(t) = 1$, while in S'_1 its function step value correspond to $f(t) = 2$. So, only the 1-sequence $([2, 4[, G)$ is extracted and $([4, 6[, G)$ is not considered as so.

Both algorithms are implemented in JAVA language using a *PrefixSpan* version[1] proposed in [5]. The implementation is done on a Windows 7(64) machine, Intel(R) Core(TM) 3 CPU 2.40 GHz with 3 GB RAM.

  We compare both extraction results using synthetic data. Data sequences have 7 different events, the average deviation between successive transactions is equal to 3 time units and a sequence average length equal to 15 transactions. During extraction executions the time constraints *mingap* (respectively *maxgap*, *min_whole_interval* and *max_whole_interval*) are fixed to 0 (resp. 1, 0 and 15). Synthetic sequences database contains 12 sequences since we focus our experimentation on the nature and the number of results and not on the execution time, that is why we choose a small sequences database. Actually, in this paper, our goal is focused on validating our algorithm by checking the relevance of its extracted frequent patterns regards to our interested application domain. Considering the time constraints relaxation employed by our approach, we expect that the *ITS-PS* algorithms provide more information. figure 1 shows provided results regards to some parameters variation. For each one of the parameters values combination, the number of patterns extracted by both methods is measured and for each result maximal sequences are computed. figures 1(a) (respectively 1(b), 1(c) and 1(d) illustrate the variation of results size according to different

---

[1] http://www.philippe-fournier-viger.com/spmf/index.php

grouping values. They show that the number of results provided by *ITS-PS* is greater than the number of patterns extracted by *GSPM*. Actually, the application of the sliding window gradually groups successive transactions and then considers all possible merging combinations. It also allows longer sequences extraction since more events combinations are considered as frequent in the data sequences. On the other hand, the backward projection employed by *ITS-PS* takes into account more continuation possibilities and so some events see their support growing up.

Table 1. i-sequences (L_i) extracted number by varying the window size, the step function depth and fixing *minsupp* to 0.4

	maximal GSPM patterns			STI-PS maximal						STI-PS patterns				
ws	L_1	L_2	L_3	L_1	L_2	L_3	L_4	L_5	L_6	L_2	L_3	L_4	L_5	L_6
1	13	21	1	17	39	14	0	0	0	21	0	14	0	0
2	11	16	5	7	47	44	3	0	0	3	19	3	0	0
3	9	12	5	7	53	96	26	3	0	0	30	26	3	0
4	8	12	6	7	53	108	62	9	1	0	23	34	8	1
5	9	13	2	7	55	133	75	9	1	0	26	42	13	1
6	9	14	4	7	52	98	88	38	7	0	26	20	27	7
7	9	19	3	7	51	115	88	21	4	0	24	29	12	4

table 1 details the number of k-patterns extracted by *ITS-PS* and *GSPM* for a fixed *minsupp* value (equal to 0.4) and different grouping values. We notice that when both methods provide the same patterns length results (correspondence between figure 1(a) and table 1), maximal sequences extracted by our approach are fewer than maximal patterns obtained by *GSPM*. Such situation is illustrated in Example 9. However, when the sequences returned by *ITS-PS* are longer than those provided by *GSPM*, *ITS-PS* maximal sequences are more than *GSPM*'s ones and majority represent longer patterns then those from maximal *GSPM* result. Finally, notice that the number of maximal sequences extracted by our approach is still similar to those extracted by *GSPM*.

Example 9. If we consider Example 8 then the longest maximal sequences extracted by *GSPM* are: $\langle([0,0[,B)([2,4[,F)\rangle, \langle([0,0[,G)\rangle, \langle([0,0[,A)\rangle, \langle([0,0[,C)\rangle$. The only one extracted by *STI_PS* is $\langle([0,2],ABC)([3,4],F)([5,6],G)\rangle$. The sequence $\langle([0,0[,B)([2,4[,F)\rangle$ extracted by *GSPM* means that "*F appears randomly in* $[2,4[$ *after B*". However, the sequence $\langle([0,2],ABC)([3,4],F)([5,6],G)\rangle$ provided by *STI_PS* means, among others, that *F appears in an* $[3-2=1,4-0=4]$ *after B*. Given that $[1,4]$ contains $[2,4[$, so we can say that the maximal sequence provided by our approach includes all maximal sequences extracted by *GSPM* by tolerating more uncertainty.

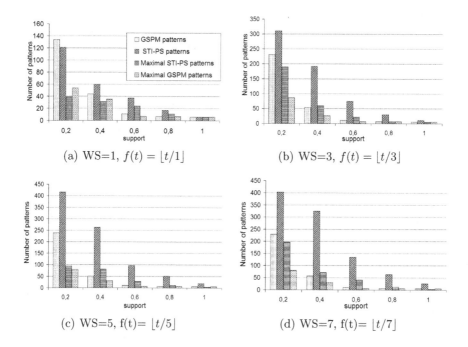

(a) WS=1, $f(t) = \lfloor t/1 \rfloor$ (b) WS=3, $f(t) = \lfloor t/3 \rfloor$

(c) WS=5, f(t)= $\lfloor t/5 \rfloor$ (d) WS=7, f(t)= $\lfloor t/7 \rfloor$

Fig. 1. Comparability of the number of extracted sequences by varying *minsupp*, the window size *ws* and the step function depth

6   Conclusion

This paper presents *ITS-PS*, a sequences extraction algorithm based on a sliding window and allowing time constraints relaxation. The sliding window gradually merges close transactions events by considering several merging combinations. The algorithm extracts interval temporal sequences from a collection of discrete temporal sequences. The interval timestamps express an uncertainty of the exact moment of transaction events occurrences. The uncertainty magnitude is managed by the size of sliding window fixed by the user. The implementation of our algorithm is inspired by that of [10]. We compared qualitatively the results of our method to those provided by the *GSPM* algorithm proposed in [9]. It turns that our algorithm provides more and longer sequences than *GSPM*.

Future work will first concern the optimization of maximal patterns extraction process. Indeed, due to our relaxation of the chronological sequence of events occurrences, we extract more sequences than other approaches. However, if we restrict the result to the maximal sequences, not only the size of our result is less than that of the other approaches but it encompasses it. From a practical viewpoint, it is not relevant to first extract all patterns and then select the maximal ones. Second, we plan to validate our method on an industrial application. It concerns the prognostic of complex system failure by extracting frequent patterns from operational data.

References

1. Allen, J.F.: Maintaining knowledge about temporal intervals. Communications of ACM 26 (1983)
2. Agrawal, R., Srikant, R.: Fast algorithms for mining association rules in large databases. In: Proceedings of VLDB Conference (1994)
3. Agrawal, R., Srikant, R.: Mining sequential patterns. In: Proceeding of ICDE Conference. IEEE Computer Society Press (1995)
4. Chen, Y., Jiang, J.C., Peng, W.C., Lee, S.: An efficient algorithm for mining time interval-based patterns in large database. In: Proceedings of the 19th ACM International Conference on Information and Knowledge Management (CIKM), pp. 49–58 (2010)
5. Fournier-Viger, P., Nkambou, R., Nguifo, E.M.: A knowledge discovery framework for learning task models from user interactions in intelligent tutoring systems. In: Proceeding of the 7th Mexican International Conference on Artificial Intelligence, pp. 765–778 (2008)
6. Giannotti, F., Nanni, M., Pedreschi, D., Pinelli, F.: Mining sequences with temporal annotations. In: Proceedings of the 2006 ACM Symposium on Applied Computing, SAC 2006, 593–597. ACM (2006)
7. Guyet, T., Quiniou, R.: Mining temporal patterns with quantitative intervals. In: Proceedings of The 4th International Workshop on Mining Complex Data. IEEE Computer Society (2008)
8. Guyet, T., Quiniou, R.: Extracting temporal patterns from interval-based sequences. In: Proceedings of IJCAI Conference, pp. 1306–1311 (2011)
9. Hirate, Y., Yamana, H.: Generalized sequential pattern mining with item intervals. JCP. Journal of Computers 1(3), 51–60 (2006)
10. Pei, J., Han, J., Mortazavi-Asl, B., Pinto, H., Chen, Q., Dayal, U., Hsu, M.: Prefixspan: Mining sequential patterns by prefix-projected growth. In: Proceedings of ICDE Conference, pp. 215–224 (2001)
11. Pham, Q., Raschia, G., Mouaddib, N., Saint-Paul, R., Benatallah, B.: Time sequence summarization to scale up chronology-dependent applications. In: Proceedings of CIKM Conference, pp. 1137–1146 (2009)
12. Rabatel, J., Bringay, S., Poncelet, P.: SO_MAD: SensOr Mining for Anomaly Detection in Railway Data. In: Perner, P. (ed.) ICDM 2009. LNCS, vol. 5633, pp. 191–205. Springer, Heidelberg (2009)
13. Srikant, R., Agrawal, R.: Mining sequential patterns: Generalizations and performance improvements. In: Proceedings of EDBT Conference, pp. 3–17 (1996)
14. Wu, S., Chen, Y.: Mining non-ambiguous temporal patterns for interval-based events. IEEE Trans. on Knowl. and Data Eng. 9, 742–758 (2007)

Enterprise Knowledge Management System: A Multi Agent Perspective

Deepak Dahiya[1], Mohit Gupta[2], and Pooja Jain[1]

[1] Jaypee University of Information Technology,
Waknaghat, Solan
{deepak.dahiya,pooja.jain}@juit.ac.in
[2] Infosys Ltd.,
mohit.gupta@infosys.com

Abstract.. In today's scenario, handling and managing of fast growing knowledge is very difficult which results in consuming more time for knowledge serving and therefore degrading the overall productivity. Therefore decision of choosing Multi-Agent system for implementing enterprise Knowledge Management (KM) results in reducing the time overhead for serving the relevant knowledge to the end-user by automatic communication between the agents. The main aim of this paper is to propose knowledge management system architecture for multi agents that will be helpful in disseminating knowledge to public sector organizations in a better way and thus enhancing the productivity. The knowledge management system architecture described in this paper also provides scalability, reusability and supports system adaptability. The paper proposes Multi Agent Enterprise KM System (MAEKMS) architecture.

Keywords: Knowledge Management (KM), Multi-Agent System, MAEKMS, Enterprise, Public Sector Unit (PSU), JADE.

1   Introduction

Knowledge Management (KM) [1, 2] is defined as to provide relevant information to the right people at right time. An agent can be defined as a software and/or hardware component of system which accomplishes tasks on behalf of its user. Agents are reactive, autonomous and co-operative in nature. They have the ability of knowledge based reasoning.

The knowledge management lifecycle starts with the create phase where new knowledge is created. Then the newly created knowledge is formalized and therefore stored in knowledge base according to the knowledge organizing mechanism. When knowledge is required, it can be searched and use relevant knowledge by accessing knowledge base. Finally knowledge is applied and further evolved into new knowledge. It also leads to further knowledge creation and completing the lifecycle.

Engineering can be considered as a knowledge-oriented industry. Even low weighted projects need thought, knowledge and skills from many sources which may

S. Dua et al. (Eds.): ICISTM 2012, CCIS 285, pp. 271–281, 2012.

include electronic media, documents, and people. Various Engineering firms are there who have been managing knowledge informally for years but the industry who is facing challenges today mean that most of the organizations now required a more structured and consistent approach to knowledge management[3]. Industries implementing projects are usually organized into stages with deadlines and there are various teams assigned to those projects. The problem is that capturing and reusing of knowledge learning from projects is measured to be difficult because teams are of dynamic in nature and may be dismissed before finishing point of the project and therefore gathered to the next project. These types of problems generally bound the information flow and can create obstacle to knowledge learning. This paper outlines an approach to assessing and implementing Knowledge Management using Multi-Agents. It highlights the importance of aligning KM initiatives to the business goals.

The rest of the paper is organized as follows. Section 2 provides the literature review and current techniques, comparisons of different KM frameworks and research related to implementing multi-agent KMS. This section also discusses the various tools for implementing multi-agents and then shows the features of JADE when compared with others. Section 3 discusses the proposed work on Multi Agent Enterprise Knowledge Management System (MAEKMS). It also discusses the motive of implementing the proposed architecture. In Section 4, detailed design of a multi agent knowledge management system for a Public Sector Unit (PSU) is described. This section also described how the functionalities like knowledge creation, knowledge extraction, knowledge reusability are working in the MAEKMS architecture. Section 5 discusses the implementation of new MAEKMS architecture for PSU. Section 6 contains the result and observations after implementing the proposed architecture. Finally, section 7 summarizes the conclusion and future work anticipated in this direction.

2   Related Work

Individual knowledge plays the important role in an organization. Individual knowledge management should be supported by the organizations by monitoring at knowledge workers' actions and move toward to manage their personal knowledge. Encouragement must be there for efficient KM behaviors in the organization. KM tool should help in enhancing the efficiency at work and should be able to help in managing time. KM tools consist of communities of practice by which people create networks of personal significant knowledge. KM within an organization can be empowered with coordination, collaboration, and cooperation.

A lot of researchers have proposed various KM frameworks where most of the frameworks are prescriptive in nature. Juan[4] described the framework by dividing into two parts:-Knowledge Agency and User Agency. Meso and Smith KMS Architecture[5] consists of functions, technology and knowledge. Nonaka and Takeouchi [6] Proposed on the basis of knowledge conversion(tacit-explicit). Hahn and Subramani [7] suggested two important considerations for managing knowledge i.e. locus of the knowledge and level of priori structure. Different techniques have been used to implement KMS. Intelligent agents are one of them [8]. Agents are proactive in nature as they can take the initiative at their own and complete their own goals. The autonomous behavior of the agents meets the required goal of this research because it can minimize the amount of work done by the employees when using a KM system. Another important issue is that agents can learn from their own experience. Consequently, agent systems are required to be more efficient because the agents get experience from their previous knowledge.

An agent can be defined as a software and/or hardware component of system who accomplishes tasks on behalf of its user [9-12]. Agents are reactive, autonomous and co-operative in nature. They have the ability of knowledge based reasoning. Agent technology is one of the best technologies when dealing with distributed and collaborative environment in knowledge management. Software agents are being used widely in software applications which range from small systems to large complex systems. Agent technology is the suitable technology for designing and implementing distributed system for KM.

Different agent-based architectures have been proposed to support activities related to KM [9-13]. Some architecture has been designed for the development of KMS. However, most of them focus on a particular domain and can only be used under specific circumstances. A lot of research and commercial organizations are involved in the realization of agent applications and a   considerable number of agent construction tools have been realized [10]. Some of the most interesting are Cougaar, JACK, 3APL, and Agent Factory, JADE[1,14,15].

3   Proposed Work on Multi Agent Enterprise Knowledge Management System (MAEKMS)

Our proposed multi agent enterprise knowledge management (MAEKM) system architecture is based on serving knowledge with the help of multi-Agent System. The salient feature of this architecture is its simplicity in nature. Our new architecture minimizes the time overhead required for knowledge serving. It provides smooth communication between agents which will guarantee to produce the desired result.

3.1   Motivation for the Work on MAEKMS for Public Sector

Traditionally, in generalized Public Sectors, it is very difficult to handle and manage the organization's   knowledge which results in:-

- More time consuming for knowledge serving queries
- Lack of appropriate knowledge
- Degradation of overall quality
- Lack of effective communication when dealing with customer knowledge queries

Therefore it has been decided to implement KM for Public Sector using Multi Agent System in a way such that to get rid of all the problems above and to produce the following result after implementation:-

- Smooth communication between agents
- Knowledge reusability by agent's past experience
- Reducing time overhead for knowledge serving

- Serve relevant knowledge at correct time
- Provides best possible solutions

3.2   Proposed Architecture of MAEKMS

In this architecture, agents communicate with each other and produce the result and serve the knowledge as fast as possible which results in enhancing the quality of services. In brief, our architecture's is unique in the following aspects:-

- **Simplicity in Nature:** Our proposed architecture is simple in the sense that management of the knowledge by the agents is done in a very simple and smooth manner and can be understand very easily.
- **Reducing Time Overhead for Knowledge Serving:** In the architecture, most of the work of knowledge serving is done automatically by the agents. Therefore knowledge will be served in rapid manner.
- **Automatic Computation Between Agents:** Automatic computation is done in this architecture at Agent's Inter-communication layer.
- **Reusability of the Knowledge by Agents:** In our proposed architecture, agents reuse their personal knowledge for the related queries if the requested query is very similar to the past queries.

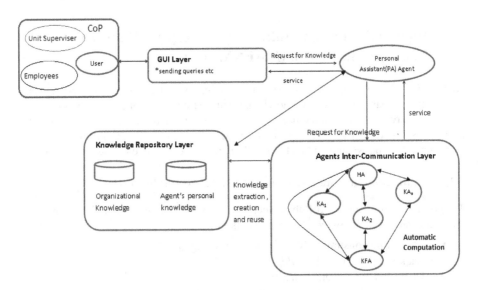

Fig. 1. General MAEKMS Architecture

The architecture consists of 4 layers:

    CoP Layer: Community of Practice layer consists of users, public employees etc.
    GUI Layer: It is the layer where information is send and receive by the user. At this layer, user interacts with the system to retrieve, create, share, use the knowledge etc. Personal Assistant (PA) Agent serves to user and act as an interface between user and the system.

Agent Inter Communication Layer: It is the main layer of the architecture. At this layer, Multi-Agents remains active all the time. Agents communicate to each other regarding knowledge processing, retrieval, creation etc and produce the result in lesser time. In this layer, automatic computation is done between the agents.

Knowledge Repository Layer: It is the lower most layer. It contains organization's overall knowledge and agent's personal knowledge where all the information is store, retrieve and reuse.

The different agents are:-

- **Head Agent (HA):-** It handles and manages all other agents which take part in some KM activity.

- **Personal Assistant (PA) Agent: -** This agent serves to the users and therefore handles the user's queries regarding the knowledge processing. PA Agent collaborates with the other agents and act according to the user's queries.

- **Knowledge Agent (KA):-**This agent processed the required query and produces the relevant information for the given request. It also manages and updates the Knowledge Repository.

- **Knowledge Filter Agent (KFA):-** This agent filters the irrelevant data from the useful data which results in producing the accurate knowledge for the related request query.

4   Detailed Design of a MAEKMS for a Public Sector Unit (PSU)

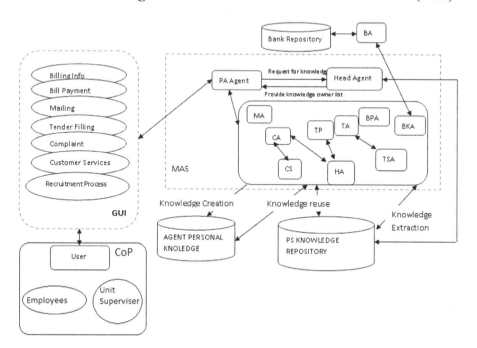

Fig. 2. Multi Agent KMS for PSU

Based on MAEKMS architecture, PSU Knowledge Management is implemented using Multi Agent System to exchange knowledge with each other, in a way that preserves the knowledge, and therefore reaches to the knowledge seeker in a just in time. One of the main tasks of this implementation is to support and encourage collaboration and knowledge sharing. This implementation defines various services like billing information, payment services, complaint services, tender filling services, complaint services, customer support services etc.

The following scenario illustrates the functionality of the knowledge market: A customer wants to apply for a new connection of electricity. Customer requires an analysis regarding the new connection schemes which are best suited according to his need. That is not directly available in the knowledge repository. Via the user interface, he communicates his needs and conditions to his personal assistant (PA) agent. The conditions set by the customer like type of connection etc. His assistant will serve the request and contacts the head agent (HA) in order to find out required agent. HA may use its own internal information about knowledge owners in the system, or possibly, referring to the knowledge repository to find out required agents matching the request and thus provide a list of required agents to the PA agent. Following its own strategy and the preferences specified by the customer, his personal assistant will then contact the required agent and try to get the best deal for his request.

Abbreviations Used

BA:- Bank Agent **BKA:-** Bill Knowledge Agent **BPA:-** Bill Payment Agent **TA:-** Tender Agent **HA:-** HRD Agent **MA:-** Mailing Agent **CSA:-** Customer Services Agent **CA:-** Complaint Agent **TSA:-** Tender Sanction Agent **TPA:-** Training & Placement Cell **PA:-** Personal Assistant

4.1 Inter Agent Communication

In figure 3, interaction between Personal Assistant Agent, Head Agent and Customer Service Agent is depicted. This is actually an agent interaction model diagram. These types of diagrams are very useful to see, at first glance, as agents interact with each other.

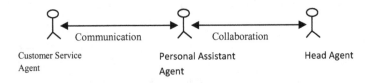

Communication   Collaboration

Customer Service   Personal Assistant   Head Agent
Agent   Agent

Fig. 3. Interaction between Agents

A customer wants to buy a new electricity connection. Then according to the figure:-

- Firstly PA Agent interacts with Head Agent for serving query for new connection on behalf of its user.
- Head Agent then replies to PA agent with the list of Agents serving for the related query.
- PA Agent then interacts with Customer Service Agent (CSA) and request for the related query.
- Finally CSA serves the required knowledge to the PA Agent

4.2   Knowledge Creation

Knowledge is created by the Customer Service Agent by monitoring that which connection plan is preferred by most of the customers. Therefore by monitoring the user's activities about to purchase a new connection, Customer Service Agent stores the knowledge of most preferred connection plan in its personal database.

4.3   Knowledge Re-use

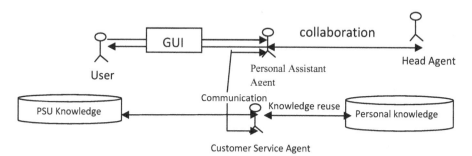

Fig. 4. Knowledge Re-use

The above figure can be described as follows:-

After successful creation of knowledge about connection plan, if another customer request for the similar query about connection plan then Customer Service Agent will re-use its knowledge and serve the required knowledge to the PA agent. The steps are as follows:-

a)   User requests for some query related to connection plan.
b)   PA Agent forward this request by asking the list of agents responsible for the query from the head Agent
c)   Head Agent then fetches the list of agents of related query from its personal database and sends back to PA Agent.
d)   PA Agent then contact to the customer service agent and request for the result of that query.
e)   Customer Service agent (CSA) first checks that whether the requested query is the similar query from the past   requested queries or not from its personal knowledgebase.
f)   If yes then CSA will reuse that knowledge and bring out the result to the PA Agent
g)   Otherwise CSA Agent will fetch the possible result from PSU knowledge base and send back to the PA Agent.

5   Implementation

PSU Multi Agent KM architecture is implemented using Java Agent Communication Language with JADE [1] under Eclipse Environment, Oracle 10g database and UML.

A 'yellow pages' service allows agents to publish descriptions of one or more services they provide in order that other agents can easily discover and exploit them. Any agent can both register (publish) services and search for (discover) services. Registrations, deregistrations, modifications and searches can be performed at any time during an agent's lifetime. Coding for CustomerServiceAgent publishing their services in yellow pages is given below:-

```
DFAgentDescription dfd = new DFAgentDescription ();
dfd.setName (getAID ());
ServiceDescription sd = new ServiceDescription ();
sd.setType ("Customer-Services");
sd.setName ("PSU KNOWLEDGE MANAGEMENT");
dfd.addServices (sd);
try {
    DFService.register (this, dfd);
    }
    catch (FIPAException fe)
    {
    fe.printStackTrace ();
    }
```

5.1   Implementation Snapshots

Figure 5 shows the communication between PA Agent and Customer Service Agent in which PA Agent sends the requested query of the User to the Customer Sercvice Agent.

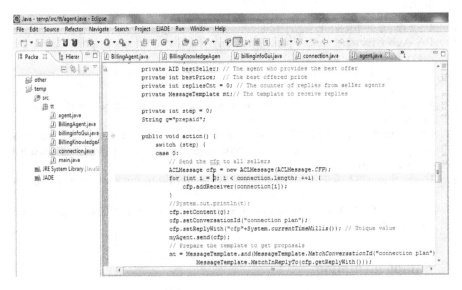

Fig. 5. PA Agent send requested query to Customer Service Agent

In Fig 6, Customer Service Agent reuses knowledge from its personal knowledgebase and therefore serves the requested query to the PA Agent.

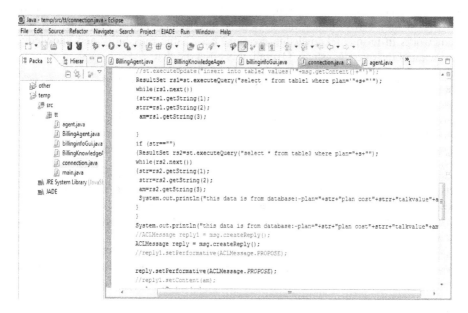

Fig. 6. Customer Service Agent reuses its knowledge and serves for the requested query

6   Results and Observations

Based on the architecture and the detailed design proposed on MAEKMS and the subsequent implementation of some of the modules, a framework comparison was carried of the following frameworks: Juan P Suto Framework and MAEKMS Framework, Hahn and Subramani Framework and MAEKMS Framework

Table 1. Comparison between the Frameworks

Item/Framework	Juan P.Suto framework	Meos and Smith Architecture	Hahn and Subramani Framework	Proposed MAEKM Architecture
Application	YES	NA	NA	YES
Knowledge Reusability	YES	YES	NA	YES
Repository	NA	NA	YES	YES
KM Process	YES	YES	NA	YES
Multi Agent Collaboration	YES	NA	NA	YES

7   Conclusion and Future Work

This paper has proposed the architecture, detailed design and implementation of MAEKMS for a PSU. Further, the work done has been compared with other existing frameworks in terms of knowledge creation, knowledge reusability and knowledge retrieving of the overall system. Overall, it is observed that:-

- MAEKMS architecture is reusing, retrieving the knowledge in a good manner
- MAEKMS architecture is providing smooth communication between agents
- MAEKMS architecture is providing automatic computation between agents.
- Providing best possible solutions according to the related queries.

After successfully implementation it will be able to provide smooth communication between agents, Knowledge reusability will be done by using agent's past experience, reducing time overhead for knowledge serving, able to serve relevant knowledge at correct time, able to provide best possible solutions etc which subsequently enhances the system productivity and quality of services

The future work on this paper will incorporate complete implementation of this architecture to fulfill the primary goal of organizational productivity enhancement.

References

1. Bellifemine, F., Caire, G., Greenwood, D.: Developing Multi agent System with JADE, Wiley Series, England (2007)
2. Soto, J.P., Vizcaíno, A., Portillo, J., Piattini, M.: Modelling a Knowledge Management System Architecture with INGENIAS Methodology. In: IEEE Proceedings of the 15th international Conference on Computing (2006)
3. Nonaka, I., Takeouchi, H.: The knowledge-creating company. Oxford University Press, NY (1995)
4. Meso, P., Smith, R.: A Resource-Based View of Organizational Knowledge Management Systems. Journal of Knowledge Management 4(3), 224–234 (2000)
5. Hahn, J., Subramani, M.: A Framework of Knowledge Management System: Issues and Challenges For Theory and Practice. In: Proceedings of the Twenty First International Conference on Information Systems. ACM, Brisbane (2000)
6. Kephart, J., Chess, D.: The Vision of Autonomic Computing. IEEE Computer 36(1), 41–50 (2003)
7. Kawamura, T., Yoshioka, N., Hasegawa, T., Ohsuga, A., Honiden, S.: Bee-agent: Bonding and Encapsulation Enhancement Agent Framework for Development of Distributed Systems. In: Proceedings of the 6th Asia-Pacific Software Engineering Conference (1999)
8. van Elst, L., Dignum, V., Abecker, A.: Agent- Mediated Knowledge Management. In: Proceedings of the Agent-Mediated Knowledge Management, Stanford, USA, pp. 1–30 (2003)
9. Helsinger, A., Thome, M., Wright, T.: Cougaar: a scalable, distributed multi-agent architecture. In: Proceedings of the IEEE Systems, Man and Cybernetics Conference, Hague, The Netherlands, pp. 1910–1917 (2004)

10. Winikoff, M.: JACK intelligent agents: an industrial strength platform. In: Bordini, R.H., Dastani, M., Dix, J., El Fallah Seghrouchni, A. (eds.) Multi-Agent Programming: Languages, Platforms and Applications, pp. 175–193. Springer, Heidelberg (2005)

11. Constructing Excellence, Demystifying Knowledge Management a Best Practice Guide for the Construction Industry (2004),
    `http://www.constructingexcellence.org.uk/resourcecentre/`
    `publications/document.jsp?documentID=116179` (accessed July 17, 2004)

12. Rao, A.S., Georgeff, M.: BDI agents: from theory to practice. In: Proceedings of the 1st International Conference on Multi-Agent Systems, San Francisco, CA, pp. 312–319 (1995)

13. Marwick, A.D.: Knowledge management technology. IBM Systems Journal (2001)

Developing a Template
for Organizational Knowledge Management

Akhilesh Bajaj and Meredith Bates

The University of Tulsa, 800 S. Tucker Dr., Tulsa, OK, USA
{akhilesh-bajaj,meredith-bates}@utulsa.edu

Abstract. Organizational knowledge is an invaluable resource for business intelligence. However in practice it has not been easy to capture organizational knowledge and to apply it intelligently in future events. Based upon previous research within the field, we have identified the elicitation and codification of context as an area of research which could be highly beneficial to enhancing the application of a knowledge management system within an organization. Context, from a knowledge management system standpoint, provides a shared background that allows users to have a better idea of why a decision was made and increases the chances of an intelligent decision being made in the future. In this work, we propose a template which creates a uniform method to elicit and codify tacit knowledge from organizational players, within its context.

Keywords: Knowledge Management, Decision Making, Business Intelligence, Context.

1 Introduction

Geographical and economies-of-scale barriers to competition are diminishing as it becomes easier for organizations to use technology to compete globally and/or cross over into new domestic markets [1]. Organizations are increasingly aware that business intelligence will decide the winners and losers [2]. Business intelligence can be derived from external, customer focused data, and internally, from the knowledge owned and used by expert employees. Many organizations have begun to realize that human capital represents a significant asset that must be actively mined for information [3]. As mentioned in [4], "Knowledge is embedded and flows through multiple entities including individuals with domain expertise, specific best known methods, or lessons learned". The process of capturing tacit organizational knowledge that has the ability to create a sustainable competitive advantage for the organization is called knowledge management [5].

Knowledge management (KM) is a mature area of study. Extensive research into elements of knowledge management such as the actual construct of knowledge and how best to structure knowledge management systems has been conducted both by academia and corporate practitioners [3]. Many different methods and constructs have been created to attempt to encapsulate the knowledge management process. However, there is still a lack of a standardized template to allow the practical elicitation and

S. Dua et al. (Eds.): ICISTM 2012, CCIS 285, pp. 282–291, 2012.

codification of knowledge within its context. In this work, we propose a template that takes context explicitly into account when eliciting and codifying organizational knowledge.

2   Background

Prior research indicates that internally defining both knowledge and knowledge management is critical to the successful incorporation of knowledge management within an organization [6]. The definitions create a common understanding so that system participants can determine what knowledge is useful and within the scope of the system. However, developing this definition may be difficult. The term *knowledge* has many definitions which can vary significantly across disciplines and even within disciplines.

To create a shared understanding of knowledge requires the users understand the distinction between *explicit* knowledge and *tacit* knowledge [7]. Explicit knowledge is knowledge that has been communicated or is commonly known and is easily codified [7]. Tacit knowledge is generally considered to be expertise, experience and assumptions gathered by personal experience and subsequently cannot be easily codified or converted into a communicable form [8, 9]. Tacit knowledge exists in many places within organizations both within acknowledged subject matter experts and more obscure sources. The unspoken nature of tacit knowledge inherently makes it difficult to identify and retain. Tacit knowledge represents a loss to the company if it is not communicated. Tacit knowledge can also be referred to as human capital which is viewed an integral component of intellectual capital [3].

The most basic form of explicit knowledge is data which can be described as facts or figures. However, data does not possess context. Information is the interpretation of data [10]. Information is seen as the result or output of a process. Data is stored in databases and accessed through reports, while tacit knowledge is seen as the process that creates information by employing data [8].

Knowledge alone, without context, is not sufficient to create a competitive advantage. Value to the organization is derived from understanding the logic of how or why data is turned into information. In order to innovate or enact change effectively, an organization must understand *why* current decisions are made.

The Value of Context
As described earlier, tacit knowledge represents a sum of experiences and insights applied to a task which creates information that can be of value to the firm [10]. Why certain elements of tactic knowledge are drawn upon during the analysis of the task, can be answered by developing a picture of the decision environment or the "context" of how the decision was formulated. Possessing context in regards to why a decision was made is especially important when exceptions or aberration arise.   When incorporated into a knowledge management system, context provides a shared background or understanding of the topic that is being accessed; thereby allowing

knowledge within the system to flow from point to point within an organization [11]. When people share a similar background or knowledge, they are able to share knowledge more similarly [12]. Without context, the flow with the system would simply be that of data or explicit knowledge which does not provide value to the user.

All KMS's require a mechanism through which participants can develop and share context [11]. However, context is not straightforward and easily transferrable. Context is comprised of many explicit and implicit inputs. Explicit inputs, such as deadlines or budgets, can impact context. Implicit inputs, such as perceived importance (both internal and external to the organization) or personal feelings can impact the context of a given scenario. Capturing these elements within a KMS in a consistent manner that is applicable to all knowledge is problematic.

The importance of context in knowledge management is articulated in [13] where they analyze the evolution of *Ba* as previously presented by Nonaka [7]. "Ba is described as the shared space that serves as the foundation for knowledge management" [7]. Choo and Neto [13] look at the factors that contribute to the development of context for knowledge creation. Context is created by conditions such as social/behavioral (norms, collaboration, interactions), cognitive/epistemic (exposure to varied mix of data inputs and outputs), information systems, and strategy/structure. If these elements are required for knowledge creation then at least portions of these elements should be captured in knowledge management systems in order for the knowledge to be transferable.

Numerous knowledge management systems are examined in [14] where the assertion is made that "it is the task of KM to work toward the management of the organization context in a way that the accomplishment of the core KM activities is enabled....Critical factors in creating a successful system include human factors (culture, people, leadership), organizational aspects (structures and processes), informational technology, and management processes." Knowledge management should seek to manage these factors to enable knowledge exchange.

Current research acknowledges the importance of context in knowledge management. However, context has not been fully explored as current research does not encapsulate how to incorporate environmental inputs into an IT system. Currently, research does not propose a method of linking "context" or criterion which influences decision making with the explicit information being captured in knowledge systems. To truly capture the "tactic" element of organizational knowledge, a method of recording the decision making process must be incorporated.

2.1 Knowledge Management Systems (KMS)

Most research into the structure of knowledge management systems tends to focus on the "acquisition, transfer, sharing, and storing of knowledge, regardless of the differences in nomenclature used to describe it" [1].

Acquisition: During the acquisition phase, the organization must define the knowledge assets it wishes to acquire in a manner which complements its mission and objectives [7]. Acquisition methods exist in both formal or purposive channels as well as informal channels [9]. Prior research has found that while informal channels such as mentoring are the most effective methods of knowledge acquisition [10], formal methods such as interviews and training programs are the most applicable to acquiring data for input into technology systems [9].

Knowledge acquisition may seem basic; simply gather knowledge that is not yet recorded and stored. However, many problems can arise in the acquisition process. Experts may be tempted to hoard knowledge or provide basic procedures rather than provide insight into decision making [15]. Another problem may be the presentation of conflicting knowledge gathered from subject matter experts [15]. Additionally, information overload can occur limiting the ability of the system to encode and retain knowledge [16].

Codification: Codification is the process by which knowledge is made explicit. When knowledge is explicit, it becomes transferable [12]. "Codification must be in a form and a structure that will build the knowledge base, by making knowledge accessible, explicit and easy to access" [17]. Depending on the purpose of the system, the knowledge base created might then allow users to perform diagnosis of problems, perform training of less expert employees, perform decision planning, perform interpretations of data, and create predictions of results. Codification can be conducted in several ways, such as visually using a knowledge map [17] or verbally using an interview [12].

Several problems can occur which hinder the codification process. As mentioned in [12], communication problems can occur in interviews when acronyms, shortcuts, and other elements pertaining to the knowledge holder's environment are inadequately communicated to intermediaries that codify the knowledge. Additionally, the encoding scheme used to codify the knowledge can limit the input and processing capacity of available organizational knowledge creating bottlenecks.

Storage: The repositories of data in KMSs most often exist as databases or archives [11]. Repositories are structured based upon the type of knowledge stored and are often linked to create integrated repositories [17]. The ability to dynamically change knowledge artifacts stored and the ability to limit inaccurate knowledge storage (whether intentionally or unintentionally incorrect) are of interest to researchers [18]. Additionally, integrated repositories must be monitored for validity and reliability problems; clear validity procedures should be in place to protect the integrity of the data [17].

Dissemination: To achieve the "knowledge management goal of getting data dispersed across the firm to those who need it, when they need it and in the format they need it" [1], a user friendly interface must exist. Features of the user interface that determine the success of the user in accessing correct knowledge include consistency, relevancy, visual clarity, navigation and usability [17]. Prior work has shown that access to knowledge is improved when users receive training on interface, filters and classifications are continuously refined, and users are incentivized to provide feedback or ratings of the quality of knowledge found [4].

Benefits of KMSs: At a macro level, the KMS acts as a tool to bring organization members closer to meeting the goals of the firm [19]. The ability to articulate a process and integrate a system in which knowledge sharing becomes routine will provide a continued advantage over current and future competitors [8]. The process of eliciting and codifying (inputting) what the company knows but has not recorded provides a solid foundation for identifying the strengths and weaknesses within an organization. The repository of both knowledge and data that is built by a knowledge management system can be invaluable if done properly as it creates resources that can stimulate organizational knowledge creation [16].

KMS Shortfalls: Despite the extensive research on KMSs, many of the existing systems are simply repositories for explicit information that exists within an organization [16]. While this information adds value to an organization, it is not the type of knowledge which is thought to create competitive advantages for organizations. Successful KMSs must acknowledge the dynamic nature of knowledge. In order for the system to respond in a timely manner to changes in knowledge, it must be an integrated component of organizational culture. This requires a commitment throughout the company to be actively engaged in knowledge management.

Based upon the literature reviewed it is clear that further research is required to more accurately capture the "context" that is a necessary component of tacit knowledge. Context is highly dynamic and the ability to elicit and codify it must be presented in a manner which captures its dynamic nature in a consistent manner. The ability to understand why a successful or unsuccessful decision is made and having a system capable of cataloging that information for future use will provide the type asset which sets an organization apart.

3   Tacit Knowledge Template (TKT)

In order to capture all the necessary variables that feed into the decision making process, we first evaluated how work flows through an organization. Typically, data is provided and information is needed. The task or the decision making process that leads to that information being formulated normally has an ideal path to completion. However, variables exist which may impact how tasks are completed. Attempting to identify these variables led us to build the rough template shown below in Figure 1. This figure includes the four high level components we have identified as critical to capturing context: the task itself, the overall work environment, the input factors, and the output factors. The input, the output and the environment components will each capture a separate area of context which may influence a work task.

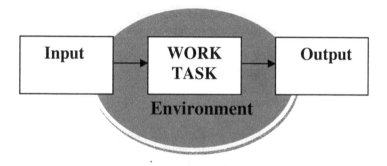

Fig. 1. High Level Components in TKT

Task: The task is the process during which decisions are made or knowledge is applied to create required information. Within the field, a brief description of the task to be completed is required. For example, a task could be *Enter a sales order.* The explicit input required for a task is then captured under the label "Documents/Information required." The task should then be described through a step-by-step process using an if/then heuristic. This heuristic is describing the most basic steps towards the completion of the task. For instance, if the task is processing a sales order, the heuristic listed could be similar to the following illustration:

- If a customer calls to order a product, then I check availability of the product.
- If the product is available, then I give the customer a price.
- If the customer accepts the price, then I input the sale into the computer.
- If the sale is in the computer, then I forward the sale to my manager for approval

The task description is the first component required for the template and the component upon which decision making context will be captured. Context of a task is operationalized in TKT using the input, output and environment. These are described below.

Input: Inputs required in a knowledge management system can be both implicit and explicit. This template includes explicit inputs such as the input source and data required to complete task. These are inputs that, while required to complete the task, are most likely explicit or previously known. In contrast, implicit inputs such as perceived importance and respect of source are variables to decision making which should vary across respondents based upon expertise and experience. Our template places an emphasis on capturing implicit inputs. To capture implicit inputs, we have created three separate fields within the template. The first field is the Input Source. This field is designed to capture from where or from whom data is obtained to complete the task. Based upon the number of input sources that exist, multiple templates for a single task may be required. The second field is labeled Input Variables. This field identifies several variables which may influence how a decision is made. Based upon previous readings and work experience, we included the following variables; each of which can be rated high or low:

- Respect of the source
- Integrity of the Input Information
- Liking of the source
- Importance of the source

The initial draft version of the template included only the input source field and the input variable fields. However, when attempting to complete the template, we found that an additional field would be beneficial to capture the respondents' reasoning as to why the variables listed above impact a decision. To provide an area for this type of response, a third free form box labeled "Variation of task due to input factors" was added. The boxes are listed vertically to visually assist the respondent to answer in appropriate order.

Output: The next major component of the template is identified as output. We feel that it is relevant for third parties to know where the information is going when viewing the knowledge required for completing a task. This portion of the template attempts to capture how decisions to complete a task may vary based upon the recipient of the output produced. Like the Input component of the template, output is captured through three separate fields. The first field identifies the recipient of the output and multiple templates may be required based upon the variation of recipients for a specific task. The second field is comprised of variables that when applied to the source may impact decision making. The output variables include the following factors, each of which can be rated high or low:

- Respect of the recipient
- Importance of integrity of the output information
- Liking of the recipient
- Importance of the recipient

The last field allows the respondent to provide additional feedback as to why or why not one of the listed variables changes how the respondent would perform the task identified. Including the output recipient on the template is vital to understanding how the task identified is completed and adds significant value to the viewer of the task within a knowledge management system.

Environmental Context: The last component of the template is the overall work environment. This component encompasses variables within the organization that are not required to complete the task identified but which may influence how decisions are made while completing the task. These variables are *time pressure, job security*, and *personal gain*. These are variables which we felt may be pertinent to capture and may be more likely to influence how a decision was made during the completion of a task. The template allows each of these criteria to be ranked as either high or low.

After initial review of the template, we also added a *variations* field in which respondents can explain their high or low ranking of why or why not the listed variables impact their decision making for a particular task.

Template Design Discussion: The process of developing the template involved a gradual refinement of the high level components shown in Figure 1. During the development, we were conscious that participation is consistently listed in knowledge management research as one of the biggest hurdles to overcome [15]. To negate complaints that the template was hard to follow, efforts were made to make the layout and fields user friendly and easy to understand. The fields were arranged to flow in a manner which stimulates the respondents to analyze variables that are included in their decision making process. The layout chosen is essentially allowing respondents to build a decision making story. The heuristic defines when a specific input is required to complete the task identified. The first fields in the input and output component identify what/who the respondents will be analyzing. The variables identify how the respondents will be analyzing the input source and the output recipient, while the variations field allows the respondent to describe why the variables are important. By building a template which includes each of these basic questions, we feel that third parties will be more likely to understand the knowledge captured and apply it when needed to create equivalent results. The final version of the template which was developed and finalized after extensive pilot testing, and on which our discussion will be based can be found in Appendix A.

4   Discussion and Conclusion

In our research and development of the TKT artifact, we utilized a systems approach to knowledge management to address what we felt was an under developed area in the field. Previous research showed no one had extensively employed a systems approach to capture context within a knowledge management system. Each work task is viewed as a system with inputs, outputs and an environment. The template formalizes the importance of context by explicitly stating that context is derived from three components which consist of inputs, outputs and the overall environment. It captures if these components affect a work task and why or why not. In our ongoing research, we hope to validate the template by testing in varying work environments and receiving feedback as to whether the TKT would be useful. We believe that the TKT will lead to the development of an easy-to-use knowledge management elicitation tool which highlights context as significant to understanding tacit organizational knowledge. While we have developed TKT for tacit knowledge, we believe a similar approach would also work for explicit knowledge.

References

1. Gabberty, J.W., Thomas, J.D.E.: Driving Creativity: Extending Knowledge Management into the Multinational Corporation. Interdisciplinary Journal of Information, Knowledge & Management 2, 2–13 (2007)

2. McAfee, A., Brynjolfsson, E.: Investing in the IT That Makes a Competitive Difference. Harvard Business Review 86(7-8), 98–107 (2008)

3. Mohammad, A.H., Hamdeh, M.A., Sabri, A.T.: Developing a Theoretical Framework for Knowledge Acquisition. European Journal of Scientific Research 42(3), 439–449 (2010)

4. Kulkarni, U.R., Ravindran, S., Freeze, R.: A Knowledge Management Success Model: Theoretical Development and Empirical Validation. Journal of Management Information Systems 23(3), 309–347 (2006-2007)

5. McCall, H., Arnold, V., Sutton, S.G.: Use of Knowledge Management Systems and the Impact on the Acquisition of Explicit Knowledge. Journal of Information Sciences 22(2), 77–101 (2008)

6. Fahey, L., Prusak, L.: The Eleven Deadliest Sins of Knowledge Management. California Management Review 40(3), 265–276 (1998)

7. Nonaka, I., Toyama, R., Nagata, A.: A Firm as Knowledge-Creating Entity: A New Prespective on the Theory of the Firm. Industrial and Corporate Change 9(1), 1–20 (2000)

8. McInerney, C.: Knowledge Management and the Dynamic Nature of Knowledge. Journal of the American Society for Information Science and Technology 53(12), 1009–1018 (2002)

9. Ipe, M.: Knowledge sharing in organizations: A conceptual framework. Human Resource Development Review 2(4), 337–359 (2003)

10. Blair, D.: Knowledge Management: Hype, Hope or Help? Journal of American Society for Information Science & Tecnology, 1019–1028 (2002)

11. Tiwana, A.: The Knowledge Management Toolkit: Orchestrating IT, Strategy, and Knowledge Platform, 2nd edn. Prentice Hall, Upper Saddle River (2002)

12. Hall, M.: Knowledge Management and the limits of knowledge codification. Journal of Knowledge Management 10(3), 117–126 (2006)

13. Choo, C.W., de Alvarenga Neto, R.C.D.: Beyond the ba: managng enabling contexts in knowledge organizations. Journal of Knowledge Management 14(4), 592–610 (2010)

14. Heisig, P.: Harmonisation of knowledge management - comparing 160 KM frameworks around the globe. Journal of Knowledge Management 13(4), 4–31 (2009)

15. Okafor, E.: The Underlying Issues in Knowledge Elicitation. Interdisciplinary Journal of Information, Knowledge & Management 1(1), 95–108 (2006)

16. McCall, H., Arnold, V., Sutton, S.G.: Use of Knowledge Management Systems and the Impact on the Acquisition of Explicit Knowledge. Journal of Information Sciences 22(2), 77–101 (2008)

17. Awad, E.M., Ghaziri, H.M.: Knowledge Management. Prentice Hall, New Saddle River (2004)

18. Wagoner, C.: Breaking the Knowledge Acquisition Bottleneck Through Conversational Knowlede Management. Information Resources Management Journal 19(1), 70–82 (2006)

19. Firestone, J.: Estimating Benefits of Knowledge Management Initiatives: Concepts, Methodology and Tools. Knowledge and Innovation:Journal of the KMCI 1(3), 110–129 (2001)

Appendix A: Tacit Knowledge Template (TKT)

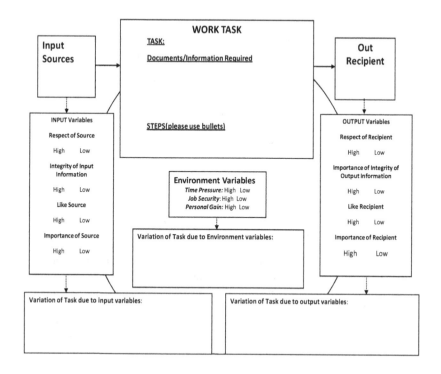

Towards of E-Learning Quality Standards for Electrical Engineers

Nadezhda Kunicina, Anastasija Zhiravecka, Antons Patlins,
Yelena Chaiko, and Leonids Ribickis

Riga Technical University/ Faculty of Power and Electrical Engineering
Institute of Industrial Electronics and Electrical Engineering
Riga, Latvia
kunicina@latnet.lv, zhiravecka@eef.rtu.lv,
{Antons.Patlins,Jelena.Caiko,Leonids.Ribickis}@rtu.lv

Abstract. The application of e – learning approach for electrical engineers could be beneficial for all types of graduates. The specific models of 3D virtual laboratories are proposed as a pre standard tool for e-learning of electrical engineers. Effective integration of 3D virtual laboratories into education process will bring benefits to higher education, as for vocational as for standard academic programs. The simple embedding of 3D virtual laboratories in education and training systems will make high quality trainings possible from distance for university branches as well. The common education programs and courses, developed in cooperation with several partners are the steps forward to international education programs as well as quality standards of e-learning for electrical engineers. The same tool will bring benefits in education of experienced engineers it terms of lifelong learning education concept. The application of Project-based learning methodology is widely used in specific education courses in Riga Technical University study program of „Computerized control of electrical technologies". The application of "Kolb's experiential learning theory" represents sufficiently the educational cycle for case of synthesis of new technology.

Keywords: Electrical Engineering; e-learning; education; Kolb's Experiential Learning Cycle; flexible integrated simulation system; virtual laboratory.

1 Introduction

The development and usage of different virtual laboratories is useful for education of electrical engineers at all stages. For standard education, the 3D virtual laboratories could be beneficial as additional education tool, for training students in especially for testing. For such education concept as vocational or part time education usage of such embedded tools are critical. The case of additional education needed or new challenges and responsibilities in the carrier to be taken up during the carrier some additional qualification is requested and 3D virtual laboratories could help engineers at this stage also.

S. Dua et al. (Eds.): ICISTM 2012, CCIS 285, pp. 292–303, 2012.

The successful career of engineers is strongly related with the market needs and the qualification of engineers to be ready to cover this interest from market. The description of job duties for electrical engineers are common and there is not much new abilities in the list added in last year's, however in reality the successful career of engineers, especially in the case of discrepancies of economics are strongly related with their flexibility and ability to learn. The observation of means of standard training as well as specific tools for electrical engineers is beneficial at all stages of the carrier as an additional embedded education instrument.

This article deals with e – learning approach analysis the identification of specific scope and needs, as well with quality analysis in learning outcomes for Electrical Engineers and experienced technicians. The availability of additional professional courses or trainings is very limited due to specific requirement and area of interest, high price of general education and time limits. It is not possible to reach the full qualification of electrical engineer without systematic approach and using only ICT tools. The e – learning approach could be successfully used as additional tools and embedded in structured education, which covered all three pillars of success in technical education: expertise of mentors, equipment of technical laboratories and availability of support during synthesis of new solutions. The new 3D virtual laboratory application development for education of electrical engineers is discussed.

2   The Engineering Education in RTU

The largest technical university of Latvia - Riga Technical University (RTU) is a leader of education of electrical engineers in Latvia.

Every year up to 180 students apply for studies in electrical and power engineering. The education is available in capital city Riga as well as in the regional branches in the biggest cities of Latvia: Daugavpils, Liepaja and Ventspils. Riga Technical University [1] takes a leading position in the development of educational materials for engineers in Latvia.

There is a strong cooperation between the lecturers during the preparation of teaching materials between technical colleges and other higher education establishments in Latvia and in the world. The cooperation with other universities, in common education activities for example with Tallinn University of Technology within the frames of doctoral schools gives a good background to enlarge such cooperation for other groups of students. It also gives an opportunity to use such programs like Erasmus Mundus to implement and enlarge the best practice.

The usage of IT tools is wide for the administrative and content storing sake in the university.

The introduction of IT applications and the administrative requirements leads to sufficient steps forward the general application of IT environment.

The main administrative e-education tool of RTU (fig.1) allows making sufficient and structured content of lectures available for all groups of students simultaneously. This tool allows giving students information, but does not allow working in special 3D mode, as well as not suitable for remote testing. The implementation of such IT tools is helpful for structuring of some studies and common approach for information storage and availability for all different groups of students; however it does not solve the standardization of content in the different specific branches of engineering science.

At the moment in RTU there are no standards for e – learning, as the e – learning approach is not formally applied for the educational programs of engineers. From other hand the amount of different IT tools, used for the education of all students at all study levels increases, so the voluntary standardization for the specific study programs is the first step in the whole standardization process.

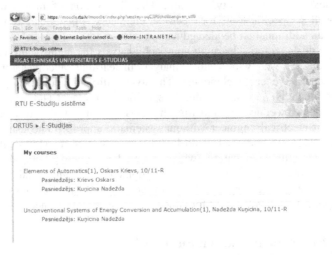

Fig. 1. General view of RTU e -education tool

The case studies for study program „Computerized control of electrical technologies" are discussed in the article. The study program covers the fields of industrial electronics and electrical engineering with the specializations in power electronics, electric drive, automation of electrical technologies and electric transport, which meet the needs of industry and the graduates of which are competitive.

The main challenges for using IT tools for education of electrical engineers make available the analysis of industrial systems via simulation of parameters as well as the design of feedback for control systems via several simulation tools.

There is specific research and measuring equipment available for the students during the studies as well as during the development of final thesis.

The study program „Computerized control of electrical technologies" covers all stages of education from bachelor to doctor. The several possibilities of vocational education are available.

3   The Education Needs

The educational needs of electrical engineers could be divided into three categories:

- General education;
- Specific education/ Training;
- Synthesis of new technology.

The ICT tools are successfully applied for academic (general) education; however there is a lack of common methodological approach in the case of specific education and training for experienced engineers. In the case of academic education the special case of vocational as well as education in branch schools are separated.

There are no possibilities to install the central laboratory corpus and equipment available for academic students in branches. For example, the industrial production line (figure 2) is not possible to transfer to other branches, but such solution like 3D model could be useful to achieve the required skills.

Fig. 2. During training demonstrations on industrial production line

For the Specific education/ Training categories the specific courses, provided by equipment suppliers, are available. For engineers and technicians, who just started career in electrical engineering a wide range of initial training is provided on the basis of regular specific training centres, such as Latvenergo training centre [2].

Fig. 3. Experience exchanging seminar for IEEI stuff in Latvenergo training centre

For Synthesis of new technology category there is a lack of educational and training opportunities. At the moment the qualified engineers can apply for some specific courses in Riga Technical University at vocational basis through existing vocational learning scheme, however this scheme allows to attend only specific courses together with regular students groups. This type of education is not popular in engineering, as it does not meet the requirements of the market. This type of knowledge is helpful only for general skills, such as project management, management of intellectual property, etc., but does not cover the needs of engineers in the case of lack of technical expertise and structural knowledge in the case of new technological solutions.

4   The Specific Methodology for Education

The application of Project-based learning methodology [3, 4, 5] is widely used in specific education courses in Riga Technical University programme of „Computerized control of electrical technologies". The application of this methodology is especially useful for synthesis tasks of new technology. Some case studies are described in [6, 7]. Project-based learning methodology application is sufficient for classical education; however for the specific technological issues application of this method in not fully covered the educational needs from sector.

The application of specific methodology to meet the requirements of educational needs for synthesis of new technology case is required.

The development of regional competence centres may meet the market requirements in this field of education.

The application of "Kolb's experiential learning theory" [8] represents sufficiently the educational cycle for case of synthesis of new technology.

A four-stage cyclical theory of learning, Kolb's experiential learning theory is a holistic perspective that combines experience, perception, cognition, and behaviour.

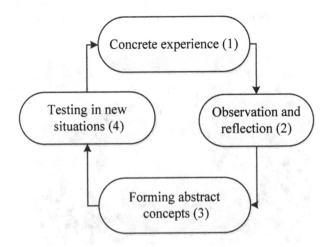

Fig. 4. Kolb's Experiential Learning Cycle

The theory presents a cyclical model of learning, consisting of four stages shown below. One may begin at any stage, but must follow each other in the sequence:

- concrete experience (or "DO")
- reflective observation (or "OBSERVE")
- abstract conceptualization (or "THINK")
- active experimentation (or "PLAN")

Kolb's four-stage learning cycle (Fig. 4) shows how experience is translated through reflection into concepts, which in turn are used as guides for active experimentation and the choice of new experiences. The stage of concrete experience (CE) is where the learner actively experiences an activity such as a lab session or field work. The stage of reflective observation (RO) is when the learner consciously reflects back on that experience. That of abstract conceptualization (AC) is where the learner attempts to conceptualize a theory or model of what is observed. The stage of active experimentation (AE) is where the learner is trying to plan how to test a model or theory or plan for a forthcoming experience.

In this connection Kolb identified four learning styles which correspond to these stages. The styles highlight conditions under which the learners study better. These styles are: a) assimilators, who learn better when presented with sound logical theories to consider; b) convergers, who learn better when provided with practical applications of concepts and theories; c) accommodators, who learn better when provided with "hands-on" experiences; d) divergers, who learn better when allowed to observe and collect a wide range of information.

There is no doubt that in the changing world of high technologies and sharp competition the representatives of all professions, particularly engineering and engineering research, need permanent development not in theory or getting information on new technologies from literature and periodicals but also in the area of studying and examining of their practical application and operation with the ideas of their further development. A particular assistance in it could be rendered by means of some kind of lifelong learning systems that could be available not only for the present students but for the graduated specialists with professional experience as well as for their further professional growth. With this aim it seems possible to create such flexible distance learning and research simulation tool that could be easily applied by representatives of all four learning styles identified by Kolb as well as integrate the four stages of its learning cycle providing an opportunity to start the learning or research at any stage.

The application of Kolb's principles in electrical engineering covers needs for sufficient research environmental for geographically distributed researchers group. Such solutions will lead to aim of promoting socially-oriented informal acquisition processes enhancing potential learning and research possibilities encouraging self-learning through project – oriented learning approach, informal peer learning and e-skills.

Promoting competence exchange processes (skills bartering) promotion, at local, national and all research projects levels as well as support of geographically distributed groups of researchers.

5   The Development of Specific IT Applications Flintes for Education of Electrical Engineers

Considering the e-learning opportunity in life-long education it seems possible to create such educational tool in the field of electrical engineering, accepting industrial processes automation as a basis of the simulation and 3D-simulation for distance learning and research - flexible integrated simulation system. For simplification and general view of the system organization representation a block diagram can be used (fig.5) where each block is also a separate independent enough kind of the system.

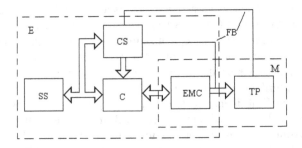

Fig. 5. Example of simulation for distance learning

The system consists of electrical (E) and mechanical (M) parts. The unit connecting these two parts is EMC – electric-mechanical converter that in most of the cases is a motor of a necessary type or a set of those depending on the technology. In the diagram the blocks are: SS – supply system, C – power converter for EMC regulation providing therefore the regulation of the process itself; TP – the block could simulate any kind of technological process. CS is control system, FB - feedback providing CS with the necessary current information within the system and its elements. The flexibility of the system is achieved with the flexibility of each block. Each block is easily transformable in order to provide the required process. Each block is active with the opportunity to vary its parameters in wide range. Each block is equipped with input elements to change these parameters and output elements for the possibility to investigate the processes in this or that block or in the system as a whole and its influence on the other elements of the system. The students are provided with tasks for laboratory works and studies, researchers and specialists in their turn are provided with the opportunity of output data and processes analysis and comparison. Each element is presented either visually or mathematically. The system of the results output is compatible with the conventional PC environment tools - MS Office, etc. Naturally there is an opportunity of any necessary measurements, electric and power parameters calculations, evaluation of influence on the network.

Such tool will enlarge possibilities to use e – learning for education of electrical engineers. It will cover additional vocation education groups, as well as groups of students in the branches of RTU.

Within the existing experience a professor (mentor) arrives to a branch of the University (e.g. to Liepaja) and during the period of 2 – 3 days conducts lectures and tutorials for students, but during other time, students have no special tools or methods to be involved into study process simultaneously. The same problem is with vocational students, they have classes 3 – 4 time per semester, in comparison normally foul time students have 16 possibilities to meet professor during lectures. The problem we are facing, that the percentage of vocational students which are finishing education is very low. Such special 3D laboratories will bring additional flexibility in education process, which is curtail for vocational and students from RTU branches.

6   The Requirements for Competences of Mentors

The introduction of elements of e – learning in a daily basis education requires also the new skills for the mentors and professors. The two different patterns are applied nowadays for this approach.

The most popular approach is that the responsible professor for study subject is responsible also for all teaching stages, including the communication with students and other applicants in web environment.

The second approach is to invite the mentors for the e – content and to leave to the responsible professor's only part of responsibilities in the study process.

Both approaches are sufficient; however for the sake of standardization, the competence of mentors in e – learning is not fully equivalent of the standard description of the duties of academic staff.

The additional competencies and specific methodology of the e – learning are requested during the studies. The continuous monitoring of the quality of e – tools and analysis of their impact in learning outcomes quality is initially requested.

The ability of developing wider educational innovation, based on the capacity of ICT to support new pedagogies and their adaptation to social and economic changes.

The use of ICT to support innovation and lifelong learning for all due to European vide initiatives, such as Lifelong learning initiative: ICT Multilateral Projects - Priority 2: ICT as a catalyst for innovation and creativity in learner by implemented specific learn-by-doing through experiments virtual settings, developed specifically for electrical engineers.

The benchmarking from ongoing studies related to development of methodologies for assessment of ICT indicators.

7   The Steps beyond – Stat-of-the-Art

The development of specific IT tools for engineers in RTU is continuous activity.

The current competence of Researchers and involvement in many bilateral and international researches requires the development of new IT tools, which could be effectively used for research and engineering for geographically distributed group of researchers.

Nowadays only for the specific training during the first stage of education the special self – made virtual laboratories are used. In the topic of analyses of control system qualitative parameters the several virtual laboratories (fig. 6) are used on daily basis.

The practical work in simulation environment helps the students to train themselves and get basic skills in system design as well as in daily work.

For the future the creation of specific tools for distance learning and research in the field of computer control in electrical engineering and power electronics - Flexible integrated simulation system (Flintes).

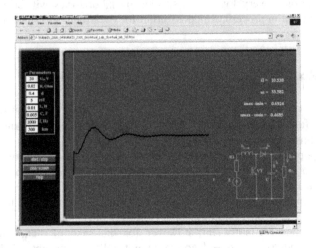

Fig. 6. Example of virtual laboratory

The web based engineering and research platform should be created. The extranet principle, and secured access will be granted to all researchers on project – based approach.

The usage of such IT tool will lead to collecting and structuring of working information from all research projects in institute. In the same time the secured access provided will allow to keep high confidentiality level, if needed. The results of several projects, when finished will become a good material for students and researchers as library of existing examples.

The concept of Flintes will cover such needs:

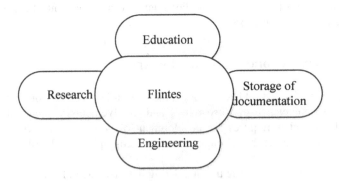

Fig. 7. Scope of Flintes application

The usage of Flintes will bring such benefits for researchers:

- The common space for development;
- The tool for working in geographically distributed researchers group;
- The visualization platform as stage 4 according Kolb's cycle;
- The validation tool.

The usage of Flintes will bring such benefits for students:

- Project – based learning.

The usage of Flintes will bring such benefits for other groups:

- Structural knowledge and systematic library;
- The easy reporting system;
- The flexible experimental base.

8   Development

Development of Flintes will be performed by following steps:

- Collection of concrete experience from research, education, and engineering
- Reflective observation of similarities, identification of similar needs between research, education, and engineering
- Design of Flintes concept
- Application of Flintes, extension of application scope

The main development stages are:

- Analysis of state – of – the art: collection of experience from geographically distributed research groups, education programs, and some best practice from engineering companies.
- Reflective observation of similarities.
- Design of Flintes concept, choosing web/ desktop alternatives, design of technical specification.
- Development of Flintes.
- Development of content and basic features, extension of application scope.

The concept of Flintes is specific and covers electrical engineering area the design of specific schemes could be made/ uploaded from Matlab, however the web application will be necessary, to cover needs of geographically distributed groups of researchers.

The implementation of Flintes will bring such benefits for different target groups:

- For education organizations, will be used as voluntary standardized approach for laboratory works and studies. It will bring the best practice from industry to new generation of engineers;
- For researchers implementation of Flintes will allow to develop closer cooperation with in geographically distributed groups;

- For engineers such tool will allow to link geographically distributed branches of companies;
- For all categories of target groups Flintes could be successfully used as storage of information – data base of previous experience.

For the successful development of Flintes such main steps will be done:

- Analysis of state-of-the-art-will include the collection of expert opinions, about market needs, current expertise of electrical engineers, skills of future engineers. The specially developed questioner will be used for formalizing opinions of experts. The pseudo 360-degree feedback approach [9] will be used for this survey. The target group of experts will include such categories, which will covers all categories, such as students, researchers, engineers, and heads of companies.

For this case classical 360 Feedback Survey Measures should be modified accordingly:

- measures of behaviours and competencies
- 360 assessments of market needs, and provide feedback on how skills of engineers fit to market requirements and identification of "weak points" in the skills.
- 360 feedbacks addresses skills such as engineering - developing of technical solutions, project management, planning, and goal setting – achieving.
- A pseudo 360 evaluation focuses on subjective areas such as teamwork, skills and leadership effectiveness.

The survey will cover so – called "Customer satisfaction surveys', with the aim to get feedback from customers to find out what you need to change to create loyal customers, to strengthen study programme „Computerized control of electrical technologies", and to prepare the basis for evolutionary standardization of content of education.

The surveying of experts will be done, using Delphi technique, which as public policy-making technique is successfully applied and brings a number of methodological innovations. In this case keen methodological approach is anonymity of experts [10].

The analysis of expert's feedback will make clear impute for formalizing technical requirements of Flintes. This feedback is necessary to formalize context and scope of Flintes, including dilemma between web – desktop concept of Flintes.

The implementation and usage of Flintes will be useful for several stages of education: for academic, vocational, geographically separated education in universities, as well as for training of experienced engineers in case of additional expertise needed from market.

9   Conclusions

The implementation and continuous development of e – learning approach for electrical engineers, and in particular for subjects covered by study programme „Computerized control of electrical technologies" will bring useful results for other education modes. The usage of such simulators like Flintes will be useful also for life learning activities different training centres for students and engineers. The development of the content in native language, the qualification of moderators will bring step forward in the development of the sufficient content. The evaluation of the results and adjustments of the study programs made by mentors will bring the qualitative evaluation of IT tool. The usage of such approach for different groups, including lifelong education approach will enlarge the group of users. The development of specific IT simulators for research and study sake will enlarge the user groups, and will cover professionals and researchers. The development and application of different IT tools will bring the benefits for all three categories:

• General education;
• Specific education/ Training;
• Synthesis of new technology.

The synergy of different EU organizations, during the development of IT tools and approaches will bring additional value, due to international expertise and "hands – on cooperation", which will bring us step closer towards of e-learning quality standards for Electrical Engineers.

References

1. http://www.rtu.lv
2. http://www.st.latvenergo.lv/portal/page?_pageid=73,419757&_d
   ad=portal&_schema=PORTAL
3. Donnelly, R., Fitzmaurice, M.: Collaborative project – based learning and problem – based learning in higher education: a construction of tutor and students roles in learning focused strategies. In: O'Neill, G., Moore, S., McMullin, B. (eds.) Emerging Issues in the Practice of University Learning and Teaching, p. 12. AISHE, Dublin (2005),
   http://www.aishe.org/readings/2005-1/
4. Thomas, J.W.: A review of research on project – based learning, p. 46 (2000)
5. Checklists to support Project Based Learning and evaluation in,
   http://pblchecklist.4teachers.org/
6. Yelena, C., Nadezhda, K., Antons, P., Leonids, R., Anastasija, Z.: Research-based approach application for electrical engineering education of bachelor program students in Riga Technical University. In: IEEE EDUCON 2010 IEEE Engineering Education 2010 – The Future of Global Learning in Engineering Education Madrid, Spain (2010)
7. Baltiņš, E., Kuņicina, N., Ribickis, L.: Improvement of Doctoral studies in Riga Technical University for Sustainable Development of Economy Engineering Education in Sustainable Development, Austrija, Graz, September 22-24, pp. 320–326 (2008)
8. Kolb, D.: Experiential Learning: Experience as the Source of Learning and Development, p. 246. Prentice Hall, New Jersey (1983)
9. Edwards, M.R., Ewen, A.J.: 360° Feedback: The powerful new model for Employee Assessment & performance improvement. AMACOM American Management Association, New York (1996)
10. Colton, S., Hatcher, T.: The Web-based Delphi Research Technique as a Method for Content Validation in HRD and Adult Education Research (2004)

A Comparative Study of Recognition of Speech Using Improved MFCC Algorithms and Rasta Filters

Lavneet Singh and Girija Chetty

Faculty of ISE, University of Canberra, Australia
{Lavneet.singh,Girija.Chetty}@canberra.edu.au

Abstract. Automatic Speech Recognition has been an active topic of research for the past four decades. The main objective of the automatic speech recognition task is to convert a speech segment into an interpretable text message without the need of human intervention. Many different algorithms and schemes based on different mathematical paradigms have been proposed in an attempt to improve recognition rates. Cepstral coefficients play an important part in speech theory and in automatic speech recognition in particular due to their ability to compactly represent relevant information that is contained in a short time sample of a continuous speech signal. The goal of this paper is to discuss comparison of speech parameterization methods: Mel-Frequency Cepstrum Coefficients (MFCC) and improved Mel-Frequency Cepstrum Coefficients (MFCC) using RASTA filters. Thus, in this study, we try to improve the MFCC algorithms to achieve much accuracy reducing the error rates in Automatic Speech Recognition. First, we remove signal correlation through normalization, then we use RASTA filter to filtering the cepstral coefficients. Finally, we reduce dimension of the cepstral coefficients by the variances of cepstral coefficients in different dimension and obtain our features. By using various classifiers, we try to simulate the speech feature extraction at much optimal and least error rate providing robust method for Automatic Speech Recognition (ASRs).

Keywords: Automatic Speech Recognition, Mel frequency Cepstrum Coefficients (MFCC's), ERB Gammatone Filtering, Hidden Markov Model.

1 Introduction

Automatic Speech Recognition has been an active topic of research for the past four decades. The main objective of the automatic speech recognition task is to convert a speech segment into an interpretable text message without the need of human intervention. Many different algorithms and schemes based on different mathematical paradigms have been proposed in an attempt to improve recognition rates. Since the problem of speech recognition is complex, under certain circumstances, recognition rates are far from optimal. In addition other constraints such as computational complexity and real-time constraints come into play in the design and implementation of a working product. Computer hardware and software have significantly improved in terms of speed, memory, cost and availability, which have enabled the use of more sophisticated and computationally demanding algorithms to be implemented even on

S. Dua et al. (Eds.): ICISTM 2012, CCIS 285, pp. 304–314, 2012.

low-power low-cost handheld electronic devices. However, we prefer algorithms with low computational and memory requirements since they can be implemented easily and at lower cost. Due to improvements both in algorithms and in hardware, automatic speech recognition has become more affordable and available. Automatic speech recognition is still an open topic of research, where improvement and changes are constantly made in a hope for better recognition rates(J.C. Junqua and J.P. Haton)[1].

Automatic speech recognition (ASR) attempts to map from a speech signal to the corresponding sequence of words it represents. To perform this, a series of acoustic features are extracted from the speech signal, and then pattern recognition algorithms are used. Thus, the choice of acoustic features is critical for the system performance. If the feature vectors do not represent the underlying content of the speech, the system will perform poorly regardless of the algorithms applied. This task is not easy and has been the subject of much research over the past few decades. The task is complex due to the inherent variability of the speech signal. The speech signal varies for a given word both between speakers and for multiple utterances by the same speaker. Accent will differ between speakers. Changes in the physiology of the organs of speech production will produce variability in the speech waveform. For instance, a difference in height or gender will have an impact upon the shape of the spectral envelope produced. The speech signal will also vary considerably according to emphasis or stress on words. Environmental or recording differences also change the signal. Although humans listeners can cope well with these variations, the performance of state of the art ASR systems is still below that achieved by humans (H.G. Hirsh and D. Pearce) [2].

As the performance of ASR systems has advanced, the domains to which they have been applied have expanded. The first speech recognition systems were based on isolated word or letter recognition on very limited vocabularies of up to ten symbols and were typically speaker dependent. The next step was to develop medium vocabulary systems for continuous speech, such as the Resource Management (RM) task, with a vocabulary of approximately a thousand words. Next, large vocabulary systems on read or broadcast speech with an unlimited scope were considered. Recognition systems on these tasks would use large vocabularies of up to 65,000 words, although it is not possible to guarantee that all observed words will be in the vocabulary. An example of a full vocabulary task would be the Wall Street Journal task (WSJ) where passages were read from the Wall Street Journal. Current state of the art systems have been applied recognizing conversational or spontaneous speech in noisy and limited bandwidth domains. An example of such a task would be the Switchboard corpus. The most common approach to the problem of classifying speech signals is the use of hidden markov model. Before delving into the worlds of phonology, we present an overview of automatic speech recognition and give insight to some commonly used techniques that attempt to solve this formidable task.

A speaker recognition system mainly consists of two main modules, speaker specific feature extractor as a front end followed by a speaker modeling technique for generalized representation of extracted features as defined by (S. Saha and D. Bobbert and M. Wolska) [3, 4]. Since long time MFCC is considered as a reliable front end for a speaker recognition application because it has coefficients that represents audio based on perception mentioned by (K. Fujita et al and D. OShaughnessy) [5, 6]. In MFCC the frequency bands are positioned logarithmically (on the Melscale) which approximates the human auditory systems response more closely than the linear spaced frequency bands of FFT or DCT. This allows for better processing of data. Fig.1 shows the speaker recognition system used in this investigation. Accuracy of automatic speaker recognition is known to degrade severely when there is acoustic mismatch between the training and testing material which is clearly defined by (Renals S. et. al and B.H. Juang and L.R. Rabiner) [7,8].

1.1   Mel Frequency Cepstral Coefficients

Cepstral coefficients play an important part in speech theory and in automatic speech recognition in particular due to their ability to compactly represent relevant information that is contained in a short time sample of a continuous speech signal (N. Morgan and Bourlard) [9]. The definition for real Cepstral coefficients is given by the following equation:

$$Cepstrum\ (x) = IDFT\ (log\ (DFT(x))) \tag{1}$$

We also note that

$$Cepstrum\ (x*y) = Cepstrum\ (x) + Cepstrum\ (y) \tag{2}$$

Equation 2 can be easily derived from equation 1 and is useful in case we model the speech signal as a result of an excitation convolved with an impulse response of the vocal tract filter. DFT is the Discrete Fourier Transform often implemented by the Fast Fourier Transform algorithm. The Mel Frequency Cepstral Coefficients (MFCCs) are obtained by converting the result of the log- absolute value frequency spectrum to a Mel perceptually-based spectrum and taking an inverse discrete cosine transform of the result. Using Cepstral terminology we regard the Mel mapping to be a rectangular low frequency filter followed by a discrete cosine transform. The result is a smoothed cepstrum which can be further sampled to a specific number of coefficients. Qfrequency is a cepstrum value ('cepstrum frequency value') while a lifter is a weighted cepstrum or in other words a filter for the cepstrum coefficients.

$$MFCC_i = \sum_{k=1}^{13} Cos\left[\frac{\left(k-\frac{1}{2}\right)\pi}{13}\right] \tag{3}$$

$$i = 1, 2\ldots\ldots M$$

M is the number of Cepstral Coefficients and Σ n represents the log energy output of the kth Mel filter. The triangular lifters are linearly spaced up to 1000 Hz and logarithmically spaced afterwards up to 4000 Hz. The hidden assumption is that more important speech information is encapsulated in the low frequency band of 0 - 1000 Hz while the higher 1000-4000 Hz band contains less information per Hz. The triangular lifters can be regarded as a possibility function which serves as an upper bound to a symmetrical distribution where only the mean and variance are known. The possibility function entails all the possible distributions that might occur and is the coarsest upper bound we can obtain knowing only the mean and variance of a stochastic process. The human ear filters sound linearly for lower frequencies and logarithmically for higher frequencies. Partitioning the frequency range into two different spacing schemes that also resemble the Bark scale yields an efficient representation of the spectrum.

MFCC's are based on the known variation of the human ears critical bandwidths with frequency, filters spaced linearly at low frequencies and logarithmically at high frequencies have been used to capture the phonetically important characteristics of speech. The characteristics are expressed on the mel-frequency scale, which is linear frequency spacing below 1000 Hz and a logarithmic spacing above 1000 Hz. In addition, rather than the speech waveforms themselves, MFCC's are shown to be less susceptible to the above mentioned variation of the speakers voice and surrounding environment.

1.2   Rasta Filters

Speech is produced by movements of the vocal tract at changing rates. These movements and their rates of change are reflected in speech components (linguistic components) of speech signals. Non-speech components of such signals often have rates of change that lie outside the range of speech components. RASTA filtering takes advantage of these differences. It aims to suppress spectral components of a speech signal that change more slowly or quickly than the normal rate of change of speech components defined by (M. S. Shi, Y. M. Cheng and X. L. Pu) [10]. Frequency characteristics of communication channels are often fixed or slowly varying, i.e. their rates of change are outside that of speech in a signal. Applied on a communication channel speech, RASTA filtering attempts to attenuate these frequencies (frequency band-stopping). It is based on principles of the PLP feature extraction method defined by (L. Zhao) [11]. In doing RASTA filtering, the power spectrum of a given frame of speech is computed. From this power spectrum an auditory spectrum is derived which is then transformed by using some form of a compression function. The logs of the resulting transform are taken and put through a RASTA filter. The output of the RASTA filter is decompressed using an inverse of the compression function applied on the auditory spectrum.

Temporal RASTA processing for channel normalization any stationary convolutive distortion will be an additive component in the logarithmic spectral energy domain. If a stationarity of a transmission channel or a microphone characteristic is assumed, it is easy to show that any convolutive distortion of the signal affects the mean of the time trajectory of logarithmic spectral energy cited in (B. Zhen, X. H. Wu, Z. M. Liu and H. S. Chi) [12]. Methods for processing temporal trajectories of logarithmic energies have already been proven to be effective in dealing with channel variability and RASTA (Relative Spectra) processing was introduced as an alternative to mean subtraction (W. Wang, F. Liu and S. Z. Wu) [13]. In this paper we propose temporal RASTA processing of log filter-bank magnitudes. The RASTA filter is a band-pass filter with the following transfer function.

Each log filter-bank magnitude component f[m,i], where i=1,2,.... . NumChan is filtered with HRASTA(z) and RASTA filtered log filter-bank magnitudes fRASTA[m,i] are produced. The presented RASTA filter attenuates modulation frequency components below 1Hz and above 10Hz. Slow-varying components, corresponding to the frequency characteristics of a communication channel, are suppressed, and a robust representation more insensitive to environmental effects is obtained. The low-pass filtering also helps to smooth spectral changes present in adjacent frames as a result of analysis artifacts, like position of the window with respect to the pitch period.

The RASTA filter removes variations in the signal that are outside the rate of change of speech by filtering the log-spectrum at each frequency band. Both very slow and very fast changes in sound are ignored by the human ear, so RASTA processing attempts to filter these components out. The filter also helps to eliminate noise due to channel variation in the data such as when various microphones are used for recording.

In the literatures (H. Hermansky and N. Morgan) [14] and (S. V. Vuuren and H. Hermansky)[15], their authors both mention that they take the measures that they filtering the signals of features in the time domain with the independent component analysis transformation to process the speech features, their purpose is to remove the correlation of each frame amongst them. We consider that the speech feature vectors actually exist some certain degree correlation amongst frames and to eliminate the correlation may not be reasonable choice and one voice generally include between 300 and 400 frames feature vectors. The computation will greatly increase the consumption of system resources. So we use above those methods to filtering the feature signals in time-domain is not easy, and we give up dealing with the features in time domain. According to the above some considerations, we cite simpler and relatively better filtering technology for time domain filtering.

RASTA Filtering of MFCC

Hermansky had made some improvements in what he proposed perceptual linear prediction (PLP, this feature improve linear prediction coefficients) with the relative spectral (RASTA) technology. The robustness of PLP after RASTA filtering shows better improving performance. Because RASTA is based on human auditory perception, this technology was taken to MFCC in recent years. In fact that human perception tends to tract the relative value of input rather than to its absolute values is very obvious in vision. Similarly, we can take knowledge of this fact in human auditory perception. Some circumstantial evidence indicates that there is a preference for sounds with a certain rate of change too. The RASTA filtering technique suppresses the spectral components that change more slowly or quickly than typical range of change of speech, and enhance the dynamic parts of noisy speech. The low cut-off frequency of the filter determines the fastest spectral change of the log spectrum, which is ignored in the output, whereas the high cut-off frequency determines the fastest spectral change that is preserved in the output parameters. The high-pass portion of the equivalent bandpass filter is expected to alleviate the effect of convolution noise introduced in the channel. The lowpass filtering helps to smooth some of the fast frame-to frame spectral changes present in the short term spectral estimate due to analysis artifacts. Because Mel frequency domain also is nonlinear frequency domain, we can filter the cepstral domain with RASTA filtering technique, in other word, we can append a filtering processing after DCT. And the DCT essentially is a linear transformation, it is not distinct between before the DCT and after, that means it is equivalent to filtering in the cepstral domain.

Transformation for the Feature Extraction when we use MFCC feature extraction, the recognition correct has been very good. However, we find that the recognition accuracy is disappointing and the insertion errors are very high. In order to decrease the insertion errors, and filtering features signals in the time domain, we use the RASTA filtering technique proposed by Hermansky after MFCC.

2   Experimental Results

The feature extraction and classification algorithm was implemented using Matlab with TIMIT databases. In Matlab, we make an audio function folder for root directory for accessing the matlab files and functions. The various functions created and scripted in matlab were used to extract the features from the wav files of TIMIT database and then classify using various classifiers. MFCC function is used to create Cepstral coefficients. Finally, the Cepstral Coefficients are classified according to various classification algorithms. In this study, we have use Hidden Markov Model as classifiers using HTK tools. The following results show the whole implementation.

This phase includes converting the speech waveform into a parametric representation with a considerably low information rate for further analysis and processing. This phase is often referred to as the signal processing front end. The speech signal can be described as a slowly timed varying signal, or quasistationary. A sample of speech from the well known speech database TIMIT, in this case from a version of TIMIT with noise added and a sample rate of 8000 Hz, can be seen below.

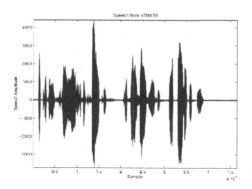

Fig. 1. Speech data from TIMIT, Fs = 16000Hz, 16-bits, telephone noise added

2.1   Frame Blocking

The first step of the feature extraction is to frame the speech into frames of approximately 30 msec (30 msec at Fs = 16000Hz gives 312 samples). To be able to extract as much features as possible from a speech sample, the technique of overlapping frames is used. The speech is blocked into frames of N samples (N = 312 in our case). With a overlapping of 50% one will get M number of frames out of a speech sample consisting of S samples:

2.2   Windowing

The next step in the processing is to window each individual frame so as to minimize the signal discontinuity at the beginning and end of each frame. The concept here is to minimize the spectral distortion by using the window to taper the signal to zero at the beginning and end of each frame. A typical window utilized for speaker verification is the Hamming window.

2.3   Fast Fourier Transform (FFT)

The next step is to apply a Fourier Transform on the windowed speech frame. Radix-4 Fast Fourier Transform is utilized, converting each frame from the time domain into the frequency domain. The FFT is a fast algorithm to implement the Discrete Fourier Transform (DFT). To get a better display of the Fourier Transform, the process of zero padding is applied. It is important to note that zero padding does not provide any additional information about the spectrum Y(w) of the sequence {x(n)}.

2.4   Mel-Frequency Wrapping

As mentioned above, studies have been conducted that show that the human perception of the frequency contents of sounds for speech signals does not follow a linear scale. Thus for each tone with an actual frequency, f, measured in Hz, a subjective pitch is measured on a scale called the Mel scale. The Mel-frequency scale is linear frequency spacing below 1000 Hz and a logarithmic spacing above 1000 Hz. As a reference point, the pitch of a 1 kHz tone, 40 dB above the perceptual hearing threshold, is defined as 1000 mels. Our approach to simulate the easier way of extracting the power from the speech is to apply a filterbank to the Power Spectrum. This filterbank is uniformly spaced on the mel scale, has a triangular bandpass frequency response, and the spacing as well as the bandwidth is determined by a constant mel frequency interval. The number of Mel spectrum coefficients, K, is typically chosen as 13, but will vary a little depending on the sampling frequency. To be observed is that we are applying these filters in the frequency domain; therefore we simply multiply those triangle-shape windows in figure 7 on the Power Spectrum.

2.5   Cepstral Coefficients

The next step is to convert the log Mel spectrum back to time. The result is called the Mel frequency cepstral coefficients (MFCC). The cepstral representation of the speech spectrum provides a good representation of the local spectral properties of the signal for the given frame analysis. Because the Mel spectrum coefficients are real numbers, we can convert them to the time domain using the Discrete Cosine Transform (DCT)-

$$MFCC_i = \sum_{k=1}^{13} Cos\left[\frac{\left(k-\frac{1}{2}\right)\pi}{13}\right] \qquad (4)$$

$$i = 1, 2\ldots\ldots\ldots M$$

The filter bank is constructed using 13 linearly-spaced filters (133.33Hz between center frequencies,) followed by 27 log-spaced filters (separated by a factor of 1.0711703 in frequency.) Each filter is constructed by combining the amplitude of FFT. The outputs from this routine implemented in Matlab are the MFCC coefficients and several optional intermediate results and inverse results. reqresp the detailed fft magnitude used in MFCC calculation, 256 rows. fb the mel-scale filter bank output, 40 rows. Here is the result of calculating the cepstral coefficients of the 'A huge tapestry hung in her hallway' utterance from the TIMIT database (TRAIN/DR5/FCDR1/SX106/ SX106.ADC) spoken by 7 speakers. The utterance is 50189 samples long at 16kHz, and all pictures are sampled at 100Hz and there are 312 frames. Note, the top row of the mfcc-cepstrum, ceps is known as C_0 and is a function of the power in the signal. Since the waveform in our work is normalized to be between -1 and 1, the C_0 coefficients are all negative. The other coefficients, C_1-C_{12}, are generally zero-mean.

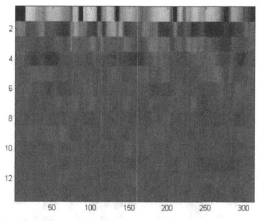

Fig. 2. Spectrogram of sample audio signal with power spectrum

After combining several FFT channels into a single Mel-scale channel, the result is the filter bank output. This is shown below (the fb output of the mfcc command includes the log10 calculation.)

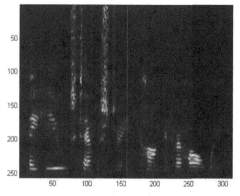

Fig. 3. MFCC's histrogram

The RASTAOUT function implements the RASTA (Relative Spectra) algorithm. The RASTA algorithm is a common piece of a speech-recognition system's front-end processing. It originally was designed to model adaptation processes in the auditory system, and to correct for environmental effects. Broadly speaking, it filters out the very low-frequency temporal components (below 1Hz) which are often due to a changing auditory environment or microphone. High frequency temporal components, above 13 Hz, are also removed since they represent changes that are faster than the speech articulators can move.

The first input to this routine in Matlab is an array of spectral data, as produced by the MFCC routines. Each row contains one "channel" of data; each column is one time slice. The fs parameter specifies the sampling rate, 100Hz in many speech recognition systems. The original RASTA filter is defined only for a frame rate of 100Hz. This code is equal to the original at 100Hz, but scales to other frame rates. Here the RASTA filter is approximated by a simple fourth order Butterworth bandpass filter.

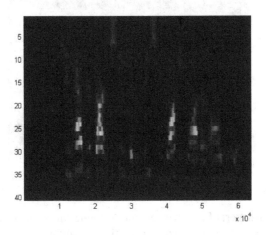

Fig. 4. MFCC's after RASTA Filtering with more sharpen spectrum images

3   Feature Matching

In our experiments, we take voice sets of TIMIT databases. The various functions of feature extraction and filters and classification are done in Matlab. For each voice in the test sets, we added Gaussian white noise to them, SNR level is from- 5db to 20db, interval 5db, and reserve the clean voices. The size of each frame is 30ms, and frame shift is 15ms. We pre-emphasis each frame after enframing the speech, pre-emphasis formula is:

$$H(z) = 1 - \mu z - 1$$

Where pre-emphasis factor $\mu = 0.9372$, because the frame length is 30ms and the sampling frequency is 16 kHz, we can use the 512-point FFT to obtain speech power spectrum. After Mel sub-band filtering, we obtain the cepstral coefficients of each frame and use the RASTA filtering technique to process the cepstral coefficients, then we get the features coefficients which we need. We select the front 13 coefficients of feature vector which has been sorted descend according to the variance, and we discard the other coefficients. What's more, the logarithmic energy of each frame is very important to reflect characteristic of voice, we append it as the supplement of feature vectors. At the same time, in order to obtain the dynamic characteristics of voice, we calculate the first and second order differential as a supplementary factor in the end of feature vector. Finally, the feature vector of each frame is consisted with 39 dimensional feature parameters. The recognition model is constructed with the non-jump from left to right continuous Hidden Markov Model (HMM). Each HMM has five states, the probability density function of the values observed under each state is the mixed Gaussian probability density function, and the transfer matrix is diagonal. Model is trained and tested by HTK.

Table 1. Classification Results

x	SNR	Clean	20dB	15dB	10dB	5Db	0dB	-5dB	Average
	Corr	85.43	85.43	81.64	37.86	27.12	21.03	9.92	**49.77**
PLP	Accurate	-3.6	-3.6	-0.5	26.82	26.33	21.03	9.92	**10.91**
	Correct	0.00	0.00	0.00	0.00	0.00	0.00	0.00	**0.36**
	Corr	98.96	82.12	75.35	59.49	22.15	8.55	8.55	**50.73**
MFCC	Accurate	65.28	-7.14	-7.40	2.80	13.42	8.55	8.55	**12.00**
	Correct	32.50	0.00	0.00	0.00	0.00	0.00	0.00	**4.64**
	Corr	100.00	99.32	96.33	82.62	49.65	23.78	9.31	**65.85**
MFCC+ RASTA	Accurate	82.55	90.26	67.13	1.05	-25.17	4.90	9.31	**32.86**
	Correct	58.75	71.25	40.00	5.00	0.00	0.00	0.00	**25.00**

In Table 1, we compare the word recognition correct, recognition accuracy and the sentence recognition correct under different SNR level, they can be indicated with Corr, Acc and Correct respectively. RA means RASTA, "+" means combing two methods. The most of the experiment results show us that the whole robustness the RASTA+MFCC method is much higher than classical PLP and classical MFCC method. Although compared the MFCC method, its average value of Corr slightly increased while its average value of Acc and Correct is also much higher than that of the MFCC and PLP method. The improving performance is obvious compared some classical feature extraction, and especially under slight high level SNR (>10db), we can get more robust feature for ASR, when we can use enhance speech method.

4   Conclusions

There are several motivations for using spectral-peak or formant features. Formants are considered to be representative of the underlying phonetic content of speech. They are also believed to be relatively robust to the presence of noise, and useful in low-bandwidth applications. Additionally, it has been hypothesized that formants or spectral peak positions can be easily adapted to different speakers. However, the extraction of robust and reliable formant estimates is a nontrivial task. Recently, there has been increased interest in other methods for estimating spectral peaks, for example, using the HMM or gravity centroid features.

We use a combination RASTA filtering technique for MFCC feature extraction in this study. One way is to replace Mel filters with ERB Gammatone filters, and another is to append a RASTA filtering in time domain after transformation. By two methods we obtain more robust feature, and we also refer that the speech enhancement can help improving robustness. Finally, because Rasta filtering used in this model is based on a linear assumption, and the voice is only similar to a linear model, in fact it is still nonlinear, we believe that the nonlinear filtering is potential, and the nonlinear filtering will become our direction in future.

References

1. Junqua, J.C., Haton, J.P.: Robustness in utomatic Speech Recognition. Kluwer Academic Publishers, Norwell (1996)
2. Hirsh, H.G., Pearce, D.: The AURORA Experimental Framework for the Performance Evaluations of Speech Recognition Systems under Noisy Conditions. In: ISCA ITRW ASR 2000, Paris, France (September 2000)
3. Saha, S.: The new age electronic patient record system. In: Proceedings of the 1995 Fourteenth Southern Biomedical Engineering Conference, April 7-9, pp. 134–137 (1995)
4. Bobbert, D., Wolska, M.: Dialog OS: An Extensible Platform for Teaching Spoken Dialogue Systems. In: Decalog 2007: Proceedings of the 11th Workshop on the Semantics and Pragmatics of Dialogue, Trento, Italy, pp. 159–160 (June 2007)
5. Fujita, K., et al.: A New Digital TV Interface Employing Speech Recognition. IEEE Trans. on Consumer Electronics 49(3), 765–769 (2003)
6. OShaughnessy, D.: Speech Communication. Addison-Wesley Publishing Company (1987)
7. Renals, S., et al.: Connectionist Probability Estimators in HMM Speech Recognition. IEEE Tran. on Speech and Audio Processing 2(1), Part 11, 161–174 (1994)
8. Juang, B.H., Rabiner, L.R.: Spectral representations for speech recognition by neural networks-a tutorial. In: Proceedings of the 1992 IEEE-SP Workshop Neural Networks for Signal Processing [1992] II, pp. 214–222 (September 1992)
9. Morgan, N., Bourlard, H.A.: Neural Networks for Statistical Recognition of Continuous Speech. Proceedings of the IEEE 83(5), 742–772 (1995)
10. Shi, M.S., Cheng, Y.M., Pu, X.L.: Probability and Statistics Tutorial, 1st edn., vol. 1, pp. 226–237. Higher Education Press, Beijing (2004)
11. Zhao, L.: Speech Signal Processing, 1st edn., vol. 1, pp. 54–55. China Machine Press, Beijing (2003)
12. Zhen, B., Wu, X.H., Liu, Z.M., Chi, H.S.: On the importance of Components of the MFCC in speech and speaker recognition. Acta Scientiarum Universitatis Pekinensis 37, 371–378 (2001)
13. Wang, W., Liu, F., Wu, S.Z.: A study for the application of RASTA on objective communication speech quality evaluation. Acta Scientiarum Universitatis Pekinensis 39, 697–702 (2003)
14. Hermansky, H., Morgan, N.: RASTA processing of speech. IEEE Transactions and Audio Processing 2, 578–589 (1994)
15. Vuuren, S.V., Hermansky, H.: Data-driven design of RASTA-like filters. In: Proceeding EUROSPEECH 1997, Rhodes. Greece, pp. 409–412 (September 1997)

Fuzzy-Based Simulation Model to Predict Flow Rate in Water Distribution Network System

Olayiwola Ojo[1], Ayodeji Oluwatope[2], Adesola Oke[3], and Adesola Aderounmu[2]

[1] Department of Computer Science Osun State College of Education, Ilesa, Nigeria
[2] Department of Computer Sci. and Engr., Obafemi Awolowo University, Ile-Ife, Nigeria
[3] Department of Civil Engineering, Obafemi Awolowo University, Ile-Ife Nigeria
steveolang@yahoo.com
{aoluwato,gaderoun,okeia}@oauife.edu.ng

Abstract. In this paper, an intelligent system using fuzzy logic was proposed to improve on the prediction of flow rate despite uncertainty in input parameters and nodal demand. This method simulates the effect of operating conditions (pipe diameter, length of pipe and frictional factor) on the flow rate. Obtained results were compared using the total error, model of selection criterion. The results revealed that fuzzy logic performed better with total error 0.033 and 0.057 Newton-Raphson respectively. It was concluded that fuzzy logic is an improved water flow rate prediction model than newton-Raphson.

Keywords: Network analysis, flow rate, frictional factor, head loss, fuzzy logic.

1   Introduction

Water is essential to life on earth. One of the most vital services to mankind is an adequate water supply, without which our society cannot survive. Humans, livestock, industrial plant and so on are all depend on water for survival. However, how to ensure adequate supply taking all factors (Population, diseases outbreak, linkages and uncertainties in input values) taking water system into consideration remains a challenge. During the last two decades, water demand increased rapidly in developing countries as a result of high population growth, improvement of living standards, rapid urbanization, industrialization and improvement of economic conditions while accessibility to source of water is decreasing [1]. Water is poorly distributed within countries and between seasons. Hence, practical distribution concerned with time, space and affordability lead to a widening gap between demand and supply in many parts of the world.

As water networks are large scale and non-linear systems, human operators are faced with the need to take right decisions, such as pumping more water or closing a valve, within a short period of time and quite frequently in the absence of reliable measurement information such as pressure and flow values [2]. This then becomes a modeling scenario so that all the factors (pipe flows, pipe length, internal diameter of pipe, velocities, nodal demand, head losses, pressures and heads, reservoir levels, reservoir inflows and outflows etc) can be brought together and modeled. Simulation

S. Dua et al. (Eds.): ICISTM 2012, CCIS 285, pp. 315–324, 2012.
© Springer-Verlag Berlin Heidelberg 2012

of water distribution network system (pressure at any point, pipe sizes, and flow rate) is germane because it can not be easily altered like water production. This therefore shows the importance of pipe network analysis, which is the technique commonly used for pipe network analysis (sizing the pipe, flow rate, discharge pressure, and headloss [3].

Various approaches have been used in the time past to address water distribution problems particularly pipe network analysis, such approaches include loop equations, numerical minimization methods, Newton-Raphson algorithm, Artificial Neural Network (ANN) [2] Linear programming, Hardy Cross equation for balanced discharges, Integer programming, non-linear programming, automatic loop extraction and dynamic programming have been applied to the optimization of small pipe network problems.

Although results from aforementioned modeling were encouraging but due to the complexity in water distribution network most of the existing modeling are developed using simpler version with precise crisp input values. Models with uncertainty are not popular in engineering practice due to complexity and duration of calculation []. Uncertainty may be as a result of inaccuracy in measuring instrument, lack of information or knowledge about the input variable, inherent stochastic variability, fluctuations in instantaneous demands and it may be due to simplifying assumptions used to model the hydraulics or water quality in the system [6];[7] . Therefore there is a need to develop a model that would adequately incorporate the uncertainty inherent in the data set of water distribution for effective network analysis. In this study, the potential applicability of fuzzy logic for analysis of water distribution network system was explored.

In the recent time, fuzzy logic approach became a preferable tool for dealing with a complex system and system with nonlinearities or uncertainties [8, 9]. Fuzzy Logic being a simple yet very powerful problem solving technique has extensive applicability. It is currently used in the fields of business, systems control, electronics and traffic engineering. The technique can be used to generate solutions to problems based on vague, ambiguous, qualitative, incomplete or imprecise information [10]. Fuzzy logic are fundamental tools for nonlinear complex system modeling [11] providing mathematical framework for expressing linguistic variables and rules, and inheriting the same ambiguity and imprecision, which follows human reasoning. The focus of this study is to develop a fuzzy-logic model for predicting the flow rate in water distribution system. In addition, we compared results obtained with prediction using Newton-Raphson method.

2   Water Distribution System

Water distribution system is an interconnection of water distribution elements for efficient distribution among its member [13]. Water distribution system are (WDS) are large scale and spatially extensive, composed of multiple pipe loops to maintain satisfactory levels of redundancy, governed by nonlinear hydraulic equations, designed with inclusion of complex hydraulic devises such as valves and pumps and complicated by numerous layout, pipe sizing and pumping alternatives[14]. The water distribution network diagram of Ede South was obtained from Osun State Water Works, South-West Nigeria. Figure 1 is the map of tthe water distribution network of the case – study was extracted from original copy. It has seven loops. In figure 2, the pipe and loop label, pipe diameter, and length were assigned, and withdrawals at each node were shown. figure 3 shows estimated value of Q for entire network and arbitrary values Q assigned at each node such that continuity is satisfy at each junction (nodes), assumed direction of flow (Q is positive if assumed direction of flow is clockwise and Q is negative if the assumed direction of flow is anticlockwise)

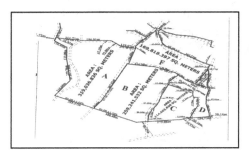
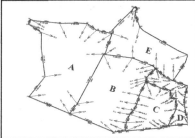

Fig. 1. Ede South water distribution network diagram

Fig. 2. Ede South water distribution showing pipe and loopanalysis

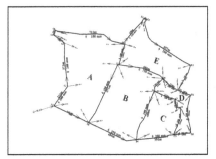
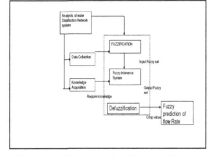

Fig. 3. Ede South water distribution Showing estimated value of Q

Fig. 4. Conceptual Model for water distribution analysis

2.1   Water Distribution Network Analysis

One of the most common but important steps in water resources engineering is water distribution network analysis (pipe network analysis). Computational methods for water distribution network analysis include linear theory, Hardy Cross and Newton-Raphson [4]. It has been shown statistically that Newton-Rapson has the highest correlation expression, reliability and higher accuracy, validity and good fitness. Therefore, it was concluded that the Newton-Raphson method should be the first method of choice when making pipe network analysis [4]. Newton-Rapson method is generally accepted the best method but the uncertainty in the input parameters were not adequately addressed. For instance nodal demand and frictional factor may be a source of uncertainty. Significant amount of uncertainties may be incorporated with model simplification and conceptualization. However, representing uncertainty using fuzzy set, theory, estimating uncertainty of model output parameters may, under certain conditions, be significantly simplified, and cover a wider range of input parameters. Although, it can not give us statistical information about uncertainty appearance (phenomenon), fuzzy set information about uncertainty quantity is more significant. Therefore, in this study, fuzzy logic approach was considered and results were compared with the Newton- Raphson. In pipe network analysis, it is normally assumed that water withdrawal takes place at the node, with a fixed and known value. The first assumption is aimed at simplifying the mathematical solution of the problem, while the second has been a standard practice, since water consumption is a function of pressure at the point, although not always adequate [4].

The combined conservation of flow and energy equations are the basis of modeling and simulating water distribution systems. The general expression for conservation of flow at each node in the network is:

$$\Sigma Q_{in} - \Sigma Q_{out} = \Sigma Q_{ext} \qquad (1)$$

Where $Q_{ij} = flow$ from node i to node j.

A conservation of energy equation is required for each loop in the network:

$$\Sigma h_l = 0 \qquad (2)$$

[ ]

The amount of flow that enters to a node equal the amount that leaves the node plus the consumption in the respective node. Then From the figure 3 diagram above, we arrived at the following equations.

$$Q_a + Q_h + 0.002 = 0.07 \qquad (3)$$

$$Q_a + Q_h = 0.068. \qquad (4)$$

$$Q_a + Q_b = 0.004. \qquad (5)$$

Thirty equations were formulated from the network diagram and were solved using matlab. The Population of people living in Ede - South (case study) area was obtained from National Population Commission, Ede. Figure 3 above is summarized in table 1 consisting of five complete loops and the initial parameters of control variables . Therefore, estimated quantity of water for the entire network, Q (l/s) equals population of people in Ede south multiplied by assumed quantity of water to be taken by an individual per day.

Q = 75,489* 80 = 6039120 liters /day
   = 70 liter/second or = 0.07 m³/s

3   Fuzzy – Based Model for Water Distribution Analysis

An intelligent system using fuzzy logic is developed for water distribution network analysis. The proposed system helps to reduce time require for effective analysis of water distribution network and the uncertainty inherent in the input data were adequately addressed. In short the fuzzy model consists of six stages including situation analysis, knowledge acquisition, data collection, fuzzification, a fuzzy inference engine and defuzzification   Figure 4 shows the model diagram.

3.1   Analysis of Water Distribution Network System

The first stage is situation analysis which is concerned with the investigation of the problem to be dealt with. Better analysis of the water distribution network system is the key to success at this stage, which provides essential information to support the design of the fuzzy system as well as the selection of the linguistic values.

3.2   Data Collection

Data are collected from different data classifications as mentioned above. Classified raw data need to be mapped into the relevant category with the right format prior to being delivered to the fussy system as the input data set. These input data received from the external world may exist in dissimilar formats, such as crisp numeric data, bivalent data, linguistic data, statistical data and a set of crisp values. Some data can be put into the fuzzy system directly while other data may not be format-compatible. For example, some sets of data represent the form of diagrams are obviously not supported for direct data integration [17]. Auto-CAD map was used to find the length of pipe (m), area in m^2 and reduce the original network to a smaller size   .

3.3   Knowledge Acquisition

Acquired knowledge needs to be extracted from the related domain follow by the procedure to turn it to IF - THEN statements which form part of the fuzzy system. Knowledge acquisition can be conducted in different ways such as interview of domain expert and data mining of historical data. Interview of domain expert was adopted for this study.

3.4   Fuzzification and Inference Engine

Fuzzification is the first stage of operation in the fuzzy system. It is mainly concerned with the conversion of the input data set (from the data collection process) into fuzzy sets. Universe of discourse included frictional factor, x, x ϵ (0.00-0.03), diameter, y, y ϵ (0.0-0.35), pipe length, z, z ϵ(0.0-720) and membership function used triangle with trapezoidal function were used for the input variables (see fig 5.). The fuzzy inference engine is the second stage of the fuzzy system. Its main operation is to convert the input fuzzy set into an output fuzzy set through an inference process which includes rule block formation, rule composition, rule firing implication and aggregation. The rule block consists of a number of fuzzy rules which are interrelated and normally operate bases on certain set criteria. Mamdani fuzzy inference system with three inputs and only one output were used. The inputs are: pipe length L (m), internal diameter of the pipe D (m), frictional factor, F. While the output is the flow rate (Discharge) m^3/s as shown in figure 5. For each input, a number of membership functions are assigned. The control variables defined are: Diameter = {Small, Medium, Large}, Frictional Factor = {Low, Medium, High} and Length = {low, Average, Long,}. Figure 6 presents the surface diagram of the effect of pipe diameter and length on the flow rate

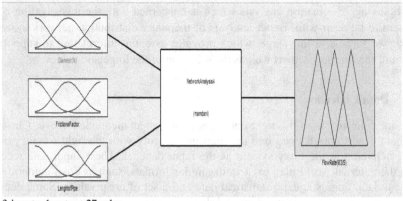

3 inputs, 1 output 27 rules

Fig. 5. Fuzzy Inference System Simulating the whole Process

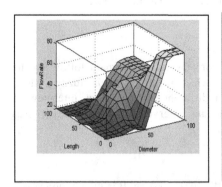

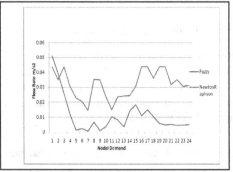

Fig. 6. Fuzzy Surface Diameter and length versus flow rate

Fig. 7. A graph comparing fuzzy output with Newton- Raphson results

3.5   Performance Evaluation of the Model

For the purpose of evaluating the model, total error, and model of selection criterion were chosen as performance statistics with which the model can be assessed in terms of accuracy and reliability. The total error is the sum of the squares of the errors between the obtained values and the predicted values, can be interpreted as a measure of variation in the values predicted unexplained by the values obtained data [19]. The lower the value of total error the higher the accuracy, validity, and good fitness of the method. Total error (Err^2) can be computed using Equation (7): The MSC is interpreted as the proportion of expected data variation that can be explained by the obtained data. The higher the value of MSC, the higher the accuracy, and validity of the method. MSC can be computed using Equation (8) The fuzzy-based and Newton – Raphson method for pipe network models were subjected to the same conditions and the performance evaluation statistics, total error coefficient of determination and model of selection criterion were used to determine the accuracy.

$$Err^2 = \sum_{i=1}^{n}\left(Y_{obsci} - Y_{cali}\right)^2 . \tag{7}$$

$$MSC = \ln\frac{\sum_{i=1}^{n}\left(Y_{obsci} - \overline{Y}_{obs}\right)^2}{\sum_{i=1}^{n}\left(Y_{obsci} - Y_{cali}\right)^2} - \frac{2p}{n}. \tag{8}$$

$$CD = \frac{\sum_{i=1}^{n}\left(Y_{obsci} - \overline{Y}_{cali}\right)^2 - \sum_{i=1}^{n}\left(Y_{obsci} - Y_{cali}\right)^2}{\sum_{i=1}^{n}\left(Y_{obsci} - Y_{cali}\right)^2} \tag{9}$$

[18] Where n is the number of observations and p is the number of parameters used. Y_{obsci} and Y_{cali} are the observed and calculated values respectively and $\overline{Y}_{obs}$ is the mean of the observed.

4   Discussions of Results

Table1 shows the initial parameters used for the model. Table2 shows the summary of performance evaluation. The total errors are 0.0338 and 0.0570 for fuzzy logic and Newton-Rapson respectively. These results indicate that fuzzy logic presents prediction with lower error than Newton – Raphson. Coefficient of determination values are 0.56 and 0.30 for the fuzzy logic and Newton-Raphson methods respectively (Table 2) which presents fuzzy logic predictions are more accurrate that Newton-Raphson predictions. Also Model of Selection Criterion values are 0.36 and 0.35 for the fuzzy logic approach and Newton-Raphson respectively (Table2). These results indicate that fuzzy logic predictions slightly higher MSC than Newton-Raphson predictions value is very close to Newton Raphson. The reasons adduced for the closeness is that there were some parameters, such as gravitational force and π which included for the Newton-Raphson model and were excluded from fuzzy logic because it was impossible to fuzzy constants.

Table 1. Initial parameters

LN	LL	D (m)	LP(m)
A1A2	a.	0.2	211
A2A3	b.	0.2	373
A3A4	c.	0.2	126
A4A5	d.	0.15	42
A5A6	e.	0.15	711
A6A7	f.	0.1	185
A7A8	g.	0.1	571
A1A8	h.	0.2	355
A8B4	i.	0.25	484
B2B4	j.	0.1	480
B1B2	k.	0.1	144
A7B1	l.	0.15	486
B4C3	m.	0.1	356
C2C3	n.	0.1	244
C1C2	o.	0.15	105
B2C1	p.	0.2	216
C3D3	q.	0.2	155
D2D3	r.	0.2	346
D1D2	s.	0.2	107
B1D1	t.	0.2	174
D1E3	u.	0.15	247
E3E2	v.	0.2	657
E2E1	w.	0.15	29
E1A6	x.	0.15	258

LN=Loop Number, LL=Loop Label, D= Diameter and Lp= Length

Table 2. Statistical table for performance evaluation

MT	FL	NR
Total error (Err^2)	0.033	0.057
Model of selection criterion	0.36	0.35
Coefficient of determine	0.56	0.30

MT=Model Type, FL=Fuzzy Logic, NR=Newton Raphson

4.1   Conclusion

The best performance of any model requires that the models should be allowed to run under various conditions repeatedly so that the parameter that gave best result from the model can be adopted. Once this is done, the model accuracy can be assessed to determine whether the model can be used for real life operation. The fuzzy logic has been successfully used to capture nonlinear relationship and address the uncertainty in water distribution model. Fuzzy model demonstrated an improved accuracy over the Hard cross and linear theory. Therefore, its use should be adopted.

Acknowledgement. This work is being partly sponsored by the STEP-B(Science and Technologoy Education at the Post-Basic Level) funding through a World Bank grant for the establishment of Center of Excellence in Software Engineering, Obafemi Awolowo University, Ile-Ife. Nigeria. (Grant No. 4304-UNI).

References

1. Abderrahman, W.A.: Urban Water Management in Developing Arid Countries. Water Resources Development 16, 7–20 (2002)
2. Makropoulos, C.K., Butler, D.: Spatial Decisions under Uncertainty: Fuzzy Inference in Urban Water Management. Journal of Hyroinformatics, 3–18 (2004)
3. Arsene, C.T.C., Bargiela, A.: Modeling and Simulation of Water System Based on Loop Equations. I.J. of Simulation 5, 61–72 (2004)
4. Oke, I.A.: Reliability and Statistical Assessment of Methods for Pipe Network Analysis. Environmental Engineering Science 24, 1481–1490 (2007)
5. Maskey, S., Guinot, V., Price, R.: Treatment of Precipitation Uncertainty in Rainfall-Runoff Modelling. Advance in Water Resources 27, 889–898 (2004)
6. Despic, O., Simonovic, S.: Methods in Evaluating Qualitative Criteria in Water Resources Multi-Criteria Decision-Making. Water Resources Research Report no. 37, Dept. of Civil and Geological Engineering, University of Manitoba. Dubois, D. & Prade, H, Operations on fuzzy numbers. Int. (1978)
7. Vankayala, P.: Contaminant Source Identification in Water Distribution Networks under the Conditions of Uncertainty. Msc Thesis in Department of civil Engineering, North Carolina State University (2007)
8. Ureigho, R.J., Oshoiribhor, E., Ogbogbo, G.: Contribution of Fuzzy logic to artificial Intelligence (AI). International Journal of Computer Science 2, 57–59 (2010)
9. Abdou, M.A., Konsowa, A.H., Ossman, M.A.: Fuzzy- Based Simulation Model For Declorization of Industrial Waste Water. Journal of Applied Sciences Research 4, 178–187 (2008)
10. Jim, M.: Applications of fuzzy logic in operational meteorology. Scientific Services and Professional Development Newsletter. In: Canadian Forces Weather Service, pp. 42–54 (1995)
11. Castillo, O., Melin, P.: Intelligent systems with interval type-2 fuzzy logic. International Journal of innovative Computing, Information and Control 4, 771–783 (2008)
12. Bardossy, Y., Duckstein, C.A.: Fuzzy Rule-Based Modelling with Applications to Geophysical, Biological and Engineering Systems. CRC Press, Boca Raton (1995)

13. Aderounmu, G.A., Adagunodo, E.R., Akintola, A.A., Adetoye, A.O.: An Agent –Based Approach to Water Distribution System Control. Journal of Agricultural Engineering and Technology 6, 39–46 (1998)
14. Kulshrestha, S., Khosa, R.: Clips Based Decision Support System for Water Distribution Networks. Drink. Water Eng. Sci. Discuss. 4, 1–38 (2011), http://www.drink-water-eng-sci-discuss.net/4/1/2011/doi:10.5194/dwesd-4-1-2011
15. Magdy, A.R., Berge, D., Nageh, G.E., Ahmed, H.: Optimization of Potable Water Network. In: Seventh International Water Technology Conference, Egypt, pp. 506–521 (2003)
16. Leung, R.W.K., Lau, H.C.W., Kwong, C.K.: On A Responsive Replenishment SystemA Fussy Logic Approach. Journal of Expert System 20, 20–32 (2003)
17. Oke, I.A., Akindahunsi, A.A.: A Statistical Evaluation of Methods of Determining BOD Rate. J. Appl. Sci. Res. 1, 223–232
18. Babatola, J.O., Oguntuase, A.M., Oke, I.A., Ogedengbe, M.O.: An Evaluation of Frictional Factors in Pipe Network Analysis Using Statistical Methods. Environmental Engineering Science 25, 1–9 (2008)

An FPGA Noise Resistant Digital Temperature Sensor with Auto Calibration

Brandon A. Brown*, Todd R. Andel, and Yong Kim

Air Force Institute of Technology, WPAFB, OH 45234, USA

Abstract. This paper presents a noise resistant, auto calibrated all digital temperature sensor for circuit protection applications. The sensor uses a variable pulse-based design, allowing one-temperature-point calibration, significantly reducing time and costs for mass production and deployment. Since a digital temperature sensor is meant to serve an auxiliary role alongside a main circuit, the sensor is designed to filter out the noise and retain accuracy while an RSA circuit is encrypting. The proposed digital temperature sensor and RSA circuit are implemented on a Field Programmable Gate Array and tested using a temperature controlled chamber. The result is a low cost, low power temperature sensor resistant to noise and suitable for quick deployment in digital devices.

1 Introduction

In the past decade, thermal sensing in digital devices has become increasingly important. In the commercial realm, increasing processing power has led to increased heat and the need for thermal management schemes to ensure system reliability. From a security perspective, thermal detection has become necessary to protect against recent thermal-based attacks on digital devices. As demonstrated in [1], freezing dynamic random access memory significantly lengthens the time data is readable after loss of power, leaving critical memory contents vulnerable to attackers. Thus, there has been an escalating demand for low-cost, low power temperature sensors that can be seamlessly integrated onto digital devices.

Traditional temperature sensors measure the base-emitter voltages of bipolar transistors, which varies with temperature [2,3]. The voltages must be measured using an analog-to-digital (ADC) converter. While these analog sensors have proven reliability and a high degree of accuracy, the expense is large area and significant power consumption due to the ADC, preventing their adoption in mobile devices. These sensors also require separate external design and fabrication since they are not compatible with the Complementary Metal Oxide Semiconductor (CMOS) process. These problems are additionally compounded if many sensors are desired to characterize a larger area on the chip.

---

* The views expressed in this article are those of the authors and do not reflect the official policy or position of the United States Air Force, Department of Defense, or the U.S. Government. This work is performed with support from the Air Force Office of Scientific Research under grant number F1ATA01103J001.

S. Dua et al. (Eds.): ICISTM 2012, CCIS 285, pp. 325–335, 2012.

Fully digital temperature sensors based on the correlation between integrated circuit propagation delay and core temperature are much more suitable for circuit protection applications. It has generally been assumed that while a digital temperature sensor is smaller and more efficient than its analog counterparts, that it does so at the expense of accuracy [4]. However, many of the latest designs have accuracies within reach of a typical analog sensor and are more than adequate for circuit protection applications. A digital temperature sensor's small size and low power allow for many sensors to be placed on a single chip, even in mobile devices. An all digital approach allows for easy integration with Very Large Scale Integration (VLSI) systems and even dynamic insertion and removal in programmable logic devices such as Field Programmable Gate Arrays (FP-GAs). In the case of security systems, digital sensor implementations are much more difficult to detect and disable since they are integrated and dispersed within the device.

One of the earliest designs in [5] uses a ring oscillator to measure propagation delay, where the the number of oscillations in a given time is proportional to temperature. With this approach, extensive calibration is required over the expected operating temperature range. More recent designs, such as in [6,7,8,4,9,10,11], use more advanced time-to-digital converters to increase accuracy. These sensors measure delay at two different temperatures to calibrate out process variation, stemming from device fabrication. While more efficient than a complete calibration over an entire temperature range, two-point calibration is still too tedious and time consuming, especially if a large number of sensors are utilized on a chip.

The latest designs attempt to operate with one-point calibration. One-point calibration loses some accuracy, but the trade-off is much easier and results in quicker calibration, substantially decreasing the time and cost of calibrating many sensors. A digital temperature sensor using dual-delay-locked-loops (DLLs) to calibrate at one-point is proposed in [6]. However, the DLLs require a substantial increase in chip area and power. In addition, the device is custom fabricated, negating much of the time and cost benefits of one-point calibration since fabrication is significantly more expensive and time consuming than implementation on an FPGA.

All of these prior designs have not been tested in the presence of additional circuitry. Since digital temperature sensors are designed to supplement a main circuit on the same chip, they must be resistant to noise and power fluctuations resulting from other components. It is expected that a digital temperature sensor sensitive to delay is likely to be negatively affected by other circuitry on the same device.

The goal of this research is to study the effects of additional components and implement measures to mitigate any adverse effects. In addition, auto calibration is developed to enable rapid mass calibration of many sensors outside the lab environment, reducing the time and cost of high volume deployment and permitting operation in the field. The sensor builds upon the work of [6,7,11], retaining the benefits of small size, low power, and one-point calibration. The addition of noise resistance and auto calibration provide a sensor suitable for circuit protection applications.

2   Digital Temperature Sensor Design

The proposed digital temperature sensor design is shown in Figure 1. The pulse based design measures the time for a ring oscillator to reach a variable number of circulations, rather than count the number of oscillations in a given time period. The former is more precise since it eliminates potential residual delay not counted if the circulation has not completed.

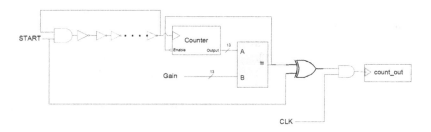

Fig. 1. Proposed design of the digital temperature sensor

The sensor is comprised of two main components - a delay generator and a time-to-digital converter. The delay generator uses a fixed ring oscillator and a counter to generate a circulation period sensitive to delay. The total circulation time is measured by creating a pulse: the START initiates the pulse and the counter terminates the pulse when the counter has reached the variable pre-set number of oscillations. The variable number of oscillations, known as the gain, allows for easy adjustment of the pulse width, an important aspect for calibration.

The time-to-digital converter digitally encodes the pulse width using the system clock as a reference. An AND gate continually increments a counter as long as the pulse is high, so that the measured time is effectively the number of clock cycles of the system.

2.1   Auto Calibration

An important feature of the sensor is auto calibration, which allows the device to be calibrated dynamically at its current temperature. Auto calibration, utilizing one-point calibration, offers several advantages over previous methods of calibration. Full calibration, taking numerous measurements over the range of expected use, is far too tedious and requires precision equipment to produce the desired temperatures. Two-point calibration is more practical. However, even two-point calibration still requires external equipment to achieve two significantly different temperature points. For thermal sensing applications, where many sensors are placed on a chip, each sensor is required to be independently calibrated. Thus, two-point calibration is not feasible for a digital temperature sensor.

One-point calibration allows for calibration at room temperature without external equipment. Auto calibration is made possible since the device is easily able to re-calibrate at any given temperature, without user intervention. While one-point calibration is not as accurate as two-point calibration, the trade-off is significant cost and time savings, especially since precision and accuracy requirements may vary. For example, to detect the freezing attack mentioned previously, sensing a large change in temperature may be more important than the precision or accuracy of the exact temperature points.

One point calibration is made possible by the variable gain input, which effectively adjusts the pulse width of each sensor. Since each temperature sensor will be unique at the physical level, the delay of each sensor on the device is also unique. The variable gain allows the calibration to normalize all temperature sensors to a reference device. The reference device is usually an analog sensor or another digital temperature sensor. The following explains the calibration process.

Propagation delay for an equal strength CMOS inverter is given by the following equation:

$$D = \frac{L}{W} \frac{C_L}{C_{ox}} * \frac{1}{\mu} * \frac{ln(3 - 4V_{th}/V_{dd})}{V_{dd}(1 - V_{th}/V_{dd})}$$

Only two variables within this equation are affected by temperature: μ, the electron mobility, and V_{th}, the threshold voltage. It is estimated that the temperature dependence due to V_{th} is only a few percent of that due to μ and therefore negligible [6]. We assume, at a loss of accuracy, that μ varies linearly with temperature. Since the supply voltage V_{dd} is kept constant, the equation can be simplified to the following:

$$D = P * T * C$$

Here, P is the process variation, T is the temperature dependence, and C is the remaining constants. Since the length of the ring oscillator is fixed (but not the number of circulations), the delay represents one circulation of the ring oscillator. The digital output $DOUT$ of the reference digital temperature sensor, known as the master sensor, is now:

$$Dout_M(T) = N_M * D_M = P_M * T * C * N_M$$

The term N_M is the gain (the number of oscillations required), chosen empirically or based on previous research. The master sensor is fitted to actual

temperatures by multiple point calibration and least-squares regression. This
tedious portion is only required once to find the general correlation between
delay and temperature. The calibration temperature point T_C is chosen, usually
room temperature, and the master $DOUT$ is recorded.

$$Dout_M(T_C) = N_M * D_M = P_M * T_C * C * N_M$$

For any other digital temperature sensor, one-point calibration is now possible.
At the same calibration temperature, the $DOUT_I$ is recorded. The only unknown
is P_I, the process variation due to unique device fabrication.

$$Dout_I(T_C) = N_I * D_M = P_I * T_C * C * N_I$$

The process variation is compensated by adjusting the gain value for each individual sensor. At the calibration temperature, the gain is found by the difference
in the process, reflected by the difference in the $DOUT$ values.

$$N_I = \frac{N_M * Dout_M}{Dout_I}$$

After this one-point calibration, each sensor will ideally have the same $DOUT$
value for any given temperature, regardless of the physical differences and the
unique delays.

2.2   Noise Resistance

Another key feature of the proposed digital temperature sensor is its resistance
to digital component noise. The digital temperature sensor is meant to provide
a critical auxiliary role alongside a main component. Implemented alone, the
temperature sensor is clumsy and expensive at best. However, most previous
research does not include a main computational activity in the implementation
and experimentation. Because digital temperature sensors rely on the delay of
integrated circuits, it is expected that additional circuitry running concurrently
may effect this delay, and consequently the calibration and accuracy of the sensors. While ignoring additional circuitry may provide a more accurate sensor, it
is not realistic and does not support the original intent of the sensor. Thus, it is
imperative that the sensor be immune to noise from other circuits. Two methods
are proposed to filter out noise from the main activity:

Noise Lock. A lock is placed on the device while the digital temperature sensor
is taking a sample, forcing the main circuit to remain idle during a temperature
read, ensuring the sensor is free from noise. However, the obvious loss of computational time leads to slower devices, depending on the sensor sampling rate.
It also may not be possible to lock a main circuit via an interrupt in the middle
of a long main process.

Noise Calibration. A more elegant solution is calibrating the sensor to account for the extra noise present. One-point calibration, as discussed earlier, is used twice - once with the main circuit and once without, storing two gain vales for each sensor. The sensor is calibrated during the execution of the main circuit to filter out the noise generated. When sampling after calibration, the sensor checks whether the main activity is occurring and selects the correct calibration. Using this method, the main activity is not modified, and the circuit does not sacrifice speed or area. If the main circuit is modified, a quick recalibration is all that is required to maintain an accurate sensor.

3   Experimental Results

To evaluate the design, six temperature sensors are implemented on a Xilinx Virtex 5 XC5VFX70T FPGA. The number of inverters in the delay line is set at 35, based on previous research [12] and empirical data. The baseline gain from which all digital temperature sensors are calibrated is set at 8192. The high gain and relatively short delay line ensures a very fine calibration resolution without a substantial increase in size or power consumption. The temperature sensors are measured from 0 °C to 80 °C ambient temperature in 10 °C increments using a programmable temperature chamber. The FPGA is given five minutes at each point to reach thermal equilibrium, at which the core temperature is approximately 15 °C higher than the ambient temperature. All calibrations are done at room temperature (23 °C). While this may not be the most accurate point, it is the most practical since no temperature chamber is required for operation outside the lab environment.

Although all six temperature sensors are implemented on the same FPGA, each has their own process variation, and must be individually calibrated. To show the need for calibration, the measurement results for each sensor before calibration is shown in Figure 2. Here, the process variation is incorrectly assumed to be the same for all sensors, and each uses the same calibration of one sensor. So, the gain of each sensor is fixed at 8192.

Next, each sensor is simultaneously calibrated at room temperature (one-point calibration) using the onboard System Monitor ADC sensor as a reference. The gain of each sensor is now unique to account for the process variation among the sensors. The gain values are stored locally on the FPGA, and the device theoretically never needs calibration again. However, if the device will be used in a different temperature range, re-calibration is recommended to ensure the highest accuracy. After one-point calibration, the same measurement is repeated, shown in Figure 3.

The average error of each sensor is shown in Figure 4, where the maximum error of all the sensors is about 4 °C. Taking the average of all the sensors at each temperature point yields a maximum error of 3 °C. The error here is due to the assumptions made earlier. Firstly, we assumed that μ varies linearly with temperature based on experimentally fitted data. As shown in Figure 4, the error increases the further the temperature point is from the calibration temperature.

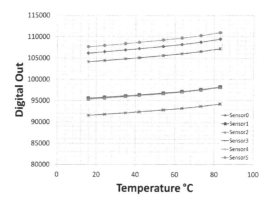

Fig. 2. Digital temperature sensor response without calibration

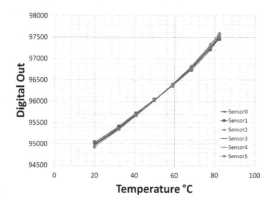

Fig. 3. Digital temperature sensor response after calibration at room temperature

Another source of error is ignoring the effect of V_{th} on temperature. Although the effect is small, the process variation is not completely removed, adding to the error. While these assumptions due cause a decrease in accuracy, the simple equation allowing for one-point calibration translates to significant cost and time savings, as mentioned previously.

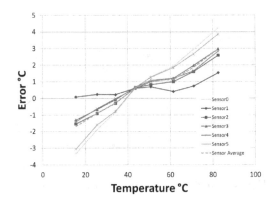

Fig. 4. Digital temperature sensor response error vs System Monitor ADC on a single FPGA after auto calibration

To evaluate the noise resistance of the sensor, a 512-bit RSA circuit is implemented on the FPGA alongside the six temperature sensors. The 512-bit RSA circuit utilizes over 50% of the FPGA resources, providing a good workload to represent a highly computational circuit. Measurement results with the RSA circuit disabled and encrypting are shown in Figure 5. The results are measured after one-point calibration. Clearly, RSA impacts the accuracy of the sensor. The higher digital out values with RSA running indicate the sensors took longer to complete, and hence were slower.

In order to filter out the apparent effects of the RSA circuit, noise calibration is performed on the digital temperature sensor. Similar to the one-point calibration previously discussed, the noise calibrating performs this same procedure, except with RSA encrypting during the calibration. Two gain values are now stored for each sensor, one with RSA, and one without. After noise calibration, the device selects the appropriate gain value when reading the temperature. Using this approach, measurement results are once again performed.

From Figure 6, it appears the noise calibration is able to correct the offset from the RSA noise. Looking at the error in Figure 7, the sensor performs no worse in the presence of noise after noise calibration compared with calibration without noise. Thus, the digital temperature sensor is able to run alongside a main circuit without a substantial loss of accuracy, so long as a separate calibration is run simultaneously with main computational circuit.

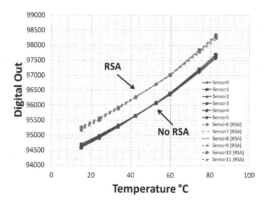

Fig. 5. Digital temperature sensor response with 512-bit RSA computing

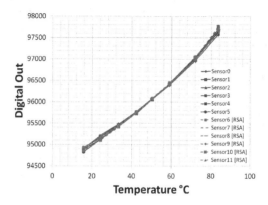

Fig. 6. Digital temperature sensor response with 512-bit RSA computing after noise calibration

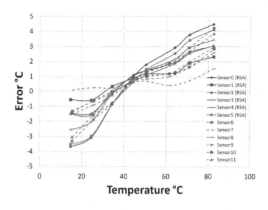

Fig. 7. Digital temperature sensor error with 512-bit RSA computing after noise calibration

It is difficult to point to the exact source of noise from the additional RSA circuit. Since the circuit and sensors are implemented on an FPGA, the specific details of the design are left to the Xilinx synthesizer. However, it is speculated that the noise may result from a slight drop in voltage when running both circuits. Since voltage also affects delay, any change in voltage would affect the delay and thus the reported temperature. Noise calibration would in effect be calibrating out the change in voltage. Initially, voltage was assumed to be kept constant, which means any change in voltage requires a recalibration. Regardless of the specific reason, the recalibration with the inclusion of noise allows the sensor to operate with no worse accuracy than calibration without the noise.

4   Conclusion

In this paper, an auto calibrated, noise resistant digital temperature sensor is presented. It retains the specification of many other digital temperature sensors, such as low power and low area, while also being noise resistant to a computationally intensive circuit. Two methods are presented to filter out the noise. A simple solution is to halt any main computing activity while the sensing is occurring. A more practical and robust solution is to calibrate out the effects of noise by storing two gain values for each sensor. Auto calibration allows the sensor to quickly calibrate and operate in the field, reducing mass deployment costs and time. The result is a digital temperature sensor able to fulfil its auxiliary role as a practical, efficient temperature sensor for digital circuit protection.

References

1. Halderman, J.A., Schoen, S.D., Heninger, N., Clarkson, W., Paul, W., Cal, J.A., Feldman, A.J., Felten, E.W.: Least we remember: Cold boot attacks on encryption keys. In: USENIX Security Symposium (2008)
2. Bakker, A., Huijsing, J.H.: Micropower CMOS temperature sensor with digital output 31(7), 933–937 (1996)
3. Bakker, A.: CMOS smart temperature sensors - an overview. In: Proc. IEEE Sensors, vol. 2, pp. 1423–1427 (2002)
4. Chen, P., Shie, M.-C., Zheng, Z.-Y., Zheng, Z.-F., Chu, C.-Y.: A fully digital time-domain smart temperature sensor realized with 140 FPGA logic elements. IEEE Transactions on Circuits and Systems I: Regular Papers 54(12), 2661–2668 (2007)
5. Lopez-Buedo, S., Garrido, J., Boemo, E.: Thermal testing on reconfigurable computers. IEEE Design & Test of Computers 17(1), 84–91 (2000)
6. Woo, K., Meninger, S., Xanthopoulos, T., Crain, E., Ha, D., Ham, D.: Dual-DLL-based CMOS all-digital temperature sensor for microprocessor thermal monitoring. In: Proc. IEEE Int. Solid-State Circuits Conf. - Digest of Technical Papers ISSCC 2009, pp. 68–69 (2009)
7. Chung, C.-C., Yang, C.-R.: An autocalibrated all-digital temperature sensor for on-chip thermal monitoring. IEEE Transactions on Circuits and Systems II: Express Briefs 58(2), 105–109 (2011)

8. Chen, P., Chen, C.-C., Tsai, C.-C., Lu, W.-F.: A time-to-digital-converter-based CMOS smart temperature sensor. IEEE Journal of Solid-State Circuits 40(8), 1642–1648 (2005)
9. Chen, P., Wang, K.-M., Peng, Y.-H., Wang, Y.-S., Chen, C.-C.: A time-domain SAR smart temperature sensor with inaccuracy for on-chip monitoring. In: Proc. 34th European Solid-State Circuits Conf. ESSCIRC 2008, pp. 70–73 (2008)
10. Chen, P., Chen, T.-K., Wang, Y.-S., Chen, C.-C.: A time-domain sub-micro watt temperature sensor with digital set-point programming. IEEE Sensors Journal 9(12), 1639–1646 (2009)
11. Chen, P., Chen, S.-C., Shen, Y.-S., Peng, Y.-J.: All-digital time-domain smart temperature sensor with an inter-batch inaccuracy of-0.7 to 0.6 after one-point calibration. IEEE Transactions on Circuits and Systems I: Regular Papers 58(5), 913–920 (2011)
12. Franco, J.J.L., Boemo, E., Castillo, E., Parrilla, L.: Ring oscillators as thermal sensors in FPGAs: Experiments in low voltage. In: Proc. VI Southern Programmable Logic Conf (SPL), pp. 133–137 (2010)

Twisting Additivity in Program Obfuscation

Mila Dalla Preda[1], Wu Feng[2,*], Roberto Giacobazzi[3],
Richard Greechie[2], and Arun Lakhotia[4]

[1] University of Bologna, Bologna, Italy
dallapre@cs.unibo.it
[2] Louisiana Tech University, Ruston, LA, USA
{greechie,wfe002}@latech.edu
[3] University of Verona, Verona, Italy
roberto.giacobazzi@univr.it
[4] University of Louisiana, Lafayette, LA, USA
arun@louisiana.edu

Abstract. Additivity plays a key role in program analysis. It is the basis for designing Galois connection based abstract interpretations, it makes a Data-Flow Analysis (DFA) problem easy being convertible into a Kildall's general form, and provides a lattice-theoretic model for disjunctive analysis. In this paper we consider reversible transformers respectively making any monotone function additive and maximally non-additive. We show that, under non restrictive hypothesis, these transformers exist and that they provide a theoretical foundation for the obfuscation of DFA.

Keywords: Program analysis, distributive DFA framework, code obfuscation.

1 Introduction

Additive functions play a key role in programming languages and systems. They provide a model for transfer functions in what is known as *distributive framework* in Kildall's Data-Flow Analysis (DFA) [22], they provide order-theoretic models for predicate transformers in program and system verification methods such as *a la Hoare* verification logic, model checking and trajectory evaluation, and they constitute one of the key ingredients in Galois-connection based abstract interpretation [6]. In this latter case, additivity provides both the essence in having a Galois connection [9] and in case of both adjoint functions are additive, the essence of having a disjunctive analysis [17].

Functions can be modified by other functions, later called *transformers*. Modifying functions in order to obtain their additive counterparts, and conversely modifying them in order to make them maximally non-additive, provides an in-depth understanding of the role of additivity in programming languages and systems, unveiling how much of our understanding of programs and their semantics depends on additivity. For this reason we consider two basic transformers that return respectively the *residuated approximation* and the *residuated ceiling* of a given function f. The residuated approximation of a function f is the additive function that is closest to f [1], while the residuated

---

* Funded by AFOSR grant FA9550-09-1-0715.

S. Dua et al. (Eds.): ICISTM 2012, CCIS 285, pp. 336–347, 2012.
© Springer-Verlag Berlin Heidelberg 2012

ceiling of f is the largest function with the same residuated approximation of f. Thus, the residuated approximation of f represents the least modification of f in order to induce additivity, while the residuated ceiling of f represents the largest modification of f with the same residuated approximation. We prove that under non restrictive hypothesis these two transformers exist and can be computed easily for arbitrary functions on completely distributive lattices. This generalizes a previous result on closure operators [16,17] to arbitrary functions.

We apply these transformations to static program analysis by showing that these transformers provide simple methods for understanding some known code obfuscation strategies defeating DFA in the distributive framework. Obfuscating a program with respect to an analysis corresponds to deform the program in such a way that a maximum loss of precision is induced in the analysis [14]. When considering the obfuscation of a distributive DFA, this corresponds precisely to deform the transfer function of a program P in order to make it maximally non-additive. We show that this can be modeled precisely as the residuated ceiling of the semantics of P. The proposed application of the residuated ceiling to code obfuscation is language independent, and relies upon pure lattice-theoretic arguments on program semantics and analysis.

The paper is structured as follows: Section 2 recalls some background notions from lattice theory. In Section 3 we summarize the previous results on the transformers that modify functions in order to gain or loose additivity. We study the existence if these transformers by generalizing a previous result on closures. Section 4 shows how these transformers can implement an obfuscating algorithm defeating DFA for imperative programs.

2   Background

Mathematical notation. The notation $(C, \leq)$ denotes a *poset C* with ordering relation $\leq_C$, or when no confusion entails, simply $\leq$. The *down-set* of x in C is defined to be $\downarrow x := \{y \in C \mid y \leq x\}$. For $S \subseteq C$, we define $\downarrow S = \bigcup_{s \in S} \downarrow s$. A function $f : C \to C$ is *monotone* if $x \leq y$ implies $f(x) \leq f(y)$ for all $x, y \in C$. For a function $f : C \to A$ between two posets, the function $f^{-1} : A \to C$ is defined as $f^{-1}(\downarrow a) := \{c \in C \mid f(c) \leq a\}$ for $a \in A$. For two functions $f, g : C \to A$, $f \sqsubseteq g$ denotes the pointwise ordering between f and g, i.e., $f(x) \leq_A g(x)$ for all $x \in C$, in this case we say f is *under* g. Given two functions $f : C \to B$ and $g : B \to A$ between posets A, B and C, we use $g \circ f : C \to A$ to denote the *composition of functions f and g*, i.e., $g \circ f(x) := g(f(x))$ for $x \in C$. Let $f : C \to A$ and $g : A \to C$ be monotone functions between two posets C and A; thus the pair functions (f, g) is a *monotone Galois connection* (alias a residuated-residual pair), for short a *Galois connection*, iff, for all $c \in C$ and all $a \in A$, $f(c) \leq_A a \Leftrightarrow c \leq_C g(a)$, or equivalently $c \leq g \circ f(c)$ for all $c \in C$, $f \circ g(a) \leq a$ for all $a \in A$, and for any $a \in A$, there exists $c \in C$ such that $f^{-1}(\downarrow a) = \downarrow c$.

A *complete lattice* is denoted by $(C, \leq, \vee, \wedge, \top, \bot)$ with ordering relation $\leq$, least upper bound $\vee$, greatest lower bound $\wedge$, top element $\top$ and bottom element $\bot$. A complete lattice C is *completely distributive* if it satisfies, for all index sets I and for all sets of selection functions sets F where $f(i)$ is some element in non-empty set $S(i)$ for each $i \in I$, $\bigvee_{i \in I} \bigwedge_{s \in S(i)} x_{i,s} = \bigwedge_{f(i) \in F} \bigvee_{i \in I} x_{i,f(i)}$. For example, the power set lattice $(\wp(X), \subseteq)$ for any set X is a completely distributive lattice [12]. It is *infinitely (join) distributive* if it satisfies that $x \wedge (\bigvee Y) = \bigvee_{y \in Y} (x \wedge y)$ for all $x \in C$ and $Y \subseteq C$. $x \ll y$ if for any chain $D \subseteq C$: $y \le \bigvee D$ implies there exists $d \in D$ such that $x \le d$. An element $x \in C$ is *compact* if $x \ll x$. The set of compact elements in a complete lattice C is denoted $K(C)$. C is *algebraic* if it is complete and for any $x \in C$: $x = \bigvee(\downarrow x \cap K(C))$ [18]. Dual-algebraic lattices are defined by duality. In algebraic lattices, every element can be generated from compact elements by disjunction. A function $f : C \to A$ between two complete lattices is *additive* (resp. *co-additive*) if, for any $X \subseteq C$, $f(\bigvee_C X) = \bigvee_A f(X)$ (resp. $f(\bigwedge_C X) = \bigwedge_A f(X)$).

3   Inducing and Removing Additivity

In this section we follow Andréka et al. [1] introducing the notion of residuated approximation of a generic monotone function on complete lattices and consider the case when residuated approximation is *join-uniform* [16], guaranteeing the existence of residuated ceilings.

Residuated Approximation: Making Functions Additive. It is easy to see that there exists the largest additive function ρ_f under a monotone mapping $f : C \to A$ where C and A are complete lattice, formally $\rho_f := \bigvee\{g : L \to Q \mid g \text{ is additive and } g \le f\}$. Following Andréka et al. [1] we call the function ρ_f the *residuated approximation* of f. They introduce a function $\sigma_f : C \to A$, called the *shadow* of f, that for any $c \in C$ is defined as follows:

$$\sigma_f(c) := \bigwedge\{a \in A \mid c \le \bigvee f^{-1}(\downarrow a)\}$$

In [1] the authors prove that $\rho_f \le \sigma_f \le f$ and that σ_f is monotone. Su et al. [13] define the *umbral mappings* $\sigma_f^{(\alpha)}$ of f: for any ordinal number α,

$$\sigma_f^{(\alpha)} := \begin{cases} f, & \alpha = 0, \\ \sigma_{\sigma_f^{(\alpha-1)}}, & \text{for a successor ordinal } \alpha, \\ \bigwedge_{\beta < \alpha} \sigma_f^{(\beta)}, & \text{for a limit ordinal.} \end{cases}$$

They also proved that: (1) $f \ge \sigma_f \ge \sigma_f^{(2)} \ge \dots \ge \rho_f$, (2) there exists a least ordinal α such that $\sigma_f^{(\alpha)} = \rho_f$, and (3) as the ordinal number α becomes larger, the decreasing sequence $\sigma_f^{(\alpha)}$ converges to ρ_f. The least ordinal number α in point (2) is called the *umbral number*, u_f, of f. Point (3) shows that the residuated approximation ρ_f of f can be calculated by iteration of the shadow of f and the least iteration number is u_f. Of course u_f might be larger than 1. The efficiency of the iterative computation of umbral mapping is measured by the iterative number u_f. Andréka et al. prove a theorem in [1] which implies the following proposition.

Proposition 1. *Let $f : C \to A$ be a monotone mapping between two complete lattices. If A is completely distributive, then $u_f = 1$, i.e., $\sigma_f = \rho_f$.*

Residuated Ceilings: Removing Additivity. Let us consider the problem of removing additivity by considering the largest function having the same residuated approximation of a given (additive) function. Following [16], a function $f : C \to C$ on a complete lattice C is *join-uniform* if for any nonempty subset $S \subseteq C$, if all the elements of S are mapped by f to some c, then $\bigvee S$ is mapped by f to c. We note that a monotone function f is join-uniform if and only if $f(\bigvee f^{-1}(\downarrow f(x))) = f(x)$ for all $x \in C$, i.e., there is a largest element of C mapping to $f(x)$ for all $x \in C$. The residuated approximation of this function collapses to the given (additive) function if and only if the residuated approximator is join-uniform. Let C be a complete lattice. An element x in C is *completely join-irreducible* if $x = \bigvee S$ for $S \subseteq C$ implies that $x \in S$. Let $JI(C)$ be the set of completely join-irreducible elements in C, i.e. $JI(C) := \{x \in C \mid \forall S \subseteq C, x = \bigvee S \Rightarrow x \in S\}$. An element x in C is *completely join-reducible* if there is $S \subseteq C$ such that $x = \bigvee S$ and $x \notin S$. It has been proved that when C is a dual-algebraic complete lattice. Then, for all $x \in C$, it holds that $x = \bigvee((\downarrow x) \cap JI(C))$ [3]. We need the following two results in order to characterize the residuated approximation of a function in terms of the elements join-irreducible.

Lemma 1. *Let C be an infinitely distributive complete lattice and let $S \subseteq C$. If $x \leq \bigvee S$ and $x \in JI(C)$, then $x \in \downarrow S$. Hence $(\downarrow S) \cap JI(C) = (\downarrow \bigvee S) \cap JI(C)$ holds.*

Lemma 2. *Let $f : C \to A$ be a monotone mapping from an infinitely distributive complete lattice C to a complete lattice A. Then, for all $x \in JI(C)$, $f(x) = \sigma_f(x) = \rho_f(x)$.*

The following Theorem provides a setting in which there is a much simpler formula for the shadow. Moreover, in this setting the shadow of a monotone function f is, in fact, the residuated approximation of f. Thus, in this setting, we have a quite simple formula for calculating the residuated approximation of f. Recall that, if f is a function with domain C and $S \subseteq C$, then $f(S) := \{f(s) \mid s \in S\}$.

Theorem 1. *Let $f : C \to A$ be a monotone mapping from a dual-algebraic infinitely distributive complete lattice C to a complete lattice A. Then, for all $x \in C$,*

$$\rho_f(x) = \sigma_f(x) = \bigvee f((\downarrow x) \cap JI(C))$$

Let $\mathcal{M}_{C,A}$ denote the complete lattice of all monotone functions between the complete lattices C and A, where functions are ordered by the usual pointwise ordering. The *residuated approximator* $\rho : \mathcal{M}_{C,A} \to \mathcal{M}_{C,A}$ is a transformer that computes the residuated approximation of a given monotone function f, i.e., $\rho(f) := \rho_f$. Given a function $f \in \mathcal{M}_{C,A}$, we define the *residuated ceiling of f* as the largest function that has the same residuated approximation of f:

$$\omega_f := \bigvee \{g \in \mathcal{M}_{C,A} \mid \rho(g) = \rho(f)\}$$

This gives rise to another transformer $\omega : \mathcal{M}_{C,A} \to \mathcal{M}_{C,A}$ called the *residuated ceiling* defined by $\omega(f) = \omega_f$, for each $f \in \mathcal{M}_{C,A}$. Observe that the residuated approximator ρ is join-uniform if and only if for every monotone function $f : C \to A$ we have that $\rho(\bigvee \{g \in \mathcal{M}_{C,A} \mid \rho_g = \rho_f\}) = \rho_f$, i.e., $\rho(\omega_f) = \rho(f)$.

Theorem 2. *Let C be a dual-algebraic complete lattice and A be a complete lattice. If C is infinitely distributive, then ρ is join-uniform.*

In the setting of the last Theorem, we see that $\mathcal{M}_{C,A}$ can be partitioned into intervals $[\rho_f, \omega_f]$ in such a way that the transformers ρ and ω exchange the bounds of each of the intervals $[\rho_f, \omega_f]$ in the sense that $\rho(\omega_f) = \rho_f$ and $\omega(\rho_f) = \omega(f)$. In this sense, they are reversible transformers. The following example demonstrates that ω need not be join-uniform if it were to be defined on A^C (all functions from C to A). This is the reason we restrict the definition of ω to $\mathcal{M}_{C,A}$.

Example 1. Let C be the complete boolean lattice isomorphic to 2^3 with atoms a, b and c. Define $f_c : C \to C$ by $f_c(b \vee c) = a$, $f_c(a \vee c) = b$, $f_c(a \vee b) = 1$ and $f_c(x) = x$ for $x \in \{0, a, b, c, 1\}$. Since $f_c(c) = c \nleq a = f_c(b \vee c)$, the function f_c is not monotone. Using the symmetry of C we may define f_a and f_b similarly. One easily calculates that, for each $f \in \{f_a, f_b, f_c\}$, $\rho_f = \sigma_f = 0_C$ and if $h := \bigvee\{g : C \to C \mid \rho_g = \rho_f\}$, then $h(x) = 1$ for $x \in \{a \vee b, b \vee c, c \vee a\}$, otherwise $h(x) = x$. It follows that $\rho_h(x) = x$ for $x \in C$. Thus $\rho(\bigvee\{g : C \to C \mid \rho_g = \rho_f\}) \neq \rho_f$.

The following example shows that, if C is not distributive, then ω may not be join-uniform.

Example 2. Let M_3 be the 5-element lattice with 0, 1 and atoms a, b and c (see [12]). Define $f : M_3 \to M_3$ by $f(0) = f(a) = f(b) = 0$ and $f(c) = f(1) = 1$. Obviously f is monotone. One easily calculate that $\rho_f = 0$ and $\omega_f(0) = 0$ and $\omega_f(x) = 1$ for $x \in M_3 - \{0\}$. Since ω_f is additive, we have $\omega_f = \rho_{\omega_f}$. Thus $\rho_{\omega_f} = \omega_f \neq f = \rho_f$.

4   Systematic Obscuring of DFA Problems

Obfuscating a program P with respect to an analysis (or attacker) means to transform P into a functionally equivalent program P' such that the result of the analysis on P' is less precise than the result of the analysis on P. In fact, obfuscation with respect to an analysis can be elegantly formalized as a loss of precision of the analysis [14]. In the rest of this section we consider the standard data-flow analysis framework of Kildall and we instantiate it to the case of *reaching definition analysis*. Next we show that the reaching definition analysis is additive and, since the residuated ceiling of an additive function precisely corresponds to the maximal loss of precision with respect to additivity, we derive an obfuscating algorithm for the reaching definition analysis which is based on its residuated ceiling. This confirms the intuition that code obfuscation for an analysis is making the analysis maximally imprecise.

4.1   Kildall's Monotone Distributive Framework for DFA

All the existing forward (backward) data-flow analyses, such as reaching definition, live variables, available expression, etc., consider the CFG of a program and are defined in terms of a pair of functions that specify the information that is true respectively at the entry and at the exit of each block (or program point) of the CFG. More specifically, these forward (resp. backward) data-flow analyses proceed as follows: (1) specify the information that holds at the start (resp. end) of a program; (2) if a node has more than one incoming (resp. outgoing) edge then combine the incoming (resp. outgoing) information; (3) describe how the execution of a node changes the information which is propagated forward (reps. backward) from that node. Thus, a general framework for DFA consists of a domain D of data-flow facts that express the information of interest; an operator $\bigsqcup$ on the domain D for combining the information coming from multiple predecessors (successors); and a set $\mathcal{F}$ of (transfer) functions on D that describe how a node modifies the information flowing forward (res. backward) through that node. We consider here the general monotone and distributive framework for DFA introduced by Kildall [22] that put some additional requirements on the domain D and on the set of functions $\mathcal{F}$ in order to guarantee the correctness of the analysis.

Definition 1 ([22]). *A monotone distributive framework for DFA consists of:*

- *A complete lattice $(D, \leq)$ that satisfies the ascending chain condition, with least upper bound $\bigsqcup$;*
- *A set $\mathcal{F}$ of monotone functions form D to D that contains the identity function and that is closed under function composition. Moreover, each function f in $\mathcal{F}$ is distributive, which means that for every pair of elements d_1 and d_2 in D we have that $f(d_1 \sqcup d_2) = f(d_1) \sqcup f(d_2)$.*

Reaching Definition Analysis: Let us instantiate the general framework of Killdal at the case of reaching definition (RD) analysis. RD analysis is a forward DFA that for each node of the CFG is interested in characterizing the assignments that may have been made and not overwritten when reaching this node. We consider a program P as consisting of a sequence of instructions. Each node in the CFG of P represents an elementary block of P, namely a (maximal) sequence of instructions of P that are executed sequentially. We associate an unique location to every block of a program and write $[stmt_1; \ldots; stmt_n]^l$ to specify that the block at location l contains the sequence of statements $stmt_1; \ldots; stmt_n$. We consider the following set $Stmt$ of possible program statements:

$$stmt ::= x := e \mid x := R \mid \mathsf{case}\{(b_1, l_1), \ldots, (b_n, l_n)\} \mid \mathsf{ret}\ x \mid \mathsf{skip} \mid stmt; stmt$$

where $x := e$ assigns the value of expression e to variable x, $x := R$ assigns a random value from the set R to variable x; $\mathsf{case}\{(b_1, l_1), \ldots, (b_n, l_n)\}$ implements a guarded multiple branch that redirects the flow of computation to the location l_i associated to the boolean condition b_i that evaluates to true. The other statements have the standard meaning. Let us denote with $Loc[P]$ the locations of the blocks of program P (where $|Loc[P]| \geq 2$); with $init[P]$ and $final[P]$ be the locations of the initial and final blocks of P; with $Block[P] \subseteq Stmt^* \times Loc[P]$ be the set of elementary blocks of program P, and with $Var[P]$ be the variables of P. Let $succ[P] : Stmt^* \times Loc[P] \to \wp(Loc[P])$ be a function that computes the locations of the possible successors of a block at a given location in a program P. Since the statements in a block are executed sequentially the successors of a block are determined by the forward flow of its last statement that is usually a case construct (except for the final block that has no successors). Let S denote a sequence of sequential statements.

- $succ[P]([S ; \mathsf{case}\{(b_1, l_1), \ldots, (b_n, l_n)\}]^l) = \{l_1, \ldots, l_n\}$;
- $succ[P]([S ; stmt]^l) = \emptyset$ when $stmt$ is not a case construct.

The RD analysis is based on functions $kill$ and gen that compute the pairs of variables and labels that are $killed$ and $generated$ by the execution of each block:

- $kill([x := a]^l) = kill([x := R]^l) = \{(x, ?)\} \cup \{(x, l') \mid [S]^{l'}$ contains an assignment to $x\}$;
- $kill([S_1 ; S_2]^l) = kill([S_1]^l) \cup kill([S_2]^l)$;
- $kill([stmt]^l) = \emptyset$ in all the other cases;
- $gen([x := a]^l) = gen([x := R]^l) = \{(x, l)\}$;
- $gen([S_1 ; S_2]^l) = gen([S_1]^l) \cup gen([S_2]^l)$;
- $gen([stmt]^l) = \emptyset$ in all the other cases;

Since each block in a program is uniquely identified by its location, sometimes we write $kill(l)$ for $kill([S]^l)$, and $gen(l)$ for $gen([S]^l)$. The RD analysis of program P is defined by the pair of functions $RD_{entry}[P], RD_{exit}[P] : Loc[P] \rightarrow \wp(Var[P] \times Loc[P])$ that given a program location l, return respectively the locations that contain the definition of a variable that reaches the entry or the exit of the block at location l.

$$RD_{entry}[P](l) = \begin{cases} \{(x, ?) \mid x \in Var[P]\} & \text{if } l = init[P] \\ \bigcup \{RD_{exit}[P](l') \mid l \in succ[P](l')\} & \text{otherwise} \end{cases}$$

$$RD_{exit}[P](l) = (RD_{entry}[P](l) \setminus kill(l)) \cup gen(l)$$

By specifying function $RD_{exit}[P]$ with respect to a program location l we obtain function $RD_{exit}[P, l] : \wp(Var[P] \times Loc[P]) \rightarrow \wp(Var[P] \times Loc[P])$ that, by definition, behaves as follows:

$$RD_{exit}[P, l] = \lambda X. (X \setminus kill(l)) \cup gen(l).$$

Thus, when instantiating the general DFA framework to RD we have that the domain D of data-flow facts of interest is given by the complete lattice $\wp(Var[P] \times Loc[P])$, and the set $\mathcal{F}$ of monotone functions, that specify how the execution of a block modifies the analysis, is given by $\{RD_{exit}[P, l] \mid l \in Loc[P]\}$.

Example 3. Let us consider a program P that randomly assigns a value between 0 and 1 to variable b and then computes the sum of 9 and 5 if b is equal to 1, or the product of 9 and 2^5 if b is equal to 0. In Fig. 1 on the left we report the CFG of program P. The number at the top left of each block of the CFG of P denotes the location of the block. The RD analysis of P has the following solution:

- $RD_{entry}[P](1) = \{(x, ?), (y, ?), (b, ?), (t, ?)\}$
- $RD_{exit}[P](1) = \{(x, 1), (y, 1), (b, 1), (t, ?)\}$
- $RD_{entry}[P](2) = \{(x, 1), (x, 3), (y, 1), (y, 3), (b, 1), (t, ?)\} = RD_{exit}[P](2) = RD_{entry}[P](3)$
- $RD_{exit}[P](3) = \{(x, 3), (y, 3), (b, 1), (t, ?)\}$
- $RD_{entry}[P](4) = \{(x, 1), (x, 5), (y, 1), (y, 5), (b, 1), (t, ?)\}$
- $RD_{exit}[P](4) = \{(x, 1), (x, 5), (y, 1), (y, 5), (b, 1), (t, 4)\} = RD_{entry}[P](5)$
- $RD_{exit}[P](5) = \{(x, 5), (y, 5), (b, 1), (t, 4)\}$
- $RD_{entry}[P](6) = \{(x, 1), (x, 3), (x, 5), (y, 1), (y, 3), (y, 5), (b, 1), (t, ?), (t, 4)\} = RD_{exit}[P](6)$

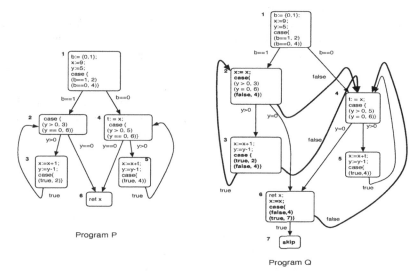

Fig. 1. The CFG of program P and of its obfuscated variant Q

4.2 Obfuscating RD Analysis

The RD analysis is clearly additive. More precisely, given a program location l, we have that function $RD_{exit}[P, l] : \wp(Var[P] \times Loc[P]) \to \wp(Var[P] \times Loc[P])$ is additive:

$$
\begin{aligned}
RD_{exit}[P, l](X_1 \cup X_2) &= ((X_1 \cup X_2) \setminus kill(l)) \cup gen(l) \\
&= (X_1 \setminus kill(l)) \cup gen(l)) \cup ((X_2 \setminus kill(l)) \cup gen(l)) \\
&= RD_{exit}[P, l](X_1) \cup RD_{exit}[P, l](X_2)
\end{aligned}
$$

This means that in order to make the RD analysis imprecise we have to become imprecise for disjunction when computing function $RD_{exit}[P, l]$. Thus, if we want to obfuscate a program P in order to make the analysis of RD imprecise at location l we have to transform P into a program Q such that the computation of function $RD_{exit}[Q, l]$ is maximally imprecise every time that, at the entry of location l, we have that a variable could have been defined in more than one location. This means that we have to design a program Q such that the computation of function $RD_{exit}[Q, l]$ corresponds to the maximal loss of additivity of function $RD_{exit}[P, l]$, namely we want a function $RD_{exit}[Q, l]$ to behave precisely like the residuated ceiling of $RD_{exit}[P, l]$. Observe that from Theorem 2 the existence of the residuated ceiling of function $RD_{exit}[P, l]$ is guaranteed by the fact that the domain $\wp(Var[P] \times Loc[P])$ is a dual algebraic and infinitely distributive complete lattice. For simplicity in the following we consider the RD analysis of a single variable x at a given location l of a program P, denoted $RD_{entry}[P, l, x]$ and $RD_{exit}[P, l, x]$. In particular: $RD_{exit}[P, l, x] = \lambda X.(X \setminus kill(x, l)) \cup gen(x, l)$ where $kill(l, x)$ and $gen(l, x)$ restrict the computation of functions $kill(l)$ and $gen(l)$ to the definition of the single variable x.

Following the definitions of the RD functions we have that if the block at location l of a given program P contains an assignment to variable x then $RD_{exit}[P, l, x] = \lambda X.\{(x, l)\}$, which means that at the exit of the block the analysis is precise and returns the singleton $\{(x, l)\}$. Following this observation, we can obfuscate the RD analysis only for those variables that are not defined in the block that we want to obfuscate. Under this hypothesis, loosing precision in the computation of function $RD_{exit}[P, l, x]$ by loosing its additivity means that every time that the input X to the above function is not a singleton set then the analysis returns a "I do not know" value: *Any variable may reach that block.* Following this intuition, we define function $k[P, l, x] : \wp(Var[P] \times (Loc[P] \setminus \{l\})) \to \wp(Var[P] \times (Loc[P] \setminus \{l\}))$ as follows:

$$k[P, l, x] = \lambda X. \begin{cases} RD_{exit}[P, l, x](X) & \text{if } |X| \leq 1 \\ \top_l & \text{otherwise} \end{cases}$$

where $\top_l$ corresponds to the set $\{(x, i) \mid i \in Loc[P] \setminus \{l\}\}$, namely $\top_l$ means that variable x could have been defined in every block of the program but not in the one that we are currently analyzing. Observe that $k[P, l, x]$ is defined on $\wp(Var[P] \times (Loc[P] \setminus \{l\}))$ and this follows from the hypothesis that we are obfuscating the RD analysis for variable x that is not defined at location l. Function $k[P, l, x]$ is clearly non-additive:

$$k[P, l, x](\{(x, j)\}) \cup k[P, l, x](\{(x, i)\}) = RD_{exit}[P, l, x](\{(x, j)\}) \cup RD_{exit}[P, l, x](\{(x, i)\})$$
$$\subset k[P, l, x](\{(x, j), (x, i)\}) = \top_l$$

The next result shows that $k[P, l, x]$ is precisely the residuated ceiling of $RD_{exit}[P, l, x]$.

Theorem 3. *Consider a program P and assume that variable x is not defined in the block at location l of a given program P. Function $k[P, l, x]$ is the residuated ceiling of $RD_{exit}[P, l, x]$, i.e., $k[P, l, x] = \omega(RD_{exit}[P, l, x])$. Namely $k[P, l, x]$ is the most abstract function such that $\rho(k[P, l, x]) = \rho(RD_{exit}[P, l, x]) = RD_{exit}[P, l, x]$.*

This means that if we want to obfuscate the RD analysis of a program P at a given location l for a given variable x, we have to modify the program in such a way that the RD analysis at l of x of the transformed program Q behaves like the residuated ceiling $\omega(RD_{exit}[P, l, x]) = k[P, l, x]$. This allows us to state the following result that proves optimality and provides a mathematical foundation of the intuitive obfuscation of RD.

Theorem 4. *Let P be a source program. A transformed program Q (with the same functionality of P) maximally obfuscates the RD analysis with respect to variable x at location l of program P if $RD_{exit}[Q, l, x] = \omega(RD_{exit}[P, l, x])$.*

Example 4. Let us design a program Q that obfuscates the RD analysis of the variable x at the block 4 of the program P presented in Example 3, namely we want that $\omega(RD_{exit}[P, 4, x]) = RD_{exit}[Q, 4, x]$. Since $RD_{entry}[P, 4, x] = \{(x, 1), (x, 5)\}$ then we want that $RD_{exit}[Q, 4, x] = \top_4$. In order to obtain this we have to design the program Q in such a way that every block (except for the one at location 4) contains a definition of x and that this definition reaches the block at location 4 of program Q. In Fig. 1 on the right we show a program Q that satisfies these requirements. In fact, the RD analysis of program Q with respect to variable x at program point 4 returns

$RD_{exit}[Q, x, 4] = \{(x, 1), (x, 2), (x, 3), (x, 5), (x, 6)\} = \top_4$. Observe that the two programs have the same functionality since the modifications made to P to obtain Q preserve program functionality.

Following the previous example we can derive an algorithm that maximally obfuscates the RD analysis of a program in a given location with respect to a particular variable. Given a block $[S]^l$, which is not final, we denote with $[S \oplus \mathtt{case}\{(b, l')\}]^l$ the block that we obtain from $[S]^l$ by adding the pair (b, l') to the $\mathtt{case}$ construct at the end of the sequence of statements inside the elementary block.

Optimal RD-obfusaction

1 : **input**: $Block[P]$, l, x;
2 : $A := Block[P] \setminus \{[S]^l\} \cup \{[S]^j \mid (x, j) \in RD_{exit}[P, l, x]\}$;
3 : **while** $A \neq \emptyset$ **do**
4 :   select a block $[S]^i$ from A;
5 :   **if** $i \in final[P]$
6 :   **then** $Block[P] := Block[P] \setminus \{[S]^i\} \cup \{[x := x; S; \mathtt{case}\{(true, l_{new}), (false, l)\}]^i, [skip]^{l_{new}}\}$
7 :   **else** $Block[P] := Block[P] \setminus \{[S]^i\} \cup \{[x := x; S \oplus \mathtt{case}\{(false, l)\}]^i\}$;
8 : $A := A \setminus [S]^i$;
9 : **output**: $Block[P]$

The algorithm **Optimal RD-obfusaction** takes as inputs a program P in the form of its elementary blocks, a program location l and a variable x (not defined in the block l) and returns the blocks of a program with the same functionality of P that maximally obfuscates the RD analysis of variable x at location l. In order to do this, the algorithm defines at line 2 the set A of the elementary blocks of P that are not at the location that we want to obfuscate and that do not already contain a definition of variable x that reaches location l. The algorithm modifies each block in A in order to ensure that it contains a definition of variable x that reaches location l. We distinguish two cases. At line 7 of the algorithm we consider the case when the block $[S]^i$ is not final and we add (at the beginning of the block) the assignment $x := x$ (which is clearly a semantic nop), and we enrich the $\mathtt{case}$ construct that terminates the block with the pair $(false, l)$ which makes the block at location l reachable from the current block (even if at execution time this never happens thus preserving the semantics of the program). At line 6 of the algorithm we consider the case when the block $[S]^i$ is final (namely it has no successors). In this case the block $[S]^i$ does not end with a $\mathtt{case}$ construct and therefore we add (at the beginning of the block) the assignment $x := x$ and at the end of the block a case construct $\mathtt{case}\{(true, l_{new}), (false, l)\}$, where l_{new} is a new program location. By doing this the block at location i is no longer final and therefore we add a final block at the new location l_{new} that contains only the $skip$ statement.

The above algorithm for the obfuscation of RD analysis is very simple and easy to break. In order to make it more resilient we could use sophisticated opaque predicates instead of the always false condition $false$, and more complex obfuscations for the insertion of the semantic nop instead of the simple $x := x$. In the literature we can find many obfuscation techniques for opaque predicates insertion and semantic nops insertion, such as in [5,23,29,30].

5   Conclusion

We introduced basic function transformers that respectively induce and remove additivity from functions. These operations have been proved to play a key role in modeling an important aspect in static program analysis, which is additivity. In particular we proved that the residuated ceiling provides a mathematical foundation of standard code obfuscation strategies defeating distributive data-flow analysis problems, such as reaching definitions (RD) analysis. This confirms the intuition in [14]: *Making a program obscure for an analysis is making the same analysis imprecise for the transformed code.*

Residuated ceilings express here the imprecision in disjunction, which is distributivity in monotone frameworks. Other algorithms exist for breaking distributivity. Wang et al. [30] present a code obfuscation technique based on control flow flattening and variable aliasing that drastically reduces the precision of static analysis. Their basic idea is to make the analysis of the program control flow dependent on the analysis of the program data-flow, and then to use aliasing to complicate data-flow analysis. In particular, the proposed obfuscation transforms the original control flow of the program into a flattened one where each elementary block can be the successor/predecessor of any other elementary block in the CFG of the program. In order to preserve the semantics of the program, the actual program flow is determined dynamically by a dispatcher. This obfuscating transformation clearly also obfuscates the RD analysis. However, it is not the simplest obfuscation for disjointness in RD. Theorem 4 proves that this can be achieved by the residuated ceiling of RD analysis. A far more elementary analysis (an therefore a wider number of attacks) is obscured in Wang's transformation, as recently proved in [15], which is precisely the Control-Flow Graph extraction analysis, which is used in RD analysis. This of course obscures RD in the sense of lack of precision. In fact, it makes every elementary block of the CFG reachable from every other one, so the RD analysis of a flattened program would conclude that the definition of a variable reaches all the elementary blocks of the program. This means that for every location l we have that $RD_{entry}[P^f](l) = \top_l$, and this means that for every variable x that is not defined in the block at location l we have that $RD_{exit}[P^f, l, x] = \omega(RD_{exit}[P, l, x])$, where P is the original program (before the control flow flattening obfuscation).

References

1. Andréka, H., Greechie, R.J., Strecker, G.E.: On Residuated Approximations. In: Kreowski, H.-J., Herrlich, H., Preuß, G., Ehrig, H. (eds.) Categorical Methods in Computer Science. LNCS, vol. 393, pp. 333–339. Springer, Heidelberg (1989)
2. Balasundaram, V., Kennedy, K.: A technique for summarizing data access and its use in parallelism enhancing transformations. In: PLDI, New York, NY, pp. 41–53 (1989)
3. Birkhoff, G.: Subdirect unions in universal algebra. Bull. Amer. Math. Soc. 50, 764–768 (1944)
4. Blyth, T., Janowitz, M.: Residuation theory. Pergamon Press (1972)
5. Collberg, C., Thomborson, C., Low, D.: Manufacturing cheap, resilient, and stealthy opaque constructs. In: 25th POPL, pp. 184–196. ACM Press (1998)
6. Cousot, P., Cousot, R.: Abstract Interpretation: A Unified Lattice Model for Static Analysis of Programs by Construction of Approximation of Fixed Points. In: 4th POPL, pp. 238–252 (1977)

7. Cousot, P., Cousot, R.: Abstract Interpretation framework. Journal of Logic and Computation 2(4), 511–547 (1992)
8. Cousot, P., Cousot, R.: Static determination of dynamic properties of programs. In: Proc. 2nd Int. Symp. on Programming, Dunod, pp. 106–130 (1976)
9. Cousot, P., Cousot, R.: Systematic design of program analysis frameworks. In: 6th POPL, San Antonio, TX, pp. 269–282. ACM Press (1979)
10. Cousot, P., Halbwachs, N.: Automatic discovery of linear restraints among variables of a program. In: 5th POPL, Tucson, AZ, pp. 84–97. ACM Press (1978)
11. Dalla Preda, M., Giacobazzi, R.: Semantics-based code obfuscation using abstract interpretation. Journal of Computer Security 17(6), 855–908 (2009)
12. Davey, B.A., Priestly, H.A.: Introduction to Lattices and Order. Cambridge University Press (2002)
13. Feng, W., Su, J., Greechie, R.: On calculating residuated approximations. Algebra Universalis (to appear)
14. Giacobazzi, R.: Hiding information in completeness holes - New perspectives in code obfuscation and watermarking. In: 6th IEEE International Conference SEFM, pp. 7–20 (2008)
15. Giacobazzi, R., Jones, N.D., Mastroeni, I.: Obfuscation by Partial Evaluation of Distorted Interpreters. In: Proc. ACM SIGPLAN Partial Evaluation and Program Manipulation (PEPM 2012), Philadelphia, USA (to appear, 2012)
16. Giacobazzi, R., Ranzato, F.: Uniform Closures: Order-Theoretically Reconstructing Logic Program Semantics and Abstract Domain Refinements. Information and Computation 145(2), 153–190 (1998)
17. Giacobazzi, R., Ranzato, F.: Optimal domains for disjunctive abstract interpretation. Science of Computer Programming 32(1-3), 177–210 (1998)
18. Gierz, G., Hofmann, K.H., Keimel, K., Lawson, J.D., Mislove, M., Scott, D.S.: A Compendium of Continuous Lattices. Springer, Berlin (1980)
19. Granger, P.: Static analysis of arithmetic congruence. Int. J. Comput. Math. 30, 165–190 (1989)
20. Granger, P.: Static Analysis of Linear Congruence Equalities Among Variables of a Program. In: Abramsky, S., Maibaum, T.S.E. (eds.) CAAP 1991 and TAPSOFT 1991. LNCS, vol. 493, pp. 169–192. Springer, Heidelberg (1991)
21. Greechie, R.J., Janowitz, M.F.: Personal communication (2005)
22. Kildall, G.A.: Global expression optimization during compilation. In: 1st POPL, Boston, MA, pp. 194–206. ACM Press (1973)
23. Majumdar, A., Thomborson, C.: Manufactoring opaque predicates in distributed systems for code obfuscation. In: 29th Australasian Computer Science Conference (ACSC 2006), vol. 48, pp. 187–196 (2006)
24. Masdupuy, F.: Semantic Analysis of Interval Congruences. In: Pottosin, I.V., Bjorner, D., Broy, M. (eds.) FMP&TA 1993. LNCS, vol. 735, pp. 142–155. Springer, Heidelberg (1993)
25. Mauborgne, L.: Tree Schemata and Fair Termination. In: Palsberg, J. (ed.) SAS 2000. LNCS, vol. 1824, pp. 302–319. Springer, Heidelberg (2000)
26. Nielson, F., Nielson, H., Hankin, C.: Principles of Program Analysis. Springer (2004)
27. Plaisted, D.A.: Theorem proving with abstraction. Artificial Intelligence 16, 47–108 (1981)
28. Su, J., Feng, W., Greechie, R.J.: Disitributivity conditions and the order-skeleton of a lattice. Algebra Universalis 66(4), 337–354 (2011)
29. Szor, P.: The Art of Computer Virus Research and Defense. Addison-Wesley Professional (2005)
30. Wang, C., Hill, J., Knight, J., Davidson, J.: Software tamper resistance: obstructing static analysis of programs, Technical Report CS-2000-12, Department of Computer Science, University of Virginia (2000)

Automatic Simplification
of Obfuscated JavaScript Code
(Extended Abstract)[*]

Gen Lu, Kevin Coogan, and Saumya Debray

Department of Computer Science,
The University of Arizona,
Tucson, AZ 85721, USA
{genlu,kpcoogan,debray}@cs.arizona.edu

Abstract. Javascript is a scripting language that is commonly used to create sophisticated interactive client-side web applications. It can also be used to carry out browser-based attacks on users. Malicious JavaScript code is usually highly obfuscated, making detection a challenge. This paper describes a simple approach to deobfuscation of JavaScript code based on dynamic analysis and slicing. Experiments using a prototype implementation indicate that our approach is able to penetrate multiple layers of complex obfuscations and extract the core logic of the computation.

1 Introduction

A few years ago, most malware was delivered via infected email attachments. As email filters and spam detectors have improved, however, this delivery mechanism has increasingly been replaced by web-based delivery mechanisms, e.g., where a victim is lured to view an infected web page from a browser, which then causes malicious payload to be downloaded and executed. Very often, such "drive-by downloads" rely on JavaScript code; to avoid detection, the scripts are usually highly obfuscated [8]. For example, the Gumblar worm, which in mid-2009 was considered to be the fastest-growing threat on the Internet, uses Javascript code that is dynamically generated and heavily obfuscated to avoid detection and identification [11].

Of course, the simple fact that a web page contains dynamically generated and/or obfuscated JavaScript code does not, in itself, make it malicious [5]; to establish that we have to figure out what the code does. Moreover, the functionality of a piece of code can generally be expressed in many different ways. For these reasons, simple syntactic rules (e.g., "*search for* 'eval(' *and* 'unescape(' *within 15 bytes of each other*" [11]) turn out to be of limited efficacy when dealing with obfuscated JavaScript. Current tools that process JavaScript typically rely on such syntactic heuristics and so tend to be quite imprecise.

---

[*] This work was supported in part by the National Science Foundation via grant nos. CNS-1016058 and CNS-1115829, the Air Force Office of Scientific Research via grant no. FA9550-11-1-0191, and by a GAANN fellowship from the Department of Education award no. P200A070545.

S. Dua et al. (Eds.): ICISTM 2012, CCIS 285, pp. 348–359, 2012.

A better solution would be to use semantics-based techniques that focus on the behavior of the code. This is also important and useful for making it possible for human analysts to easily understand the inner workings of obfuscated JavaScript code so as to deal quickly and effectively with new web-based malware. Unfortunately, current techniques for behavioral analysis of obfuscated JavaScript typically require a significant amount of manual intervention, e.g., to modify the JavaScript code in specific ways or to monitor its execution within a debugger [13,17,22]. Recently, some authors have begun investigating automated approaches to dealing with obfuscated JavaScript, e.g., using machine learning techniques [3] or symbolic execution of string operations [20]; Section 5 discusses these in more detail. This paper takes a different approach to the problem: we use run-time monitoring to extract execution trace(s) from the obfuscated program, apply semantics-preserving code transformations to automatically simplify the trace, then reconstruct source code from the simplified trace. The program so obtained is observationally equivalent to the original program for the execution considered, but has the obfuscation simplified away, leaving only the core logic of the computation performed by the code. The resulting simplified code can then be examined either by humans or by other software. The removal of the obfuscation results in code that is easier to analyze and understand than the original obfuscated program. Experiments using a prototype implementation indicate that this approach is able to penetrate multiple layers of complex obfuscations and extract the core logic of the underlying computation. Some of the details of this work have been omitted from this paper due to space constraints; interested readers are referred to the full version of the paper, which is available online [12].

In addition to obfuscated JavaScript code, web-based malware may also use other techniques, such as DOM interactions, to hamper analysis [8]. In such situations, simplification of obfuscated JavaScript code, while necessary, may not be sufficient to give a complete picture of what the malware is doing. This paper focuses on dealing with obfuscations involving dynamic constructs in JavaScript core language; additional issues, such as objects provided by DOM and the interactions between JavaScript and DOM, are beyond the scope of this paper and are considered to be future work.

2 Background

2.1 JavaScript

Despite the similarity in their names and their object-orientation, JavaScript is a very different language than Java. A JavaScript object consists of a series of name/value pairs, where the names are referred to as *properties*. Another significant difference is that while Java is statically typed and has strong type checking, JavaScript is dynamically typed. This means that a variable can take on values of different types at different points in a JavaScript program. JavaScript also makes it very convenient to extend the executing program. For example, one can "execute" a string s using the construct **eval(s)**. Since the string s can itself be constructed at runtime, this makes it possible for JavaScript code to be highly dynamic in nature.

There are some superficial similarities between the two languages at the implementation level as well: e.g., both typically use expression-stack-based byte-code interpreters, and in both cases modern implementations of these interpreters come with JIT compilers. However, the language-level differences sketched above are reflected in low-level characteristics of the implementations as well. For example, Java's static typing means that the operand types of each operation in the program are known at compile time, allowing the compiler to generate type-specific instructions, e.g., **iadd** for integer addition, **dadd** for addition of double-precision values. In JavaScript, on the other hand, operand types are not statically available, which means that the byte code instructions are generic. Unlike Java, the code generated for JavaScript does not have an associated class file, which means that information about constants and strings is not readily available. Finally, JavaScript's **eval** construct requires runtime code generation: in the SpiderMonkey implementation of JavaScript [15], for example, this causes code for the string being **eval**ed to be generated into a newly-allocated memory region and then executed, after which the memory region is reclaimed.

The dynamic nature of Javascript code makes possible a variety of obfuscation techniques. Particularly challenging is the combination of the ability to execute a string using the **eval** construct, as described above, and the fact that the string being executed may be obfuscated in a wide variety of ways. Howard discusses several such techniques in more detail [8]. Further, dynamic code generation via **eval** can be multi-layered, e.g., a string that is **eval**-ed may itself contain calls to **eval**, and such embedded calls to **eval** can be stacked several layers deep. Such obfuscation techniques can make it difficult to determine the intent of a JavaScript program from a static examination of the program text.

2.2   Semantics-Based Deobfuscation

Deobfuscation refers to the process of simplifying a program to remove obfuscation code and produce a functionally equivalent program that is simpler (or, at least, no more complex) than the original program relative to some appropriate complexity metric. To motivate our approach to deobfuscation, consider the semantic intuition behind any deobfuscation process. In general, when we simplify an obfuscated program we cannot hope to recover the code for the original program, either because the source code is simply not be available, or due to code transformations applied during compilation. All we can require, then, is that the process of deobfuscation must be semantics-preserving: i.e., that the code resulting from deobfuscation be semantically equivalent to the original program.

For the analysis of potentially-malicious code, a reasonable notion of semantic equivalence seems to be that of *observational equivalence*, where two programs are considered equivalent if they behave—i.e., interact with their execution environment—in the same way. Since a program's runtime interactions with the external environment are carried out through system calls, this means that two programs are observationally equivalent if they execute identical sequences of system calls (together with the argument vectors to these calls).

This notion of program equivalence suggests a simple approach to deobfuscation: identify all instructions that directly or indirectly affect the values of the arguments to system calls. Any remaining instructions, which are by definition semantically irrelevant, may be discarded (examples of such semantically-irrelevant code include dead and unreachable code used by malware to change their byte-signatures in order to avoid detection). The crucial question then becomes that of identifying instructions that affect the values of system call arguments: for the JavaScript code considered in this paper, we use dynamic slicing, applied at the byte-code level, for this.

3   JavaScript Deobfuscation

3.1   Overview

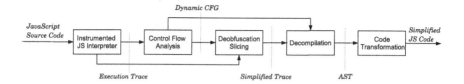

Our approach to deobfuscating JavaScript code, shown above, consists of the following steps:

1. Use an instrumented interpreter to obtain an execution trace for the JavaScript code under consideration.
2. Construct a control flow graph from this trace to determine the structure of the code that is executed.
3. Use our dynamic slicing algorithm to identify instructions that are relevant to the observable behavior of the program. Ideally, we would like to compute slices for the arguments of the system calls made by the program. However, the actual system calls are typically made from external library routines that appear as native methods. As a proxy for system calls, therefore, our implementation computes slices for the arguments passed to any native function.
4. Decompile excution trace to an abstract syntax tree (AST), and label all the nodes constructed from resulting set of relevant instructions.
5. Eliminate **goto** statements from the AST, then traverse it to generate deobfuscated source code by printing only labeled syntax tree nodes.

3.2   Instrumentation and Tracing

We instrument the JavaScript interpreter to collect a trace of the program's execution. Each byte-code instruction is instrumented to print out the instruction's address, operation mnemonic, and length (in bytes) together with any additional information about the instruction that may be relevant, including expression stack usage, encoded constants, variable names/IDs, branch offets and object related data. Due to the space constraints, detailed description of the format and processing of the execution trace is not presented.

3.3   Control Flow Graph Construction

In principle, the (static) control flow graph for a JavaScript program can be obtained fairly easily. The byte-code for each function in a JavaScript program can be obtained as a property of that function object, and it is straightforward to decompile this byte-code to an abstract syntax tree. In practice, the control flow graph so obtained may not be very useful if the intent is to simplify obfuscations away. The reason for this is that dynamic constructs such as **eval**, commonly used to obfuscate JavaScript code, are essentially opaque in the static control flow graph: their runtime behavior—which is what we are really interested in—cannot be easily determined from an inspection of the static control flow graph. For this reason, we opt instead for a dynamic control flow graph, which is obtained from an execution trace of the program. However, while the dynamic control flow graph gives us more information about the runtime behavior of constructs such as **eval**, it does so at the cost of reduced code coverage.

The algorithm for constructing a dynamic control flow graph from an execution trace is a straightforward adaptation of the algorithm for static control flow graph construction, found in standard compiler texts [2,16], modified to deal with dynamic execution traces.

3.4   Deobfuscation Slicing

As mentioned in Section 2.2, we use dynamic slicing to identify instructions that directly or indirectly affect arguments passed to native functions, which has been investigated by Wang and Roychoudhury in the context of slicing Java byte-code traces [21].We adapt the algorithm of Wang and Roychoudhury in two ways, both having to do with the dynamic features of JavaScript used extensively for obfuscation. The first is that while Wang and Roychoudhury use a static control flow graph, we use the dynamic control flow graph discussed in Section 3.3. The reason for this is that in our case a static control flow graph does not adequately capture the execution behavior of exactly those dynamic constructs, such as **eval**, that we need to handle when dealing with obfuscated JavaScript. The second is in the treatment of the **eval** construct during slicing. Consider a statement **eval**(s): in the context of deobfuscation, we have to determine the behavior of the code obtained from the string s; the actual construction of the string s, however—for example, by decryption of some other string or concatenation of a collection of string fragments—is simply part of the obfuscation process and is not directly relevant for the purpose of understanding the functionality of the program. When slicing, therefore, we do not follow dependencies through **eval** statements. We have to note that because an **eval**ed string s depends on some code v doesn't automatically exclude v from the resulting slice; if the real workload depends on v, then v would be added to slice regardless of the connection with **eval**. In other words, only code which is solely used for obfuscation would be eliminated. Therefore, an obfuscator cannot simply insert **eval**s into the pragram's dataflow to hide relevant code. We refer to this algorithm as deobfuscation-slicing, the pseudocode is shown in Algorithm 1.

Input: A dynamic trace T; a slicing criterion C; a dynamic control flow graph G;

Output: A slice S;

```
 1  S := ∅;
 2  currFrame := lastFrame := NULL;
 3  LiveSet := ∅;
 4  stack := a new empty stack;
 5  I := instruction instance at the last position in T;
 6  while true do
 7  │   inSlice := false;
 8  │   Uses := memory addresses and property set used by I;
 9  │   Defs := memory addresses and property set defined by I;
10  │   inSlice := I ∈ C ;                      /* add all instructions in C into S */
11  │   if I is a return instruction then
12  │   │   push a new frame on stack;
13  │   else if I is an interpreted function call then
14  │   │   lastFrame := pop(stack);
15  │   else
16  │   │   lastFrame = NULL;
17  │   end
18  │   currFrame := top frame on stack;
    │   // inter-function dependence: ignore dependency due to eval
19  │   if I is an interpreted function call ∧ I is not eval then
20  │   │   inSlice := inSlice ∨ lastFrame is not empty;
21  │   else if I is a control transfer instruction then
    │   │   // intra-function control dependency
22  │   │   for each instruction J in currFrame s.t. J is control-dependent on I do
23  │   │   │   inSlice := true;
24  │   │   │   remove J from currFrame;
25  │   │   end
26  │   end
27  │   inSlice := inSlice ∨ (LiveSet ∩ Defs ≠ ∅) ;                    // data dependency
28  │   LiveSet := LiveSet − Defs;
29  │   if inSlice then                                  // add I into the slice
30  │   │   add I into S;
31  │   │   add I into currFrame;
32  │   │   LiveSet := LiveSet ∪ Uses;
33  │   end
34  │   if I is not the first instruction instance in T then
35  │   │   I := previous instruction instance in T;
36  │   else
37  │   │   break;
38  │   end
39  end
```

Algorithm 1. d-slicing

3.5   Decompilation and Code Transformation

The slicing step described in Section 3.4 identifies instructions in the dynamic trace that directly or indirectly affect arguments to native function calls, which includes functions that invoke system calls. This slice is used to transform the control flow graph of the program to an abstract syntax tree (AST) representation. We do this in two stages. In the first stage, we construct an AST that may sometimes contain explicit **goto** nodes that capture lower-level control flow. Such **goto** nodes are created in two situations: (*i*) at the end of basic blocks that do not end with a brach instruction, and (*ii*) when an explicit branch instruction is encountered. In addition to storing information of target block in **goto** nodes, we also keep track of a list of preceding **goto** nodes in each target node. Loops in the control flow graph are identified using dominator analysis [2] and represented in the AST as an indefinite loop structure of the form **while (1)** {...}, with branches out of the loop body represented using explicit **goto**s that reflect the control flow behavior of the low-level code. In the second stage, this AST is transformed using semantics-preserving **goto**-eliminating code transformations that generate valid JavaScript soure code, as described below.

Joelsson proposed a **goto** removal algorithm for decompilation of Java byte-code with irreducible CFGs, the algorithm traverses the AST over and over and applies a set of transformations whenever possible [9]. We adapt this algorithm to handle JavaScript and the instruction set used by the SpiderMonkey JavaScript engine [15]. The basic idea is to transform the program so that each **goto** is either replaced by some other construct, or the **goto** and its target are brought closer together in a semantics-preserving transformation. Space constraints preclude a detailed description of our transformation rules; interested readers are referred to the full version of the paper [12]. The fact that SpiderMonkey always generates byte-code with reducible CFGs (due to the lack of an aggressive code optimization phase) and the difference between JavaScript byte-code and Java byte-code, makes it possible for our algorithm to have a smaller set of tranformation rules. But it would be straightforward to add more rules, if necessary, to handle highly optimized JavaScript byte-code with possibly irreducible CFGs.

After this transformation step, the syntax tree is traversed again, for each **goto** node n, we examine its target node t, if t is the node immediately following n, then n is removed from syntax tree. The resulting syntax tree is then traversed one last time and, for each node labeled by the decompiler described above, the corresponding source code is printed out.

4   Experimental Results

We evaluated our ideas using a prototype implementation based on Mozilla's open source JavaScript engine SpiderMonkey [15]. Here we present results for two versions of Fibonacci number computation program. We chose them for two reasons: first, because it contains a variety of language constructs, including conditionals, recursive function calls, and arithmetic; and second, because it is small (which is important given the space constraints of this paper) and familiar (which makes it easy to assess the quality of deobfuscation). The first of these, P_1, is shown in Figure 1(a); this program was hand-obfuscated to incorporate multiple

```
function f(n){                              function fib(i){
    var t1=n;var t2=n;var k;                    var k;var x = 1;var f1 = "fib(";
    var s4 = "eval('k=t1+t2;');";               var f2 = ")";var s1 = "i-";
    var s3 = "t1=f(t1-1);eval(s4);";            var s2 = "x";
    var s2 = "t2=f(t2);eval(str3);";           if(i<2)
    var s1 = "if(n<2){k=1;}\                        eval("k="+eval("s"+
        else{t2=t2-2;eval(s2);}";                         (x*2).toString()));
    eval(s1);                                   else
    return k;                                       eval("k="+f1+s1+x.toString()+
}                                                       f2+"+"+f1+s1+(x*2).toString()
var x = 3;                                              +f2);
var y = f(x);                                   return k;
print(y);                                   }
                                            var y = fib(3);
                                            print(y);
```

| (a) Program P_1 | (b) Program P_2 |

Fig. 1. The test programs P_1 and P_2

nested levels of dynamic code generation using **eval** for each level of recursion. The second program, P_2, as shown in Figure 1(b), is also hand-obfuscated, in which we added dependency between real workload and the value used by **eval** (local variable x in function **fib**). Three versions of each of these programs are used—the program as-is as well as two obfuscated versions—one using an obfuscator we wrote ourselves that uses many of the obfuscation techniques described by Howard [8]; and an online obfuscator [1]. Figures 2 and 3 show the obfuscated programs corresponding to input programs P_1 and P_2 respectively.

The output of our deobfuscator for these programs is shown in Figure 4. Figure 4(a) shows the deobfuscated code for all three versions of program P_1 (the original code, shown in Figure 1(a), as well as the two obfuscated versions shown in Figure 2). Figure 4(b) shows the deobfuscated code for all three versions of the program P_2 (the original, shown in Figure 1(b), as well as the obfuscated versions shown in Figure 3). For both P_1 and P_2, the deobfuscator outputs are the same for each of the three versions. It can be seen that the recovered code is very close to the original, and expresses the same functionality. The results obtained show that the technique we have described is effective in simplifying away obfuscation code and extracting the underlying logic of obfuscated JavaScript code. This holds even when the code is heavily obfuscated with multiple different kinds of obfuscations, including runtime decryption of strings and multiple levels of dynamic code generation and execution, in particular, from simplified code of P_2 (Figure 4(b)), we could see that our approach handles those code intented to be "hidden" by **eval** correctly.

5   Related Work

Most current approaches to dealing with obfuscated JavaScript typically require a significant amount of manual intervention, e.g., to modify the JavaScript code in specific ways or to monitor its execution within a debugger [13,17,22]. There

```
var cl=[168,183,176,165,182,171,177,176,98,168,171,164,106,176,107,189,184,163,180,98,182,
   115,127,176,125,184,163,180,98,182,116,127,176,125,184,163,180,98,173,125,184,163,180,
   98,181,182,180,118,98,127,98,100,167,184,163,174,106,105,173,127,182,115,109,182,116,125,
   105,107,125,100,125,184,163,180,98,181,182,180,117,98,127,98,100,182,115,127,168,171,164,
   106,182,115,111,115,107,125,167,184,163,174,106,181,182,180,118,107,125,100,125,184,163,
   180,98,181,182,180,116,98,127,98,100,182,116,127,168,171,164,106,182,116,107,125,167,184,
   163,174,106,181,182,180,117,107,125,100,125,184,163,180,98,181,182,180,115,98,127,98,100,
   171,168,106,176,126,116,107,189,173,127,115,125,191,167,174,181,167,189,182,116,127,182,
   116,111,116,125,167,184,163,174,106,181,182,180,116,107,125,191,100,125,75,167,184,163,174,
   106,181,182,180,115,107,125,75,180,167,182,183,180,176,98,173,125,191,184,163,180,98,186,
   98,127,98,117,125,184,163,180,98,187,98,127,98,168,171,164,106,186,107,125,178,180,171,
   176,182,106,187,107,125];
var ii=0;
var str=';';
for(ii=0;ii<cl.length;ii++){
   str+= String.fromCharCode(cl[ii]-66);
}
eval(str);
```

(a) Obfuscated code using our obfuscator.

```
eval(function(p,a,c,k,e,d){e=function(c){return
   c};if(!''.replace(/^/,String)){while(c--){d[c]=k[c]||c}k=[function(e){return
   d[e]}];e=function(){return'\\w+'};c=1};while(c--){if(k[c]){p=p.replace(new
   RegExp('\\b'+e(c)+'\\b','g'),k[c])}}return p}('17 8(9){0 6=9;0 4=9;0 7;0
   11="5(\'7=6+4;\')";0 10="6=8(6-1);5(11);";0 13="4=8(4);5(10);";0
   15="18(9<2){7=1;}20{4=4-2;5(13);}";5(15);19 7}0 14=3;0
   12=8(14);16(12);',10,21,'var||||t2|eval|t1|k|f|n|str3|str4|y|str2|x|str1
   |print|function|if|return|else'.split('|'),0,{}))
```

(b) Obfuscated code using online obfuscator.

Fig. 2. Obfuscated versions of the program P_1

are also approaches, such as Caffeine Monkey [6], intended to assist with analyzing obfuscated JavaScript code, by instrumenting JavaScript engine and logging the actual string passed to **eval**. Similar tools include several browser extensions, such as the JavaScript Deobfuscator extension for Firefox [18]. The disadvantage of such approaches is that they show all the code that is executed and do not separate out the code that pertains to the actual logic of the program from the code whose only purpose is to deal with obfuscation.

Recently a few authors have begun looking at automatic analysis of obfuscated and/or malicious JavaScript code. Cova *at al.* [3] and Curtsinger *et al.* [5] describe the use of machine learning techniques based on a variety of dynamic execution features to classify Javascript code as malicious or benign. Such techniques typically do not focus on automatic deobfuscation, relying instead on the heuristics based on behavioral characteristics. A problem with such approaches is that, given that obfuscation can also be found in benign code and really is simply an indicative of a desire to protect the code against casual inspection, classfiers that rely on obfuscation-oriented features may not be reliable indicators of malicious intent. Our technique of automatic deobfuscation can potentially increase the accuracy of such machine learning techniques by exposing the actual logic of the code. Saxena *et al.* discuss dynamic symbolic execution of JavaScript code using constraint-solving over strings [20]. Hallaraker and Vigna describe an approach to detecting malicious JavaScript code by monitoring the execution of the program and comparing the execution to a set of high-level policies [7]. All of these works are very different from the approach discussed in this paper.

```
var cl=[168,183,176,165,182,171,177,176,98,168,171,164,106,171,107,189,184,163,180,98,173,
   125,184,163,180,98,186,98,127,98,115,125,184,163,180,98,168,115,98,127,98,100,168,171,164,
   106,100,125,184,163,180,98,168,116,98,127,98,100,107,100,125,184,163,180,98,181,115,98,127,
   98,100,171,111,100,125,184,163,180,98,181,116,98,127,98,100,186,100,125,171,168,106,171,
   126,116,107,167,184,163,174,106,100,173,127,100,109,167,184,163,174,106,100,181,100,109,
   106,186,108,116,107,112,182,177,149,182,180,171,176,169,106,107,107,107,125,167,174,181,
   167,189,167,184,163,174,106,100,173,127,100,109,168,115,109,181,115,109,186,112,182,177,
   149,182,180,171,176,169,106,107,109,168,116,109,100,109,100,109,168,115,109,181,115,109,
   106,186,108,116,107,112,182,177,149,182,180,171,176,169,106,107,109,168,116,107,125,191,180,
   167,182,183,180,176,98,173,125,191,184,163,180,98,187,98,127,98,168,171,164,106,117,107,125,
   178,180,171,176,182,106,187,107,125];
var ii=0;
var str=';';
for(ii=0;ii<cl.length;ii++){
   str+= String.fromCharCode(cl[ii]-66);
}
eval(str);
```

(a) Obfuscated code using our obfuscator.

```
eval(function(p,a,c,k,e,d){e=function(c){return
   c.toString(36)};if(!''.replace(/^/,String)){while(c--)
   {d[c.toString(a)]=k[c]||c.toString(a)}k=[function(e){return
d[e]}];e=function(){return'\\w+'};c=1};while(c--){if(k[c])
   {p=p.replace(new RegExp('\\b'+e(c)+'\\b','g'),k[c])}}return p}
   ('f a(i){0 k;0 4=1;0 6="a(";0 8=")";0 9="i-";0 d="4";c(i<2)7("k="+7
   ("e"+(4*2).5()));g 7("k="+6+9+4.5()+8+"+"+6+9+(4*2).5()+8);h k}0
   b=a(3);j(b);',21,21,'var||||x|toString|f1|eval|f2|s1|fib|y|
   if|s2|s|function|else|return||print|'.split('|'),0,{}))
```

(b) Obfuscated code using online obfuscator.

Fig. 3. Obfuscated versions of the program P_2

```
function f (arg0) {
   local_var0 = arg0;
   local_var1 = arg0;
   if((arg0<2))
      local_var2 = 1;
   else {
      local_var1 = (local_var1-2);
      local_var1 = f(local_var1);
      local_var0 = f((local_var0-1));
      local_var2 =
         (local_var0+local_var1);
   }
   return local_var2;
}
(x = 3);
(y = f(x));
print(y);
```

(a) Deobfuscated P_1

```
function fib (arg0) {
   (local_var1=1);
   if((arg0<2))
      (local_var0=local_var1);
   else
      (local_var0=
         (fib((arg0-1))+fib((arg0-2))));
   return local_var0;
}
(y=fib(3));
print(y);
```

(b) Deobfuscated P_2

Fig. 4. Deobfuscator outputs for programs P_1 and P_2

There is a rich body of literature dealing with dynamically generated ("unpacked") code in the context of conventional native-code malware executables [14,19,4,10]. Much of this work focuses on detecting the fact of unpacking and identifying the unpacked code; because of the nature of the code involved, the techniques used are necessarily low-level, typically relying on detecting the execution of a previously-modified memory locations (or pages). By contrast, the work described here is not concerned with the identification and extraction of dynamically-generated code *per se*, but focuses instead on identifying instructions that are relevant to the externally-observable behavior of the program.

6   Conclusions

The prevalence of web-based malware delivery methods, and the common use of JavaScript code in infected web pages to download malicious code, makes it important to be able to analyze the behavior of JavaScript programs and, possibly, classify them as benign or malicious. For malicious JavaScript code, it is useful to have automated tools that can help identify the functionality of the code. However, such JavaScript code is usually highly obfuscated, and use dynamic language constructs that make program analysis difficult. This paper describes an approach for dynamic analysis of JavaScript code to simplify away the obfuscation and expose the underlying logic of the code. Experiments using a prototype implementation indicate that our technique is effective even against highly obfuscated programs.

References

1. Online Javascript obfuscator,
   http://www.daftlogic.com/projects-online-javascript-obfuscator.html
2. Aho, A.V., Sethi, R., Ullman, J.D.: Compilers – Principles, Techniques, and Tools. Addison-Wesley, Reading (1985)
3. Canali, D., Cova, M., Vigna, G., Kruegel, C.: Prophiler: A fast filter for the large-scale detection of malicious web pages. In: Proceedings of the 20th International Conference on World Wide Web, pp. 197–206. ACM (2011)
4. Coogan, K., Debray, S., Kaochar, T., Townsend, G.: Automatic static unpacking of malware binaries. In: Proc. 16th IEEE Working Conference on Reverse Engineering, pp. 167–176 (October 2009)
5. Curtsinger, C., Livshits, B., Zorn, B., Seifert, C.: Zozzle: Fast and precise in-browser JavaScript malware detection. In: USENIX Security Symposium (2011)
6. Feinstein, B., Peck, D., SecureWorks, Inc.: Caffeine monkey: Automated collection, detection and analysis of malicious JavaScript. Black Hat USA (2007)
7. Hallaraker, O., Vigna, G.: Detecting malicious JavaScript code in mozilla. In: Proc. 10th IEEE International Conference on Engineering of Complex Computer Systems, pp. 85–94 (June 2005)
8. Howard, F.: Malware with your mocha: Obfuscation and antiemulation tricks in malicious JavaScript (2010)
9. Joelsson, E.: Decompilation for visualization of code optimizations (2003)
10. Kang, M.G., Poosankam, P., Yin, H.: Renovo: A hidden code extractor for packed executables. In: Proc. Fifth ACM Workshop on Recurring Malcode (WORM 2007) (November 2007)

11. Kirk, A.: Gumblar and more on Javascript obfuscation. Sourcefire Vulnerability Research Team (May 22, 2009),
    http://vrt-blog.snort.org/2009/05/gumblar-and-more-on-javascript.html
12. Lu, G., Coogan, K., Debray, S.: Automatic simplification of obfuscated JavaScript code. Technical report, Dept. of Computer Science, The University of Arizona (October 2011),
    http://www.cs.arizona.edu/~debray/Publications/js-deobf-full.pdf
13. Markowski, P.: ISC's four methods of decoding Javascript + 1 (March 2010),
    http://blog.vodun.org/2010/03/iscs-four-methods-of-decoding.html
14. Martignoni, L., Christodorescu, M., Jha, S.: OmniUnpack: Fast, Generic, and Safe Unpacking of Malware. In: Proc. 21st Annual Computer Security Applications Conference (December 2007)
15. Mozilla. Spidermonkey JavaScript engine,
    https://developer.mozilla.org/en/SpiderMonkey
16. Muchnick, S.S.: Advanced compiler design and implementation (1997)
17. Nazario, J.: Reverse engineering malicious Javascript. CanSecWest (2007),
    http://cansecwest.com/csw07/csw07-nazario.pdf
18. Palant, W.: JavaScript deobfuscator 1.5.7,
    urlhttps://addons.mozilla.org/en-US/firefox/addon/javascript-deobfuscator/
19. Royal, P., Halpin, M., Dagon, D., Edmonds, R., Lee, W.: Polyunpack: Automating the hidden-code extraction of unpack-executing malware. In: ACSAC 2006: Proceedings of the 22nd Annual Computer Security Applications Conference, pp. 289–300 (2006)
20. Saxena, P., Akhawe, D., Hanna, S., Mao, F., McCamant, S., Song, D.: A symbolic execution framework for JavaScript. In: Proc. IEEE Symposium on Security and Privacy, pp. 513–528 (2010)
21. Wang, T., Roychoudhury, A.: Dynamic slicing on java bytecode traces. ACM Transactions on Programming Languages and Systems (TOPLAS) 30(2), 10 (2008)
22. Wesemann, D.: Advanced obfuscated JavaScript analysis (April 2008),
    http://isc.sans.org/diary.html?storyid=4246

Improved Malware Classification through Sensor Fusion Using Disjoint Union

Charles LeDoux[1], Andrew Walenstein[2], and Arun Lakhotia[1]

[1] Center for Advanced Computer Studies, University of Louisiana at Lafayette,
Lafayette, LA, U.S.A.
{cal,arun}@louisiana.edu
[2] School of Computing and Informatics, Computer Science Program,
University of Louisiana at Lafayette, Lafayette, LA, U.S.A.
walenste@ieee.org

Abstract. In classifying malware, an open research question is how to combine similar extracted data from program analyzers in such a way that the advantages of the analyzers accrue and the errors are minimized. We propose an approach to fusing multiple program analysis outputs by abstracting the features to a common form and utilizing a *disjoint union* fusion function. The approach is evaluated in an experiment measuring classification accuracy on fused dynamic trace data on over 18,000 malware files. The results indicate that a naïve fusion approach can yield improvements over non-fused results, but the disjoint union fusion function outperforms naïve union by a statistically significant amount in three of four classification methods applied.

1 Introduction

A fundamental problem encountered in the automatic classification of malware is constructing features extracted from the malicious programs such that accurate classification is achieved. A significant, underlying cause of this difficulty is the fact that program analysis has general limits to accuracy and that weaknesses are often exploited by malware through *program obfuscation* [8]. Thus, all malware classification work that utilizes features generated from program analysis face the threat of inaccurate or missing features that can lead to inaccurate generalization and misclassifications. Effective methods are therefore needed to address this omnipresent problem for malware classification. One such promising method is using *data fusion* [10]. Data fusion involves combining data from disparate sources such that the information is in some sense "better" (more complete or accurate, say) than would be possible if the sources are considered independently. *Sensor fusion* is a type of data fusion that combines data outputs from multiple *sensors* which, in the case of malware, are often program analyzers such as disassemblers or tracers.

In order to perform any data fusion, a *fusion function* must be defined. This task is relatively simple when the types of information extracted by the different program analyzers are fundamentally different, since the information can be

S. Dua et al. (Eds.): ICISTM 2012, CCIS 285, pp. 360–371, 2012.

combined independently. The issue, however, is not so simple when the sensors measure similar but not identical types of information, with differing levels of accuracy. Consider the problem of fusing program behavior data extracted by two different program tracers: one generating system call traces by intercepting system calls and another generating instruction traces by running the program in a specially-instrumented emulator. Both tracers extract information about behavior, but with many potential differences; they are not perfectly substitutable. Additionally, the tracers are susceptible to different obfuscations, so that an obfuscated program might successfully hide salient behaviors from one tracer but not the other. Moreover, while fusing the results might yield a more complete picture, how can we know that the fusion does not serve to multiply the errors of both and lead to decreased accuracy? Thus, an important open problem in malware classification is knowing how to fuse outputs from program analyzers generating related information.

In this paper, we propose a two step approach to solving the problem of fusing similar data in malware classification. We first find a common abstraction that permits combination, and then use a *disjoint union* fusion function. The key insight is the realization that the commonalities and differences in the outputs of the program analyzers may provide useful information for malware classification. That is, apart from the direct benefit of combining two sources of data for a more complete picture, we propose that there is *additional useful information* to be mined from how sensors agree and disagree. The proposed disjoint union approach is utilized to fuse results of the program tracers CWSandbox [9] and Anubis [2]. We report on an experimental evaluation of the proposed fusion approach using over 18,000 malicious files and four machine learning classifiers. The results show that accuracy improved by a statistically significant amount for three of four classifiers when using the disjoint union fusion as compared to either a naïve union of features or using any single tracer output.

2   Fusing Related, Imperfect Program Data

To achieve the promises of sensor fusion, important problems must be solved in terms of finding a suitable common basis for fusion and in defining a fusion function that yields maximal benefit and minimizes potential problems.

2.1   The Unreliable Sensor Problem

Malware classification faces a unique set of difficulties. First, extracting a complete and accurate set of relevant features about programs is impossible in the general since many of the program attributes that may identify related malware are not generally computable [8]. Second, analyzers attempting to extract similar results can have a myriad of variances in models and assumptions resulting in outputs containing varying information with differing qualities. For example, program tracers running different versions of operating systems (patched versus unpatched, for example) can generate traces that are different even for identical programs.

The problem is further compounded by the existence of an adversarial context. Malware authors frequently utilize techniques know as *obfuscations* to prevent complete or accurate extraction of program properties. For example, Chen et al. [7] found that 40% of the 6,700 malicious files they examined utilize "anti-VM" or "anti-debugger" evasion methods. This adversarial context is distinct from the classic adversarial classification problem [14] in which adversaries attack the learning algorithms that utilize the features rather than feature extraction itself. Thus, taken in the context of both the limitations of feature extraction and the adversarial element, sensor fusion appears to be particularly advantageous.

2.2   Fusing Sensors for Robustness and Completeness

In this paper we are specifically concerned with what Boudjemaa et al. [6] classify as "fusion across sensors." Fusion across *sensors* combines information obtained from multiple sensors measuring the *same* attribute. In malware, a possible example is fusing results from two different disassemblers in order to combine the strengths of both. Given the limitations of program analysis reviewed above, one can expect several benefits due to fusion across sensors:

1. **Completeness of Information.** Two different traces of a program collected under different execution conditions can yield a more complete profile of its possible behaviors. For example, a more complete set of system calls might be collected.

2. **Combination of Strengths.** All obfuscations necessarily target some class of sensors [8] due to the impossibility of perfectly obfuscating all properties to all data collectors [4]. So, in a heterogeneous collection of sensors, a given set of obfuscations may negatively affect only a portion of the collection. For example, a junk byte insertion obfuscation can prevent correct disassembly by a linear sweep disassembler, but does not affect a recursive traversal disassembler [13].

3. **Decoupled Integration.** While it is possible to create new tools which combine the strengths of existing tools (Kruegel et al. [13] combine aspects of recursive traversal and linear sweep disassembly, for example), it is generally difficult to create such new tools on a continual and ongoing basis. It would advantageous to instead be able to define a fusion function that combines the strengths of existing tools in a fully decoupled manner not requiring repeated algorithm revision and combination of current best-of-breed implementations.

2.3   Sensor Fusion Function Problem

In the domain of program analysis, combining multiple analyzers can be a difficult problem because the models of program information generated by the program analyzers often differ between analyzers, even analyzers measuring the same property. For example, consider the case of the tracers CWSandbox and Anubis. Both tracers generate reports of interactions with the system. Anubis, however, reports registry keys that are "created or opened", whereas CWSandbox reports registry key opens and creates separately. Some method for resolving the differences between models must be adopted.

A second important problem for defining a sensor fusion function is to define one that combines the strengths and not the weaknesses of individual sensors. If this problem is not handled correctly, it is possible that composing an accurate sensor with a less accurate sensor will result in a loss of improvement due to the inaccuracies introduced.

3   Sensor Fusion Using Disjoint Union

We describe a general method for fusing the outputs of program analyzers in cases where the analyzers extract the same class of attributes but have differences in their outputs. The heart of the approach is the construction of a feature set using a disjoint union. We illustrate the approach by deriving a fuser for two dynamic program tracers.

3.1   Approach through Disjoint Union of Features

The proposed approach fuses *features* as illustrated in Figure 1. For this form of fusion, the main design questions are how to assure the features can be combined, and deciding on a fusion function. In our approach, we ensure the ability to combine features by defining a *feature abstraction* and use *disjoint union* as our fusion function.

Definition. Let I be an ordered set indexing a set of program analyzers run on some input program. Let $\Theta = \{\sigma_i \| \forall i \in I\}$ be the sets of outputs corresponding to the program analyzers in I. A *feature abstraction* for Θ is then defined as the pair (F, A) where F is a set of features, and A is the family of functions $A = \{\alpha_i \| \forall i \in I, \alpha_i(\sigma_i) \subset F\}$ such that $\forall i, j \in I, s_i \in \alpha_i(\sigma_i), s_j \in \alpha_j(\sigma_j), [(s_i = s_j) \rightarrow (\sigma_i \approx_{s_i} \sigma_j)]$, where $x \approx_z y$ means analyzer output x is similar to analyzer output y according to some attribute z.

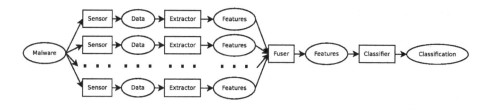

Fig. 1. Feature fusion in malware classification

Example Given disassembler D and program tracer T which both provide information about the set of function calls the program may perform, let the output of the disassembler, σ_D, be a list of system calls with abstract parameter types, and the output of the tracer, σ_T, be a sequence of calls with their concrete parameters. Let us assume that the system calls in σ_D and σ_T are represented by their symbolic names. We define a feature abstraction (F, A) over $\Theta = \{\sigma_D, \sigma_T\}$ such that F is the set of all symbolic names contained in either σ_D or σ_T and both α_D and α_T are functions which remove the parameters of the system calls and leave only the symbolic names. We then consider that $\sigma_D \approx_f \sigma_T$ if a call to function f is present in both σ_D and σ_T. In Figure 1, each of the Extractor components implements one of the α_i abstraction functions.

Definition. Let $\{S_i \| i \in I\}$ be the sets of features extracted via the feature abstraction function from the program analyzers indexed by I. That is, $S_i = \alpha_i(\sigma_i)$. Then, *fusion by disjoint union* is defined as $\bigsqcup_{i \in I} = \bigcup_{i \in I}\{(f, i)\| \forall f \in S_i, i \in I\}$. This gives us a set containing the ordered pairs (f, i) where f is a feature extracted from the output of sensor i.

Example Let there be three sensor which generate outputs σ_1, σ_2, and σ_3. Feature abstraction functions α_i are applied to each σ_i to generate $S_1 = \{f_1, f_2\}$, $S_2 = \{f_2, f_3\}$, and $S_3 = \{f_1\}$. The fused feature set, $\bigsqcup_{i \in I} = \{(f_1, 1), (f_2, 1), (f_2, 2), (f_3, 2), (f_1, 3)\}$, indicates that feature f_1 was extracted from the outputs of sensors 1 and 3, feature f_2 was extracted from the output of sensors 1 and 2, and feature f_3 was extracted only from the output of sensor 2. In Figure 1, the Fuser component implements the fusion function.

The proposal to use disjoint union is based on the following hypothesis: the information about which sensors generate which output is additional information that will assist in correct classification, so preserving it in the fusion will aid classifiers. There are two intuitions underlying this hypothesis.

1. **Information Present in Differences.** Programs that are related are likely to generate similar sets of commonalities and differences in the outputs of sensors. Consider two programs x, y, both containing an obfuscation against sensor 1. If sensor 2 is not susceptible to this obfuscation, then S_2 will contain certain system calls that S_1 does not. Since the disjoint union records that the hidden system calls are found by sensor 2 and not by sensor 1, this information can be used to determine both x and y use the obfuscation.

2. **Reputation.** Not all program analyzers for a given attribute will generate equally reliable information. For example, classification accuracy might be significantly higher using one sensor rather than another simply because one sensor generates more consistent sets of features for related inputs than the other does. By labeling which sensor generates which feature, this is information the classification algorithms can use to factor (in some way) the reliability of input sensors into account.

If the above hypothesis is true, then fusion using disjoint union should tend to result in better classification performance than either naïve union or classification with individual sensors.

3.2   Trace Fusion Example

Our example fusion is of two web-based behavioral analysis systems, Anubis (formerly TTAnalyze) [2] and CWSandbox [9]. Both of these sensors trace program execution and report on program behavior, particularly interactions with the operating system through system calls. Anubis and CWSandbox collect data at different system layers and run programs in differing runtime environments. Anubis runs in a modified version of the system emulator Qemu and works by inserting itself between the operating system and the hardware [19]. Instead of the operating system directly communicating with and controlling the hardware, it instead communicates with the virtualized hardware provided by Anubis through Qemu. CWSandbox, on the other hand, uses DLL hooking to insert itself between the Application Binary Interface (ABI) and the operating system [5]. In Windows, the ABI is contained in a collection of DLL files. Whenever one these DLLs are loaded into memory CWSandbox modifies the functions in the DLL so that system calls are first "hooked" and control flow redirected to CWSandbox instead of directly going to the operating system.

These two analyzers are appropriate choices to illustrate the fusion approach because there must be both expected overlap and differences between the sensor outputs. The hypothesis behind using disjoint union as the fusion function is that the differences between sensor outputs provide additional information. If there are either no differences or no commonalities, then this hypothesis will not hold true. Since Anubis and CWSandbox collect similar but not identical data using two different methods susceptible to different obfuscations, these requirements are held.

In order to fuse the outputs of Anubis and CWSandbox, we first need to define the abstract features and the abstraction function. The abstract features used are an adaptation of those presented in [5] and [17]. A feature is an action taken upon a resource, divided into three parts: category, action, and data. The category of a feature corresponds to the type of object that an action was taken upon. These are things such as DLLs, files, processes, etc. For example, the data stored for files is the path to the file and the data stored for registry actions is the registry key. The abstraction function removed all actions unique to a single sensor and converted a few actions to a common abstract feature. For example, in the case of CWSandbox, file open events are turned into file read events, and file copy events are turned into file create events. Actions unique to a single sensor were not included because our focus in the paper is on the in case where sensor information is nominally the same. Thus eliminating these actions ensure measured improvements in classification accuracy are due to combining strengths of the tracers rather than provision of a more comprehensive collection of features. The list of possible features together with some example concrete data are given in Table 1.

Table 1. List of possible features with concrete examples

Possible feature types			Concrete example	
Category	Actions	Data	Action	Concrete Data
DLL	load	path	load	c:\windows\system32\mlang.dll
Mutex	create	name	create	aashea
Registry	create, modify, read	key	read	hklm\software\classes\chkfile
File	create/modify, read	path	read	c:\windows\winvrn.exe
Process	create	name	create	c:\windows\charmapnt.exe

4   Evaluation

An experiment was conducted to evaluate the hypothesis that fusion by disjoint union can succeed in improving classification, and that the additional information in the pattern of sensor responses helps combine strengths of sensors without combining weaknesses. The essential test is to compare trained classifier performance for statistically significant differences when using different feature sets on three treatments: single sensor, regular union fusion, and disjoint union fusion. Specifically, the experiment tests the following:

1. **Increased Performance.** The application of sensor fusion using disjoint union is expected to increase the accuracy of malware classification. This is tested by comparing the accuracies obtained when no feature fusion is used to the accuracies obtained when feature fusion is used. If the fusion function increases accuracy, we should be able to observe statistically significant differences in the dependent variable of classifier accuracy.

2. **Increased Performance Due to Patterns of Differences.** It is possible that any increase in accuracy observed in the fusion case is due solely to the composition of information from multiple sensors and no additional improvement is made through the use of patterns of sensor differences. We test against this by comparing accuracies obtained using disjoint union as the fusion function to accuracies obtained using regular set union as the fusion function. If the disjoint union provides additional useful information to the classifiers, we should be able to observe a statistically significant increase in the dependent variable of classifier accuracy.

4.1   Data Set

The sample of malware used contained 18,422 executables and was composed of six malware families plus a set of benign (non-malicious) executables gathered from three different sources. The files belonging to the Agent, Parite, PcClient, and the Benign families were obtained from a commercial anti-virus vendor. The Banker and SDBot families were provided by OffensiveComputing.net. The Storm class was self-collected from the Storm botnet. The benign files were collected from system and third party executables from clean Windows 2000 and Windows Vista systems. Table 2 gives the number of malware files in each family.

Table 2. Malware files in sample, organized by family

Family	# Files	% of Collection	Source
sdbot	5,956	32.33%	OffensiveComputing.net
agent	1,930	10.48%	Commercial AV
benign	5,460	29.64%	Clean Systems
banker	1,118	6.07%	OffensiveComputing.net
pcclient	1,562	8.49%	Commercial AV
parite	1,841	9.99%	Commercial AV
storm	575	3.12%	Self Collected

4.2   Procedure

The overall procedure followed was to submit the malware files to the sensors and retrieve the raw data, extract the features from the raw data, create the fused and non-fused feature sets, determine classification accuracies, and perform statistical analysis. The feature set reductions, cross validation, and the classifications for the paired t-tests were performed using the open source tool RapidMiner [16]. The dependent pairs t-tests were performed using the Data Analysis ToolPak in Microsoft Excel 2007.

Feature Set Generation. There were four types of feature sets extracted. The Anubis feature set contained only features that were detected by Anubis, the CWSandbox feature set contained only features detected by CWSandbox, the Union feature set was created using union as the fusion function, and the Disjoint feature set was created using disjoint union as the fusion function. The total number of features for each feature type are given in Table 3. Information gain was used to reduce the features used to a manageable subset. The number of features detected by each sensor are given in Table 4

Accuracy Measure Collection. The learning algorithms used for classification are: Naïve Bayes, Rule Induction, Decision Tree, and K-Nearest Neighbor (KNN) as implemented by the RapidMiner [16] application. 10-Fold Cross Validation was used to obtain accuracy estimations for all combinations of classifier and feature set types. Hold-Out classification was performed to obtain measurements for the statistical tests. This was due to limitations of RapidMiner as it did not provide mechanisms to collect the needed data using Cross Validation.

Statistical Tests. Paired t-tests were performed only against combinations of feature sets using the same classifier. The experiment was focused on how the feature sets rather the classifier affected classification accuracy. In the same way, statistical tests were not performed to compare classifications using the CWSandbox feature set against those using the Anubis feature set.

Table 3. Number of features by feature set

Feature Type	Before Reduction	After Reduction
Anubis	24,767	661
CWSandbox	40,854	906
Union	58,924	1,363
Disjoint Union	58,924	1,265

Table 4. Number of features by sensor

Detected By	Number of Features
Only Anubis	18,070
Only CWSandbox	34,157
Anubis and CWSandbox	6,697
Anubis or CWSandbox	58,924

4.3   Results

The overall accuracies obtained from Cross Validation are given in Table 5. The bold accuracies indicate the feature type with the highest accuracy for each classifier. For the Naïve Bayes classifier, the CWSandbox feature set achieved the highest accuracy with 81.40%. For the Rule Induction, Decision Tree, and KNN classifiers, Disjoint Union had the highest accuracies with 91.30%, 92.83%, and 95.30% respectively.

Table 5. Classification accuracies

Feature Type	Naïve Bayes	Rule Induction	Decision Tree	KNN
Anubis	67.78%	75.32%	78.20%	86.29%
CWSandbox	**81.40%**	86.98%	88.91%	91.65%
Union	76.45%	84.11%	90.48%	92.85%
Disjoint	79.88%	**91.30%**	**92.83%**	**95.30%**

The p-values from the paired t-tests are given in Table 6. The difference in accuracies between the two feature sets is statistically significant if the p-value is less than 0.05. The places where statistical significance is *not* achieved are indicated by bold text. This is only between the Union and CWSandbox feature sets for the KNN classifier (6.11×10^{-2}), the Disjoint and CWSandbox feature sets using the Naïve Bayes classifier (2.02×10^{-1}), and the Disjoint and Union feature sets using the Decision Tree classifier (8.41×10^{-2}).

4.4   Discussion

The results support the hypothesis that sensor fusion using disjoint union improves the accuracy of malware classification. As can be seen in Table 5, disjoint union obtained a statistically significant increase in accuracy over the classifications performed without feature fusion in all but one case. For the Naïve Bayes classifier, the CWSandbox feature set had an accuracy of 80.40%, while disjoint union had an accuracy of only 79.88%. However, according to Table 6, the p-value for these two classifications is 0.202 indicating this difference in not statistically significant. All increases in accuracy disjoint union obtained over one of the non-fused feature sets, however, were statistically significant. For the Rule

Table 6. P-values from the paired t-tests

Feature Types	Naïve Bayes	Rule Induction	Decision Tree	KNN
Union & Anubis	1.00×10^{-16}	1.00×10^{-16}	1.00×10^{-16}	1.00×10^{-16}
Disjoint & Anubis	1.00×10^{-16}	1.00×10^{-16}	1.00×10^{-16}	1.00×10^{-16}
Union & CWSandbox	2.29×10^{-6}	1.11×10^{-4}	1.33×10^{-4}	6.11×10^{-2}
Disjoint & CWSandbox	2.02×10^{-1}	9.42×10^{-7}	8.58×10^{-9}	1.63×10^{-9}
Disjoint & Union	1.00×10^{-15}	1.00×10^{-13}	8.41×10^{-2}	1.02×10^{-6}

Induction, Decision Tree, and KNN classifiers, the CWSandbox feature set obtained accuracies of 86.98%, 88.91%, and 91.65%, while disjoint union obtained higher accuracies of 91.30%, 92.83%, 95.30%. The p-values for these classifications were 9.42×10^{-7}, 8.58×10^{-9}, and 1.63×10^{-9}.

The results also lend evidence to support the hypothesis that the additional information captured by disjoint union contributes to the improvement in classification accuracy. This can be seen by comparing the accuracies of Disjoint features to Union features. Looking at Table 5, we find that Disjoint consistently achieves a higher accuracy than Union (79.88% vs. 76.45%, 91.30% vs. 84.11%, 92.83% vs. 90.48%, 95.30% vs. 92.85%) and these increases are statistically significant, except when using the Decision Tree classifier (p-values of 1×10^{-15}, 1×10^{-13}, 1.02×10^{-6}, and 8.41×10^{-2}). Lending further evidence is the fact that while Disjoint consistently achieved higher accuracies than no fusion, Union only performed better than the CWSandbox feature set when using the Decision Tree and KNN classifiers (90.48% vs. 88.91% and 92.85% vs. 91.65%), and only the increase using the Decision Tree classifier was statistically significant with a p-value of 1.33×10^{-4} (KNN had p-value of 6.11×10^{-2}).

5   Relations to other Work

The concept of utilizing patterns of differences in sensor outputs to understand malware was previously explored in several prior works. Kang et al. [12] and Balzarotti et al. [3] use divergences in the execution behavior of the same malware running on both reference hardware and an emulation environment to automatically detect circumstances where the malware is detecting the emulated environment and modifying its behavior as a result. Allen et al. [1] describe a method called cross-view diff which uses discrepancies between different views of the same data structure to detect malware attempting to hide by modifying the data structure. While these three works cleanly illustrate the promise of exploiting the patterns of differences between sensor outputs, they only used these differences to identify malware which contains a specific type of obfuscations. The present work instead utilizes the insight to improve machine learning classifiers.

The idea of using data fusion in malware classification has also been explored by previous works. Islam et al. [11] combine function length frequency and printable string features. While Islam et al. did not have a specified motivation for the features chosen to combine, Lu et al. [15] combine features which are meant to be complementary, specifically static and dynamic features. Walenstein et al. [18] provide a review of work combining program metadata with various other data. None of these works address the problems associated with fusion across sensors.

6   Conclusion

In this paper, we have introduced a method of performing sensor fusion using disjoint union to combine the strengths of program analyzers ("sensors") while minimizing their weaknesses in the context of malware classification. We present an implementation of our approach and evaluate it through an experimental case study. We found that the application of sensor fusion using disjoint union typically increased the accuracy of classification by a statistically significant amount. Additionally, the results from the case study lend evidence to the additional information provided through the use of disjoint union rather than a naïve union contributing to this increase in accuracy.

One question left by this paper to be addressed in later work is the nature of the additional information provided through the use of disjoint union. It is evident that it is useful to provide the classifier with provenance information on the features, but the question still remains: Why? There are several possible answers to this question. It could be that obfuscations are affecting the sensors differently, or perhaps the provenance information helps the classifier decide which features are trustworthy from which sensor. It is worthwhile to explore this question further.

Acknowledgments. This research work was sponsored in part by funds from Air Force Research Lab and DARPA (FA8750-10-C-0171) and from Air Force Office of Scientific Research (FA9550-09-1-0715). We would like to thank Craig Miles, Anshuman Singh, and Daniel Hefner for help with test design and implementation.

References

1. Allen, W.H., Ford, R.: How not to be seen II: The defenders fight back. IEEE Security & Privacy 5(6), 65–68 (2007)
2. Anubis: Analyzing unknown binaries (June 2011), http://anubis.iseclab.org
3. Balzarotti, D., Cova, M., Karlberger, C., Kruegel, C., Kirda, E., Vigna, G.: Efficient detection of split personalities in malware. In: Network and Distributed System Security, NDSS (2010)
4. Barak, B., Goldreich, O., Impagliazzo, R., Rudich, S., Sahai, A., Vadhan, S.P., Yang, K.: On the (Im)possibility of Obfuscating Programs. In: Kilian, J. (ed.) CRYPTO 2001. LNCS, vol. 2139, pp. 1–18. Springer, Heidelberg (2001)
5. Bayer, U., Kruegel, C.: TTAnalyze: A tool for analyzing malware. In: Proceedings of the 15th European Institute for Computer Antivirus Research (EICAR 2006) Annual Conference (2006)

6. Boudjemaa, R., Forbes, A.: Parameter estimation methods for data fusion. NPL Report CMSC 38(04) (2004)
7. Chen, X., Andersen, J., Mao, Z., Bailey, M., Nazario, J.: Towards an understanding of anti-virtualization and anti-debugging behavior in modern malware. In: Proceedings of the IEEE International Conference on Dependable Systems and Networks, Anchorage, AK, U.S.A., pp. 177–186 (2008)
8. Collberg, C., Nagra, J.: Surreptitious Software: Obfuscation, Watermarking, and Tamperproofing for Software Protection. Addison-Wesley Professional (2009)
9. CWSandbox: behavior-based malware analysis (June 2011),
   http://mwanalysis.org
10. Hall, D., Llinas, J.: An introduction to multisensor data fusion. Proceedings of the IEEE 85(1), 6–23 (1997)
11. Islam, R., Tian, R., Batten, L., Versteeg, S.: Classification of malware based on string and function feature selection. In: Cybercrime and Trustworthy Computing, Workshop, pp. 9–17 (2010)
12. Kang, M.G., Yin, H., Hanna, S., McCamant, S., Song, D.: Emulating emulation-resistant malware. In: Proceedings of the 1st ACM Workshop on Virtual Machine Security, pp. 11–22. ACM, Chicago (2009)
13. Kruegel, C., Robertson, W., Valeur, F., Vigna, G.: Static disassembly of obfuscated binaries. In: Proceedings of the 13th USENIX Security Symposium, pp. 255–270. Usenix (2004)
14. Laskov, P., Lippman, R.: Machine learning in adversarial environments. Machine Learning 81, 115–119 (2010)
15. Lu, Y., Din, S., Zheng, C., Gao, B.: Using multi-feature and classifier ensembles to improve malware detection. Journal of C.C.I.T. 39(2) (November 2010)
16. Mierswa, I., Wurst, M., Klinkenberg, R., Scholz, M., Euler, T.: Yale: Rapid prototyping for complex data mining tasks. In: Ungar, L., Craven, M., Gunopulos, D., Eliassi-Rad, T. (eds.) Proceedings of the 12th ACM SIGKDD International Conference on Knowledge Discovery and Data Mining, pp. 935–940. ACM (2006)
17. Trinius, P., Willems, C., Holz, T., Rieck, K.: A malware instruction set for behavior-based analysis. Tech. Rep. TR-2009-07, University of Mannheim (2009)
18. Walenstein, A., Hefner, D., Wichers, J.: Header information in malware families and impact on automated classifiers. In: Proceedings of the 5th International Conference on Malicious and Unwanted Software, pp. 15–22. IEEE CSP (2010)
19. Willems, C., Holz, T., Freiling, F.: Toward automated dynamic malware analysis using CWSandbox. IEEE Security & Privacy 5(2), 32–39 (2007)

Dynamic Architectural Countermeasure to Protect RSA against Side Channel Power Analysis Attacks

John Barron*, Todd R. Andel, and Yong Kim

Air Force Institute of Technology, WPAFB OH 45433, USA

Abstract. The modular exponentiation operation used in popular public key encryption schemes such as RSA, has been the focus of many side channel analysis (SCA) attacks in recent years. Current SCA attack countermeasures are largely static. Given sufficient signal to noise ratio and a number of power traces, static countermeasures can be defeated as they merely attempt to mask or hide the power consumption of the system under attack. This paper introduces a dynamic countermeasure which constantly varies the timing and power consumption of each operation, making correlation between traces more difficult than for static countermeasures.

1 Introduction

In the seminal 1999 paper [1], Kocher et al. present a method to recover a secret key from cryptographic hardware by monitoring the hardware's power consumption. In recent years, these so called side channel analysis (SCA) attacks have become a focus of the cryptographic community. These attacks are conducted by collecting power consumption data of the hardware, referred to as power traces, over many cryptographic cycles and statistically correlating this data to the likely cryptographic key. These attacks allow an attacker to recover keys much faster than traditional cryptanalysis. The RSA public key encryption algorithm [2] has been the target of many of these attacks. Current methods of SCA protection fall into main two categories: masking and hiding [3]. Masking introduces randomness into the input text to introduce independence between intermediate calculations and power consumption. Hiding obscures any correlation by introducing electrical noise or designing the hardware in such a way that minimizes the signal an attacker wishes to capture, thus making successful attacks more difficult. The goal of both methods is to lower the signal to noise ratio (SNR) discernible by the attacker to a level that makes the attack infeasible. However,

* The views expressed in this article are those of the authors and do not reflect the official policy or position of the United States Air Force, Department of Defense, or the U.S. Government. This work performed with support from the Air Force Office of Scientific Research under grant number F1ATA01103J001.

S. Dua et al. (Eds.): ICISTM 2012, CCIS 285, pp. 372–383, 2012.

these static countermeasures are insufficient because they can be broken by collecting more, higher fidelity power traces and by improved post processing using better algorithms.

This paper introduces a dynamic countermeasure that incorporates randomness into operations, intermediate calculated values, power consumption, and timing. This constantly changing architecture drives side channel attackers to perform a "brute force" search to achieve the correlation needed for successful attacks. The paper is organized as follows: Section 2 provides a short background on RSA, Booth multiplication, and modular exponentiation methods. Section 3 introduces the dynamic architectural countermeasure. Sections 4 and 5 discuss several well known side channel attacks and currently existing countermeasures. Section 6 presents simulated results of the countermeasure. Lastly, Section 7 provides conclusions and future implementation plans.

2   Background

Modern cryptographic algorithms use very large integers for keys, e.g., 4096-bit RSA. Many public key cryptographic algorithms, including RSA, rely on the modular exponentiation operation for encryption. RSA decryption, as seen in Equation 1, raises the ciphertext C to the power of the private key d modulo the modulus N. The result is the plaintext message M.

$$M = C^d \pmod{N} \tag{1}$$

Naively computing C^d via $d - 1$ multiplications of C is impractical because of memory and timing constraints [4]. Therefore, algorithms are required to decrease storage requirements and the number of steps required for the modular exponentiation operation. These algorithms are known as square-and-multiply algorithms. The algorithms represent the exponent (i.e., key) in binary and repeatedly compute modular multiplication operations. These algorithms keep the memory space limited as they perform modular reduction during exponentiation and complete after $\log_2 d$ iterations. Additionally, exponentiation methods can operate on a single bit of the exponent (binary) or multiple bits of the exponent (k-ary) for a given iteration.

2.1   Modular Exponentiation

Binary exponentiation is the most straightforward method for exponentiation; operating on a single bit of the binary representation of the exponent at a time. This process can be performed either from the left-to-right (MSB to LSB) or right-to-left (LSB to MSB). The square-and-multiply algorithm for left-to-right can be seen in Algorithm 1.

It is also possible to operate on multiple bits of the exponent at once. For maximum efficiency, the goal is to compute C^d using the fewest number of operations,

---

Algorithm 1. Left-to-Right Binary Exponentiation [4]

INPUT: Base C, Modulus N, and Exponent $d = (d_t, d_{t-1}...d_1, d_0)_2$
OUTPUT: $C^d \pmod{N}$
$R := 1$;
for $i = t - 1$ downto 0 **do**
   $R := R^2 \pmod{N}$; —Square
   if $d_i = 1$ **then**
      $R := R \cdot C \pmod{N}$; —Multiply
   end if
end for
return R

---

given that it is only possible to multiply two already computed powers of C [5]. Since multiple bits are being operated on at once, there are fewer total operations needed. This approach, referred to as windowing, provides some speedup. This speedup comes as trade off of higher memory requirements. As seen in Algorithm 2, precomputation and storage of additional powers of C are needed. The higher the window size k, the less multiplication operations needed and more memory space required.

Algorithm 2. Window Method [4]

INPUT: Base C, Modulus N, Window Size k, Exponent $d = (d_t, d_{t-1}...d_1, d_0)_2$
OUTPUT: $C^d \pmod{N}$
PRECOMPUTE:
$c_0 := 1$;
for $i = 1$ to $2^k - 1$ **do**
   $c_i := c_{i-1} \cdot C$; — Compute Powers For Window
end for
$R := 1$;
for $i = k - 1$ downto 0 **do**
   $R := R^{2^k} \pmod{N}$;
   $R := R \cdot c_{d_i} \pmod{N}$; —Use Precomputed Powers
end for
return R

In order to complete the modular multiplications $R^2 \pmod{N}$ and $R \cdot C \pmod{N}$, referred to as squaring and multiplying respectively, we must implement a multiplier. Basic binary multiplication is accomplished by repeated addition and shift operations. In contrast, Booth encoded multiplication [6] recodes operands in such a way to reduce the number of costly addition steps. This paper focuses on a modification of the Booth concept to dynamically randomize the calculation, which provides a level of SCA protection to RSA.

2.2 Booth Multiplication

As shown in the flowchart in Figure 1, Booth multiplication tests the LSBs of the multiplier to determine whether adding or subtracting the multiplicand is needed in each iteration. Booth's approach has a speedup benefit since arithmetic logic unit (ALU) operation is only required on 0-to-1 and 1-to-0 transitions. For each iteration, the LSBs of the multiplier are tested, ALU operation is completed (if needed), and multiplier and product registers are shifted. To complete modular multiplication, the product of Booth multiplication must be reduced via a modulo operation. There are two main classes of reduction techniques for modular multiplication: multiply-then-reduce and reduce-as-you-go [7]. In this paper, we implement the reduce-as-you-go approach. Using the simple method outlined in Algorithm 3 keeps the product within the bounds of the modulus. This algorithm is left-to-right (MSB to LSB), which forces Booth encoding to be preformed left-to-right also. However, the architecture presented in this paper does not preclude implementing the popular Montgomery reduction [8].

Algorithm 3. Modular Reduction

INPUT: Multiplier A, Multiplicand B, Modulus N
OUTPUT: $A \cdot B$ (mod N)
Double the product register
If product register is $> |N|$ modulus, Add/subtract to adjust
Add/Subtract via Booth operation
If product register is $> |N|$ modulus, Add/subtract to adjust

---

3 Dynamic Architectural Countermeasure

3.1 Randomized Radix Encoding Booth Multiplier

This paper proposes a design for a Booth multiplier with randomized radix encoding. Increasing the radix of Booth encoding causes more bits to be encoded each cycle, thus further decreases the number of required cycles to complete multiplication. The Booth encoding for radix 2, 4, and 8 are shown in Table 1. We note that all multiples of the multiplier M are trivial (shifts and 2's complements) except the multiple of three. However, the multiple of three is easily precomputed and stored for later use.

To provide protection against SCA we vary the radix of Booth encoding. Driven by a pseudorandom number generator, henceforth referred to as random, the multiplier hardware randomly selects a radix at each iteration. This dynamic architecture induces randomness into the timing of operand use, randomizes intermediate operands, randomizes power consumption, and multiplication completes in a nondeterministic number of clock cycles. Additionally this causes alignment of traces to be lost, making correlation much more difficult.

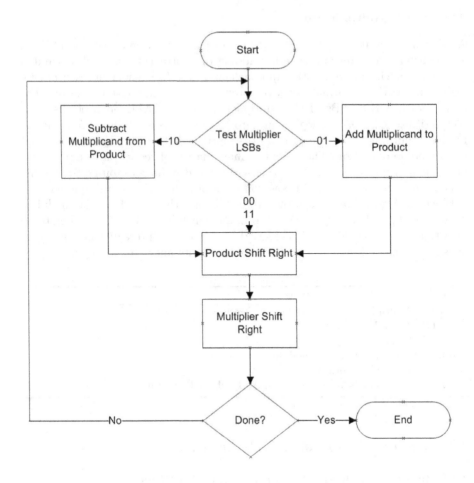

Fig. 1. Flowchart of Booth Multiplication [9]

Table 1. Table of Booth Encoding For Given Radix

Radix-2	M	Radix-4	M	Radix-8	M
00	0	000, 111	0	0000, 1111	0
01	M	001, 010	M	0001, 0010	M
10	$-M$	011	$2M$	0011, 0100	$2M$
11	0	100	$-2M$	0101, 0110	$3M$
		101, 110	$-M$	0111	$4M$
				1000	$-4M$
				1001, 1010	$-3M$
				1011, 1100	$-2M$
				1101, 1110	$-M$

3.2   Variable Window Exponentiator

Building upon the randomness introduced via the randomized radix encoding Booth multiplier, we also randomize the window size of the exponentiator. Starting with the general windowing Algorithm 2, we complete the precomputations needed for a maximum window size of 2. Continuing on into the second loop, we randomly vary the window size k between 1 and 2 each iteration. If window size 1 is chosen, the algorithm simplifies to simple binary exponentiation. If window size of 2 is chosen, $R = R^4$ is computed and $R = R \cdot c_{d_i}$ is calculated using the precomputed powers of c. Similar to randomizing the radix in Booth multiplication, randomizing the window size in exponentiation further introduces timing, operations, and calculated intermediate value randomness. Although this paper presents an architecture with window sizes of 1 and 2, it is possible to increase the window size further for added randomization. However, this is a storage trade off since increasing the window size exponentially increases the number of precomputations and storage needed for very large integers.

4   Side Channel Attacks

As mentioned throughout this paper, the goal of adding randomness to timing and operations is to decrease the side channel attack susceptibility of the modular exponentiation operation. There are many known side channel attacks. We highlight a few well known attacks and reasons why our architecture is expected to thwart them.

4.1   Simple Power Analysis

SPA involves directly observing power traces to gather information about the secret key[1]. SPA leaks are caused by programming conditional branch decisions based on secret keys or intermediate values. For example, in binary exponentiation as described in Algorithm 1, if there is a distinguishable difference between a squaring operation and a multiplying operation (time or power), the implementation is vulnerable to SPA. The dynamic countermeasure introduced in this paper uses a single set of hardware for multiplication. For this research, squaring and multiplication are both completed as simple modular multiplication operations using the same hardware; there will be no distinction between operations. Also, any possible timing or power variations causing SPA leakages will be difficult to discern as the operation or the randomness introduced by this dynamic countermeasure.

4.2   Differential and Correlation Power Analysis

Differential power analysis (DPA), presented by Kocher [1], is a very common and very powerful side channel attack. Based on key guesses, an attacker calculates an expected intermediate bit, and checks whether the difference between the mean traces partitioned according to this bit differ. Similarly in correlation power analysis, attackers calculate an expected intermediate value and check for statistical correlation within the captured power traces. There are many variants of this attack using either the Hamming weight of the intermediate value, Hamming distance, zero value model, etc [3]. All of these attacks depend heavily upon first being able to calculate the correct intermediate values. With our randomly changing architecture there are many possible intermediate values for each multiplication and exponentiation bit. Secondly, DPA attacks require these intermediate values to be correlated to the power traces. Even in the instances when our architecture calculates the same intermediate values, there is randomization in the way they are calculated. Different methods of calculation will drive different switching activity which draws different power, also decreasing correlation. Lastly, DPA relies on trace alignment to correlate operations at the same slice in time. While there are advanced algorithms to aid in trace alignment, all the randomness heretofore discussed makes this task more difficult.

4.3   Comparative Power Analysis

Another popular class of side channel attacks are comparative power analysis attacks[10,11,12]. Many of these attacks are chosen message attacks where the message is purposely chosen such that it generates a collision within two traces at some point during modular exponentiation. Because the attacker chooses the message to be encrypted, they know where in each trace the collision occurs. Using advanced pattern matching algorithms they are able to determine bit(s) of the key using these collisions. The same randomness that increases protection against DPA also applies here. First, the collision may not occur since there is a randomness to the calculated intermediate values. Secondly, the timing and power consumption randomness will make it very difficult for the pattern matching algorithms to recognize a collision since even though the intermediate values may have collided, they arrived at the collision in different ways, which have different power signatures.

5   Existing Countermeasures

As previously mentioned, current SCA countermeasures are largely static. Many existing countermeasures rely on hiding the signal from an attacker. Two common ways this is attempted is dual rail logic [13] and bit balancing [14]. These countermeasures concurrently calculate a result and its inverse, with the goal of hiding the true switching activity based on Hamming weights. The problem with these countermeasures are imperfections in ASIC fabrication or FPGA synthesis. It is nearly impossible to fabricate a device that perfectly balances switching power consumption [15]. The security of these countermeasures rely only on the quality of the probe and the signal attackers are able to capture.

6   Simulation Results

Our design was developed in VHDL and simulated using Mentor Graphics' ModelSim. The following sections discuss simulated execution of both our randomized radix encoding Booth multiplier and variable window exponentiator.

6.1   Randomized Modular Multiplication Simulation

Three computations of $146 \cdot 85$ (mod 207) were simulated to show the induced randomness in timing and operations. The simulation results are presented in Figure 2. It is clearly seen that all three computation's *output* arrive at the correct answer of $146 \cdot 85$ (mod 207) = 197. However, the simulations complete in 9, 5, and 6 iterations respectively.

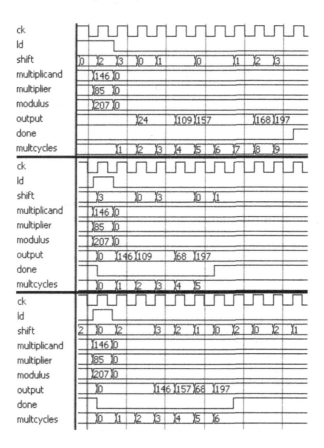

Fig. 2. Three Simulations of $146 \cdot 85$ (mod 207)

Table 2 presents the computations in tabular form in order to show the randomness in the calculations, where the multiplier 85 is represented in binary.

Table 2. Three Computations of $146 \cdot 85$ (mod 207) [Entire Table (mod 207)]

Multiplier		1st Run	Radix	2nd Run	Radix	3rd Run	Radix
MSB	0	$P = 0$				$P = 0$	
		$2^2 \cdot P = 2^2 \cdot 0 = 0$	$2 = 00\underline{0}$	$P = 0$		$2^2 \cdot P = 2^2 \cdot 0 = 0$	$2 = 00\underline{0}$
	0	$P + 0 = 0$		$2^3 \cdot P = 2^3 \cdot 0 = 0$	$3 = 000\underline{1}$	$P + 0 = 0$	
	0			$P + M = 146$		$2^2 \cdot P = 2^2 \cdot 0 = 0$	
		$2^3 \cdot P = 2^3 \cdot 0 = 0$				$P + M = 0 + 146 = 146$	$2 = 01\underline{0}$
	1	$P + 3M = 0 + 3 \cdot 146 = 24$	$3 = 010\underline{1}$				
	0			$2^3 \cdot P = 2^3 \cdot 146 = 133$			
				$P - 3M = 133 - 3 \cdot 146 = 109$	$3 = 101\underline{0}$	$2^3 \cdot P = 2^3 \cdot 146 = 133$	
	1	$2 \cdot P = 2 \cdot 24 = 48$				$P + 3M = 133 + 3 \cdot 146 = 157$	$3 = 010\underline{1}$
		$P - M = 48 - 146 = 109$	$1 = 1\underline{0}$				
	0	$2 \cdot P = 2 \cdot 109 = 11$					
		$P + M = 11 + 146 = 157$	$1 = 0\underline{1}$				
	1	$2 \cdot P = 2 \cdot 157 = 107$		$2^3 \cdot P = 2^3 \cdot 109 = 44$		$2 \cdot P = 2^2 \cdot 157 = 7$	
		$P - M = 107 - 146 = 168$	$1 = 1\underline{0}$	$P + 3M = 44 + 3 \cdot 146 = 68$	$3 = 010\underline{1}$	$P - M = 7 - 146 = 68$	$2 = 10\underline{1}$
	0	$2^2 \cdot P = 2 \cdot 168 = 51$					
		$P + M = 51 + 146 = 197$	$2 = 01\underline{0}$	$2 \cdot P = 2 \cdot 68 = 136$		$2 \cdot P = 2 \cdot 68 = 136$	
LSB	1			$P - M = 136 - 146 = 197$	$1 = 1\underline{0}$	$P - M = 136 - 146 = 197$	$1 = 1\underline{0}$

We notice as each "run" works from MSB to LSB of the multiplier, horizontal lines show which bit(s) each cell operates on. Notice where cells end on the same bit (horizontal lines line up), the calculated value is the same, but where iterations end on different bits of the multiplier (horizontal lines do not line up) the addition operation and results are different. This effect is significant because although the algorithm is computing the same answer, the power signature will be vastly different, not only because of the induced timing variance, but also the switching activity from different operands in each iteration.

6.2 Randomized Exponentiation Using Randomized Modular Multiplication Simulation

To further randomize the modular exponentiation operation, this architectural countermeasure combines the randomized Booth multiplier and the randomized exponentiator. A simulation of three calculations of 146^{187} (mod 207) is presented in Figure 3. It is verified that all three iterations arrive at the correct answer of 146^{187} (mod 207) = 47. Notice the combined timing variance of the randomized multiplication and exponentiation lead to completion in 133, 136, and 119 cycles respectively.

Window	I2				I1		I2						I1			
Output	I1				I202	I25	I131	I187	I193	I77	I133	I94	I62	I118		I47
Cycles	I15	I20	I27	I38	I42	I51	I57	I64	I72	I82	I92	I100	I108	I114	I121	I133
Window	I2		I1				I2					I1				
Output	I1				I146	I202	I25	I4	I185	I70	I139	I133	I94	I62	I118	I47
Cycles	I15	I20	I27	I38	I43	I51	I57	I63	I71	I81	I90	I99	I107	I113	I120	I136
Window	I1				I2											
Output	I1				I146	I202	I25	I4	I185	I70	I139	I133	I94	I142	I47	
Cycles	I15	I20	I26	I37	I42	I50	I56	I62	I70	I80	I89	I98	I106	I111	I119	

Fig. 3. Three Simulations of 146^{187} (mod 207)

Table 3. Three Computations of 146^{187} (mod 207) [Entire Table (mod 207)]

	Exponent	1st Run	Window	2nd Run	Window	3rd Run	Window
MSB	0	$R = 1$		$R = 1$		$R = 1$	
		$R^2 = 1^2 = 1$	2	$R^2 = 1^2 = 1$	2	$R^2 = 1^2 = 1$	1
	0	$R^2 = 1^2 = 1$		$R^2 = 1^2 = 1$		$R^2 = 1^2 = 1$	1
		$R^2 = 1^2 = 1$		$R^2 = 1^2 = 1$		$R^2 = 1^2 = 1$	
	1	$R^2 = 1^2 = 1$		$R \cdot M = 1 \cdot 146 = 146$	1	$R \cdot M = 1 \cdot 146 = 146$	1
	0	$R \cdot M^2 = 1 \cdot 202 = 202$	2	$R^2 = 146^2 = 202$	1	$R^2 = 146^2 = 202$	1
	1	$R^2 = 202^2 = 25$		$R^2 = 202^2 = 25$		$R^2 = 202^2 = 25$	
		$R \cdot M = 25 \cdot 146 = 131$	1	$R^2 = 25^2 = 4$	2	$R^2 = 25^2 = 4$	2
	1	$R^2 = 131^2 = 187$		$R \cdot M^3 = 4 \cdot 98 = 185$		$R \cdot M^3 = 4 \cdot 98 = 185$	
		$R^2 = 187^2 = 193$	2	$R^2 = 185^2 = 70$		$R^2 = 185^2 = 70$	
	1	$R \cdot M^3 = 193 \cdot 98 = 77$		$R^2 = 70^2 = 139$	2	$R^2 = 70^2 = 139$	2
	0	$R^2 = 77^2 = 135$		$R \cdot M^2 = 139 \cdot 202 = 133$		$R \cdot M^2 = 139 \cdot 202 = 133$	
		$R^2 = 135^2 = 94$	2	$R^2 = 133^2 = 94$	1	$R^2 = 133^2 = 94$	
	1	$R \cdot M^1 = 94 \cdot 146 = 62$		$R \cdot M = 94 \cdot 146 = 62$		$R^2 = 94^2 = 142$	2
		$R^2 = 62^2 = 118$		$R^2 = 62^2 = 118$		$R \cdot M = 142 \cdot 98 = 47$	
LSB	1	$R \cdot M = 118 \cdot 146 = 47$	1	$R \cdot M = 118 \cdot 146 = 47$	1		

More interestingly, the tabular calculation shown in Table 3 is inspected to see its effect on intermediate calculations. Because intermediate calculations, power consumption, and timing are of such importance to DPA attacks, this architecture for implementing the popular modular exponentiation operation incorporates countermeasures to defeat attacks. Again take notice where cells end on the same bit (horizontal lines line up), the calculated value is the same, but where iterations end on different bits of the exponent (horizontal lines do not line up) results are different. This result validates via simulation that this proposed dynamic architectural countermeasure successfully randomizes switching activity.

7 Conclusions

As stated previously, this research is driven by the fact that current static SCA countermeasures rely on hiding the signals, not protecting them. These countermeasures' success are based upon the quality of equipment and quality of signal an attacker is able to capture. In contrast to the existing countermeasures, the dynamic architectural countermeasure presented in this paper does not rely on hiding signals. This approach is much more in line with Kerckhoffs's principle [4], which states that a cryptosystem should be secure even if everything about the system, except the key, is public knowledge. The new countermeasure presented in this paper makes no attempts to mask or hide power consumption, only to randomize it. This forces an attacker into a brute force side channel attack in which the attacker must calculate every possible combination of intermediate values for every trace. Therefore, this research lays a foundation for exponential difficulty side channel attack protection. Assuming the correct trade off choices are made with respect to performance and hardware area, it is conceivable that large enough pools of radixes and window sizes could lead to a future system with brute force side channel attack difficulty no worse than the underlying encryption algorithm's brute force security, thus rendering side channel attacks impractical.

The randomized algorithms and simulation results presented here are the product of VHDL code. This research is being carried forward and physically implemented on a Xilinx Virtex-5 FPGA for real world analysis. Using noninvasive electromagnetic probes to collect power emanations, attacks will be attempted and provide a measure of real world side channel attack protection. The results of these future tests will provide concrete validation to the preliminary simulated results provided here. Preliminary results show very little execution time costs. The precalculations are offset by large windows. Preliminary attacks also show correlation spikes from correlation power analysis attacks are many orders of magnitude lower than baseline binary exponentiation.

References

1. Kocher, P.C., Jaffe, J., Jun, B.: Differential Power Analysis. In: Wiener, M. (ed.) CRYPTO 1999. LNCS, vol. 1666, pp. 388–397. Springer, Heidelberg (1999)
2. Rivest, R.L., Shamir, A., Adleman, L.: A method for obtaining digital signatures and public-key cryptosystems. Commun. ACM 21, 120–126 (1978)
3. Mangard, S., Oswald, E., Popp, T.: Power Analysis Attacks: Revealing the Secrets of Smart Cards (Advances in Information Security). Springer-Verlag New York, Inc., Secaucus (2007)
4. Menezes, A.J., Oorschot, P.C.V., Vanstone, S.A., Rivest, R.L.: Handbook of Applied Cryptography (1997)
5. Nedjah, N., Mourelle, L.: Efficient hardware for modular exponentiation using the sliding-window method with variable-length partitioning. In: Proc. 9th Int. Conf. for Young Computer Scientists ICYCS 2008, pp. 1980–1985 (2008)
6. Booth, A.D.: A signed binary multiplication technique. The Quarterly Journal of Mechanics and Applied Mathematics 4(2), 236–240 (1951)
7. Daly, A., Marnane, W.: Efficient architectures for implementing montgomery modular multiplication and RSA modular exponentiation on reconfigurable logic. In: Proceedings of the 2002 ACM/SIGDA Tenth International Symposium on Field-Programmable Gate Arrays, FPGA 2002, New York, NY, USA, pp. 40–49. ACM (2002)
8. Montgomery, P.L.: Modular multiplication without trial division. Math. Computation 44, 519–521 (1985)
9. Patterson, D.A., Hennessy, J.L.: Computer organization & design: the hardware/software interface. Morgan Kaufmann Publishers Inc., San Francisco (1993)
10. Homma, N., Miyamoto, A., Aoki, T., Satoh, A., Samir, A.: Comparative power analysis of modular exponentiation algorithms. IEEE Trans. Comput. 59, 795–807 (2010)
11. Fouque, P.-A., Valette, F.: The Doubling Attack – Why Upwards Is Better than Downwards. In: Walter, C.D., Koç, Ç.K., Paar, C. (eds.) CHES 2003. LNCS, vol. 2779, pp. 269–280. Springer, Heidelberg (2003)

12. Yen, S.-M., Lien, W.-C., Moon, S.-J., Ha, J.C.: Power Analysis by Exploiting Chosen Message and Internal Collisions – Vulnerability of Checking Mechanism for RSA-Decryption. In: Dawson, E., Vaudenay, S. (eds.) Mycrypt 2005. LNCS, vol. 3715, pp. 183–195. Springer, Heidelberg (2005), doi:10.1007/11554868_13
13. Popp, T., Mangard, S.: Implementation aspects of the DPA-resistant logic style MDPL. In: Proc. IEEE Int. Symp. Circuits and Systems ISCAS (2006)
14. Ambrose, J.A., Parameswaran, S., Ignjatovic, A.: MUTE-AES: A multiprocessor architecture to prevent power analysis based side channel attack of the AES algorithm. In: IEEE/ACM International Conference on Computer-Aided Design, ICCAD 2008, pp. 678–684 (November 2008)
15. Sauvage, L., Guilley, S., Danger, J.-L., Mathieu, Y., Nassar, M.: Successful attack on an FPGA-based WDDL DES cryptoprocessor without place and route constraints. In: Design, Automation Test in Europe Conference Exhibition, DATE 2009, pp. 640–645 (April 2009)

Deployable Classifiers for Malware Detection

Anshuman Singh, Sumi Singh, Andrew Walenstein, and Arun Lakhotia

University of Louisiana at Lafayette, USA
{asingh,sxs5729,arun}@louisiana.edu,
walenste@cacs.louisiana.edu

Abstract. The application of machine learning methods to malware detection has opened up possibilities of generating large number of classifiers that use different kinds of features and learning algorithms. A straightforward way to select the best classifier is to pick the one with best holdout or cross-validation performance. Cross-validation or holdout gives a point estimate of generalization performance that varies with training data and learning algorithm parameters. We propose a classifier selection criterion that considers bounds on the performance estimates using confidence intervals in conjunction with a performance target. Performance targets are commonly used in practice, particularly in security applications like malware detection, for classifier selection. The proposed criterion, called *deployability*, selects a classifier as *deployable* if the cost target lies within or above the classifiers expected cost confidence interval. We conducted an experiment with machine learning based malware detectors to evaluate the criterion. We found that for a given confidence level and cost target, even the classifier with least expected cost may not be deployable and classifiers with higher expected cost may also be deployable.

1 Introduction

Machine learning based methods have been proposed for malware detection as an alternative and complementary approach to static and dynamic analysis based methods [8]. The space of classifiers for malware detection is quite large. The choice of feature type for malware detection includes bytecode n-grams, bytecode n-perms, opcode n-grams, opcode n-perms. Each of these feature types can be efficiently extracted for $n = 1, 2, \ldots, 6$. For each choice of n, one can choose the type of weights applied to each n-gram. The weights typically considered are count, term frequency, TFIDF, etc [11]. There are also many learning algorithms to choose from.

The standard method of selecting the best classifier is to pick the one with best holdout or cross validation performance. The cross validation performance is a point estimate with high variance that depends on the training data and the initial parameters of the learning algorithms. The variability of point estimates can be determined using interval estimates like confidence intervals. The classifier selection criterion can be modified to explicitly incorporate the high variance of

S. Dua et al. (Eds.): ICISTM 2012, CCIS 285, pp. 384–395, 2012.
© Springer-Verlag Berlin Heidelberg 2012

point estimates in conjunction with performance target to select classifiers with better generalization performance that meets the given targets.

In this paper, we explicitly incorporate interval estimation in the classifier selection criterion. We propose the criterion that if a given target of expected consequential cost of misclassification (per input) lies in the confidence interval of point estimate of the expected cost of the classifier on a dataset, then the classifier is said to be *deployable*. We call this criterion the *deployability* of a classifier. The deployability criterion also incorporates performance targets, more commonly used in malware detection, to select the classifiers. For example, expected cost (per input) target of 0.25 utils (unit of utility) may be required for the selected classifier to be deployed.

We conducted an experiment with machine learning based malware detectors to compare deployable classifiers with the least expected cost classifier. We found that even the least expected cost classifier may not be deployable under some given cost targets and classifiers with high expected costs may be deployable for a given cost target.

We discuss related work in section 2. We give some background on performance measures, confidence intervals and text categorization based features in section 3. In section 4, the notion of deployability is formally defined and the method of selecting deployable classifiers is outlined. Section 5 describes the setup, methodology and results of the experiment conducted to evaluate the method of selecting deployable classifiers. This is followed by a discussion of the experimental evaluation in section 6. We conclude the paper in section 7.

2   Related Work

The concept of deployability in our work is related to the concept of *actionability* introduced by Kleinberg *et al.* [6] and defined in a decision-theoretic framework by Elovici *et al.* [2]. A decision of a classifier is actionable if it maximizes the utility to the entity using that decision. A deployable classifier can be thought of as a generalization of an actionable decision of a meta-classifier that decides whether an input classifier satisfies the cost constraints of the setting in which the classifier has to be deployed. Deployability is a generalization because it considers bounded cost model instead of utility maximization or cost minimization model of decision theory.

Applicability of a classifier was introduced by Brazdil *et al.* [1,4]. A meta-classifier labels an input classifier as applicable if the input classifier minimizes the error rate for a given test data set. The meta-classifier can be trained to learn rules that give a bound or a range on the number of features, the value of parameters of a classifier, the number of training samples, etc. for an input classifier to be applicable. The deployability criteria for classifier selection can be thought of as a meta-classifier but it does not learn the cost constraint rules. So, in that sense it does not give the applicability of the classifier when there is incomplete information about the cost constraint rules of the environment.

Gaffney & Ulvila [3] use the difference in expected cost at optimal operating point as a criterion to select the best intrusion detection system. In their work, the operating point is assumed to be directly tunable for each IDS to obtain the optimal operating point. This assumption of direct tunability does not hold for machine learning systems where the notion of operating point is more complicated. For machine learning based systems, the optimal parameters of a classifier are first determined by the model selection method used by the learning algorithm. The optimal parameters and the training data then determine a point estimate of the operating point of the classifier depending on the method used for evaluation (e.g. cross-validation, holdout, etc.). Since there is a variability in the point estimate due to the training data and parameters chosen by the model selection method of the learning algorithm, a bound on the estimate in the form of confidence intervals is required to select the best machine learning based detection system. The criterion of deployability proposed in this paper takes into account the bounds on the estimate explicitly along with the performance target.

3   Background

3.1   Performance Measures

The simplest way to describe the test performance of a classifier is to construct a *confusion matrix*. The elements of this matrix are commonly used in measures like detection rate and false positive rate [5].

Confusion Matrix. Given a binary classifier $C : \{P, N\} \rightarrow \{P, N\}$, the performance of C can be described using a 2×2 matrix $M = [n_{ij}]$ where n_{ij} is the number of instances of input with true class i that were classified as class j for $i, j = 1, 2$ (See Table 1).

Table 1. Confusion matrix

Classified Label	True Label		
	Positive	Negative	Row Total
Positive	TP	FP	TP+FP
Negative	FN	TN	FN+TN
Column Total	TP+FN	FP+TN	N=TP+TN+FP+FN

Detection Rate. The proportion of actual positives that were correctly classified. Also called *true positive rate*, *recall*, or *sensitivity*.

$$P_D = \frac{TP}{TP + FN}$$

False Positive Rate. The proportion of actual negatives that were incorrectly classified. Also called *false alarm rate*.

$$P_F = \frac{FP}{FP + TN}$$

3.2 Generalization Performance

A classifier's performance on unseen data (data other than training and test data) is called its generalization performance. The generalization performance of a classifier can be estimated by evaluation methods like holdout and cross validation. Holdout and cross validation give a point estimate of the chosen performance measure (e.g. accuracy, detection rate, etc.). This point estimate varies with the training and test data as well as the initial parameters of the learning algorithms. Interval estimates in the form of confidence intervals are more useful in real world as they give a bound on the estimates of generalization performance.

Performance measures like detection rate and false positive rate are proportions that can be can be estimated for unseen data using their holdout or cross validation values. The *Wald interval* for detection rate P_D can be written as [10]:

$$\bar{P}_D \pm z_{1-\alpha/2}\sqrt{\frac{\bar{P}_D(1 - \bar{P}_D)}{n}}$$

where $\bar{P}_D$ is the holdout detection rate of the classifier on a test data with proportion of actual positives $n = TP + FN$ and $(1 - \alpha)\%$ is the confidence level. The confidence interval for P_F can be computed similarly by taking n as the proportion of actual negatives $(n = FP + TN)$. Another interval used for cross validation is the *Wilson interval* [7]:

$$\frac{2n\bar{P}_D + z_{\alpha/2}^2 \pm z_{\alpha/2}^2\sqrt{z_{\alpha/2}^2 + 4n\bar{P}_D - 4n\bar{P}_D^2}}{2(n + z_{\alpha/2}^2)}$$

3.3 Text Categorization Features

In our experiment, we use n-grams as features for machine learning based malware detectors. n-grams are widely used in text categorization (see [12]) and have also been used in malware detection [9]. Based on the relative importance of different n-grams in a file, they can be weighted using different criteria. Some of the commonly-used weights for n-grams are count, term frequency, document frequency, and inverse document frequency [12]. *Term count* is the number of times a particular term (e.g. bytecode n-gram, opcode n-gram) appears in a document. *Term frequency* is count normalized by document size or the total number of terms in a document ($TF_i = TC_i/|D|$). *Document frequency* (DF_i) is the number of documents containing the term. *Inverse document frequency* is defined as

$$IDF1 = \log_{10}(|D|/DF_i)$$

An alternative definition of inverse document frequency is

$$IDF2 = \log_{10}(|D| - DF_i/DF_i)$$

TFIDF1 and *TFIDF2* are defined as TF*IDF1 and TF*IDF2, respectively.

4   Deployable Classifiers

In this section, we set up the model, give definitions of deployability and provide a method for deployable classifier selection.

4.1   The Model

The expected cost of classification of an input by a classifier depends on two factors: the misclassification costs and the probability of classification into malicious and benign. We use the true positive rate (P_D) and one minus false positive rate ($1 - P_F$) of the classifier as the probability of classification into malicious and benign, respectively. There are two kinds of misclassifications: false positives and false negatives. The consequential cost of a false positive is the cost of response r required to respond to the alarm. The consequential cost of a false negative is the cost of damage d done by the malware. The consequential costs are usually asymmetric with cost of damage greater than the cost of response i.e. $d > r$.

The costs and probabilities are shown in figure 1. In figure 1, λ is the proportion of inputs that are malware. The class of malware is denoted as + and benign input as -. It can be seen from the figure that if the input to the classifier C is benign and the classifier incorrectly labels it as malware with probability P_F, then the cost of this misclassification is r. Similarly, if the input to the classifier C is malware and the classifier incorrectly labels it as benign with probability $1 - P_D$, then the cost of this misclassification is d. The is no cost of a correct classification.

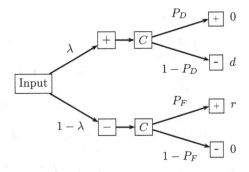

Fig. 1. Classification tree with costs and probabilities

The expected cost over decision outcomes (+ and -) of the classifier for a given P_D and P_F is the sum of probability weighted costs for all possible outcomes shown in figure 1:

$$E[C] = \lambda(1 - P_D)d + (1 - \lambda)P_F r \tag{1}$$

4.2 Strong and Weak Deployability

We now give the definition of deployable classifiers. The definition captures the intuition that a classifier is deployable if the interval estimate of generalization performance meets the performance target. We use confidence intervals for interval estimation and use expected consequential cost of misclassification (per input) as the performance measure . In other words, if a given target of expected consequential cost of misclassification (per input) lies in the confidence interval of expected cost of the classifier, then the classifier is called deployable. We denote by $u(P_D)$ and $l(P_D)$, the upper and lower end of the confidence interval, respectively. The notation for P_F is similar. The confidence interval for $E[C]$ can be obtained by substituting the upper and lower end of the confidence interval of P_D and P_F in (1). Let $E[C]_G$ denote the confidence interval of $E[C]$, then

$$u([E[C]_G) = \lambda(1 - u(P_D))d + (1 - \lambda)u(P_F)r$$

and

$$l([E[C]_G) = \lambda(1 - l(P_D))d + (1 - \lambda)l(P_F)r$$

We now give the definition of deployable classifiers.

Definition 1. *(**Strong Deployability**) Given the consequential costs of misclassification r and d, a classifier is called* strongly deployable *if the upper bound of the confidence interval the estimation of the expected cost of the classifier is bounded by k, the average consequential cost per sample that can be tolerated by the classifier deployer, i.e.,*

$$u([E[C]_G) \leq k$$

where $E[C]$ is the expectation over decision outcomes of the classifier.

Definition 2. *(**Weak Deployability**) Given the consequential costs of misclassification r and d, a classifier is called* weakly deployable *if k, the average consequential cost per sample that can be tolerated by the classifier deployer, lies in the confidence interval of the expected cost of the classifier, i.e.,*

$$l([E[C]_G) \leq k \leq u([E[C]_G)$$

where $E[C]$ is the expectation over decision outcomes of the classifier.

4.3 Condition for Existence of Non-extremal Deployable Performance

The values of P_D and P_F of deployable classifiers are called deployable performance values. The value of P_D and P_F is extremal i.e. $P_D = 1$ and $P_F = 0$ in the decision-theoretic cost minimization model which implies solving

$$\min_{P_D, P_F} E[C]$$

The bounded cost model used in deployability provides non-extremal solutions for a given cost bound if certain condition is satisfied. We derive this condition in the following.

From $E[C] < k$ and (1), we get

$$\lambda(1 - P_D)d + (1 - \lambda)P_F r < k$$

We consider the case when the classifier designer fixes the value of false positives, P_F i.e. only those classifiers will be considered whose false positive rate confidence interval consists of P_F. The target k is decided based on some resource constraints. Given the misclassification consequential costs r and d, the deployable true positive rate, P_D, is given by

$$P_D = \min \left[1 - \frac{k - (1 - \lambda)P_F r}{\lambda d}, 1 \right]$$

From above it follows that P_D will have a non-extremal value if

$$k - (1 - \lambda)P_F r > 0$$

which gives

$$\frac{k}{r} > (1 - \lambda)P_F$$

Hence, the ratio of expected cost bound and response cost should be greater than $(1 - \lambda)P_F$ for the existence of a non-extremal value of P_D.

4.4 Method of Deployable Classifier Selection

We now give the method for determining classifiers that are deployable The method is based on determining the confidence intervals of the expected cost point estimate obtained by holdout or cross validation. The method consists of following four steps:

1. Train N classifiers and evaluate their performance to obtain P_D, P_F.
2. Calculate confidence interval of P_D and P_F for each classifier.
3. Calculate confidence interval of $E[C]$ using confidence interval of P_D and P_F for each classifier.
4. Select those classifiers as deployable for which strong or weak deployability holds.

The above method can be used with performance evaluation methods like holdout, cross validation or bootstrap with appropriate formula for calculating confidence intervals.

5   Experimental Illustration

We conducted an experiment to illustrate and evaluate the method of determining deployable classifiers and then compare them against classifiers with least expected cost. We first describe the methodology of the experiment, then the setup of the experiment in terms of data sets and the tools used followed by the results obtained from the experiment.

5.1   Methodology

We followed the steps given below for deployable classifier selection. We added the validation step to the method given in section 4.4.

1. Train 16 classifiers and determine their holdout performance P_D, P_F.
2. Calculate confidence interval of P_D and P_F for each classifier.
3. Calculate confidence interval of $E[C]$, denoted as $[EC_H, EC_L]$, using confidence interval of P_D and P_F for each classifier.
4. Select those classifiers as deployable for which $k \in [EC_H, EC_L]$, respectively i.e. we determine weakly deployable classifiers. The P_D and P_F of such classifiers are considered deployable.
5. Validate the set of deployable classifiers on validation data by verifying that the expected cost of deployable classifiers is lower than the expected cost of non-deployable classifiers.

Strongly deployable classifiers can be considered analogously.

5.2   Experimental Setup

Dataset. The training and test dataset consisted of 674 assembly programs, of which 378 were benign and 296 were malicious. The validation dataset consisted of 341 assembly programs, of which 215 were benign and 126 were malicious. The malicious assembly programs were obtained from `http://www.mediafire.com/?jzymqzumnjy`. The benign assembly programs were obtained from `http://www.assembly.happycodings.com/index.html` and `http://asmsource.8k.com/source32.htm`.

Feature Extraction. The programs were preprocessed to extract all the 2-grams of opcodes (2-gram is a pair of adjacent opcodes). The extraction of mnemonic opcodes from all instructions in a program was followed by computation of weights for each opcode 2-gram. The weights considered were count, term frequency, TFIDF-1, and TFIDF-2.

Feature Selection. There were 163 unique x86 opcodes, and if all the opcodes were used for generating 2-grams, there could be 26,569 unique 2-grams. Some opcodes do not occur in a program and there are some with corresponding term frequency equal to 0. These opcodes provide negligible information while adding overhead to the classification process by increasing the size of the feature set. Therefore, there arises a need to use a function that can remove these negligibly useful features. A threshold function as discussed below was used for this purpose. If the sum of occurrence or the count of an opcode op_i in document d_i is s_i, then the total count of occurrence of this opcode over all the documents in dataset D can be given by $\psi_i = \sum_i^n s_i$. The mean occurrence of each opcode in the complete dataset D is given by $\bar{k} = \psi_i/163$. The function $\lambda(\psi_i, \bar{k})$ returns the list of opcodes op_z for which $s_z \geq \lceil 10\% of \bar{k} \rceil$. This list of op_z is used for constructing the 2-grams. For the current analysis, $\bar{k} = 77$, so the cut off value is 7. This resulted in reduction of number of relevant 2-grams from 26569 to 4625, as 85 OpCodes were discarded.

Learning Algorithms. We used Weka to train and evaluate 16 classifiers for malware detection. The following learning algorithms were used for building classifiers from the training set: Naive Bayes, Decision tree, Lazy learner K-nearest neighbor, support vector machines. Their Weka implementations are NB, J48, IBk and SVM, respectively.

5.3   Results

The performance evaluation of 16 classifiers is given in Table 2. The expected cost $(E[C])$ for $r = 1$, $d = 5$ and $\lambda = 132/229$ is given for classifier.

Table 2. Performance evaluation results for opcode 2-gram based classifiers for malware detection

Algorithm	Feature	P_D	P_F	$E[C]$
NB	Count	0.808	0.165	0.623
J48	Count	0.931	0.134	0.255
IBk	Count	0.846	0.113	0.491
SVM	Count	0.908	0.093	0.304
NB	Freq.	0.917	0.221	0.332
J48	Freq.	0.841	0.116	0.507
IBk	Freq.	0.795	0.116	0.640
SVM	Freq.	0.962	0.274	0.225
NB	TFIDF-1	0.915	0.257	0.353
J48	TFIDF-1	0.873	0.138	0.424
IBk	TFIDF-1	0.814	0.156	0.602
SVM	TFIDF-1	0.907	0.229	0.365
NB	TFIDF-2	0.905	0.218	0.366
J48	TFIDF-2	0.921	0.109	0.273
IBk	TFIDF-2	0.778	0.059	0.664
SVM	TFIDF-2	0.937	0.178	0.257

The confidence intervals of $E[C]$ for error level of $\alpha = 0.1$ for each classifier is given using errorbars in Figure 2. The cost target lines for $k = 0.2, 0.3, 0.5$ are also given. The classifiers for which the cost target lines intersect the confidence interval are considered (weakly) deployable for that α and k.

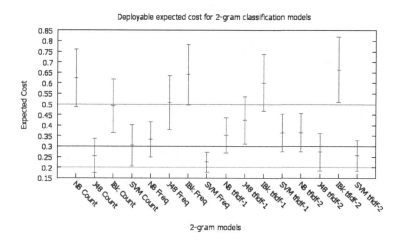

Fig. 2. Deployability of different opcode 2-gram based classifiers for malware detection

The true positive rate (P_D) and the false positive rate (P_F) of deployable classifiers is given in Table 3 for different values of cost bound (k). The P_D and P_F of classifiers that were not deployable are shown with a hyphen. The deployable classifiers that passed the validation on a validation dataset are indicated using asterisk.

6   Discussion

It can be seen from Table 3 that the classifier with minimum holdout expected cost does not turn out to be deployable. For e.g., in Table 2 SVM Freq is the lowest expected cost classifier $(E[C] = 0.225)$ but as it can be seen in Figure 2, for a confidence level of 0.9 $(\alpha = 0.1)$ and cost bound of $k = 0.15$, SVM Freq is not deployable (the expected cost confidence interval of SVM Freq lies above the line $k = 0.15$). There are also examples of classifiers that are deployable but have expected costs higher than that of SVM Freq. For e.g., NB Tfidf-2 is strongly deployable for $\alpha = 0.1$ and $k = 0.5$ even though it is not in the top one half of the lowest cost classifiers.

The results also show that the set of deployable classifiers was successfully validated with 75% accuracy on an average across different values of cost target (k). For e.g., in Table 3, for $\alpha = 0.1$ and $k = 0.2$, three out of four classifiers could be successfully validated.

Table 3. Deployable classifiers and their performance for confidence level of $\alpha = 0.1$ (non-deployable classifiers are shown with a hyphen). Validated classifiers are shown with an asterisk).

Classifier	$k = 0.2$		$k = 0.3$		$k = 0.5$	
	P_D	P_F	P_D	P_F	P_D	P_F
NB Count	-	-	-	-	0.808	0.165
J48 Count	0.931*	0.134*	0.931*	0.134*	-	-
IBK Count	-	-	-	-	0.846*	0.113*
SVM Count	-	-	0.908*	0.093*	-	-
NB Freq	-	-	0.917	0.221	-	-
J48 Freq	-	-	-	-	0.841*	0.116*
IBK Freq	-	-	-	-	0.795	0.116
SVM Freq	0.962*	0.274*	-	-	-	-
NB Tfidf-1	-	-	0.915	0.257	-	-
J48 Tfidf-1	-	-	-	-	0.873*	0.138*
IBK Tfidf-1	-	-	-	-	0.814*	0.156*
SVM Tfidf-1	-	-	0.907*	0.229*	-	-
NB Tfidf-2	-	-	0.905*	0.218*	-	-
J48 Tfidf-2	0.921	0.109	0.921	0.109	-	-
IBK Tfidf-2	-	-	-	-	-	-
SVM Tfidf-2	0.937*	0.178*	0.937*	0.178*	-	-

The deployability analysis can also be used to determine the right cost target, k, in situations where target is not previously known. In this case, choose the least k for which the classifiers with least resource requirements are deployable.

7   Conclusions

Deployability is an effective classifier selection criterion that is novel in two respects: a) it takes into account the variance of holdout or cross validation point estimates of performance by considering confidence intervals of the performance estimates; and b) it takes into account performance target usually determined by cost constraints of the classifier deployer. This makes the selected classifier(s) (deployable classifier(s)) more suitable for deployment in security applications like malware detection since it will be expected to meet the the cost constraints of the deployer with a high probability.

Acknowledgments. This research work was sponsored in part by funds from Air Force Research Lab and DARPA (FA8750-10-C-0171) and from Air Force Office of Scientific Research (FA9550-09-1-0715). We would also like to thank Craig Miles for reviewing the manuscript and providing feedback on our work.

References

1. Brazdil, P., Gama, J., Henery, B.: Characterizing the Applicability of Classification Algorithms Using Meta-Level Learning. In: Bergadano, F., De Raedt, L. (eds.) ECML 1994. LNCS, vol. 784, pp. 83–102. Springer, Heidelberg (1994)
2. Elovici, Y., Braha, D.: A decision-theoretic approach to data mining. IEEE Transactions on Systems, Man and Cybernetics, Part A: Systems and Humans 33(1), 42–51 (2003)
3. Gaffney Jr., J., Ulvila, J.: Evaluation of intrusion detectors: A decision theory approach. In: Proc. of IEEE Symposium on Security and Privacy, pp. 50–61 (2001)
4. Gama, J., Brazdil, P.: Characterization of classification algorithms. In: Progress in Artificial Intelligence, pp. 189–200 (1995)
5. Han, J., Kamber, M.: Data mining: concepts and techniques. Morgan Kaufmann (2006)
6. Kleinberg, J., Papadimitriou, C., Raghavan, P.: A microeconomic view of data mining. Data Mining and Knowledge Discovery 2(4), 311–324 (1998)
7. Kohavi, R.: A study of cross-validation and bootstrap for accuracy estimation and model selection. In: International Joint Conference on Artificial Intelligence, vol. 14, pp. 1137–1145 (1995)
8. Kolter, J., Maloof, M.: Learning to detect malicious executables in the wild. In: Proc. of the Tenth ACM SIGKDD Intl. Conf. on Knowledge Discovery and Data Mining, pp. 470–478 (2004)
9. Kolter, J., Maloof, M.: Learning to detect and classify malicious executables in the wild. The Journal of Machine Learning Research 7, 2721–2744 (2006)
10. Miller, I., Miller, M.: John E. Freund's mathematical statistics with applications. Prentice Hall (2004)
11. Moskovitch, R., Feher, C., Tzachar, N., Berger, E., Gitelman, M., Dolev, S., Elovici, Y.: Unknown Malcode Detection Using OPCODE Representation. In: Ortiz-Arroyo, D., Larsen, H.L., Zeng, D.D., Hicks, D., Wagner, G. (eds.) EuroISI 2008. LNCS, vol. 5376, pp. 204–215. Springer, Heidelberg (2008)
12. Sebastiani, F.: Machine learning in automated text categorization. ACM Computing Surveys 34(1), 1–47 (2002)

Interconnecting Workflows Using Services: An Approach for "Case Transfer" with Centralized Control

Saida Boukhedouma[1], Zaia Alimazighi[1], Mourad Oussalah[2], and Dalila Tamzalit[2]

[1] USTHB - FEI - Department of Computer Science- LSI Laboratory – ISI Team
El Alia BP n°32, Bab Ezzouar, Alger, Algérie
{sboukhedouma,zalimazighi}@usthb.dz
[2] Nantes University - LINA Laboratory – MODAL Team
2, Rue de la Houssinière, BP 92208, 44322 – Nantes, cedex 3- France
{Mourad.oussalah,Dalila.tamzalit}@univ-nantes.fr

Abstract. In this paper, we are interested in structured cooperation based on workflow (WF). The current work proposes an approach based on **services** for WF interconnection particularly obeying to the "case transfer" architecture. This late defines a form of cooperation in Inter-Organizational WF involving a range of partners with common business goals, exercising the same business. All partners share the same WF model implemented at each location and a transfer policy to manage transfer for process instances from one partner to another. By the use of services, our goal is to obtain IOWF models flexible enough so they remain easily adaptable to support process changes. The proposed approach is based on centralized control for transfers.

Keywords: IOWF, Process model, Service, SOA, Transfer policy, Coordinator.

1 Introduction

The B2B cooperation was initially supported by concepts and tools of *Inter-Organizational workflow* (IOWF). In our research, we focus on structured inter-organizational processes mainly based on architectures of cooperation well defined in the literature of IOWF [1].

Also, in a context of unstable environment, businesses often face stressful situations like a breach of contract with a partner or needs of additional resources. Thus, these companies must revise their systems, their business processes and their cooperation with other business partners in order to make the necessary adjustments. These adjustments can cover three complementary aspects of the system: data, process and organization where the central aspect is the *process* one. Therefore, our final objective is to define mechanisms for adaptation of IOWF models in order to support process changes. Because the adaptation of a process model depends on the entities composing it and links between these entities, we focus first on the question of *interconnection of workflows* so that they remain flexible enough and easily

S. Dua et al. (Eds.): ICISTM 2012, CCIS 285, pp. 396–401, 2012.

adaptable. Thus, for WF interconnection, we adopt an approach based on *services* because of their characteristics: loosely coupled, easily invoked and business oriented.

This paper deals with the *case transfer* architecture [1] where several business partners share the *same WF model* implemented at each partner and define conjointly a *transfer policy* implementing rules to govern transfers of process instances from one location (partner) to another, at runtime. To develop our approach, we focus on two main questions: the *structuring* of the WF process in terms of services and the *control* of transfer of instances. In the following, section 2 defines the context of the work and basic concepts. Section 3 talks about some related works and explains the motivation of this paper. Section 4 describes conceptual and technical aspects of our approach. Section 5 concludes the work and talks about future works.

2   Context of the Work

An inter-organizational workflow (IOWF) can be defined as a manager of activities involving two or more WFs (affiliated with business partners) autonomous, possibly heterogeneous and interoperable in order to achieve a common business goal [1].

Several architectures of IOWF have been defined; we talk about the *capacity sharing*, the *chained execution*, the *subcontracting*, the (extended) *case transfer*, and the *loosely coupled* architectures [1].

The "*case transfer*" defines a form of cooperation fairly widespread in B2B, especially between partners engaged in the same profession and aiming to satisfy promptly many potential customers. In the "*case transfer*" architecture, business partners share the same WF model implemented at each partner and hosted by a local WFMS (WF management system). Their cooperation consists of transfer of process instances (cases) from one partner to another in order to achieve their execution.

For example, one can envisage an IOWF involving a set of partners in a process of production of medicines to meet many potential customers. A customer's order may arrive at partner x but it is not completely performed by the WF of this partner; the order may be transferred to other partners. The transfer can occur for example for load balancing or because of the lack of skills or resources at partner x.

At any moment, a process instance is at a single location. Each transfer is done at a *stable point* of the process in order to avoid any incoherence of execution. Also, transfers take into account the *state data* of instances.

3   Related Works and Motivation

With the emergence of SOA (Service Oriented Architectures) [2] and web services [3] standards, many research works deal with orchestration and choreography of web services in order to build business processes by service composition [4], [5]. Other research works such as [6], [7], [8] show the interest of combining BPM, WF and SOA for the re-use of services to construct dynamic business processes.

Also, many platforms and approaches based on WF and SOA have been proposed in the context of structured B2B cooperation, we cite as examples: *CoopFlow* [9], *CrossWork* [10] and *Pyros* [11]. These approaches provide a certain degree of flexibility since they allow internal adaptation of WF processes.

The principal motivation of our works is to achieve the adaptation of IOWF process models, by providing mechanisms to support process changes in context of *structured* cooperation in order to improve them or to satisfy new constraints imposed by the environment. Assuming that the ability of a model to be adaptable depends heavily on its components, we focus first on the question of WF interconnection and we propose *an approach based on services*, since services are software components loosely coupled, easily invoked and business oriented. For structured IOWF models, we rely on patterns defined in [1] because they cover various forms of cooperation that can link business partners together. In [12], we have proposed an approach for interconnecting workflows according to the *subcontracting* architecture. The current paper deals with the *case transfer* architecture, we propose an approach with *centralized* control of transfer which is well adapted for complex transfer policy.

4   Our Approach for WF Interconnection

Our approach focuses on two main questions: (i) How to *structure* the WF process into services? (ii) How to *control* the transfer of instances? To answer these two questions, we must define the notions of *transfer point* and *transfer policy*.

4.1   Transfer Point and Transfer Policy

- A **Transfer point** can be each state of the process that guarantees the coherence of execution of instances when a transfer is done. In fact, a transfer point should verify the following conditions: (i) It must be before the beginning or after the end of an activity. (ii) It should not interrupt the execution of an activity. (iii) It should not be between a routing operator *Split* and the corresponding operator *Join*; whether a parallel or an alternative branch is involved, the transfer may only occur after *Join*.

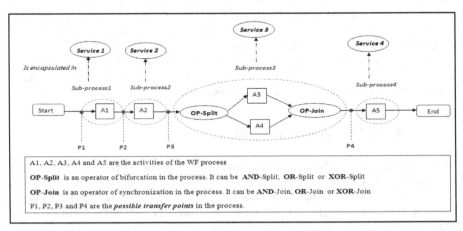

Fig. 1. Illustration of transfer point and Structuring of a WF process in services

Fig.1. illustrates the notion of *transfer points* on a WF process schema. We can see four transfer points (P1, P2, P3, P4) in the process. Let's notice that transfer points are the states of the process where a *case transfer* can eventually occur, they are fixed by the designers of IOWF at build time.

-    A ***Transfer policy*** is conjointly defined by all partners at build time. It defines the set of *transfer points* and expresses a set of *rules* governing the transfer of process instances from one location to another. A rule is associated to a *transfer point* and can be defined by a pair (condition, action) meaning that if the condition is verified, an action of transfer is done to another location; otherwise the instance continues its execution at its current location.

4.2   Structuring of the Process into Services

Our basic idea is to consider each WF process as a composition of *sub-processes* and then to encapsulate each *sub-process* within a *service* so it becomes easily invoked. A sub-process is a part of a global WF process composed by a single activity, a single bloc of activities delimited by a *Split* operator and the corresponding *Join* operator or a sequence of several activities and/or blocs. The cutting of the WF process into sub-processes is done according to the transfer policy defined. Hence, *transfer points* delimit the *sub-processes* encapsulated into *services* (see Fig. 1).

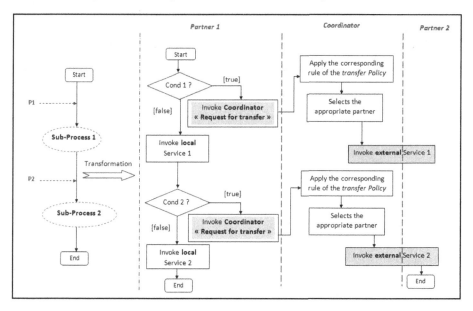

Fig. 2. Schema of WF interconnection with central coordinator

Also, for WF interconnection with *centralized* control of transfers, an additional component (the *coordinator*) is needed in order to manage all transfers to be done through the partners implied in the IOWF process. So, workflows don't interact directly with each other but they must do this through the *coordinator*. This mode is appropriate in case of a complex transfer policy (non deterministic rules), this can usually occur when transfers are done for load balancing in the system. The process model is transformed to an IOWF model based on *services*. At each partner, the WF process is implemented as a set of *local services* (on Fig.2, Service 1 and Service 2) encapsulating the *sub-processes*. Hence, the execution of an instance is done through *invocations* of services: local invocation if no transfer is necessary and external invocation if a transfer is necessary. Thus, at each transfer point, the appropriate transfer condition (on Fig.2, cond1 or cond2) is evaluated by the system hosting the current instance, if it is true the *coordinator* is invoked (*Request for transfer*). According to the transfer policy and the state of the global system, the coordinator selects the partner to receive the instance and thus invokes it for a transfer with the *state data* of the instance and necessary *artifacts*.

4.3   Technical Aspects

Each partner implements the specification of the WF process locally, a local WFMS interprets the specification, a local DBMS manages local data bases containing state data of all instances locally executed and all artifacts necessary to perform services. The system of each partner implements local applications and services especially those which encapsulate the sub-processes of the WF (see Fig. 3). The *coordinator* is implemented as a service "*Service coordinator*" based on a transfer policy. Also, the coordinator maintains a local data base containing a global view of process instances in the system (this is particularly needed for load balancing). This architecture implies more interactions in the system comparatively to the architecture with decentralized control described in [13], but it is inevitable when the transfer policy is complex.

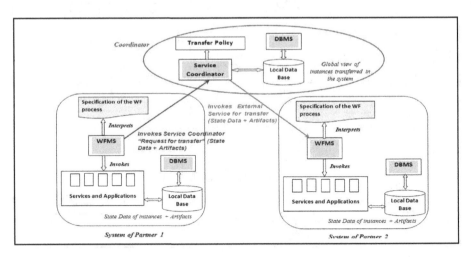

Fig. 3. Architecture of the system

5   Conclusion

In this work, we have presented an approach based on *services* for WF interconnection according to the *case transfer* architecture [1]. The use of *services* for interconnecting workflows is motivated by the fact that services are software components loosely coupled, easily invoked and business oriented. Thus, the IOWF models obtained remain easily adaptable which is the principal issue of our research.

The proposed approach relies on two main questions related to the *structuring of the WF process into services* and the *control of execution*. In this paper, we have proposed an approach with *centralized control* for transfer which is particularly appropriate to complex transfer policy that implements non deterministic rules. Thus, the systems of the partners interact through an additional component called *coordinator*. We have exhibited only conceptual aspects and general architecture of the system. This work should be completed by improving technical aspects mainly specification of the IOWF based on services (i.e specification of the WF process and the coordinator) using an appropriate specification language like BPEL or YAWL.

Currently, we are working on the question of adaptability of process models, we must inventory all possible changes (or the most important and frequent ones) in the IOWF process and we must formalize them as *adaptation patterns*. After that, we aim to develop a tool that helps the designer of the IOWF process in doing adaptation.

References

1. Aalst, W.V.D.: Process-oriented architectures for electronic commerce and inter-organizational workflow, Journal of IS, Copyright Elsevier Sciences (1999)
2. Papazoglou, M.P., Heuvel, W.: Service Oriented Architectures: approaches, technologies and research issues. The VLDB Journal 16, 389–415 (2007)
3. Alonso, G., Casati, F., Kuno, H.: Web services: concepts, architectures and applications. Springer, Heidelberg (2004)
4. Decker, G., Kopp, O., Leymann, F., Weske, M.: Bpel4chor:Extending BPEL for modeling choreographies. In: Proceedings of the 2007 IEEE International Conference on Web Services (ICWS 2007), pp. 296–303. IEEE Computer Society (2007)
5. Amirreza, T.: Web Service Composition Based Interorganizational Workflows, Sudwestdeutscher Verlag fur Hochschulschriften edition (2009) ISBN 9783838106700
6. Leymann, F., Roller, D., Schmidt, M.T.: Web Services and Business Process Management. IBM Systems Journal 41(2) (2002)
7. Gorton, S., Montangero, C., Reiff-Marganiec, S., Semini, L.: StPowla: SOA, Policies and Workflows. In: Di Nitto, E., Ripeanu, M. (eds.) ICSOC 2007. LNCS, vol. 4907, pp. 351–362. Springer, Heidelberg (2009)
8. Pedraza Ferrera, G.R.: An extensible Framework for the Construction of Process-Oriented Applications. PhD Thesis, University of Grenoble I, France (2009)
9. Chebbi, I.: CoopFlow: An approach for workflow ascending cooperation in virtual enterprises. PhD thesis-National Institute of Telecoms, France (2007)
10. Mehandjiev, N., Stalker, I., Fessl, K., Weichhart, G.: Interoperability contributions of Crosswork. In: Invited Short Paper to Proceedings of INTEROP-ESA 2005 Conference. Springer, Heidelberg (2005)
11. Belhajjame, K., Vargas-Solar, G., Collet, C.: Pyros - an environment for building and orchestrating open services. In: SCC 2005: Proceedings of the 2005 IEEE International Conference on Services Computing, USA, pp. 155–164. IEEE Computer Society (2005)
12. Boukhedouma, S., Alimazighi, Z., Oussalah, M., Tamzalit, D.: SOA Based Approach for Interconnecting Workflows According to the Subcontracting Architecture. In: Proceedings of IADIS- Collaborative Technologies 2011- Rome, Italy, July 22-24 (2011)
13. Boukhedouma, S., Alimazighi, Z., Oussalah, M., Tamzalit, D.: Une approche basée SOA pour l'interconnexion de workflows: Application au transfert de cas. In: Proceedings of INFOSID 2011, Lille, France, May 24-27 (2011)

Assessing Key Success Factors in an ERP Implementation Project: A Case Study in Automotive Industry

Iskander Zouaghi[1] and Abderrazak Laghouag[2]

[1] CNRS/Grenoble University CERAG, Grenoble, France
iskander.zouaghi@upmf-grenoble.fr
[2] Management Department, M'sila University, M'sila, Algeria
laghouag.abderrazak@univ-msila.dz

Abstract. Business integration that improves inter-functional cooperation among departments, or even inter-organizational integration could be supported by the implantation of an ERP system. Consequently, in these last five years, more and more companies are implementing ERP system but lots of them fail so far. We try to understand in this research, from a project management perspective, the reasons that bring the ERP implementation project to succeed or to fail. We provide in this paper a brief overview of the literature dealing with ERP implementation key success factors (KSFs), then we study a case of an ERP implementation project in a company operating in automotive industry using a quail-metric methodology, to better deepen the reasons success or failure of such projects.

Keywords: ERP Implementation, Key Success Factors, Case Study, Quali-Metric Approach.

1 Introduction

ERP implementation presents important investments regarding the significant human, material and financial assets committed, as well as informational and time resources devoted in order to succeed. This issue has attracted not only the interest of managers and professionals, but also academics and consultants. ERP implementation has been defined by Keller and Teufel (1998) as the configuration of the ERP software followed by a set of organizational and technical changes, such as the definition of new responsibilities or the design of new interfaces. For Hasan et al. (2011, p.132), it represents the implementation of "a set of best practices, procedures and tools that different functions of a company can utilize to accomplish total organizational excellence through integration".

In addition, Esteves and Bohórquez (2007) show in their works that implementation presents the most important issue from 449 contributions that have been provided about the ERP system from 1997 to 2005. However, Al-Mudmigh et al. (2011) stipulate that a widespread inclusive ERP implementation approach has not yet been settled. Moreover, the literature review of Moon (2007) shows that there are six main areas about ERP project, and more than 40% of research articles related to ERP covered the area of implementation.

S. Dua et al. (Eds.): ICISTM 2012, CCIS 285, pp. 402–407, 2012.

ERP systems can effectively generate significant benefits for companies. But at the same time, it can bring organizations to disaster if the implementation process fails. Accordingly our research question revolves around: what are the KSFs that should be taken into account in order to successfully implement an ERP system, namely in automotive industry? To answer this question, we will present first a brief overview of the literature dealing with ERP implementation project success factors in a first section. In the second section, we will present our methodology used to tackle our research question. In a third section, we will present results of our case study and related discussion. Finally, we will draw conclusion and present further research perspectives.

2   ERP Implementation KSFs: The Standish Group Model Revisited

Implementing successfully ERP system is generally based on a set of objective factors that contribute greatly to the project success. The identification of these KSFs has been the subject of several studies, joining interests of researchers and professionals (cf. Gargeya and Brady, 2005). This growing attention to this issue was supported by the literature review of Esteves and Bohórquez (2007). In our work, we have adopted the Standish Group KSFs for practical and effective concerns (see Table1). As reported by Gemino et al. (2008), and based on Hartmann (2006), Standish Group covered twelve years of data collection with over 50 000 accomplished IT projects. The Standish Group has provided a list of ten essential factors that the company should take into account in order to maximize the success of its software implementation. Even if the model was severely criticized by some authors, like Eveleens and Verhoef (2010), but we just mention arguments of Highsmith (2009) who stipulates that surely the Standish group data are not good indicators of poor software development performance. But, they represent indicators of systemic failure of planning and measurement processes.

3   The Methodology Used

The methodology used is a case study based on a quail-metric approach (Savall and Zardet, 2004), an intermediate approach between qualitative and quantitative approaches. First, open but oriented exploratory interviews were conducted within different departments of "SCOM Company"[1], a company operating in automotive industry, specialized in trucks and buses assembling and commercialization. The purpose of these interviews is the exploration of the existing system of SCOM Company, but also the assessment of the nature and the extent of problems that will possibly been encountered during the implementation process of the ERP system.

---

[1] This is not the real name of the company. For confidentiality concerns, we give it the name of SCOM Company.

Table 1. Standish Group IS projects KSFs in the literature

Key success factor	Characteristics	Authors
Users' Involvement (UI)	Identify future users of the ERP, involve them in the project as soon as possible, develop channels of communication in order to ensure a permanent exchange with the project team and adapt the ERP system depending on their needs.	Kansal (2007), Dagher and Kuzic (2011).
Top Management Support (TMS)	Identify key leaders in the company, who are able to mostly support the ERP implementation project and motivate and convince them by providing a detailed plan about the project so that they can make decision.	Yusuf et al., (2004), Kansal (2007), Finney and Corbet (2007).
Clear Definition of Needs (CDN)	Lead functional and cross-functional needs analysis and risks and assessment. Elaborate a return on investment plan and define metrics, measures and milestones that determine success.	Soja and Paliwoda-Pękosz (2009).
Developing Clear Planning (DCP)	Prepare a synthetic document describing the project issues and benefits, with expectations and possible solutions. Select the right people and assign to each one a proper role. Planning must allow changes and adjustments.	Mandal and Gunasekaran (2003), Somers and Nelson (2004), Finney and Corbet (2007)
Realistic Expectations (RE)	Prepare a document describing a realistic project, containing necessary arguments to demonstrate its practicality. Systematically eliminate unrealistic initiatives.	Esteves (2009), Ganesh and Mehta (2010).
Division Project into Steps (DPSS)	Devising the project into several steps has a significant importance. Start addressing broad issues and, then, discussing progressively the details of each one.	Chen et al. (2009).
Project Team Competency (PTC)	Settle on clearly required skills. Develop structured and oriented training for project team by both internal staff and external professionals.	Stratman and Roth (2002), Kansal (2007), Finney and Corbet (2007).
Ownership of Project by Stakeholders (OPS)	Clearly define roles and responsibilities of all stakeholders of the project. Determine the organizational structure that allows coordinating all members. Link specific rewards to project outcomes.	Newell et al. (2004).
Clear visions on Project objectives (CVPO)	Formally clarify short, medium and long term vision, goals and objectives. Ensure the fit between predetermined objectives, strategy and overall goals of the company.	Mandal and Gunasekaran (2003), Kansal (2007).
Motivation and focus of the Project Team (MPT)	Motivate the team by a set of means, such as premiums, bonuses, promotions, etc. Create a culture of ownership and collective work that creates a homogeneous atmosphere.	Barker and Frolick (2003), Finney and Corbet (2007).

Subsequently, 14 Directors of several departments and divisions were questioned, including Head Office, Production Department, Purchasing and Supply Department, Financial Department, IT Department, Scheduling Department, Methods Department, Accounting Department, Maintenance Department, as well as other departments and services. The questions were adopted from Standish Group model, and subsequently customized according to SCOM Company specification. Then, they were categorized in ten groups characterizing ten major variables (KSFs) mentioned above, with five items for each variable. Afterward, a Likert scale (5 levels) has been applied in order to have more precise answers.

4   Results and Discussion

The research results consist in analyzing the stakeholders' answers in order to determine the risk factors aiming to reduce their impact. According to existing system, the technological culture is somewhat ubiquitous in the company. SCOM Company had and still has several information systems whose the most important is the MM/3000 (Materials Management/3000) provided by HP. However, all existing systems are not interconnected. So, adopting an ERP system was a real need as it was affirmed by Scheduling Methods Department manager who said: "actually, the implementation of an ERP system is not a choice but a necessity". From this, SCOM Company's goal is to implement an ERP system that will ensure the integration at least among the most important functions. As the ERP project has started in recent years, SCOM Company is now in the step of effective ERP system implementation.

Globally, the Standish Group method shows that the risk rate is 52.75%, with a standard deviation of 15.56% which is significant in terms of dispersion. For some, the risk related to the project can reach 80%, while for others it can border 25%. However, it's quite clear that most respondents found the project risky while only two (2) respondents don't. Also, results analysis shows that three variables, which are the OPS, MPT and CDN, present mainly a high risk. And that explains the fact that roles are not clearly defined, and that incentives and rewards do not greatly contribute to achieve defined targets. Productivity and Motivation Project Team (MPT) presents also a risk element; and also other variables that present fairly large risk, namely UI, CVPO as well as PTC. Results analysis put in plain words that some entities have not been involved in the ERP project. This means that some future users didn't participate in the process of the definition of their needs. Consequently, they are not in accordance with ERP specifications, and this adaptation could extend over time and budget. Also, ERP project objectives in terms of definition of expected features and measures tools to assess the evolution of ERP project are not clearly defined. This can expose the company to the fact that it can't define problems that can likely encounter during ERP project implementation. Moreover, several training seminars were programmed for some managers, but were not scheduled in convenience with all stakeholders. That reflects the difficulties of future users to understand the ERP software. Two other variables present a moderate risk, namely DPSS and DCP. Finally, two variables don't present a significant risk according to respondents, and present relatively opportunities for the ERP implementation project, these factors are TMS and RE. When deepening our analysis, some key leaders are relatively mobilized in the implementation project. For them, a successful ERP implementation is an important. However, failure is not acceptable at all. This may be due to the fact that there is no detailed project plan that can reduce the information asymmetry between managers and project team. Also, incentives proposed by leaders to motivate the project team are not very interesting. According to realistic expectations, SCOM Company has relatively realistic expectations about the project evolution. However, the specifications for these expectations are not sufficiently clear and quite formal as well as the priority of needs is not clear. Finally, no simulation has been performed so far, either because it is too early to make one, or because it is not planned.

5   Conclusion

Generally speaking a literature review reveals that the omnipresent nature of ERP system usually leads companies to come across complex organizational and technical difficulties that bring, in the most cases, the ERP project to fail. The Standish group provides a list of the most important KSFs that help greatly companies successfully implement an ERP system. By assessing them within SCOM Company, We find that some factors present strengths because they are correctly perceived and assimilated by stakeholders, such as TMS, while others present vice versa.

The hereby article reveals a considerable potential of further research that could focus, for example, on the examination of the applicability of the Standish group model to other companies in different industries. Another perspective research can revolve around an exploratory study about the status of the utilization ERP software in this kind of industry in order to improve their global performance. Finally, the study of the measurement and valorization of the return on investment (ROI) of information system projects in general, and especially those of the ERP presents an important and strategic research field.

References

1. Al-Mudimigh, A.S., Ullah, Z., Alsubaie, T.A.: A framework for portal implementation: A case for Saudi organizations. International Journal of Information Management 31(1), 38–43 (2011)
2. Barker, T., Frolick, M.N.: ERP implementation failure: A case study. Information Systems Management 20(4), 43–49 (2003)
3. Chen, C.C., Law, C.C.H., Yang, S.C.: Managing ERP implementation failure: a project management perspective. IEEE Transactions on Engineering Management 56(1), 157–170 (2009)
4. Dagher, J., Monash, J.K.: Factors Influencing ERP Implementation in Australia. In: Ariwa, E., El-Qawasmeh, E. (eds.) Digital Enterprise and Information Systems, pp. 197–205. Springer, Heidelberg (2011)
5. Esteves, J., Bohorquez, V.: An Updated ERP Systems Annotated Bibliography: 2001-2005. The Communications of the Association for Information Systems 19(1), 18 (2007)
6. Esteves, J., Pastor, J.: Enterprise resource planning systems research: an annotated bibliography. Communications of the Association for Information Systems 7(8), 1–52 (2001)
7. Esteves, J.: A benefits realisation road-map framework for ERP usage in small and medium-sized enterprises. Journal of Enterprise Information Management 22(1/2), 25–35 (2009)
8. Eveleens, J., Verhoef, C.: The rise and fall of the Chaos Report figures. IEEE Software 27(1), 30–36 (2010)
9. Finney, S., Corbett, M.: ERP implementation: a compilation and analysis of critical success factors. Business Process Management Journal 13(3), 329–347 (2007)
10. Ganesh, L., Mehta, A.: A Survey Instrument for Identification of the Critical Failure Factors in the Failure of ERP Implementation at Indian SMEs. International Journal of Managing Public Sector Information and Communication Technologies 1(2), 10–22 (2010)

11. Gargeya, V.B., Brady, C.: Success and failure factors of adopting SAP in ERP system implementation. Business Process Management Journal 11(5), 501–516 (2005)
12. Gemino, A., Reich, B.H., Sauer, C.: Examining IT Project Performance. In: ASAC, pp.180-195 (2008)
13. Hartmann, D.: Interview: Jim Johnson of the Standish Group. Infoqueue, August 25 (2006)
14. Hasan, M., Trinh, T.N., Chan, F.T.S., Chan, H.K., Chung, S.H.: Implementation of ERP of the Australian manufacturing companies. Industrial Management & Data Systems 111(1), 132–145 (2010)
15. Highsmith, J.: Agile Project Management: Creating Innovative Products, 2nd edn. Addison Wesley Professional (2009)
16. Kansal, V.: Systemic Analysis for Inter-Relation of Identified Critical Success Factors in Enterprise Systems Projects. Contemporary Management Research 3(4), 331–346 (2007)
17. Keller, G., Teufel, T.: SAP R/3 Process Oriented Implementation. Addison-Wesley, Reading (1998)
18. Mandal, P., Gunasekaran, A.: Issues in implementing ERP: a case study. European Journal of Operational Research 146, 274–283 (2003)
19. Moon, Y.B.: Enterprise resource planning (ERP): a review of the literature. International Journal of Management and Enterprise Development 4(3), 235–264 (2007)
20. Newell, S., Tansley, C., Huang, J.: Social capital and knowledge integration in an ERP Project team: the importance of Bridging and Bonding. British Journal of Management 15 (2004)
21. Savall, H., Zardet, V.: Recherche en sciences de gestion: approche qualimétrique - Observer l'objet complexe. Economica (2004)
22. Soja, P. and Paliwoda-Pękosz, G.: What are real problems in enterprise system adoption? Industrial Management & Data Systems, 109(5), 610-627 (2009)
23. Somers, T.M., Nelson, K.G.: A taxonomy of players and activities across the ERP project life cycle. Information & Management 41(3), 257–278 (2004)
24. Stratman, J.K., Roth, A.V.: Enterprise resource planning (ERP) competence constructs: two-stage multi-item scale development and validation. Decision Sciences 33, 601 (2002)
25. Yusuf, Y., Gunasekaran, A., Wu, C.: Implementation of enterprise resource planning in China. Technovation 26(12), 1324–1336 (2006)

Automatic Light Control for White Marker Board in Conference/Seminar Hall Using Ultrasound Sensor via RF Wireless Communication

Hema N., Krishna Kant, and Hima Bindu Maringanti

JIIT, A-10, Sector-62, Noida, Uttar Pradesh
{hema.n,k.kant,hima.bindu}@jiit.ac.in
www.jiit.ac.in

Abstract. In any conference/seminar hall, whenever a speaker/presenter wants to switch over from projected presentation to white maker board due to some audience query, someone has to physically monitor the speaker activity and then control the lights accordingly. This paper tries to automate this activity by using Projector Light Controller Module (PLCM) which consists of 180^0 continuous rotating ultrasound sensor that senses the presence of the speaker near the white marker board and send this information via RF wireless communication to the light control system for decision making to automatically turn ON the light. As the speaker moves away from the white marker board, lights will be automatically turned off. This design will take care of two adjacent white markers board in the conference/seminar hall, to turn ON the lights of respective white marker board.

Keywords: Microcontroller (MCU), Ultrasound sensors, RF wireless communication, 180^0 servo motors, Solid State Relays.

1   Introduction

Recently, home automation has become integral part of our day-to-day life; as we need more accurate, trust-worthy and autonomous system. Introduction of various sensors measuring light, sound, temperature, pressure, chemical property, physical property and various other characteristics helped to bring out more sophisticated automated systems in the real life. Advances in wireless technology have made such automation systems handier for user and also cost efficient.

The combination of sensors, wireless technology and low power MCU can bring many good automated designs. The presented paper is going to discuss one such automation system designed for white board light control in conference hall.

Y. W. Bai and Y. T. Ku (2008) [1] discusses a similar automation system to control the light intensity of entire room depending upon the environmental lighting conditions to save energy. Our paper also discusses about light control but for the selected area of a conference hall, especially the white marker board usage. There can be different solutions for this kind of problem such as touch sensitive lamps, touch projector and sound based light control, which are very expensive and not accurate for

S. Dua et al. (Eds.): ICISTM 2012, CCIS 285, pp. 408–413, 2012.

conference hall environment. In our design, when speaker/presenter shows the gesture of using white marker board then lights will be automatically controlled. Also this design is cost effective; approximately 5 times lesser then touches projectors.

In a conference hall, speaker will be well equipped with resources for his/her presentation. At times, audience get anxious to clarify their doubts instantly without waiting for the question/answer time, where speaker need to switch over form power point projection to white maker board. In the traditional method, one person has to physically monitor the speaker activity to switch ON/OFF the lights. In this paper, we propose a design of PLCM to automate the whole scenario. For the PLCM implementation, we are using microcontroller that is interfaced with ultrasound sensor, which is mounted on the 180° continuous rotation motor to sense the speaker's presence near white marker board.

When ultrasound sensor senses the presence of speaker near white marker board, microcontroller sends the signal via transmitter and receiver RF module to the light control module. The white board light controlled by PLCM has microcontroller, relay module to control the 240volt bulb, transmitter and receiver RF module and decision-making system. Light Control module can handle two white maker boards.

As show in Fig 1, ultrasound sensor mounted on 180° continuous rotating servo motor will be placed in the middle of the left side of white marker board. Whenever the ultrasound sensor detects the human's presence near the white marker board, it sends signal from PLCM to light control module via RF wireless communication through the microcontroller. Now, light control module will decide which white marker board is selected for usage, accordingly that relay will be selected to turn ON the light.

This paper has been organized as follows. Section 2 introduces PLCM while section 3 describes the white marker board light control used in our design. Section 4 summarizes the implementation and Section 5 concludes the paper.

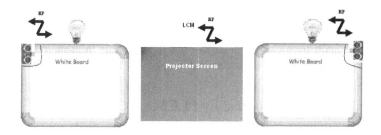

Fig. 1. Design of Automated Light Control for White Marker Board

2   Design of PLCM

The PLCM is made up of the Ultrasound sensor mounted on 180° rotating servomotor, the RF module and the low-power microcontroller. We also provide a DC power supply from AC power to every component.

In this design, we are using an ultrasound sensor mounted on servomotor, as we have to detect the speaker's presence in detection area irrespective of the light conditioning. The ultrasonic sensors [2] are commonly used for a wide variety of non-contact presence, proximity, or distance measuring applications. These devices typically transmit a short burst of ultrasonic sound toward a target, which reflects the sound back to the sensor. The system then measures the time for the echo to return to the sensor and computes the distance to the target using the speed of sound in the medium. The ultrasound sensor provides precise and stable non-contact distance measurements from about 2cm to 4 meters with very high accuracy. Servo motors are DC motors with built in gearing, feedback control loop circuitry and a shaft that can be precisely controlled. And no motor drivers are required. The servo motor that we are using is the standard rotation one, which can rotate between 0 to 180 degrees.

The advantage of mounting the ultrasound sensor on servomotor is to increase the coverage of detection area, as the servomotor continuously rotates covering 180°. An alternative to increase the detection coverage area is by increasing the number of ultrasound sensors.

Microcontroller Atmega 328 [4] is used and wireless module that we are using in our design is Zigbee that has Indoor/Urban range up to 133 ft. (40m), Outdoor RF line-of-sight range up to 400 ft. (120m), RF Data Rate 250 Kbps, Frequency ISM 2.4 GHz, Dimensions 0.0960" x 1.087", Power-down Current 1 μA and they can be programmed as the Coordinator /Router/End-device. Since, the application doesn't require complex wireless communication; we need only three wireless modules. One module is used by central decision making system, second one is used by the PLCM and third one is used for white board light control.

Once the power is on, ultrasound sensor starts rotating to sense the presence of the speaker in the detection area. Depending upon need of accuracy, we can set the values of ultrasound sensor reading as low as possible. This data will be picked up by the Microcontroller to make a decision for the turning lights on/off. Microcontroller decision marking for PLCM is as show in Figure 2.

Depending upon the decision, microcontroller sends this information to the light control module via RF wireless communication.

3   Design of Light Control by PLCM

Once the PLCM detect that speaker needs to use the board, relay will turn ON the corresponding white marker board light. As the speaker moves away from the board, relay will turn OFF the lights.

The relay allows our relatively low voltage MCU to easily control higher power circuits. A relay accomplishes this by using the 5V output from an MCU pin to energize an electromagnet which in-turn closes an internal, physical switch attached to the below mentioned high power relay circuit figure 3.

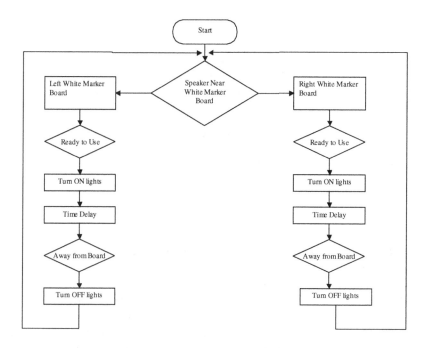

Fig. 2. The Control Flow chart of the PLCM

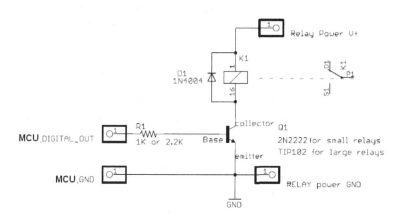

Fig. 3. Relay circuit for MCU

Light Control module will continuously receive instruction wireless from the PLCM to turn ON/OFF the lights. Algorithm for the light control is show below.

```
{
  if (Serial.available() > 0){
          incomingByte = Serial.read();
          if(incomingByte=='Y')
          digitalWrite(RELAY_PIN, HIGH);
          else
          {
             digitalWrite(RELAY_PIN, LOW);
          }
          delay(5);

  }

}
```

4   Implementation and Experimental Setup

Figure 4 shows the implementation of PLCM and White Marker Board Light Controller.
We are using relay of 6V with 10 Amps at 240V AC power, this means that we can handle 2400 VA and enough to brighten the white marker board. If you are having two white
marker boards beside the projector we will need two PLCM's. There has to be communication among PLCM's and their corresponding light control module. The necessity of
using separate PLCMs and light control module is that location and position of detection
area and light control can be used as per the flexibility of the end user. The ultrasound
sensor is able to cover maximum distance of 4 meters with very high accuracy. Since,
ultrasound is mounted on 180° rotating servo motors the maximum coverage area will be
25.133 meters. In our experiment ultrasound is connected to digital pin 7, motor to digital
pin 9 and relay to pin 13 of MCU. For servo motor to take position, 15ms delay was
given. In light control module, 30ms time delay was given for switch over.

For wireless communication XBee Series-2 module is used, where DIN and DOUT
is connected to Tx and Rx pin of MCU. Remote XBee modules may be manually
configured for different addresses. The address of the XBee defines its place on the
network. It can be used to specify data to a particular node (destination) and the sender's address (source) in some cases. By default, all XBee's have an address of 0 (the
MY address) and a destination low address of 0 (DL).

In loop-back testing, the XBee modules used the default configuration and both
were sending data from address 0 to address 0 being able to communicate with each
other. In our design of PLCM has MY address as 0, DL address as 406EC9DD and
DH address as 13A200 (address of White Marker Board Light Control). Where as
White Marker Board Light Control has MY address as FFFE, DL as 0 and DH as
FFFF for the broadcast purpose. In addition to node addresses, sometimes we may
want different group of XBee modules in the same area to be isolated from one another for communications—different networks in the same physical area. This may be
done by using either unique Personal Area Network (PAN) IDs (ID setting), or by
placing them on different channel frequencies (CH). In our design we are using PAN
ID is set as 3 for both the PLCM's and White Marker Board Light Control module.

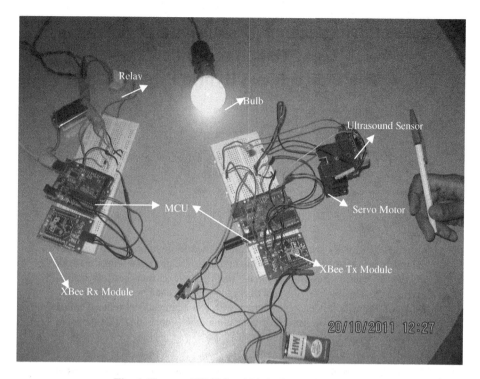

Fig. 4. Picture of PLCM and Light Controller Module

5   Conclusion

In this paper we have proposed a design to automate the light control for the white marker board in the conference/seminar hall. PLCM has been installed near white marker board which detects the speaker's need for marker board usage and turns ON the lights. To increase the coverage area, ultrasound is mounted on 180° rotating servo motor so that the maximum coverage area can go upto 25.133 meters. There is wireless communication between the PLCM and Light Control module so that depending upon the need and location of user, position of PLCM and Light control module can be changed. The future work includes centralized monitoring of the various conference halls white marker board usage.

References

1. Bai, Y.W., Ku, Y.T.: Automatic Room Light Intensity Detection And Control Using A Microprocessor And Light Sensors. IEEE Transactions on Consumer Electronics 54, 1173–1176 (2008)
2. Shirley, P.A.: An Introduction to Ultrasonic Sensing. Sensors 6 (November 1989)
3. Getting Started with XBee RF Modules- A Tutorial for BASIC Stamp and Propeller Microcontrollers by Martin Hebel and George Bricker with Daniel Harris
4. http://www.atmel.com/dyn/products/product_card.asp?part_id=4720
5. http://www.digi.com/support/kbase/kbaseresultdetl.jsp?id=2213

Wireless Environmental Monitoring System (WEMS) Using Data Aggregation in a Bidirectional Hybrid Protocol

Tapan Jain

Jaypee University of Information Technology,
Waknaghat, Solan
tapan.jain@juit.ac.in

Abstract. A wireless sensor network can be used to monitor the environment and warns for a mishappening occurring in future. The proposed sensor network protocol is hybrid and bi-directional. The dynamic cluster head formation increases the network life. Efficient data aggregation techniques are used so that the data transmission is energy efficient, with less aggregation overhead and is reliable. The concept of distributed computing is also applied so that the work of the sink node is made easy and fast.

Keywords: Environmental monitoring system, wireless sensor network, cluster head, data aggregation, reactive, proactive, bi-directional, hybrid.

1 Introduction

The Wireless Environment Monitoring System(WEMS) monitors critical environmental conditions, such as temperature, humidity, intrusion, and smoke. When the sensed attribute goes out of the range of a threshold, the system will notify using an alarm. The sensor network measures the attribute which it asked to, like temperature, pressure etc, at a particular point and pass on this information to the application processor. The user can get his desired information directly from the application processor in the form of a topographic map. The end user might be interested in extracting a variety of topographic information about the metadata in the network. He might want to know the boundaries of all regions where the temperature exceeds a certain threshold, or just the numbers of disjoint regions where temperature exceeds a threshold, or might want the complete topographic map of the terrain where contours correspond to temperature levels.

The proposed network is capable of monitoring more than one physical attribute as opposed to a single attribute detection in most of the research papers. The paper talks about mobile sensor nodes, whose position is calucalted by the cluster head through triangulation method. The benefit of data aggregation can be maximized by implementing it at each cluster head till the BS or the sink. The data need not be concealed or made private, so the overhead of encryption and decryption is avoided. The base station uses distrubuted computing to make the processing of the sensed data

S. Dua et al. (Eds.): ICISTM 2012, CCIS 285, pp. 414–420, 2012.

fast and more efficient. The protocol discussed is bi-directional and a hybrid protocol, which is a combination of reactive and proactive approaches.

Data aggregation(DA) collects the most critical data from the sensors and make it available to the BS in an energy efficient manner with minimum data latency[3]. The advantage of it is that the data transmissions are minimized as the data is first aggregated at a node and then it is send to the BS.

This paper talks about a wireless sensor network used to monitor the environment so that it can detect tsunami to be occurring in the near future. The remainder of this paper is organized as follows: Section 2 provides background in the areas of wireless sensor network, data aggregation, cluster head formation and query processing. Section 3 deals with the proposed architecture in detail. Section 4 deals with the simulation and results. Section 5 concludes the paper and talks about the future work.

2   Related Work

There are many routing protocols discussed in various research papers [1]. After comparing the existing routing protocols with the consideration of several design factors like Scalability, Power Usage, Mobility, Over-heads, Query-based, Data Aggregation and Localization, the parameters to be included in designing a new routing protocol are listed in Table 1. Ideally the new proposed routing protocol should follow the parameters listed below, but due to the interdependency of parameters, it's not possible to achieve all the ideal characteristics in a routing protocol.

Table 1. Design Factor for Protocol

Data delivery model	Hybrid
Data aggregation	Possible
Power usage	Low
Mobility	Possible
Scalability	Good
Security	Possible
Topology	Self organizing and random

3   Architecture of the Proposed System

The protocol is bi-directional and hybrid. In addition to getting the value at regular intervals, it can also react to any absurd, emergency condition. The application processor can ask the sensing unit to send the data at a particular instant and it can even change the time interval at which data is being transmitted by the sensing unit. Thus the time critical data can reach the user on time without any delay.

The protocol facilitates the sensing of more than one parameter by the sensor network. The sensor node passes the complete data to the BS. It sends the value of the attribute along with the sensed attribute, so that the BS knows which parameter is sensed by the sensor node.

3.1   Cluster Head Selection

The first step in transmitting the data in the WEMS is the selection of cluster heads and the creation of the clusters. The following steps are followed:-

Step 1: Sensors are randomly deployed on the sensor field and the base station is fixed to transmit the sensed information to the application processor.

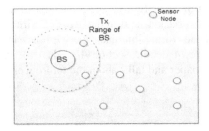

Fig. 1. step 1 of cluster head selection   **Fig. 2.** step 2 of cluster head selection

Step 2: BS transmits the Cluster Head Selection message (CHS_msg) to the entire sensor within its transmission range. It assigns a hop_ID of 1 to all the sensor nodes. In the figure 1 the two nodes coming within the transmission range of BS are A and B. The CHS_msg consists of the following parameters:-

1. hop_ID, the number of hops from the current node to the BS.
2. msg_ type, the type of message send by the BS to the sensor network. It can be a cluster head selection message or it can be a query processing message.
3. ch_ID, the id of the previous cluster head or the BS.

Step 3: In above figure, Sensor node A only send the CHS_msg to C and D, so in this case A become cluster head CH. After each CH transmit the message to child sensors in the network and then decide the CH selection.

Step 4: The transmission range of A sends the CHS_msg to n number of nodes than the selection criteria of cluster head as follows

```
if (!CH)
{
        if (! CH in last n-1 rounds)
        {
                if (! Receive CHS_msg in current round)
                {
                Calculate R_n = generate random between 0 to1;
                        if (R_n < T(n))
                        {
                                Nodes become CH;
                                Broadcast CHS_msg to child sensor;
}       }       }       }
```

Initially, when clusters are formed, each node decides whether it's the cluster head for the current round or not. This decision is based on the percentage of the CH for the network (determined a priori). This decision is based on random generator value between 0 to 1, if the number is less than a threshold T(n), node become CH for the current round. The T(n) = Threshold value can calculated by given formula [10]

$$T(n) = \frac{p}{1 - p * (r \bmod(1/p))} \qquad n \epsilon G \qquad (1)$$

where p = the desired percentage of cluster heads, r = the current round, and G is the set of nodes that have not been CH in the last 1/p rounds.

Step 5: Once all the CH are formed in the given network and on the basis of hop_ID, decide the routing path having minimum number of hops. In the given network node A, C, F behave as CH and all other nodes are needed hop_ID+1 hop to send the data from source node to sink node.

In this way the cluster heads are selected and cluster formation is complete. The black circles in the diagram represent the cluster heads. The sensors know their cluster heads, the ones which have minimum hop_id. E.g. if a sensor node is in the transmission range of two cluster heads, it received the CHS_msg from two cluster heads as (3, CHS_msg, CH$_4$) and (5, CHS_msg, CH$_6$), where 3 is the hop_id,

CHS_msg is the message type and CH$_4$ is the cluster head id. Then the sensor knows that its cluster head is CH$_4$ and not CH$_6$ because the number of hops required sending the data from the node to the sink in the former case is 3 and in the latter casing its 5.

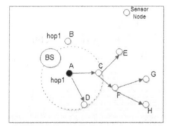 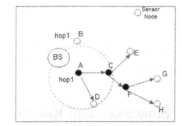

Fig. 3. step 3 of cluster head selection   **Fig. 4.** cluster head selected

3.2   Data Transmission from the Sensor to the Sink

The reactive part of the protocol deals with the transfer of data from the sensor node to the BS whenever there is some absurd behavior sensed by the sensor. The proactive part of the protocol deals with transmission of data from the sensor to the BS at regular time intervals. This time interval can be changed by the application processor as and when required. The sensors send their unique identification number (S_{id}), the value of the parameter to be measured (V_iA), and the time of measurement (t) to the cluster head selected earlier. The data transmitted would be of the form (S_{id}, V_iA, t)

The sensor sends the data to the cluster head assigned to it. The cluster head sends the information to the BS through the minimum number of hops as designated by the hop_id of the cluster head. The cluster head and consequently the BS are aware of the position of the mobile transceivers through the triangulation method. Using the signal strength the cluster head performs triangulation to determine the exact location of the sensor. And correspondingly it adds the coordinates of the sensor in the message to be send to the next cluster head (next hop) or to the BS. The format of the information is

$$(S_{id}, V_iA, t, (X_i, Y_i), CH_{id}), \text{ Where } CH_{id} \text{ is the cluster head id.}$$

The BS would use the above information to process any type of application. In this task it may generate spatial and temporal data, process the desired parameters and predict events like cyclone, Tsunami etc and the affected areas.

3.3   Data Aggregation

As discussed earlier the proposed protocol deals with the sensing of multiple attributes by the sensor network. Most of the research papers talk about data aggregation techniques for single attribute data. Jiao Zhang talks about attribute aware data aggregation, which deals with multiple attributes being sensed by the network and their values being aggregated.

In the case of WEMS, a physical quantity is sensed. In real world, the environmental factors (e.g., temperature, humidity) change continuously instead of flipping over along the space field. According to this natural phenomenon, there exists kind of correlation in the data gathered from natural environment. Hence in WEMS, data aggregation can be done by exploiting the correlation among the data. This would save time and energy. One way to exploit correlation is a linear transform in which the statistically dependent data will be mapped into a set of more independent coefficients and then compressed and transmitted. 3D-DCT (Discrete Cosine Transform) algorithm is used to exploit the spatial-temporal correlation in a regularly deployed network to achieve significant aggregation performance [5, 6]. The DCT transform function for N data sequence, f, is defined in [8].

4   Simulation and Results

The network is simulated in OMNet++[11]. OMNeT++ is a component-based, modular and open-architecture discrete event simulation framework. The simulation results show that the proposed protocol is good in energy conservation by effectively selecting the cluster heads. The data can flow in both the directions with the minimal loss and time delay. It has been observed that there can be an effective hybrid bidirecional protocol for the transmission of sensed data in a wireless sensor network. Sensing multiple attributes, increases the complexity of the system and the size of the message passed by the BS to the sensor network also becomes more as compared to a single sensed attribute. The WEMS can analyse the parameters of the environment and can produce alarm in adverse conditions.

Table 2. Simulation Results

	First Node Die (Rounds)	Network Lifetime(Rounds)	Packet delivery efficiency (%)
Without DA	50	60	47
DA- Node near BS	63	94	64
DA- All Hops	120	147	92

From the simulation results of a given network, It is evident that the Network Lifetime increses with the help of data aggregation technique. These are the primitive level results and some strong conclusion can be drawn as we progress on this problem through more simulations.

5   Conclusion and Future Work

This paper discusses an approach of sensing multiple attributes in an environment and then producing an alarm if any absurd condition is predicted. The protocol used is hybrid and bidirectional. The use of data aggregation has minimized the data transmissions and also made it fast. The parallel processing in the application processor has fastened up the data analysis.

The future work corresponds to dealing with a hybrid bidirectional protocol for tree based wireless sensor network. Then have a comparison between the two approaches based on energy consumption and time delay. The author plans to simulate both the approaches in OMNet++ and then come up the comparison chart between the two approaches.

References

1. Akyildiz, I.F., Su, W., Sankarasubramaniam, Y., Cayirci, E.: A survey on sensor networks. IEEE Comm. Magazine 40(8) (2002)
2. Manjeshwar, A., Agarwal, D.P.: TEEN: a routing protocol for enhanced efficiency in wireless sensor networks. In: IPDPS (April 2001)
3. Rajagopalan, R., Varshney, P.K.: Syracuse university, Data aggregation techniques in sensor networks:A survey. IEEE Communications Surveys & Tutorials, 4th Quarter, The Electronic Magazine of Original Peer Reviewed Survey Articles (2006)
4. Zhang, J.-H., Peng, H., Yin, T.-T.: Tree-Adapting: an Adaptive Data Aggregation Method for Wireless Sensor Networks. In: WiCOM (2006)
5. Bai, F., Jamalipour, A.: 3D-DCT Data Aggregation Technique for Regularly Deployed Wireless Sensor Networks. In: Proc. IEEE International Conference on Communication (ICC), Beijing, China (May 2008)
6. Rao, K.R., Yip, P.: Discrete Cosine Transform: Algorithms, Advantages and Applications. Academic Press (1990)

7. Ahmed, N., Natarajan, T., Rao, K.R.: Discrete Cosine Transfom. IEEE Transactions on Computers C-23, 90–93 (1974)
8. Pham, T., et al.: On Data Aggregation Quality and Energy Efficiency of Wireless Sensor Network Protocols - Extended Summary. In: BROADNETS 2004 (2004)
9. Choi, J.-Y., Lee, J.-H., Chung, Y.-J.: Minimal Hop Count Path Routing Algorithm for Mobile Sensor Networks. In: IMSCCS 2006 (2006)
10. http://ce.sharif.ir/courses/
    87-88/2/ce657/resources/root/OMNet/OMNet++.pdf

Detecting Healthcare Fraud through Patient Sharing Schemes

Aryya Gangopadhyay, Song Chen, and Yelena Yesha

University of Maryland Baltimore County (UMBC)
Baltimore, MD 21250
gangopad@umbc.edu, songchencs@gmail.com, yeyesha@cs.umbc.edu

Abstract. The United States loses at least $60 billion in health-care fraud every year, and some estimates put the cost as high as 10% of the nation's total health-care spending, which exceeds $2 trillion. The federal government is putting tremendous efforts in combating health frauds and safeguard the two largest government sponsored programs: Medicare and Medicaid. Using data analysis techniques to discover and prevent health care frauds is an important focus in all of the efforts. In this paper, we propose a new method for identifying patient sharing schemes that are prevalent in many parts of this country. Our proposed method is based on the PageRank algorithm that has been used by Google's Web search engine. We describe our approach, discuss the similarities and differences with PageRank, and demonstrate the applicability of this method by applying it to datasets simulated from real-life scenarios.

1 Introduction

The Medicare program offers health and financial protections to 48 million seniors and younger people with disabilities. However, the high cost of premiums, cost-sharing requirements, and gaps in the Medicare benefit packages can result in beneficiaries spending a substantial share of their household budgets on health care. According to a recent study by Kaiser Family Foundation, health expenses accounted for nearly 15 percent of Medicare household budgets in 2009. Most doctors, health care providers, suppliers, and private companies who work with Medicare are honest. However, there are a few who are not. Fraud costs the Medicare Program millions of dollars every year, and taxpayers end up paying for fraud with higher health care costs. Fraud schemes may be carried out by individuals, companies, or groups of individuals. Fraud, waste, and abuse take critical resources out of the country's health care system, and contribute to the rising cost of health care. Both the government and the private insurance companies are working together to help eliminate fraud by investigating fraudulent Medicare and Medicaid operators who are cheating the system.

The federal government has collected a vast of amount health care data, especially in the public health area and the majority of them are in Medicare and Medicaid programs. With large amounts of data available, it is possible to perform data analyses in large scales and discover abnormal billing patterns. A

S. Dua et al. (Eds.): ICISTM 2012, CCIS 285, pp. 421–426, 2012.

Patient Sharing Scheme is one that fraudsters frequently use to scoop money easily from the Medicare trust funds. In one latest news release, a Miami chiropractor used a "runner" to hire patients and forge false claims. The same group of patients could be hired to go to other physicians who want to make similar false claims. This is known as *patient sharing scheme*. Such a scheme can exist in any of the health programs.

In this paper, we adapt a dataset from the prescription drugs program or the Medicare Part D Program. This prescription drugs program, or Medicare Part D, was initiated in 2003 by Medicare Modernization Act (MMA) and began its operations in 2006. It mainly administers pharmacy claims managed by private health plans. Pharmacies dispense prescriptions to patients and then submit claims to private health plans. All claims are centralized in a vast data repository, which makes it possible for further data analysis. Pharmacies that bill false claims usually need to obtain a list of patient insurance numbers or hire a group of patients who are willing to lend their identify information for personal profits. The list of insurance numbers are shared among fraudulent pharmacies. Pharmacies that are set up for false claims or that only exist on paper are sometimes called *false front pharmacies* or *phantom pharmacies*. In the method described in this paper we propose to identify such pharmacies by analyzing the patients shared by pharmacies and ranking pharmacies according to the likelihood of their involvement in fraudulent schemes.

The rest of the paper is organized as follows: in Section 2 we briefly review the PageRank algorithm, followed by our proposed method in Section 3, experimental results in 4, and conclusions in Section 5.

2   The PageRank Algorithm

The PageRank algorithm was originally proposed in [2] and was subsequently analyzed, elaborated, and implemented in numerous other papers such as [4,1,3]. The purpose of the PageRank algorithm is to rank webpages according to their importance so that when a query is submitted by a searcher the relevant pages are identified based on matching search terms and presented in order of their importance. The importance of a page is determined by its link structure and those of the pages that have inlinks and outlinks from and to the page in question. It starts by allocating every page the same "importance" by giving each page one vote that it distributes equally to all pages to which it has a hyperlink. Thus, a page is considered important if other "important" pages have a hyperlink to it. Interestingly since a webpage is likely to have hyperlinks to other pages that are relevant to its content, synonyms and homonyms of search terms are effectively incorporated without any explicit linguistic analysis. Using the recursive definition of the importance of webpages the importance of each webpage can be written as a linear combination of the votes of all pages that hyperlink to it. Listing the importance of all webpages gives rise to a system of linear equations of the form $x = Ax$, where x is the vector of webpages and A is the coefficient matrix that captures the vote distribution of all pages. It is obvious that the vector x is an eigenvector of the matrix A with the corresponding eigenvalue 1. The matrix A is column stochastic but is not a regular Markov matrix as the web is likely to contain dangling nodes leading to multiple connected components. A connected matrix P is obtained from A by adding a probability matrix whose every entry is p, which is the probability that a surfer will randomly land on a webpage. P is a regular Markov matrix because it is connected. If P is raised to a sufficiently high power it will converge to a rank-1 matrix where every column represents the eigenvector that corresponds to the eigenvalue 1. We describe below how the PageRank algorithm can be used to rank pharmacies in order of their likelihood of being involved in a patient sharing scheme.

3   Proposed Method

The proposed method is inspired by the PageRank algorithm originally proposed in [2]. In our method we start with an $m \times n$ (typically $m \gg n$) matrix of patients versus pharmacies (called *PatientPharmacy* $\mathbb{P}$ matrix) where each entry $p_{ij} \in \mathbb{P}$ is 1 if a patient i goes to pharmacy j and 0 otherwise. Note that the orientation of the matrix is just for convenience and its transpose will work just as well with our algorithm. The first step of our algorithm involves obtaining *PharmacyPharmacy* matrix $\mathcal{P}$ that simply counts the number patients shared by any pair of pharmacies. The matrix $\mathcal{P}$ is obtained by $\mathbb{P}^T \times \mathbb{P}$ (see Table 1 for an example of the matrix $\mathcal{P}$). Note the diagonal elements of $\mathcal{P}$ represent the number of unique patients that are sole customers of the pharmacy in question. In the next step we column-normalize the matrix $\mathcal{P}$ so that the sum of each of its column equals 1. Once normalized, if $\mathcal{P}$ is a column stochastic regular Markov matrix, it will converge to a rank-1 matrix if it is raised to a high enough power. Once converged, each column of $\mathcal{P}$ represents the eigenvector corresponding to the eigenvalue of 1. There is one possible realistic situation where the column-stochastic matrix $\mathcal{P}$ will not converge to a rank-1 matrix: when there are pharmacies that do share patients with any other pharmacy. This is similar to the case of a dangling node in the PageRank algorithm where there are multiple connected components in the graph $\mathcal{G}$. We handle this situation by adding a small probability value p_{ij} to every entry of the matrix $\mathcal{P}$. The algorithm for computing the ranking of the pharmacies is shown in Algorithm 1.

Algorithm 1 starts with an adjacency matrix $\mathcal{P}$ as an input and returns a vector that ranks all pharmacies in the order of their likelihood of participating in a patient sharing scheme. The rationale behind the algorithm is that pharmacies where a high percentage of patients are shared with another pharmacy are likely participants in a patient sharing scheme. However, this information cannot be directly gleaned by just looking at the percentages of patients shared between any pair of pharmacies. Rather, if *pharmacy 1* shares a significant number of their patients with *pharmacy 2* and *pharmacy 2* in turn shares a significant number of patients with *pharmacy 3* and so forth, then it might be an indication that these pharmacies are potentially colluding with each other in a patient sharing scheme. Hence there may be indirect relationships among pharmacies in a patient sharing scheme. We capture all direct and indirect relationships in algorithm 1.

Algorithm 1. Algorithm for ranking pharmacies

Input: An $n \times n$ adjacency matrix $\mathcal{P}$
Output: Ranking vector $\mathcal{V}$.

    Generate a random n-dimensional vector s with each entry equal to $\frac{1}{n}$;
    Generate a random scalar $m \in [0, 1]$;
    Generate a random n-dimensional vector x_0 such that $\|x_0\|_1 = 1$;
    $i = 0$;
    repeat
        $x_{i+1} = (1 - m).\mathcal{P}.x_i + m.s$;
        $i = i + 1$;
    until $x_{i+1} - x_i \leq \tau$
    $\mathcal{V} = x_i$;
    return $\mathcal{V}$

The input adjacency matrix ($\mathcal{P}$) is a doubly stochastic Markov matrix where the sum of each column (and row) is 1. However, $\mathcal{P}$ may not be a regular Markov matrix as there could be some pharmacies that do not share patients with any other pharmacy. In order to create a regular Markov matrix we add another matrix $\mathcal{S}$ to $\mathcal{P}$ and obtain another Markov matrix $\mathcal{M}$, which is regular as all of its values are strictly positive. All entries of $\mathcal{S}$ have the same value $\frac{1}{n}$ indicating that there is a probability that any pharmacy can potentially be a participant to a patient sharing scheme. Note that the probability function is uniformly distributed across all pharmacies and is typically very small given that n is large. A subsequent column normalization is done so that $\mathcal{M}$ is column stochastic. Because $\mathcal{M}$ is positive definite, all of its eigenvalues are > 0. Furthermore, it can be shown that all entries of $\mathcal{M}$ are also ≤ 1.

In graph $\mathcal{G}$ each pharmacy is a node and the edge between pharmacy $\mathcal{P}_i$ and $\mathcal{P}_j$ represents the number of patients shared between $\mathcal{P}_i$ and $\mathcal{P}_j$ as a percentage of the total number of patients for each pharmacy $\mathcal{P}_i$ and $\mathcal{P}_j$. Figure 1 shows a the graph structure of pharmacies and patients. The colors of the nodes indicate their degrees, ranging deep blue where the degree is 1 to deep red where the degree is 700 or above.

4   Experiments and Results

We adapted a test dataset from a real-world dataset. The test dataset contained 30 pharmacies (including two injected pharmacies) and 3,825 patients (including 20 injected patients). The total number of claims is 4,631. The result is a matrix of the 30 pharmacies as shown in Table 1. Each cell in Table 1 indicates the number of unique patients shared between a pair of pharmacies. The diagonal elements represent the number of patients for each pharmacy. This matrix is further normalized by the number of patients and the diagonal elements are removed.

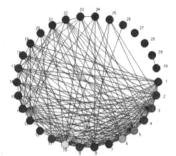

Fig 1. Graph Structure

Table 2. Ranks of Pharmacies

Pharmacy ID	Eigenvector	Ranks
1	0.2552	4
2	0.3775	3
3	0.0913	9
4	0.0454	14
5	0.0529	11
6	0.1040	8
7	0.0175	21
8	0.0519	13
9	0.0058	25
10	0.0102	24
11	0.0235	19
12	0.2187	5
13	0.0346	15
14	0.0010	28
15	0.0274	17
16	0.0000	29
17	0.0036	26
18	0.0000	30
19	0.0146	23
20	0.0522	12
21	0.1269	7
22	0.0173	22
23	0.0178	20
24	0.0314	16
25	0.1386	6
26	0.0256	18
27	0.0782	10
28	0.0020	27
29	0.5786	1
30	0.5774	2

Table 1. Part of the sharing matrix

Pharmacy ID	1	2	3	4	5	6	7	8	9	10
1	850	57	13	6	8	16	1	14	1	2
2	57	798	15	10	7	41	8	12	1	2
3	13	15	130	3	4	10	1	2	0	0
4	6	10	3	181	1	2	0	0	0	1
5	8	7	4	1	102	2	0	2	0	2
6	16	41	10	2	2	224	0	1	0	0
7	1	8	1	0	0	0	40	0	0	0
8	14	12	2	0	2	1	0	200	0	0
9	1	1	0	0	0	0	0	0	19	0
10	2	2	0	1	2	0	0	0	0	30

4.1   Ranking and Interpretation

The ranks of the 30 pharmacies are shown in Table 2. As we see from Table 2, the top two pharmacies are Pharmacy 29 and 30. These are the two pharmacies we injected into the test dataset. These two pharmacies share 20 patients and the shared patients represent 100% of the total patients each pharmacy.

Pharmacy 1 and 2 are ranked at numbers 3 and 4. These are the two largest pharmacies in this community that also share many patients with other pharmacies in this community. The high ranks of these two pharmacies may be due to their large patient bases. However, their scores are significantly lower than those of Pharmacies 29 and 30.

The lowest ranking pharmacies are Pharmacy 16 and 18. These two pharmacies do not share any patient with other pharmacies. They have their exclusive group of patients who do not go to other pharmacies. From investigative standpoints, these two pharmacies are also suspicious as their patient sharing patterns are abnormally different from the rest of the group.

Based on the results pharmacies 29 and 30 are suspicious pharmacies due to fact that these share a significant percentage of their patients with other pharmacies. Pharmacy 16 and 18 are also suspicious due to the fact that they do not share any of their patients with other pharmacies.

5   Conclusions

In this paper we present a novel approach to detect fraudulent activities in the pharmacy claims by using a method based on the PageRank algorithm. Our test results demonstrate the applicability of this method to successfully identify pharmacies that exhibit abnormal patients sharing patterns. We are currently working on scaling the proposed method to larger number of pharmacies.

We can further develop a customized scoring system to facility fraud detection in other fraudulent schemes with the same methodology. For example, if we want to find pharmacies that are dispensing compounding drugs in abnormal patterns we can develop a scoring system and rank pharmacies by the customized scores. The pharmacies with the top rank will have the most fraud potentials in this specific fraud scheme.

We are currently developing methods for co-clustering patients and pharmacies using spectral analysis. While we describe one form of fraudulent scheme in this paper, it is by no means the only form of fraud in practice. Further research into identifying fraudulent schemes is an area with far-reaching potential.

References

1. Berry, M.W., Browne, M.: Understanding Search Engines: Mathematical Modeling and text retrieval. SIAM, Philadelphia (2005)
2. Brin, S., Page, L.: The anatomy of a large-scale hypertextual web search engine. In: Seventh International World-Wide Web Conference, WWW 1998 (1998)
3. Moler, C.B.: Cleve's corner: The world's largest matrix computation: Google's pagerank is an eigenvector of a matrix of order 2.7 billion. Technical note (October 2002)
4. Mostafa, J.: Seeking better web searches. Scientific American 292, 66–73 (2005)

Software Security by Obscurity
A Programming Language Perspective

Roberto Giacobazzi

Dipartimento di Informatica, University of Verona, Italy
roberto.giacobazzi@univr.it

Abstract. In this paper we present recent achievements and open problems in software security by obscurity. We consider the problem of software protection as part of the Digital Asset Protection problem, and develop a formal security model that allows to better understand and compare known attacks and protection algorithms. The ultimate goal is to provide a comprehensive theory that allows a deeper understanding and systematical derivation of secured code against specific attacks.

1 The Scenario

Protecting digital assets represent an inescapable condition for the development of modern society. This becomes more and more critical in the current "pervasive computing" scenario, where ICT is ubiquitously integrated into everyday objects and people's life. Digital assets include traditional data objects such as keys, personal infos, pictures, movies, sound tracks, medical data, as well as more complex software (and hardware) systems. The latter case is definitively the less explored in the context of Digital Asset Protection (DAP), in particular in the case of software systems. In information-rich products, in contrast with more traditional manufactured goods where much of the know-how required to make the goods is located inside the factory, most of the know-how is located in the product itself. Piracy, terrorism, Intellectual Property (IP) theft over a wide scale market of software products make urgent the development of solutions for software protection which has to be widely recognized and accepted as sound and fair. Cryptography represents a possible solution which however has to cope with the peculiar nature of software product and systems: programs must be executable and analyzable in some or all (e.g., in an open source context) of its parts. Software, by its own, is indeed a very malleable engineering product, especially if expressed in modern widespread languages such as the Java bytecode or in the .Net environment. On the one hand, it easily takes the shape of the content it carries, so it is hard to dissimulate specific information within it, for instance to perfectly prevent information leakage or reverse engineering. On the other hand, software quickly lends itself to any kind of transformations, so it is easy to *deform* it in order to thwart accurate information retrieval in a *security by obscurity* approach (e.g., [17]): This makes problematic, for example, to dam up malware infection. These issues are well understood by the ICT community,

S. Dua et al. (Eds.): ICISTM 2012, CCIS 285, pp. 427–432, 2012.

as proved by the growing number of patents and ad-hoc algorithms for code protection, e.g., on software watermarking and fingerprinting, tamper-proofing, and more in general obfuscation (see [3] for a comprehensive account on the state of the art in the field). Negative results on the impossibility of perfect and universal protection by obscurity, such as [1], did not dishearten researchers in developing methods and algorithms for hiding sensitive information in programs. As well as Rice's theorem represented the greatest challenge for the development of automatic program analysis and verification tools, the impossibility of obfuscation against malicious host attacks is a major challenge for developing concrete techniques which are sufficiently robust that an attacker is in trouble for a sufficient amount of time in trying to defeat them (e.g., see [4,5,6]). The main problem is the lack of a recognized security model, i.e., models of attack and provably secure protection mechanisms for software, similarly to what is known in cryptography. Provable security assumes that crackers cannot violate a secure system unless some known *hard* computational problems become affordable or equivalently some specific computational capability is assumed. The importance of this problem in the future of cyberspace security is proved by the growing interest of scientist and companies in the developing of solid security models for software (e.g., see [2] and the recent establishment of D.A.P.A. – Digital Asset Protection Association [12]). Developing a security model means having a widely recognized model of attack and provably secure countermeasures, the whole set up in the most formal and mathematically sound framework.

2   Attack Models

Software can be defined as something turning a multi-purpose machine into a machine with a specific purpose [16]. Perception and comprehension of code's structure and behavior are deep semantics concepts, which depend on the relative degree of abstraction of the observer, which corresponds precisely to observable semantics. An *observer* is typically an *interpreter*. This includes both static and dynamic attacks, e.g., via monitoring, slicing, debugging, profiling, static and dynamic analysis, as well as in Man-At-The-End (MATE) attacks [2] for information disclosure and reverse engineering. The semantics of a program is a too complex, often undecidable, object. In all cases, approximation is mandatory to make program understanding feasible. According to the aims and the degree of abstraction of an observer, we can have a lot of different observable semantics. For an anti-virus scanner, the observable semantics is whether it includes or not any *virus signature*, i.e., a fixed sequence of bytes from a sample of a virus [18,10]. For an analyzer looking for similarities between two software applications, observable semantics is its birthmark, i.e., a sequence of unique characteristics used to identify the code [21]: If two applications have the same birthmark, they are likely to derive from the same source. For a verification tool aimed at checking safety-critical software for embedded systems (e.g., [9]), observable semantics may be whether it terminates or not when executed or it does not exhibit run-time errors. Furthermore, imaginative observers may devise unconventional ways of interpreting code, so that e.g., code structure and semantics may become themselves covert channels for information exchange. An attacker is therefore an approximate interpreter. Abstract interpretation [7,8] provides here the adequate model for reasoning about semantics, and interpreters, at different levels of abstraction and provides the most general setting in order to develop both a theoretic understanding of the basic aspects of security by obscurity in programming languages and the description of measures for the quality of protection measures (e.g., capacity, complexity, stealthiness, and resilience) as a basis for a rigorous cost-benefit analysis in a well-defined formal setting. We will concentrate in automatic code attacks, namely in the set of tools that assist and determine the quality of any MATE attack to code. Consider a programming language as a set of all well formed programs $\mathbb{P}$ over a domain of semantic objects $\mathcal{D}$ and a semantics specified as a partial function $[\![\cdot]\!] : \mathbb{P} \times \mathcal{D} \longrightarrow \mathcal{D}$. Typical semantic objects include registers and memory states, code, variables, program points, execution traces, probabilistic distributions etc. Once $\mathcal{D}$ is fixed, the semantics of a program $P \in \mathbb{P}$ in an initial (input) configuration $d \in \mathcal{D}$ is $[\![P]\!](d)$. Semantic objects can be approximated by abstraction [8]. Abstractions map concrete semantic objects into abstract ones, which are semantic properties– the ones specified (extracted) by the abstraction. Abstractions α and β can be compared with respect to their relative degree of precision: $\alpha \sqsubseteq \beta$ *if α is more precise than (at least extracts the properties of) β*. The properties of semantic objects are elements in $\wp(\mathcal{D})$. An abstract interpretation for abstraction α is a partial (total in case of decidable approximation) function $[\![\cdot]\!]^\alpha : \mathbb{P} \times \mathcal{D} \longrightarrow \wp(\mathcal{D})$. The construction of $[\![\cdot]\!]^\alpha$ may involve interpretation of *concrete* operations on approximate abstract objects and complex fix point iteration strategies in order to ensure convergence in decidable abstractions or to extract, by induction, invariant properties of code parts [7].

An attacker is therefore an (abstract) interpreter $\mathtt{Attack}^\alpha$ which may employ a number of program transformations and analysis all devoted to extract properties about the behavior of the input program. An attack always corresponds to fix the set of properties involved in the attack, which is the abstraction α. As an interpreter it satisfies the main property of interpreters: For any program $P \in \mathbb{P}$: $[\![\mathtt{Attack}^\alpha]\!](P)(\alpha(d)) = [\![P]\!]^\alpha(d)^1$.

3   Protection Mechanisms

As well as standard protection and concealment techniques in traditional digital media, such as video and audio media, are all characterized by the exploitation of the limitations of human/technology perception and understanding system [20], security by obscurity in programming languages means making the attacker unable to extract the desired informations form the input program, by exploiting the limitations of its approximate perception of program semantics. In this context this corresponds precisely in transforming the input program P in such a way that the property extracted by the attacker is as much imprecise

---

[1] Here a function $f : A \longrightarrow B$ is naturally lifted additively to sets of objects by defining $f(X) = \{f(x) \mid x \in X\}$ for any $X \subseteq A$.

as possible with respect to the property of the true program execution: $\alpha(\llbracket P \rrbracket)$. This phenomenon is precisely captured by the notion of *completeness* of an abstract interpretation [15]. Completeness expresses precisely the accuracy of the approximate semantics in modeling program behavior. This corresponds to the possibility of replacing, with no loss of precision, concrete computations with approximate ones. The lack of completeness of the attacker corresponds here to its poor understanding of the obscured program's semantics. Consider the simple statement $P : x = a * b$, multiplying a and b, and storing the result in x [13] and an attacker willing to extract the property of the sign computed by C. A straightforward abstract interpretation is possible by implementing the *rule of sign* which is an abstraction σ which is complete for integer multiplication. In this case, for any $a, b \in \mathbb{Z}$: $\sigma(\llbracket P \rrbracket(a, b)) = \llbracket \texttt{Attack}^\sigma \rrbracket(P)(\sigma(a), \sigma(b))$. A clear loss of completeness can be obtained by transforming P into $\mathfrak{O}(P)$:

```
x = 0;
if b ≤ 0 then {a = −a; b = −b};
while b ≠ 0 {x = a + x; b = b − 1}
```

In this case, the sign analysis is unable to extract any information concerning the computed sign, because the rule of signs is incomplete for integer addition. This is a simple case of code obfuscation relatively to the attacker σ:

$$\forall a, b \in \mathbb{Z} : \ \sigma(\llbracket P \rrbracket(a, b)) \sqsubseteq \llbracket \texttt{Attack}^\sigma \rrbracket(\mathfrak{O}(P))(\sigma(a), \sigma(b))$$

A far more refined abstraction than σ is necessary in order to extract the desired information from $\mathfrak{O}(P)$, which is interval analysis [15]. Of course also interval analysis can be defeated by transforming $\mathfrak{O}(P)$ (see [13] for an example) and so on. We can therefore state that *protection by obscurity in programming is making the attacker (maximally) incomplete*:

$$\forall d \in \mathcal{D} : \ \llbracket \texttt{Attack}^\alpha \rrbracket(P)(\alpha(d)) \sqsubseteq \llbracket \texttt{Attack}^\alpha \rrbracket(\mathfrak{O}(P))(\alpha(d))$$

The more $\llbracket \texttt{Attack}^\alpha \rrbracket(\mathfrak{O}(P))(\alpha(d))$ is vague (i.e., provides weak properties about the behavior of P) the more the protection is effective. Because abstractions can be combined, and the result is also an abstraction, this approach can scale easily to complex attack models, involving a number of different program analyses, both dynamic and static. The very first semantic-based model for code obfuscation was in [11], where the notion of potency was described in terms of the impossibility for an abstract interpreter to extract the desired property form the input program. This notion has been refined into completeness in [13] and recently applied in the systematic derivation of obfuscated code by partial evaluation of distorted interpreters in [14]. In this latter case, the obfuscated program $\mathfrak{O}(P)$ is systematically derived by specializing a distorted interpreter that acts on code structures on which $\texttt{Attack}^\alpha$ is incomplete. A number of known obfuscation methodologies have been systematically derived by specializing a distorted interpreter, defeating specific and well isolated attackers (viz., abstractions).

4   Open Problems in PLDAP

The framework described above provides an initial step in formally understanding security by obscurity in programming languages. A number of open questions and problems remain and deserve further investigation. In the following we describe some of the major challenges in the field.

Theory. The use of abstract interpreters as attack models is promising in order to derive an *impossibility result* a la Barack et al., [1] based on simple recursive theoretic results, without probabilistic models. To the best of our knowledge this possibility is still an open problem in security by obscurity.

Methodology. The bridge between the structure of Attack^α and $\mathfrak{D}(P)$ is still unclear. In [13] and [14] an important step forward in understanding this link has been set up, but still there is a missing link between the form of the attack and the form of protection. Both are facets of the notion of interpretation, the first running the code the second distorting the run towards maximal imprecision. This is clearly a game which is not yet clearly understood (see [19] for a recent interesting account of this perspective).

Pragmatics. The idea of using program specialization of distorted interpreters as in [14] is extremely promising in order to move forward in the direction of the systemic design and production of secured code by obfuscation. Open questions here concern the complexity overhead introduced by partial evaluation of one level of interpretation and the industrial applicability of this technology in large scale applications, e.g., on specific code portions for key concealment and watermarking.

Measure. The above security model is based on a qualitative comparison of relative precision of abstract interpreters in their capabilities in extracting program properties. The possibility of providing adequate and well recognized metrics for measuring the security is an essential aspect for its practical usability [2]. This can involve the measure of the increased entropy relatively to a probabilistic abstract interpreter or more specifically the amount of information necessary in order to refine the abstraction for extracting the desired properties out of $\mathfrak{D}(P)$.

Unifying software and traditional digital media technologies in security by obscurity is in this perspective a major challenge in DAP. This can be achieved both by strengthening the impact of software technologies in this context and by providing provable secure methodologies for information hiding in programming. The standard theory for digital media obfuscation and steganography is based on Shannon information theory, where the gain provided by source compression and natural or artificial noise is used for hiding. We plan to expand this theory with a new dimension concerning semantics and abstraction in order to handle code as a new media. The long term vision is that of having a unifying theory with a number of tools and metrics for handling the problem of information hiding and disclosure in the digital era, where complexity, semantics and information theory coexist and interact in order to provide adequate tools for provable secure concealing systems.

References

1. Barak, B., Goldreich, O., Impagliazzo, R., Rudich, S., Sahai, A., Vadhan, S.P., Yang, K.: On the (Im)possibility of obfuscating programs. In: Kilian, J. (ed.) CRYPTO 2001. LNCS, vol. 2139, pp. 1–18. Springer, Heidelberg (2001)
2. Collberg, C., Davidson, J., Giacobazzi, R., Xiang Gu, Y., Herzberg, A., Wang, F.-Y.: Toward digital asset protection. IEEE Intelligent Systems 26(6), 8–13 (2011)
3. Collberg, C., Nagra, J.: Surreptitious Software. Addison Wesley (2010)
4. Collberg, C., Thomborson, C.D.: Software watermarking: models and dynamic embeddings. In: 26th ACM SIGPLAN-SIGACT POPL 1999, pp. 311–324. ACM (1999)
5. Collberg, C., Thomborson, C.D., Low, D.: Manufactoring cheap, resilient, and stealthy opaque constructs. In: 25st ACM SIGPLAN-SIGACT POPL 1998, pp. 184–196. ACM (1998)
6. Collberg, C., Thomborson, C.D., Townsend, G.M.: Dynamic graph-based software fingerprinting. ACM Trans. Program. Lang. Syst. 29(6), 35 (2007)
7. Cousot, P., Cousot, R.: Abstract interpretation: A unified lattice model for static analysis of programs by construction or approximation of fixpoints. In: 4th ACM SIGPLAN-SIGACT POPL 1977, pp. 238–252. ACM (1977)
8. Cousot, P., Cousot, R.: Systematic design of program analysis frameworks. In: 6th ACM SIGPLAN-SIGACT POPL 1979, pp. 269–282. ACM (1979)
9. Cousot, P., Cousot, R., Feret, J., Mauborgne, L., Miné, A., Monniaux, D., Rival, X.: The ASTREÉ Analyzer. In: Sagiv, M. (ed.) ESOP 2005. LNCS, vol. 3444, pp. 21–30. Springer, Heidelberg (2005)
10. Dalla Preda, M., Christodorescu, M., Jha, S., Debray, S.: A semantics-based approach to malware detection. In: 34th ACM SIGPLAN-SIGACT POPL 2007, pp. 377–388. ACM (2007)
11. Dalla Preda, M., Giacobazzi, R.: Semantic-based code obfuscation by abstract interpretation. Journal of Computer Security 17(6), 855–908 (2009)
12. Digital Asset Protection Association (2012), http://www.d-a-p-a.org
13. Giacobazzi, R.: Hiding information in completeness holes - new perspectives in code obfuscation and watermarking. In: Proc. of The 6th IEEE SEFM 2008, pp. 7–20. IEEE (2008)
14. Giacobazzi, R., Jones, N.D., Mastroeni, I.: Obfuscation by partial evaluation of distorted interpreters. In: ACM PEPM 2012. ACM (to appear, 2012)
15. Giacobazzi, R., Ranzato, F., Scozzari, F.: Making abstract interpretation complete. Journal of the ACM 47(2), 361–416 (2000)
16. Hoare, C.A.R.: Private communication (September 2007)
17. Kerckhoffs, A.: La cryptographie militaire. J. des Sciences Militaires IX(5-38), 161–191 (1883)
18. Lakhotia, A., Mohammed, M.: Imposing order on program statements to assist Anti-Virus scanners. In: WCRE, pp. 161–170 (2004)
19. Pavlovic, D.: Gaming security by obscurity. CoRR, abs/1109.5542 (2011)
20. Petitcolas, F.A.P., Anderson, R.J., Kuhn, M.G.: Information hiding – A survey. Proc. of the IEEE 87(7), 1062–1078 (1999)
21. Tamada, H., Nakamura, M., Monden, A., Matsumoto, K.: Detecting the theft of programs using birthmarks. Information Science Technical Report NAIST-IS-TR2003014, Graduate School of Information Science, Nara Institute of Science and Technology (November 2003) ISSN 0919-9527

System-Level Methods to Prevent Reverse-Engineering, Cloning, and Trojan Insertion

Sylvain Guilley[1], Jean-Luc Danger[1],
Robert Nguyen[2], and Philippe Nguyen[2]

[1] TELECOM-ParisTech, COMELEC departement,
(CNRS LTCI, UMR 5141), 46 rue Barrault, 75 013 Paris, France
[2] Secure-IC S.A.S., 80 avenue des Buttes de Coësmes, 35 700 Rennes, France

Abstract. The reverse-engineering (RE) is a real threat on high-value circuits. Many unitary solutions have been proposed to make RE difficult. Most of them are low-level, and thus costly to design and to implement. In this paper, we investigate alternative solutions that attempt to deny the possibility of RE using high-level methods, at virtually no added cost.

Keywords: Reverse-engineering (RE), Cloning, Trojans.

1 Introduction

The field of protection against reverse-engineering (RE) has developed recently, especially in the field of software (where it is called digital forensic [11]). Those techniques have extended to hardware, because the design of circuits is more and more outsourced (for fabrication, packaging, assembly, *etc.*). Some governments have additionally enforced anti-RE laws, to force industrialists take this risk into consideration. This article is a position paper about non-technical ways to resist RE and derived attacks that span from mere cloning to Trojan insertion.

The rest of this paper is structured as follows. A detail analysis of the threats categories and of the typical attack protections against them is covered in Sec. 2. Some technologies, mainly proposed by the academia, suitable to fight RE, have emerged. They are reviewed in Sec. 3. Solutions that aim at preventing RE and related attacks at a system-level are discussed in Sec. 4. Eventually, the conclusions are given in Sec. 5.

2 Threats

Reverse engineering consists in recovering the design by analyzing its implementation. It can serve *per se* to gain illegitimate information. The motivation is typically acquiring the knowledge about industrial design secrets embedded in a system, or cloning a design by extracting its masks or its netlist, in a view to producing compatible chips (albeit without paying for the research/development cost). Also, it

S. Dua et al. (Eds.): ICISTM 2012, CCIS 285, pp. 433–438, 2012.

can be a first step for Trojan [15] insertion. A Trojan (or a backdoor) is a piece of software or of hardware that is added to the circuit. It is designed not to interfere with its nominal operation, and to allow for the leakage of some secrets when activated by a secret sequence of inputs. Sometimes, the Trojan is an added functionality, that will not be detectable by the test; sometimes, it can alter one functionality. For instance, the bug attack of Shamir [3] can be seen as an exploitation of a Trojan. The idea of this Trojan is that the integer multiplier of the circuit returns one incorrect value, which allows the attacker that knows the data that causes this error to craft a message that will sign properly modulo p (resp. q) but incorrectly modulo q (resp. p), which makes it possible to carry out a remote Bellcore attack on CRT-RSA [5].

Accessing the design can be obtained by several means. The first one consists in simply getting the whole design, if the source is accessible or can be easily stolen. To avoid this risk, recommended design practices consist in concealing the design, by good practices of development. For instance, the class ALC[1] of the common criteria formally addresses [1] this point.

But even when organizational measures are enforced, the design can still be reversed. Indeed, the binaries can be extracted from memories, and subsequently decompiled to recover its functionality. Nonetheless, as this threat is very pregnant, the designers usually encrypt the memory contents. This doctrine is commonplace in the military objects, where different kind of data exist:

1. insensitive data, called black, that are either public or encrypted variables,
2. sensitive data, called red, that consist in secret material manipulated unencrypted (*i.e.* plain).

Thus, as a countermeasure, the data that is intended to be stored in easy dumpable memories is encrypted (*i.e.* turned to black). We talk about a secure bus architecture [10], *a.k.a.* a protection about the so-called bus probing attacks. The attacker can target the bus encryption mechanism, that can be for instance a side-channel attack or a fault attack (corruption of a data when writing to memory).

Now, secrets can be recovered from a circuit by various means:

- Non-invasive means: for instance, RE using side-channel attacks, *aka* SCARE [8];
- Semi-invasive means [19]; for instance, RE using fault injection attacks, *aka* FIRE [18];
- Invasive means; for instance, the delayering of circuits.

3   State-of-the-Art Technical Solutions

The protection of circuits against RE has been appropriated by the scientific community (CHES, FDTC, *etc.*). Many technical solutions, that most of the time assume *optimistically* that an attacker is omnipotent, have been put forward and studied. The most relevant are detailed in the next subsections.

---

[1] In version $\geqslant 3.1$ of the CC, ALC details the requirements associated with the developer's site.

3.1   Physically Unclonable Functions (PUFs)

Physically Unclonable Functions (PUFs [20]) consist in devices that produce a stable yet unique per chip output. They can be used to deter RE by producing internally a key. This key is known by nobody, and thus there is less chance that it is compromised.

Also, as the PUF is unique per chip, it does not prevent to extract the encrypted data (common to a product line), but it prevents from the alteration (by a remote Trojan patch) of all the product line. Indeed, an attacker can only forge the data for the device whose key (PUF result) is known.

3.2   Obfuscation

Obfuscation consists in turning a straightforward implementation into a complex description, that is hard to unravel. It has been proved that there is no universal obfuscation technique, that can apply to any algorithm [2]. Nonetheless, in theory, a concrete obfuscator for RSA, AES, *etc.* can exist. This method exists for both the pure hardware modules as well as for the pure software.

At the hardware-level, the typical impediments are:

- Covering of the chip with a top-level metal to prevent seeing the layers underneath, and to fight probing;
- Spaghetti routing, for evident control wires not to clearly stand out;
- Standard cells scattering, which comes down to the previous item.

At the software-level, the typical impediments are:

- Adding an intermediate virtual machine operating with unknown opcodes;
- Call graph re-engineering;
- Addition of florid tautologies.

3.3   Whitebox Cryptography

Whitebox cryptography is a scientific domain that aims at providing a description of an algorithm that embeds a secret (for instance an AES with a constant key), but from which the key cannot be recovered. Some examples exist:

- A PIN code or password verification algorithm, in which the PIN code or the password is stored hashed;
- A block cipher that is implemented as its codebook (hence as a huge memory, that is unrealistic in practice).

Concrete implementations of whitebox cryptography make of secret tables much smaller than the codebook [7]. This solution is attractive in hardware also, since EEPROM memories are much more difficult to read by invasive means than RAM or ROM.

3.4 Backend-Level Decoiling

Circuits can be reversed by the analysis of their layout. Advanced techniques exist for state-of-the-art circuits [21]. But on various occasions, older designs have been exposed with much lower technology tools. For instance,

- CRYPTO1, the encryption algorithm of the NXP MyFare card [16], and
- DSC, the encryption algorithm of the DECT [17],

have between disclosed by the observation of the chip. Incidentally, those algorithms have been cryptanalysed almost as soon as they were known, which is a brilliant example of the danger of security by obscurity mechanisms.

Optical dissimulation against delayering consists in making difficult the analysis of the images, by:

- adding dummy wires, dummy interconnections, dummy gates, *etc.*
- scrambling the memories [6],
- using custom cells that resemble despite their function differ; For instance the SecLib cells are all derived from a common template, and are customized by the addition of vias [12].

4 More Solutions

In this section, we promote prospective solutions, most of which do not rely on a technical mechanism. The primary goal of the electronic design industry is to sell products that accomplish a given function. Preventing RE is thus usually only a secondary goal. Thus, the anti-RE mechanisms shall be as less costly as possible. Therefore, the state-of-the-art techniques listed in Sec. 3 are often not suitable. Indeed, they answer (fully or partially) to the issue of preventing RE, but are a cost center. In addition, it can be noticed that they are *ad hoc* solutions that attempt to fix a local problem.

Now, the goal of the protection against RE is to protect the whole circuit, and not only some parts in a unitary manner. Therefore, global solutions can be thought about. The next subsection details some recommendations. They might not cover all the problems of RE, but still already provide some hints for good design practices at low cost.

4.1 Leaving No Secret in the Weakest Link

In some communication systems, one party is weaker than the other. For instance, in the case of a smartcard talking to a terminal, the smartcard is the easiest party to attack. Indeed, it is depends on the environment for its power supply and time reference, and it is cost-constrained.

Thus, it shall contain as few secrets as possible. This is indeed possible using public-key cryptography [9], for instance. The terminal generates a signature, and the smartcard verifies it. The verification requires no secret, thus there is no reason to attack the smartcard. This technique allows typically to deny virused code (*e.g.* containing a Trojan) to be executed on the smartcard.

4.2   Providing a Minimalist API

The more rich the API, the more attack scenarios an attacker can write. At the opposite, if the API is minimalist, most of the operations are realized internally, at an unknown pace. They leave fewer control for the attacker to understand what the circuit is actually computing.

4.3   Randomizing the Protocols

If the protocols are deterministic, then they can be replayed, which enables some training. Also, differential attacks (such as DFA [4]) require a correct and at least one [22] faulty cryptogram. This approach is similar to resilient countermeasures: the secret is made volatile [14], as well as the data [13]. We emphasize that for this class of countermeasure to be efficient, a tamper-resistant TRNG (True Random Number Generator) shall be available.

5   Conclusions

Fighting RE can be done by dedicated means that have been widely discussed in the scientific literature. Nonetheless, they are costly in general, because they consider a very powerful attacker that is able to play with the target at her will. The solutions we sketch in this article do not have this drawback. They are designed not to give the opportunity for the attacker to be in a favourable position, for instance by ascertaining the attack is impossible to setup. The resulting countermeasures, being only "organizational", are thus also low cost, hence acceptable in an industrial context. Nonetheless, they require to define new specific high-level communication protocols that are low-level security oriented.

References

1. Common Criteria (*aka* CC) for Information Technology Security Evaluation (ISO/IEC 15408), http://www.commoncriteriaportal.org/
2. Barak, B., Goldreich, O., Impagliazzo, R., Rudich, S., Sahai, A., Vadhan, S.P., Yang, K.: On the (Im)possibility of Obfuscating Programs. In: Kilian, J. (ed.) CRYPTO 2001. LNCS, vol. 2139, pp. 1–18. Springer, Heidelberg (2001)
3. Biham, E., Carmeli, Y., Shamir, A.: Bug Attacks. In: Wagner, D. (ed.) CRYPTO 2008. LNCS, vol. 5157, pp. 221–240. Springer, Heidelberg (2008)
4. Biham, E., Shamir, A.: Differential Fault Analysis of Secret Key Cryptosystems. In: Kaliski Jr., B.S. (ed.) CRYPTO 1997. LNCS, vol. 1294, pp. 513–525. Springer, Heidelberg (1997), doi:10.1007/BFb0052259
5. Boneh, D., DeMillo, R.A., Lipton, R.J.: On the Importance of Checking Cryptographic Protocols for Faults. In: Fumy, W. (ed.) EUROCRYPT 1997. LNCS, vol. 1233, pp. 37–51. Springer, Heidelberg (1997)
6. Brier, E., Handschuh, H., Tymen, C.: Fast Primitives for Internal Data Scrambling in Tamper Resistant Hardware. In: Koç, Ç.K., Naccache, D., Paar, C. (eds.) CHES 2001. LNCS, vol. 2162, pp. 16–27. Springer, Heidelberg (2001)

7. Chow, S., Eisen, P.A., Johnson, H., van Oorschot, P.C.: White-Box Cryptography and an AES Implementation. In: Nyberg, K., Heys, H.M. (eds.) SAC 2002. LNCS, vol. 2595, pp. 250–270. Springer, Heidelberg (2003)

8. Clavier, C.: An Improved SCARE Cryptanalysis Against a Secret A3/A8 GSM Algorithm. In: McDaniel, P., Gupta, S.K. (eds.) ICISS 2007. LNCS, vol. 4812, pp. 143–155. Springer, Heidelberg (2007)

9. Diffie, W., Hellman, M.E.: New Directions in Cryptography. IEEE Transactions on Information Theory 22(6), 644–654 (1976)

10. Elbaz, R., Champagne, D., Gebotys, C.H., Lee, R.B., Potlapally, N.R., Torres, L.: Hardware Mechanisms for Memory Authentication: A Survey of Existing Techniques and Engines. Transactions on Computational Science 4, 1–22 (2009)

11. Garfinkel, S.: Anti-Forensics: Techniques, Detection and Countermeasures. In: ICIW, 2nd International Conference on i-Warfare and Security, Naval Postgraduate School, Monterey, California, USA, March 8-9, pp. 77–84 (2007)

12. Guilley, S., Flament, F., Mathieu, Y., Pacalet, R.: Security Evaluation of a Balanced Quasi-Delay Insensitive Library. In: DCIS, Grenoble, France, IEEE. Session 5D – Reliable and Secure Architectures (November 2008), http://hal.archives-ouvertes.fr/hal-00283405/en/ ISBN: 978-2-84813-124-5

13. Guilley, S., Sauvage, L., Danger, J.-L., Selmane, N.: Fault Injection Resilience. In: FDTC, August 21, pp. 51–65. IEEE Computer Society, Santa Barbara (2010), doi:10.1109/FDTC.2010.15

14. Kocher, P.C.: Leak-resistant cryptographic indexed key update, March 25, United States Patent 6,539,092 filed on July 2nd, 1999 at San Francisco, CA, USA (2003)

15. Lin, L., Kasper, M., Güneysu, T., Paar, C., Burleson, W.: Trojan Side-Channels: Lightweight Hardware Trojans through Side-Channel Engineering. In: Clavier, C., Gaj, K. (eds.) CHES 2009. LNCS, vol. 5747, pp. 382–395. Springer, Heidelberg (2009)

16. Nohl, K., Starbug, D.E., Plötz, H.: Reverse-Engineering a Cryptographic RFID Tag. In: USENIX Security Symposium, San Jose, CA, USA, July 31, pp. 185–193 (2008)

17. Nohl, K., Tews, E., Weinmann, R.-P.: Cryptanalysis of the DECT Standard Cipher. In: Hong, S., Iwata, T. (eds.) FSE 2010. LNCS, vol. 6147, pp. 1–18. Springer, Heidelberg (2010)

18. San Pedro, M., Soos, M., Guilley, S.: FIRE: Fault Injection for Reverse Engineering. In: Ardagna, C.A., Zhou, J. (eds.) WISTP 2011. LNCS, vol. 6633, pp. 280–293. Springer, Heidelberg (2011), doi:10.1007/978-3-642-21040-2_20

19. Skorobogatov, S.P.: Semi-Invasive Attacks — A new approach to hardware security analysis. PhD thesis, Cambridge University / Computer Laboratory, Security Group, TAMPER laboratory, Technical Report UCAM-CL-TR-630 (April 2005), http://www.cl.cam.ac.uk/techreports/UCAM-CL-TR-630.pdf

20. Edward Suh, G., Devadas, S.: Physical unclonable functions for device authentication and secret key generation. In: DAC, pp. 9–14 (2007)

21. Torrance, R., James, D.: The State-of-the-Art in IC Reverse Engineering. In: Clavier, C., Gaj, K. (eds.) CHES 2009. LNCS, vol. 5747, pp. 363–381. Springer, Heidelberg (2009)

22. Tunstall, M., Mukhopadhyay, D., Ali, S.: Differential Fault Analysis of the Advanced Encryption Standard Using a Single Fault. In: Ardagna, C.A., Zhou, J. (eds.) WISTP 2011. LNCS, vol. 6633, pp. 224–233. Springer, Heidelberg (2011)

The Grand Challenge in Metamorphic Analysis

Mila Dalla Preda

Department of Computer Science/INRIA, University of Bologna, Italy
dallapre@cs.unibo.it

Abstract. Malware detection is a crucial aspect of software security. Malware typically recur to a variety of disguise and concealing techniques in order to avoid detection. Metamorphism is the ability of a program to mutate its form yet keeping unchanged its functionality and therefore its danger in case of malware. A major challenge in this field is the development of general automatic/systematic detection techniques that are able to catch the possible variants of a metamorphic malware. We take the position that the key for handling metamorphism relies in a deeper understanding of the semantics of the metamorphic malware. By applying standard formal methods we aim at proving that metamorphic analysis is a special case of program analysis, where the object of computation is code interpreted as a mutational data structure.

1 Metamorphic Malware Analysis

Detecting and neutralizing malware is a major challenge in computer security involving both sophisticated intrusion detection strategies and code manipulation tools and methods. Traditional misuse (or signature-based) malware detectors are syntactic in nature: They use pattern matching to compare the byte sequence comprising the body of the malware against a signature database [23]. Metamorphism emerged in the last decade as an effective strategy to foil misuse malware detectors. Metamorphic malware apply semantics preserving transformations (e.g. code obfuscation techniques) to modify their own code so that one instance of the malware bears very little resemblance to another instance even though semantically their functionality is the same. Thus, a metamorphic malware is a malware equipped with a metamorphic engine that takes the malware, or parts of it, as input and morphs it at run-time to a syntactically different but semantically equivalent variant, in order to foil signature matching. The quantity of metamorphic variants possible for a particular piece of malware makes it impractical to maintain a signature set that is large enough to cover most or all of these variants, making standard signature-based detection ineffective [5]. The reason for this vulnerability to metamorphism lies upon the purely syntactic nature of most exiting and commercial detectors that ignore program functionalities. Following this observation researchers began to develop detection techniques that take into account properties of the malware behavior instead of properties of its syntax. This naturally needs sophisticated program and behavioral analysis techniques, that rely upon known and new formal methods for reasoning about programs that mutate their code during execution.

S. Dua et al. (Eds.): ICISTM 2012, CCIS 285, pp. 439–444, 2012.

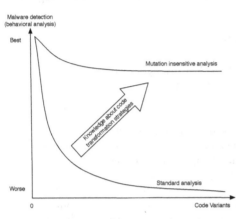

As far as data/control flow analysis is concerned, program and behavioral analysis are standard in programming languages and system [20]. The situation changes when metamorphism is considered. The main difficulties in applying these techniques to metamorphic code analysis relies upon the fact that code mutation and data/control behavior are interleaved. This makes the first interfering with the second making the analysis impossible or imprecise enough to let malware be indistinguishable from good software.

The reason of this difficulty is twofold: (1) The code of the malware is not fixed, it mutates during execution or may take on extremely different shapes when caught in the wild or executed in an emulator or debugger. An adequate semantics, on which any sound analysis has to be based, has to cope with this aspect of metamorphic code, either by keeping track of code mutations in order to model similarities or being insensitive to these mutations in order to understand malware attacks; (2) It is extremely difficult to isolate the code portions devoted to code mutations, the so called *metamorphic engine*, being this code hardly obfuscated and interleaved into the malware payload. The analysis has therefore to cope with mixed (hybrid) computations involving standard data structures (the payload) as well as the code itself as a data structure.

2   Behavioral Approaches to Metamorphism

Nowadays, in the literature we can find a variety of detection algorithms that use standard formal methods and program analysis tools to model the malicious behavior in order to detect malware. Most of these tools and methods are based on the idea that a model of the behavior of a malware may be a valid signature for catching it. This is indeed in the tradition of intrusion detection systems (IDS), where an attack is essentially captured by understanding the attacker behavior in terms of which and how data are manipulated. Christodorescu et al. [6] put forward a very first semantics-aware malware detector that is able to handle some of the metamorphic transformations commonly used by hackers. Singh and Lakhotia specify malicious behaviors through a formula in linear temporal logic (LTL), expressing temporal properties of malware behavior relatively to some state properties, and then use the model checker SPIN to check if this property is satisfied by the control flow graph of a suspicious program [22]. Kinder et al. [15] introduce an extension of the CTL temporal logic, which is able to express some malicious properties that can be used to detect malware through standard model checking algorithms. Christodorescu and Jha [4] describe a malware detection system based on language containment and unification. The malicious code and the possibly infected program are modeled here as automata. In this setting, a program presents a malicious behavior if the intersection between the language of the malware automaton and the one of the program automaton is not empty. Beaucamps et al. [2] approximate the set of possible execution traces of a program with a regular language. They define an abstraction of this regular language with respect to some predefined behavioral patterns that express a certain property of the malware behavior (an invariant of the metamorphic transformations used by the malware). This leads to a description of a program as a regular language of abstract symbols that can be compared to the one of known malware to detect infection. A similar approach has been considered more recently in [1], where a tree automata is derived from system call data-flow dependency graphs, which is insensitive on code mutation. Lo et al. [18] develop a programmable static analysis tool, called MCF (Malicious Code Filter), that uses program slicing and flow analysis to detect malicious code. Lakhotia et al. [17] propose a methodology based on program semantics and abstract interpretation for making context-sensitive analysis of assembly programs even when the call and ret instructions are obfuscated. Jacob et al. [14] propose a model of malware based on the *Join Calculus* and they identify a fragment of the Join calculus where the malware detection problem becomes decidable. All these approaches share a common pattern: They consider a set T of metamorphic transformations commonly used by malware (e.g. variable renaming, code permutation, junk insertion) and then they develop an abstract behavioral model for programs that ideally captures the maliciousness of a program while abstracting form those details that are susceptible to metamorphism, namely that can be changed by the transformations in T (for example symbolic names can be used to handle variable/location renaming). Thus, the design of the abstract model is driven by the considered set T of code transformation. Of course, researchers can recur to any existing tool for the static analysis of programs in order to define the abstract behavioral model of the malware (e.g. model checking, program semantics, abstract interpretation, language theory, data mining). In this context, the process of detecting a malware based on some given behavioral model can be viewed as the process of abstracting its semantics. It is known that abstract interpretation [7,8] can be used to characterize the obfuscating behavior of any metamorphic transformation in terms of the most concrete semantic property it preserves [11]. Moreover, any abstract behavioral model of programs obtained through static analysis can be expressed as an abstract interpretation of standard trace semantics [7]. This observation lead us to the definition of a general purpose framework based on a formal model of program semantics (trace semantics) and abstract interpretation for proving soundness (no false positives) and completeness (no false negatives) of malware detectors in the presence of metamorphism [10]. This means that the detection strategy and the metamorphic transformation can both be characterized as proper abstractions of program trace semantics. The idea is to use standard trace semantics to describe the concrete behavior of programs and malware, and abstract interpretation to model both the semantic properties preserved by the metamorphic transformation and the behavioral model employed by the detection strategy. Related works that address the analysis of self-modifying code with respect to a different semantics model based on Hoare Logic are the ones of Cai et al. [3] and Myreen [19].

One of the main limits of all the these formal behavioral approaches to metamorphic malware detection resides in the fact that they all assume to know the metamorphic transformations used by the malware. In fact, the design of the abstract model that specifies the behavior of programs is always driven by the obfuscating transformations used by the metamorphic engine. This makes the analysis mutation insensitive. Of course, a malware writer who has access to the detection algorithm, or who is aware of the set of basic transformations T used for deriving the abstract semantics, can exploit this knowledge in order to design new and ad-hoc obfuscation technique to bypass detection, even by simple modifications of the existing ones. As the malware detection problem is in general undecidable, for any given malware detector it is always possible to design an obfuscation that defeats that detector. We believe that a deeper understanding of the semantics of metamorphic malware, involving both the payload and the metamorphic engine could lead to a more robust detection system that is not based on the knowledge of the metamorphic techniques used by the malware and is mutation insensitive. The idea is to consider the metamorphic malware as a unique program, acting both as a standard program which modifies memory, and as a program modifying the code structure, which is also a data-structure.

3   Semantics-Based Learning Metamorphism

The *grand challenge* in metamorphic malware detection is to make behavioral analysis mutation insensitive. This means catching a signature which is durable and specific for a wide range of mutations of the malware. In [9] we propose a different approach to metamorphic malware detection based on the idea that extracting metamorphic signatures is approximating malware semantics, where the term metamorphic signature refers to any (possibly decidable) approximation of the properties of code evolution. The code is therefore viewed as a mutational data-structure, and approximating its shape consists in approximating the possible mutations of the malware. We face the problem of determining how code mutates, yet catching properties of this mutation, without any a priori knowledge about the implementation of the metamorphic transformations. We use a formal semantics to model the execution behavior of self-modifying code commonly encountered in malware. Using this as the basis, we developed a theoretical model for statically deriving, by abstract interpretation, an abstract specification of all possible code variants that can be generated during the execution of a metamorphic malware. The mixed computations on code and data are represented, and separated, in the so called *phase semantics*. The idea is to partition each possible execution trace of a metamorphic program into phases, each collecting the computations performed by a particular code variant. Thus, the sequence of phases (once disassembled) represents the sequence of possible code mutations. This means that the phase semantics of a program provides a precise description of the evolution of its code during execution. Indeed, phase semantics can be graphically represented as a set of traces of program representations, e.g., program control-flow graphs, such that two programs P ad P' are consecutive along the trace τ if during the execution, the program P can evolve to program P'. The phase semantics is a sound abstract interpretation of standard program trace semantics. The main advantage of the phase semantics is in modeling code mutations without isolating the metamorphic engine from the rest of the viral code. The phase semantics provides here the basis in order to let standard program analysis methods and algorithms to extract invariant properties of code mutations. Decidable approximations of phases allow to extract an approximate semantics of the metamorphic engine, without knowing a priori any features of the metamorphic engine itself, providing the adequate knowledge in order to make behavioral analysis mutation insensitive. The information extracted by approximating the phase semantics is indeed precisely the information which is necessary in behavioral analysis for designing the appropriate abstractions making the analysis mutation insensitive. At the same time, the information extracted from the phase semantics may provide a signature (the *metamorphic signature*) of the possible evolution of the code. Observe that in this setting abstract domains approximating semantics objects represent properties of the code shape in phases, namely the abstractions capture properties of the evolution of the code rather than of the evolution of program states (e.g., memory or stack), as usual in abstract interpretation. Indeed, the design of such abstract domains for the analysis of code properties (rather than semantic properties) where the code is the object of abstraction and the way it is generated is the object of abstract interpretation, represents a new and interesting research field. This is an aspect of a semantics based learning technique acting at the metamorphic engine level, which is unknown. Indeed, abstract phase semantics expresses both the set of possible code variants generated during execution and the mechanisms of generation of such variants. For example, in [9] we introduce the notion of regular metamorphism that approximates phase semantics of a metamorphic malware M with an automata on the language of abstract instructions Q whose recognized language represents all possible (regular) sequence of instructions in the program evolutions of M. In this case the language recognized by the automata Q represents the regular metamorphic signature for the metamorphic malware M, while the automata Q represents the mechanism of generation of the metamorphic variants and therefore it provides a model of the metamorphic engine of M. Other learning strategies can be used. Metamorphic engines can be modeled as grammars or term rewriting systems. In this case existing algorithms for learning grammars, inductive logic programming, and term rewriting systems from positive examples [21,12,13,16] can be used for implementing more expressive abstarct phase semantics. In this case the idea is that positive examples can be derived from the possible code evolutions expressed by the program evolution graph, i.e., the phase semantics, of the metamorphic program, while the metamorphic transformations are modeled as productions, or rewriting rules.

References

1. Babić, D., Reynaud, D., Song, D.: Malware Analysis with Tree Automata Inference. In: Gopalakrishnan, G., Qadeer, S. (eds.) CAV 2011. LNCS, vol. 6806, pp. 116–131. Springer, Heidelberg (2011)
2. Beaucamps, P., Gnaedig, I., Marion, J.Y.: Behavior Abstraction in Malware Analysis. In: Barringer, H., Falcone, Y., Finkbeiner, B., Havelund, K., Lee, I., Pace, G., Roşu, G., Sokolsky, O., Tillmann, N. (eds.) RV 2010. LNCS, vol. 6418, pp. 168–182. Springer, Heidelberg (2010)
3. Cai, H., Shao, Z., Vaynberg, A.: Certified self-modifying code. In: ACM PLDI, pp. 66–77 (2007)
4. Christodorescu, M., Jha, S.: Static analysis of executables to detect malicious patterns. In: USENIX Security Symp., pp. 169-186. USENIX Association (2003)
5. Christodorescu, M., Jha, S.: Testing malware detectors. In: ISSTA 2004, pp. 34–44 (2004)
6. Christodorescu, M., Jha, S., Seshia, S.A., Song, D., Bryant, R.E.: Semantics-aware malware detection. In: Proc. of the IEEE Security and Privacy, pp. 32–46 (2005)
7. Cousot, P., Cousot, R.: Abstract interpretation: A unified lattice model for static analysis of programs by construction or approximation of fixpoints. In: ACM POPL, pp. 238–252 (1977)
8. Cousot, P., Cousot, R.: Systematic design of program analysis frameworks. In: ACM POPL, pp. 269–282 (1979)
9. Dalla Preda, M., Giacobazzi, R., Debray, S., Coogan, K., Townsend, G.M.: Modelling Metamorphism by Abstract Interpretation. In: Cousot, R., Martel, M. (eds.) SAS 2010. LNCS, vol. 6337, pp. 218–235. Springer, Heidelberg (2010)
10. Dalla Preda, M., Christodorescu, M., Jha, S., Debray, S.: A semantics-based approach to malware detection. In: ACM POPL, pp. 377–388 (2007)
11. Dalla Preda, M., Giacobazzi, R.: Semantics-based Code Obfuscation by Abstract Interpretation. J. of Computer Security 17(6), 855–908 (2009)
12. de la Higuera, C.: Grammatical Inference Learning Automata and Grammars. Cambridge University Press (2010)
13. Eyraud, R., de la Higuera, C., Janodet, J.C.: LARS: A Learning Algorithm for Rewriting Systems. Machine Learning 66(1), 7–31 (2007)
14. Jacob, G., Filiol, E., Debar, H.: Formalization of Viruses and Malware Through Process Algebras. In: ARES 2010, pp. 597–602. IEEE Computer Society (2010)
15. Kinder, J., Katzenbeisser, S., Schallhart, C., Veith, H.: Detecting Malicious Code by Model Checking. In: Julisch, K., Krügel, C. (eds.) DIMVA 2005. LNCS, vol. 3548, pp. 174–187. Springer, Heidelberg (2005)
16. Krishna Rao, M.R.K.: Some classes of term rewriting systems inferable from positive data. Theoretical Computer Science 397(1-3), 129–149 (2008)
17. Lakhotia, A., Boccardo, D.R., Singh, A., Manacero, A.: Context-sensitive analysis of obfuscated x86 executables. In: Proc. of ACM PEPM 2010, pp. 131-140 (2010)
18. Lo, R.W., Levitt, K.N., Olsson, R.A.: MCF: A malicious code filter. Computers & Security 14, 541–566 (1995)
19. Myreen, M.O.: Verified just-in-time compiler on x86. In: Proc. of the 37th ACM POPL 2010, pp. 107-118 (2010)
20. Nielson, F., Nielson, H., Hankin, C.: Principles of Program Analysis (2004)
21. Plotkin, G.: A note on inductive generalization. Machine Intell. 5, 153–163 (1970)
22. Singh, P., Lakhotia, A.: Static verification of worm and virus behaviour in binary executables using model checking. In: Proc. of the 4th IEEE Information Assurance Workshop. IEEE Computer Society, Los Alamitos (2003)
23. Ször, P.: The Art of Computer Virus Research and Defense. Addison-Wesley Professional (2005)

The Art and Science of Obfuscation

Clark Thomborson

Computer Science Department,
The University of Auckland,
Private Bag 92019, New Zealand
cthombor@cs.auckland.ac.nz
http://www.cs.auckland.ac.nz/~cthombor

Abstract. Obfuscation is fundamentally both an art and a science, implying that its competent practitioners must be crafty as well as intelligent, and clever as well as precise.

Keywords: Obfuscation, fuzzy security, well-defined security, requirements engineering, trustworthy systems, trusted systems.

1   Introduction

In 2001, Boaz Barak et al. published the first scientific results on obfuscation [2]. Their theorems established hard limits on what an automated obfuscation process could acheive in a well-defined security model. In their model, an obfuscating process must be *uniformly successful* over a broad range of input programs, where success is defined as preventing the adversary from learning anything useful by inspecting the obfuscated program that they couldn't learn (within a polynomial time bound) by executing it on sample inputs. They proved that obfuscation is impossible in this model, if we insist that the obfuscated program must always be

- *efficient*: with no more than a polynomial slowdown, and
- *correct*: with no differences in its input-output map,

in comparison to the original program.

Barak subsequently web-published an informal discussion of the implications of these results [1] regarding fundamental questions such as "can we obfuscate programs?" and "can obfuscators enjoy well-defined security?"

With the benefit of ten years of hindsight and subsequent publications, I revisit Barak's informal questions. I argue that his distinction between well-defined security and fuzzy security is nicely framed and still relevant. However his dismissive attitude toward fuzzy security is poorly supported, and I argue that this attitude is inappropriate except in formal scientific work. I conclude with an appeal for a middle-path, that the "artists" of obfuscation must continue to communicate with the "scientists" in order for our discipline to continue developing.

S. Dua et al. (Eds.): ICISTM 2012, CCIS 285, pp. 445–450, 2012.

2   A Philosophy of Obfuscation?

For millennia, philosophers have pontificated on the subject of epistemology. They developed, and published, many interesting and plausible theories about the nature of knowledge, and about the limits on our ability to acquire knowledge. It is far beyond the scope of this paper to adequately describe any of these theories, or to discuss any of the ongoing controversies in epistemology. However some epistemological grounding is necessary for any science of obfuscation.

An obfuscator is attempting to impede the adversary's quest for knowledge about the information being obfuscated, without unduly impairing the rightful user's quest for the relevant knowledge about this information. In this light, an obfuscation process is an art rather than a science, for the successful obfuscater will find clever ways to befuddle their adversaries while still enlightening their allies. The artistic obfuscater will not expect any adversary or ally to attain, or even to desire, complete knowledge of all aspects of the underlying information. However – to the delight of magicians and their audiences – a skilled obfuscater can perform amazing feats, dissembling and misdirecting with a very high probability of success.

In the formal treatment of Barak et al. [2], the adversary is assumed to desire knowledge of the value of a predicate: a "secret bit" of information. This knowledge is assumed to be readily available, to the adversary, in the source code of the original program. This secret bit must also be expressed somehow in the execution semantics of the program, otherwise it would be merely a comment or other inessential information which would normally be suppressed by the compilation process. This is a very attractive definition for the adversary's goal, and it is certainly precise enough to support a scientific theory of obfuscation. However this formal definition of obfuscation does not cover any of the commercially-important forms of obfuscation which target the lexical structure of a program, in particular the names of its variables, objects, and interfaces.

In a standalone program, as assumed in the model of [2], all object names can be fully obfuscated by a trivial process. Note that this doesn't disprove any of Barak's theorems, because knowledge about object names is excluded from the (assumed) goals of the (likely) adversaries.

C-language compilers have been performing lexical-level obfuscation for decades, partly to avoid shipping bulky name tables, but also to avoid revealing information which may help a competitor or unlicensed user to gain a better understanding of the programmer's intent. One of the basic tenets of security is to release information only on a "need to know" basis – because in practical settings, we cannot predict all of an adversary's goals. As a case in point: the inadvertent release of a debugging build recently became a public-relations problem for its developer, when one of its program objects was discovered to have an offensive name [7].

Because internal names do not affect program behaviour, they can be obfuscated very easily except in interpreted languages, such as Java bytecode, which use these names for internal linkages. However even when this is a trivial form of obfuscation, it is not always an appropriate one. When internal names are suppressed, error traces are much more difficult to interpret. Finding, then linking, all of the relevant symbol tables to the trace of a crash dump that involves code from different program builds can be a tedious and error-prone process.

I conclude that a critically important part of the "art" of obfuscation is for the obfuscater to develop an adequate understanding of the (often quite disparate) goals of all of their important white-hat and black-hat stakeholders. If debugging support is very important, as in alpha and beta testing, then either internal names must be retained or some special "deobfuscation" support must be provided to the testers and debuggers. When program performance is important, then preparing a release with an appropriate level of support for the testers and debuggers poses some difficult technical challenges [4]. The benefits of such support must be balanced, somehow, against the risks of opening an information leakage vulnerability as defined (for example) in the nascent OWASP taxonomy:

> *Information Leakage*: Revealing system data or debugging information helps an adversary learn about the system and form a plan of attack. An information leak occurs when system data or debugging information leaves the program through an output stream or logging function. [6]

Increasingly, codes are dynamically linked – implying that we cannot trivially obfuscate the names of any externally-accessible variables, objects, or functions. The model of Barak et al. [2] treats only the case of a standalone program, and is silent about the problem of obfuscating sets of cooperating programs. Recent advances in homomorphic encryption suggest that this technology may someday become feasible for a wider range of computations than those computable by simple finite state machines; and it seems possible (in the absence of a theorem to the contrary) that these techniques might find a suitable application in the obfuscation of a dynamic linking.

3   Information Systems Security versus Cryptographic Security

Much of the argumentation in Barak's essay on program obfuscation [1] is directed at the difference between what he calls "well-defined security" and "fuzzy security". The former is the province of cryptoprotocol analysis, where the analyst makes some (often quite plausible) assumptions about the secrecy of cryptographic keys, the opacity of the cryptographic apparatus which manipulates the keys and produces the plaintext or signs the documents, and the unbreakability of the underlying cipher.

Fuzzy security is the province of information systems analysts and software engineers, who practice the difficult art of balancing stakeholder requirements for knowledge against security risks, cost constraints, performance requirements, usability considerations, as well as a host of other non-functional requirements such as maintainability and extensibility. Only some of these requirements can be captured in a model with sharp definitions; and even when there is a clear definition of a metric, for example of a development cost or a probability of a specific type of system failure after a specific type of event, sharply-specified requirements are often found to be infeasible during development. In this light, Barak's deprecation of "fuzzy security" is the stance of a theoretician who is not addressing some of the most difficult problems facing a practitioner. A competent practitioner will happily use a sharply-defined concept, if one is available, when designing a system to meet a sharply-defined requirement. However when communicating requirements to stakeholders who don't already know the sharp concepts, and who aren't willing to learn them, we must resort to "fuzzy security".

I also note that there is a dark art of obfuscating security requirements, and other forms of information about a system, whenever an open release of information about vulnerabilities, exploits, and their remediations would pose unacceptable security risks.

4   Confidence versus Trust

Niklas Luhmann was a prominent sociologist who studied the processes of communication. He nicely distinguished confidence from trust [5].

Confidence, in Luhmann's meaning, is attained through a cognitive process: this would generally involve a formal proof if it is conducted by a cryptographic researcher such as Boaz Barak. Trust is, for Luhmann, inherently immediate and unthinking. A continued growth in Luhmannian trust is, he argues, necessary for the continued development of the modern world because its ever-increasing level of complexity makes our confident assessments ever-more restricted in their scope and utility. The pursuit of modernity, in this view, is a fraught enterprise with ever-increasing risk – one which can only be mitigated, never eliminated. We "assume it away" at our peril!

I note that the inexpert stakeholder is exhibiting a Luhmannian trust in any system they are using.

I also note that the expert analyst is exhibiting a Luhmannian trust in any axiom they are employing for their confidently-made decisions. My reasoning here is that the axiomatic grounding of any well-defined security property is the result of a trusting decision, one which is not amenable to proof. The argument is by contradiction: if any axiom were provable from the other axioms, then it is a lemma and not an axiom. It is possible, of course, for an axiom in one model to be supported by proof based on axioms in another model; but such cross-validations merely make a more complex axiomatic structure, and do not do away with the requirement for a Luhmannian ("fuzzy") trust in the appropriateness of this structure for use in our epistemological quests.

5   Obfuscaters versus Obfuscators

The art of an obfuscater is to pick an appropriate set of obfuscations for the task at hand. If the obfuscater restricts their attention to any clear, well-defined, set of security objectives they will be unable to capture requirements (such as maintainability and debuggability) which are expressible only vaguely. The "artistic" obfuscater will probably adopt a "soft" definition such as the one proposed in 1998 by Collberg et al.:

> Unlike server-side execution, code obfuscation can never completely protect an application from malicious reverse engineering. Given enough time and determination, [the adversary] Bob will always be able to dissect Alice's application to retrieve its important algorithms and data structures... Existing obfuscation tools (such as Crema) are based on the assumption that the original and obfuscated program must have identical behavior. In the present paper we assume that under certain circumstances it will be possible to relax this constraint. In particular, we allow must of our obfuscating transformations to make the target program slower or larger than the original. In special cases we may even allow the target program to have different side-effects than the original, or not to terminate when the original program terminates with an error condition... [3]

The science of obfuscation is the study of the limits to obfuscators as exemplified in Barak et al. [2], and of the assessable performance of specific obfuscators, in well-defined models. The assumptions in these models may be contrary to, or silent on, some stakeholder requirements for practical obfuscation – for example in the suppression of variable names in standalone programs (where perfect obfuscation is trivially achievable), or in the obfuscation of the linkages in a dynamic computational environment.

6   The Art/Science Divide

As a member of the program committee for PPREW, I was very pleased to see strong contributions to both the "art" and "science" of obfuscation as defined in this essay. This is a healthy sign: we're making progress on both fronts!

At PPREW, the practitioners and the theorists of obfuscation will have an unprecedented opportunity to communicate across the art/science divide which is – I believe – inevitable whenever a "fuzzy" thinker meets a "precise" one.

Any difficulty in communication can easily be considered an obfuscation by either party, and as such, our art/science divide becomes an essential piece in our shared puzzles:

- What epistemology will support obfuscations of practical utility?
- How can we be appropriately confident in our obfuscations?
- How can we discuss our obfuscators with our stakeholders, in ways that will inspire appropriate levels of trust?

References

1. Barak, B.: Can we obfuscate programs? (2003),
   http://www.math.ias.edu/~boaz/Papers/obf_informal.html
2. Barak, B., Goldreich, O., Impagliazzo, R., Rudich, S., Sahai, A., Vadhan, S.P., Yang, K.: On the (Im)possibility of Obfuscating Programs. In: Kilian, J. (ed.) CRYPTO 2001. LNCS, vol. 2139, pp. 1–18. Springer, Heidelberg (2001)
3. Collberg, C., Thomborson, C., Low, D.: Manufacturing cheap, resilient, and stealthy opaque constructs. In: POPL 1998: Proceedings of the 25th ACM SIGPLAN-SIGACT Symposium on Principles of Programming Languages, pp. 184–196. ACM Press, New York (1998)
4. Hanselman, S.: Release IS NOT debug: 64bit optimizations and C# method inlining in release build call stacks (October 2007), http://www.hanselman.com/blog/ReleaseISNOTDebug64bitOptimizationsAndCMethodMethodInliningInReleaseBuildCallStacks.aspx
5. Luhmann, N.: Familiarity, confidence, trust: Problems and alternatives. In: Gambetta, D. (ed.) Trust: Making and Breaking Cooperative Relations, pp. 94–107. Blackwell, Malden (1998)
6. OWASP: Information leakage (March 2011),
   https://www.owasp.org/index.php/Information_Leakage
7. Westbrook, L.: Steam user finds misogynistic "joke" buried in dead island code [updated] (September 2011), http://www.escapistmagazine.com/news/view/112870-Steam-User-Finds-Misogynistic-Joke-Buried-in-Dead-Island-Code-UPDATED

Capturing the Essence of Practical Obfuscation

J. Todd McDonald

School of Computer and Information Sciences,
University of South Alabama, Mobile, AL USA
jtmcdonald@usouthal.edu

Abstract. In the realm of protecting programs from illegitimate use, obfuscation offers a modicum of defense against malicious reverse engineering and tampering. As a field of study, obfuscation would benefit from a unifying framework that has solid theoretical foundation yet provides value in empirical study and implementation. The essence of obfuscation (in practice) is best described as a measurable loss of abstraction. We argue that mathematical frameworks such as abstract interpretation and Boolean algebras may provide an ideal marriage of theory and practice, providing focused direction for future research.

1 Background

Obfuscation is a transformation process that produces semantically equivalent versions of a given program or circuit, with a definable security goal related to hiding or understandability of an original program. Notable obfuscation results prove that virtual black-box (VBB) simulation as an information theoretic goal is impossible for *all* functions [1] or for *all* functions with cryptographic applications [2]. Other theoretic models relate security to the distributions produced by the obfuscator itself [3,4]. A steady stream of positive results over the last decade show that security can be proven in specific contexts or for specific families of programs: access control [5], point functions [6], re-encryption [7,8], probabilistic encryption [9], private-key schemes [10], straight-line arithmetic programs [11], single use programs with hardware support [12], and time-limited obfuscation [13]. Formal expressions for obfuscation have also grown to include term rewriting systems [14] and abstract interpretation [15,16].

Real-world obfuscators focus on preventing reverse engineering or tampering [17,18,19] to guard intellectual property investment. Successful reverse engineering aims to correctly identify system components, component interrelationships, or system representations at higher levels of abstraction [20], whether for beneficial or malicious purposes. Deobfuscation finds relevance in malware analysis and virus detection research [21,22]. Circuits and embedded hardware protection [23] have likewise seen positive results, particularly where fully trusted [24,25] or partially trusted hardware [26] is leveraged. Copy prevention through digital fingerprinting and watermarking [27,28] and hiding of circuit features have been demonstrated empirically or proven generally [29,30].

S. Dua et al. (Eds.): ICISTM 2012, CCIS 285, pp. 451–456, 2012.

2   Practical Obfuscation as Loss of Abstraction

Two (often divergent) paths have shaped the meaning of obfuscation. In one approach, the obfuscator is defined mathematically with a corresponding security requirement that must be met for all possible programs: VBB, computational indistinguishability, best possible, non-malleability, etc. Based on the security test, proofs typically demonstrate negative results by producing a counter-example. Weakened definitions and specific contexts often provide positive results. Lifting specific constraints, such as semantic equivalence, can provide greater possibilities as well [31,32]. Alternatively, creating obfuscators and making observations about their capabilities provides real-world context. In this paradigm, practical metrics or formal characterizations are in view: targeting steps in the reverse engineering process, computing loss of abstraction, preventing specific attack vectors, increasing cost-complexity for an adversary, relating adversarial tasks to known hard problems, or measuring heuristics that relate security to program attributes. Practitioners have a harder road to travel because characterization is not an exact science. Defining an adversary's power and correlating those to security objectives may require intuition or experience. Metrics and attack vectors may be valid today but change tomorrow as adversaries employ new strategies.

Real-world obfuscators operate primarily on the syntax/structural level (supporting real-world application) whereas theoretic definitions operate at the functional/semantic level (supporting statements about entire families). The fundamental property of obfuscation, from either perspective, is the characterization of *change*. White-box polymorphic variation is a structural transformation process that preserves functional semantics. Using program diversity itself (creating large numbers of functionally equivalent variants) can have stand-alone value as a remedy to piracy [33] and limiting impact of exploitable vulnerabilities. Obfuscation may best be described as the hiding of one or more semantic level properties, which is to say, achieving a measurable loss of abstraction. To mature the definition of obfuscation and lend credence to practical techniques, we need quantitative measures that adequately describe this loss and a framework that allows comparison of algorithms themselves.

The use of abstract interpretation (AI) [34] has shown promise as a method to achieve obfuscation [35,16] and to support deobfuscation for malware detection [36,37]. Following [16], a syntactic transformer (or variation process) is an *obfuscator* if it meets requirements for *potency, semantic equivalence*, and *conservative transformation*. The AI framework provides a method to clearly identify loss of abstract information by defining adversaries as properties that are either preserved or obfuscated. It also provides the tools for quantitative analysis of obfuscating transforms, whereby conservative transformations formally express the more fuzzy notion of obscurity. Abstract interpretation represents one contender for strengthening analytical studies, giving a rigorous, formal methodology that separates description of the variation engine from quantitative assessments of obfuscation.

3   Logic Programs: Bridging Theory and Practice

Boolean logic circuits are ideal for studying obfuscation because they bridge the gap between the often disparate worlds of theory and practice. They have rich history in theoretic study related to computational complexity, proof systems, logic algebras, and computational models. They rival Turing machines (TM) in answering fundamental questions of computability and possibility. Circuits have only one polynomial representation space (size), while Turing machines have two (size and running time). It is possible to show that all (physical) machines with bounded memory are constructible via sequential circuits and binary memory units. Further, we can completely simulate machines (whose computations terminate) with circuits. As an observation, many theoretical obfuscation results are expressed as proofs on circuit classes versus Turing machines.

Circuits also have real-world manifestations that are foundational to every day computing tasks, giving them the unique ability for practical realization. Focusing on logic circuits that derive from Boolean algebra may help establish foundational principles for obfuscation research. In addition, lessons learned from polymorphic circuit variation can be applicable to general programs: if the essence of obfuscation can be captured at this level, it may support an ideal marriage of theory and practice.

Circuit Representation and Variation: Circuits have a well studied semantic in the form of Boolean algebras and reasoning systems. Natural representation of Boolean algebras as lattices supports their evaluation under abstract interpretation. For example, a Boolean algebra β defines a lattice $\langle B, \leq \rangle$ where for any x and y in B, the set $\{x, y\}$ has a least upper bound defined as $x \vee y$ and a greatest lower bound defined as $x \wedge y$. Boolean algebras have clear relationships between syntax and semantics: physical circuits (traditionally AND, OR, NOR, $NAND$, XOR, $NXOR$, NOT gates) can be derived from logic statements (semantics) and logical expressions have multiple equivalent structural implementations. For example, the logical $\wedge$ operation maps to a physical OR gate and has a precise semantic, with the same holding true for the logical $\vee$. Given a complete basis set of operators $\{\vee, \wedge, \neg\}$, where $\neg$ represents negation, we can express any programmatic functionality. In addition, the lattice $\langle B, \leq \rangle$ immediately derives laws for idempotence, commutativity, associativity, absorption, partial orders for equivalence, and partial orders for implication. Circuit variation (a structural concept) is ultimately a reflection of Boolean logic variation (a semantic concept). We can formally define any variation technique as an application of one or more logic theorems.

Logical Redundancy and Reduction: In digital logic applications, considerable research has been geared at reducing circuits to their smallest (logical) form for efficiency and cost. Theoretically, obfuscators are allowed a polynomial overhead in circuit features such as size or depth. Practically, any overhead introduced might be viewed as a step backwards. Assuming that circuit candidates for obfuscation are in a minimally reduced form to begin with, circuit variation effectively introduces logical redundancy. Variation (aiming to achieve obfuscation) would essentially work backwards from the viewpoint of Boolean logic reduction. Laws of idempotence, identity (0 and 1), complementation, and involution would provide the necessary generation mechanism for expanding terms. For example, reduction would replace the function $F_0 = (A \vee B \vee C) \wedge \neg(A \wedge \neg B \wedge \neg C) \wedge \neg C$ with its reduced form $F_0 = B \wedge \neg C$ via repeated application of logic laws. Going in reverse, variation would expand the function $F_0 = B \wedge \neg C$ forward and $F_0 = (A \vee B \vee C) \wedge \neg(A \wedge \neg B \wedge \neg C) \wedge \neg C$ represents one possible expansion. As a key observation, redundancy introduced by variation algorithms *should* be reducible. From empirical study [38,30], any single transformation (an aspect of confusion) is trivially reducible; however, combinations of overlapping redundancies (an aspect of diffusion) may not be removable via heuristic methods. These observations validate Cohen's [39] original approach to programmatic transformation using confusion/diffusion primitives. Redundancy and reduction form a primary analysis aspect of circuits, where Boolean logic reduction serves as an adversarial analysis vector. Other circuit features such as topology, signals, components, and control provide primary means for assessing loss of abstraction.

4   Conclusions

Empirical study of practical obfuscation can be a trial and error method. Defining security properties of interest and developing variation algorithms that obscure those properties in a quantitative approach would serve to validate practical techniques. Several questions of interest arise in this pursuit:

1. How do we characterize the polymorphic white-box variation process?
2. How do we know when variation becomes obfuscation (a loss of abstraction)?
3. How do we compare different obfuscation algorithms?
4. How do we quantitatively asses the overhead of introduced redundancy with the protection gained?

As a way forward, formal analysis frameworks such as abstract interpretation and Boolean logic algebras provide a good starting point that may ultimately bring theory and practice closer together.

References

1. Barak, B., Goldreich, O., Impagliazzo, R., Rudich, S., Sahai, A., Vadhan, S., Yang, K.: On the (im)possibility of obfuscating programs. Electronic Colloquium on Computational Complexity 8 (2001)
2. Goldwasser, S., Kalai, Y.T.: On the impossibility of obfuscation with auxiliary input. In: Proc. of the 46th Annual IEEE Symposium on Foundations of Computer Science (FOCS 2005), Washington, DC, USA, pp. 553–562. IEEE Computer Society (2005)
3. Goldwasser, S., Rothblum, G.N.: On Best-Possible Obfuscation. In: Vadhan, S.P. (ed.) TCC 2007. LNCS, vol. 4392, pp. 194–213. Springer, Heidelberg (2007)
4. Yasinsac, A., McDonald, J.T.: Tamper resistant software through intent protection. Intl. Journal Network Security 7, 370–382 (2008)

5. Lynn, B.Y.S., Prabhakaran, M., Sahai, A.: Positive Results and Techniques for Obfuscation. In: Cachin, C., Camenisch, J.L. (eds.) EUROCRYPT 2004. LNCS, vol. 3027, pp. 20–39. Springer, Heidelberg (2004)
6. Wee, H.: On obfuscating point functions. In: Proc.of the 37th Annual ACM Symposium on Theory of Computing (STOC 2005), pp. 523–532. ACM, New York (2005)
7. Hohenberger, S., Rothblum, G.N., Shelat, A., Vaikuntanathan, V.: Securely Obfuscating Re-encryption. In: Vadhan, S.P. (ed.) TCC 2007. LNCS, vol. 4392, pp. 233–252. Springer, Heidelberg (2007)
8. Chandran, N., Chase, M., Vaikuntanathan, V.: Collusion resistant obfuscation and functional re-encryption. IACR Cryptology ePrint Archive 2011, 337 (2011)
9. Hofheinz, D., Malone-Lee, J., Stam, M.: Obfuscation for cryptographic purposes. Journal of Cryptology 23, 121–168 (2010), doi:10.1007/s00145-009-9046-1
10. Hada, S., Sakurai, K.: A Note on the (Im)possibility of Using Obfuscators to Transform Private-Key Encryption into Public-Key Encryption. In: Miyaji, A., Kikuchi, H., Rannenberg, K. (eds.) IWSEC 2007. LNCS, vol. 4752, pp. 1–12. Springer, Heidelberg (2007), doi:10.1007/978-3-540-75651-4
11. Narayanan, S., Raghunathan, A., Venkatesan, R.: Obfuscating straight line arithmetic programs. In: Proceedings of the Nineth ACM Workshop on Digital Rights Management. DRM 2009, pp. 47–58. ACM, New York (2009)
12. Goldwasser, S., Kalai, Y.T., Rothblum, G.N.: One-Time Programs. In: Wagner, D. (ed.) CRYPTO 2008. LNCS, vol. 5157, pp. 39–56. Springer, Heidelberg (2008)
13. Beaucamps, P., Filiol, E.: On the possibility of practically obfuscating programs towards a unified perspective of code protection. Journal in Computer Virology 3, 3–21 (2007)
14. Walenstein, A., Mathur, R., Chouchane, M.R., Lakhotia, A.: Normalizing metamorphic malware using term rewriting. In: SCAM 2006: Proceedings of the Sixth IEEE, pp. 75–84. IEEE Computer Society, Washington, DC (2006)
15. Dalla Preda, M., Giacobazzi, R., Debray, S., Coogan, K., Townsend, G.M.: Modelling Metamorphism by Abstract Interpretation. In: Cousot, R., Martel, M. (eds.) SAS 2010. LNCS, vol. 6337, pp. 218–235. Springer, Heidelberg (2010)
16. Dalla Preda, M., Giacobazzi, R.: Semantic-Based Code Obfuscation by Abstract Interpretation. In: Caires, L., Italiano, G.F., Monteiro, L., Palamidessi, C., Yung, M. (eds.) ICALP 2005. LNCS, vol. 3580, pp. 1325–1336. Springer, Heidelberg (2005)
17. Majumdar, A., Thomborson, C.: Manufacturing opaque predicates in distributed systems for code obfuscation. In: ACSC 2006: Proceedings of the 29th Australasian Computer Science Conference, pp. 187–196. Australian Computer Society, Inc., Darlinghurst (2006)
18. Collberg, C., Thomborson, C.: Watermarking, tamper-proofing, and obfuscation - tools for software protection. IEEE Transactions on Software Engineering 28, 735–746 (2002)
19. Madou, M., Anckaert, B., Moseley, P., Debray, S., De Sutter, B., De Bosschere, K.: Software Protection Through Dynamic Code Mutation. In: Song, J.-S., Kwon, T., Yung, M. (eds.) WISA 2005. LNCS, vol. 3786, pp. 194–206. Springer, Heidelberg (2006)
20. Chikofsky, E., Cross I, J.H.: Reverse engineering and design recovery: a taxonomy. IEEE Software 7, 13–17 (1990)
21. Lakhotia, A., Kumar, E.U., Venable, M.: A method for detecting obfuscated calls in malicious binaries. IEEE Transactions on Software Engineering 31, 955–968 (2005)

22. Christodorescu, M., Jha, S., Seshia, S.A., Song, D., Bryant, R.E.: Semantics-aware malware detection. In: Proceedings of IEEE Symposium on Security and Privacy, pp. 32–46. IEEE Computer Society, Washington, DC (2005)

23. Kim, Y.C., McDonald, J.T.: Considering software proteciton for embedded systems. Crosstalk: The Journal of Defense Software Engineering 22, 4–8 (2009)

24. Chandran, N., Goyal, V., Sahai, A.: New Constructions for UC Secure Computation Using Tamper-Proof Hardware. In: Smart, N. (ed.) EUROCRYPT 2008. LNCS, vol. 4965, pp. 545–562. Springer, Heidelberg (2008), doi:10.1007/978-3-540-78967-3

25. Ding, N., Gu, D.: A General and Efficient Obfuscation for Programs with Tamper-Proof Hardware. In: Bao, F., Weng, J. (eds.) ISPEC 2011. LNCS, vol. 6672, pp. 401–416. Springer, Heidelberg (2011)

26. Bitansky, N., Canetti, R., Goldwasser, S., Halevi, S., Kalai, Y.T., Rothblum, G.N.: Program obfuscation with leaky hardware. Cryptology ePrint Archive, Report 2011/660 (2011), http://eprint.iacr.org/

27. Castillo, E., Meyer-Baese, U., García, A., Parrilla, L., Lloris, A.: Ipp@hdl: Efficient intellectual property protection scheme for ip cores. IEEE Trans. Very Large Scale Integr. Syst. 15, 578–591 (2007)

28. Charbon, E., Torunoglu, I.: Watermarking Techniques for Electronic Circuit Design. In: Petitcolas, F.A.P., Kim, H.-J. (eds.) IWDW 2002. LNCS, vol. 2613, pp. 147–169. Springer, Heidelberg (2003)

29. Chakraborty, R.S., Bhunia, S.: Hardware protection and authentication through netlist level obfuscation. In: Proc. of the IEEE/ACM Int"l Conference on Computer-Aided Design, ICCAD 2008, pp. 674–677. IEEE Press, Piscataway (2008)

30. McDonald, J.T., Trias, E.D., Kim, Y.C., Grimaila, M.R.: Using logic-based reduction for adversarial component recovery. In: Proc. of the 25th ACM Symposium on Applied Computing, SAC (2010)

31. Sander, T., Tschudin, C.: On Software Protection via Function Hiding. In: Aucsmith, D. (ed.) IH 1998. LNCS, vol. 1525, pp. 111–123. Springer, Heidelberg (1998), doi:10.1007/3-540-49380-8

32. McDonald, J.T., Kim, Y.C., Yasinsac, A.: Software issues in digital forensics. ACM Operating Systems Review 42 (2008)

33. Anckaert, B., Sutter, B.D., Bosschere, K.D.: Software piracy prevention through diversity. In: DRM 2004: Proceedings of the 4th ACM Workshop on Digital Rights Management, pp. 63–71. ACM, New York (2004)

34. Cousot, P.: Constructive design of a hierarchy of semantics of a transition system by abstract interpretation. Theor. Comput. Sci. 277, 47–103 (2002)

35. Dalla Preda, M., Giacobazzi, R., Visentini, E.: Hiding Software Watermarks in Loop Structures. In: Alpuente, M., Vidal, G. (eds.) SAS 2008. LNCS, vol. 5079, pp. 174–188. Springer, Heidelberg (2008)

36. Dalla Preda, M., Madou, M., De Bosschere, K., Giacobazzi, R.: Opaque Predicates Detection by Abstract Interpretation. In: Johnson, M., Vene, V. (eds.) AMAST 2006. LNCS, vol. 4019, pp. 81–95. Springer, Heidelberg (2006)

37. Dalla Preda, M., Christodorescu, M., Jha, S., Debray, S.: A semantics-based approach to malware detection. SIGPLAN Not. 42, 377–388 (2007)

38. McDonald, J.T., Kim, Y.C., Grimaila, M.R.: Protecting reprogrammable hardware with polymorphic circuit variation. In: Proc. of the 2nd Cyberspace Research Workshop 2009 (2009)

39. Cohen, F.B.: Operating system protection through program evolution. Comput. Secur. 12, 565–584 (1993)

Author Index